Educational Research

Educational Research

Planning, Conducting, and Evaluating Quantitative and Qualitative Research

FOURTH EDITION

John W. Creswell
University of Nebraska-Lincoln

Boston Columbus Indianapolis New York San Francisco Upper Saddle River
Amsterdam Cape Town Dubai London Madrid Milan Munich Paris Montreal Toronto
Delhi Mexico City São Paulo Sydney Hong Kong Seoul Singapore Taipei Tokyo

Vice President and Editor-in-Chief: Paul A. Smith
Development Editor: Christina Robb
Editorial Assistant: Matthew Buchholtz
Marketing Manager: Joanna Sabella
Production Editor: Karen Mason
Production Coordination: TexTech International
Text Design and Illustrations: TexTech International
Cover Design: Jodi Notowitz

This book was set in Garamond by TexTech. It was printed and bound by Edwards Brothers, Inc. The cover was printed by Phoenix Color Corp.

Between the time website information is gathered and then published, it is not unusual for some sites to have closed. Also, the transcription of URLs can result in typographical errors. The publisher would appreciate notification where these errors occur so that they may be corrected in subsequent editions.

If you purchased this book within the United States or Canada you should be aware that it has been imported without the approval of the Publisher or the author.

10 9 8 7 6 5 4 3 2 1

ISBN-10:   0-13-261394-8
ISBN-13: 978-0-13-261394-1

This text is dedicated to Karen, who provided caring editorial help and support through four editions of this book. You have been my inspiration and thoughtful advocate throughout this project. Thanks for standing beside me.

Brief Contents

Contents

Chapter 13   *Grounded Theory Designs   422*

Chapter 14   *Ethnographic Designs   461*

Chapter *Narrative Research Designs 501*

Chapter *Mixed Methods Designs 534*

Preface

NEW TO THE FOURTH EDITION

You will find several key changes in this edition as a result of reader feedback and the careful review of the last edition by anonymous external reviewers.

◆ Increased coverage of ethical issues—this edition includes an expanded treatment of ethical issues that occur throughout the research process, from the inception of the idea, through data collection, analysis, reporting, and the use of the research. These ethical discussions incorporate many new ideas, references, and authors who have focused attention on the developing field of the ethics of conducting research.

◆ Ethical issues are highlighted throughout the specific research design chapters of Part III. For example, ethical concerns unique to experimental research, survey research, narrative research, and mixed methods research—to name a few of the design chapters—are given specific attention. In addition, these design chapters now include a new boxed feature called "Ethical Dilemma" in which the reader is introduced to a specific ethical issue that may arise in using the design. The reader is also asked to consider how to resolve the issue.

◆ Most of the sample articles used throughout the book are new. They present recently published journal articles so that the issues presented in the articles address timely concerns (and recent methods ideas) that educational researchers need to know. As with past editions, these articles are annotated with marginal notes to help readers locate key passages of research and important characteristics of research.

◆ The references used in this edition have been extensively updated from past editions of this book. Key writers in research methods have issued new editions of books, and readers need to be introduced to these new editions. Also, new books on research methods are continually being published, and readers need to be informed of the latest writings. At the end of each chapter are suggestions for additional resources to consider for more information about certain topics. Also, references to software and their Web sites have been updated when needed.

◆ The text has been streamlined to focus on key content that needs to be mastered. Chapters 1 and 2 have been combined to focus attention on important ideas from the outset. Also, the objectives at the start of chapters now match the central topics in the chapter and the summary at the end of the chapter.

◆ Quantitative and qualitative research approaches continue to be seen as forms of research that lie along a continuum (instead of two completely separate approaches). In this book, the discussion about the characteristics of both quantitative and qualitative research now better reflects this continuum. Often in educational research, studies are not entirely either quantitative or qualitative but contain some elements of both approaches. The design chapters on mixed methods and action research reinforce this emerging trend in research.

THE PHILOSOPHY OF THE TEXT

The philosophy that guided the development of this text is twofold. First, research involves a process of interrelated activities rather than the application of isolated, unrelated concepts and ideas. Educators practice research following a general sequence of procedures—from the initial identification of a research problem to the final report of research. This means that understanding the sequence or flow of activities is central to inquiry. Thus, the text begins with specific chapters devoted to each step in the process of research and the inclusion of concepts and ideas within this process.

Second, the educational researcher today needs a large toolbox of approaches to study the complex educational issues in our society. No longer can we, as educators, use only experiments or surveys to address our research problems. Educators in this new century—whether conducting research or reading research to self-inform—need to know about quantitative, qualitative, and combined approaches to inquiry and to have an indepth understanding of the multiple research designs and procedures used in our studies today. In each step in the process of research, this text will introduce you to quantitative, qualitative, and combined approaches. Throughout the text, you will learn about the differences and similarities of qualitative and quantitative research. In the last section of the text, you will be introduced to eight distinct quantitative and qualitative research designs or procedures that comprise the repertoire of the educational researcher in the quantitative, qualitative, and combined applications of research.

KEY FEATURES

This text offers a truly balanced, inclusive, and integrated overview of the field as it currently stands. As you will see from the table of contents, the book's coverage is unique in its balanced presentation of quantitative and qualitative research. Moreover, it consistently examines foundational issues of research—for example, determining how to approach a project and understanding what constitutes data and how to analyze them—from quantitative, qualitative, and mixed perspectives. This approach helps students understand fundamental differences *and* similarities among these approaches. This text has three main purposes:

- ◆ It provides balanced coverage of quantitative and qualitative research.
- ◆ It helps students learn how to begin to conduct research.
- ◆ It helps students learn how to read and evaluate research studies.

Let's look at each of these in detail to see how each can help you achieve your course objectives.

Balances Coverage of Quantitative and Qualitative Research

This text provides balanced coverage of all types of research designs. This provides readers with a complete picture of educational research as it is currently practiced. The text begins with an overview in part I of the general nature of educational research and the specific quantitative and qualitative approaches to educational research. Next, in part II, chapters 2 through 9, the book examines in depth the steps in the research process:

1. Identifying a research problem
2. Reviewing the literature
3. Specifying a purpose and research questions or hypotheses
4. Collecting either quantitative or qualitative data
5. Analyzing and interpreting either quantitative or qualitative data
6. Reporting and evaluating the research

Looking at the process simultaneously from both quantitative and qualitative perspectives helps students understand what choices a researcher has available and what meaning exists for a particular choice.

After this discussion, in part III, students will learn the procedures for conducting specific types of quantitative, qualitative, and mixed methods studies. Chapters 10 through 17 provide balanced coverage and examples of each of these types of educational research designs: experimental, correlational, survey, grounded theory, ethnographic, narrative, mixed methods, and action research.

Helps Students Learn How to Begin to Conduct Research

Both the research process and design chapters offer the researcher step-by-step guidance in the basic aspects of planning, conducting, and evaluating research. A number of features guide readers through the steps and procedures of research. For example, a fictional beginning researcher, Maria, who is also a high school teacher and new graduate student, is followed throughout part II and part III to illustrate one researcher's efforts and to provide students with a realistic perspective of the process of research and the selection of specific research designs. Other features include, but are not limited to:

◆ Tips on planning and conducting research in "Useful Information for Producers of Research"

◆ Checklists that summarize key points such as evaluation criteria used to assess the quality of a quantitative or qualitative study

◆ In-text examples of actual and hypothetical studies that illustrate the correct and incorrect ways of reporting research

◆ Follow-up activities in "Understanding Concepts and Evaluating Research Studies" to help students apply the concepts they've just learned

◆ A "Think-Aloud" feature that describes practices the author has found useful

Helps Students Learn How to Read and Evaluate Research Studies

Direct guidance on reading research is offered throughout the text. To further help students become more skilled at interpreting and evaluating research, the text offers a number of features. Most important among these are the many articles included in the text and the "Useful Information for Consumers of Research" feature.

◆ The text provides annotated research articles in each of the design chapters in part III. Two other articles—one qualitative, one quantitative—appear at the end of chapter 1. All of these complete articles (there are numerous other, shorter article excerpts in the book) include highlighted marginal annotations that help students understand the structure of articles and the key issues with which a reader should be concerned when evaluating the quality and the applicable scope of each particular piece of research.

◆ The "Useful Information for Consumers of Research" feature appears at the end of every chapter and offers concrete guidance in interpreting and evaluating research.

NEW! COURSESMART eTEXTBOOK AVAILABLE

CourseSmart is an exciting new choice for students looking to save money. As an alternative to purchasing the printed textbook, students can purchase an electronic version of the same content. With a CourseSmart eTextbook, students can search the text, make notes online, print out reading assignments that incorporate lecture notes, and bookmark important passages for later review. For more information, or to purchase access to the CourseSmart eTextbook, visit **www.coursesmart.com**.

SUPPLEMENTARY MATERIALS

A number of ancillaries are available to complement the text:

MyEducationLab

Prepare with the Power of Practice   MyEducationLab is an online learning tool that provides contextualized interactive exercises and other resources designed to help develop the knowledge and skills researchers need. All of the activities and exercises in MyEducationLab are built around essential learning outcomes. The Web site provides opportunities to both study course content and to practice the skills needed to understand and carry out research.

For each topic covered in the course you will find most or all of the following features and resources:

Assignments and Activities   Designed to enhance student understanding of concepts covered in class and save instructors preparation and grading time, these assignable exercises give students opportunities to apply class content to research scenarios. (Feedback for the assignments is available to the instructor only.)

Building Research Skills   These exercises help students develop skills that are essential for understanding and carrying out research.

Study Plan   A MyEducationLab Study Plan consists of multiple choice assessments tied to learning outcomes, supported by study material. A well-designed Study Plan offers multiple opportunities to fully master required course content as identified by learning outcomes:

◆ *Learning outcomes* identify the learning outcomes for the topic and give students targets to shoot for as they read and study.

◆ *Multiple Choice Assessments* assess mastery of the content. These assessments are mapped to learning outcomes, and students can take the multiple choice pretests as many times as they want. Not only do these assessments provide overall scores for each outcome, but they also explain why responses to particular items are correct or incorrect.

◆ *Study Material: Review, Practice, and Enrichment* give students a deeper understanding of what they do and do not know related to topic content. This material includes activities that include hints and feedback.

Visit **www.myeducationlab.com** *for a demonstration of this exciting new online teaching resource.*

Instructor Supplements

The following resources are available for instructors to download at **www.pearson highered.com/educators**:

Online Test Bank and MyTest   The Test Bank contains various types of items—multiple choice, matching, short essay, and fill in the blank—for each chapter. Questions ask students to identify and describe research processes and design characteristics they have learned about and to classify and evaluate quantitative and qualitative studies and research situations. Offered along with the *Test Bank* is Pearson *MyTest* a powerful assessment generation program that helps instructors easily create and print quizzes and exams. Questions and tests are authored online, allowing ultimate flexibility and the ability to efficiently create and print assessments anytime, anywhere! Instructors can access Pearson MyTest and their test bank files by going to **www.pearsonmytest.com** to log in, register, or request access.

PowerPoint Slides   These slides include key concept summarizations and other graphic aids to help students understand, organize, and remember core concepts and ideas.

Web CT and BlackBoard Course Content Cartridges   The online course cartridges contain the content of the Test Bank, available for use on either online learning application.

ACKNOWLEDGMENTS

This book is a culmination of 30 years of experience in conducting both quantitative and qualitative research in education and the social sciences. It could not have been written without the capable assistance of numerous individuals such as graduate students, research assistants, and colleagues at the University of Nebraska–Lincoln. Dr. Dana Miller assisted in a timely and thorough review of many chapters. Dr. Vicki Plano Clark provided editorial assistance and a key conceptual eye for missing details as well as useful leads for sample illustrative articles. Amanda Garrett has provided invaluable assistance in locating up-to-date materials and in conceptualizing ideas. Dr. Ron Shope developed the initial PowerPoint presentation. Others have been helpful as well. Dong Dong Zhang provided inspiration for many applied ideas and support at critical phases of the project. Other graduate students offered useful ideas, including Michael Toland, Kathy Shapely, and many other students in my graduate program area, quantitative and qualitative methods of education, as did students in my classes on the foundations of educational research. Dr. Bill Mickelson served as a statistics consultant and quantitative analysis reviewer.

I am also indebted to Kevin Davis at Pearson for initiating this book and providing the vision to launch it as the "next-generation" research methods text in education. Christina Robb, my excellent development editor at Pearson for this edition, provided patience, support, and useful insights throughout the project.

Numerous reviewers helped to shape this book: Patricia L. Busk, University of San Franciso; Julita G. Iambating, California State University at Sacramento; Hari Koirala, Eastern Connecticut State University; Rene Parmar, St. John's University; John Rogutt, Illinois State University; Christine Anne Royce, Shippensburg University; Linda Shepard, Indiana University at Bloomington; and Stephen Whitney, University of Missouri at Columbia.

PART ONE

An Introduction to Educational Research

Consider research your personal journey. It will be challenging but also exciting. Pack along for your journey a toolkit. In chapter 1 you will be introduced to the basic supplies. In your pack, place a solid understanding of "research." Also include a map—the six steps in the process of conducting research. Realize that on this journey you need to respect people and the places you visit. Enjoy the process using your natural skills such as the ability to solve puzzles, use library resources, and write. After learning the process of research, decide on which of two major paths—quantitative or qualitative research—you will follow. Each is viable, and, in the end, you may choose to incorporate both, but as you begin a study consider one of the paths for your research journey.

Let us begin.

The Process of Conducting Research Using Quantitative and Qualitative Approaches

*W*hat is research? Research is a process in which you engage in a small set of logical steps. In this chapter, we define research, discuss why it is important, advance six steps for conducting research, and identify how you can conduct research ethically by employing skills that you already have. You can approach research in two ways—through a quantitative study or a qualitative study—depending on the type of problem you need to research. Your choice of one of these approaches will shape the procedures you use in each of the six steps of research. In this chapter, we explore the many ways these two approaches are similar and different.

By the end of this chapter, you should be able to:

◆ Define and describe the importance of educational research.
◆ Describe the six steps in the process of research.
◆ Identify the characteristics of quantitative and qualitative research in the six steps.
◆ Identify the type of research designs associated with quantitative and qualitative research.
◆ Discuss important ethical issues in conducting research.
◆ Recognize skills needed to design and conduct research.

To begin, consider Maria, a teacher with 10 years of experience, who teaches English at a midsized metropolitan high school. Lately, a number of incidents in the school district have involved students possessing weapons:

◆ A teacher found a 10th grader hiding a knife in his locker.
◆ A 12th-grade student threatened another student, telling him "he wouldn't see the light of day" unless he stopped harassing her.
◆ At a nearby high school, a student pointed a handgun at another student outside the school.

These incidents alarm district officials, school administrators, and teachers. The principal forms a committee made up of administrators and teachers to develop guidelines about how the school should respond to these situations. In response to a call for teachers to serve on this committee, Maria volunteers immediately.

Maria sees the school committee assignment and her graduate program's research study requirement as mutual opportunities to research school violence and weapon possession and to have a positive impact on her school. Where does she begin?

Maria's situation of balancing the dual roles of professional and graduate student may be familiar to you. Let's assess her present research situation:

◆ Maria recognizes the need to closely examine an important issue—school violence and weapons at school—although she is new to research. However, she is not a stranger to looking up topics in libraries or to searching the Internet when she has a question about something. She has occasionally looked at a few research journals, such as the *High School Journal,* the *Journal of Educational Research,* and *Theory into Practice,* in her school library, and she has overheard other teachers talking about research studies on the subject of school violence. Although she has no research background, she expects that research will yield important findings for her school committee and also help her fulfill the requirement to conduct a small-scale research study for her graduate degree.

◆ To complete the required research for her graduate program, Maria must overcome her fears about planning and conducting a study. To do this, she needs to think about research not as a large, formidable task, but as a series of small, manageable steps. Knowing these smaller steps is key to the success of planning and completing her research.

Your situation may be similar to Maria's. At this stage, your concerns may start with the question "What is research?"

A DEFINITION OF RESEARCH AND ITS IMPORTANCE

Research is a process of steps used to collect and analyze information to increase our understanding of a topic or issue. At a general level, research consists of three steps:

1. Pose a question.
2. Collect data to answer the question.
3. Present an answer to the question.

This should be a familiar process. You engage in solving problems every day and you start with a question, collect some information, and then form an answer. Although there are a few more steps in research than these three, this is the overall framework for research. When you examine a published study, or conduct your own study, you will find these three parts as the core elements.

Not all educators have an understanding and appreciation of research. For some, research may seem like something that is important only for faculty members in colleges and universities. Although it is true that college and university faculty members value and conduct research, personnel in other educational settings also read and use research, such as school psychologists, principals, school board members, adult educators, college administrators, and graduate students. Research is important for three reasons.

Research Adds to Our Knowledge

Educators strive for continual improvement. This requires addressing problems or issues and searching for potential solutions. **Adding to knowledge** means that educators undertake research to contribute to existing information about issues. We are all aware of pressing educational issues being debated today, such as the integration of AIDS education into the school curriculum.

Research plays a vital role in addressing these issues. Through research we develop results that help to answer questions, and as we accumulate these results, we gain a deeper understanding of the problems. In this way, researchers are much like bricklayers who build a wall brick by brick, continually adding to the wall and, in the process, creating a stronger structure.

How can research specifically add to the knowledge base and existing literature? A research report might provide a study that has not been conducted and thereby fill a void in existing knowledge. It can also provide additional results to confirm or disconfirm results of prior studies. It can help add to the literature about practices that work or advance better practices that educators might try in their educational setting. It can provide information about people and places that have not been previously studied.

Suppose that you decide to research how elementary schoolchildren learn social skills. If you study how children develop social skills, and past research has not examined this topic, your research study addresses a gap in knowledge. If your study explores how African American children use social skills on their way home from school, your study might replicate past studies but would test results with new participants at a different research site. If your study examines how children use social skills when at play, not on the school grounds, but on the way home from school, the study would contribute to knowledge by expanding our understanding of the topic. If your study examines female children on the way home from school, your study would add female voices seldom heard in the research. If your study has implications for how to teach social skills to students, it has practical value.

Research Improves Practice

Research is also important because it *suggests improvements* for practice. Armed with research results, teachers and other educators become more effective professionals. This effectiveness translates into better learning for kids. For instance, through research, personnel involved in teacher education programs in schools of education know much more about training teachers today than they did 20 years ago. Zeichner (1999) summarized the impact of research on teacher training during this period (see Table 1.1). Teacher trainers today know about the academic capabilities of students, the characteristics of good teacher training programs, the recurring practices in teacher training programs, the need to challenge student beliefs and worldviews, and the tensions teacher educators face within their institutions. But before these research results can impact teacher training or any other aspect of education, individuals in educational settings need to be aware of results from investigations, to know how to read research studies, to locate useful conclusions from them, and to apply the findings to their own unique situations. Educators using research may be teachers in preschool through Grade 12, superintendents in school district offices, school psychologists working with children with behavioral problems, or adult educators who teach English as a second language. Research may help these individuals improve their practices on the job.

Research offers practicing educators *new ideas* to consider as they go about their jobs. From reading research studies, educators can learn about new practices that have been

TABLE 1.1	
Zeichner's (1999) Summary of Major Research Results in Teacher Education	
Research Conducted	**What Researchers Have Learned**
Surveys about students in teacher education programs	• From academic, social class, racial, ethnic, and gender characteristics of both teacher educators and their students, the research has challenged the misconception that students who go into teaching are academically inferior to those who go into other fields. • Despite changing U.S. demographics, teacher education programs admit mostly students who are white, monolingual English speakers.
Specific case studies of individual teacher education programs	• Successful teacher education programs have a coherent vision of good teaching and close links to local schools. • Researchers need to spend time living in teacher education programs to understand them.
Conceptual and historical research on teacher education programs	• Teacher education programs differ in their approaches, such as the importance of disciplinary knowledge versus students learning versus critiquing societal inequalities in schooling practices. • Programs throughout the 20th century have emphasized recurring practices such as performance-based teacher education.
Studies of learning to teach in different settings	• It is difficult to change the tacit beliefs, understandings, and worldviews that students bring to teacher education programs. • The impact of a program on students can be increased through cohort groups, portfolio development, case studies, and narratives in which they examine their beliefs.
Nature and impact of teacher education activities and self-studies	• Despite the sometimes unfavorable structural conditions of teacher educators' work, their voices are being heard. • Teachers, in these self-studies, describe the tensions and contradictions involved in being a teacher educator.

tried in other settings or situations. For example, the adult educator working with immigrants may find that small-group interaction that focuses on using cultural objects from the various homelands may increase the rate at which immigrants learn the English language.

Research also helps practitioners *evaluate approaches* that they hope will work with individuals in educational settings. This process involves sifting through research to determine which results will be most useful. This process is demonstrated in Figure 1.1, which focuses on three steps that a classroom teacher might use (Connelly, Dukacz, & Quinlan, 1980). As shown in Figure 1.1, a teacher first decides what needs to be implemented in the classroom, then examines alternative lines of research, and finally decides which line of research might help accomplish what needs to be done.

For example, a reading teacher decides to incorporate more information about cultural perspectives into the classroom. Research suggests that this may be done with classroom interactions by inviting speakers to the room (line A) or by having the children consider and think (cognitively) about different cultural perspectives by talking with individuals at a local cultural center (line B). It may also be accomplished by having the children inquire into cultural messages embedded within advertisements (line C) or identify the cultural subject matter of speeches of famous Americans (line D). A line of research is then chosen that helps the teacher to accomplish classroom goals. This teacher might be Maria, our teacher conducting research on weapon possession in schools and its potential for violence. Maria hopes to present options for dealing with this issue to her committee and needs to identify useful research lines and consider approaches taken by other schools.

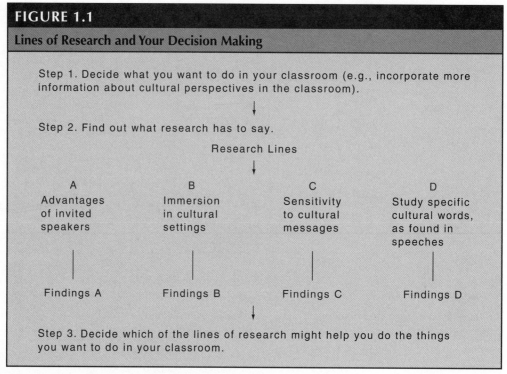

FIGURE 1.1

Lines of Research and Your Decision Making

Step 1. Decide what you want to do in your classroom (e.g., incorporate more information about cultural perspectives in the classroom).

Step 2. Find out what research has to say.

Research Lines

A	B	C	D
Advantages of invited speakers	Immersion in cultural settings	Sensitivity to cultural messages	Study specific cultural words, as found in speeches
Findings A	Findings B	Findings C	Findings D

Step 3. Decide which of the lines of research might help you do the things you want to do in your classroom.

Source: Adapted from Connelly, Dukacz, & Quinian, 1980.

At a broader level, research helps the practicing educator *build connections* with other educators who are trying out similar ideas in different locations. Special education teachers, for example, may establish connections at research conferences where individuals report on topics of mutual interest, such as using small-group strategies for discipline management in classrooms.

Research Informs Policy Debates

In addition to helping educators become better practitioners, research also provides information to policy makers when they research and debate educational topics. Policy makers may range from federal government employees and state workers to local school board members and administrators, and they discuss and take positions on educational issues important to constituencies. For these individuals, research offers results that can help them weigh various perspectives. When policy makers read research on issues, they are informed about current debates and stances taken by other public officials. To be useful, research needs to have clear results, be summarized in a concise fashion, and include data-based evidence. For example, research useful to policy makers might summarize the alternatives on:

◆ Welfare and its effect on children's schooling among lower income families
◆ School choice and the arguments proposed by opponents and proponents

Several Problems with Research Today

Despite the importance of research, we need to realistically evaluate its contributions. Sometimes the results show contradictory or vague findings. An education aide to the

Education and Labor Committee of the U.S. House of Representatives for 27 years expressed this confusion: "I read through every single evaluation . . . looking for a hard sentence—a declarative sentence—something that I could put into the legislation, and there were very few" (Viadero, 1999, p. 36). Not only are policy makers looking for a clear "declarative sentence," many readers of educational research search for some evidence that makes a direct statement about an educational issue. On balance, however, research accumulates slowly, and what may seem contradictory comes together to make sense in time. Based on the information known, for example, it took more than 4 years to identify the most rudimentary factors about how chairpersons help faculty become better researchers (Creswell, Wheeler, Seagren, Egly, & Beyer, 1990).

Another problem with research is the issue of questionable data. The author of a particular research report may not have gathered information from people who are able to understand and address the problem. The number of participants may also be dismally low, which can cause problems in drawing appropriate statistical conclusions. The survey used in a study may contain questions that are ambiguous and vague. At a technical level, the researcher may have chosen an inappropriate statistic for analyzing the data. Just because research is published in a well-known journal does not automatically make it "good" research.

To these issues we could add unclear statements about the intent of the study, the lack of full disclosure of data collection procedures, or inarticulate statements of the research problem that drives the inquiry. Research has limits, and you need to know how to decipher research studies because researchers may not write them as clearly and accurately as you would like. We cannot erase all "poor" research reported in the educational field. We can, however, as responsible inquirers, seek to reconcile different findings and employ sound procedures to collect and analyze data and to provide clear direction for our own research.

THE SIX STEPS IN THE PROCESS OF RESEARCH

When researchers conduct a study, they proceed through a distinct set of steps. Years ago these steps were identified as the "scientific method" of inquiry (Kerlinger, 1972; Leedy & Ormrod, 2001). Using a "scientific method," researchers:

◆ Identify a problem that defines the goal of research
◆ Make a prediction that, if confirmed, resolves the problem
◆ Gather data relevant to this prediction
◆ Analyze and interpret the data to see if it supports the prediction and resolves the question that initiated the research

Applied today, these steps provide the foundation for educational research. Although not all studies include predictions, you engage in these steps whenever you undertake a research study. As shown in Figure 1.2, the **process of research** consists of six steps:

1. Identifying a research problem
2. Reviewing the literature
3. Specifying a purpose for research
4. Collecting data
5. Analyzing and interpreting the data
6. Reporting and evaluating research

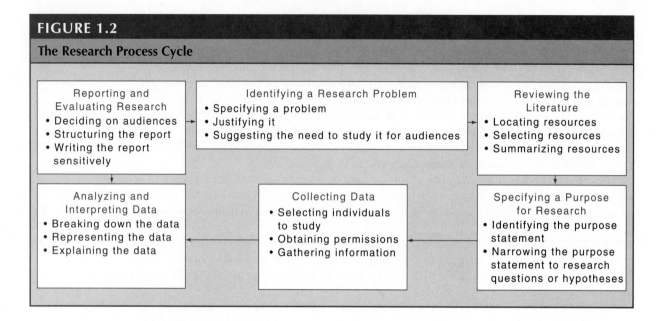

FIGURE 1.2

The Research Process Cycle

Reporting and Evaluating Research
- Deciding on audiences
- Structuring the report
- Writing the report sensitively

Identifying a Research Problem
- Specifying a problem
- Justifying it
- Suggesting the need to study it for audiences

Reviewing the Literature
- Locating resources
- Selecting resources
- Summarizing resources

Analyzing and Interpreting Data
- Breaking down the data
- Representing the data
- Explaining the data

Collecting Data
- Selecting individuals to study
- Obtaining permissions
- Gathering information

Specifying a Purpose for Research
- Identifying the purpose statement
- Narrowing the purpose statement to research questions or hypotheses

Identifying a Research Problem

You begin a research study by identifying a topic to study—typically an issue or problem in education that needs to be resolved. **Identifying a research problem** consists of specifying an issue to study, developing a justification for studying it, and suggesting the importance of the study for select audiences that will read the report. By specifying a "problem," you limit the subject matter and focus attention on a specific aspect of study. Consider the following "problems," each of which merits research:

◆ Teens are not learning how to connect to others in their communities
◆ Teenage smoking will lead to many premature deaths

These needs, issues, or controversies arise out of an educational need expressed by teachers, schools, policy makers, or researchers, and we refer to them as *research problems*. You will state them in introductory sections of a research report and provide a rationale for their importance. In a formal sense, these problems are part of a larger written section called the "statement of the problem," and this section includes the topic, the problem, a justification for the problem, and the importance of studying it for specific audiences such as teachers, administrators, or researchers.

Let's examine Maria's research to see how she will specify her study's research problem.

> Maria plans to study school violence and weapon possession in schools. She starts with a problem: escalating weapon possession among students in high schools. She needs to justify the problem by providing evidence about the importance of this problem and documenting how her study will provide new insight into the problem.

In her research, Marie will need to identify and justify the research problem that she is studying.

Reviewing the Literature

It is important to know who has studied the research problem you plan to examine. You may fear that you will initiate and conduct a study that merely replicates prior research.

However, faculty and advisors often fear that you will plan a study that does not build on existing knowledge and does not add to the accumulation of findings on a topic. Because of these concerns, reviewing the literature is an important step in the research process. **Reviewing the literature** means locating summaries, books, journals, and indexed publications on a topic; selectively choosing which literature to include in your review; and then summarizing the literature in a written report.

The skills required for reviewing the literature develop over time and with practice. You can learn how to locate journal articles and books in an academic library, access computerized databases, choose and evaluate the quality of research on your topic, and summarize it in a review. Library resources can be overwhelming, so having a strategy for searching the literature and writing the review is important. Let's examine Maria's approach to reviewing the literature.

> To inform her committee about the latest literature on school violence and to plan her own research, Maria needs to conduct a literature review. This process will involve becoming familiar with the university library holdings, spending time reviewing resources and making decisions about what literature to use, and writing a formal summary of the literature on school violence. She consults the library catalog at her university and plans to search the computerized databases.

In order to review the literature, Maria will need to become familiar with the literature and visit her university library.

Specifying a Purpose for Research

If your research problem covers a broad topic of concern, you need to focus it so that you can study it. A focused restatement of the problem is the *purpose statement*. This statement conveys the overall objective or intent of your research. As such, it is the most important statement in your research study. It introduces the entire study, signals the procedures you will use to collect data, and indicates the types of results you hope to find.

The **purpose for research** consists of identifying the major intent or objective for a study and narrowing it into specific research questions or hypotheses. The purpose statement contains the major focus of the study, the participants in the study, and the location or site of the inquiry. This purpose statement is then narrowed to research questions or predictions that you plan to answer in your research study. Let's check again with Maria to see how she will write a purpose statement and research questions.

> Maria now needs to write down the purpose of her study and formulate the questions she will ask of the individuals selected for her study. In draft after draft, she sketches this purpose statement, recognizing that it will provide major direction for her study and help keep her focused on the primary aim of her study. From this broad purpose, Maria now needs to narrow her study to specific questions or statements that she would like her participants to answer.

Maria will need to write a good purpose statement and the research questions for her study.

Collecting Data

Evidence helps provide answers to your research questions and hypotheses. To get these answers, you engage in the step of collecting or gathering data. **Collecting data** means identifying and selecting individuals for a study, obtaining their permission to study them, and gathering information by asking people questions or observing their behaviors. Of paramount concern in this process is the need to obtain accurate data from individuals and places. This step will produce a collection of numbers (test scores, frequency of behaviors) or words (responses, opinions, quotes). Once you identify these individuals and places, you write *method* or *procedure sections* into your research studies. These sections offer detailed, technical discussions about the mechanics and administration of data collection. Many decisions, however, go into creating a good data collection procedure. Let's see how Maria will address data collection.

> At this point in the research process, Maria needs to think about where she will conduct her study of school violence and weapon possession, who will participate in the study, how she will obtain permission to study them, what data she will collect, and how she will gather the data. She needs to decide whether she will have students fill out forms or talk to them directly to gather data to answer her research questions. Whichever course she chooses, she will need permission from the high school students and, because the students are minors, from their parents.

Maria will engage in the steps of data collection to gather the data she needs to address her research questions.

Analyzing and Interpreting the Data

During or immediately after data collection, you need to make sense of the information supplied by individuals in the study. Analysis consists of "taking the data apart" to determine individual responses and then "putting it together" to summarize it. **Analyzing and interpreting the data** involves drawing conclusions about it; representing it in tables, figures, and pictures to summarize it; and explaining the conclusions in words to provide answers to your research questions. You report analysis and interpretation in sections of a research report usually titled *Results, Findings,* or *Discussions.* How will Maria analyze and interpret the data in her research?

> If Maria collects information on a written questionnaire from students across the school district, she will need to enter the questionnaire responses into a computer program, choose a statistical procedure, conduct the analyses, report the results in tables, and draw conclusions about (or interpret) whether the data confirm or disconfirm her expected trends or predictions. If she conducts face-to-face interviews, she will collect audiotapes of students talking about weapon possession at school and transcribe these tapes to obtain a written record. With her transcriptions, she will engage in making sense of student comments by selecting specific sentences and paragraphs and by identifying themes of information. From these themes, she will interpret the meaning of student comments in light of her own personal stance and the suggestions found in past studies.

For help in the data analysis and interpretation phase of her study, Maria will need to analyze her data and make an interpretation to answer her research questions.

Reporting and Evaluating Research

After conducting your research, you will develop a written report and distribute it to select audiences (such as fellow teachers, administrators, parents, students) that can use your information. **Reporting research** involves deciding on audiences, structuring the report in a format acceptable to these audiences, and then writing the report in a manner that is sensitive to all readers. The audiences for research will vary from academic researchers who contribute and read journal articles, to faculty advisors and committees that review master's theses and dissertations, to personnel in educational agencies and school districts who look for reports of research on timely topics. Your structure for the research report will vary for each audience, from a formal format for theses and dissertations to a more informal document for in-house school reports. In all types of reports, however, researchers need to be respectful and to avoid language that discriminates on the basis of gender, sexual orientation, race, or ethnic group.

The audience for your report will have its own standards for judging the quality and utility of the research. **Evaluating research** involves assessing the quality of a study using standards advanced by individuals in education. Unfortunately, there are no iron-clad standards for evaluating educational research in the academic research community; in school districts; or in local, state, or federal agencies. Still, we need some means of determining the quality of studies, especially published research or reports presented to practitioner audiences. Let's look at how Maria thinks about organizing her research report.

> Maria thinks about how she will organize her final report to her school committee and to her university graduate committee. Her graduate committee likely has a structure in mind for her graduate research study, and she needs to consult her faculty advisor about the format that students typically use. She should have a general idea about what the major sections of the study will be, but the contents of the specific paragraphs and ideas will take shape as her data analysis and interpretation progress.
>
> Her school report will likely be different from her research report. The school report will be informative and concise, will offer recommendations, and will include minimal discussions about methods and procedures. Whatever the audience and structure for her report, it must be respectful of the audience and be devoid of discriminatory language.

Maria will need to organize and report her research in ways suitable for different audiences.

THE CHARACTERISTICS OF QUANTITATIVE AND QUALITATIVE RESEARCH IN EACH OF THE SIX STEPS

Conducting educational research is more than engaging in the major steps in the process of research. It also includes designing and writing the research in one of the two major tracks: quantitative research or qualitative research. The way that this unfolds is illustrated in the flow of the research process as shown in Figure 1.3.

Based on the nature of the research problem and the questions that will be asked to address the problem (and accompanying review of the literature that establishes the importance of the problem), the researcher chooses either the quantitative or qualitative research track. The problem, the questions, and the literature reviews help to steer the researcher toward either the quantitative or qualitative track. These, in turn, inform the specific research design to be used and the procedures involved in them, such as sampling, data collection instruments or protocols, the procedures, the data analysis, and the final interpretation of results.

What are the characteristics of quantitative and qualitative research tracks at each step in this research process? As each characteristic is discussed, it is helpful to first examine two sample journal articles at the end of this chapter because these articles will be cited with illustrations for each characteristic. Marginal notes have been inserted into the articles to identify the specific passage containing the quantitative and qualitative

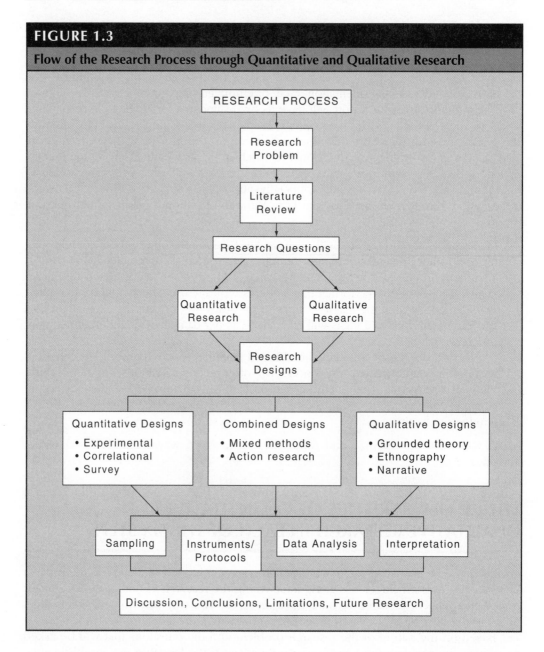

FIGURE 1.3

Flow of the Research Process through Quantitative and Qualitative Research

characteristics. The first article is quantitative research while the second is qualitative research. These two articles were chosen because they are good representatives of both tracks of research and they illustrate within them good procedures of research. They will become a frame of reference for each step in the process of research for the quantitative and qualitative tracks. The two articles are:

◆ *Quantitative:*   Deslandes, R., & Bertrand, R. (2005). Motivation of parent involvement in secondary-level schooling. *Journal of Educational Research, 98*(3), 164–175.
◆ *Qualitative:*   Shelden, D. L., Angell, M. E., Stoner, J. B., & Roseland, B. D. (2010). School principals' influence on trust: Perspectives of mothers of children with disabilities. *Journal of Educational Research, 103,* 159–170.

Quantitative Research Characteristics

In quantitative research the major characteristics are:

◆ Describing a research problem through a description of trends or a need for an explanation of the relationship among variables
◆ Providing a major role for the literature through suggesting the research questions to be asked and justifying the research problem and creating a need for the direction (purpose statement and research questions or hypotheses) of the study
◆ Creating purpose statements, research questions, and hypotheses that are specific, narrow, measurable, and observable
◆ Collecting numeric data from a large number of people using instruments with preset questions and responses
◆ Analyzing trends, comparing groups, or relating variables using statistical analysis, and interpreting results by comparing them with prior predictions and past research
◆ Writing the research report using standard, fixed structures and evaluation criteria, and taking an objective, unbiased approach

In *quantitative research,* the investigator *identifies a research problem* based on trends in the field or on the need to explain why something occurs. Describing a trend means that the research problem can be answered best by a study in which the researcher seeks to establish the overall tendency of responses from individuals and to note how this tendency varies among people. For example, you might seek to learn how voters describe their attitudes toward a bond issue. Results from this study can inform how a large population views an issue and the diversity of these views.

However, some quantitative research problems require that you explain how one variable affects another. *Variables* are an attribute (e.g., attitude toward the school bond issue) or characteristic of individuals (e.g., gender) that researchers study. By explaining a relation among variables, you are interested in determining whether one or more variables might influence another variable. For example, quantitative researchers may seek to know why certain voters voted against the school bond issue. The variables, gender and attitude toward the quality of the schools, may influence individuals' vote on the bond issue.

For example, examine the sample quantitative article—the parent involvement study—at the end of this chapter. The authors in the parent involvement study (Deslandes & Bertrand, 2005) are less interested in describing the level of parent involvement in secondary-level schooling and more interested in examining the relationship between four factors—parents' role construction, self-efficacy, perceptions of teacher invitations, and perceptions of adolescent invitations—as predictors of parent involvement at home and at school. To examine this relation, they collect survey data from 770 parents of children in Grades 7, 8, and 9 (American system equivalents to Canadian schools). Thus, the problem being addressed is that we know little about what factors relate to parental involvement in secondary-level schooling. Assessing whether certain factors predict an outcome is best suited to quantitative research.

In *reviewing the literature* in quantitative research, you will typically see a substantial literature review at the beginning of the study. Thus, the literature plays a major role in two ways: justifying the need for the research problem and suggesting potential purposes and research questions for the study. Justifying the research problem means that you use the literature to document the importance of the issue examined in the study. To accomplish this, you search the literature, locate studies that identify the problem as important to examine, and then cite this literature in the opening sections of a research report.

The literature also creates a need for the study, as expressed specifically in the purpose statement and the research questions or hypotheses. You identify in the literature key variables, relations, and trends, and use these to provide direction for your research questions and hypotheses. A literature review on college students, for example, may show that we know little about the problem of binge drinking. Existing literature, however, may identify the importance of peer groups and styles of interacting among student peer groups. Thus, important research questions might address how peers and their interaction styles influence binge drinking on college campuses. In this way, the literature in a quantitative study both documents the need to study the problem and provides direction for the research questions.

In the quantitative parent involvement study (Deslandes & Bertrand, 2005), the authors cite extensive literature at the beginning of the article. In these paragraphs, the authors rely on the model of the parent involvement process, and they discuss the literature surrounding each of the four major factors that are expected to influence parental involvement. They begin by reviewing the literature about the demographic or personal factors such as family size and educational level, then they proceed to review the literature about the major factors in the study that they predict will influence parental involvement—parents' role construction, parents' self-efficacy, parents' perceptions of teacher invitations, and parents' perceptions of student invitations. In this way, the introduction establishes the research that has been reported in the literature on each of the four factors in the study and foreshadows the research questions that will be addressed in the study.

In *quantitative research questions,* you ask specific, narrow questions to obtain measurable and observable data on variables. The major statements and questions of direction in a study—the purpose statement, the research questions, and the hypotheses—are specific and narrow because you identify only a few variables to study. From a study of these variables, you obtain measures or assessments on an instrument or record scores on a scale from observations. For example, in a study of adolescent career choices, the variable, the role of the school counselor, narrows the study to a specific variable from among many variables that might be studied (e.g., role of parents, personal investment by student). To examine the impact of the school counselor on adolescent career choices, data must be obtained from the students.

In the quantitative parent involvement study (Deslandes & Bertrand, 2005), the authors narrow and select a few factors that they predict will explain parental involvement. They state their purpose of the study and the major research questions. They say that they will examine four factors that influence parental involvement at home and at school, and then they identify the four factors that they predict will influence this involvement. Thus, their research questions are specific to four factors, and later in the method section, they explain how they will measure these factors.

In *quantitative data collection,* you use an instrument to measure the variables in the study. An *instrument* is a tool for measuring, observing, or documenting quantitative data. It contains specific questions and response possibilities that you establish or develop in advance of the study. Examples of instruments are survey questionnaires, standardized tests, and checklists that you might use to observe a student's or teacher's behaviors. You administer this instrument to participants and collect data in the form of numbers. For instance, you might collect responses based on students checking boxes on a form, or from checklists you complete as you watch a student perform a task in the classroom. The intent of this process is to apply the results (called *generalizing the results*) from a small number of people to a large number. The larger the number of individuals studied, the stronger the case for applying the results to a large number of people. For example, on a survey sent to 500 parents in a school district, the researcher seeks information about parents' attitudes toward the educational needs of pregnant teenagers in the schools. The researcher selects an instrument, "Attitudes toward Education of Pregnant

Teenagers," found through a search of library resources. The 500 parents who receive this instrument represent a cross section of people from all socioeconomic levels in the school district. After collecting and analyzing this data, the investigator will draw conclusions about all parents in this school district based on the representative sample studied.

Data collection is also an integral part of the quantitative parent involvement study (Deslandes & Bertrand, 2005). The authors study a large number of parents (i.e., 770) of children in Grades 7, 8, and 9. They survey parents using an adaptation of the instrument, "Sharing the Dream! Parent Questionnaire," as well as items on a questionnaire designed by other researchers to assess parents' perceptions of student invitations. The survey items are translated into French to fit the Quebec context, and they gather quantifiable data (scores) on the survey. They discuss the scales used to collect the data and how they are scored (i.e., from 1 = *disagree very strongly* to 6 = *agree very strongly*).

In *quantitative data analysis,* you analyze the data using mathematical procedures, called *statistics*. These analyses consist of breaking down the data into parts to answer the research questions. Statistical procedures such as comparing groups or relating scores for individuals provide information to address the research questions or hypotheses. You then interpret the results of this analysis in light of initial predictions or prior studies. This interpretation is an explanation as to why the results turned out the way they did, and often you will explain how the results either support or refute the expected predictions in the study.

For example, in the parent involvement study (Deslandes & Bertrand, 2005), the authors collect responses from the parents of secondary-level students who provide scores on the survey instrument. The survey has questions relating to each of the eight factors (or constructs) and the outcome measures as shown in Table 2. To examine the relation of factors to parental involvement, the researchers do not use all of the items on the survey because some were not good measures of the factors. They use a statistical program (i.e., factor analysis) to help them identify the most important questions for each of the four scales composed of items (or factors) in the study. With this reduced set of questions for each of the four factors in the study, they then conduct descriptive analysis (i.e., means and standard deviations as shown in Table 3), and use the statistical program of regression statistical analysis to predict whether the control or personal items or four predictors best explain the variation in scores for parent involvement. From Tables 4 and 5, we see what variables best explain the variation for each grade level (7, 8, 9) and for the two outcome measures of parent involvement at home and parent involvement at school. In short, the authors use statistical analysis consisting of three phases: factor analysis, descriptive analysis, and regression analysis. The ultimate goal was to relate variables to see what predictors (demographics or the four factors) best explain parental involvement. Then, in the implication section of the article, the authors discuss the main results of the study and compare their results with those found in other studies in the literature.

In *reporting and evaluating* quantitative research, the overall format for a study follows a predictable pattern: introduction, review of the literature, methods, results, and discussion. This form creates a standardized structure for quantitative studies. In addition, it also leads to specific criteria that you might use to judge the quality of a quantitative research report. For example, you examine a quantitative study to see if it has an extensive literature review; tests good research questions and hypotheses; uses rigorous, impartial data collection procedures; applies appropriate statistical procedures; and forms interpretations that naturally follow from the data.

In quantitative research, you also use procedures to ensure that your own personal biases and values do not influence the results. You use instruments that have proven value and that have reliable and valid scores from past uses. You design studies to control for all variables that might introduce bias into a study. Finally, you report research without referring to yourself or your personal reaction.

In the quantitative parent involvement study (Deslandes & Bertrand, 2005), the authors subdivide the research into standard sections typically found in quantitative studies. The study begins with an introduction that includes the literature review, purpose statement, and research questions; the methods; the results; the discussion; and, finally, the implications and limitations. The entire study conveys an impersonal, objective tone, and they do not bring either their biases or their personal opinions into the study. They use proven instruments to measure variables, and they employ multiple statistical procedures to build objectivity into the study.

Qualitative Research Characteristics

In qualitative research, we see different major characteristics at each stage of the research process:

- ◆ Exploring a problem and developing a detailed understanding of a central phenomenon
- ◆ Having the literature review play a minor role but justify the problem
- ◆ Stating the purpose and research questions in a general and broad way so as to the participants' experiences
- ◆ Collecting data based on words from a small number of individuals so that the participants' views are obtained
- ◆ Analyzing the data for description and themes using text analysis and interpreting the larger meaning of the findings
- ◆ Writing the report using flexible, emerging structures and evaluative criteria, and including the researchers' subjective reflexivity and bias

Qualitative research is best suited to address a *research problem* in which you do not know the variables and need to explore. The literature might yield little information about the phenomenon of study, and you need to learn more from participants through exploration. For example, the literature may not adequately address the use of sign language in distance education courses. A qualitative research study is needed to explore this phenomenon from the perspective of distance education students. Unquestionably, using sign language in such courses is complex and may not have been examined in the prior literature. A *central phenomenon* is the key concept, idea, or process studied in qualitative research. Thus, the research problem of the difficulty in teaching children who are deaf requires both an exploration (because we need to better know how to teach these children) and an understanding (because of its complexity) of the process of teaching and learning.

The authors in the sample article on mothers' trust in school principals (Shelden et al., 2010) build a case for the importance of trust in the opening passages of the article. They suggest that it is an important issue, and that it has a positive effect on student outcomes. They then narrow the discussion to trust of school leaders and then to parents of children with disabilities, and then finally to the relationships between home and school partnerships for students with disabilities. They point out the problem of possible discrepant viewpoints between parents and schools—a potential problem that needs to be addressed. They then discuss the need for exploring further the critical role of principals in establishing trust in the relationships between families of children with disabilities and education professionals. In sum, they open the article by discussing the important central phenomenon of trust and exploring the potential discrepant viewpoints between mothers of individuals with disabilities and principals. They say that they view trust as the "central phenomenon requiring exploration and understanding" (p. 161).

In qualitative research, the *literature review* plays a less substantial role at the beginning of the study than in quantitative research. In qualitative research, although you may review the literature to justify the need to study the research problem, the literature does not provide major direction for the research questions. The reason for this is that qualitative research relies more on the views of participants in the study and less on the direction identified in the literature by the researcher. Thus, to use the literature to foreshadow or specify the direction for the study is inconsistent with the qualitative approach of learning from participants. For example, one qualitative researcher who studied bullying in the schools cited several studies at the beginning of the research to provide evidence for the problem but did not use the literature to specify the research questions. Instead, this researcher attempted to answer in the research the most general, open question possible, "What is bullying?," and to learn how students constructed their view of this experience.

In the illustrative sample qualitative study by Shelden et al. (2010), the authors begin the article by citing numerous studies from the literature. This literature review is not to identify specific questions that need to be answered; instead, the literature review establishes the meaning and importance of the central phenomenon of trust—why it is important and the relationships needed in schools that involve parents and educational teams, including principals. In this article, there is no separate literature review section, and the literature is used to justify the importance of studying the potential problem of the relationships between parents (i.e., mothers) and the schools (i.e., principals).

In qualitative research, the *purpose statement* and the *research questions* are stated so that you can best learn from participants. You research a single phenomenon of interest and state this phenomenon in a purpose statement. A qualitative study that examines the "professionalism" of teachers, for example, asks high school teachers, "What does it mean to be a professional?" This question focuses on understanding a single idea—being a professional—and the responses to it will yield qualitative data such as quotations.

In the qualitative study of mothers' trust in school principals (Shelden et al., 2010), the authors say that the study emerged from a broader study of the perspectives of mothers of children with disabilities on trust in education personnel. The authors raise this question, "What are the perspectives of mothers of children with disabilities on trust in school principals?" (p. 161). This is a general and broad question that seeks to understand (or "gain insight into," p. 161) the perspectives of the mothers.

In qualitative research, you *collect data* to learn from the participants in the study and develop forms, called *protocols,* for recording data as the study proceeds. These forms pose general questions so that the participants can provide answers to the questions. Often questions on these forms will change and emerge during data collection. Examples of these forms include an *interview protocol,* which consists of four or five questions, or an *observational protocol,* in which the researcher records notes about the behavior of participants. Moreover, you gather text (word) or image (picture) data. Transcribed audio recordings form a database composed of words. Observing participants in their work or family setting, you take notes that will become a qualitative database. When researchers ask young children to write their thoughts in a diary, these diary entries, too, become a text database. With each form of data, you will gather as much information as possible to collect detailed accounts for a final research report.

In our sample qualitative study by Shelden et al. (2010), the authors recruited a sample of mothers of school-age children with disabilities, and conducted interviews with 16 of these parents. In the journal article, the authors provide the eight open-ended questions that they asked. These interviews enabled them to probe for further information, elaboration, and clarification of responses, while maintaining a "feeling of openness" to the participants' responses.

In qualitative research typically you gather a text database, so the *data analysis* of text consists of dividing it into groups of sentences, called *text segments,* and determining the meaning of each group of sentences. Rather than using statistics, you analyze words or pictures to describe the central phenomenon under study. The result may be a description of individual people or places. In some qualitative studies, the entire report is mostly a long description of several individuals. The result may also include themes or broad categories that represent your findings. In qualitative studies in which you both describe individuals and identify themes, a rich, complex picture emerges. From this complex picture, you make an interpretation of the meaning of the data by reflecting on how the findings relate to existing research; by stating a personal reflection about the significance of the lessons learned during the study; or by drawing out larger, more abstract meanings.

In the study of mothers' perspectives of trust in school principals (Shelden et al., 2010), we can see these data analysis steps. The authors analyzed text data based on audiotaped and transcribed verbatim passages as mentioned in the section on interviews. In their section on data analysis, they talk about the "line-by-line coding" of their data in which they used the words of the participants to form categories. They provide in Table 1 a detailed descriptive portrait of participants in their study, noting the ethnicity, type of disability, grade level, and other personal information. In the results section we find the various themes that they identified, such as principal attributes and principal actions. In the conclusion section, they review all of these findings, thereby creating a complex picture of the relationship between mothers and school leaders. Although their personal reflections are minimal in this study, the authors discuss their challenges in recruiting participants to the study and how they sought to protect the identity of the participants.

In *reporting* qualitative research you employ a wide range of formats to report your studies. Although the overall general form follows the standard steps in the process of research, the sequence of these "parts" of research tends to vary from one qualitative report to another. A study may begin with a long, personal narrative told in story form or with a more objective, scientific report that resembles quantitative research. With such variability, it is not surprising that the standards for evaluating qualitative research also are flexible. Good qualitative reports, however, need to be realistic and persuasive to convince the reader that the study is an accurate and credible account. Qualitative reports typically contain extensive data collection to convey the complexity of the phenomenon or process. The data analysis reflects description and themes as well as the interrelation of themes. In addition, you discuss your role or position in a research study, called *being reflexive.* This means that you reflect on your own biases, values, and assumptions and actively write them into the research. This may also involve discussing personal experiences and identifying how you collaborated with participants during phases of the project. You may also discuss how your experiences and cultural backgrounds (e.g., Asian American perspectives) affect the interpretations and conclusions drawn in the study.

In the sample study of mothers' trust in school principals (Shelden et al., 2010), the authors used more of a scientific structure than a literary structure for writing their article. This may have been done because of the requirements of the journal to address certain aspects (e.g., methods, results, discussion). However, the article did depart from the traditional structure by not having a separate literature review section; instead, the literature review was incorporated into the introduction to establish the importance of the central phenomenon—trust—and to develop a need for the study. The authors did employ the personal pronoun "we" in referring to themselves in the study, a subjective orientation typically associated with qualitative, literary writing. As mentioned earlier, references to themselves, and especially how their backgrounds shaped their interpretation, were absent.

Similarities and Differences between Quantitative and Qualitative Research

At this point you may be asking how quantitative research and qualitative research are similar and different. In terms of similarity, both forms of research follow the six steps in the process of research. There are minor differences, as well, in the introduction to a study—the research problem section—in that both sections need to establish the importance of the problem. In quantitative research the research problem section is used to direct the types of questions or hypotheses asked in the study, whereas in qualitative research the research problem discussion is typically used to establish the importance of the central idea. These differences are apparent in the comparison of the introduction to the quantitative parent involvement study (Deslandes & Bertrand, 2005) and the qualitative mothers' trust in school principals study (Shelden et al., 2010).

Another similarity exists in the data collection procedures. Both quantitative and qualitative data collection may employ similar approaches, such as interviews or observations. However, quantitative approaches use more closed-ended approaches in which the researcher identifies set response categories (e.g., strongly agree, strongly disagree, and so forth), whereas qualitative approaches use more open-ended approaches in which the inquirer asks general questions of participants, and the participants shape the response possibilities (e.g., in an interview with a teacher, a qualitative researcher might ask: What does professional development mean to you?).

There are distinct differences that go beyond the forms of gathering data. In data analysis, the procedures are quite different. In quantitative research, the investigator relies on statistical analysis (mathematical analysis) of the data, which is typically in numeric form. In qualitative research, statistics are not used to analyze the data; instead, the inquirer analyzes words (e.g., transcriptions from interviews) or images (e.g., photographs). Rather than relying on statistical procedures, the qualitative researcher analyzes the words to group them into larger meanings of understanding, such as codes, categories, or themes. The reporting formats are also typically different, with the quantitative structure following the typical introduction, literature review, methods, results, and conclusion sections. In qualitative research, some of these sections may be missing (e.g., the literature review in the Shelden et al., 2010 study), and the format may be more of a literary opening with a personal vignette or passage, an unfolding story, the use of extensive quotes from participants, and personal reflections from the researcher.

It should also be mentioned that rather than viewing quantitative and qualitative as two end points in a dichotomy, but rather as different points on a continuum. Studies may contain some elements of the characteristics of quantitative research and some elements of qualitative research. However, studies do *tend* to lean toward one approach or the other, and knowing the characteristics associated with each type of research enables a researcher to assess whether a particular study favors either quantitative or qualitative research.

How do you choose whether to use a quantitative or a qualitative approach? Three factors are important. First, match your approach to your research problem. Remember that the problems best suited for quantitative research are those in which trends or explanations need to be made. For qualitative research, the problems need to be explored to obtain a deep understanding. Second, your approach needs to fit the audience(s) for the research report. Educators write for several audiences, such as policy makers, faculty and graduate committees, editors and review boards, evaluators of grant proposals, and individuals in schools or educational settings. It is important that the audience(s) be familiar with the approach used in a study. Third, relate your approach to your personal experience and training. A quantitative researcher typically has taken some courses or training in measurement, statistics, and quantitative data collection, such as experiments, correlational designs, or survey techniques. Qualitative researchers need experience in field studies in which they practice gathering information in a setting and learning the skills of observing or interviewing individuals. Coursework or experience in analyzing text data is helpful, as well as in research designs such as grounded theory, ethnography, or narrative research. Some individuals have experience and training in approaches to research that combine both quantitative and qualitative methods, such as mixed methods research or action research.

Research Designs Associated with Quantitative and Qualitative Research

It is not enough to know the steps in the process of research, and that quantitative and qualitative procedures differ at each step. This text will also go into detailed procedures involved in quantitative, qualitative, and combined research. **Research designs** are the specific procedures involved in the research process: data collection, data analysis, and report writing. Figure 1.4 illustrates how the steps in the research process relate to quantitative and qualitative research and advances eight different research designs, used by educational researchers, discussed in this book.

Experimental Designs

Some quantitative researchers seek to test whether an educational practice or idea makes a difference for individuals. Experimental research procedures are ideally suited for

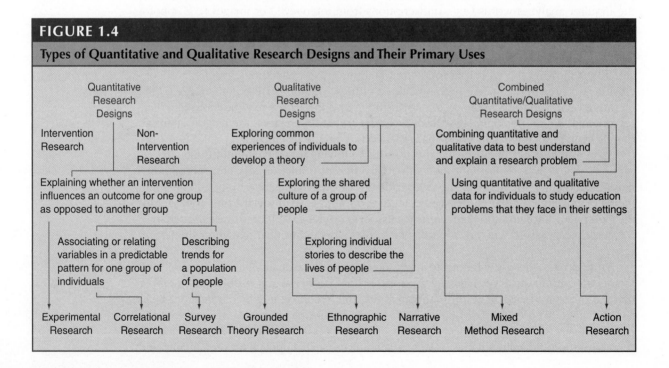

FIGURE 1.4

Types of Quantitative and Qualitative Research Designs and Their Primary Uses

this study. *Experimental designs* (also called intervention studies or group comparison studies) are procedures in quantitative research in which the investigator determines whether an activity or materials make a difference in results for participants. You assess this impact by giving one group one set of activities (called an *intervention*) and withholding the set from another group.

Correlational Designs

In some studies, you may be unable to provide an intervention or to assign individuals to groups. Moreover, you focus more on examining the association or relation of one or more variables than in testing the impact of activities or materials. *Correlational designs* are procedures in quantitative research in which investigators measure the degree of association (or relation) between two or more variables using the statistical procedure of correlational analysis. This degree of association, expressed as a number, indicates whether the two variables are related or whether one can predict another. To accomplish this, you study a single group of individuals rather than two or more groups as in an experiment.

Survey Designs

In another form of quantitative research, you may not want to test an activity or materials or may not be interested in the association among variables. Instead, you seek to describe trends in a large population of individuals. In this case, a survey is a good procedure to use. *Survey designs* are procedures in quantitative research in which you administer a survey or questionnaire to a small group of people (called the *sample*) to identify trends in attitudes, opinions, behaviors, or characteristics of a large group of people (called the *population*).

Grounded Theory Designs

Instead of studying a single group, you might examine a number of individuals who have all experienced an action, interaction, or process. *Grounded theory designs* are systematic, qualitative procedures that researchers use to generate a general explanation (grounded in the views of participants, called a *grounded theory*) that explains a process, action, or interaction among people. The procedures for developing this theory include primarily collecting interview data, developing and relating categories (or themes) of information, and composing a figure or visual model that portrays the general explanation. In this way, the explanation is "grounded" in the data from participants. From this explanation, you construct predictive statements about the experiences of individuals.

Ethnographic Designs

You may be interested in studying one group of individuals, in examining them in the setting where they live and work, and in developing a portrait of how they interact. An ethnographic study is well suited for this purpose. *Ethnographic designs* are qualitative procedures for describing, analyzing, and interpreting a cultural group's shared patterns of behavior, beliefs, and language that develop over time. In ethnography, the researcher provides a detailed picture of the culture-sharing group, drawing on various sources of information. The ethnographer also describes the group within its setting, explores themes or issues that develop over time as the group interacts, and details a portrait of the group.

Narrative Research Designs

You may not be interested in describing and interpreting group behavior or ideas, or in developing an explanation grounded in the experiences of many individuals. Instead, you wish to tell the stories of one or two individuals. *Narrative research designs* are qualitative procedures in which researchers describe the lives of individuals, collect and tell stories about these individuals' lives, and write narratives about their experiences. In education, these stories often relate to school classroom experiences or activities in schools.

Mixed Methods Designs

You decide to collect both quantitative data (i.e., quantifiable data) and qualitative data (i.e., text or images). The core argument for a mixed methods design is that the combination of both forms of data provides a better understanding of a research problem than either quantitative or qualitative data by itself. *Mixed methods designs* are procedures for collecting, analyzing, and mixing both quantitative and qualitative data in a single study or in a multiphase series of studies. In this process, you need to decide on the emphasis you will give to each form of data (priority), which form of data you will collect first (concurrent or sequential), how you will "mix" the data (integrating or connecting), and whether you will use theory to guide the study (e.g., advocacy or social science theory).

Action Research Designs

Like mixed methods research, action research designs often utilize both quantitative and qualitative data, but they focus more on procedures useful in addressing practical problems in schools and the classrooms. *Action research designs* are systematic procedures used by teachers (or other individuals in an educational setting) to gather quantitative and qualitative data to address improvements in their educational setting, their teaching, and the learning of their students. In some action research designs, you seek to address and solve local, practical problems, such as a classroom-discipline issue for a teacher. In other studies, your objective might be to empower, transform, and emancipate individuals in educational settings.

IMPORTANT ETHICAL ISSUES IN CONDUCTING RESEARCH

Respect for audiences and the use of nondiscriminatory language are ethical issues that Maria must observe. Like Maria, all educational researchers need to be aware of and anticipate ethical issues in their research. Such a need stems from the research horrors of treatment of individuals in Nazi Germany and the inappropriate Tuskegee syphilis studies (Mark & Gamble, 2009). From these and other violations of treatment of participants developed federal guidelines for conducting research as announced in the 1978 National Commission for the Protection of Human Subjects on Biomedical and Behavioral Research and its *Belmont Report* (Department of Health, Education, and Welfare, 1978). The three basic principles of this *Report* involve the beneficence of treatment of participants (maximizing good outcomes and minimizing risk), respect for participants (protecting autonomy and ensuring well-informed, voluntary participation), and justice (a fair distribution of risk and benefits).

Institutional Review Boards

Campus offices developed to monitor adherence to these three principles, and offices of institutional review boards emerged. Federal funds could be withheld from campuses if research conducted on those campuses did not protect the treatment of participants. Accordingly, on campuses that receive federal funds, educational researchers need to learn about the procedures involved in applying for approval from their institutional review board offices, and follow guidelines in developing applications for approval and in designing consent forms for participants to complete that guarantee their protection.

Professional Associations

Ethical standards are also available from professional associations. Examples of professional associations that offer helpful guidelines include the American Educational Research Association (AERA; *Ethical Standards of the American Educational Research Association,* Strike et al., 2002), the American Psychological Association (APA; *Ethical Principles of Psychologists and Code of Conduct,* 2003), the American Anthropological Association (AAA; *Code of Ethics,* 1998), and the Joint Committee on Standards for Educational Evaluation (*Program Evaluation Standards,* adopted November 21, 1980; amended through September 20, 1995).

According to these guidelines, individuals who participate in a study have certain rights. Before participating in research, individuals need to know the purpose and aims of the study, how the results will be used, and the likely social consequences the study will have on their lives. They also have the right to refuse to participate in a study and to withdraw at any time. When they participate and provide information, their anonymity is protected and guaranteed by the researcher. Individuals are not to be offered excessive financial inducements to participate in a project. Participants also have the right to gain something from a study. Researchers need to actively look for ways to "give back" (or reciprocate) to participants in a study because the participants have freely provided their time. For example, in one study involving individuals with HIV, the author shared book royalties with the participants in the study. In another study, a researcher volunteered to help supervise lunchroom activities in exchange for information from students in the school.

Ethical Practices throughout the Research Process

In all steps of the research process, you need to engage in ethical practices. Practicing ethics is a complex matter that involves much more than merely following a set of static guidelines such as those from professional associations or conforming to guidelines from campus institutional review boards. Ethics has become a more pervasive idea stretching from the origins of a research study to its final completion and distribution. Ethics should be a primary consideration rather than an afterthought, and it should be at the forefront of the researcher's agenda (Hesse-Bieber & Leavy, 2006). Of all of the steps in the research process, it does tend to relate closely to the data collection and reporting and distribution of reports than any of the other phase of research. A few of some of these issues will be mentioned here.

Some Ethical Issues in Data Collection

It is important to respect the site in which the research takes place. This respect should be shown by gaining permission before entering a site, by disturbing the site as little as possible during a study, and by viewing oneself as a "guest" at the place of study. Lincoln Public Schools (n.d.) in Lincoln, Nebraska, provides illustrative guidelines to follow for conducting research with minimal disruption to a school district. Their guidelines list several reasons why a project may not be approved. Disapproved projects are those that take away considerable amounts of instructional time; require large amounts of teacher, administrator, or office time (the district may ask to be reimbursed for the costs of compiling information, staff time, or materials); interfere with district data collection or the work of current research projects; are planned for the first or last month of the school year; or are received too late in the year to be adequately reviewed.

Another strategy for respecting the research site with minimal disruption is to gain access through gatekeepers (or officials). Researchers may need to consult with different gatekeepers at multiple levels in an organization. For example, in a study in one high school classroom, the researcher sought permission from several individuals, including the school board responsible for ensuring that the rights of human participants were protected, the research official in the school district, the principal of the school, the teacher in a government class, and the actual students who participated in the study and their parents.

Other ethical issues arise in data collection and are associated with specific types of research designs. You need to not purposefully deprive some participants of helpful treatments, only publish positive results, or fail to disclose the purpose of the study to participants. It is helpful to involve stakeholders in assessing risk to participants, and to not pressure participants into signing consent forms (S. Levy, personal communication, May 3, 2010), to not engage in practices that create power imbalances, and to respect norms of indigeneous cultures (Lincoln, 2009).

Some Ethical Issues in Data Reporting

You need to show respect to audiences who read and use information from studies. Data should be reported honestly, without changing or altering the findings to satisfy certain predictions or interest groups. It may, however, be appropriate for the primary investigator to provide those at the research site with a preliminary copy of any publications. In addition, studies completed by others should not be plagiarized, and credit should be given for material quoted from other studies. This credit involves citing the authors and the date of the publication, and listing the publication in the reference section of the study. In addition, research should be free of jargon and be understandable to those being studied. As ethical educators, we need to make every effort to communicate the practical significance of our research to the community of researchers and practitioners so inquiry will be encouraged and used. Educational researchers have an ethical mandate to produce research that is of high quality, and to report their results that convey basic assumptions they are making. This also means that research should not sit unpublished and that researchers should openly share their findings (Brown & Hedges, 2009). Results should be published and disseminated, even though they may present findings contrary to accepted standards (S. Levy, personal communication, May 3, 2010).

SKILLS NEEDED TO DESIGN AND CONDUCT RESEARCH

As a new researcher, you may wonder whether you have the ability to read, evaluate, and actually conduct research. Knowing the process of research, you may say, does not guarantee an adequate research study. Certainly Maria, who is new to research, has these concerns.

Let me set your mind at ease. You have already learned valuable research skills through your life experiences. These skills include solving puzzles, employing a long attention span, using a library, and, of course, writing out your thoughts.

Solving Puzzles

Researchers look at problems as puzzles to solve. The steps in the research process are viewed as a series of puzzle pieces that the inquirer assembles. You already have skills in solving puzzles. You fit together the debits and credits to balance your checkbook. As a parent (or prospective parent), you engage in multiple roles during the day that require juggling of different tasks. These are puzzles that we work out by breaking them down into manageable parts ("What will be the demands on my time today?"), setting obtainable objectives ("I will have a busy day at work, so I will focus on my job today"), and possibly writing them down ("I need to make a list of what I must accomplish today"). As you examine research studies or engage in the process of inquiry, assembling these parts of the puzzle—such as first working on a research problem and then specifying a purpose for a study—will require that all of the pieces fit together, as with the many puzzles that we solve in daily living.

Lengthening Your Attention Span

Although we generally make time to complete the tasks we love, our attention span certainly varies from task to task. The process of research involves six steps that may span a period of 6 months or more. To read through a journal article and identify each of these steps, for example, requires patience as well as knowledge about what to look for. We all bring attention spans of varying lengths to the process of research. But if we consider the tasks we love and the amount of time we devote to them, we can see that we have already developed an attention span long enough to spend considerable time at research.

Learning to Use Library Resources

The step in the research process that requires you to review the literature means spending time in an academic library. For most of us, going to the library probably began in grade school with trips to the school library. Engaging in research requires spending time with library resources, a process that is facilitated by home computers and Internet connections to library catalogs. But the process of research requires that you use skills in locating studies, summarizing them, and writing a review of the literature. These skills are developed during research, if you do not already have them. They develop from our comfort level with a library and with experiences that began early in our schooling and continue today.

Writing, Editing, and More Writing

Researchers cannot escape the ever-present aspect of writing as a key facet of research. As writers, we work through numerous drafts, receive reactions from others, and develop new drafts. Research involves writing the study for an audience. Do you enjoy writing and communicating your thoughts? Do you like to write in a journal or a diary? Do you get satisfaction from completing projects? You have probably written several essays in college already or worked on a research report with other students or a faculty member. In short, you have experience in writing. As you know, writing is more than recording ideas on paper or in a computer file. It is also organizing ideas, preparing interview questions, jotting down notes during an observation, and writing for permission to use someone else's questions or articles. Writing exists in all phases of the creative process of planning and in conducting research.

KEY IDEAS IN THE CHAPTER

The Definition and Importance of Educational Research

Research involves asking a question, collecting data, and analyzing data to determine the answer to the question. It helps educators understand problems or issues through the accumulation of knowledge. It can assist educators in improving practice, and it focuses attention on important policy issues being discussed and debated by decision makers. Also, engaging in research provides valuable conceptual writing and presenting skills for students.

The Six Steps in the Process of Research

Six steps are followed when conducting a research study. The study begins with identifying a research problem or issue of study. It then consists of reviewing the literature; advancing direction through research questions and statements; and collecting, analyzing, and interpreting the data. This process culminates in a research report presented, evaluated, and potentially used by the educational community.

The Characteristics of Quantitative and Qualitative Research

In quantitative research the major characteristics are: describing a research problem through a description of trends or a need for an explanation of the relationship among variables; providing a major role for the literature through suggesting the research questions to be asked and justifying the research problem and creating a need for the direction (purpose statement and research questions or hypotheses) of the study; creating purpose statements, research questions, and hypotheses that are specific, narrow, measurable, and observable; collecting numeric data from a large number of people using instruments with preset questions and responses; analyzing trends, comparing groups, or relating variables using statistical analysis, and interpreting results by comparing them with prior predictions and past research; and writing the research report using standard, fixed structures and evaluation criteria, and taking an objective, unbiased approach.

In qualitative research, we see different major characteristics at each stage of the research process: exploring a problem and developing a detailed understanding of a central phenomenon; having the literature review play a minor role but justify the problem; stating the purpose and research questions in a general and broad way so as to the participants' experiences; collecting data based on words from a small number of individuals so that the participants' views are obtained; analyzing the data for description and themes using text analysis and interpreting the larger meaning of the findings; writing the report using flexible, emerging structures and evaluative criteria, and including the researchers' subjective reflexivity and bias.

Although quantitative and qualitative characteristics need to be seen as points on a continuum rather than opposites, the choice of research between the two is based on matching the approach to a research problem, fitting the approach to your audience, and relating the approach to your experiences.

The Types of Research Designs Associated with Quantitative and Qualitative Research

Researchers tend to employ specific procedures for data collection, analysis, and report writing within the quantitative and qualitative approaches. This text emphasizes eight research designs: experimental, correlational, survey, grounded theory, ethnographic, narrative, mixed methods, and action research designs.

The Important Ethical Issues

A need for attention to ethical issues arose out of the inhumane treatment of participants in past years. As a result, the federal government issued legislation and reports governing good ethical practices. These guidelines have been supplemented by professional organizational reports. As a result, educational researchers need to anticipate ethical issues throughout the research process, but they are especially important during data collection and in writing and disseminating reports.

The Skills Needed to Design and Conduct Research

Research often mirrors the practices found in everyday life, such as solving puzzles, focusing attention on topics, and practicing good writing and editing. It also involves learning how to use the academic library and to locate useful literature for a study.

USEFUL INFORMATION FOR PRODUCERS OF RESEARCH

- ◆ As you plan and conduct a study, keep in mind that research needs to be valuable to educators. Include comments in your study that convey the value to specific educational audiences.
- ◆ Use the general framework of the six steps for thinking about your plans and the conduct of research. These six steps make research manageable, help ensure that you conduct thorough inquiries, and provide a useful strategy for the design and writing of the research.
- ◆ As you plan and conduct a study, discuss specifically the characteristics of the quantitative and qualitative approach you are using.
- ◆ Recognize that research is not either all quantitative or all qualitative, but tends toward one or the other (on a continuum).
- ◆ Be ethical in conducting research. Respect the rights of participants, research sites, and individuals who will be readers of your study.
- ◆ Consider the skills that you need to develop to be a researcher. You may already have developed the skills of reading and writing, using library resources, solving puzzles, and focusing in on a topic of interest.

USEFUL INFORMATION FOR CONSUMERS OF RESEARCH

- ◆ As you examine a study, recognize that authors emphasize different reasons for undertaking their study. Look for suggestions by the author for practical applications of a study.
- ◆ Recognize that researchers proceed through a process of research and then construct sections of a study that reflect different steps in this process. For the research problem, examine the "introduction" to a study; for the literature review, explore the "literature review" section. For the data collection discussion, visit the "method" or "procedure" section, and for the data analysis and interpretation, see the "results" or "findings" as well as the "discussion" sections.

> ◆ Expect that a quantitative study and a qualitative study will not look the same, because they differ in many of the steps of the research process. At the same time, they adhere to the same general steps of the overall research process.
> ◆ Look for statements in the study where the researcher discusses ethical issues that arose in the study and how they were addressed.

UNDERSTANDING CONCEPTS AND EVALUATING RESEARCH STUDIES

You can test your knowledge of the content of this chapter by answering the following questions that relate to the parent involvement study and the mothers' trust in school principals study. Answers to the questions are found in appendix A so that you can assess your progress.

1. What preconceptions do you bring to the study of research? List three advantages and three disadvantages of conducting research.
2. Assume that you are Maria in the introductory scenario in this chapter. List three steps that you might take to begin your research study.
3. How would the parent involvement study (Deslandes & Bertrand, 2005) be different if you presented it as a *qualitative* study? How would the mothers' trust in school principals study (Shelden et al., 2010) be different if you presented it as a *quantitative* study?

Go to the Topic "Introduction to Educational Research" in the MyEducationLab (**www.myeducationlab.com**) for your course, where you can:

- ◆ Find learning outcomes for "Introduction to Educational Research."
- ◆ Complete Assignments and Activities that can help you more deeply understand the chapter content.
- ◆ Apply and practice your understanding of the core skills identified in the chapter with the Building Research Skills exercises.
- ◆ Check your comprehension of the content covered in the chapter by going to the Study Plan. Here you will be able to take a pretest, receive feedback on your answers, and then access Review, Practice, and Enrichment activities to enhance your understanding. You can then complete a final posttest.

Sample Quantitative Study

Motivation of Parent Involvement in Secondary-Level Schooling

Rollande Deslandes
Université du Québec à Trois-Rivières, Canada
Richard Bertrand
Université Laval, Quebec, Canada

Quantitative Characteristics in Marginal Annotations

Abstract

Inspired by K. V. Hoover-Dempsey and H. M. Sandler's (1995, 1997) model of the parent involvement process, the authors examined 4 psychological constructs of parent involvement: (a) relative strength of parents' role construction, (b) parents' self-efficacy for helping adolescents succeed in school, (c) parents' perceptions of teacher invitations to become involved, and (d) parents' perceptions of students' invitations to become involved. The authors obtained survey responses from 770 parents of adolescents in 5 Quebec secondary schools—354 parents of 7th graders, 231 parents of 8th graders, and 185 parents of 9th graders. Results emphasize that it is important that researchers distinguish parent involvement at home and at school when examining the predictive power of the 4 psychological constructs. Findings also provide evidence of grade-level differences in the predictive models of parent involvement at home and at school. Parents' perceptions of students' invitations was the most powerful predictor of parent involvement at home models across the 3 grade levels. Parents' role construction made important contributions to the prediction of their involvement at Grades 7 and 9; parents' perceptions of teacher invitations were associated with parent involvement at school across the 3 grade levels. Whether at home or at school, parents became involved if they perceived that teachers and students expected or desired their involvement.
Key words: parent involvement, parent motivation, secondary schools

In past decades, a wealth of studies showed that parent involvement is essential in children's educational process and outcomes (Henderson & Mapp, 2002). Parent involvement refers to parents' roles in educating their children at home and in school (Christenson & Sheridan, 2001). Involvement can take different forms, including discussions about school, help with homework, or volunteering at school. Parent involvement appears to have lasting benefits even through high school. When parents are involved, secondary students tend to earn higher grades (Deslandes, Royer, Turcotte, & Bertrand, 1997; Dornbusch & Ritter, 1988; Lee, 1994; Steinberg, Lamborn, Dornbusch, & Darling, 1992), show higher aspirations (Trusty, 1996), and have fewer disciplinary problems (Deslandes & Royer, 1997; Eccles, Early, Frasier, Belansky, & McCarthy, 1997).   (01)

Even though the benefits associated with parent involvement at the secondary level seem to be well understood, educators still know little about what factors lead parents to decide to become involved in their adolescents' schooling. In the present study, we explored how the psychological constructs, as defined in Hoover-Dempsey and Sandler's model (1995, 1997), influence the parent involvement process at the secondary level, and more precisely, at the first three grade levels in Quebec secondary schools. We addressed the following research question: What are the relative contributions of parents' (a) role construction, (b) self-efficacy, (c) perception of teacher invitations, and (d) perception of adolescent invitations to predict parent involvement at home and at school in Grades 7, 8, and 9? (Because the invitation for parents to become involved is presented by teachers and students, we considered, as did Walker, Hoover-Dempsey, Reed, and Jones [2000], teacher invitations and student invitations as two difference constructs, thus leading to four psychological constructs related to parent involvement.) Previous research on the evolution of adolescents' autonomy and parent involvement in secondary schools led us to expect some differences across grade levels in the predictive models of parent involvement at home and at school (Deslandes, 2003).   (02)

Address correspondence to Rollande Deslandes, Education Department, Université du Québec à Trois-Rivières, C. P. 500, Trois-Rivières, Québec, Canada, G9A 5H7. (E-mail: Rollande_Deslandes@uqtr.ca)

Influences on Parent Involvement

(03)

The literature
plays a major role

Jordan, Orozco, and Averett (2001) identified factors that influence levels and aspects of parent involvement. Family (e.g., education level, family structure, family size, parent gender, work outside the home) and child characteristics (e.g., age, gender, grade level, academic performance) are of particular relevance in this study. Research has shown that undereducated parents and single parents are less involved in certain types of involvement activities. For instance, Deslandes, Potvin, and Leclerc (1999) found that adolescents from traditional families and well-educated parents report more affective support (parent encouragement and praise, help with homework, frequent discussions about school, and attendance at school performances or sports events) than do adolescents from nontraditional families and less educated parents. Astone and McLanahan (1991) also indicated that adolescents who live with single parents or stepparents report that their homework is monitored less than the homework of adolescents from traditional families. Deslandes and Cloutier (2000) reported that mothers are more involved with homework than are fathers. Dauber and Epstein (1989) argued that well-educated parents and those who do not work outside the home (Eccles & Harold, 1996) are more likely to be involved at school. Eccles and Harold concluded that parents with fewer children provide more help with homework than do parents with more children.

(04)   Child characteristics also may influence parent involvement. For example, Deslandes and Potvin (1999) observed that mothers of adolescent boys communicated with teachers more often than did mothers of adolescent girls. Parents tend to become more involved when their children experience their first learning or behavior difficulties. According to Eccles and Harold (1996), parents of high-achieving children tend to participate more in school activities than do parents of low-achieving children. Epstein (2001) showed that parent involvement decreases dramatically as children move into secondary school. When Deslandes (2003) compared parent involvement in Grades 8, 9, and 10, he found a steady decline in parent involvement, but a steady increase in adolescent autonomy.

Parents' Role Construction

(05)   Parents need to understand their roles because that understanding identifies the activities that they believe are necessary and part of their responsibilities as parents. In other words, parents are more likely to become involved if they view their participation as a requirement of parenting. Hoover-Dempsey, Jones, and Reed (1999) hypothesized three components of role construction, depending on whether parents focused responsibility for children's education on themselves as parents, on the school, or on parent–school partnerships.

Parents' Self-efficacy for Helping Children Succeed in School

(06)   Parent self-efficacy is rooted in Bandura's (1997) self-efficacy theory and suggests that parents are more likely to be involved if they believe that they have the skills and knowledge to help their children. In other words, parents become involved if they believe that their actions will improve learning and academic performance (Hoover-Dempsey, Bassler, & Brissie, 1992; Stevenson, Chen, & Uttal, 1990). Prior research has indicated that parents believe that they will have more influence over their children's schooling when their children are in the elementary grades than they will when their children are in the upper grades (Freedman-Doan, Arbreton, Harold, & Eccles, 1993). In general, the stronger their self-efficacy, the more persistence parents exhibit in their involvement (Hoover-Dempsey et al., 2001).

Parents' Perceptions of Teacher Invitations

(07)   Research also has shown that teachers' demands and opportunities for involvement, coupled with an inviting school climate, are related significantly to level of parent involvement (Comer & Haynes, 1991; Dauber & Epstein, 1993; Eccles & Harrold, 1996; Epstein, 1986). Parents tend to be more involved if they perceive that teachers and students both want and expect their involvement (Hoover-Dempsey et al., 2001).

Parents' Perceptions of Student Invitations

(08)   Parents will become involved if they perceive that their young children or adolescents want them to do so. Students' invitations are either implicit or explicit and emerge as a function of their age,

their press for independence, and their performance level (Hoover-Dempsey et al., 2001; Walker et al., 2000). For instance, when young children or adolescents ask for help with homework, they are expressing explicit invitations. On the other hand, if they express the desire to work alone, parents might respond by reducing their involvement. If children bring a poor report card home, they might be conveying implicit invitations. Seeking parental help does not necessarily mean that young children or adolescents are having academic difficulties. For example, Zimmerman and Martinez-Pons (1986) found that high-achieving students wanted more parental assistance than did low-achieving students.

Reflecting on three of the four psychological constructs to involvement cited in the preceding paragraphs (i.e., parents' role construction, self-efficacy, and perceptions of teacher invitations), Reed, Jones, Walker, and Hoover-Dempsey (2000) found that parents' role construction, self-efficacy for helping the child succeed in school, and perceptions of teacher invitations represent motivators of parents' involvement in their children's education at the elementary level. Role construction was the first predictor of parent involvement; perception of teachers' invitations was the second predictor. Parent self-efficacy seemed less influential. The authors suggested that role construction may be a mediator of efficacy's influence on involvement (Reed et al.).

(09)

The literature justifies the research problem and provides direction for the study

In a study that compared 5th, 8th, and 11th graders' self-reported invitations to parent involvement in homework, Walker and Hoover-Dempsey (2001) revealed decreased levels of parent homework involvement across adolescence. Across the three age groups, students' invitations for parents' homework involvement was steady, but the authors found that parents of younger students tend to help without being asked.

(10)

Investigations are needed to better understand what motivates parents to become involved in their young children's education and, more particularly, in their adolescents' educational process. Researchers need to examine differences in parents' motivation to become involved across secondary-grade levels. To our knowledge, no study has yet examined the individual and combined contributions of Hoover-Dempsey and Sandler's (1995, 1997) four psychological constructs to predict parent involvement decisions across secondary-grade levels.

(11)

We targeted adolescents in the first 3 years of secondary school in Quebec (equivalent to Grades 7, 8, and 9 in the American school system). Prior work (Deslandes, 2003) showed that parent involvement is significantly lower, and adolescent autonomy level is significantly higher, in the fourth year of secondary school in Quebec (Grade 10 in the American school system) than in the second and third years of secondary school.

(12)

To examine how the four psychological constructs influence parent-involvement decisions across the three secondary grade levels, we posed the following research question: What are the relative contributions of parents' role construction, self-efficacy, perceptions of teacher invitations, and perceptions of adolescent invitations to predict parent involvement at home and at school in Grades 7, 8, and 9?

(13)

Purpose statements, research questions and hypotheses are specific and narrow

Method

Participants

Participants were 770 parents of secondary-level students attending five public schools located in urban and rural areas in the Mauricie and Centre du Quebec and Monteregie regions. The regions are representative of the general Quebec population. Forty-six percent (354) of the participants were parents of Secondary I students (equivalent to Grade 7 students in the American school system), 30% (231) were parents of Secondary II students (equivalent to Grade 8 students in the American system), and 24% (185) were parents of Secondary III students (equivalent to Grade 9 students in the American system). Nearly 51% of the students were girls and 49% were boys. Forty-seven percent of the students were first born in their family, 37% second born, 13% third born, and 3% fourth and fifth born, respectively.

(14)

The demographics of the sample were as follows: Approximately 84% of the respondents were mothers, and 13% were fathers. The other respondents were either stepmothers or stepfathers, or others. Seventy percent of the participants were employed outside of the home. Seventy percent lived in a traditional family, and 30% lived in a nontraditional one, which corresponds exactly to what is being reported in the Quebec population in general (Quebec Statistics Institute. 2001). The majority of the families (37%) had two children, 25% had one child, 21% had three children, and the remainder of the sample (17%) had four or more children. About 3% of the respondents had

(15)

less than a high school education, 65% had a high school diploma or a secondary-level trade formation, and 32% had a college or university education. Seventy-two percent of the participants had
a job outside the home environment. Table 1 presents the characteristics of the whole sample and
of the three subsamples.

Measures

(16)

Purpose state-
ments, research
questions, or
hypotheses seek
measurable,
observable data
on variables

Among the eight constructs that we used, parents' role construction, self-efficacy, perception of
teacher invitations, and reports of parent practices of involvement were adapted from the Sharing
the Dream! Parent Questionnaire (Jones, Gould, Brown, Young, & The Peabody Family School Partnership Lab of Vanderbilt University, 2000). They are grounded in Hoover-Dempsey and Sandler's
(1995, 1997) model of the parent-involvement process. The parents' perceptions of student invitations and their reports of involvement activities include items from questionnaires designed by
Epstein and her colleagues (Epstein, Connors, & Salinas, 1993; Epstein, Connors-Tadros, Horsey, &
Simon, 1996). The items have been translated in French, adapted in the Quebec context, and used in
previous studies on the basis of adolescents' perceptions (Deslandes, 2000; Deslandes & Cloutier,
2002; Deslandes et al., 1997; Deslandes & Potvin, 1999).

(17)

We used classical item analysis and factor analysis to evaluate the psychometric properties of
the eight constructs (see the list of constructs presented as the predictors and the outcomes with
the control variables in Table 2). The final decision of keeping or rejecting some of the items was
based mostly on the eigenvalues greater than 1 criterion and on the scree test. For all the analyses,
we used only those items loaded at least .30 on the factor to interpret the factors. We computed
Cronbach's alpha reliability coefficient for each scale. We obtained all scores by calculating the
mean score of the items of the same constructs, which are described in the following paragraphs.

(18)

Parents' role construction. This construct measured the extent to which parents believed that
it is their responsibility to help the school educate their adolescent (Hoover-Dempsey & Sandler,
1995, 1997). We based the construct on Hoover-Dempsey's work that suggests three types of parent
role construction: parent focused (six items), school focused (five items), and partnership focused

TABLE 1
Demographic Characteristics of the Sample and Subsamples (in Percentages)

Characteristic	N	Grade 7	Grade 8	Grade 9
Adolescent gender	Female (51)	Female (44)	Female (52)	Female (60)
	Male (49)	Male (56)	Male (48)	Male (40)
Rank in family	1 (47)	1 (46)	1 (46)	1 (49)
	2 (37)	2 (36)	2 (39)	2 (36)
	3 (13)	3 (13)	3 (13)	3 (12)
	Others (3)	Others (5)	Others (2)	Others (3)
Participant gender	Mothers (84)	Mothers (84)	Mothers (83)	Mothers (87)
	Fathers (13)	Fathers (12)	Fathers (15)	Fathers (13)
	Others (3)	Others (4)	Others (2)	Others (0)
Participant education level				
Primary level	3	2	2	3
High school or equivalent	65	63	68	65
College or university	32	35	30	32
Participant outside work	Yes (73)	Yes (76)	Yes (69)	Yes (69)
	No (27)	No (24)	No (31)	No (31)
Family structure				
Traditional	70	68	71	74
Nontraditional	30	32	29	26
Family size				
One child	25	31	26	27
Two children	37	33	37	43
Three children	21	23	23	17
Four or more children	17	13	15	13

TABLE 2
Control Variables, Predictors, and Outcome Measures

Control variable	Predictor	Outcome
Participant gender	Parents' role constructions	Parent involvement at home
Participant outside work	Parents' self-efficacy for helping	Parent involvement at school
Participant education level	adolescents succeed in school	
Family size	Relative parent influence	
Family structure	Impact of parent efforts	
Adolescent gender	Parents' perceptions of teacher	
Rank in family	invitations	
Results in French	Parents' perceptions of adolescent	
	invitations	
	Invitations in academic domain	
	Invitations in social domain	

Data collection involves studying a large number of individuals, gathering numeric data, and using instruments identified prior to the study

(six items; Hoover-Dempsey et al., 1999; Reed et al., 2000). Principal axis factor analysis revealed a single-factor solution that corresponded to a combination of the three types of role construction with a predominance of items related to the partnership-focused role construction. We used a construct that comprised 10 items ($\alpha = .72$) that measure behaviors that are parent focused, school focused, and mainly partnership focused in accordance with the adolescents' education. The parents had to respond to items, for exmple, "It's important that I let someone at school know about things that concern my teenager," and "I make it my business to stay on top of things at school") by using a 6-point, Likert-type scale that ranged from (1) *disagree very strongly* to (6) *agree very strongly.* One possible explanation for obtaining only one scale instead of three could be a cultural one. Another explanation could be associated with the fact that Hoover-Dempsey and her colleagues developed the constructs on the basis of pilot work with a small sample of 50 parents of elementary school children, reported in Reed et al. (2000).

Parents' self-efficacy for helping adolescents succeed in school. We assessed this construct with (19) Hoover-Dempsey and colleagues' scale after adaptations for parents of high school students (Jones et al., 2000). Factor analysis revealed a two-factor solution that accounted for 49% of the total variance in parents' self-efficacy for helping adolescents succeed in school. The first factor, relative parent influence, contained four items ($\alpha = .68$) and measured the extent to which parents believed that they could help their adolescent succeed in school compared with other sources of influence (e.g., "Other adolescents have more influence on my adolescent's motivation to do well in school than I do"). The second factor, impact of parent efforts, estimated the level of influence that parents' perceptions had on their adolescents' education. We assessed perceptions with five items ($\alpha = .63$; e.g., "I feel successful about my efforts to help my adolescent learn"). Participants used a 6-point, Likert-type scale that ranged from 1 (*disagree very strongly*) to 6 (*agree very strongly*).

Parents' perceptions of teacher invitations. This construct provided an assessment of parents' (20) perceptions of teacher invitations to become involved in their adolescents' schooling at home. We based the measure on an eight-item scale created by Hoover-Dempsey and her colleagues (Jones et al., 2000; Reed et al., 2000). In the present study, principal axis factoring analysis yielded a one-factor solution that was composed of four items ($\alpha = .70$; e.g., "One or more of my teenager's teachers has spoken with me about homework"). We asked parents to rate the frequency of teachers' invitations on a 6-point, Likert-type scale that ranged from 1 (*never*) to 6 (*once or more per week*).

Parents' perceptions of student invitations. This construct is a modification of a similar construct (21) for adolescents (Deslandes & Cloutier, 2002) that we derived from Epstein et al., (1993) and Epstein et al. (1996). Principal axis factor analysis revealed the presence of two factors that explained 50% of the total variance in parents' perceptions of student invitations. The first factor, invitations in the academic domain, included five items ($\alpha = .79$; e.g., "My adolescent has asked me to . . . listen to him/her read something he/she wrote"). The second factor, invitations in the social domain, consisted of four items ($\alpha = .71$; e.g., "My adolescent has asked me to . . . talk with me about current events"). All items were answered on a 6-point, Likert-type scale that ranged from 1 (*disagree very strongly*) to 6 (*agree very strongly*).

(22)   *Parent reports of involvement activities.* This measure was a modified version of the question-naires elaborated by Epstein and colleagues (1993; 1996) and used in prior studies on the basis of adolescents' perceptions (e.g., Deslandes, 2000; Deslandes & Cloutier, 2002; Deslandes et al., 1997) and those designed by Hoover-Dempsey and her colleagues (e.g., Jones et al., 2000). Principal axis factoring analysis followed by varimax rotation revealed a two-factor solution that accounted for 35% of the total variance. The first factor, parent involvement at home, was composed of 16 items and assessed how often parents get involved in educational activities at home with their adoles-cents ($\alpha = .87$; sample items: ". . . encourage my adolescent about school," ". . . help my adolescent study before a test"). The second factor, parent involvement in school, included eight items and measured how often parents were at school and how often they interacted with their adolescents at school and with the teachers ($\alpha = .67$; sample items: ". . . go to school to attend an extracurricular event," ". . . have a conference with one or more of my adolescent's teachers"). Parents were asked to answer on a 6-point, Likert-type scale that ranged from 1 (*never*) to 6 (*once or more per week*).

(23)   *Demographics.* We collected information on family and student individual characteristics from the parents. Participants reported on their gender (mother, father, or other), education level (pri-mary, secondary, college or university levels), family structure (traditional, nontraditional), family size (number of children living at home), and outside work (yes/no). They also provided informa-tion on their adolescents' gender (female, male), rank in the family, grade level (7, 8, or 9), and grades in French, their mother tongue, as reported in the last report card (see Table 2).

Procedures

(24)   We collected all the data from survey respondents by means of questionnaires in late spring 2001. Following the school principals' acceptance to participate in the study, we mailed nearly 2,560 parent questionnaires to the schools. Forty-five classroom teachers from five schools volunteered to send the questionnaires to 1,500 parents via the students. The package included a letter that explained the purpose of the study and requested voluntary participation. The participation rate was approximately 51% (770 parents accepted from the 1,500 questionnaires that were sent home). The classroom council received a token payment of thanks ($1) for each returned questionnaire, and the classroom teachers received a token payment of thanks ($10) for their collaboration and support. (The token payments were considered as costs associated with the collaboration and were paid through the research grant.)

Results

Predicting Parent Involvement

(25)   The primary question in the study focused on the relative strength of parents' role construction, self-efficacy, and perceived teacher and student invitation measures for predicting parent involve-ment at home and at school. We performed separate stepwise regression analyses to examine the best predictive models at Grades 7, 8, and 9 in Quebec secondary schools. We computed Mallow's C(P) statistic[1] for each final model and grade level. Descriptive statistics of the measures are illus-trated in Table 3.

Parent Involvement at Home for Seventh-Grade Students

(26)   First, eight family and individual adolescent characteristics,[2] used as control variables, were intro-duced as a block and forced into the regression equation. Together, the control variables explained 4% of the variance in parent involvement at home. After the introduction of the control variables, the analyses yielded a final five-variable model that explained an additional 42% (total $R^2 = 46\%$; total R^2 adj. $= 42.5\%$) of the variance in parent involvement at home, F(13, 232) = 15.47, $p < .001$ (see Table 4). The variable corresponding to parents' perception of student invitations in the aca-demic domain was the best predictor of parent involvement in schooling at home, $\Delta R^2 = .28$; $\beta = .31$, $p < .001$. The variable was followed by parents' role construction, $\Delta R^2 = .07$; $\beta = .18$, $p < .001$, parents' perceptions of student invitations in the social domain, $\Delta R^2 = .04$; $\beta = .25$, $p < .001$, and parents' self-efficacy, that is, perceived impact of efforts, $\Delta R^2 = .02$; $\beta = .15$, $p < .01$, and perceived relative influence $\Delta R^2 = .01$; $\beta = .12$, $p < .05$.

TABLE 3
Means and Standard Deviations for all Predictors and Outcome Measures

Variable	Grade 7 (n = 246)		Grade 8 (n = 156)		Grade 9 (n = 112)	
	M	SD	M	SD	M	SD
Parents' role constructions	4.52	.56	4.40	.59	4.30	.67
Parents' self-efficacy for helping adolescents succeed in school						
Relative parent influence	4.14	.87	4.13	.94	4.14	.90
Impact of parent efforts	4.41	.66	4.32	.71	4.19	.73
Parents' perceptions of teacher invitations	1.55	.61	1.40	.52	1.31	.48
Parents' perceptions of adolescent invitations						
Invitations in academic domain	3.96	1.06	3.82	1.04	3.39	1.04
Invitations in social domain	3.80	1.06	3.61	1.0	3.65	1.0
Parent involvement at home	4.67	.73	4.45	.83	4.13	.87
Parent involvement at school	2.28	.70	2.12	.71	2.00	.66

Data analysis consists of describing trends, comparing groups, or relating variables and using statistical analysis.

Parent Involvement at Home for Eighth-Grade Students

We observed a somewhat different pattern of relations in analyses conducted at the eighth-grade (27) level; control variables explained 10% of the variance. Regression analysis revealed a three-variable model that accounted for an additional 38% of the total variance (total $R^2 = 48\%$; total R^2 adj. = 43%) in the level of parent involvement at home, $F(11,144) = 11.69$, $p < .001$. Parents' perceptions of students' invitations in the social domain was the most powerful predictor; it accounted for an additional 28% of the variance ($\beta = .35$, $p < .001$). Parents' perceptions of student invitation in the academic domain was the second strongest predictor, $\Delta R^2 = .07$; $\beta = .26$, $p < .01$, followed by parents' self-efficacy, that is, impact of efforts ($\Delta R^2 = .03$; $\beta = .19$, $p < .01$).

TABLE 4
Final Regression Models for Each Grade Level Predicting Parent Involvement at Home

Variable	ΔR^2	β
Grade 7		
Control variables	.04	
Parents' perceptions of adolescent invitations in the academic domain	.28	.31***
Parents' role constructions	.07	.18***
Parents' perceptions of adolescent invitations in the social domain	.04	.25***
Parents' self-efficacy		
Impact of parent efforts	.02	.15**
Impact of parent influence	.01	.12*
Grade 8		
Control variables	.10	
Parents' perceptions of adolescent invitations in social domain	.28	.35***
Parents' perceptions of adolescent invitations in academic domain	.07	.26**
Parents' self-efficacy		
Impact of parent efforts	.03	.19**
Grade 9		
Control variables	.11	
Parents' perceptions of student invitations in academic domain	.26	.44***
Parents' perceptions of student invitations in social domain	.03	.20*

Note. $\Delta R^2 = R^2$ change. Grade 7: Mallow's C(P) = 14.385; P = 14 (independent variables, including constant); Grade 8: Mallow's C(P) = 10.335; P = 12 (independent variables, including constant); Grade 9: Mallow's C(P) = 9.769; P = 11 (independent variables, including constant). $p < .05$. **$p < .01$. ***$p < .001$.

Parent Involvement at Home for Ninth-Grade Students

(28)   The control variables accounted for 11% of the variance in the first step. A two-variable model explained an additional 30% of the variance (total $R^2 = 41\%$; total R^2 adj. = 34%) in the level of parent involvement at home, $F(10,101) = 6.81$, $p < .001$. Parents' perceptions of student invitations in the academic domain emerged as the first predictor in the final model, accounting for 26% of the variance ($\beta = .44$, $p < .001$); parents' perception of student invitation in the social domain was the second predictor, explaining 3% of the variance ($\beta = .20$, $p < .05$).

Parent Involvement at School for Seventh-Grade Students

(29)   As shown in Table 5, control variables explained 9% of the variance in parent involvement at school. A three-variable model explained an additional 17% of the variance (total $R^2 = 26\%$; total R^2 adj. = 23%) for level of parent involvement at school, $F(11,234) = 7.51$, $p < .001$. Parents' role construction explained the greatest part of the variance, $\Delta R^2 = .13$, $\beta = .31$, $p < .001$. Parents' perceptions of teacher invitations ($\beta = .14$, $p < .05$) and parents' perceptions of student invitations in the social domain explained an additional 2% of the variance ($\beta = .15$, $p < .01$).

Parent Involvement at School for Eighth-Grade Students

(30)   For eighth-grade students, introducing the demographic variables resulted in a small contribution to the model ($\Delta R^2 = .05$). Parents' perceptions of teacher invitations ($\Delta R^2 = .12$; $\beta = .31$, $p < .001$), and parents' perceptions of student invitations in the social domain, $\Delta s R^2 = .08$; $\beta = .29$, $p < .001$, added significance to the final model (total $R^2 = 25\%$; total R^2 adj. = 19%), $F(10,145) = 4.61$, $p < .001$.

Parent Involvement at School for Ninth-Grade Students

(31)   For ninth-grade students, the control variables first introduced explained 9% of the variance in parent involvement at school. Subsequently, parents' role construction appeared as the stronger predictor of parent involvement at school (b = .36, $p < .001$), accounting for 22% of the variance. The second predictor was parents' perceptions of teacher invitations, explaining an additional 8% of the variance, which resulted in a final model (total $R^2 = 39\%$; total R^2 adj. = 33%), $F(10,101) = 6.48$, $p < .001$.

Discussion

(32)   We investigated the contribution of Hoover-Dempsey and Sandler's (1995, 1997) four psychological constructs—parents' role construction, self-efficacy, perceived student invitations, and perceived teacher invitations—to predict parent involvement at home and at school. We addressed whether predictive models might differ across the first three grade levels in Quebec secondary schools. The following paragraphs summarize the overall results.

(33)   Of great importance were our findings that extended beyond family and adolescent characteristics—two different models that predicted secondary-level parent involvement at home and parent involvement at school. In similar research conducted with 1,227 parents of elementary students, Deslandes and Bertrand (2003) also reported two different parent involvement models—a home-based model and a school-based model.

Parent Involvement at Home

(34)   With respect to seventh-grade students, after we controlled for family and individual characteristics, our findings showed that parents decided to become involved at home mostly because of their adolescents' specific academic invitations, such as asking (a) for ideas for a story or a project, (b) that a parent listen to the student read an original writing, (c) that a parent observe something learned or done well, or (d) for help to study or practice for a test. When personally invited by the adolescents, parents tended to perceive their involvement as expected and desired. Also predictive at a much lesser degree were parent beliefs that their responsibility was, for example, to closely watch their adolescents' progress and to keep abreast of activities at school (parents' role construc-

TABLE 5
Final Regression Models for Each Grade Level Predicting Parent Involvement at School

Variable	ΔR^2	β
Grade 7		
Control variables	.09	
Parents' role constructions	.13	.31***
Parents' perceptions of teacher invitations	.02	.14*
Parents' perceptions of student invitations in the social domain	.02	.15**
Grade 8		
Control variables	.05	
Parents' perceptions of teacher invitations	.12	.31***
Parents' perceptions of student invitations in social domain	.08	.29***
Grade 9		
Control variables	.09	
Parents' role constructions	.22	.36***
Parents' perceptions of teacher invitations	.08	.31***

Note. $\Delta R^2 = R^2$ change. Grade 7: Mallow's C(P) = 12.199; P = 12 (independent variables, including constant); Grade 8: Mallow's C(P) = 12.845; P = 11 (independent variables, including constant); Grade 9: Mallow's C(P) = 8.138; P = 11 (independent variables, including constant). $p < .05$. **$p < .01$. ***$p < .001$.

tion). Similarly, adolescents' personal invitations in the social domain, like talking with a parent about a TV show or current events or interviewing a parent for information or opinions, contributed to parent involvement at home. Contributing to a much lesser extent were significant parents' beliefs that their involvement could make a difference in their adolescents' school performance and that their help was better than any other sources of influence (parents' self-efficacy). Parents subsequently responded with high levels of involvement at home manifested by their help with homework when asked, discussions about school, future plans, course options, and so forth. Findings at the seventh-grade level supported a five-variable, predictive model of parent involvement at home that explained a significant portion of the variance (42.5%).

Concerning eighth-grade students, the full model comprised three variables that included, as the   (35) major predictors, (a) parents' perceptions of student invitations in the social domain (i.e., ask for opinion or information, discuss current events, exchange information on trends during parents' youth), (b) parents' perception of student invitations in the academic domain, and (c) parents' self-efficacy. One especially striking result in our prediction of parent involvement at home was the importance of adolescents' personal invitations in the social domain, such as talking with a parent about a TV show or current event or interviewing a parent for information or opinions. Those findings suggest that positive parent–adolescent interactions might contribute to adolescents' personal invitations to parents to become involved, which is related to subsequent parent involvement at home.

According to Belsky (1981) and Sameroff's (1975) transactional model, our results highlight   (36) the importance of reciprocal influences in the parent–adolescent relationship regarding schooling. Obviously, the quality of parent–adolescent relationships is key to a better understanding of parent involvement at home for secondary-level students. The quality of those relationships seems to be of paramount importance for eighth-grade students. The results are consistent with those of previous studies conducted in Quebec that provide evidence of the positive relation between authoritative parenting style characterized by high levels of warmth, supervision, and psychological autonomy (Steinberg, Elmen, & Mounts, 1989; Steinberg, Lamborn, Darling, Mounts, & Dornbusch, 1994), parent involvement in schooling (Epstein et al., 1993), perceived autonomy (Greenberger, Josselson, Knerr, & Knerr, 1975), and adolescent school grades (Deslandes et al., 1997; Deslandes, 2000; Deslandes & Potvin, 1999). Similarly, Deslandes and Cloutier (2002) found with a sample of 872 eighth-grade students in Quebec that specific invitations to involve parents requires that the adolescents are willing and open to work and exchange ideas with parents. The authors concluded that adolescents with a high level of autonomy, and more precisely, those who are highly work oriented and self-confident are more likely than adolescents without these traits to invite parent involvement.

(37)   Concerning ninth-grade students, analyses revealed a two-variable predictive model: (a) Parent perception of student invitations in the academic domain made the most significant contribution and (b) parent perception of student invitations in the social domain was a less powerful predictor. Whether parents believe that their involvement will have a positive impact on their adolescents' school performance is not significant at Grade 9. Rather, parents wait for their adolescents' invitations before they become involved at home. One possible explanation is that parents may consider that Grade 9 students have developed self-responsible behaviors toward school and schoolwork (see Xu & Corno, 2003). Consequently, parents rely on the adolescents to initiate the requests for parent involvement at home. That behavior somewhat reinforces the perspective that differences in adolescent autonomy modulate the degree of parent involvement at home (Deslandes, 2000).

Parent Involvement at School

(38)   At the Grade 7 level, after the introduction of controlled variables, the addition of the four psychological constructs resulted in a three-variable model that predicted parent involvement at school. Across various family and individual characteristics, the more that parents of Grade 7 students believed their involvement was part of their parenting responsibilities (e.g., teacher conferences are helpful to parents; parents should call the school with concerns about their adolescents' progress), the more they perceived invitations from the teachers (e.g., one of the teachers spoke with them about homework; a school employee has asked the parents to have a conference about their adolescent), and the more they perceived invitations from their adolescents in the social domain (e.g., interview parents for information or opinions), the more they reported involvement at school (e.g., having a conference with one or more of their adolescents' teachers, attending an extracurricular event at school). Noteworthy is the more significant contribution of parents' role construction to the predictive model at the Grade 7 level. Parents reported that they would be more involved at school if they believed that it is their duty.

(39)   Once we controlled for demographics, regression analyses yielded a two-variable predictive model at the Grade 8 level. Parents of Grade 8 students are involved at school if they perceive invitations from the teachers and from their adolescents in the social domain. The question of whether parents of Grade 8 students are involved at school seems to be primarily an issue of relations and parent–teacher and parent–adolescent relationships. We think of the development of trust in teachers (Adams & Christenson, 2000) and of positive parent–adolescent interactions as prerequisites to parents' decisions to become involved at school, and more important, at the Grade 8 level (see Christenson & Sheridan, 2001).

(40)   For Grade 9, adding the four psychological constructs yielded a two-variable model that contributed significantly to the prediction of parent involvement at school. Parents' understanding that involvement at school is part of their responsibilities (parents' role construction) was by far the best predictor, followed by parents' perceptions of teacher invitations.

(41)   To summarize, our findings clearly identify two categories of predictive models: (a) parent involvement at home and (b) parent involvement at school. Contrary to Hoover-Dempsey and Sandler's (1995) measures, parents' self-efficacy in its francophone version comprised two factors: (a) relative parent influence and (b) impact of parent efforts, whereas parents' role construction consisted of only one factor. Our findings confirmed the relevance of Hoover-Dempsey and Sandler's model mainly for the seventh graders' parent involvement at home model, in which perceived teacher invitations was the only missing construct (one of four). Parents' role construction contributed more significantly to seventh and ninth graders' parent involvement at school models. Parents' self-efficacy contributed significantly only in the seventh and eighth graders' parent involvement at home models, and its overall contribution was marginal.

(42)   Of major interest in this study is the powerful contribution exerted by parents' perception of student invitations in the models of parent involvement at home at the three secondary-grade levels. As adolescents mature, parent involvement at home becomes more a question of parent–adolescent relationships, which is particularly important at the eighth-grade level. Parents of students in Grades 7, 8, and 9 appear to be involved more proactively (e.g., in response to invitations) than reactively (e.g., in reaction to prior school grades, adolescent gender). The links between perceived adolescents' invitations and parent involvement at home are robust across various individual and family characteristics.

Two notable patterns stand out in our results regarding parent involvement at school. The most outstanding pattern is the greater influence of parents' role construction. Parents must comprehend that parent involvement at school is part of their responsibilities before they decide to become involved. Also of interest in this study are the perceived invitations from the teachers to motivate parents to become involved at school.   (43)

Implications and Limitations

The main implication derived from this study relates to the two identified categories of parent involvement predictive models. First, if the objective of the school interventions is to enhance parent involvement at home, the findings suggest the need to work directly with adolescents. That effort could be undertaken by (a) sensitizing adolescents to the importance of their inviting parents to become involved at home and by (b) coaching them on how to involve a family member in homework, discussions, or other tasks (Balli, Demo, & Wedman, 1998). For example, adolescents could ask their families to offer feedback about the assignments. Evidently, if parent involvement at home is the objective of school interventions, the involvement should focus on increased adolescent acceptance of and openness to developmentally appropriate parent involvement in schooling activities. Our findings also suggest that parent education programs should enhance parents' skills and self-efficacy. Parents should be aware of the importance of sustained parent–adolescent communication about schooling, and career and work planning over time. Parents could regularly attend workshops or meetings (e.g., parenting classes) to increase their parenting skills and their knowledge of different types of parent involvement, including less intensive involvement.   (44) Researchers report in an objective and unbiased approach

Second, if the objective is increased parent involvement at school, the implications are fairly straightforward: school interventions should first focus on individualized contacts that teachers initiate with parents. Our finding regarding perceived invitations involved specific requests from teachers, such as "One or more of my teenager's teachers has spoken with me about homework," ". . . has asked me to encourage my teenager to read," and so forth. Parents responded to teachers' specific invitations by attending an extracurricular event, by volunteering at school, and so forth. The findings call attention to the value of personal teacher–parent contacts for building trusting relationships that will be manifested subsequently by parent involvement activities at school and by other forms of parents' willingness to help. Those results suggest that preservice and inservice teachers could benefit from training programs that offer the opportunity to develop knowledge and skills needed to initiate first contacts with parents and foster parent involvement (Hiatt-Michael, 2001; Shartrand, Weiss, Kreider, & Lopez, 1997).   (45)

There are limitations of this study that suggest directions for future investigations. First, the sample used in our investigation included only students in Grades 7, 8, and 9, and the subsamples were of various sizes. Future investigations need to expand across the secondary levels. We collected data only from parents of adolescents. Past research focused primarily on adolescents' perceptions; researchers should endeavor to use both adolescent and parent reports.   (46)

Research findings indicate the need for further research on parent–adolescent and parent–teacher relationships to better understand parents' decision to become involved at home and at school. In addition, more research is needed on the relationship between parents' self-efficacy, role construction, and involvement. Some issues remain unclear. For instance, what is the explanation for the marginal contribution of parents' self-efficacy in the parent involvement at home model? As Hoover-Dempsey and colleagues (2000) suggested, is it possible that parents' self-efficacy is distal to parents' involvement decisions, whereas parents' role construction and perceived teacher and student invitations are more proximal? Researchers need to replicate this study in other settings by comparing different age categories to determine greater "generalizability" of the findings. Longitudinal research would help clarify the extent to which each of the studied psychological constructs changes over time and in different settings. To fully understand parents' motivation to become involved, educators need more qualitative studies that focus on the subject.   (47)

Conclusions

The results of this study highlight the importance of researchers considering parent involvement at home and parent involvement at school separately as opposed to their examining parent involvement in terms of global involvement. For example, parents' perception of student invitations in the   (48) academic domain made a significant contribution to the prediction of parent involvement at home but did not appear as a predictor of parent involvement at school. In addition, parents' perceived teacher invitations were associated with parent involvement at school, but not with parent involvement at home. Thus, the findings would have been missed had parent involvement been assessed in global terms. Obviously, the different models obtained in this study require more research that examines the influences on parent involvement at home and at school separately. In terms of practical implications, our research suggests that use of one of the psychological constructs should depend on whether parent involvement at home or parent involvement at school is the target. To enhance parent involvement at home, school administrators and teachers should work mainly with adolescents. To improve parent involvement at school, the results suggest the importance of sensitizing parents to their duties and responsibilities and of regarding the role of the school and the teachers when motivating parents to become involved.

(49)   The results of this study provide evidence of grade-level differences in the predictive models of parent involvement at home and at school. For instance, at Grade 7, the parent involvement at home predictive model included three constructs: (a) perceived student invitations, (b) parents' role construction, and (c) parents' self-efficacy. At Grade 9, only one construct made a significant contribution—perceived student invitations. Regarding parent involvement at school, the predictive power of parents' role construction at Grade 9 was nearly twice as important as that at Grade 7. Overall, the pattern of results differs to some extent by grade levels. Analogous to those results, one might focus on the specific influences of each grade level that seem to be used in parents' involvement decisions. Further longitudinal research is needed to test changes in the models across all secondary grade levels.

Notes

This research was supported by grants to the first author from the Fonds québécois de la recherche sur la société et la culture (FQRSC) and to both authors from the Centre de Recherche et d'Intervention sur la Réussite Scolaire (CRIRES).

1. One can use Mallow's C(P) statistic to evaluate the amount of mean square error (bias and random error) in the model. We sought values of C(P) near or below p (number of independent variables in the model; Neter, Wasserman, & Kutner, 1990, p. 448). We obtained all statistics with SPSS 11.0 (e.g., the stepwise regression method and the SELECTION keyword [for the Mallow's statistic]).

2. Merging the 770 parents' file with the students' file totaled 514 cases.

References

Adams, K. S., & Christenson, S. L. (2000). Trust and the family-school relationship examination of parent-teacher differences in elementary and secondary grades. *Journal of School Psychology, 38*, 477–497.

Astone, N. M., & McLanahan, S. S. (1991). Family structure, parent practices and high school completion. *American Sociological Review, 56*, 309–320.

Balli, S. J., Demo, D. H., & Wedman, J. F. (1998). Family involvement with children's homework: An intervention in the middle grades. *Family Relations, 47*, 142–146.

Bandura, A. (1997). *Self-efficacy in changing societies.* New York: Freeman.

Belsky, J. (1981). Early human experience: A family perspective. *Developmental Psychology, 17*, 2–23.

Christenson, S. L., & Sheridan, S. M. (2001). *Schools and families: Creating essential connections for learning.* New York: Guilford Press.

Comer, J. P., & Haynes, N. M. (1991). Parent involvement in schools: An ecological approach. *The Elementary School Journal, 91*, 271–277.

Dauber, S. L., & Epstein, J. L. (1989). *Parents' attitudes and practices of involvement in inner-city elementary and middle schools* (CREMS Report 33). Baltimore: Johns Hopkins University, Center for Research on Elementary and Middle Schools.

Dauber, S. L., & Epstein, J. L. (1993). Parents' attitudes and practices of involvement in inner-city elementary and middle schools. In

N. F. Chavkin (Ed.), *Families and schools in a pluralistic society* (pp. 53–71). Albany: State University of New York Press.

Deslandes, R. (2000, April). *Direction of influence between parenting style and parent involvement in schooling practices, and students autonomy: A short-term longitudinal design.* Paper presented at the 10th International Roundtable on School, Family, and Community Partnerships, New Orleans, LA. (ERIC Document Reproduction Service No. ED441586)

Deslandes, R. (2003). Evolution of parenting and parent involvement in schooling practices and Canadian adolescents' autonomy over a three-year span. In S. Castelli, M. Mendel, & B. Ravns (Eds.), *School, family, and community partnerships in a world of differences and change* (pp. 89–104). Poland: Gdansk University.

Deslandes, R., & Bertrand, R. (2003). *Raisons qui motivent les parents à participer au suivi scolaire de leur enfant du primaire.* [Reasons that motivate parents to be involved in their child's schooling at the elementary level]. Manuscript submitted for publication.

Deslandes, R., & Cloutier, R. (2000). Engagement parent dans l'accompagnement scolaire et réussite des adolescents à l'école. [Parent involvement in their adosescent's schooling and success in school]. *Bulletin de Psychologie Scolaire et d'Orientation, 2*, 1–21.

Deslandes, R., & Cloutier, R. (2002). Adolescents' perception of parent-school involvement. *School Psychology International, 23*(2), 220–232.

Deslandes, R., & Potvin, P. (1999, April). *Autonomy, parenting, parent involvement in schooling and school achievement: Perception of*

Quebec adolescents. Paper presented at the annual meeting of the American Educational Research Association, Montreal, Canada. (ERIC Document Reproduction Service No. ED430697)

Deslandes, R., Potvin, P., & Leclerc, D. (1999). Family characteristics predictors of school achievement: Parent involvement as a mediator. *McGill Journal of Education, 34*(2), 133–151.

Deslandes, R., & Royer, É. (1997). Family-related variables and school disciplinary events at the secondary level. *Behavioral Disorders, 23*(1), 18–28.

Deslandes, R., Royer, E., Turcotte, D., & Bertrand, R. (1997). School achievement at the secondary level: Influence of parenting style and parent involvement in schooling. *McGill Journal of Education, 32*(3), 191–208.

Dornbusch, S. M., & Ritter, P. L. (1988). Parents of high school students: A neglected resource. *Educational Horizons, 66*(2), 75–77.

Eccles, J. S., Early, D., Frasier, K., Belansky, E., & McCarthy, K. (1997). The relation of connection, regulation, and support for autonomy to adolescents' functioning. *Journal of Adolescent Research, 12,* 263–286.

Eccles, J. S., & Harold, R. D. (1996). Family involvement in children's and adolescents' schooling. In A. Booth & J. Dunn (Eds.), *Family–school links: How do they affect educational outcomes?* Hillsdale, NJ: Erlbaum.

Epstein, J. L. (1986). Parents' reactions to teacher practices of parent involvement. *Elementary School Journal, 86,* 277–294.

Epstein, J. L. (2001). *School, family, and community partnerships: Preparing educators and improving schools.* Boulder, CO: Westview Press.

Epstein, J. L., Connors-Tadros, L., Horsey, C. S., & Simon, B. S. (1996). *A report from the School, Family & Community Partnership Project.* Baltimore: Johns Hopkins University, Center on Families, Communities, Schools and Children's Learning.

Epstein, J. L., Connors, L. J., & Salinas, K. C. (1993). *High school and family partnerships: Questionnaires for teachers, parents, and students.* Baltimore: Johns Hopkins University, Center on Families, Communities, Schools and Children's Learning.

Freedman-Doan, C., Arbreton, A. J., Harold, R. D., & Eccles, J. S. (1993). Looking forward to adolescence: Mothers' and fathers' expectations for affective and behavioral change. *Journal of Early Adolescence, 13,* 472–502.

Greenberger, E., Josselson, R., Knerr, C., & Knerr, B. (1975). The measurement and structure of psychosocial maturity. *Journal of Youth and Adolescence, 4,* 127–143.

Henderson, A. T., & Mapp, K. L. (2002). *A new wave of evidence. The impact of school, family, and community connections on student achievement. Annual synthesis.* Austin, TX: National Center for Family & Community Connections with Schools. Southwest Educational Development Laboratory. Retrieved from http://www.sedl.org/connections

Hiatt-Michael, D. (Ed). (2001). *Promising practices for family involvement in school.* Greenwich, CT: Information Age Publishing, Inc.

Hoover-Dempsey, K. V., Bassler, O. C., & Brissie, J. S. (1992). Explorations in parent–school relations. *The Journal of Educational Research, 85,* 287–294.

Hoover-Dempsey, K. V., Battiato, A. C., Walker, J. M. T., Reed, R. P., DeJong, J. M., & Jones, K. P. (2001). Parent involvement in homework. *Educational Psychologist, 36,* 195–209.

Hoover-Dempsey, K. V., Jones, K. P., & Reed, R. (1999, April). *"I wish I were a bird in the window": The voices of parents seeking children's school success.* Paper presented at the annual meeting of the American Educational Research Association, Montréal, Canada.

Hoover-Dempsey, K. V., & Sandler, H. M. (1995). Parent involvement in children's education: Why does it make a difference? *Teachers College Record, 95,* 310–331.

Hoover-Dempsey, K. V., & Sandler, H. M. (1997). Why do parents become involved in their children's education? *Review of Educational Research, 67,* 3–42.

Jones, K., Gould, D., Brown, A., Young, J., & The Peabody Family School Partnership Lab of Vanderbilt University. (2000). *"Sharing the dream" parent questionnaire.* Retrieved from http://www.Vanderbilt.edu/Peabody/family-school

Jordan, C., Orozco, E., & Averett, A. (2001). Emerging issues in school, family, & community connections. Austin, TX: National Center for Family & Community Connections with Schools. Southwest Educational Development Laboratory. Retrieved from http://www.sedl.org/connections

Lee, S. (1994). *Family-school connections and students' education: Continuity and change of family involvement from the middle grades to high school.* Unpublished doctoral dissertation, Johns Hopkins University, Baltimore, MD.

Neter, J., Wasserman, W., & Kutner, M. H. (1990). *Applied linear statistical models.* Homewood, IL: Irwin.

Quebec Statistics Institute. (2001). *Portrait social du Québec. Données et analyses.* Quebec, Canada: Publications governementales du Québec.

Reed, R. P., Jones, K. P., Walker, J. M., & Hoover-Dempsey, K. V. (2000, April). *Parents' motivations for involvement in children's education: Testing a theoretical model.* Paper presented at the annual meeting of the American Educational Research Association, New Orleans, LA.

Sameroff, A. J. (1975). Early influences on development: Fact or fancy. *Merrill-Palmer Quarterly, 21,* 267–294.

Shartrand, A. M., Weiss, H. B. Kreider, H. M., & Lopez, M. E. (1997). *New skills for new schools: Preparing teachers in family involvement.* Harvard Family Research Project. Cambridge, MA: Harvard Graduate School of Education. Retrieved from http://www.ed.gov/pubs/New Skills

Steinberg, L., Elmen, J. D., & Mounts, N. S. (1989). Authoritative parenting, psychosocial maturity, and academic success among adolescents. *Child Development, 60,* 1424–1436.

Steinberg, L., Lamborn, S. D., Darling, N., Mounts, N. S., & Dornbusch, S. M. (1994). Over-time changes in adjustment and competence among adolescents from authoritative, authoritarian, indulgent, and neglectful families. *Child Development, 65,* 754–770.

Steinberg, L., Lamborn, S. D., Dornbusch, S. M., & Darling, N. (1992). Impact of parenting practices on adolescent achievement: Authoritative parenting, school involvement, and encouragement to succeed. *Child Development, 63,* 1266–1281.

Stevenson, H. W., Chen, C., & Uttal, D. H. (1990). Beliefs and achievement. A study of Black, White, and Hispanic children. *Child Development, 6,* 508–523.

Trusty, J. (1996). Relationship of parent involvement in teens' career development to teens' attitudes, perceptions, and behavior. *Journal of Research and Development in Education, 30,* 317–323.

Walker, J. M. T., & Hoover-Dempsey, K. V. (2001, April). *Age-related patterns in student invitations to parent involvement in homework.* Paper presented at the annual meeting of the American Educational Research Association, Seattle, WA.

Walker, J. M., Hoover-Dempsey, K. V., Reed, R. P., & Jones, K. P. (2000, April). *"Can you help me with my homework?" Elementary school children's invitations and perspectives on parent involvement.* Paper presented at the annual meeting of the American Educational Research Association, New Orleans, LA.

Xu, J., & Corno, L. (2003). Family help and homework management reported by middle school students. *The Elementary School Journal, 103,* 503–536.

Zimmerman, B. J., & Martinez-Pons, M. P. (1986). Development of a structured interview for assessing student use of self-regulated learning strategies. *American Educational Research Journal, 23,* 614–628.

Sample Qualitative Study

School Principals' Influence on Trust: Perspectives of Mothers of Children with Disabilities

Qualitative
Characteristics
in Marginal
Annotations

Debra L. Shelden
Maureen E. Angell
Julia B. Stoner
Bill D. Roseland
Illinois State University

Abstract

The authors employed a qualitative research design to explore issues of trust in family–professional relationships. They specifically focused on the nature of trust between mothers of children with disabilities and school principals. Analysis of the mothers' responses to face-to-face interview questions yielded two primary categories related to their perspectives regarding principals: (a) personal and professional principal attributes and (b) principal actions within the education system, with students, and with students' families. Subcategories were developed that further delineated the relationships participants had with the principals of their children's educational programs. The authors address implications for school leadership and the establishment of trustworthy family–professional relationships, especially as they impact the lives of students and families in need of special education support.
Key words: parents of children with disabilities, school principals, trust

(01)   Parents are meant to be included as fundamental participants in educational organizations. Decades of research have supported the role of parent involvement in positive educational outcomes for students (Colarusso & O'Rourke, 2007; Freiberg, 2006). Recent legal mandates require school systems to engage parents in meaningful ways. The No Child Left Behind Act of 2001 (NCLB; 2002) calls for school systems to facilitate parent involvement (Keller, 2006) and the Individuals with Disabilities Education Improvement Act (IDEIA; 2004) mandates parental involvement in all aspects of assessment and service delivery for students who receive special education support (Fletcher, Coulter, Reschly, & Vaughn, 2004). In light of these legal mandates and underlying fundamental principles of family–school relationships, trust between parents and educational professionals has emerged as a critical factor (Bryk & Schneider, 2003; Dunst, Johanson, Rounds, Trivette, & Hamby, 1992). Trust may influence student achievement because of its role in establishing and maintaining collaborative relationships between home and school, and trust may shape parents' attitudes toward educational systems and influence their engagement in their children's educational programs (Dunst et al.; Tschannen-Moran, 2004). Bryk and Schneider found that was not only trust associated with greater gains in student achievement, but also with longer lasting gains in achievement.

(02)   Consequently, not only is trust between parents and education professionals necessary for effective partnerships stipulated by legal mandates, but also, and more importantly, it appears to have a positive effect on student outcomes, and it is the students themselves who are the true beneficiaries of trusting relationships between parents and education professionals. However, if trust is valuable to parents, teachers, and students, it is incumbent on school principals to foster it, maintain it, and exemplify trusting relationships with all parents, including parents of children with disabilities. Indeed, trust is "increasingly recognized as a critical element of leadership" (Tschannen-Moran, 2003, p. 162) and the leadership of schools, the principals, must understand their vital role in establishing trust.

(03)   Many definitions of trust exist in the literature. In their review of literature on trust, Hoy and Tschannen-Moran (1999) found 16 definitions of trust. They identified five facets of trust reflected in those definitions, including benevolence, reliability, competence, honesty, and openness. Based on those facets of trust, Hoy and Tschannen-Moran proposed that trust is "an individual's or

---

Address correspondence to Debra L. Shelden, Illinois State University, Department of Special Education, Campus Box 5910, Normal, IL 61790-5910. (E-mail: dlsheld@ilstu.edu)

group's willingness to be vulnerable to another party based on the confidence that the latter party is benevolent, reliable, competent, honest, and open" (p. 189). In this definition, they established vulnerability as a precursor to the need for trust. The need for trust rests on the recognition of the potential for betrayal or harm from another person. When that risk does not exist, we have no need to trust (Tschannen-Moran, 2004). The latter part of the definition identifies five facets, or dimensions, that influence the extent of trust. This definition served as a conceptual foundation for the present report of a study of the perspectives of mothers of children with disabilities on the role of school principals in facilitating or inhibiting the establishment and maintenance of trust between parents of children with disabilities and education professionals. Hoy and Tschannen-Moran's facets of trusts, particularly benevolence, openness, and competence, were reflected in the principal attributes and actions that emerged from the present study as facilitators of trust.

Trust and School Leaders

On a systems level, trust is identified as a critical factor in school reform (Bryk & Schneider, 2003). School leaders can influence the nature of trust within educational systems (Kochanek, 2005; Tschannen-Moran, 2004). The significance of teachers' and parents' trust in school principals is strong and can influence trust among other constituents (Hoy & Tschannen-Moran, 1999). Among school leaders, principals in particular can influence the overall school climate and thereby influence trust (DiPaola & Walther-Thomas, 2003; Hoy, Smith, & Sweetland, 2002; Soodak & Erwin, 2000). Collegial leadership, or the openness of the leadership behavior of the principal, is a predictor of school climate, which in turn also influences overall trust (Hoy et al.).   (04)

Literature justifies the problem

As leaders who set the tone in schools, principals are responsible for building and maintaining trusting relationships (Whitener, Brodt, Korsgaard, & Werner, 1998). To demonstrate how principals might fulfill this responsibility, Tschannen-Moran (2004) offered a three-dimensional Trustworthy Leadership Matrix (p. 176). She emphasized the usefulness of considering not only five facets of trust (i.e., benevolence, honesty, openness, reliability, and competence) in relation to five constituencies of schools (i.e., administrators, teachers, students, parents, and the public), but also five functions of school leadership in understanding how school principals' behavior can significantly influence school climate and culture. These functions of leadership, as applied to trust, include (a) developing a vision of a trustworthy school, (b) serving as a role model for trustworthiness through language and action, (c) facilitating teacher competence through effective coaching, (d) improving school discipline among students and teachers through effective management, and (e) mediating conflict and repair in a constructive and honest manner. Administrator trustworthiness, then, is demonstrated by nurturing and balancing relationships among facets of trust, constituencies of schools, and the functions of leadership.   (05)

Bryk and Schneider (2003) discussed the demonstration of respect as one critical facet of the trust definition for school principals. They claimed that respect is closely related to other facets of trust, particularly openness, benevolence, and reliability. Bryk and Schneider defined respect as part of the social discourse within school communities. When educators in a school system demonstrate respect in their social exchanges, they contribute to the development of trust. Principals serve as models of these social exchanges for other school personnel (Kochanek, 2005). Openness, as a part of the trust definition, refers to the perception of one party that another party is forthcoming with relevant information and one party's confidence that another party does not withhold relevant information (Butler & Cantrell, 1984; Mishra, 1996). This openness signals a kind of reciprocal trust (Tschannen-Moran & Hoy, 2000). Benevolence, as demonstrated by caring and support, also influences reciprocal trust (Tschannen-Moran & Hoy) and is valued by principals' constituents (Bryk & Schneider; Tschannen-Moran, 2004). Finally, reliability is demonstrated not only through predictability but also through commitment and dedication. These facets of trust are principal characteristics valued by parents. As Bryk and Schneider noted, "Almost every parent and teacher we spoke with at this school commented effusively about the principal's personal style, his openness to others, and his willingness to reach out to parents, teachers, and students" (p. 42).   (06)

Although the research cited above applies to all relationships of trust within a school, there is a growing body of research that has focused on these issues as related to parents of children with disabilities. Parents of children with disabilities may have increased interaction with educational administrators simply by the nature of special education delivery. Administrators and parents of children with disabilities are part of an Individualized Education Program (IEP) team. Parents and   (07) administrators are integral to team decisions and, through stipulations in the IDEIA, parents are to be considered equal and active team members. Beyond the legal requirements of parental involvement with children with disabilities, recent research has investigated parent perspectives regarding various aspects of interactions with education professionals (Angell, Bailey, & Stoner, 2008; Bailey, Parette, Stoner, Angell, & Carroll, 2006; Stoner & Angell, 2006; Stoner, Angell, House, & Bock, 2007; Stoner et al., 2005). This research has revealed that trust is a major factor in the complex relationship between parents of children with disabilities and education professionals (Lake & Billingsley, 2000; Stoner & Angell; Stoner et al., 2005).

(08)   Parents of children with disabilities also have the right to implement due process proceedings if they disagree with the decisions of the IEP team (IDEIA, 2004). Due process safeguards "afford parents a basic right of protest when they disagree with the educational decisions and actions of the school district" (Fiedler, Simpson, & Clark, 2007, p. 207). These due process safeguards provide for increased opportunities between parents and educational administrators and hence provide additional opportunities for trust to be influenced. If due process is lengthy and involves hiring attorneys, it can be quite costly to the school district and parents. The IDEIA encourages but does not require mediation prior to the implementation of due process. Lake and Billingsley (2000) investigated perspectives of parents and education professionals involved in due process cases. Nearly 90% of their parent participants reported the initiation or escalation of conflict as a result of discrepant perceptions between parents and other team members' differing perceptions of children's needs. In their study, parents reported dissatisfaction with school teams who did not recognize children's individuality (i.e., did not recognize individual strengths and limitations separate from a disability label). In addition, parents felt as though schools operated from a deficit perspective, placing too much emphasis on what children cannot do as opposed to focusing on or recognizing the strengths of each child (Aigne, Colvin, & Baker, 1998; Lake & Billingsley). It should be noted that the discrepant perspectives between parents and education professionals developed over time as parents perceived negative interactions with school teams.

(09)   In addition, when parents and educational teams operate from discrepant viewpoints with regard to assessment and service delivery, parents are more likely to distrust future exchanges when their expectations are not met (Stoner & Angell, 2006). Principals can influence the impact of these discrepant viewpoints through their influence on school climate. Tschannen-Moran (2004) described the relationship among principals, overall school trust and climate, and parents' trust:

> Principals play an important role in creating the context for trust to develop between parents and the school and between teachers and parents. The school leader creates the framework and structure for these relationships and, by example, may set the tone for these interactions as well. (p. 136)

(10)   More specifically, principals' interactions with individual students and families can influence the overall child-centeredness of schools (DiPaola & Walther-Thomas, 2003; Kochanek, 2005; Soodak & Erwin, 2000).

(11)   Establishing and maintaining trust does not ensure that school districts never face a due process hearing; however, a trusting relationship has the potential to minimize conflict and lead to resolution. Consequently, principals have a major responsibility to positively contribute to the establishment of trust with all parents, including parents of children with disabilities, who may be interacting with great frequency with education professionals, including teachers, related service personnel, and principals.

Purpose of the Study

(12)   The role of the principal in establishing or influencing overall organizational trust in schools has emerged from extant research (e.g., Hoy et al., 2002; Hoy & Tschannen-Moran, 1999). More recent research has addressed characteristics and actions that can be taken by principals to improve organizational trust (e.g., Kochanek, 2005). The importance of trust in establishing effective home–school partnerships for students with disabilities is also strongly supported in recent research (Lake & Billingsley, 2000; Stoner & Angell, 2006; Stoner et al., 2005; Turnbull, Turnbull, Erwin, & Soodak, 2006). Given the critical role principals can assume in establishing trust, further research is needed on how they influence levels of trust in relationships between families of children with disabilities and education professionals.

Problem is exploratory

The present study emerged from a broader study of the perspectives of mothers of children with disabilities on trust in education personnel (Angell, Stoner, & Shelden, 2009). Although we did not inquire specifically about the role of administrators, the strong influence of administrators, particularly school principals, was apparent during interviews with 16 mothers of children of varying disabilities, ages, and geographical settings. We then re-examined our data to address the following research question:

What are the perspectives of mothers of children with disabilities on trust in school principals?

Method

Research Design

We employed a qualitative research methodology to gain insight into the nature of trust of mothers of children with disabilities in school principals. We viewed trust as the central phenomenon requiring exploration and understanding (Creswell, 2002). Considering the nature of our target phenomenon (i.e., trust), we followed the advice of Strauss and Corbin (1998) who explained that "qualitative methods can be used to obtain the intricate details about phenomena such as feelings, thought processes, and emotions that are difficult to extract or learn about through more conventional methods" (p. 11).

The method used for the present study was the collective case study as described by Stake (2000). Collective case study involves the study of more than one case in order to "investigate a phenomenon, population, or general condition" (p. 437). This approach assumes that investigating a number of cases leads to better comprehension and better theorizing (Brantlinger, Jimenez, Klingner, Pugach, & Richardson, 2005). Miles and Huberman (1994) contended that studying multiple cases gives the researcher reassurance that the events in only one case are not "wholly idiosyncratic" (p. 172). Further, studying multiple cases allowed us to see processes and outcomes across all cases and enabled a deeper understanding through more powerful descriptions and explanations.

Participants

We used a purposive sampling technique that included snowballing methods to recruit a heterogeneous group of mothers of school-aged children with disabilities as participants in this study, basing the rationale for our maternal focus on research indicating that mothers have more contact with education professionals than do fathers (e.g., David, 1998; Nord, Brimhall, & West, 1997; Nord & West, 2001; Thomson, McLanahan, & Curtin, 1992). We purposefully included a range of mothers who had children with various disabilities across various grade levels in schools from several school districts that represented a range of settings (e.g., rural, suburban, urban). We expected this sampling methodology to afford us maximum opportunities for comparable analysis (Strauss & Corbin, 1998) of mothers from a variety of backgrounds and experiences with schools, as well as having children with a variety of disabilities and at various ages.

Participants were recruited using three techniques: (a) district-level administrators' distribution of recruitment materials; (b) individual school personnel's distribution of recruitment materials; and (c) a participant referral snowballing technique, whereby participants distributed recruitment materials to other mothers who might express different perspectives or had had different experiences with education professionals. This sampling method facilitated our attaining as much variation as possible within our sample (Patton, 1980). In our initial recruitment phase, after obtaining university approval to conduct the research, we mailed explanatory and invitational letters to several school district administrators in a Midwestern state, asking them to distribute the letters to potential participants if they approved of our interviewing mothers with children in their schools. In the invitational letters, mothers were asked to return permission-to-contact forms if they were interested in participating in the study. Although it was designed to protect potential participants' identities until they agreed to meet with us for interviews, this method of recruitment proved to be minimally effective, yielding only 2 participants. We tentatively attributed administrators' or mothers' reluctance to participate to the nature of the study (i.e., the investigation of trust) and consequently asked school principals and various school personnel (e.g., therapists and special education teachers) to assist us in recruiting participants.

Margin annotations:

(13) Purpose and question focuses on participants' experiences

(14) Literature plays a minor role in shaping question

(15)

(16)

(17)

(18)

The researcher is reflexive

(19)   During the second phase of recruitment, school personnel sent permission-to-contact forms to potential participants with whom they had regular contact. On receipt of this approval, we scheduled one-on-one, face-to-face interviews with the mothers, explained the study, and obtained informed consent. We tentatively attributed the success of this recruitment method to the nature of the relationships participants had with the education professionals who contacted them or to the personal contact. Personal contact from familiar individuals within their schools or districts may have influenced the mothers' willingness to participate.

(20)   Our second and third recruitment phases yielded an additional 14 participants. Our final participant pool consisted of 16 mothers of children with various disabilities. They ranged in age from 18 to 55 years. In all, 12 mothers were Caucasian, I was African American, and 3 were Hispanic. One of the Hispanic mothers had limited English proficiency, so a Spanish-speaking interpreter assisted during her interview. Most of the mothers were from urban and suburban areas and 2 were from rural areas. These mothers and their children represented eight school districts, varying grade levels, and a range of geographical areas (i.e., rural, suburban, and urban). See Table 1 for participant demographics.

Data are based on small numbers

Interviews

(21)   Data were collected via semistructured interviews, which Fontana and Frey (2000) described as "one of the most powerful ways in which we try to understand our fellow human beings" (p. 645). Face-to-face interviews occurred in the mothers' homes or at places the mothers designated (e.g., restaurants, coffee shops) and ranged in length from 60 to 90 min. The interview questions, which focused on trust, relationships with education professionals, and situations where trust was either enhanced or diminished, are provided in the Appendix. Each interview was audio-taped and transcribed verbatim to facilitate subsequent data analysis.

Text data are collected

(22)   Each interview was conducted by one of the first three authors. The 16 single-participant interviews consisted of broad, open-ended questions designed to investigate mothers' perspectives on their trust in education professionals. As we interviewed the mothers, we probed for further information, elaboration, or clarification of responses as we deemed appropriate. Semistructured interviews permitted us to address the issue of trust while maintaining a feeling of openness (Kvale, 1996).

Descriptive analysis is presented

TABLE 1
Participant Demographics

Parent name	Ethnicity	Child's name	Disability/Diagnosis	Grade level	Instructional setting	School location
Mary	Caucasian	Alex	ASD	Preschool	Self-contained	Rural
Olivia	Caucasian	Emily	Sensory integration dysfunction	Preschool	Inclusive	Suburban
Terri	Hispanic	Frankie	Developmental delay	Preschool	Inclusive	Urban
Vickie	Caucasian	Larry	Mental retardation	Elementary	Self-contained	Rural
Yvonne	Caucasian	George	ASD	Elementary	Inclusive	Suburban
Noreen	Caucasian	Roger	Other health impaired	Elementary	Inclusive with pull-out services	Urban
Nicole	Caucasian	Oscar	ADHD-PI	Elementary	Inclusive with pull-out services	Urban
Monica	Caucasian	Tommy	ADHD-PI	Elementary	Inclusive with pull-out services	Urban
Lisa	Caucasian	Hank	Learning disability	Elementary	Inclusive	Urban
DeDe	African American	Victor	Deaf	Middle	Inclusive	Urban
Teresa	Hispanic	Selena	Deaf	Middle	Self-contained	Urban
Dolorita	Hispanic	Josefina	Deaf	Middle	Self-contained	Urban
Ursula	Caucasian	Charlie	ADHD	Middle	Inclusive	Suburban
Valerie	Caucasian	Tad	Nonverbal learning disability	High	Inclusive	Suburban
Carole	Caucasian	Sam	Cerebral palsy	High	Inclusive	Suburban
Pat	Caucasian	Mike	Learning disability	High	Inclusive	Suburban

Note. Dolorita used an English–Spanish interpreter during her interview. ASD = autism spectrum disorder; ADHD-PI = attention-deficit hyperactivity disorder predominantly inattentive; ADHD = attention-deficit hyperactivity disorder.

Data Analysis

The findings related to mothers' trust in school principals actually emerged as one of several categories or themes we identified as we analyzed our interview data. Besides reporting the findings related to overall trust in education professionals (Angell et al., 2009), we decided to report separately on other emergent themes, such as mothers' trust in school principals, issues related to communication, and teaming factors. Once we had analyzed all the interview data and identified the major themes, we then focused more closely on specific themes and developed concept maps that guided our reports. For example, when we reported on our overall findings (Angell et al.), we did not have the journal space to delve into and discuss our findings related to mothers' trust in school principals. We took all the data that were categorized as *administrator perspectives* from our larger study and conducted additional analysis by revisiting the data, recoding the data, and categorizing the themes. Therefore, we selected this set of data for its own in-depth analysis and discussion due to the perspectives of our participants that principals had a significant impact on their trust in education professionals.

(23)

Text data are analyzed

We used cross-case analysis as described by Miles and Huberman (1994) to study each mother (i.e., case) as a whole entity, using line-by-line coding of each mother's interview responses, followed by a comparative analysis of all 16 cases. Each researcher independently line-by-line coded each interview and all codes were entered in NVivo7 software (Richards, 2002). Next, we met as a team on several occasions to discuss the codes, identify emergent themes, and reach concordance on the development of a concept map (shown in Figure 1) that represents the study's findings.

(24)

We used a flexible standard of categories, meaning we adjusted our categories as additional data from each case was analyzed in depth (Coffey & Atkinson, 1992). As categories emerged, we used a constant comparative method (Charmaz, 2000) to compare cases and to refine, expand, or delete categories as needed. This type of coding procedure helped us stay in tune with the mothers' views as we continually studied our interview data (Charmaz). As we discussed any disagreements we had about emergent categories, we returned to the verbatim data to again ascertain the participants' viewpoints, and continued this process until we agreed on all categories. This process of cross checking coding of the major categories provided "thoroughness for interrogating the data" and allowed for discussion that enhanced insights of the coding (Barbour, 2001, p. 1116).

(25)

Confirmability

We engaged in methods of respondent validation (Creswell, 2002) and member checking (Janesick, 2000) to confirm our findings. To secure respondent validation, we presented a summary of our findings to the interviewees by telephone or e-mail, asking them if they concurred with any or all of the emergent perspectives, that is, if they saw their personal perspectives represented in any or all of the reported findings. We also conducted member checks as a means of confirming the findings. Through member checking, we asked participants to comment on the accuracy of verbatim quotes and obtained their approval to use their direct personal quotes in written or verbal reports of the study. All 16 participants confirmed that the summary of findings adequately and accurately represented their perspectives on trust in school principals and all the mothers whose direct quotes appear in the report gave permission to cite them.

(26)

Limitations and Scope of the Study

Although we used accepted qualitative research methods for this study, we recognize that the validity of the findings may be affected by certain limitations. The first limitation of this study was that we did not explicitly plan to gather data on mothers' trust in school principals. Rather, these data emerged from the data gathered for broader research questions about mothers' trust in education professionals. The use of a semistructured interview protocol allowed us to probe further when participants discussed their trust in principals. However, we did not explicitly ask all participants about their trust in school principals or their perspectives on how those principals might influence their trust in other education professionals.

(27)

The second limitation of this study was that we did not establish extended relationships with the participants. We interviewed each mother once. Multiple interviews would have been ideal. However, we feel that the initial data and our analysis of them provided a strong foundation for more

(28)

FIGURE 1
Concept Map of Findings

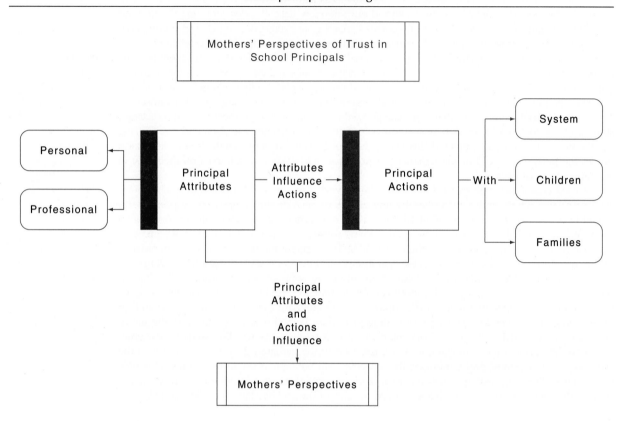

in-depth examinations of trust between parents of children with disabilities and school principals. We also recognize that the generalizability of the findings might have been limited by the nature of our participants. Although these findings are based on the perceptions of only 16 mothers from one state, these participants reflected ethnic, racial, and economic diversity and were mothers of children of various ages and disabilities. The recruitment of participants through school personnel might have also limited the generalizability of the findings, in that school personnel might have identified mothers with whom they felt they had positive, established relationships.

(29)   **Results**

Interviews centered on the issue of trust and the perspectives of the participants regarding their relationships with education professionals. Relationships with administrators, primarily school principals, emerged from all participants as one of the education professionals who had a strong effect on the trust of the mothers of children with disabilities. Two primary categories were identified as affecting the participants' perspectives of principals: (a) principal attributes (personal and professional) and (b) principal actions within the education system, with students, and with students' families. Additionally, within each of these primary categories, subcategories were developed that further delineated the relationships participants had with the principals at their children's schools.

Principal Attributes

(30)

Theme analysis is
presented

Principal attributes can be viewed as those *individual* characteristics that participants identified as affecting their trust. Attributes were categorized as either personal or professional. Within each of those two categories, the attributes could positively or negatively affect the relationship participants had with principals.

Personal attributes. All participants had interacted at one time or another with administra-   (31)
tors, primarily principals. Interactions might have been brief but participant perspectives were
developed over a long period of time. Participants might have had numerous relationships with
their children's teachers but relationships with principals were consistent over a longer period of
time. Principal personal attributes were part of principals' characters that participants perceived
during their interactions. We categorized these personal attributes as approachability and authentic
caring.

Approachability was identified as a positive influence on the trust of the participants in princi-   (32)
pals. Principals who were perceived as approachable were those who not only took the time to
listen but also conveyed an accepting attitude that resulted in parents comfortably approaching
them with their concerns. For example, Norine stated,

> You know, I had talked to him earlier in the year about how I thought it would really be important that
> those end-of-the-year awards that the kids all get, that every kid could get an award. And I didn't want to
> speak just about my son but obviously that's where it's coming from. But he just dreads those awards. He
> would have no reason to think that he could attain an art award, a music award, a scholastic award, noth-
> ing. He has nothing to shoot for . . . He [the principal] was, you know, very approachable about that and
> he has substituted some reading awards. So, now I just have to read with T. I feel like I have to do it now
> because I was the one that planned this.

However, not all participants described their principals as approachable. For example, Nicole   (33)
described her son's principal as "personable, but not to the point where I feel I could sit down and
talk to her on a personal level at all." Even if a principal was accessible, approachability was identified as the key to a mother's connecting and developing trust in the principal.

Similarly, another key to developing trust was the perception that the principal authentically   (34)
cared for the children and their parents. Authentic caring can be viewed as actions and behaviors
that participants identified as genuine, voluntary, child-focused, and benefiting children or the
parents themselves. Ursula exemplified this concept when she described her son's principal: "He
knew that my son had problems, so he would actually be checking out his assignment book as
he left."

Authentic caring did not have to necessarily result in actions; it was often a perception of   (35)
warmth that parents described from their interactions with principals. Dolorita talked about the
principal from her son's school who had retired in the previous year: "Yes, very good [referring to
her relationship with the principal]. She was always welcoming the parents. Really warm."

Principals who were trusted by participants were described as warm, respectful, and exhibiting   (36)
caring for children that was perceived as authentic.

Professional attributes. Attributes that were categorized as professional also affected the trust par-   (37)
ticipants had in principals. These professional attributes included accessibility and knowledge of
disabilities.

Principal accessibility was highly valued by all participants. Teresa spoke of the accessibility of   (38)
her son's principal: "She was very nice, she was so helpful with me any time that I need anything.
She was there and if I needed to talk to her she was right there." Participants recognized how busy
principals were and perhaps that recognition made them value the time principals offered even
more, illustrated by Monica's comment: "Even if she was busy she would take the minutes off."
Vickie highly valued the principal time given to her when she had concerns:

> I just called her and she sat on the phone with me for like a half an hour. And she had me come out and
> she gave me some books and, I mean, they are all, I think they are all wonderful.

Mary related an incident concerning programs for her son with Autism Spectrum Disorder   (39)
(ASD). She had expressed concern about her child's placement in a new program to the special
education administrator.

> So I said I'd go ahead and try it out and I kinda wanted him to stay where he was. She's like "Well, you
> know, you want to go with it and you can try it out and then we can pull him out if you don't like it or feel
> comfortable with it." So I said, "Okay." And we went ahead and tried it and then I called her up saying that
> I wasn't comfortable with him going there and just for all the happenings that were going on and we'd like
> him to go back to the first school and she said, "Okay, we can make some calls."

(40)   This incident illustrates the value of accessibility when participants feel a strong need to speak with principals. Accessibility was a necessary prerequisite for the establishment of trust and was mentioned by all participants. Participants were also keenly aware of the knowledge principals had about their children's disabilities. Valerie spoke of the knowledge a new principal had of her son's disability and the subsequent effect on the entire school staff.

> They also have a new principal, who I think is a little bit more aware of that [the disability]. I think the staff, whether they know it or not, takes cues from the principal as to whether the principal's going to follow up, whether this is something serious that we need to take note of. Is this really important, or is it something I can put a second priority on?

(41)   One incident in which the principal and staff had no knowledge of her daughter's disorder prompted Olivia to offer to provide an in-service session to the entire school staff. The principal readily agreed and this was appreciated by the parent.

> So I did a lot of reading on the issue, prepared a presentation. It was a good hour long, and they even stayed after to ask questions. I was really surprised. You know, we're talking an in-service that is in the evening, when people can be freed up from the classroom. It was 6–7:30 in the evening, and they made it mandatory.

(42)   The lack of knowledge of the disability was not viewed as an inhibitor to trust unless it was accompanied by a lack of desire to learn. Terri withdrew her child from a parochial school when she perceived that the staff was unwilling to address her son's disability. This perception appeared to contrast directly with the principal's words indicating that her son should remain at the school.

> Right, it is like I am, you know, I am very into the school. And the principal said "No we will leave him here." You know, and I said "No" because I am not going to force somebody on him. I am not going to do that to them just like I am not going to force that person onto my son.

(43)   One participant, Yvonne, spoke of the benefit of having the same principal during her son's vertical transition from preschool through elementary school. Yvonne was in an unusual situation in which her son's principal had moved from the preschool to the elementary school attended by her son. She spoke of the benefit of the principal's and the staff's continuous knowledge of her son's development and progress:

> I think again it's just been continuity and it's been more than just the principal that's been continually in his case; each time we meet people they seem to be amazed, everyone that is sitting around the table seems to be amazed at the progress that he's made. Yeah so they take great pride in him as do I and I don't know if he does yet, but he should.

(44)   Unfortunately, participants also recalled instances when principals did not recognize their children's disabilities, did not know their children, and at times appeared to dismiss parents' concern for their children. Ursula stated,

> The only thing I do want to add is I think the principals of each school should be more involved in IEP meetings. I know they're invited to it, but they never show up. So they might know this child is in special education but if they don't sit down and listen to everything, they really don't know the child.

(45)   Principals who were approachable, exhibited authentic caring, were accessible, and had knowledge of disabilities were identified as enhancing trust between participants and principals. Conversely, when these attributes were perceived as lacking, trust was negatively affected. Participants were aware that if principals valued their children and themselves, an example was set for the staff to follow.

Principal Actions

(46)   Actions spoke loudly to the participants. They identified actions that were categorized into three subcategories: (a) actions within the system, (b) actions with children, and (c) actions with families. These actions, or, at times, lack of action, had a significant effect on the trust participating mothers had in principals.

Actions within the system involved actions that were focused on issues such as encouraging (47)
teachers' involvement with parents and attendance at IEP meetings. When participants experienced
or observed these actions, they felt principals truly were concerned about the student body and
about their students with disabilities as well. Monica illustrated this by comparing the new principal
of her son's school with the previous one, illustrating the issue of teacher involvement with parent
fundraising efforts.

> And Mrs. F [the previous principal] was pushing the teachers to join, and pushing the teachers to do things.
> When we [Parent-Teacher Organization] did a pizza fundraiser she made every teacher order lunch with the
> kids for the room. She just was so involved in supporting all that stuff. And she knew we would in turn,
> money would go back to her. Whatever money we raised would go back to the school. I don't think he [the
> new principal] sees that. So, she was very much into everything.

Several participants indicated that principal attendance at IEP meetings was an action that facili- (48)
tated trust. Attendance not only affected the participants but the staff that was directly involved
with the child. Valerie spoke of the significance of her son's principal attending the IEP meeting:
"And I just think, especially at the IEP meetings, even if they're only there for 5–10 minutes, especially at the middle school, at least what I saw, it made a quite a difference . . . quite a difference."

While attendance at IEP meetings was appreciated, if it did not occur on a regular basis, prin- (49)
cipal attendance became an indicator of a problem. Carole recalled that the only IEP meeting
her son's principal attended was one that was contentious. The principal attended only when
the conflict had grown to a point where she was considering filing due process. Carole felt that
once the principal fully recognized her son's disability, his perception of her and her son changed
drastically.

> He actually saw my son then, and saw that these parents are not making this up. He [her son] has trouble
> speaking, too, so that people can't understand him, it's not just that he has trouble writing, everything is
> delayed to some degree. He can do everything but it just takes longer and he needs assistance. Before that
> the principal just thought I was a complaining parent.

It should be noted that most of our participants indicated that principals did not attend IEP (50)
meetings. Participants also reported there was significantly less principal involvement in IEP meetings at the middle and secondary levels.

Principal actions with students that affected parent trust were numerous. When the principals (51)
took a personal interest in their children, parents noticed. Ursula reported that one of her son's
principals was very involved with all the students in the school, including those with disabilities.

> My son had a principal in fifth and sixth grade, Mr. L, he was on top of it. He was a very good principal.
> He would be checking the kids out. He was just very—he was not just a principal that stays in his office.
> He would get there and be involved with all the kids. He knew that my son had had problems so he would
> actually be checking out his assignment book as he left.

Involvement with students, and especially involvement that included students with disabilities, (52)
was appreciated and recognized by our participants and had a positive effect on their establishment of trust in education professionals. Conversely, ignoring students or a perceived nonaction
by principals was perceived negatively and had an inhibiting effect on the establishment of trust.
Carole described this perception as, "A few times they've [principals] been involved. I don't feel
like they ever took a stand on anything. They just kind of were there."

Principals' actions with parents directly also had the potential of positively affecting trust. DeDe (53)
related a conversation with a vice principal:

> Because when last year my son was in it was his first year and he's mainstreamed. So she was . . . I was
> going to get his grades and she said, "How did he do?" And I said he did fine, but he was in fourth grade
> and doing fifth grade math and I was like well, he got a "C" in math, that was the only thing. She was like
> but you should be proud of him and I said I am proud of him. She kinda like, she was encouraging me to
> encourage him. She said "'cause you have to think he's in fourth grade, he's doing fifth grade math; he got a
> 'C' so that's wonderful." So I was like you know for a vice principal to come and talk to the parents is really
> good. So she talked to me and you know they are very encouraging and I think if I ever needed anything or
> needed to talk to one of them I could go up there and talk to them.

(54)   Actions with parents that were positively perceived were a focus on actively listening to parents and offering advice or assistance when needed, resulting in an enhancement of trust. However, not all principal actions with participants were positive.

(55)   Pat related an incident of requesting an evaluation for her son, who was having significant difficulties in school. Pat had spoken with a special educator, who had advised her to ask for an assessment for her son:

> She [the special educator] said "there is something not right here. And I can see this and you can deal with this. Go to the principal and tell him that he has to have him tested." And so I went and I told him and he [the principal] is like, "No, he is just a disruptive little boy."

(56)   Participants related other incidents that decreased trust, similar to the one stated above. These incidents were ones that did not respect or acknowledge parent perspectives.

(57)   Participants identified principal attributes and actions that enhanced trust and spoke strongly of times when these same attributes and actions were absent and inhibited their trust in principals. Participants wanted to trust principals; they appreciated principals who were accessible and evidenced authentic caring for their children and they described principal actions within the educational system, with their children, and with their families that facilitated their trust.

Discussion

(58)   Through an examination of the perspectives of mothers of children with disabilities, the present study findings revealed insights into the critical role school administrators, specifically principals, may assume in establishing and maintaining trust between schools and families. After a consideration of the limitations of this study, we discuss key findings from a school leadership framework. We then discuss implications for practice and future research.

Researchers interpret the larger meaning of findings

Principals' Influence on Trust

(59)   As depicted in Figure 1, the mothers we interviewed identified principals' attributes and actions that can have positive and negative influences on trust. They spoke primarily of school principals rather than special education administrators when they discussed school leaders. The findings on influential attributes and actions that emerged from these interviews were consistent with previous research on trust, particularly on trust in and as facilitated by school leaders (Bryk & Schneider, 2003; Kochanek, 2005; Tschannen-Moran, 2004). However, these findings extend past research by illuminating how trustworthy leadership may connect to the educational experiences of students with disabilities and their families.

(60)   Through her leadership matrix, Tschannen-Moran (2004) presented a framework for school leadership that promotes trust. The framework identified facets of trust, constituencies of schools, including parents, and functions of instructional leadership. The functions of leadership in the framework—visioning, modeling, coaching, managing, and mediating—can be demonstrated in a manner that inhibits or facilitates trust. We discuss our key findings in relationship to this framework for trustworthy school leadership.

Facets of Trust

(61)   Five facets of trust are included in Tschannen-Moran's (2004) leadership matrix, including benevolence, honesty, openness, reliability, and competence. Past research has confirmed the centrality of these facets to building trusting relationships in schools (see Bryk & Schneider, 2003; Hoy & Tschannen-Moran, 1999; Tschannen-Moran & Hoy, 1998, 2000). The personal and professional attributes that emerged in the present study as influences on mothers' trust in school principals reflect aspects of the facets of trust, specifically benevolence, openness, and competence.

(62)   Benevolence involves demonstrating caring, support, and respect. It may be the most critical facet of trust (Tschannen-Moran, 2004) and is valued by constituencies of school leaders (Bryk & Schneider, 2003; Tschannen-Moran). Mothers in this study identified the personal attribute of authentic caring, perceived as warmth and respect, as a critical influence on trust. Authentic caring also involves acceptance of a child (Noddings, 1992). For parents of children with disabilities,

schools: Its measure and relationship to faculty trust. *High School Journal, 86*(2), 38–49.

Hoy, W. K., & Tschannen-Moran, M. (1999). Five facets of trust: An empirical confirmation in urban elementary schools. *Journal of School Leadership, 9,* 184–208.

Individuals with Disabilities Education Improvement Act of 2004, Pub. L. No. 108-446, 118 Stat. 2647 (2004).

Janesick, V. (2000). The choreography of qualitative research design. In N. K. Denzin & Y. S. Lincoln (Eds.), *Handbook of qualitative research* (pp. 379–399). Thousand Oaks, CA: Sage.

Keller, B. (2006). Views differ over NCLB rules on involving parents. *Education Week, 26*(4), 12–13.

Kochanek, J. R. (2005). *Building trust for better schools: Research-based practices.* Thousand Oaks, CA: Corwin Press.

Kvale, S. (1996). *Interviews: An introduction to qualitative research interviewing.* Thousand Oaks, CA: Sage.

Lake, J. F., & Billingsley, B. S. (2000). An analysis of factors that contribute to parent-school conflict in special education. *Remedial and Special Education, 21,* 240–251.

Miles, M., & Huberman, A. (1994). *Qualitative data analysis.* Thousand Oaks, CA: Sage.

Mishra, A. (1996). Organizational responses to crisis: The centrality of trust. In R. M. Kramer & T. R. Tyler (Eds.), *Trust in organizations* (pp. 261–287). Thousand Oaks, CA: Sage.

No Child Left Behind Act of 2001, Pub. L. No. 107-110, 20 U. S. C. 70 (2002).

Noddings, N. (1992). *The challenge to care in schools: An alternative approach to education.* New York: Teachers College Press.

Nord, C. W., Brimhall, D., & West, J. (1997). *Fathers' involvement in their children's schools. NCES 98-091.* Washington, DC: National Center for Education Statistics.

Nord, C. W., & West, J. (2001). *Fathers' and mothers' involvement in their children's schools by family type and resident status* (NCES 2001-032). Washington, DC: National Center for Education Statistics.

Patton, M. Q. (1980). *Qualitative evaluation methods.* Beverly Hills, CA: Sage.

Richards, L. (2002). NVivo [Computer software]. Victoria, Australia: Bundoora.

Soodak, L. C., & Erwin, E. J. (2000). Valued member or tolerated participant: Parents' experiences in inclusive early childhood settings. *Journal of the Association for Persons with Severe Handicaps, 25*(1), 29–41.

Stake, R. (2000). Case studies. In N. K. Denzin & Y. S. Lincoln (Eds.), *Handbook of qualitative research* (pp. 435–454). Thousand Oaks, CA: Sage.

Stoner, J. B., & Angell, M. E. (2006). Parent perspectives on role engagement: An investigation of parents of children with ASD and their self-reported roles with education professionals. *Focus on Autism and Other Developmental Disabilities, 21,* 177–189.

Stoner, J. B., Angell, M. E., House, J. J., & Bock, S. J. (2007). Transitions: A parental perspective from parents of young children with Autism Spectrum Disorder (ASD). *Journal of Developmental and Physical Disabilities, 19,* 23–39.

Stoner, J. B., Bock, S. J., Thompson, J. R., Angell, M. E., Heyl, B., & Crowley, E. P. (2005). Welcome to our world: Parent perspectives of interactions between parents of young children with ASD and education professionals. *Focus on Autism and Other Developmental Disabilities, 20,* 39–51.

Strauss, A., & Corbin, J. (1998). *Basics of qualitative research: Techniques and procedures for developing grounded theory.* Thousand Oaks, CA: Sage.

Thomson, E., McLanahan, S. S., & Curtin, R. B. (1992). Family structure, gender, and parental socialization. *Journal of Marriage and the Family, 54,* 368–378.

Tschannen-Moran, M. (2003). Fostering organizational citizenship in schools: Transformational leadership and trust. In W. K. Hoy & C. Miskel (Eds.), *Studies in leading and organizing schools* (pp. 157–180). Greenwich, CT: Information Age Publishing.

Tschannen-Moran, M. (2004). *Trust matters: Leadership for successful schools.* San Francisco, CA: Jossey-Bass.

Tschannen-Moran, M., & Hoy, W. K. (1998). Trust in schools: A conceptual and empirical analysis. *Journal of Educational Administration, 36,* 334–352.

Tschannen-Moran, M., & Hoy, W. K. (2000). A multidisciplinary analysis of the nature, meaning, and measurement of trust. *Review of Educational Research, 70,* 547–570.

Turnbull, A., Turnbull, R., Erwin, E., & Soodak, L. (2006). *Families, professionals, and exceptionality: Positive outcomes through partnerships and trust* (5th ed.). Upper Saddle River, NJ: Merrill/ Prentice Hall.

Whitener, E. M., Brodt, S. E., Korsgaard, M. A., & Werner, J. M. (1998). Managers as initiators of trust: An exchange relationship framework for understanding managerial trustworthy behavior. *Academy of Management Review, 23,* 513–530.

Authors Note

Debra L. Shelden, PhD, is an Associate Professor in the Department of Special Education at Illinois State University in Normal, Illinois. Her research interests include perspectives of parents of children with disabilities, trust in educational professionals, and the transition from school to adult life for individuals with disabilities.

Maureen E. Angell, PhD, Professor of Special Education, is the Special Education Doctoral Program Coordinator at Illinois State University. Her research interests include systematic instruction for learners with disabilities, parents' perspectives, effective management of school-based dysphagia programs, issues of trust and parental advocacy, and self-determination in individuals with disabilities.

Julia B. Stoner, EdD, CCC-SLP, is an Associate Professor in the Department of Special Education at Illinois State University in Normal, Illinois. Her research interests include augmentative and alternative communication, perspectives of parents of children with disabilities, trust in educational professionals, and communication intervention strategies for young children with disabilities.

Bill D. Roseland, MA, is the Executive Director of an urban special education cooperative in Illinois in addition to being a doctoral student in the Department of Special Education at Illinois State University. His research interests include trust in educational professionals, and leadership self-efficacy.

Appendix

Trust Study Interview Questions

[Advise interviewee that she can apply most of these questions to ANY education professionals in her child's life—administrators, teachers, assistants, related services personnel like SLPs, OTs, PTs . . .]

1. Tell me about your child.
2. How would you generally describe your relationship with (child's name)'s teacher? [teachers]
3. Describe the trust you have in the professionals who work with your child. [Do you trust the education professionals who work with your child? . . . Probe: Please describe this trust/lack of trust . . .]
4. Have there been situations or experiences that have increased your level of trust in the professionals who work with your child? [Tell me about this/these . . .]
5. Have there been situations that have decreased the trust you have in the professionals who work with your child? [Tell me about this/these . . .]
6. Do you tend to trust other people or distrust them? Does it take time for you to develop trust in someone?
7. How much contact have you had with your child's education professionals? Have you had contact on a regular basis, occasionally, seldom . . . ? Have your interactions been generally positive? Generally negative? Please describe some . . .
8. Do you think that your cultural background (your race, ethnicity, education, income level) in any way influences your level of trust in others or in education professionals? If so, how?

PART TWO

The Steps in the Process of Research

Now that you have the general road map for your journey, we will start the trip and proceed through each step. Not all researchers go through each step in the order presented here, but many do. By proceeding down the research path, step by step, you will enhance your ability to read, evaluate, and conduct research using both quantitative and qualitative approaches.

The chapters in Part II are:

- Chapter 2 Identifying a Research Problem
- Chapter 3 Reviewing the Literature
- Chapter 4 Specifying a Purpose and Research Questions or Hypotheses
- Chapter 5 Collecting Quantitative Data
- Chapter 6 Analyzing and Interpreting Quantitative Data
- Chapter 7 Collecting Qualitative Data
- Chapter 8 Analyzing and Interpreting Qualitative Data
- Chapter 9 Reporting and Evaluating Research

CHAPTER

Identifying a Research Problem

*R*esearchers begin a study by identifying a research problem that they need to address. They write about this "problem" in the opening passages of their study and, in effect, give you as a reader the rationale for why the study is important and why you need to read their study. In this chapter, you will learn about specifying a research problem and positioning it within a section that introduces a study, the "statement of the problem" section.

By the end of this chapter, you should be able to:

◆ Define a research problem and explain its importance in a study.

◆ Distinguish between a research problem and other parts of research process.

◆ Identify criteria for deciding whether a problem can and should be researched.

◆ Describe how quantitative and qualitative research problems differ.

◆ Learn the five elements in writing a "statement of the problem" section.

◆ Identify strategies useful in writing a "statement of the problem" section.

Maria begins her research project required for her graduate program. Where does she start? She starts by posing several questions and then writing down short answers to them.

◆ *"What is the specific controversy or issue that I need to address?"* Escalating violence in the schools

◆ *"Why is this problem important?"* Schools need to reduce the violence; students will learn better if violence is less a part of their lives, etc.

◆ *"How will my study add to what we already know about this problem?"* We really don't have many school plans for addressing this escalating violence

◆ *"Who will benefit from what I learn about this problem?"* Schools, anybody interested in learning how schools can respond to escalating violence (the body of literature, administrators, teachers, etc.)

For a beginning researcher, the difficulty is not developing answers to questions, but coming up with the questions to ask yourself. To do this, we need to learn how to write an introduction or "statement of the problem" section for a research study.

WHAT IS A RESEARCH PROBLEM AND WHY IS IT IMPORTANT?

One of the most challenging aspects of conducting research is to clearly identify the "problem" that leads to a need for your study. Individuals do not seem to give enough attention to why they are conducting their studies. **Research problems** are the educational issues, controversies, or concerns that guide the need for conducting a study. Good research problems can be found in our educational settings, such as:

1. The disruptions caused by at-risk students in classrooms
2. The increase in violence on college campuses
3. The lack of parental involvement in schools for students with challenging behaviors

These problems concern personnel in our schools, classrooms, and college campuses. In writing about the research problem, authors state it as a single sentence or several sentences in a research report. To locate the research problem in a study, ask yourself:

◆ What was the issue, problem, or controversy that the researcher wanted to address?
◆ What controversy leads to a need for this study?
◆ What was the concern being addressed "behind" this study?
◆ Is there a sentence like "The problem addressed in this study is . . ."?

You can find "problems" in the introduction to a study. They are included in a passage called the "statement of the problem" section. You can locate this passage in the opening, introductory paragraphs of a research report.

We study research problems so we can assist policy makers when they make decisions, help teachers and school officials solve practical problems, and provide researchers with a deeper understanding of educational issues. From a research standpoint, specifying a research problem in your study is important because it sets the stage for the entire study. Without knowing the research problem, readers do not know why the study is important and why they should read the study. What are some educational issues that you might research? Write down these issues.

Although you are aware of many educational problems, it is challenging to write them into a research report. This may be due to a lack of understanding about how to write them or identify them for your study.

HOW DOES THE RESEARCH PROBLEM DIFFER FROM OTHER PARTS OF RESEARCH?

To better understand research problems, you might distinguish them from other parts of the research process. The research problem is distinct from the *topic* of the study (to be addressed later in this chapter), the *purpose* or intent of the study (to be considered in the chapter on purpose statements), and specific *research questions* (also discussed in the chapter on purpose statements). The research problem needs to stand on its own and be recognized as a distinct step because it represents the problem addressed in the study.

In the brief definitions that follow, consider the differences among these parts of research:

◆ A *research topic* is the broad subject matter addressed by the study. Maria, for example, seeks to study weapon possession by students in schools.

◆ A *research problem* is a general educational issue, concern, or controversy addressed in research that narrows the topic. The problem Maria addresses is the escalating violence in schools due, in part, to students possessing weapons.

◆ A *purpose* is the major intent or objective of the study used to address the problem. Maria might state the purpose of her study as follows: "The purpose of my study will be to identify factors that influence the extent to which students carry weapons in high schools."

◆ *Research questions* narrow the purpose into specific questions that the researcher would like answered or addressed in the study. Maria might ask, "Do peers influence students to carry weapons?"

Looking at these differences, you can see that they differ in terms of breadth from broad (topic) to narrow (specific research questions). Let's examine another example, as shown in Figure 2.1, to make this point. In this example, a researcher begins with a broad topic, distance learning. The inquirer then seeks to learn about a problem related to this topic: the lack of students enrolled in distance education classes. To study this problem, our educator then reformulates the problem into a statement of intent (the purpose statement): to study why students do not attend distance education classes at one community college. Examining this statement requires that our investigator narrow the intent to specific questions, one of which is "Does the use of Web site technology

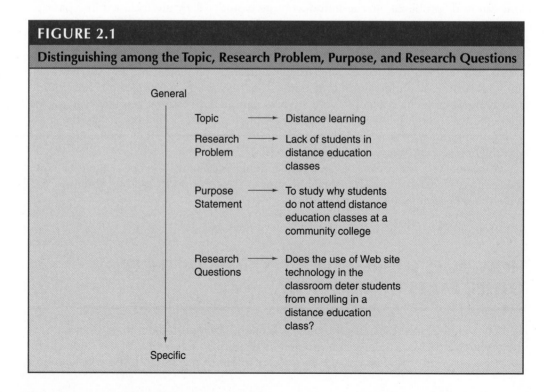

FIGURE 2.1

Distinguishing among the Topic, Research Problem, Purpose, and Research Questions

General

Topic ⟶ Distance learning

Research Problem ⟶ Lack of students in distance education classes

Purpose Statement ⟶ To study why students do not attend distance education classes at a community college

Research Questions ⟶ Does the use of Web site technology in the classroom deter students from enrolling in a distance education class?

Specific

in the classroom deter students from enrolling in distance education classes?" The process involves narrowing a broad topic to specific questions. In this process, the "research problem" becomes a distinct step that needs to be identified to help readers clearly see the issue.

A common error is stating research problems as the purpose of the study or as the research question. The following examples show how you might reshape a purpose or a research question as a research problem.

> *Poor model.* The researcher intends to identify the research problem but instead presents it as a *purpose statement:* The purpose of this study is to examine the education of women in Third World countries.
>
> *Improved model.* A revision of it as a *research problem:* Women in Third World countries are restricted from attending universities and colleges because of the culturally oriented, patriarchal norms of their societies.
>
> *Poor model.* A researcher intends to write about the research problem but instead identifies the *research question:* The research question in this study is "What factors influence homesickness in college students?"
>
> *Improved model.* An improved version as a *research problem:* Homesickness is a major issue on college campuses today. When students get homesick, they leave school or start missing classes, leading to student attrition or poor achievement in classes during their first semester of college.

As you design and conduct a study, make sure that you are clear about the distinctions among these parts of research and that your written material differentiates among a topic, the research problem, the purpose, and your research questions.

CAN AND SHOULD PROBLEMS BE RESEARCHED?

Just because a problem exists and an author can clearly identify the issue does not mean that the researcher *can* or *should* investigate it. You *can* research a problem if you have access to participants and research sites as well as time, resources, and skills needed to study the issue. You *should* research a problem if the study of it potentially contributes to educational knowledge or adds to the effectiveness of practice.

Can You Gain Access to People and Sites?

To research a problem, investigators need to gain permission to enter a site and to involve people at the location of the study (e.g., gaining access to an elementary school to study children who are minors). This access often requires multiple levels of approval from schools, such as district administrators, principals, teachers, parents, and students. In addition, projects conducted by educational agencies receiving federal funding (most colleges and universities) need to have institutional review approval to ensure that researchers protect the rights of their participants. Your ability to gain access to people and sites can help determine if you can research the issue.

Can You Find Time, Locate Resources, and Use Your Skills?

Even if you can gain access to the people and sites needed for your study, your ability to research the problem also depends on time, resources, and your research skills.

Time

When planning a study, investigators should anticipate the time required for data collection and data analysis. Qualitative studies typically take more time than quantitative studies because of the lengthy process of collecting data at research sites and the detailed process of analyzing sentences and words. Regardless of the approach used, you can gauge the amount of time needed for data collection by examining similar studies, contacting the authors, or asking researchers who are more experienced. Developing a time line for a study helps you assess whether you can reasonably complete the study within the time available.

Resources

Investigators need resources such as funds for equipment, for participants, and for individuals to transcribe interviews. Researchers need to create a budget and obtain advice from other, experienced researchers about whether the anticipated expenses are realistic. Other resources may be needed as well, such as mailing labels, postage, statistical programs, or audiovisual equipment. Dependent on these resource requirements, investigators may need to limit the scope of a project, explore funding available to support the project, or research the project in stages as funds become available.

Skills

The skills of the researcher also affect the overall assessment of whether the study of a problem is realistic. Investigators need to have acquired certain research skills to effectively study a problem—skills gained through courses, training, and prior research experiences. For those engaged in quantitative studies, these skills require using computers, employing statistical programs, or creating tables for presenting information. The skills needed for qualitative researchers consist of the ability to write detailed passages, to synthesize information into broad themes, and to use computer programs for entering and analyzing words from participants in the study.

Should the Problem Be Researched?

A positive answer to this question lies in whether your study will contribute to knowledge and practice. One important reason for engaging in research is to add to existing information and to inform our educational practices. Research adds to knowledge. Now let's examine these ways in more detail as you think about the research problem in one of your studies.

There are five ways to assess whether you should research a problem:

1. *Study the problem if your study will fill a gap or void in the existing literature.*   A study fills a void by covering topics not addressed in the published literature. For example, assume that a researcher examines the literature on the ethical climate on college campuses and finds that past research has examined the perceptions of students, but not of faculty. This is a void or gap in the body of research about this issue. Conducting a study about faculty perceptions of the ethical climate would address a topic not studied in the current literature.

2. *Study the problem if your study replicates a past study but examines different participants and different research sites.*   The value of research increases when results can apply broadly to many people and places rather than to only the setting where the initial research occurred. This type of study is especially important in quantitative experiments.

In a quantitative study of ethical climate, for example, past research conducted in a liberal arts college can be tested (or replicated) at other sites, such as a community college or major research university. Information from such a study will provide new knowledge.

3. *Study the problem if your study extends past research or examines the topic more thoroughly.*   A good research problem to study is one in which you extend the research into a new topic or area, or simply conduct more research at a deeper, more thorough level to understand the topic. For example, in our illustration on ethical climate, although research exists on ethical climates, it now needs to be extended to the situation in which students take exams, because taking exams poses many ethical dilemmas for students. In this way, you extend the research to new topics. This extension is different from replication because you extend the research to these topics rather than participants and research sites.

4. *Study the problem if your study gives voice to people silenced, not heard, or rejected in society.*   Your research adds to knowledge by presenting the ideas and the words of marginalized (e.g., the homeless, women, racial groups) individuals. For example, although past studies on ethical climate have addressed students on predominantly white campuses, we have not heard the voices of Native Americans on this topic. A study of this type would report and give voice to Native Americans.

5. *Study the problem if your study informs practice.*   By examining the problem, your research may lead to the identification of new techniques or technologies, the recognition of the value of historical or current practice, or the necessity of changing current teaching practice. Individuals who benefit from practical knowledge may be policy makers, teachers, or learners. For example, a study of ethical issues in a college setting may lead to a new honor code, new policies about cheating on exams, or new approaches to administering tests.

HOW DOES THE RESEARCH PROBLEM DIFFER IN QUANTITATIVE AND QUALITATIVE RESEARCH?

After you identify a research problem, you should also consider if it better fits a quantitative or qualitative approach. Because the two approaches differ in their essential characteristics, there should be a match between your problem and the approach you use. What factors are important in determining this match? What type of research problem is best suited for quantitative research and what type for qualitative research?

Let's look once again at the parent involvement study (Deslandes & Bertrand, 2005) and the mothers' issues of trust in school principals study (Shelden et al., 2010). We can see that each study addresses a different type of problem. In the quantitative parent involvement study, the researchers make a case that we know little about what factors lead parents to decide to (or to *explain why they*) become involved in their adolescents' schooling. Why would such a lack of involvement be important? The authors cite literature suggesting that involvement means fewer disciplinary problems and higher grades. Explaining or predicting relations among variables is an important characteristic of *quantitative* research. Alternatively, in the qualitative study of mothers' issues of trust study, the authors describe a need to gain insight into the trust of mothers of children with disabilities in school principals. This requires *exploring* and *understanding* the nature of trust. Exploring a problem is a characteristic of *qualitative* research.

These two factors—explanation and exploration—provide a standard you can use to determine whether your research problem is better suited for either a quantitative or qualitative study. Here are some additional factors to consider:

Tend to use *quantitative research* if your research problem requires you to:	Tend to use *qualitative research* if your research problem requires you to:
◆ Measure variables	◆ Learn about the views of individuals
◆ Assess the impact of these variables on an outcome	◆ Assess a process over time
◆ Test theories or broad explanations	◆ Generate theories based on participant perspectives
◆ Apply results to a large number of people	◆ Obtain detailed information about a few people or research sites

HOW DO YOU WRITE A "STATEMENT OF THE PROBLEM" SECTION?

After you have identified your research problem, determined that it can and should be researched, and specified either the quantitative or qualitative approach, it is time to begin writing about the "problem" in a statement of the problem section that introduces your research study.

The **statement of the problem** section includes the actual research problem as well as four other aspects:

1. The topic
2. The research problem
3. A justification of the importance of the problem as found in the past research and in practice
4. The deficiencies in our existing knowledge about the problem
5. The audiences that will benefit from a study of the problem

By identifying these five elements, you can easily understand introductions to research studies and write good introductions for your own research reports.

The Topic

The opening sentences of a "statement of the problem" section need to encourage readers to continue reading, to generate interest in the study, and to provide an initial frame of reference for understanding the entire research topic. Given these factors, it makes sense to start with a broad topic that readers can easily understand. In this way, you bring readers into a study slowly and encourage them to read beyond the first page.

An **educational topic** is the broad subject matter that a researcher wishes to address in a study and that creates initial interest for the reader. As shown in Figure 2.2, researchers state the topic in the title and introduce it in the first sentences. Note that the authors ease into the study with general ideas that most readers can understand (standardized tests, the education of Native Americans, the problem-solving mode of teaching elementary science). For example, assume that an author begins the topic discussion with comments about

FIGURE 2.2

Select Topics and First Sentences of Research Studies Reported in Educational Journals

The Impact of Mandated Standardized Testing on Minority Students

Richard G. Lomax, Mary Maxwell West, Maryellen C. Harmon, Katherine A. Viator, & George F. Madaus, 1995

One of the original reasons for the introduction of mandated standardized tests was to reduce the effects of patronage and thereby open educational opportunities and a range of occupations to a wider population of students (Madaus, 1991). However,. . .

Inhibitors to Implementing a Problem-Solving Approach to Teaching Elementary Science: Case Study of a Teacher in Change

Mary Lee Martens, 1992

The problem-solving mode of teaching elementary science now recommended in many states implies change for many groups of professionals including teachers, administrators, and other individuals charged with implementing educational policy. Teachers, however,. . .

Living and Working in Two Worlds
Case Studies of Five
American Indian
Women Teachers
BRENDA HILL, COURTNEY VAUGHN, AND SHARON BROOKS HARRISON, 1995

The Euro-American education of American Indians began under the auspices of missionaries and a few lay educators, with the ongoing purpose of remaking American Indians into the Euro-American image. In. . .

plagiarism on college campuses. This approach may unnecessarily narrow the topic too soon and lose readers who have not studied or read about plagiarism. Instead, writers might begin with the broader topic of dishonesty on campus and the need to explore the values students learn during their college years.

Let's examine the first sentence. We call it a **narrative hook**. It serves the important function of drawing the reader into a study. Good narrative hooks have these characteristics: cause the reader to pay attention, elicit emotional or attitudinal responses, spark interest, and encourage the reader to continue reading.

A convincing narrative hook might include one or more of the following types of information:

1. Statistical data (e.g., "More than 50% of the adult population experiences depression today.")
2. A provocative question (e.g., "Why are school policies that ban smoking in high schools not being enforced?")
3. A clear need for research (e.g., "School suspension is drawing increased attention among scholars in teacher education.")
4. The intent or purpose of the study (e.g., "The intent of this study is to examine how clients construe the therapist–client relationship.")

Although all of these represent possibilities for you to use, the key idea is that a study begins with an introduction to a topic that the reader can easily understand and with a first sentence that creates reader interest. Examine once again Figure 2.2 and assess whether the first sentence in these three studies captures your interest and encourages you to continue reading. Evaluate each based on the four types of information for a good narrative hook listed above.

The Research Problem

After stating the topic in the opening discussion, you then narrow the topic to a specific research problem or issue. Recall that a **research problem** is an educational issue, concern, or controversy that the researcher investigates. Authors may present it as a single sentence or as a couple of short sentences. Also, authors may frame the problem as a deficiency in the literature, such as we know little about the factors that lead parents to be involved in their adolescents' schooling (Deslandes & Bertrand, 2005).

What types of research problems do you study? Sometimes research problems come from issues or concerns found in schools or other educational settings. We will call these **practical research problems**. For example, can you see the practical issue in the following research problem posed about the Chinese policy toward single-child families?

> Since the late 1970s a single-child policy has been implemented by the Chinese government to control the largest population in the world. Selective abortion to choose a boy could inevitably skew the Chinese gender distribution, and is clearly prohibited by the government. As a result, although boys were valued higher than girls in traditional Chinese culture, many parents eventually have a girl as their single child. (Wang & Staver, 1997, p. 252)

The practical problem in this study was that boys were valued more than girls and the policy controls people in the population.

In other research studies the "problem" will be based on a need for further research because a gap exists or we need to extend the research into other areas. It might also be based on conflicting evidence in the literature. This type of problem is a **research-based research problem**. For example, see how the author in the next example calls for additional research that connects developmentally appropriate reading practices and teachers' approaches:

> Although both teacher beliefs about developmentally appropriate practices with young children and teacher theoretical orientation to early reading instruction have been previously studied, there is a lack of research that connects the two areas. (Ketner, Smith, & Parnell, 1997, p. 212)

The "problem" in this case is based on a research need for more information.

In some research, you can take both a practical and a research-based approach to the problem and state both types of problems. For example, consider how both play into this statement: "There is a need to better explain reading progress (the practical approach) as well as make up for a lack of research about developmentally appropriate practices and teacher orientation (the research-based approach)."

Whether you find the research problem in a practical setting, find it as a need in the research literature, or both, the point is to state it clearly in a sentence or two in the statement of the problem section. The reader simply needs to know the issue or concern that leads to a need for your study.

Justification of the Importance of the Problem

It is not enough to state the problem or issue. You also need to provide several reasons that explain why this issue is important. **Justifying a research problem** means presenting reasons for the importance of studying the issue or concern. This justification occurs

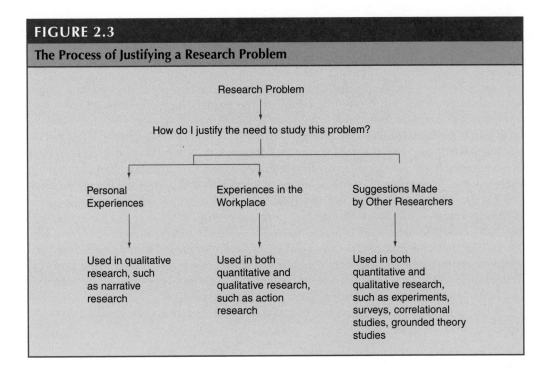

FIGURE 2.3

The Process of Justifying a Research Problem

in several paragraphs in an introduction in which you provide evidence to document the need to study the problem. As shown in Figure 2.3, you can justify the importance of your problem by citing evidence from:

◆ Other researchers and experts as reported in the literature
◆ Experiences others have had in the workplace
◆ Personal experiences

These justifications draw from different sources, are used in different types of approaches (i.e., quantitative or qualitative), and typically find expression in select research designs such as experiments, action research, or narrative research (to be addressed more specifically in the research design chapters in part III).

Justification in the Literature Based on Other Researchers and Experts

We will begin with the most scholarly justification—suggestions from other researchers that the problem needs to be studied. Authors often cite research problems that require further study in the conclusions of the literature such as journal articles. For example, note the suggestions for future research in the concluding paragraph in the mothers' trust in school principals study (Shelden et al., 2010):

> These findings also suggest a need to examine the extent to which school principal personnel preparation programs are adequately preparing school principals to build trust and effective partnerships with parents of students with disabilities. (pp. 168–169)

Using this example, you might cite Shelden et al. (2010) and use this information as justification for the changes in personnel preparation programs. Another justification from the literature consists of advancing a need for the study based on an incomplete model or theory that explains the relation among elements of the model or theory.

A theory, for example, may be incomplete because it does not address important factors that need to be considered. Thus, a leadership theory may identify the traits of the leader, the characteristics of the follower, and the elements operating in the leadership situation (e.g., congenial environment), but be lacking the element of the daily interactions that occur between the leader and the follower. A research study is needed to account for these interactions and more fully complete the model. Researchers could cite other researchers and experts who have also stated this conclusion but have not followed up on it with a research study.

Cite experts as justification for your research problem. Where do you find references to other researchers or experts who have indicated a need for a study? Often, authors of conference papers, research syntheses, or encyclopedias that report the latest research, such as the *Encyclopedia of Educational Research* (Alkin, 1992), mention the need for additional research on topics. Research experts have often studied topics for years, and they understand future research needs that will contribute to knowledge. You can identify and locate these experts through a search of library references, contact them at professional conferences, or find them through the Internet or through Web site addresses. Individuals who have spent entire careers becoming authorities on research topics or problems generally welcome student questions or requests.

When approaching these individuals, consider the questions you might ask them. Here is a short list of possibilities:

- ◆ What are you working on at present?
- ◆ Is my proposed topic and research problem worthy of study?
- ◆ Who else should I contact who has recently studied this topic and problem?

Although you may be hesitant to contact experts, such conversation yields leads for finding references, names of others interested in your topic, and names of conferences at which your research may be discussed.

Another authority on a particular research problem may be your graduate faculty advisor or your graduate committee members. Your advisor may have a long-term research agenda of examining an educational issue through a series of studies. By participating in the faculty member's research, you can learn about other studies and locate useful research to use as justification for your own research problems.

Justification Based on Workplace or Personal Experiences

You can justify your research problem based on evidence from your workplace or your personal experiences. This is the case for Maria, who based her justification for the study of students possessing weapons on the increased use of weapons in high schools in her school (or workplace) in the district.

Issues arise in educational workplaces that you can address in your research. For example, policy makers need to decide whether to mandate state standards of assessment, or principals and teachers must develop approaches to classroom discipline. Closely related are the personal experiences of our lives that provide sources for researchable problems. These personal experiences may arise from intense personal school experiences or experiences drawn from our childhood or family situations. Personal experiences provide justification especially in those studies with a practical orientation, such as solving a particular classroom dilemma in an action research study. They are also apparent in studies in which the researcher is the object of study, such as in narrative research. Researchers citing their own personal experiences as justification for a research problem need to be forewarned that some individuals (such as those trained in quantitative research) may feel that such experiences should not be the sole justification for a study. This is a fair warning, and you might consider including not only your own personal experiences, but some of the other reasons mentioned for justifying a research problem.

Consider the following two examples of researchers introducing their own experiences as justification for studying a research problem. One researcher justifies the need to study students in a multiage middle school by referring to her own experiences in school. The study begins:

> In the spring of 1992, the opportunity to conduct classroom action research was offered to Madison, Wisconsin teachers. Though my daily schedule was already full, I was drawn to this opportunity because of its emphasis on practical, classroom based research. . . . For me, multicultural curricula, cooperative learning, computer technology, and thematic education were exciting developments in classroom teaching. (Kester, 1994, p. 63)

Another researcher justifies the need for studying the ostracism of African American students in schools by tracing personal family experiences. The study starts:

> When I was growing up, there was never a thought in my mind about whether or not I would go to school. It was given that I was going to go to school every day as long as my parents were alive and the Lord woke me up in good health. (Jeffries, 1993, p. 427)

Now consider Maria's justification based on her school experiences. Provide three reasons why a need exists for research on students possessing weapons in school. As a hint, consider how the school, the teachers, and the students themselves might benefit from a better understanding of this problem.

Deficiencies in What We Know

In the "statement of the problem" section, you next need to summarize how our present state of knowledge—both from research and from practice—is deficient. Although a deficiency in the literature may be part of the justification for a research problem, it is useful to enumerate on several deficiencies in the existing literature or practice. A **deficiency in the evidence** means that the past literature or practical experiences of the researchers does not adequately address the research problem. For example, deficiencies in the research may require a need to extend the research, replicate a study, explore a topic, lift the voices of marginalized people, or add to practice. A deficiency in practice means that educators have not yet identified good and workable solutions for schools or other educational settings. As you summarize these deficiencies, identify two or three reasons why existing research and practice are deficient in addressing the research problem, and state these reasons toward the end of the introduction to the study. In the following example, a researcher indicates weaknesses in past research and reflects on personal experiences:

> The past research does not address the cultural differences of children in preschools. It also does not consider the multiple factors that explain teacher interactions with these students. From observing preschools, the need further exists to better understand how teachers interact with preschool children from different cultures.

In Maria's situation, in what areas would her school committee lack information to help them address the problem of weapons in the schools? They might not know how frequently students actually carry weapons, what types they are, and the places where they hide the weapons. State at least two other deficiencies in knowledge the school committee might have.

The Audience

The **audience** in a "statement of the problem" section needs to be identified. It consists of individuals and groups who will read and potentially benefit from the information provided in your research study. These audiences will vary depending on the nature of your study, but several often considered by educators include researchers, practitioners, policy makers, and individuals participating in the studies. One author, for example, in ending an introduction section, commented about the importance of the study for school administrators:

> By exploring the need for athletic trainers in high schools, school administrators can identify potential issues that arise when trainers are not present, and coaches can better understand the circumstances in which trainers are most needed at athletic events.

As this example illustrates, authors often enumerate multiple audiences. Passages such as these are typically found in the concluding passage in the introduction or the "statement of the problem" section and explain the importance of addressing the problem for each audience. Like the narrative hook, this information continues to draw the reader into the study and it personalizes the research so that readers can see that the study will potentially provide meaningful information. When researchers include comments about the importance of the study for audiences, they also remind themselves about the need to report useful results.

WHAT ARE SOME STRATEGIES FOR WRITING THE "STATEMENT OF THE PROBLEM" SECTION?

Writing the introduction or "statement of the problem" section as an opening passage in your research report sets the stage for readers to understand your project and appreciate the strong research orientation of your report. Several writing strategies can help you craft this section.

A Template

One strategy you can use as you write your "statement of the problem" section is to visualize this section as five paragraphs, with each paragraph addressing one of the five aspects of the section. Take sections in order beginning with the topic, the research problem, the justification, the deficiencies, and the audience. Examine the flow of ideas as shown in Figure 2.4. This figure shows that a "statement of the problem" section has five elements, and it provides a brief definition for each element and an example to illustrate the element. The researcher begins with the topic of parents' role in promoting access to college for their students of color. This is a sensitive topic and it could be difficult to study. However, the topic merits a research study. Also, from practical experiences on campuses, past literature has documented low attendance by students of color and that there has been a norm of underachievement by these students in college. Thus, parents might play a key role in encouraging college attendance, and we need evidence

FIGURE 2.4

Flow of Ideas in a "Statement of the Problem" Section

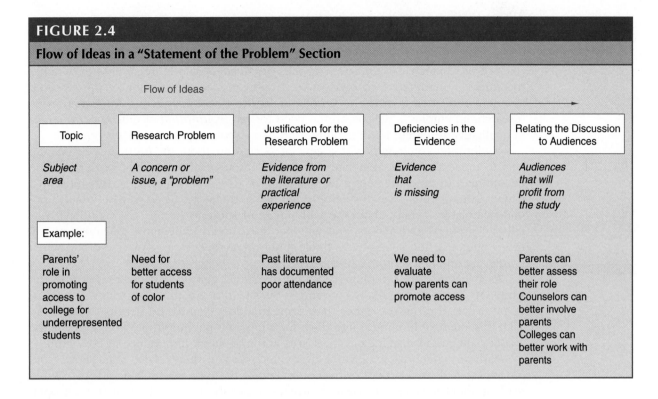

from parents about how they might construct this role. By studying this problem and gaining insight from parents, the role of parents can be better understood, school counselors can reach out to involve parents in encouraging their children, and colleges can better recruit underrepresented students to their campuses. The flow of ideas runs from the topic to the problem and its justification and deficiencies that, if studied, will aid specific audiences.

Other Writing Strategies

Another writing strategy is to use frequent references to the literature throughout this introductory passage. Multiple references add a scholarly tone to your writing and provide evidence from others, rather than relying on your own personal opinion. The use of references in your study will build credibility for your work. A third strategy is to provide references from statistical trends to support the importance of studying the research problem. How many teenagers smoke? How many individuals are HIV positive? This form of evidence is especially popular in quantitative studies. Another writing strategy is to use quotes from participants in a study or from notes obtained from observing participants to begin your "statement of the problem" introduction. This approach is popular and frequently used in qualitative studies. Finally, be cautious about using quotes from the literature to begin a study, especially in the first sentence. Readers may not extract the same meaning from a quote as the researcher does. The quotes are often too narrow to be appropriate for an introductory section in which you seek to establish a research problem and provide justification for it. To use quotes effectively, readers often need to be led "into" as well as "out of" the quote.

Think-Aloud About Writing a "Statement of the Problem"

I will model how I would write a "statement of the problem" to illustrate the actual practice of research. My approach applies the five-step model regardless of whether the study is quantitative or qualitative. However, close inspection of the research problem indicates a different emphasis in the two approaches. In quantitative research, an emphasis will be on the need for an *explanation* of outcomes, whereas in qualitative research, I will explore a *process, event,* or *phenomenon.*

My introduction begins with a general discussion about the topic of the research. I try to present the first sentence as a good "narrative hook" so that readers will be encouraged to read the report. The writing of this first sentence is difficult, and I may draft numerous revisions before I am satisfied that it will be general, timely, and understandable. I think about the wide range of students in my class who have varied backgrounds and majors, and whether they would understand and relate to my first sentence. I find it helpful to think about my audiences as a diverse group when I write the opening sentence of this passage.

As I've said, the opening paragraph needs to gently lead the reader into the study. My analogy for this is lowering a bucket into a well to get water. I hope to gently lower the bucket rather than drop it suddenly into the depths of the well. With this example in mind, I introduce the study in a paragraph or two and focus the reader's attention on a single subject area and its general importance in education.

With any given topic, several issues may present themselves. Some arise from my experiences in a school or from a review of the past research on a topic. While reading about my topic in research articles (typically in journal articles), I am open to issues that need to be studied, and am most interested in specific issues that other authors suggest need to be studied. These issues are located in future research sections at the conclusion of articles. I often make a list of these suggestions for research on a piece of paper and try to follow up on one of them. When reviewing these studies, I try to become familiar with authors who are leaders in the field. These are often individuals frequently cited in published studies or commonly heard at conferences. Because of their expertise, I may contact these authors by phone or by e-mail to discuss my proposed study.

Once I have an understanding of a problem and can adequately justify studying it through evidence from the literature, I begin the process of writing the first section of a research report, the "statement of the problem." I follow my five elements for writing this section, write the section, and check it for all five elements. My goal is to present a solid rationale for why my study is needed, and I support this need with several arguments using multiple forms of evidence. I extensively cite references in the introductory passage of my study. To ensure that the importance of the study is clear to the audience, I end the "statement of the problem" section with comments about the utility of the study for several audiences.

EXAMPLES OF "STATEMENT OF THE PROBLEM" SECTIONS

An example of a "statement of the problem" section is shown in Figure 2.5. This is from my study about teenage smoking in high schools. I introduce the topic and research problem in the first paragraph. This shows how the topic and the research problem can sometimes blend. I then cite evidence for this problem in the second paragraph. Note

FIGURE 2.5

Sample "Statement of the Problem" Section

Statement of the Problem Elements	Exploring the Conceptions and Misconceptions of Teen Smoking in High Schools: A Multiple Case Analysis
The Topic	Tobacco use is a leading cause of cancer in American society (McGinnis & Foefe, 1993). Although smoking among adults has declined in recent years, it has actually increased for adolescents. The Center for Disease Control and Prevention reported that smoking among high school students had risen from 27.5 percent in 1991 to 34.8 percent in 1995 (USDHHS 1996). Unless this trend is dramatically reversed, an estimated 5 million of our nation's children will ultimately die a premature death (Center for Disease Control, 1996).
The Research Problem	
Evidence Justifying the Research Problem	Previous research on adolescent tobacco use has focused on four primary topics. Several studies have examined the question of the initiation of smoking by young people, noting that tobacco use initiation begins as early as junior high school (e.g., Heishman et al., 1997). Other studies have focused on the prevention of smoking and tobacco use in schools. This research has led to numerous school-based prevention programs and intervention (e.g., Sussman, Dent, Burton, Stacy, & Flay, 1995). Fewer studies have examined "quit attempts" or cessation of smoking behaviors among adolescents, a distinct contrast to the extensive investigations into adult cessation attempts (Heishman et al., 1997).
	Of interest as well to researchers studying adolescent tobacco use has been the social context and social influence of smoking (Fearnow, Chassin, & Presson, 1998). For example, adolescent smoking may occur in work-related situations, at home where one or more parents or caretakers smoke, at teen social events or at areas designated as "safe" smoking places near high schools (McVea et al., in press).
Deficiencies in Evidence	Minimal research attention has been directed toward the social context of high schools as a site for examining adolescent tobacco use. During high school students form peer groups which may contribute to adolescent smoking. Often peers become a strong social influence for behavior in general and belonging to an athletic team, a music group, or the "grunge" crowd can impact thinking about smoking (McVea et al., in press). Schools are also places where adolescents spend most of their day (Fibkins, 1993) and are available research subjects. Schools provide a setting for teachers and administrators to be role models for abstaining from tobacco use and enforcing policies about tobacco use (O'Hara et al., 1999).
	Existing studies of adolescent tobacco use are primarily quantitative with a focus on outcomes and transtheoretical models (Pallonen, 1998). Qualitative investigations, however, provide detailed views of students in their own words, complex analyses of multiple perspectives, and specific school contexts of different high schools that shape student experiences with tobacco (Creswell, in press). Moreover, qualitative inquiry offers the opportunity to involve high school students as co-researchers, a data collection procedure that can enhance the validity of student views uncontaminated by adult perspectives.
The Audience	By examining these multiple school contexts, using qualitative approaches and involving students as co-researchers, we can better understand the conceptions and misconceptions adolescents hold about tobacco use in high schools. With this understanding, researchers can better isolate variables and develop models about smoking behavior. Administrators and teachers can plan interventions to prevent or change attitudes toward smoking, and school officials can assist with smoking cessation or intervention programs.

that I am not discussing any study in detail here in the introduction; in many of my studies, specific reference to individual studies will appear later in the literature review section. Following the evidence for the problem, I mention in the fourth paragraph the "deficiencies" in past studies and the need for extending past research. In the final paragraph, I appeal to various audiences (i.e., researchers, administrators, and teachers) to read and use this study.

You can learn how to write "statement of the problem" sections from reading introductions to studies, looking for the five elements, and noting sentences that capture the research problem. Examine the following two additional examples to see how an author of a *qualitative* study and an author of a *quantitative* study wrote introductory sections for their studies. Both followed the template, but the type of problem is more exploratory in the qualitative and more explanatory in the quantitative. Following each example, we will relate the passages to each of the five elements of a "statement of the problem" section. The first example is a qualitative study by Brown (1998) on distance learning in higher education, and this passage presents the entire introduction to her study.

> Distance learning is an increasingly important aspect of higher education because it meets the needs of an expanding pool of nontraditional students who find education necessary for jobs in today's information age. Distance learning provides a flexible manageable alternative for this developing segment of society. However, students in distance classes work at computers miles apart at varying times of the day and night. This feeling of being alone is overcome when students join in a community of learners who support one another (Eastmond, 1995). The process of forming a community of learners is an important issue in distance learning because it can affect student satisfaction, retention, and learning (Gabelnick, Mac-Gregor, Matthews, & Smith, 1990c; Kember, 1989; Kowch & Schwier, 1997; Powers & Mitchell, 1997). It may even affect faculty evaluations, which tend to be lower in distance education courses (Cordover, 1996).
>
> In reviewing the literature on distance learning for adults and nontraditional students in higher education, I found a decided lack of research about community building within the class and within the institution. However, other research has paved the way for the exploration of this topic. Studies discussed the need for institutional support (Dillon, Gunawardena, & Parker, 1989) and for student/student and student/faculty interaction (Hiltz, 1986, 1996; Powers & Mitchell, 1997) which appear to be steps in building a community of distance learners. (Brown, 1998, p. 2)

In this example, Brown opens with a comment about distance learning and its importance today (the topic). She then argues that there are several problems facing distance education: Students feel alone (evidence from practice) and faculty evaluations are low (evidence from past research). Next she assesses a shortcoming in past research: the need to explore community building (a deficiency in past research). Brown does not end the passage with implications for a specific audience, although she might have discussed the importance of addressing community-building in distance learning for the student, teacher, or college personnel. Overall, Brown's "statement of the problem" section contains four of the five elements.

Next you will read the complete "statement of the problem" introducing a quantitative study by Davis et al. (1997) that was reported in a journal article. The study deals with the topic of tobacco use among high school students.

> Adolescent use of all tobacco products is increasing (3–6). By age 18 years, approximately two thirds of United States teenagers have tried smoking and approximately one fourth have smoked in the last 30 days (3). In addition, more than 20 percent

of white adolescent males use smokeless tobacco products (4). Adolescent tobacco use has been reported by race/ethnicity, gender, and grade level (5); however, the relationship between sports intensity, race, and tobacco use has not been studied to the best of our knowledge. (Davis et al., 1997, pp. 97–98)

This example models the elements of the "statement of the problem" section. Contained within two opening paragraphs in a journal article, it begins with a discussion about the prevalence of smoking in high school (the topic). The authors then advance the issue of the high rate of smokeless tobacco use among athletes (the research problem) and provide evidence for this issue drawing on past studies and statistical trends (evidence from past research documenting this as a problem). Following this, the authors indicate that sports intensity (defined later in the study), race, and tobacco use have not been studied (a deficiency). They seek an explanation for the influence of sports intensity and race on tobacco use. Although the authors do not comment about the audience that will profit from this study, the intended audience is likely students, teachers, schools, coaches, and researchers who study high school students and adolescent tobacco use.

REEXAMINING THE PARENT INVOLVEMENT AND THE MOTHERS' TRUST IN SCHOOL PRINCIPALS STUDIES

Let's revisit the quantitative parent involvement study (Deslandes & Bertrand, 2005) and the qualitative mothers' trust in school principals study (Shelden et al., 2010) to examine the "statement of the problem" introductory sections to the studies. In the parent involvement study (Deslandes & Bertrand, 2005), the authors introduce the problem and integrate the literature review in the first 12 paragraphs. They mention the problem early by framing it within the existing literature: we know little about the factors that influence parents' involvement in adolescent schooling. The authors do not present the issue strongly as a "problem"; instead, they talk about the positive advantages of parent involvement. Then they review the literature about the four factors that influence parent involvement. They continue to review the literature about the four factors, and then state the deficiencies of the literature and establish a need for their study. They mention that investigations are needed (i.e., the literature is deficient) to better understand what motivates parents to become involved and that the combined contribution of the four factors has not been studied across secondary grade levels. In this opening passage, the authors do not mention the audiences who will profit from this study. However, in the concluding sections of the article, the authors mention the benefits of the study for researchers, school administrators, and teachers. In sum, the authors followed the template for a good problem statement that we have discussed.

The qualitative mothers' trust in school principals study (Shelden et al., 2010) opens with the broad topic of the role of parent involvement in their students' education. It then reviews the literature on trust and the importance of school leaders. Then we learn about the "problem" that parents of children with disabilities have the right to implement due process proceedings if they disagree with the decisions of the school staff. These proceedings, if implemented, can be quite costly and escalate conflict between parents and team members. Principals can intervene because of their important school role. Thus, further research is needed on how principals influence trust with parents. No audiences were specified in the introduction who could profit from this research, but implications for several audiences were developed at the end of the article. Thus, the authors did identify a focus for the study, specify a problem, review the literature, and make a case for deficiencies in our understanding of the problem. What characterized this introduction is that the authors brought in the problem *after* the literature review rather than before it in our order of topics learned about writing a problem statement.

KEY IDEAS IN THE CHAPTER

Define a Research Problem and Explain Its Importance

A research problem is an educational issue, concern, or controversy that the investigator presents and justifies in a research study. In a research report, the investigator introduces this problem in the opening paragraphs of a study in a section called the "statement of the problem." It may consist of a single sentence or several sentences.

Distinguish between a Research Problem and Other Parts of Research

The research problem is distinct from the topic of a study, the purpose, and the research questions. The topic is the subject matter of the study, the purpose statement sets forth the intent of the study, and the research questions raise questions that the researcher will answer based on data collected in the study.

Criteria for Deciding Whether a Problem Can and Should Be Researched

Before designing and writing about the problem, researchers need to consider whether it can and should be studied. The researcher must have access to people and sites and possess the time, resources, and skills to study the problem. The study needs to contribute to knowledge and practice. There also needs to be a match between the research problem and the approach—quantitative or qualitative—chosen for the study.

The Difference between Quantitative and Qualitative Research Problems

Research problems best studied using the quantitative approach are those in which the issue needs to be explained; problems best addressed by the qualitative approach are those that need to be explored.

The Five Elements of a "Statement of the Problem" Section

The "statement of the problem" section or the introduction to a study includes five elements: the educational topic, the research problem, a justification for the problem based on past research and practice, deficiencies or shortcomings of past research or practice, and the importance of addressing the problem for diverse audiences. This is an ideal order for these sections.

Strategies Useful in Writing the "Statement of the Problem" Section

Several writing strategies assist in this process of designing and writing a "statement of the problem" section. These strategies include writing the elements of this section in order using a template as a guide, using ample citations to the literature, and including references to statistical information in quantitative studies and quotes in qualitative studies.

USEFUL INFORMATION FOR PRODUCERS OF RESEARCH

◆ Assess whether a problem can and should be researched. Apply three criteria: (a) Can the participants and sites be studied? (b) Can the problem be researched given the researcher's time, resources, and skills? (c) Will a study of the issue contribute to knowledge and practice?

◆ Identify and write a distinct research problem. Make it separate from the topic, the purpose of the study, and the research questions.

◆ Position the research problem in the "statement of the problem" section, and present it as the opening passage of a study.

◆ When writing the "statement of the problem," introduce the reader to the topic, convey the research problem, justify the need to study the research problem, identify deficiencies in the evidence, and target audiences who will benefit from the study.

◆ Consider writing the "statement of the problem" section in five distinct paragraphs to ensure inclusion of all elements. Use extensive references, cite statistics for a quantitative study, and include quotes from participants for a qualitative study.

USEFUL INFORMATION FOR CONSUMERS OF RESEARCH

◆ The actual "problem" in a study may be hidden in the opening paragraphs. Look for the issue or concern leading to the study. Ask yourself what educational "problem" is addressed by the study.

◆ Recognize that not all research problems should and can be researched. A problem *can* be researched if the inquirer has access to people and sites and if the investigator has the time, resources, and skills to adequately study the problem. A problem *should* be researched if the investigator can claim that studying it will add to knowledge or practice.

◆ Look for five elements in the introduction to a study: the topic, the research problem, the justification for this problem, the deficiencies in this evidence, and the importance of the study for audiences. This structure can help you understand the opening passages of a study and the author's intent.

UNDERSTANDING CONCEPTS AND EVALUATING RESEARCH STUDIES

You can test your knowledge of the content of this chapter by answering the following questions that relate to the parent involvement study and the mothers' trust in school principals study. Answers to questions are found in appendix A so that you can assess your progress.

1. Examine the first sentence—the narrative hook—for each study as stated below. Evaluate whether it is an effective narrative hook.

    a. In past decades, a wealth of studies have showed that parent involvement is essential in children's educational process and outcomes (Deslandes & Bertrand, 2005).

    b. Parents are meant to be included as fundamental participants in educational organizations (Shelden et al., 2010).

2. Identify and review the research problem found in the parent involvement study and in the mothers' trust in school principals study. Why is the first problem best suited for quantitative research and the second for qualitative research?

3. A research problem should be researched if it contributes to educational knowledge or practice. Listed below are five ways a study might contribute to knowledge:
   a. Fills a void or extends existing research
   b. Replicates a study with new participants or at new sites
   c. Studies a problem that has not been studied or is understudied
   d. Gives voice to people not heard
   e. Informs practice

   Identify for both the parent involvement study and the mothers' trust in school principals study how they contribute to knowledge.

4. For both the parent involvement study and the mothers' trust in school principals study discuss a justification of each study based on personal experiences.

5. If multiple references add a scholarly tone to a "statement of the problem" section, which article, the parent involvement study or the mothers' trust in school principals study introduces a better scholarly introduction to their study? Why?

6. For an educational topic of your choice, write down the topic, the research problem, your justification for the problem based on practice or research, potential deficiencies in the knowledge about the problem, and the audiences that will benefit from your study.

CONDUCTING YOUR RESEARCH

Write a "statement of the problem" section for a research study you would like to conduct. Identify the topic, the research problem, justification for the problem, the deficiencies in knowledge about the problem, and the audience that will benefit from studying the problem.

PEARSON
myeducationlab
The Power of Classroom Practice
www.myeducationlab.com

Go to the Topic "Selecting and Defining a Research Topic" in the MyEducationLab (**www.myeducationlab.com**) for your course, where you can:

◆ Find learning outcomes for "Selecting and Defining a Research Topic."
◆ Complete Assignments and Activities that can help you more deeply understand the chapter content.
◆ Apply and practice your understanding of the core skills identified in the chapter with the Building Research Skills exercises.
◆ Check your comprehension of the content covered in the chapter by going to the Study Plan. Here you will be able to take a pretest, receive feedback on your answers, and then access Review, Practice, and Enrichment activities to enhance your understanding. You can then complete a final posttest.

CHAPTER 3

Reviewing the Literature

*W*ith so much information available, searching and locating good literature on your topic can be challenging. This chapter introduces you to five logical steps in reviewing the literature so that you can locate useful resources and write them into the literature review section of a research report.

By the end of this chapter, you should be able to:

◆ Define what a literature review is and why it is important.
◆ Identify the five steps in conducting a literature review.

Maria needs to find and review the literature for her study on the possession of weapons by students in high schools. Because she has not spent much time in the university library, she compiles a list of questions for her advisor:

1. What is a literature review?
2. Where do I begin in conducting a literature review?
3. What are the best materials to include in my review and how do I locate them?
4. Is it worth my time to search the Internet for the literature?
5. Are there any shortcuts for identifying journal articles on my topic?
6. Should I gather and summarize both quantitative and qualitative studies?
7. How long should my literature review be?
8. Do you have an example of a literature review that I might examine?

As you begin to think about reviewing the literature for a research study, you may have questions similar to Maria's.

WHAT IS A LITERATURE REVIEW AND WHY IS IT IMPORTANT?

A **literature review** is a written summary of journal articles, books, and other documents that describes the past and current state of information on the topic of your research study. It also organizes the literature into subtopics, and documents the need for a proposed study. In the most rigorous form of research, educators base this review mainly on research reported in journal articles. A good review, however, might also contain other information drawn from conference papers, books, and government documents. In composing a literature review, you may cite articles that are both quantitative and qualitative studies. Regardless of the sources of information, all researchers conduct a literature review as a step in the research process.

Why is this review necessary? Many reasons exist. You conduct a literature review to document how your study adds to the existing literature. A study will not add to the literature if it duplicates research already available. Like Maria, you conduct a literature review to convince your graduate committee that you know the literature on your topic and that you can summarize it. You also complete a literature review to provide evidence that educators need your study. You may base this need on learning new ideas, sharing the latest findings with others (like Maria and her school committee), or identifying practices that might improve learning in your classroom. Conducting a literature review also builds your research skills of using the library and being an investigator who follows leads in the literature, all useful experiences to have as a researcher. Reading the literature also helps you learn how other educators compose their research studies and helps you find useful examples and models in the literature for your own research. By conducting a literature search using computer databases, you develop skills in locating needed materials in a timely manner.

How Does the Literature Review Differ for Quantitative and Qualitative Studies?

How the review of the literature is used tends to differ between quantitative and qualitative research. Table 3.1 identifies three primary differences: the amount of literature cited at the beginning of the study, the use it serves at the beginning, and its use at the end of a study.

In a quantitative study, researchers discuss the literature extensively at the beginning of a study (see Deslandes & Bertrand, 2005). This serves two major purposes: it justifies the importance of the research problem, and it provides a rationale for (and foreshadows) the purpose of the study and research questions or hypotheses. In many quantitative studies, the authors include the literature in a separate section titled "Review of the Literature" to highlight the important role it plays. The authors also incorporate the literature into the end of the study, comparing the results with prior predictions or expectations made at the beginning of the study.

In a qualitative study, the literature serves a slightly different purpose. Similar to quantitative research, the authors mention the literature at the beginning of the study to document or justify the importance of the research problem (Shelden et al., 2010). However, authors do not typically discuss the literature extensively at the beginning of a study. This allows the views of the participants to emerge without being constrained by the views of others from the literature. In some qualitative studies, researchers use the literature to support the findings. Nevertheless, in many qualitative projects, researchers often cite the

TABLE 3.1		
Differences in Extent and Use of Literature in Quantitative and Qualitative Research		
Differences	**Quantitative Research**	**Qualitative Research**
Amount of literature cited at the beginning of the study	Substantial	Minimal
Use of literature at the beginning of the study	Justifies or documents the need for the study	Justifies or documents the need for the study
	Provides a rationale for the direction of the study (i.e., purpose statement and research questions or hypotheses)	
Use of literature at the end of the study	Confirms or disconfirms prior predictions from the literature	Supports or modifies existing findings in the literature

literature at the end of the study as a contrast or comparison with the major findings in the study. In qualitative inquiry, researchers do not make predictions about findings. They are more interested in whether the findings of a study support or modify existing ideas and practices advanced in the literature—for example, expand on the understanding of trust as mentioned in the introduction to the mothers' trust in principals qualitative study (Shelden et al., 2010).

WHAT ARE THE FIVE STEPS IN CONDUCTING A LITERATURE REVIEW?

Regardless of whether the study is quantitative or qualitative, common steps can be used to conduct a literature review. Knowing these steps helps you read and understand a research study. If you conduct your own research study, knowing the steps in the process will give you a place to start and the ability to recognize when you have successfully completed the review.

Although conducting a literature review follows no prescribed path, if you plan to design and conduct a study, you will typically go through five interrelated steps. If you are simply looking for literature on a topic for your own personal use or for some practical application (such as for Maria's school committee), only the first four steps will apply. However, learning all five steps will provide a sense of how researchers proceed in reviewing the literature. These steps are:

1. *Identify key terms* to use in your search for literature.
2. *Locate literature* about a topic by consulting several types of materials and databases, including those available at an academic library and on the Internet.
3. *Critically evaluate and select the literature* for your review.
4. *Organize the literature* you have selected by abstracting or taking notes on the literature and developing a visual diagram of it.
5. *Write a literature review* that reports summaries of the literature for inclusion in your research report.

Identify Key Terms

Begin your search of the literature by narrowing your topic to a few key terms using one or two words or short phrases. You should choose these carefully because they are important for initially locating literature in a library or through an Internet search. To identify these terms, you can use several strategies, outlined below:

◆ Write a preliminary "working title" for a project and select two to three key words in the title that capture the central idea of your study. Although some researchers write the title last, a working title keeps you focused on the key ideas of the study. Because it is a "working" title, you can revise it at regular intervals if necessary during the research (Glesne & Peshkin, 1992).

◆ Pose a short, general research question that you would like answered in the study. Select the two or three words in this question that best summarize the primary direction of the study.

◆ Use words that authors report in the literature. In some quantitative research studies, educators test a prediction for what they expect to find from the data. This prediction is an explanation for what researchers hope to find. Researchers use the term *theory* for these explanations, and they might be a theory of "social support" or "learning styles" of students. The actual words of the theory (e.g., "social support" or "learning styles") become the words to use in your search.

◆ Look in a catalog of terms to find words that match your topic. Visit online databases that are typically available in college or university libraries. For example, one database is the **ERIC database** (see Educational Resources Information Center [ERIC], 1991; **www.eric.ed.gov/**). ERIC provides free access to more than 1.2 million bibliographic records of journal articles and other education-related materials and, if available, includes links to full text. ERIC is sponsored by the U.S. Department of Education, Institute of Education Sciences (IES).

◆ Go to the bookshelves in a college or university library, scan the table of contents of education journals from the last 7 to 10 years, and look for key terms in titles to the articles. You can also examine the electronic database called *Ingenta* at your academic library. Ingenta supplies access to full-text online publications and journal publications. Especially helpful is the "browse publications" feature, in which you enter the name of the journal you wish to examine and obtain a list of the titles of articles from that journal for select years.

Maria needs to identify key terms to help her locate literature on weapon possession by high school students. After thinking about how she might get started, she writes down a working title, "Weapon Possession by High School Students." She begins by going to the ERIC Web site and enters the words *weapon possession* in the search terms procedure. She examines the articles identified in her search and feels that narrowing her search to high school students will provide more targeted references in the literature. She then uses the feature of searching within results and adds the additional term, *high school students*. She has now sufficiently narrowed her search and will closely examine the references in the literature that her search has yielded. Now try duplicating Maria's procedure yourself. Locate the ERIC Web site and insert Maria's terms into the ERIC database.

Locate Literature

Having identified key terms, you can now begin the search for relevant literature. You might be tempted to begin your search by accessing the Internet and exploring the electronic literature available on a topic. Although this process may be convenient, not all literature posted on the Internet is dependable. Sometimes individuals post articles that have not passed through standards of external reviews. However, full-text documents of high quality are available on the Internet.

You might also begin your search by asking faculty or students to recommend good articles and studies to review. This approach may be helpful, but it lacks the systematic process found in searching library resources.

Use Academic Libraries

A sound approach is to begin your search in an academic library. By physically searching the stacks, reviewing microfiche, and accessing the computerized databases, you will save time because you will find comprehensive holdings not available through other sources. Although a town or city library may yield some useful literature, an academic library typically offers the largest collection of materials, especially research studies.

Academic library resources provide online journals for easy computer access and computerized databases such as ERIC. Academic libraries typically have online catalogs of their holdings so that you can search the library materials easily. In addition, from any location, you can search the online library holdings of many large academic libraries (e.g., University of Michigan or University of California, Berkeley) to see what books are available on your topic. Another useful library to search is the Library of Congress, which contains most published books (**http://catalog.loc.gov**).

When using academic libraries, two challenges exist. First, the researcher needs to locate material—a task often made difficult because of the large and complex holdings in a library, such as journals or periodicals (recent and bound), government documents, the microfiche collection, and indexes. To help locate material, you might use the services of a reference librarian or search through the computerized library holdings. The second challenge is overcoming the frustration that arises when other library users have checked out materials you need, making them unavailable for use. When this occurs, researchers can use an interlibrary loan service as a means of obtaining the literature; however, this process takes time and requires patience.

Use Both Primary and Secondary Sources

Literature reviews often contain both primary and secondary source materials. **Primary source literature** consists of literature reported by the individual(s) who actually conducted the research or who originated the ideas. Research articles published by educational journals are an example of this type of source. **Secondary source literature**, however, is literature that summarizes primary sources. It does not represent material published by the original researcher or the creator of the idea. Examples of secondary sources are handbooks, encyclopedias, and select journals that summarize research, such as the *Review of Educational Research*. Typically, you will locate both primary and secondary sources, but it is best to report mostly primary sources. Primary sources present the literature in the original state and present the viewpoint of the original author. Primary sources also provide the details of original research better than do secondary sources. Secondary sources are helpful as you begin your review, to explore and determine the range of materials on a topic. Historically, the division into primary and secondary sources has been a useful classification for literature in fields such as law and history (Barzun & Graff, 1985).

Search Different Types of Literature

Figure 3.1 provides a useful classification system of the literature that you might consider. Modified from a classification originally developed by Libutti and Blandy (1995), the figure is a guide to resources as well as a framework for getting started in a literature search.

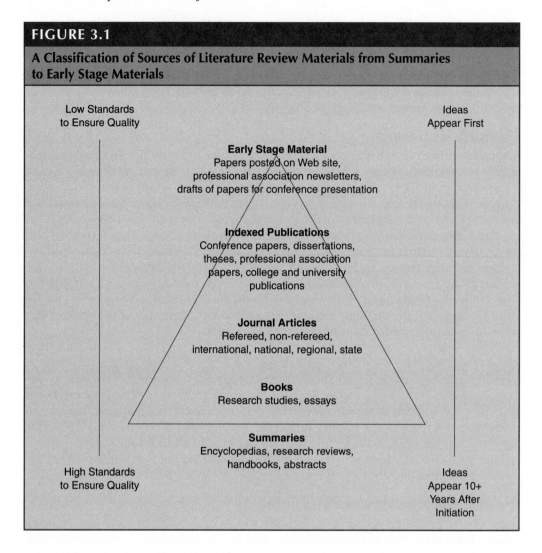

FIGURE 3.1

A Classification of Sources of Literature Review Materials from Summaries to Early Stage Materials

Low Standards
to Ensure Quality

Ideas
Appear First

Early Stage Material
Papers posted on Web site,
professional association newsletters,
drafts of papers for conference presentation

Indexed Publications
Conference papers, dissertations,
theses, professional association
papers, college and university
publications

Journal Articles
Refereed, non-refereed,
international, national, regional, state

Books
Research studies, essays

Summaries
Encyclopedias, research reviews,
handbooks, abstracts

High Standards
to Ensure Quality

Ideas
Appear 10+
Years After
Initiation

Using this framework, you might begin your search at the bottom of the triangle by consulting summaries of research that synthesize numerous studies on a topic (secondary sources of information). From these broad summaries, you can work your way up to journal articles (primary sources) and to "early stage" literature found at the top. For many beginning researchers, starting with summaries is a good idea because summaries give an overview of topics at an entry-level discussion. Summaries also have a longer "life" from the initial idea stage, and they have undergone reviews for quality.

Summaries   **Summaries** provide overviews of the literature and research on timely issues in education. A list of available summaries is shown in Table 3.2. These sources include encyclopedias, dictionaries and glossaries of terms, handbooks, statistical indexes, and reviews and syntheses. These summaries introduce a beginning researcher to a problem area, and they help locate key references and identify current issues. Leading specialists in the field of education write these summaries.

Encyclopedias   A good place to start when you know little about a topic is an **encyclopedia**, such as the *Encyclopedia of Educational Research* (Alkin, 1992). Sponsored by

TABLE 3.2
Types of Summaries Available in Academic Libraries with Examples

Encyclopedias	*Handbook of Research on Teacher Education* (Houston,
Encyclopedia of Educational Research (Alkin, 1992)	Haberman, & Sikula, 1990)
The International Encyclopedia of Education (Husen & Postlethwaite, 1994)	*The Handbook of Qualitative Research in Education* (LeCompte, Millroy, & Preissle, 1992)
Encyclopedia of American Education (Unger, 1996)	*The SAGE Handbook of Qualitative Research* (Denzin & Lincoln, 2005)
Dictionaries and Glossaries of Terms	*Educational Research, Methodology and Measurement:*
The SAGE Dictionary of Qualitative Inquiry (Schwandt, 2007)	*An International Handbook* (Keeves, 1988)
Dictionary of Terms in Statistics and Methodology: *A Nontechnical Guide for the Social Sciences* (Vogt, 2005)	**Statistical Indexes** *American Statistics Index* (Congressional Information Service, 1973–)
Glossary of postmodern terms, in *Post-Modernism and the Social Sciences* (Rosenau, 1992)	*Digest of Educational Statistics* (National Center for Educational Statistics, 1997)
Handbooks	**Reviews and Syntheses**
Handbook of Research on Multicultural Education (Banks & Banks, 1995)	*Review of Educational Research* (1931–) *Annual Review of Psychology* (1950–)

AERA, this encyclopedia provides research under 16 broad topics, including the curriculum of elementary and secondary education, education of exceptional persons, and the organizational structure and governance of education. The appendix on "Doing Library Research in Education" is especially useful (Alkin, 1992, p. 1543).

Dictionaries and Glossaries of Terms   Other useful tools in the literature review and overall research process are **dictionaries and glossaries** of terms. These dictionaries contain most of the recent educational terms. For example, the *Dictionary of Statistics and Methodology: A Nontechnical Guide for the Social Sciences,* 3rd edition (Vogt, 2005), defines statistical and methodological terms used in the social and behavioral sciences; such terms are often problematic for beginning researchers. *The SAGE Dictionary of Qualitative Inquiry,* 3rd edition (Schwandt, 2007), is a reference book of qualitative terms containing multiple and often contested points of view about definitions. *Post-Modernism and the Social Sciences* (Rosenau, 1992) provides a glossary of postmodern terms related to studying issues of inequality and oppression in our society.

Handbooks   There are numerous **handbooks** that discuss topics such as teaching, reading, curriculum, social studies, educational administration, multicultural education, and teacher education. Several handbooks are available on educational research topics. A handbook that addresses methods of research inquiry, the utilization of knowledge, measurement, and statistics is *Educational Research, Methodology, and Measurement: An International Handbook* (Keeves, 1988). Two recent handbooks are also available on topics in qualitative research: *The Handbook of Qualitative Research in Education* (LeCompte, Millroy, & Preissle, 1992) and *The SAGE Handbook of Qualitative Research* (Denzin & Lincoln, 2005). In quantitative research, handbooks are available as well, such as *The SAGE Handbook of Applied Social Research Methods* (Bickman & Rog, 2009). For research that combines both the quantitative and qualitative research approach, you might want to refer to the *Handbook of Mixed Methods in the Social and Behavioral Sciences* (Tashakkori & Teddlie, 2003, 2011).

Statistical Indexes   **Statistical indexes** such as the annual *Digest of Educational Statistics* (National Center for Educational Statistics [NCES], 1997) report educational trends useful in writing problem statements or literature reviews. The *Digest,* issued since 1933 by the U.S. government, compiles statistical information covering the broad field of American education from kindergarten through graduate school. It also reports information from many sources, including the surveys and activities carried out by the NCES.

Reviews and Syntheses   A final summary source on topics consists of timely **reviews and syntheses** in education, psychology, and the social sciences. For example, the *Review of Educational Research* (1931–) is a quarterly journal of AERA that publishes lengthy articles synthesizing educational research on various topics.

Books   Academic libraries have extensive collections of books on a broad range of educational topics. The books most useful in reviewing the literature will be those that summarize research studies or report conceptual discussions on educational topics. Textbooks used in classes are less useful because they typically do not contain reports of single research studies, but they contain summaries of the literature and useful references. The *Subject Guide to Books in Print* (1957–) and the *Core List of Books and Journals in Education* (O'Brien & Fabiano, 1990) are guides that might also be helpful in your literature search.

Journals, Indexed Publications, and Electronic Sources   Journal (or periodical) articles and conference papers that report research are prime sources for a literature review. To locate articles in journals, consider searching an abstract series, indexes to journals, or the diverse computer databases in education and the social sciences.

Abstract Series   Abstract series, which allow for a broad search of journal articles by subject area, are available in many fields. In educational administration, for example, you might examine the *Educational Administration Abstracts* (University Council for Educational Administration, 1966–), or in early childhood development, look at the *Child Development Abstracts and Bibliography* (Society for Research in Child Development, 1945–). You can usually find these abstracts by accessing the online library catalog and using key words such as *abstracts,* and the subject field or topic to determine if the library contains a specific abstract series. Another place to search for journal publications are indexes such as the *Education Index* (Wilson, 1929/32–), an index devoted primarily to periodicals and organized into subject areas and fields.

Databases   The most likely place to find journal articles is in databases that index journal articles both in print form and on CD-ROMs. A Google search can also often lead to timely articles and discussions on educational topics. A more careful and monitored approach is to examine one of the many literature databases. By examining these databases, you can easily access hundreds of journal articles on educational topics. Computerized databases also facilitate searching the literature for conference papers and miscellaneous publications, such as papers from professional associations or education agencies. You might start a computerized search of the databases with the education data, followed by the psychological and sociological sources of information. Six important databases offer easy retrieval of journal articles and other documents related to education:

   1. ERIC (1991) is a national system of information in education established in 1966 by the U.S. Department of Education and the National Library of Education (NLE). Because public monies supported the development of ERIC, you can search the ERIC database free of charge. You can search this extensive database both online (Internet) and in print forms (available on the bookshelves of academic libraries).

   Education documents allowed into the ERIC database are selected mainly by reviewers at 16 subcontent clearinghouses (e.g., Adult, Career, and Vocational Education; Assessment and Evaluation). Individuals at these clearinghouses examine the educational material, write abstracts, and assign terms or *descriptors* from the ERIC vocabulary to identify each source of information. The literature that goes into ERIC is not peer reviewed for quality, but reviewers at the clearinghouses do select it for inclusion in the database.

The ERIC database consists of two parts: journals, located in the *Current Index to Journals in Education* (CIJE; ERIC, 1969–), and documents, found in *Resources in Education* (RIE; ERIC, 1966–). *CIJE* is a monthly and cumulative index to information located in approximately 980 major educational and education related journals. It provides a subject index, an author index, and abstracts of specific studies. *RIE* is a monthly and cumulative index to current research findings, project and technical reports, speeches, unpublished manuscripts, and books. It indexes education information by subject, personal author, institution, and publication type.

A sample ERIC journal article (CIJE) summary (or resume) and a sample ERIC document (RIE) resume are shown in Figures 3.2 and 3.3. You will find these on the ERIC

FIGURE 3.2

Sample ERIC Journal Article Resume

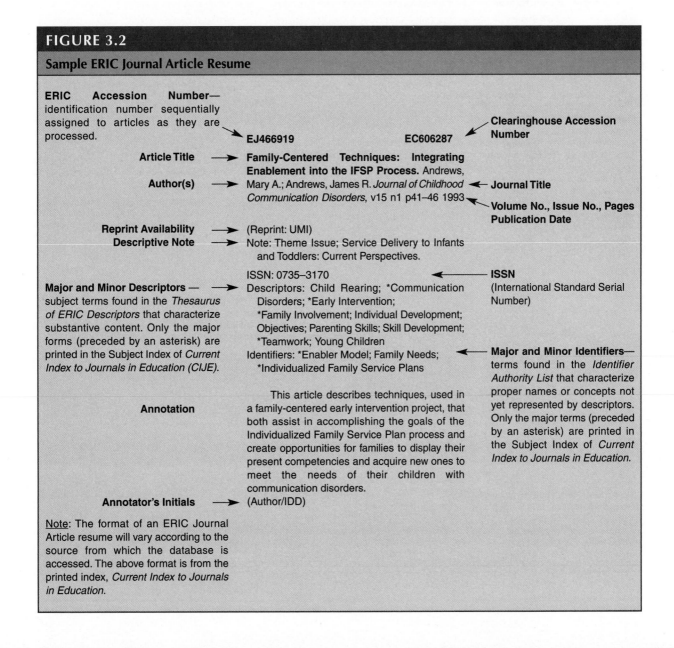

FIGURE 3.3

Sample ERIC Document Resume

ERIC Accession Number—identification number sequentially assigned to articles as they are processed.

Clearinghouse Accession Number

ED359626   EA025062

Author(s) → Fuhrman.-Susan H. Ed.

Title → **Designing Coherent Education Policy; Improving the System.**

Institution.
(Organization where document originated.)

Corporate Source—Consortium for Policy Research in Education, New Brunswick, NJ.
Sponsoring Agency—Office of Educational Research and Improvement (ED), Washington, DC.

Sponsoring Agency—agency responsible for initiating, funding, and managing the research project.

Contract or Grant Number → Contract Nos.–R117G10007; R117G10039

Date Published → Pub Date—1993

ISBN
(International Standard Book Number)

ISBN-1-55542-536-4

Available from—Jossey-Bass Publishers, 350 Sansome Street, San Francisco, CA 94104.

Alternate source for obtaining document.

None-370 p.

Descriptive Note (pagination first).

ERIC Document Reproduction Service (EDRS) Avaliability—"MF" means microfiche: "PC" means reproduced paper copy. When describes as "Document Not Available from EDRS," alternate sources are cited above. Prices are subject to change. For latest price code schedule see section on "How to Order ERIC Documents," in the most recent issue of *Resources in Education*, or call EDRS at 1-800-443-3742 for price information.

EDRS Price—MF01/PC15 Plus Postage.

Pub Type—Books (010)—Collected Works-General (020)—Guides–Non-Classroom (055)

Descriptors—Educational Change; Elementary Secondary Education; Governance; Politics of Education; Standards; *Educational Objectives; *Education Policy; *Instructional Improvement; *Policy Formation; *Public Education

Publication Type—broad categories indicating the form or organization of the document, as contrasted to its subject matter. The category name is followed by the category code

Descriptors—subject terms found in the *Thesaurus of ERIC Descriptors* that characterize substantive content. Only the major terms (proceeded by an asterisk) are printed in the Subject Index of *Resources in Education*.

Abstract

This book examines issues in designing coherent education policy for public elementary and secondary schools. It seeks to expand the policy discussion by refining the definition of coherence and considering a number of complex questions raised by the notion of coherent policy. The book offers an indepth look at systemic school reform and offers a variety of ideas as to how educators at the district, state, and federal levels may coordinate the various elements of policy infrastructure around a new set of ambitious, common goals for student achievement. Chapters include the following: (1) "The Politics of Coherence" (Susan H. Fuhrman); (2) "Policy and Practice: The Relations between Governance and Instruction" (David K. Cohen and James P. Spillanc); (3) "The Role of Local School Disctricts in Instructional Improvement" (Richard F. Elmore); (4) "Systemic Educational Policy: A Conceptual Framework" (William H. Clune); (5) "Student Incentives and Academic Standards: Independent Schools as a Coherent System" (Arthur G. Powell); (6) "New Directions for Early Childhood Care and Education Policy" (W. Steven Barnett); (7) "How the World of Students and Teachers Challenges Policy Coherence" (Milbrey W. McLaughlin and Joan E. Talbert); (8) "Systemic Reform and Educational Opportunity" (Jennifer A. O'Day and Marshall S. Smith); and (9) "Conclusion: Can Policy Lead the Way?" (Susan H. Fuhrman). References accompany each chapter. (LMI)

Abstractor's Initials

Note: The format of an ERIC Document resume will vary according to the source from which the database is accessed. The above format is from the printed index, *Resources in Education*.

Web site. Read through the marginal notations that explain the information about the document. This summary contains an accession number (*EJ* for journal and *ED* for documents). It also displays the author, the title, the major and minor descriptors assigned to the article, and a brief annotation describing the article.

2. *Psychological Abstracts* (APA, 1927–) and the CD-ROM versions, *PsycLit* (SilverPlatter Information, Inc., 1986) and *PsycINFO* (**www.apa.org**), are important sources for locating research articles on topics broadly related to psychology. In October 2000, PsycLit and PsycINFO consolidated into one database to provide a comprehensive source of psychological literature from 1887 to the present. This database is available in a print version, on CD-ROM, and on a Web site. These databases are available in libraries or through online versions leased by the libraries and networked through campus computers.

These databases index more than 850 journals in 16 categories. They provide bibliographic citations, abstracts for psychological journal articles, dissertations, technical reports, books, and book chapters published worldwide. The print version has a 3-year cumulative index. An example of a journal record from PsycINFO is shown in Figure 3.4. Similar to an ERIC record, this summary from PsycINFO includes key phrase *identifiers,* as well as the author, title, the source, and a brief abstract of the article.

3. *Sociological Abstracts* (Sociological Abstracts, Inc., 1953–) is available in a print version, on CD-ROM (*Sociofile,* SilverPlatter Information, Inc., 1974/86–), and in a library-leased Web version available to computers networked to the library. Available from Cambridge Scientific Abstracts, this database provides access to the world's literature in sociology and related disciplines. The database contains abstracts of journal articles selected from more than 2,500 journals, abstracts of conference papers presented at sociological association meetings, dissertations, and books and book reviews from 1963 to the present.

4. The *Social Science Citation Index* (SSCI; Institute for Scientific Information [ISI], 1969–) and the CD-ROM version, *Social Sciences Citation Index* (ISI, 1989–), provide a database of cited references to journal articles. The citation index allows you to look up a reference to a work to find journal articles that have cited the work. SSCI covers 5,700 journals, representing virtually every discipline in the social sciences.

5. EBSCO Information Services (**www.ebsco.com/**) is a worldwide information service that provides print and electronic subscription services, research database development and production, and online access to more than 150 databases and thousands of e-journals. Academic libraries purchase the services of EBSCO or individuals can purchase articles of interest through the pay-per-view feature. Using EBSCO, the educational researcher can view tables of contents for journals and abstracts to articles, and link directly to full text from over 8,000 titles. Researchers can also receive e-mails of the tables of contents for their favorite journals as soon as they are published.

6. *Dissertation Abstracts* (University Microfilms International [UMI], 1938–1965/66) and the CD-ROM version *Dissertation Abstracts Ondisc* (*Computer File;* UMI, 1987–) provide guides to doctoral dissertations submitted by nearly 500 participating institutions throughout the world. It is published in three sections: Section A, The Humanities and Social Sciences; Section B, The Sciences and Engineering; and Section C, Worldwide. Examining these sections, a researcher finds abstracts (350-word summaries) of dissertations. A comprehensive index permits easy access to titles, authors, and subject areas.

Early Stage Literature   The final major category of literature to review (see Figure 3.1) comprises materials at an early stage of development that may or may not be screened by reviewers (e.g., journal editors or book publishers) for quality. Such early stage literature consists of newsletters, studies posted to Web sites, professional-association newsletters, and drafts of studies available from authors. For example, electronic journals and research studies are posted to Web sites and available on the Internet. Some of

FIGURE 3.4

Sample Journal Record from PsycINFO Database
(www.apa.org/psychinfo/about/sample.html#journal)

Sample Records from the PsycINFO Database

The values in each field below vary from record to record. For a complete list of possible values for each field, plus a description of each field, please visit our Database Field Guide.

› View a Journal Record
› View a Book Record
› View a Book Chapter Record
› Review sample records representing non-article data

Sample Journal Record

Accession Number
    2000-15980-004
Author
    Dubois, Michel; Vial, I.
Affiliation
    U Pierre Mendes, Lab de Psychologie Sociale, Grenoble, France
Title
    Multimedia design: The effects of relating multimodal information.
Source
    Journal of Computer Assisted Learning. 2000 Jun Vol 16(2) 157-165
ISSN/ISBN
    0266-4909
Language
    English
UMI
URL
DOI
Release Date
    20000628
Abstract
    The are few models that describe learner behaviour during the simultaneous processing of several types of information, yet this is the defining characteristic of the use of multimedia tools, which bring together media in different informational formats (fixed or moving images, sound, text). Following studies in cognitive psychology concerning the increase in the ability to form mental images of words, this article aims at defining how different multimedia presentation modes affect the learning of foreign language vocabulary (Russian). 60 college students learned Russian phrases and then participated in a recall experiment where the multimedia presentation of the phrases was varied. An effect was observed on word memorisation in the different information presentation modes, suggesting better processing when there is co-referencing of the different sources, especially when the encoding and tests modes are the same. In addition to these experimental results, some principles for the design of multimodal learning tools are discussed. (PsycINFO Database Record (c) 2000 APA, all rights reserved)
Key Concepts
    information presentation method, recall of foreign language phrases, college students
Keywords (Thesaurus Terms)
    *Foreign Language Learning; *Instructional Media; *Recall (Learning); *Visual Display
Classification Codes
    2343 Learning & Memory
Population
    10 Human; 300 Adulthood (18 yrs & older)
Population Location
    France
Form/Content Type
    0800 Empirical Study
Table of Contents (Book Records only)
Publication Year
    2000

Source: Reprinted with permission of the American Psychological Association, publisher of the PsycINFO Database © 2004, all rights reserved.

TABLE 3.3

Advantages and Disadvantages of Using the Internet as a Resource for a Literature Review

Advantages	Disadvantages
• There is easy access to material since the researcher can search any time of the day.	• Research posted to Web sites is not reviewed for quality by "experts."
• Web sites have a breadth of information on most topics.	• The research found on Web sites may have been plagiarized without the searcher's knowledge.
• Web sites provide a network that researchers can contact about their topic and research problem.	• Research studies may be difficult to find and time-consuming to locate.
• Research posted to Web sites is typically current information.	• Web site literature may not be organized or summarized in a way that is useful.
• Web sites can be searched easily using a search engine and keywords.	• Full-text electronic journals available on the Web are new and few in number.
• Select research studies can be printed immediately from Web sites.	

the advantages and disadvantages of using these materials from the Internet appear in Table 3.3.

Unquestionably, the easy ability to access and capture this material makes it attractive; however, because reviewers may not have evaluated the quality of this information, you need to be cautious about whether it represents rigorous, thoughtful, and systematic research for use in a literature review. Ways to determine the credibility of the material include the following:

◆ See if it is a study reported in an online journal with a peer review board to oversee the quality of publications.
◆ Determine if you recognize the authors because they have published materials in quality journals or books.
◆ See if the Web site has standards for accepting the research studies and reporting them.
◆ Ask a faculty member in your graduate program if he or she feels that the article is of sufficient quality to be included in your literature review.

Critically Evaluate and Select the Literature

Let's return to the major steps in conducting a literature review. The process begins with identifying key words and locating resources. Once you locate the literature, you need to determine if it is a good source to use and whether it is relevant to your particular research.

Is It a Good, Accurate Source?

It sometimes comes as a shock to beginning researchers that even though a study has been published, it may not be worthy of including in a literature review. Some guidelines are helpful to make a careful selection of the literature. Remember, as mentioned in Figure 3.1, there are different types of literature.

◆ Rely as much as possible on journal articles published in national journals. Typically, a panel of editors (two or three editorial board members plus a general editor) reviews and critically evaluates a manuscript before it is accepted for publication. If the journal lists reviewers or editorial board members from around the country, consider it to be high quality because it is a refereed, national journal.

◆ Use a priority system for searching the literature. Start with refereed journal articles; then proceed to nonrefereed journal articles; then books; then conference papers, dissertations, and theses; and finally nonreviewed articles posted to Web sites. This order reflects the extent of external review of materials from a high level of review to minimal or no review. If you are using full-text articles from Web sites, review the quality of the material. Use articles reported in national online journals that have undergone a review through editorial boards. Information about the journals and their review process can be obtained online. Material obtained from Web sites not in national, refereed journals needs to be carefully screened to determine the qualifications of the author, the quality of the writing, and the scope and rigor of data collection and analysis.

◆ Look for "research" studies to include in your literature review. This research consists of posing questions, collecting data, and forming results or conclusions from the data. Also, the claims made by authors in their results need to be justified and supported based on the data collected.

◆ Include both quantitative and qualitative research studies in your review, regardless of the approach you might use in your own study. Each form of research has advantages and provides insight for our knowledge base in education.

Is It Relevant?

Whether a source is high quality and worthy of inclusion in a literature review is one consideration. An entirely separate question is whether the literature is relevant to use. You might read the literature you have selected, noting the titles of articles, the contents of abstracts at the beginning of the material (if they are present), and major headings in the study. This review helps determine if the information is relevant to use in a review. Relevance has several dimensions, and you might consider the following criteria when selecting literature for a review:

◆ Topic relevance: Does the literature focus on the same topic as your proposed study?

◆ Individual and site relevance: Does the literature examine the same individuals or sites that you want to study?

◆ Problem and question relevance: Does the literature examine the same research problem that you propose to study? Does it address the same research question you plan to address?

◆ Accessibility relevance: Is the literature available in your library or can you download it from a Web site? Can you obtain it easily from the library or a Web site?

If you answer yes to these questions, then the literature is relevant for your literature review.

Organize the Literature

Once you have located the literature, assessed its quality, and checked it for relevance, the next step is to organize it for a literature review. This process involves photocopying and filing the literature. At this time you might quickly read it, take notes on it, and determine how it fits into the overall literature. You might also construct a visual picture of the literature—a literature map—that helps to organize it, positions your study within the literature, and provides a framework for presenting research to audiences about your topic.

Reproducing, Downloading, and Filing

After locating books, journal articles, and miscellaneous documents (such as the education documents in ERIC available online) in a library, you should make copies of the articles, scan the articles, or download the articles (as html or pdf files) and develop some system to easily retrieve the information. Copyright laws permit the duplication of only one complete article without the permission of the author. Placing the articles in file folders (or storing them in a computer file) alphabetized by author name may be the most convenient way to organize the materials. Alternatively, you might organize the literature by sources, topic, or key words. However, using an author index may be the most convenient method because topics and key words you use in your literature review may shift as you work through drafts of the review.

Taking Notes and Abstracting Studies

During the process of reading the literature, researchers take notes on the information so that a summary of the literature is available for a written review. This note taking is often an informal procedure in which the researcher identifies important ideas about the article or material and writes rough notes about each source of information. This process may involve a citation to the article (see "Using a Style Manual" section later in this chapter) and a brief summary of the major points of the article. These points may generally include (a) the questions being addressed, (b) data collection, and (c) major results.

Instead of this informal approach, a preferred strategy is to systematically record information about each source so that you can easily insert it into a written review of the literature. This process yields useful information so that you can remember the details of the studies.

A systematic approach for summarizing each source of information is to develop an abstract for each one. An **abstract** is a summary of the major aspects of a study or article, conveyed in a concise way (for this purpose, often no more than 350 words) and written with specific components that describe the study. Be careful not to use the abstracts available at the beginning of journal articles. They may be too brief to use because of word or space limitations imposed by journal editors. Also, if you use such an abstract, you need to reference it so that you do not plagiarize someone else's work. Instead, write your own abstracts of articles and materials. This calls for identifying the topics that you need to abstract from the study.

The first step is to think about the type of literature you will be abstracting. Researchers typically emphasize research studies for abstracting and inclusion in the literature review, rather than essays or opinion papers (although you probably need to cite important essays or opinions if authors widely cite them).

To abstract elements for a *quantitative research* study such as a journal article, conference paper, or dissertation or thesis, you might identify the:

◆ Research problem
◆ Research questions or hypotheses
◆ Data collection procedure
◆ Results of the study

A complete abstract reporting these four elements for a quantitative survey study by Metzner (1989) is shown in Figure 3.5. Notice in this abstract that the summaries of each element are short and that a complete reference to the work is listed at the top so

FIGURE 3.5

Sample Abstract for a Quantitative Research Study

Metzner, B. (1989). Perceived quality of academic advising: The effect on freshman attrition. *American Educational Research Journal, 26*(3), 422–442.*

Research Problem:

Colleges and universities place emphasis on student retention, and academic advising positively intervenes to reduce dropout. However, surveys show extensive dissatisfaction with advisement. Empirical investigations of this relationship have provided equivocal results. Some studies show a positive relationship between retention and quality of advising; others have failed to discover an association.

Research Questions or Hypotheses:

No specific research questions or hypotheses were raised, but this reader can deduce them from the purpose statement. The general question was: Does the quality of advisement influence student attrition? The specific questions are: Is better advising associated with lower attrition than poor advising? Do changes in quality of advising (from good, poor, or no advising) affect retention differently?

Data Collection Procedure:

Freshmen at a public university were asked about the quality of advising they received, their intent to leave the institution, and their general satisfaction with the college experience. One thousand and thirty-three students completed questionnaires in their English Composition courses late in the fall semester of 1982.

Results:

In response to the question, "Is better advising associated with lower attrition than poor advising?", the results (of regression analysis) showed that good advising reduced dropout while poor advising failed to have any effect. Thus, levels of advising quality did impact freshman attrition differently. In response to the next question: "Do changes in the quality of advising (good, poor, none) affect retention differently?", the results showed that yes, the impact was different. Good advising helped to lower dropout more than no advising, and poor advising lowered dropout more than no advising. The implications of these results is that the best strategy for improving retention is to offer good advising to students who receive no advising.

Source: Abstracted with the assistance of Beth Caughlin, Bob Mann, Chad Abresch, Qian Geng, and Ling-Mean Heng from Education 800, University of Nebraska, Lincoln, Fall 1998.

that each abstract is fully documented. (Reference format will be addressed later in this chapter.)

For a *qualitative research* study, the topics are the same as those used in a quantitative study, but the headings reflect terms commonly used in qualitative research. Instead of using hypotheses and questions, qualitative researchers state only questions. Instead of *results, findings* is a more acceptable qualitative term.

When abstracting a qualitative research study, you might identify the:

◆ Research problem
◆ Research questions
◆ Data collection procedure
◆ Findings

These elements were used to abstract a qualitative study by Creswell and Brown (1992), shown in Figure 3.6. This study explores the role of academic chairpersons in enhancing faculty research. Again, there is a brief summary of each element and a complete reference to the article at the top of the abstract.

The elements abstracted in both the quantitative and qualitative examples illustrate typical information extracted from research studies. In other forms of abstracting, you may include additional information in which you critique or assess the strengths and weaknesses of the research.

FIGURE 3.6

Sample Abstract for a Qualitative Research Study

Creswell, J. W., & Brown, M. L. (1992). How chairpersons enhance faculty research: A grounded theory study. *The Review of Higher Education, 16*(1), 41–62.

Research Problem:

The authors mention that past research has addressed the correlates of scientific achievement and the research performance of faculty. However, an unexplored correlate is the role of the chairperson in influencing faculty scholarly performance. Since chairs are in a position to enhance and facilitate faculty scholarship, the role of the chair needs clarification.

Research Questions:

The central research question is implied in the title to the study: "How do chairpersons enhance faculty research?" More specifically, the authors asked chairs to discuss an issue involved in assisting faculty members in the department in his or her professional development. They were also asked to specify actions or roles in performing this assistance, identify reasons for assistance, note signs that the individual needed assistance, and indicate the outcomes of assistance for the individual.

Data Collection Procedure:

The authors collected semi-structured interview data from 33 chairpersons located in a variety of disciplines and types of institutions of higher education. Chief academic officers and faculty development personnel on the campuses nominated these chairs for the study. The authors used the procedures of grounded theory.

Findings:

The authors identified from the interviews seven major categories of roles engaged in by the chairpersons: provider, enabler, advocate, mentor, encourager, collaborator, and challenger. Further analysis then led to understanding how these roles played out for faculty at different stages of their careers. Four levels of faculty were used to illustrate their chair roles: beginning faculty, pre-tenured faculty, post-tenured faculty, and senior faculty. From these profiles, the authors identified a theoretical model of the chair's role and advanced propositions (or hypotheses) for future testing. These propositions related to the type of issue the faculty member experienced, the career stage issue of the faculty member, and the strategies employed by the chairperson.

Constructing a Literature Map

As you organize and take notes or abstract articles, you will begin to understand the content of your literature review. In other words, a conceptual picture will begin to emerge. Having a diagram or visual picture of this conceptualization allows you to organize the literature in your mind, identify where your study fits into this literature, and convince others of the importance of your study.

This visual picture results in a literature map, literally a map of the literature you have found. A **literature map** is a figure or drawing that displays the research literature (e.g., studies, essays, books, chapters, and summaries) on a topic. This visual rendering helps you see overlaps in information or major topics in the literature and can help you determine how a proposed study adds to or extends the existing literature rather than duplicates past studies. As a communication device, a map helps you convey to others, such as faculty committee members or an audience at a conference, the current picture of the literature on a topic.

The actual design of this map can take several forms. Figure 3.7 shows a chart in which the researcher organized the literature hierarchically. Organized in top-down fashion, this chart portrays the literature that Hovater (2000) found on the topic of preservice training for teachers on multicultural topics. At the top of the figure he lists the topic: the need for teacher education programs to train culturally responsive teachers. Next, below the top level, he identifies the two programs available, study abroad programs and U.S.

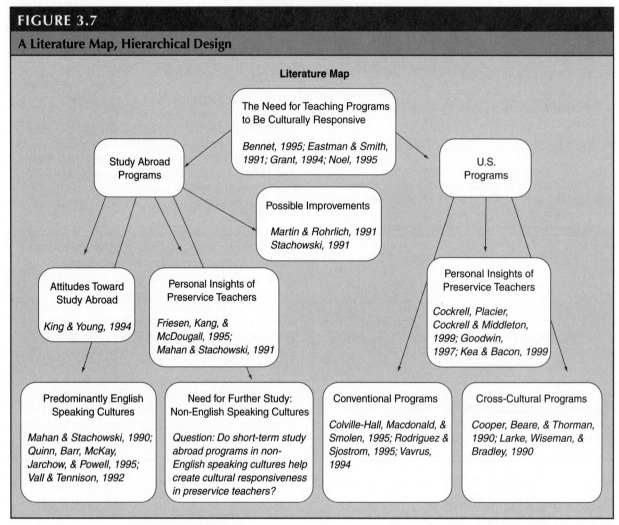

FIGURE 3.7

A Literature Map, Hierarchical Design

Source: Used by permission of Scott Hovater, 2000.

programs, and below that, specific studies that address these two types of programs. These studies relate to attitudes of students, personal insights of teachers, and possible improvements in training. At the lower left-center of the map, Hovater advances his proposed study: to extend the literature addressing the question, "Do short-term study abroad programs in non-English-speaking cultures help create cultural responsiveness in preservice teachers?"

Hovater's (2000) literature map includes several useful design features that you can include in a literature map. Here are some guidelines to follow when constructing your own literature map:

◆ Identify the key terms for your topic and place them at the top of the map. As discussed earlier, these key terms are found in draft titles, questions, or ERIC resources.

◆ Take the information for your map and sort it into groups of related topical areas or "families of studies." Think in terms of three or four groupings because these groups will likely result in major sections in a written literature review.

◆ Provide a label for each box (later this label is useful as a heading in your literature review). Also, in each box, include key sources you found in your literature search that fit the label of the box.

◆ Develop the literature map on as many levels as possible. Some branches in the drawing will be more developed than others because of the extent of the literature. In some cases, you may develop one branch in detail because it is the primary area of focus of your research topic.

◆ Indicate your proposed study that will extend or add to the literature. Draw a box at the bottom of the figure that says "my proposed study," "a proposed study," or "my study." In this box, you could state a proposed title, a research question, or the problem you wish to study. An extremely important step is to draw lines *connecting* your proposed study to other branches (boxes) of the literature. In this way, you establish how your study adds to or extends the existing literature. The map in Figure 3.8 shows a hierarchical design. Other designs, such as a circular design of interconnecting circles or a sequential design to show the literature narrowing and focusing into a proposed study, can also be used. We can see a circular design by shifting and changing Hovater's (2000) hierarchically designed map into a circular map, as shown in Figure 3.8.

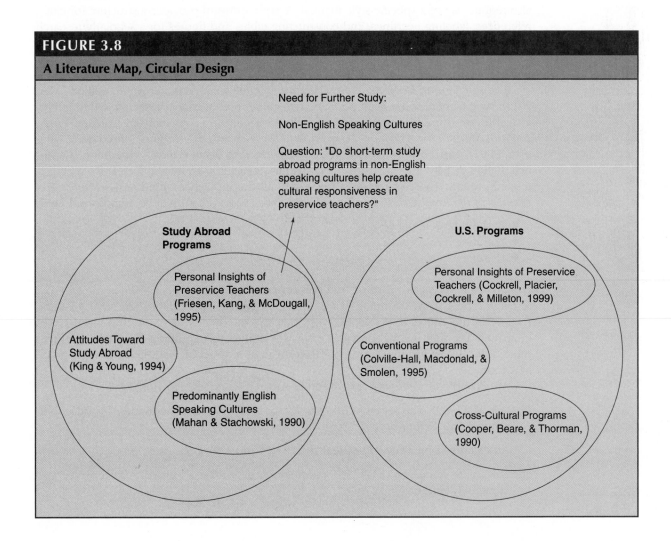

FIGURE 3.8

A Literature Map, Circular Design

Need for Further Study:

Non-English Speaking Cultures

Question: "Do short-term study abroad programs in non-English speaking cultures help create cultural responsiveness in preservice teachers?"

Study Abroad Programs

Personal Insights of Preservice Teachers (Friesen, Kang, & McDougall, 1995)

Attitudes Toward Study Abroad (King & Young, 1994)

Predominantly English Speaking Cultures (Mahan & Stachowski, 1990)

U.S. Programs

Personal Insights of Preservice Teachers (Cockrell, Placier, Cockrell, & Milleton, 1999)

Conventional Programs (Colville-Hall, Macdonald, & Smolen, 1995)

Cross-Cultural Programs (Cooper, Beare, & Thorman, 1990)

Write a Literature Review

Now that you have scanned the literature to determine its relevance, abstracted it, and organized it into a literature map, it's time to construct the actual written summary of the literature. For the most part, this literature consists of journal articles and research reports found in library resources. Researchers use procedures for summarizing each study, providing a clear reference to it, and writing the literature review. This writing requires pulling together all aspects of the review to this point, such as:

- ◆ Using an appropriate style to write complete references for these summaries (for a list at the end of your research report) and to develop headings for the literature review
- ◆ Employing specific writing strategies related to the extent of the review, the type of review, and the concluding statements in a review

Using a Style Manual

We have already seen how abstracts can include a complete reference (or citation) to the information in the literature (see Figures 3.5 and 3.6). In writing these references, you should use an accepted style manual. Headings, tables, figures, and the overall format also require use of a specific style manual. A **style manual** provides a structure for citing references, labeling headings, and constructing tables and figures for a scholarly research report. When you use a style manual, the research (and the literature review) will have a consistent format for readers and other researchers, and this format will facilitate their understanding of the study.

The *Publication Manual of the American Psychological Association,* 6th edition (APA, 2010), style manual is the most popular style guide in educational research. Other guides available are the *Chicago Manual of Style,* 15th edition (University of Chicago Press, 2003), *A Manual for Writers of Term Papers, Theses, and Dissertations,* 7th edition (Turabian, 2007), and *Form and Style: Theses, Reports, and Term Papers,* 8th edition (Campbell, Ballou, & Slade, 1990). These style manuals provide a consistent format for writing a research report. Three of the most frequently used approaches found in the *Publication Manual of the American Psychological Association* (APA, 2010) will be emphasized here:

- ◆ End-of-text references
- ◆ Within-text references
- ◆ Headings

End-of-Text References   **End-of-text references** are the references listed at the end of a research report. In APA form, they are double spaced and listed alphabetically by author. Include in the end-of-text reference list only the references mentioned in the body of the paper. The APA manual provides examples of the most common kinds of end-of-text references. Below are illustrations of three common types of references in appropriate APA form.

An example of a *journal article* end-of-text reference in APA form is:

Elam, S. M. (1989). The second Phi Delta Kappa poll of teachers' attitudes toward public schools. *Phi Delta Kappan, 70*(3), 785–798.

An example of a *book* end-of-text reference in APA form is:

Shertzer, B., & Stone, S. C. (1981). *Fundamentals of guidance* (4th ed.). Boston: Houghton Mifflin.

An example of a *conference paper* end-of-text reference in APA form is:

Zedexk, S., & Baker, H. T. (1971, May). *Evaluation of behavioral expectation scales.* Paper presented at the meeting of the Midwestern Psychological Association, Detroit, MI.

As these examples show, the first line is left adjusted and the second line is indented. We call this a *hanging indent.* Also, observe the use of all lowercase letters (noncapitals) in the titles of the articles, except for the first word and proper nouns. In the journal article example, we capitalize all words in the journal title. In the book example, we capitalize only the first word in the title of the book, the first word following a colon in the title, and proper nouns.

With increasing frequency, electronic journal publishing and materials located on the Internet are common today. Two ways to identify material obtained on the Internet are to provide a URL or a DOI (digital object identifier) number to the reference information. The **URL** is used to map digital information on the Internet. A URL contains several components: a protocol, a host name, the path to the document and the specific file name, such as **http://www.apa.org/monitor/oct09/worlplace.html**. The words "Retrieved from" precede the URL name as in the following example of a journal article reference:

Smith, J. (2008, June). Sciences vs. ideologies. *Science, 29*(3). Retrieved from **http://www.apa.org/monitor/**.

URLs are often changed on the Internet, and scholarly publishers have increasingly used the assignment of a DOI to journal articles and to documents. The **DOI System** provides a means of identification for managing information on digital networks (see **http://www.doi.org/**). A DOI is a unique alphanumeric string assigned by a registration agency to identify content and provide a persistent link to its location on the Internet. The DOI number is typically located on the first page of the electronic journal article, close to the copyright notice. When cited in a reference, this number is placed at the end of a reference, such as in this journal article example:

Smith, J. P. (2005). Mixed methods research: Its controversies and potential. *Journal of Mixed Methods Research, 3*(1), 34–50. doi: 1038/0278.6133.24.2.226

Within-Text References   **Within-text references** are references cited in a brief format within the body of the text to provide credit to authors. APA style lists several conventions for citing these in-text references. The following examples illustrate the appropriate use of APA style when you cite both single and multiple authors.

An example of a within-text reference in APA style in which the author refers to a single reference is:

Rogers (1994) compared reaction times for athletes and nonathletes in middle schools. . . .

As this reference shows, APA style requires that you use only the author's last name for within-text citations, unless first initials are needed to distinguish between authors with identical surnames. This reference also includes information about the year of the publication. These references may also appear anywhere in the sentence.

An example of a within-text reference in APA style in which the author refers to multiple references is:

Past studies of reaction times (Gogel, 1984; Rogers, 1994; Smith, 1989) showed. . . .
Entire groups of studies have addressed the difficulty of test taking and reaction times (Gogel, 1984; Happenstance, 1995; Lucky, 1994; Smith, 1989).

As illustrated by this example, semicolons separate the different studies. Also, the authors are listed in alphabetical order, as in end-of-text references, rather than in chronological order based on the date of publication.

The in-text citation of multiple authors needs to be carefully considered. When a work has only two authors, you should cite both names every time the reference occurs in the text, such as:

Kurines and Smith (2009) demonstrated . . .

However, when a work has three, four, or five authors, cite all of the authors the first time the reference occurs, but cite only the first author followed by *et al.* and the year in subsequent citations. For example,

First time citation:

The difficulty of test taking and reaction times has been examined by Smith, Paralli, John, and Langor (1994).

Subsequent citation in the same paper:

The study of test taking and reaction times (Smith et al., 1994) . . .

The *Publication Manual of the American Psychological Association,* 6th edition (APA, 2010), has a useful table to indicate how to cite references in text by one author, multiple authors, and groups.

Finally, good scholarly writing requires that authors cite original sources—where the information came from originally—rather than cite a book or article that contains the reference. For example,

Inadequate model:

Smith (1994), as reported in Theobald (1997), said that. . . .

An improved model, using the original source:

Smith (1994) said that. . . .

Levels of Headings   As you write a literature review, consider the number of topics or subdivisions in your review. **Levels of headings** in a scholarly study and literature review provide logical subdivisions of the text. Headings provide important clues for readers that help them understand a study. They also divide the material in the same way as topics in an outline.

In APA style, the maximum number of heading levels is five. As shown in Figure 3.9, these five headings differ in their use of upper- and lowercase letters; in centered,

---

FIGURE 3.9

Headings in APA Sixth Edition Style

Centered, Boldface, Uppercase and Lowercase Heading (Level 1)

Flush left, Boldface, Uppercase and Lowercase Heading (Level 2)

 Indented, boldface, lowercase paragraph heading ending with a period. (Level 3)

 Indented, boldface, italicized, lowercase paragraph heading ending with a period. (Level 4)

 Indented, italicized, lowercase paragraph heading ending with a period. (Level 5)

Source: APA (2010), p. 62

left-adjusted, and indented words; and in italics. Most educational studies include either two or three levels of headings. Authors seldom use fourth- or fifth-level headings because their research lacks the detail needed for many subdivisions. For some books, five levels of headings may be appropriate, but typically two to three levels of headings will suffice for most educational research studies.

The choice of heading levels in a literature review depends on the number of subdivisions of topics you use. Regardless of subdivisions, APA style requires that you use certain types of headings for a two-, three-, four-, and five-level heading format. The following examples illustrate these three popular forms.

When you have only two levels in a research report, use Levels 1 and 2. An example of a *two-level heading* in APA form that uses first (centered, boldface, uppercase and lowercase) and second levels (flush left, boldface, uppercase and lowercase) is:

Review of the Literature (Level 1)

Introduction (Level 2)

Social Support Research (Level 2)

If you have three levels in your research, use Levels 1 (centered, boldface, uppercase and lowercase), 2 (flush left, boldface, uppercase and lowercase), and 3 (indented, boldface, lowercase paragraph heading ending with a period.). A lowercase paragraph means that the first letter of the first word is uppercase and the remaining words are lowercase. An example of a *three-level heading* in APA form is:

Review of the Literature (Level 1)

Introduction (Level 2)

    Social support. People band together in work units. . . . (Level 3)

Sections of a paper may have different levels of headings, depending on length and complexity. The introduction to a manuscript does not carry a heading that identifies it as an introduction. It is assumed that the first part of a manuscript is the introduction. Also, the title of a manuscript should be typed in uppercase and lowercase letters, centered, and positioned in the upper half of a page. In sum, headings are not easy to describe, and they need to be short—typically two or three words—and state exactly and succinctly the content of the passage that follows.

Writing Strategies

As you write a literature review, several additional elements will need your attention: the extent of the review, the type of review, and the concluding statement of the review.

Extent of the Review   One question Maria asked her advisor was "How long should my literature review be?" There is no easy answer to this question, but you can begin by considering the type of research report you are writing. For dissertations and theses, you need an extensive review of the literature, which often comprehensively includes all sources of information identified in the classification of resources in Figure 3.1. For research plans or proposals, a less than comprehensive literature review may suffice, although guidelines may be set by advisors or reviewers. The literature review in proposals or plans for a study establishes the framework for a study and documents the importance of the research problem. Typically, literature reviews for proposals run from 10 to 30 pages in length, although this can vary. A proposal literature review summarizes the citations obtained from searching databases such as ERIC, PsycINFO, EBSCO, Sociofile, and others. For a journal article, the extent of the literature review varies, with typically more attention given to the literature review in a separate section in a quantitative study than in a qualitative study. In a journal article, researchers also tend to shorten the literature review to fit word requirements of journal editors, as compared to a more thorough and extensive review as found in proposals or plans for a study.

Also related to the *extent* of the literature review is the question "How far back in the literature do my references need to go?" When completing a dissertation or thesis, the search covers most published literature and the author examines sources back to the inception of the research topic. For research proposals and journal articles (and preliminary reviews), use as a rough guide the last 10 years, focusing on the more recent studies. An exception is to cite earlier, classical studies because they substantially influence subsequent literature published in the last decade.

Types of Literature Reviews At this point you will need to determine how to actually structure the summaries or notes taken on the articles and studies in the literature. The organization of the summaries varies depending on the type of research report and the traditions for literature reviews on different campuses. When writing a literature review for a dissertation or thesis, you might visit with an advisor to determine the appropriate format to use. However, the two models presented here—the thematic review and the study-by-study review—will serve you well. [See Cooper (1984) and Cooper & Lindsay (1998) for additional approaches.]

In a **thematic review of the literature**, the researcher identifies a theme and briefly cites literature to document this theme. In this approach, the author discusses only the major ideas or results from studies rather than the detail of any single study. Authors use this approach frequently in journal articles, but students also use it for dissertations and theses in graduate programs. You can identify this form by locating a theme and noting the references (typically multiple references) to the literature used to support the theme.

For example, in a study by Brown, Parham, and Yonker (1996), the authors reviewed the literature about racial identity development of White counselors-in-training in a course on racial identity attitudes of White women and men. This passage, appearing in an early section in the study, illustrates a thematic approach:

> Among other things, racial identity is a sense of group belonging based on the perception of a shared racial heritage with a specific group and, as such, it has an impact on personal feelings and attitudes concerning distinguishable racial groups (Helms, 1990; 1994; Mitchell & Dell, 1992). Researchers agree that White Americans generally are not challenged to ask themselves, "What does it mean to be White?" (Pope-Davis & Ottavi, 1994). . . . (p. 511)

In this case, the authors review the literature about the theme "racial identity" and briefly mention references to support the theme. The authors do not discuss each reference separately and in detail.

In contrast to a thematic review, the **study-by-study review of the literature** provides a detailed summary of each study grouped under a broad theme. This detailed summary includes the elements of an abstract shown in Figures 3.5 and 3.6. This form of review typically appears in journal articles that summarize the literature and in dissertations and theses. When presenting a study-by-study review, authors link summaries (or abstracts) by using transitional sentences, and they organize the summaries under subheadings that reflect themes and major divisions. Using the literature map concept discussed earlier in this chapter, these themes are the topics identified in boxes in the map (see Figure 3.7).

The following review of the literature about cross-cultural competency and multicultural education in the journal *Review of Educational Research* by McAllister and Irvine (2000) illustrates a study-by-study review. Here, the authors discuss the research one study at a time that addresses Helms's racial identity model.

> Brown, Parham, and Yonker (1996) employed the White Racial Identity Scale to measure change in the white racial identity of thirty-five white graduate students

who participated in a sixteen-week multicultural course. Eighty percent of the participants had previous multicultural training and most of them had had experiences with people from at least two different racial backgrounds, though the nature of these experiences is not defined. The authors designed the course based on three areas—acquisition of self knowledge, cultural knowledge, and cross-cultural skills—and they used a variety of teaching methods such as lectures, talks by guest speakers, and simulations. Results indicated that at the end of the course women endorsed more items than men did in the pseudo-independence stage on the White Racial Identity Scale, and men endorsed more items than women did in the autonomy stage. The authors draw a causal relationship between the course and those changes found in the group.

Neville, Heppner, Louie, and Thompson (1996) also examined the change in White racial identity as well. . . . (p. 8)

In this example, the authors first described the study by Brown et al. (1996) in some detail, then they described the study by Neville et al. (1996). In this way, they discussed one study at a time. They also provided a detailed description of the study to include the research problem (whether the scale measures change), an implied question (whether men and women differ on the scale), the data collection (i.e., 35 participants in the study), and a summary of the results (men and women endorse items differently depending on their stage of development).

Concluding Statement of the Review   How do you end a literature review section in a study? The concluding statement of a literature review serves several purposes. It summarizes the major themes found in the literature and it provides a rationale for the need for your study or the importance of the research problem.

First, summarize the major themes. Ask yourself, "What are the major results and findings from all of the studies I have reviewed?" Your answer to this question will result in the identification of three or four themes that summarize the literature. Then, briefly summarize each theme. The summaries should emphasize the major ideas under each major heading in the literature review and highlight what the reader needs to remember from the summary of the review.

Besides stating the major themes in a review, you also need to suggest reasons why the current literature is deficient and why educators need additional research on your topic. These reasons address ways the proposed study will add to knowledge, and they justify the importance of the research problem. Typically, writers mention three or four reasons that play a significant role in research because they often lead into the purpose statement, research questions, and hypotheses (to be addressed in the next chapter).

The example below illustrates both the summary of themes and the author's justification of the need for additional research.

The factors influencing faculty to be productive researchers found in the literature suggest three themes: early productivity (Did faculty begin publishing early in their careers?); mentoring (Did faculty apprentice under a distinguished researcher?); and support systems (Did faculty have adequate funding for their research?). These factors, although important, do not address the time faculty need to conduct research. When faculty have allotted time for scientific investigations and inquiries, it helps to focus their attention, offers sustained momentum for research, and removes distracting activities that may draw their attention away from research.

In this example, the author states three themes and, from these themes, identifies an area for future research: faculty time. Then, the author identifies three reasons for the importance of the study of faculty time.

REEXAMINING THE PARENT INVOLVEMENT AND THE MOTHERS' TRUST IN PRINCIPALS STUDIES

In both the quantitative parent involvement study (Deslandes & Bertrand, 2005) and the qualitative mothers' trust in principals study (Shelden et al., 2010), the authors begin their articles by citing literature from other studies. As you have learned in this chapter, you can identify this literature by noting when the researchers cite an author and a year. For example, see the reference to "Henderson & Mapp, 2002" (Paragraph 01) in the parent involvement study or the reference to "Colarusso & O'Rourke, 2007" (Paragraph 01) in the mother's trust in principals study. Let's take a closer look at the two studies and examine their use of the literature.

Literature Review Analysis in a Quantitative Study

In the *quantitative* parent involvement study (Deslandes & Bertrand, 2005), the citations to the literature cluster around the beginning and the end of the article. In the opening, Paragraph 01, the authors cite studies to document the importance of the problem: the need for parent involvement in their children's educational processes at home and at school. Then, in Paragraph 02, the authors explain that a model exists in the literature that might explain parent involvement—the Hoover-Dempsey and Sandler model. They also present research questions consistent with factors in this model that are expected to influence parent involvement: parents' role construction, parents' self-efficacy, perceptions of teacher invitations, and perceptions of adolescent invitations. You need to see how the authors identify, earlier in the article, the four primary factors that will be the focus of the study. The paragraphs to follow (03–10) merely summarize the literature on each of these four factors. Paragraph 03 begins with an overview of many possible factors that might influence parent involvement. Then Paragraphs 04–08 review the literature on each of the four factors. In Paragraph 09, the authors reflect on the relative importance of each of the four factors when measured together, and Paragraph 10 introduces the idea that grade level will influence parent outcomes and thereby anticipates this element being introduced into the study. Then, when you see Paragraph 13, which is the intent or purpose of the study, it makes sense because we now know that four factors and grade level will be of primary importance in this study. Finally, the authors return again to the literature in Paragraphs 34–43, in which they first state their major results and then compare their results to findings suggested by authors in the literature as well as the theory mentioned at the beginning of the article.

In summary, the literature in the parent involvement study:

◆ Documents the importance of the research problem at the beginning of the study
◆ Provides evidence for important components of the model to be tested
◆ Provides evidence for the research questions
◆ Provides an explanation for the results at the end of the study by citing other studies and by returning to the theoretical predictions

Literature Review Analysis in a Qualitative Study

Now let's turn to a qualitative study to see the role of the literature. In the *qualitative* mothers' trust in principals study (Shelden et al., 2010), the literature serves some of the same purposes and some different purposes than did the literature in the quantitative study. The overall use of the literature in this qualitative article is to establish the importance of trust in the parent–school relationship. Paragraphs 01–11 might be seen as a discussion of the importance of the problem of trust, and the literature unfolds from the broad concept of parents being involved in the schools (Paragraph 01), to the importance of trust and how it is defined (Paragraphs 02–03), how trust is critical in schools, especially for leaders (Paragraphs 04–06), to the important relevance for parents of children with disabilities and their due process needs (Paragraph 07–11). This broad-to-narrow perspective that the authors convey in the introduction establishes the importance of trust for parents of children with disabilities. As far as using literature in the introduction, we see in this qualitative study more reliance on the literature than is typically found in qualitative projects. However, it is important to see this literature as establishing the importance of the problem of trust and its consequences, rather than specifying the questions that need to be asked (as is found in a quantitative study). In this sense, this introduction is a good qualitative presentation of the opening literature for a study. In addition, the authors return to the literature on trust at the end of the study and compare the findings from their study with this literature to assess whether their findings were consistent (Paragraphs 59–68).

In summary, the literature in the qualitative mothers' trust in principals study:

◆ Documents the importance of the research problem at the beginning of the study
◆ Does not foreshadow the research questions (which are broad in scope to encourage participants to provide their views)
◆ Is used to compare with the findings of the present study at the end of the study

KEY IDEAS IN THE CHAPTER

What Is a Review of the Literature and Why Is It Important?

A literature review is a written summary of articles, books, and other documents that describes the past and current state of knowledge about a topic, organizes the literature into topics, and documents a need for a proposed study. This review serves the purpose of providing a need for a study and demonstrating that other studies have not addressed the same topic in exactly the same way. It also indicates to audiences that the researcher is knowledgeable about studies related to a topic.

Literature reviews are different in quantitative and qualitative research. In quantitative research, investigators provide a detailed review of the literature to justify the major purpose and research questions of a study. In qualitative research, the inquirers use a limited amount of literature in the beginning of the study to allow participant views, rather than perspectives from the literature, to play a major role in the study. The literature also helps to establish the importance of the research problem or issue. Then, the literature is cited again at the end of studies in both quantitative and qualitative research, but its use is again different. In quantitative research, the literature at the end compares results with predictions made at the beginning of the research. In qualitative research, researchers use the literature at the end to compare and contrast findings in the study with past literature.

The Five Steps in Conducting a Literature Review

Designing and conducting a literature review involves five interrelated steps. First, researchers identify key terms to use in their search of the literature. They look for these terms in titles, research questions, or in computer databases. Next, researchers locate literature in library resources such as summaries, books, journal publications and electronic sources, and early stage literature.

After locating the literature, the researcher then critically evaluates the materials and makes a determination of its relevance for use. Criteria for evaluating materials consist of assessing the quality of the publications and the rigor of the research as well as examining the relevance of the topic for a study.

Researchers next obtain the literature, take notes or create abstracts of it, and organize it into a visual rendering of the literature, called a literature map. This map helps to organize past literature as well as portray how a proposed study fits into the overall literature.

The final step is actually writing the literature review. Writing strategies at this point include using appropriate style manual formats and developing headings for the written literature review. Researchers need to consider the extent or length of the review for different types of research reports. The type of review will also vary, depending on the type of report. Some literature reviews are thematic reviews summarizing the major themes to appear in the literature. Other literature reviews provide a more detailed analysis of studies, a study-by-study approach in which each study is examined for its purpose and question, forms of data collected, and key results.

Researchers conclude a literature review by summarizing major themes and presenting reasons for a proposed study or the importance of studying a research problem. These reasons lead to a rationale for a study that builds naturally into the purpose statement and research questions or hypotheses.

Useful Information for Producers of Research

- ◆ Use the five-step process explained in this chapter for designing and conducting a literature review.
- ◆ Consider the different strategies for selecting key terms: choosing words from the project's title, selecting words from a brief question asked in the study, and using online databases.
- ◆ Begin a search of the literature with the most easily accessible material, such as published research studies reported in journals. Use the academic library databases or the Internet to search for literature.
- ◆ Begin with the ERIC database before using other databases to locate useful educational literature.
- ◆ Develop some means for organizing the literature you find, such as a graphic rendering of the literature into groups of studies in a literature map.
- ◆ Realize that not every source you locate may provide relevant information for your literature review. To determine which to use, remember these four criteria: the relevance of the topic, the individuals or sites, the problem, and the accessibility of the information.
- ◆ Abstract studies before you begin to write the literature review. These abstracts provide a useful summary of studies and can be included in your review. Be sure to include all of the elements that go into a good abstract.
- ◆ Use an accepted style manual such as the APA *Publication Manual,* 6th edition, for the end-of-text and within-text references as well as for the headings in your literature review. Avoid the temptation to jot down a citation any old way. Writing citations in APA-accepted form will save you many hours of extra work later. For most educational research reports, a two- or three-level heading format will suffice.
- ◆ Keep your literature review succinct and short. Decide whether a thematic or a study-by-study review is appropriate for your research report. Consider the type of review typically used by audiences for your report.
- ◆ Conclude your literature review with a summary of the major themes. Also, discuss how the literature is deficient and how your study adds to the literature.

Useful Information for Consumers of Research

◆ Recognize that a literature review in a research report will contain many types of literature. Literature syntheses provide a broad summary of research. Books are less valuable as research guides, but they may report useful research. The most popular sources for literature reviews are journal articles. Other research literature is available in publications from conferences. Of less value is research posted to Web sites because reviewers may not have evaluated it for quality.

◆ Do not assume that all literature cited by an author in a report contains good and valid information. Researchers need to choose the literature to include in a review selectively. Apply the evaluation criteria for relevance found in this chapter to determine whether an author used relevant literature.

◆ As you evaluate a study, consider whether the author has made a good case that the study adds to existing knowledge. The study should explicitly specify how and in what way it adds to knowledge. A visual literature map of sources of information helps to convey the author's case.

◆ A research study should employ a consistent form for reporting references to the literature, both in the text as well as at the end of the report. In addition, the headings should be easy to identify and be descriptive of the passage that follows.

Understanding Concepts and Evaluating Research Studies

1. Assume that you wish to conduct a literature review on the topic of the increasing incidence of teenage pregnancies in high schools today. What two or three words would you use to search for research on this topic using the ERIC database?
2. Run a search on your topic using one of the online databases (e.g., ERIC, PsycINFO, EBSCO). What criteria would you use to examine the quality of the articles that you find in your search?
3. Using a reference that emerged from your online database search in #2, write a correct APA (6th edition) end-of-text reference for the literature citation.

Conducting Your Research

Practice conducting a literature review using the educational topic of your choice. Go through the five steps in conducting a literature review, ending with a brief literature review of one or two articles: (a) *Identify key terms* to use in your search for literature; (b) *Locate literature* about a topic by consulting several types of materials and databases, including those available at an academic library and on the Internet; (c) *Critically evaluate and select* the literature for your review; (d) *Organize the literature* you have selected by abstracting or taking notes on the literature and developing a visual diagram of it; and (e) *Write a review* that reports summaries of the literature.

Go to the Topic "Reviewing the Literature" in the MyEducationLab
(**www.myeducationlab.com**) for your course, where you can:

◆ Find learning outcomes for "Reviewing the Literature."
◆ Complete Assignments and Activities that can help you more deeply understand the chapter content.
◆ Apply and practice your understanding of the core skills identified in the
chapter with the Building Research Skills exercises.
◆ Check your comprehension of the content covered in the chapter by going to
the Study Plan. Here you will be able to take a pretest, receive feedback on
your answers, and then access Review, Practice, and Enrichment activities to
enhance your understanding. You can then complete a final posttest.

4

Specifying a Purpose and Research Questions or Hypotheses

*P*urpose statements, research questions, and hypotheses provide critical information to readers about the direction of a research study. They also raise questions that the research will answer through the data collection process. As such, they deserve special attention. In this chapter you will learn about purpose statements, research questions, and hypotheses and how to write them for both quantitative and qualitative research.

By the end of this chapter, you should be able to:

◆ Distinguish among purpose statements, research questions, hypotheses, and objectives.

◆ Describe why these statements and questions are important.

◆ Write quantitative purpose statements, research questions, and hypotheses.

◆ Write qualitative purpose statements and research questions.

Maria completes her literature review on school violence and writes down a statement that represents the central direction of her study: "I would like to study the reasons why students carry weapons in high schools." This is an example of a quantitative research statement. Alternatively, she could write a qualitative statement: "I would like to study students' experiences with weapons in high school." For her research study at the university, Maria needs to write a statement that advances the overall intent of her study, a purpose statement, as well as research questions. The form of her purpose statement and her questions will reflect her decision to engage in quantitative or qualitative research.

WHAT ARE PURPOSE STATEMENTS, RESEARCH QUESTIONS, HYPOTHESES, AND OBJECTIVES?

Let's begin by defining four terms used in research to convey the intent of a study: *purpose statements, research questions, research hypotheses,* and *research objectives.* These

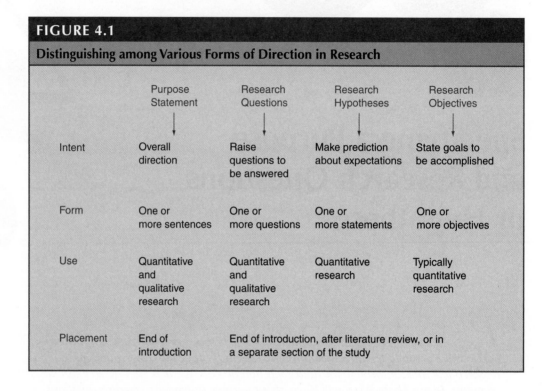

FIGURE 4.1

Distinguishing among Various Forms of Direction in Research

	Purpose Statement	Research Questions	Research Hypotheses	Research Objectives
Intent	Overall direction	Raise questions to be answered	Make prediction about expectations	State goals to be accomplished
Form	One or more sentences	One or more questions	One or more statements	One or more objectives
Use	Quantitative and qualitative research	Quantitative and qualitative research	Quantitative research	Typically quantitative research
Placement	End of introduction	End of introduction, after literature review, or in a separate section of the study		

forms differ in intent (their role in research), form (their appearance in studies), use (their application in quantitative and qualitative approaches), and placement (their location) in research reports. Knowing these differences can help you design, write, and evaluate them. Figure 4.1 illustrates the differences among these forms.

The Purpose Statement

The **purpose statement** is a statement that advances the overall direction or focus for the study. Researchers describe the purpose of a study in one or more succinctly formed sentences. It is used both in quantitative and qualitative research and is typically found in the "statement of the problem" section. It often appears as the last sentence of an introduction. You can recognize it because researchers typically state it beginning with the phrase "The purpose of this study is . . ." A *quantitative* version of this purpose statement addressing teacher–parent communications and student achievement follows:

> The purpose of this study is to examine the relationship between use of Internet communication between teachers and parents in a Midwestern school district and student achievement on tests in high school social studies.

A *qualitative* version might be:

> The purpose of this study is to explore parent stories regarding Internet communications with teachers about their students in one Midwestern school district.

Research Questions

Research questions are questions in quantitative or qualitative research that narrow the purpose statement to specific questions that researchers seek to answer. Researchers typically develop them before identifying the methods of the study (i.e., the types of data to be collected, analyzed, and interpreted in a study). Unlike the single statement found in a purpose statement, researchers typically state multiple research questions so that they can fully explore a topic. Research questions are found in both quantitative and qualitative research, but their elements differ depending on the type of research you are conducting.

In quantitative research, the questions relate attributes or characteristics of individuals or organizations. Later in the chapter you will learn that these are called *variables*. In qualitative research, the questions include the central concept being explored. You will learn that this central concept is called a *central phenomenon*. In some studies, both research questions and purpose statements appear—a good presentation style to clarify both the general and specific directions of a study. The research questions are typically at the end of the introduction of the "statement of the problem" section or immediately following the review of the literature. To locate research questions, you might look for opening passages in which authors identify the research questions they are addressing (e.g., Paragraph 02, Deslandes & Bertrand, 2005). For example, a *quantitative* research question would be:

Do parent–teacher Internet communications affect student performance in the classroom?

A *qualitative* research question is:

What types of Internet experiences do parents have with teachers about the performance of the parents' children?

Hypotheses

Hypotheses are statements in quantitative research in which the investigator makes a prediction or a conjecture about the outcome of a relationship among attributes or characteristics. Traditionally used in experiments, they serve, like research questions, to narrow the purpose statement to specific predictions. These predictions are not simply an "educated guess." Rather, researchers base them on results from past research and literature where investigators have found certain results and can now offer predictions as to what other investigators will find when they repeat the study with new people or at new sites. You will find these hypotheses stated at the beginning of a study, typically at the end of the introduction. Investigators also place them immediately after the review of the literature or in a separate section titled "Hypotheses." Usually researchers advance several hypotheses, such as three or four. An illustration of a hypothesis is:

Students in high schools in the school district in which parents and teachers communicate through the Internet will have higher grades than students whose parents and teachers do not communicate through the Internet.

Research Objectives

A **research objective** is a statement of intent used in quantitative research that specifies goals that the investigator plans to achieve in a study. Researchers often subdivide objectives into major and minor objectives. They appear frequently in survey or questionnaire studies or in evaluation research in which investigators have clearly identified objectives. Like hypotheses and research questions, objectives are found at the end of the "statement of the problem" section, after the literature review, or in a separate section of the study.

You can identify objectives by looking for phrases such as "The objectives in this study are . . ." For instance, the following represent objectives for a study:

1. To describe the frequency of Internet communication between parents and teachers regarding the parents' children in high school social studies classes
2. To describe the types (or categories) of Internet communication between parents and teachers
3. To relate (a) frequency and (b) types of communication to student achievement in the class as measured by performance on tests

Because of the limited use of research objectives in educational research today, our focus in this chapter is on hypotheses and research questions as a means of narrowing and focusing purpose statements.

WHY ARE THESE STATEMENTS AND QUESTIONS IMPORTANT?

These statements are signposts similar to a thesis statement or objectives in term papers you may have written. Without clear signposts, the readers will be lost throughout your study. They simply will not know the central ideas addressed in your study. You can also identify the most appropriate methods for collecting data from the purpose and the questions. They also provide key components for understanding the results of a project. Good research links the purpose statement and questions to major results. To write good purpose statements and research questions, we will begin with some concepts that you need to know, and then establish the building blocks for writing these statements and questions into a study.

HOW DO YOU DESIGN QUANTITATIVE PURPOSE STATEMENTS, RESEARCH QUESTIONS, AND HYPOTHESES?

To write quantitative purpose statements, research questions, and hypotheses, you need to understand the importance and use of variables. We start with their definition, talk about the various types used in quantitative research, and then discuss their use in broad theories or explanations.

Specify Variables

A **variable** is a characteristic or attribute of an individual or an organization that (a) researchers can measure or observe and (b) varies among individuals or organizations studied (see Figure 4.2). They are key ideas that researchers seek to collect information on to address the purpose of their study.

Consider the following examples of variables typically studied in educational research:

◆ Leadership style (by administrators)
◆ Achievement in science (by students)
◆ Interpersonal communication skills (of counselors)

Let's break this definition down for close inspection.

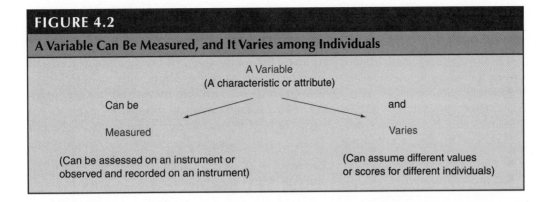

FIGURE 4.2

A Variable Can Be Measured, and It Varies among Individuals

A Variable
(A characteristic or attribute)

Can be   and

Measured   Varies

(Can be assessed on an instrument or observed and recorded on an instrument)   (Can assume different values or scores for different individuals)

Characteristics of individuals refer to personal aspects about them, such as their grade level, age, or income level. An attribute, however, represents how an individual or individuals in an organization feel, behave, or think. For example, individuals have self-esteem, engage in smoking, or display the leadership behavior of being well organized. You can measure these attributes in a study. To practice, you might take out a sheet of paper and write down three personal characteristics and three attributes about your favorite teacher.

Next, consider what it means to "measure" these attributes or characteristics. **Measurement** means that the researcher records information from individuals in one of two ways:

◆ Asking them to answer questions on a questionnaire (e.g., a student completes questions on a survey asking about self-esteem)
◆ Observing an individual and recording scores on a log or checklist (e.g., a researcher watches a student playing basketball and records scores on dribbling techniques)

In either case, student scores will probably *vary* (hence the name *variable*). When variables vary, it means that scores will assume different values depending on the type of variable being measured. For example,

◆ Gender varies by two possible scores: female = 2 and male = 1.
◆ Self-esteem varies by three possible scores: positive = 3, neither positive nor negative = 2, and negative = 1.

In the quantitative parent involvement study (Deslandes & Bertrand, 2005), the authors, for example, measured parents' role construction (see Paragraph 18), the extent to which parents believed that it was their responsibility to help the school educate their adolescent. The authors asked parents to rate on a 6-point scale from "disagree very strongly" to "agree very strongly" statements such as "It's important that I let someone at school know about things that concern my teenager" (p. 167).

Distinguish between Variables Measured as Categories and as Continuous Scores

When participants in a study complete a question, the researcher assigns a score to their response (e.g., 5 for strongly agree). This score is a value for the variable being measured, and investigators measure variables using continuous and categorical scores. Knowing this classification will help you understand the different types of variables and their use in purpose statements, research questions, and hypotheses.

Researchers score variables by grouping them into a limited number of categories or by using them to represent a value of some degree on a continuum, ranging from low to high levels (Gall, Borg, & Gall, 1996; Vogt, 2005). A **variable measured in categories** is a variable measured by the researcher as a small number of groups or categories. In research, authors sometimes call this type of measure a *discrete* or *nominal* score, and it is illustrated by these examples:

◆ *Groups of students:* males (1) and females (2), or low ability (1) and high ability (2)
◆ *Types of instruction:* groups of students who experience lectures (1), groups of students who experience discussion (2), and groups of students who experience classroom activities (3)

A second type of score is based on measuring scores along a continuum. A **variable measured as continuous** is a variable measured by the researcher on a point along a continuum of scores, from low to high scores. Sometimes authors call this type of scoring an *interval,* a *rating,* or a *scaled* score. The most typical example of a continuous score would be age (e.g., from 25 years old to 65 years old) or height (e.g., from 5 feet to 6 feet tall). Often, continuous scores indicate the extent to which individuals agree or disagree with an idea or rate the level of importance of an issue.

Distinguish Variables from Constructs

Some attributes, such as "socialization," cannot be measured because they are too abstract. Some characteristics, such as "whether the children engage in thinking in the classroom," do not vary among people. Certainly all children think; what varies is how they think differently, such as when they engage in the activity of writing. A **construct** is an attribute or characteristic expressed in an abstract, general way; a variable is an attribute or characteristic stated in a specific, applied way. For example, *student achievement* is a construct, while the more specific term *grade point average* is a variable. The trend in educational research is to use variables rather than constructs in purpose statements, research questions, and hypotheses. In this text we will use variables.

The Family of Variables

With these definitions in mind, we can now discuss the different types of variables incorporated into quantitative purpose statements, research questions, and hypotheses. Understanding the "family of variables" requires learning the definition of each type of variable and understanding its role in providing direction for a study.

This "family" is shown in Figure 4.3. In this discussion you will learn about each type of variable listed in this figure, starting with the most important variables: the dependent, independent, and intervening variables. As shown in this figure, a useful way to think about organizing these variables is to consider them in a cause-and-effect relationship (Tuckman, 1999). What variables influence outcomes? Ask yourself:

1. What outcomes in my study am I trying to explain? (the dependent variables)
2. What variables or factors influence the outcomes? (the independent variables)
3. What variables do I need to also measure (i.e., control) so that I can make sure that my major factors influence outcomes and not other factors? (the control variables and the mediating variables)
4. What variables might influence the outcomes but cannot or will not be measured? (the confounding variables)

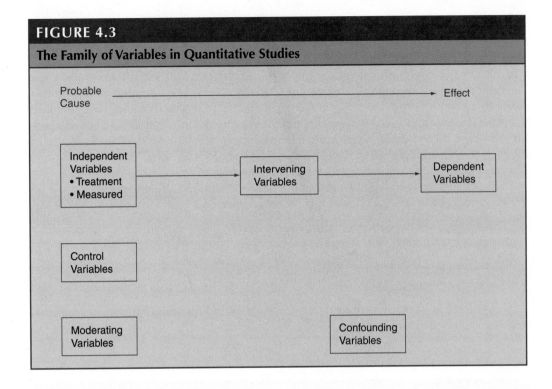

FIGURE 4.3

The Family of Variables in Quantitative Studies

Consider a fender bender car accident as an example. The outcome (dependent variable) was that you hit another car at a stop sign—rammed right into the back of it. You caused this fender bender because you were talking on your cell phone (independent variable). The cause might have been the slick pavement (control variable), but the skies were sunny and it had not rained for days. The fact that you had daydreamed might have caused the accident (confounding variable), but this fact would be difficult to measure after the accident. See how this works? Now take another situation in your life this last week, and list the dependent, independent, control, and confounding variables in your own cause-and-effect situation.

Dependent Variables

Now we will go into variables in some more depth. Look at Figure 4.3. On the right-hand side are the dependent variables. A **dependent variable** is an attribute or characteristic that is dependent on or influenced by the independent variable. You may find them labeled in the literature as the outcome, effect, criterion, or consequence variables. Researchers typically investigate multiple dependent variables in a single study (e.g., you hit another car, the other car hit the car in front of it, and so forth), although in many studies, one of the dependent variables is typically of central interest. Dependent variables can be measured using continuous or categorical scores.

Examples of dependent variables in education are achievement scores on a test, the organizational climate of a junior high school, the leadership skills of principals, or the cost effectiveness of student affairs programs in colleges. To locate dependent variables in a study, examine purpose statements, research questions, and hypotheses for outcomes that the researcher wishes to predict or explain. Ask yourself, "What is the outcome in this study?"

Independent Variables

On the left side of Figure 4.3 are the independent variables. An **independent variable** is an attribute or characteristic that influences or affects an outcome or dependent variable. In Figure 4.3, the arrows show how the independent variable influences the dependent variable through the intervening variable. Sometimes an intervening variable exists in a research study, and sometimes it does not. In research studies, you will find the independent variables called factors, treatments, predictors, determinants, or antecedent variables. Regardless of name, researchers measure this type of variable distinctly (or independently) from the dependent variable, and they identify these variables as worthy of study because they expect them to influence the outcomes.

Researchers study independent variables to see what effect or influence they have on the outcome. For instance, consider this research question:

Do students who spend more instructional time in class on math have higher math scores than students who spend less time?

Independent variable: Time on math instruction
Dependent variable: Math scores

As shown in Table 4.1, there are four types of independent variables, and each serves a slightly different purpose.

TABLE 4.1

Four Types of Independent Variables

	Measured Variable	Control Variable	Treatment Variable	Moderating Variable
Definition	An independent variable that is measured in a study	A special type of independent variable that is of secondary interest and is neutralized through statistical or design procedures	An independent variable manipulated by the researcher	A special type of independent variable that is of secondary interest and combines with another independent variable to influence the dependent variable
Type of Variable Measurement	A categorical or continuous variable that is measured or observed in the study	A variable not directly measured but controlled through statistical or research design procedures	A categorical variable actively manipulated by the researcher and composed of two or more groups	A categorical or continuous variable measured or observed as it interacts with other variables
Use in	Experiments, surveys	Experiments, correlational studies	Experiments	Experiments
Examples	Age of a child; performance on a test; attitudes assessed on a survey	Often demographic variables such as age, gender, race, socioeconomic level	Classroom learning: one group receives standard lecture and one group receives discussion; researcher assigns students to groups and thus manipulates group membership	Demographic variables such as age, gender, race, or socioeconomic level, a measured variable such as performance or attitude, or a manipulated variable such as classroom instruction

Measured Variables   The standard independent variable influences the outcome and is measured by the researcher. A **measured variable** is an independent variable that is measured or observed by the researcher and consists of a range of continuous or categorical scores. For example, consider the following research question:

How does math ability influence achievement on the final quiz in the classroom?

The independent variable is a measured variable indicating math ability scores assessed by results on an ability test.

Control Variables   A control variable is another type of independent variable that researchers measure for the purposes of eliminating it as a possibility, but it is not a central variable of concern in explaining the dependent variables or outcomes. A **control variable** is a variable that is important to consider and "neutralize" (Tuckman, 1999, p. 100) because it potentially influences the dependent variable. Typically, control variables are personal demographic attributes or characteristics (Tuckman, 1999) such as:

◆ Gender   ◆ Intelligence
◆ Socioeconomic status   ◆ Race

These variables are typically controlled through statistical procedures. Later we will learn that these variables are called *covariates* and they are statistically adjusted for their effects.

Treatment Variables

Two other specific types of independent variables can be introduced here because they will be used in educational experiments. In an experiment, a researcher treats one group of participants to specific activities and withholds them from another group. The question is whether the group that receives the activities scores differently on the dependent variable than the group without the activities. Because researchers assign individuals to these two groups, the groups are "treated" or "manipulated" by the researcher. A **treatment variable** is measured in categories (received or denied activities) to determine its effect on an outcome. In the literature you will find these variables labeled as *manipulated* variables or variables with *levels*. Experimental researchers refer to these groups as *levels* (i.e., Group 1, Group 2).

In the following example, the treatment variable is the type of instruction used by the teacher in an elementary math classroom:

In a study of student achievement outcomes in an elementary math classroom, the researcher gives one group small group discussion (Level 1) and another traditional group lecture (Level 2) to assess the independent variable, type of instruction.

Independent treatment variable: Type of instruction is considered a treatment variable because the researcher intervenes with one group, Level 1.

Moderating Variables   Moderating variables deserve our attention because they, too, are often used in educational experiments. **Moderating variables** are new variables constructed by the researcher by taking one variable times another to determine the joint impact of both variables together. This impact is called an *interaction effect*. For now, recognize that interaction effects are a special form of independent variable. A moderating variable can be illustrated in this quantitative hypothesis:

Small-group discussion for students with high prior test scores contributes to higher math quiz results than lecture discussion for students with low prior test scores.

To test this statement, the researcher takes prior test scores (independent variable) times type of discussion (small group or lecture) to determine the joint effects of both variables on math quiz results.

Locating Independent Variables   Independent variables are located in purpose statements, research questions, and hypotheses. To find them, look for the variable that exercises influence or predicts an outcome. They may be described in categories or on a continuous scale of scores. They may also be of primary interest (measured variables), controlled in a study (control variables), or have specific application to experiments (treatment variables and moderating variables).

Intervening Variables

Intervening variables are different from dependent variables or any of the types of independent variables. Look at Figure 4.3 one more time. Using cause-and-effect thinking, factors sometimes intervene between the independent variable and the dependent one to influence the outcomes. An **intervening variable** is an attribute or characteristic that "stands between" the independent and dependent variables and exercises an influence on the dependent variable apart from the independent variable. Intervening variables transmit (or mediate) the effects of the independent variable on the dependent variable. Thus, they are also called mediating variables. In some quantitative studies, intervening variables are controlled using statistical procedures.

To demonstrate how intervening variables work, consider the logic of the sequence of variables shown in Figure 4.4. In this illustration, we first see that convenient office hours for students influences whether students will seek help from faculty (Step 1). However, this situation on most college campuses is too basic. Many factors besides office hours influence student visits with faculty. Convenient office hours convey an open

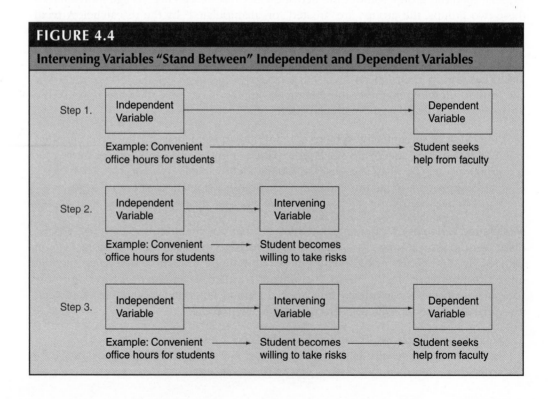

FIGURE 4.4

Intervening Variables "Stand Between" Independent and Dependent Variables

attitude toward students, and they show that faculty members care about their students. They also encourage shy and reserved students who are unable to speak up in class to visit privately with faculty. Students are willing to take risks by visiting with faculty privately in their offices (Step 2). What began as a single factor explaining the help students seek from faculty has now become more complex. When faculty members offer convenient office hours, students become willing to take risks, and they seek help from faculty (Step 3). As an intervening variable, a willingness to take risks is influenced by convenient office hours, and this, in turn, influences whether that student will seek help from a faculty member.

To locate mediating variables in purpose statements, research hypotheses, or questions:

◆ Ask yourself if any variables "stand" between the independent and dependent variables in a left-to-right sequence of events.
◆ In these statements or questions, look for the words *mediate* or *intervene*. These words provide a cue that the researcher intends to consider them as important influences on the dependent variable.
◆ Go into the "Results" section and look at the statistical analysis of the data to determine if the researcher statistically controls for variables that may "stand" between the independent and dependent variables.

Confounding Variables

The final variable listed in Figure 4.3 is the confounding variable. In this illustration, confounding variables are not directly in the probable cause-and-effect sequence but are extraneous or uncontrolled variables. **Confounding variables** (sometimes called *spurious variables*) are attributes or characteristics that the researcher cannot directly measure because their effects cannot be easily separated from those of other variables, even though they may influence the relation between the independent and the dependent variable. For example, for a high school student it may be impossible to separate an individual's race and prior discriminatory experiences as predictors of attitudes toward school. Thus, researchers measure the variables they can easily identify (e.g., race) and explain a limitation on their results (e.g., race was so interconnected with discriminatory experiences that it could not be easily separated as an independent measure).

 Think-Aloud About Identifying Variables

It is not always easy to identify variables in published studies, even with knowledge about the different types of variables and their roles. Here is a procedure I recommend to help you identify and organize variables to best understand a research report or to plan your own study.

1. Take a piece of paper and write from left to right the words *independent, intervening,* and *dependent variables.* Draw straight vertical lines between these words down the page.
2. Begin with the dependent variable. Examine a study (or consider your own project) and ask yourself: What are the outcomes the author seeks to explain in the study? Look at the title, purpose statement, questions, or hypotheses for this variable. Place the dependent variable(s) under that particular column on the sheet.
3. Next identify the independent variable(s) in the study. What factors influence this outcome? Does more than one factor influence this outcome? If so, what types of factors

are they? Is the independent variable assessed as two or more groups? Is it a variable where the author plans to intervene with one group and withhold an intervention with another group? Is some trait or characteristic of the participants being studied that influences the outcome? Does the author use language about controlling for a specific variable? List the independent variables on the sheet and write the type of independent variable in parentheses after each one (e.g., treatment, measured, or controlled).

4. Locate any intervening variables that may be used by the author. Are there any factors that mediate the influence between the independent and dependent variables in a cause-and-effect sequence? List these variables on your sheet.

With this process, you have compiled a list of major variables in the study. As a picture, this rendering will help reduce a complex study into a simple, understandable model of the research. It can help you identify and plan the variables for your own study, and it provides a useful visual for conveying the major direction of a research report to audiences such as faculty committees and conference attendees.

Theories and Testing of Variables

We need to learn one more idea that is important before we proceed directly into quantitative purpose statements, research questions, and hypotheses. Look at Figure 4.3 again and see that arrows connect the independent variable to the dependent variable. In quantitative research we seek to test whether the independent variable *influences* the outcome or dependent variable. We make this test because we have found past research that suggests that this relationship exists. Some researchers in education go one step further. They have found a theory that predicts the likely impact of the independent variable on the dependent variable. They seek to test a theory. But because this theory deals with humans in unpredictable situations, we say that the independent variable "probably causes" the dependent variable. The idea of **probable causation** is that researchers attempt to establish a likely cause-and-effect relationship between variables, rather than *prove* the relationship.

A **theory in quantitative research** explains and predicts the probable relationship between independent and dependent variables. For example, researchers test the relationship between peer groups' influence and adolescents. This relationship is tested over and over, such as with the Boy Scouts, in church groups, in middle schools, in high schools, and in other settings. Repeatedly the relationship of a positive effect holds true. Then someone comes along, calls this relationship a theory, and assigns a name to it. Smith's theory of peer influence is born, reported in the literature, and tested by other researchers. Thus, as shown in Figure 4.5, you might think about a theory as a bridge that connects the independent and dependent variables. Theories are no more than broad explanations for what we would expect to find when we relate variables.

In quantitative research, investigators locate a theory in the literature, examine the predicted relationship among variables in the theory, and then test the relationships with new participants or at new sites. To test the theory, researchers write purpose statements, research questions, and hypotheses that advance the predicted relationships. For example, a theory of leadership might predict that when principals use consensus-building decision styles, their teachers feel more supported.

Examples of theories include a theory about how students learn, a theory about what motivates people, a theory about how adults learn, a theory about leadership styles, and a theory about personality.

FIGURE 4.5

Theories as Bridges between Independent and Dependent Variables

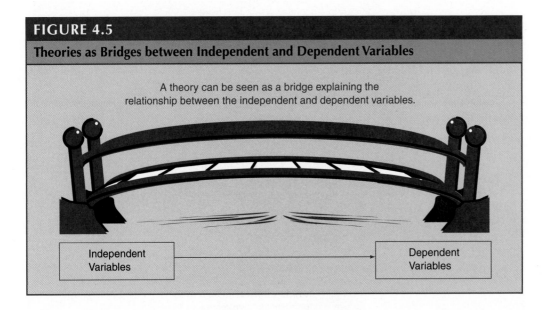

A theory can be seen as a bridge explaining the relationship between the independent and dependent variables.

Independent Variables → Dependent Variables

Not all quantitative studies employ a theory to test, but doing so represents the most rigorous form of quantitative research. It is certainly better than basing variables on your own personal hunches that are subject to challenge by other students and professors.

You might think about the test of a theory as the top of a list of reasons for studying the relationship among your variables. Look at Figure 4.6. Assume that several researchers explore the relationship between teacher respect for cultural values (the independent variable) and student performance (the dependent variable) in elementary school. In working from the bottom of the figure to the top, notice how each situation involves an increasing number of tests of studies, from a personal hunch to a sophisticated theory.

1. Some researchers have *hunches* or educated guesses as to why two variables might be related. For example, from personal experience, one researcher might feel that Hispanic children succeed in elementary school because the teacher is sensitive to cultural issues (e.g., the recognition and celebration of Hispanic holidays). Researchers have not tested this hunch, and it represents an unsophisticated approach based on the experiences of the researcher.

2. At a more rigorous level, educators can draw on a *theoretical rationale*—a logical statement for relating the variables—mentioned by authors in other studies. Assume that Jones, for example, found that Hispanic students learned best when teachers celebrated Hispanic holidays in class. With this theoretical rationale, we probably have more confidence in understanding the relationship between cultural sensitivity and performance in class (e.g., learning best).

3. Moving to an even more sophisticated level, assume that five different authors have studied this relationship and found cultural sensitivity to relate to performance. Smith, for instance, developed a *conceptual framework* (e.g., see Figure 4.6) predicting this relationship to hold true. Fox, Davis, Abel, and Sandoz tested this relationship. All found the relationship to hold true for different groups of Hispanic children. Now we have more confidence in the relationship because researchers have tested it multiple times with different Hispanic children.

4. Finally, assume that the relationship between cultural sensitivity and student performance is tested with many groups of *different* cultural orientations (e.g., Asian

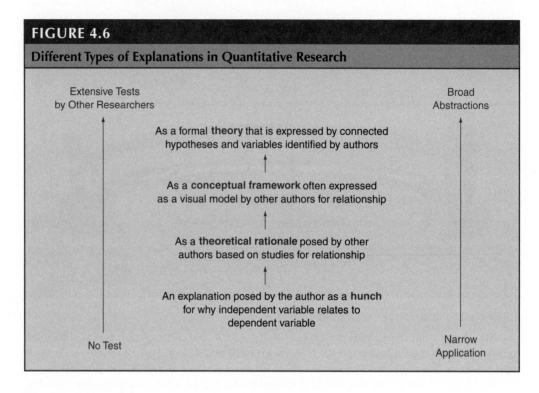

FIGURE 4.6

Different Types of Explanations in Quantitative Research

Extensive Tests
by Other Researchers

Broad
Abstractions

As a formal **theory** that is expressed by connected
hypotheses and variables identified by authors

As a **conceptual framework** often expressed
as a visual model by other authors for relationship

As a **theoretical rationale** posed by other
authors based on studies for relationship

An explanation posed by the author as a **hunch**
for why independent variable relates to
dependent variable

No Test

Narrow
Application

Americans, Native Americans, African Americans). In all of these situations, a positive relationship exists between teacher sensitivity and student performance. We now have a *theory,* a broad explanation of student performance based on cultural orientations.

What would a theory discussion look like? Here is an example, using "if . . . then" logic. *If* certain conditions are true, *then* the variables will be related. For example,

> Smith's (2000) theory of gender achievement predicts that if achievement in math is gender related, and girls are socialized to be better at math than boys, then girls will perform better in math than boys.

Where are theories located in a quantitative research report? Typically they are located in the literature review section or in the section on research questions or hypotheses. They may be called the *theoretical rationale* or a *theory-base* for the study. A good example of a theoretically driven study is the study of parent involvement by Deslandes and Bertrand (2005). In the opening paragraph of the study (Paragraph 02), they report how they will use the psychological constructs found in the Hoover-Dempsey and Sandler model as independent variables expected to influence the dependent variable, parent involvement.

Writing Quantitative Purpose Statements

With this background about variables and theory, you are ready to design and write a quantitative purpose statement, research questions, and hypotheses. To do this, first specify the elements that go into a good purpose statement, display a script that you can complete to help you design this statement, and illustrate the use of this script using examples.

Guidelines

A **quantitative purpose statement** identifies the variables, their relationship, and the participants and site for research. Several guidelines can help you prepare good purpose statements:

◆ Write the purpose statement in a single sentence.
◆ Begin the statement with key identifier words, such as "The purpose of this study," to clearly signal readers.
◆ If you plan to use a theory, introduce it in this statement by stating that you plan to "test a theory."
◆ Three options exist for using variables in this statement: You seek to relate two or more variables, to compare a variable composed of two or more groups in terms of the dependent variable, or to describe one variable. Use the words *relate* or *compare* or *describe* to indicate whether variables will be related, groups will be compared, or variables will be described.
◆ If variables are related or groups compared, specify the independent and dependent variables and any control or intervening variables.
◆ State the independent variable first (first position in the sentence), followed by the dependent variable (second position in the sentence). If control or mediating variables are used, state them last (in the third position in the sentence). The placement of these variables in this sentence is important because quantitative researchers often view variables as related from left to right, as shown in Figure 4.3.
◆ Identify the participants to be studied and the research site at which they will be studied.

Sample Scripts

To apply these guidelines, consider completing the following script by filling in the blanks:

> The purpose of this study is to test (the theory) by relating (the independent variable) to (the dependent variable) for (participants) at (the research site).

or

> by comparing (independent variable) with (group 1) and (group 2) in terms of (dependent variable) for (participants) at (the research site).

To apply this script, examine the following example for the case in which the researcher *relates* variables:

> The purpose of this study is to test Fines' theory (1996) by relating leadership style (independent variable) to autonomy (dependent variable) for teachers (participants) in high schools in State X (research site).

The next example illustrates the use of the script in which the researcher *compares* two groups (on an independent variable) in terms of one dependent variable:

> The purpose of this study is to test Smart's theory (1999) by comparing autocratic leaders (group 1) with consensus-building leaders (group 2) in terms of the satisfaction of teachers (dependent variable) in colleges in State X (research site).

Both examples begin with the phrase "The purpose of" to signal the reader. The independent variables precede the dependent variables in the statements. Also in both illustrations, the authors found theories to test, and they mentioned them at the beginning of the sentence. In other studies, a researcher may have only a hunch or a rationale and may not formally include a theory.

Maria, the high school teacher interested in studying weapon possession among high school students, might write the purpose statement with control variables in the third position:

> The purpose of this study is to relate student misbehavior factors (i.e., fighting) (independent variable—*position 1*) to attitudes toward weapon possession (dependent variable—*position 2*) for students in the district's high schools (participants—site), controlling for gender, grade level, and race (*position 3*).

In this example, the variables gender, grade level, and race will be eliminated as factors influencing weapon possession using statistical procedures.

Writing Quantitative Research Questions

Because research questions narrow and focus the purpose statement, they serve to restate the purpose in specific questions that the researcher seeks to answer. Research questions describe the participants' reactions to a single variable, compare groups on an outcome, or relate to variables. Research questions are found in all designs in quantitative research, such as in experiments, correlational studies, and surveys.

Guidelines

The basic steps in forming a research question are:

◆ Pose a question
◆ Begin with "how," "what," or "why"
◆ Specify the independent, dependent, and mediating or control variables
◆ Use the words *describe, compare,* or *relate* to indicate the action or connection among the variables
◆ Indicate the participants and the research site for the study

Three popular forms are available in quantitative research: descriptive questions, relationship questions, and comparison questions.

Descriptive Questions

Researchers use a **descriptive question** to identify participants' responses to a single variable or question. This single variable may be an independent, a dependent, or an intervening variable. The following is a script for writing a descriptive question:

> How frequently do (participants) (variable) at (research site)?

An application of this script might be:

> How frequently do African Americans feel isolated on college campuses?

Relationship Questions

In most research studies, investigators seek to learn more than responses to single variables. They may examine the relationship between two or more variables. **Relationship questions** seek to answer the degree and magnitude of the relationship between two or more variables. These questions often relate different types of variables in a study, such as independent variables to dependent variables or dependent variables to control variables. The most common case occurs when researchers relate the independent variable to the dependent variable. The following is a script for writing a relationship question:

> How does (<u>independent variable</u>) relate to (<u>dependent variable</u>) for (<u>participants</u>) at (<u>research site</u>)?

As applied to the relationship between isolation and ethnic identity, the script suggests:

> How do feelings of isolation relate to (or influence) the ethnic identity of African Americans in the United States?

Comparison Questions

Researchers might ask a **comparison question** to find out how two or more groups on an independent variable differ in terms of one or more outcome variables. Experiments employ comparison questions, and, in these studies, the researcher provides some intervention to one group and withholds it from the second group. A script for writing a comparison question would be:

> How does (<u>group 1</u>) differ from (<u>group 2</u>) in terms of (<u>dependent variable</u>) for (<u>participants</u>) at (<u>research site</u>)?

When this script is applied in a comparison of African Americans and Euro Americans, we get:

> How do African Americans and Euro Americans compare in their perceptions of ethnic identity?

Writing Quantitative Hypotheses

Similar to research questions, hypotheses narrow the purpose statement in quantitative research, but hypotheses advance a *prediction* about what the researcher expects to find. The researcher can make these predictions because of past studies in the literature that suggest certain outcomes. Also, hypotheses are not used to describe a single variable as found in the case of research questions. They also are not used as frequently as research questions because they represent a formal statement of relationships and the prediction of the relationship may not be known.

Researchers narrow the focus of the study to at least one hypothesis that provides a prediction about the outcome of the study. A prediction that Maria might make would be:

> The more students feel alienated, the more likely they are to carry weapons to school.

Can you think of other predictions about school violence that Maria might make?

Guidelines

Hypotheses need to include specific components. Guidelines for writing them are:

◆ State the variables in this order: independent (first position), dependent (second position), and control (third position).
◆ If you compare groups in your hypothesis, explicitly state the groups; if variables are related, specify the relationship among the variables.
◆ Make a prediction about changes you expect in your groups, such as less or more favorable or no changes (e.g., no difference). You will then test this prediction using statistical procedures.

TABLE 4.2		
The Null and Alternative Hypotheses		
Type of Hypothesis	**Null Hypothesis**	**Alternative Hypothesis**
Purpose	To test in the general population that there is no change, no relationship, no difference	The hypothesis that may be true if the null is rejected, it suggests a change, a relationship, or a difference
Specific Language Found in the Hypothesis	There is no difference (or relationship) between . . .	Magnitude statements such as higher, lower, more positive, more favorable
How Researchers Test the Hypothesis	A test of the hypothesis	A test of the hypothesis

◆ You may state information about the participants and the site of the study, but this information may not be necessary if it repeats information stated in your purpose statement.

There are two types of hypotheses: the null and the alternative to the null. You need both types in a research study, but authors generally write only one or the other into their reports. The basic characteristics of these two forms are shown in Table 4.2.

Null Hypotheses

The null hypothesis is the most traditional form of writing a hypothesis. **Null hypotheses** make predictions that of all possible people whom researchers might study (i.e., called the general population), there is no relationship between independent and dependent variables or no difference between groups of an independent variable or a dependent variable. To study this hypothesis, you would select a sample of all possible people and draw conclusions from the statistical analysis of this sample for the population. A null hypothesis might begin with the phrase "There is no difference between" groups or "There is no relationship between (or among)" variables.

To write a hypothesis, you can complete the following script, which employs the language "no difference":

There is no difference between (<u>independent variable, group 1</u>) and (<u>independent variable, group 2</u>) in terms of (<u>dependent variable</u>) for (<u>participants</u>) at (<u>research site</u>).

An example of the application of this script might be:

There is no difference between at-risk and non-at-risk students in terms of student achievement on math test scores for third-grade students in a Midwest school district.

Independent variable: at-risk students (members and nonmembers)
Dependent variable: student achievement test scores
Participants: third-grade students
Site: X school district
Form and language: null indicating no difference

Alternative Hypotheses

In contrast to the null hypothesis, you may write an alternative hypothesis. You will use an alternative hypothesis if you think there will be a difference based on results from past research or an explanation or theory reported in the literature.

The two types of alternative hypotheses are directional and nondirectional. In a **directional alternative hypothesis**, the researcher predicts the direction of a change, a difference, or a relationship for variables in the total population of people. A researcher selects a sample of people from a population and predicts that the scores will be higher, better, or changed in some way. This typical form for writing hypotheses is encountered in the literature more than any other type of hypothesis.

A script for a directional alternative hypothesis is:

(group 1, independent variable) at (research site) will have (some difference, such as higher, lower, greater, lesser) on (dependent variable) than (group 2 of independent variable).

An example of this script is:

Students who participate in direct learning in four elementary schools will have higher achievement scores than students who participate in whole-language learning.

Independent variable: learning (direct and whole language)
Dependent variable: achievement test scores
Participants: third-grade students
Research site: four elementary schools
Key indicator: directional, a prediction is implied

A variation on the directional hypothesis is the nondirectional hypothesis. In a **nondirectional alternative hypothesis** the researcher predicts a change, a difference, or a relationship for variables in a population but does not indicate whether the direction of this prediction will be positive or negative, or greater or less. The nondirectional alternative is not as popular as the directional alternative because the researcher does not take a stand about the direction of the relationship of the variables. A script for a nondirectional alternative hypothesis is:

There is a difference between (group 1, independent variable) and (group 2, independent variable) in terms of (dependent variable).

An illustration of this script would be:

There is a difference between varsity athletes in high school who smoke and those who do not smoke in terms of athletic accomplishments.

In this example, the author does not state whether the difference will be positive or negative. An analysis of the variables in this statement shows:

Independent variable: use of tobacco (smokers and nonsmokers)
Dependent variable: athletic accomplishments
Participants: varsity athletes
Sites: high schools
Key indicator: the words "a difference," but the direction is not specified

HOW DO YOU DESIGN QUALITATIVE PURPOSE STATEMENTS AND RESEARCH QUESTIONS?

The components of good purpose statements and research questions differ for quantitative and qualitative research. Before we learn how to write *qualitative* purpose statements and research questions, we need to understand how *qualitative* research is both similar and different from *quantitative* research.

Differentiating between Quantitative and Qualitative Purpose Statements and Research Questions

In both forms of research, inquirers use purpose statements and research questions. These statements become major signposts to alert readers to the major direction of the study. You need to write them carefully and incorporate the major elements of design into the statements of intent in your research.

However, the application differs depending on whether you conduct quantitative or qualitative research:

1. In *quantitative* research, hypotheses are used. In *qualitative* research, hypotheses are not used; instead, inquirers use only research questions. Because researchers test hypotheses using statistics, and statistics are not used in qualitative research, hypotheses in qualitative research are not appropriate.
2. In *quantitative* research, the investigator identifies multiple variables and seeks to measure them. In *qualitative* research, the term *variable* is not used, and instead the inquirer seeks to gather information on a single concept—a central phenomenon—a concept we discuss later in this chapter.
3. In *quantitative* research, researchers often test theories, broad explanations that predict the results from relating variables. In *qualitative* research, theories are typically not tested. Instead, the inquirer asks participants in a study to share ideas and build general themes based on those ideas.
4. In *quantitative* research, the investigator employs a close-ended stance by identifying variables and selecting instruments to collect data *before* the study begins. Quantitative research questions and hypotheses do not change during the study. In *qualitative* research, the inquirer uses more of an open-ended stance and often changes the phenomenon being studied or at least allows it to emerge during the study. The research questions may change based on the responses of the participants. This makes *quantitative* research more deductive and *qualitative* more inductive.
5. In *quantitative* research, the investigator seeks to measure differences and the magnitude of those differences among two or more groups or measure changes over time in individuals. In *qualitative* research, inquirers do not compare groups or relate variables. Instead, the researcher seeks a deep understanding of the views of one group or single individuals.

These factors all influence how we write qualitative purpose statements and research questions. Before we proceed, however, we need to understand two concepts in qualitative research in more detail: the central phenomenon and the emerging process.

THE CENTRAL PHENOMENON IN QUALITATIVE RESEARCH

A central component of both the purpose statement and the research questions in qualitative research is the central phenomenon. The **central phenomenon** is the concept or a process explored in qualitative research. For example, as a concept, it could be:

◆ The ethnic identity of Chinese American immigrants

As a process it might be:

◆ The process of negotiation by a female superintendent with her principals

These examples illustrate the expression of the central phenomenon in a few words. They also show a focus on a single concept or process rather than relating two or more ideas as found in quantitative research (e.g., "How do alienation and isolation relate for the female superintendent?") or comparing groups (e.g., "How do female principals and superintendents compare in their alienation?"). This comment is not to suggest that researchers may not explore comparisons or relationships in qualitative inquiry. Comparisons and relationships may emerge as the data analysis proceeds as in grounded theory, the relating of categories of information to form propositions or hypotheses, but the qualitative inquirer *begins* with a single idea, focus, or concept to explore before gathering data.

A picture might best express the differences between explaining and predicting variables in quantitative research and exploring a central phenomenon in qualitative research. As shown in Figure 4.7, one way to visualize this difference is by contrasting the explanation of an outcome (or dependent variable) by an independent variable (on

FIGURE 4.7

How Researchers Explain or Predict Variables versus Exploring or Understanding a Central Phenomenon

Quantitative

Explaining or Predicting Variables
$X \longrightarrow Y$

The independent variable (X) influences a dependent variable (Y)

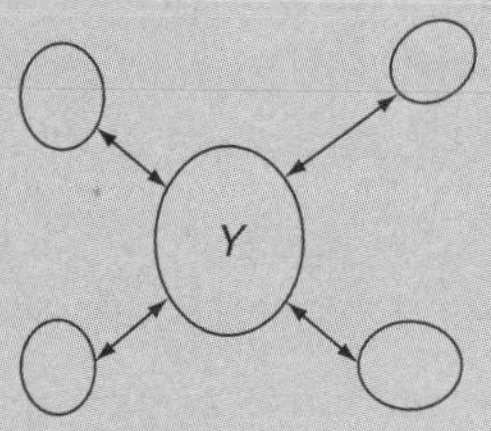

Qualitative

Understanding or Exploring a Central Phenomenon

In-depth understanding of Y; external forces shape and are shaped by Y

the left of the figure) with the different image for a central phenomenon (on the right side of the figure). Rather than using cause-and-effect logic as in quantitative research, the qualitative researcher seeks to *explore* and *understand* one single phenomenon, and to do so requires considering all of the multiple external forces that shape this phenomenon. At the beginning of a study, the qualitative researcher cannot predict the nature of external forces (i.e., Which ones will be important? How will they exercise influence?). The arrows about forces shaping the central phenomenon are multidirectional. If it is helpful for you to understand the differences better from a *quantitative* perspective, consider the central phenomenon in qualitative research to be a single variable that you would like to explore.

Emerging Processes in Qualitative Research

Another central component about purpose statements and research questions in qualitative inquiry is that these statements and questions may change during the research process. Qualitative research is an emerging design. An **emerging process** indicates that the intent or purpose of a study and the questions asked by the researcher may change during the process of inquiry based on feedback or responses from participants. Questions and purposes may change because the qualitative inquirer allows the participants to set the direction, and in doing so, the researcher learns the participants' views rather than imposing his or her own view on the research situation. One question often asked is if this means that you will be asking different questions of different people in your study. This may well be the case in qualitative research. Remember that the intent of qualitative research is to understand and explore the central phenomenon, not to develop a consensus of opinion from the people you study.

An illustration of the emerging process is shown in Figure 4.8. As you can see, the process of asking questions is a dynamic process. Researchers may start with initial questions, shape them during initial data collection, and further change them because of multiple visits to the field to gather data. Revisions may continue throughout both data collection and analysis in a qualitative project. During this process, the overall direction

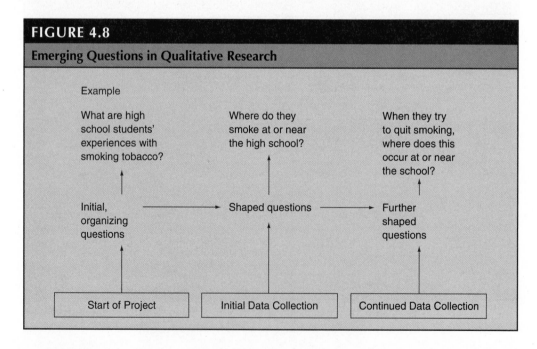

FIGURE 4.8

Emerging Questions in Qualitative Research

Example

What are high school students' experiences with smoking tobacco?

Where do they smoke at or near the high school?

When they try to quit smoking, where does this occur at or near the school?

Initial, organizing questions → Shaped questions → Further shaped questions

Start of Project | Initial Data Collection | Continued Data Collection of the study will change, and authors will rewrite their purpose statement and research questions.

In the example illustrated by Figure 4.8, the researcher may begin with the general question about the experiences high school students have with smoking tobacco. During the initial interviews, the students may discuss locations where they often smoke, such as in front of the apartment complex across the street from the school or in the neighborhood park adjacent to the school. The researcher then focuses direction by asking questions that are more detailed about where students smoke. Then through more in-depth questioning, some students begin discussing their attempts to quit smoking and how friends aide or thwart these attempts in the neighborhood park near the school. The questions change as the researcher delves deeper into the central phenomenon of high school students and smoking. Remember that the intent of qualitative research is to establish the detailed meaning of information rather than to generalize the results and standardize the responses from all participants in research.

Writing Qualitative Purpose Statements

Inquirers reflect both the nature of an emerging process and the central phenomenon in qualitative purpose statements and research questions. As a major signpost in a study, care needs to be given to writing a good purpose statement that reflects the direction of the study.

A **purpose statement in qualitative research** indicates the intent to explore or understand the central phenomenon with specific individuals at a certain research site. In quantitative research, inquirers write this purpose statement as a single sentence and typically include it in a study at the end of the introduction.

Guidelines

As you design this statement, be sure to:

◆ Use key identifier words to signal the reader, such as "The purpose of this study is . . ."
◆ Consider mentioning that the study is "qualitative" since audiences may not be familiar with qualitative research.
◆ Become familiar with qualitative research designs, and indicate the type of research design you plan to use in your study.
◆ State the central phenomenon you plan to explore.
◆ Use words that convey intent about the exploration, such as *explore, discover, understand,* and *describe*.
◆ Mention the participants in the study.
◆ Refer to the research site where you will study the participants.

Sample Script

You can use these elements in a script for writing a qualitative purpose statement. A script for a qualitative purpose statement is:

> The purpose of this qualitative study will be to (explore/discover/understand/describe) (the central phenomenon) for (participants) at (research site).

If we apply this script in the study of Internet classroom learning, we get:

> The purpose of this qualitative study is to describe classroom learning using the Internet for five high-school students participating in a sign language class.

If we analyze this example, we find:

The central phenomenon: classroom learning using the Internet
The participants: five high-school students
The research site: a class in sign language at X high school

What would be the purpose statement for Maria's study? It might be:

The purpose of this qualitative study is to explore the experiences with weapons of five high school students in the school district.

Look at this statement carefully. Can you identify the central phenomenon, the participants, and the research site? Write these down on a sheet of paper and share them with others.

Writing Qualitative Research Questions

Research questions in qualitative research help narrow the purpose of a study into specific questions. **Qualitative research questions** are open-ended, general questions that the researcher would like answered during the study.

Guidelines

The following general guidelines can help you design and write these questions [also, see Creswell (1998; 2009)]:

◆ Expect your qualitative questions to change and to emerge during a study to reflect the participants' views of the central phenomenon and your growing (and deeper) understanding of it.
◆ Ask only a few, general questions. Five to seven questions are enough to permit the participants to share information. Using only a few questions places emphasis on learning information from participants, rather than learning what the researcher seeks to know.
◆ Ask questions that use neutral, exploratory language and refrain from conveying an expected direction (or nondirectional outcome if you are thinking like a quantitative researcher). For example, use action verbs such as *generate, discover, understand, describe,* and *explore* instead of words conveying cause-and-effect relationships, such as *affect, relate, compare, determine, cause,* and *influence.*
◆ Design and write two types of qualitative research questions: the central question and subquestions.

The Central Question

The **central question** is the overarching question you explore in a research study. To arrive at this question, consider stating the most general question you can ask. The intent of this approach is to open up the research for participants to provide their perspectives and not to narrow the study to your perspective. When you write this question, place it at the end of the introduction to your study, and state it as a brief question. If you are more comfortable thinking about this question from a quantitative perspective, consider it as a single, descriptive question, such as a single dependent variable.

When designing and writing this central question, several strategies may be helpful:

◆ Begin with the word *how* or *what* rather than *why* so that you do not suggest probable cause-and-effect relationships as in *quantitative research* (i.e., "why" something influences something) but instead suggest exploration in *qualitative research.*

◆ Specify the central phenomenon you plan to explore.
◆ Identify the participants in the study.
◆ Mention the research site for the study.

Because the participants may have already been mentioned in your purpose statement, you do not need to repeat this information for your central question when you include both a purpose statement and a central question in a study.

A Sample Script

A script for a central research question that combines these elements is:

What is (the central phenomenon) for (participants) at (research site)?

The following example illustrates the application of this script to the study of creativity:

What is creativity for five students at Roosevelt High School?

Beginning word: "What"
Central phenomenon: creativity
Participants: five students
Research site: Roosevelt High School

Now consider Maria's research study. Write down the central question she might use in her study incorporating the three major elements: a central phenomenon, participants, and the research site.

Let's visit some of the challenges inherent in writing the central question. You may need to educate others about this question, especially if they are quantitative researchers and trained to "narrow down" questions and not to think in the exact opposite direction of stating the most general question possible. Also, you need to write the central question in such a way that it provides some direction for the study but does not leave the direction wide open. When a central question is too open, readers and audiences for a study will not have enough information to understand the project. Alternatively, when the central question is too specific or too laden with assumptions, it does not offer enough latitude for participants to express themselves, and it can shape too dramatically the views of participants in one direction or another.

In Table 4.3, several specific examples illustrate central questions stated in terms that are too general, too focused, or too laden with assumptions. First a poor example is given, followed by a better, improved version. In the first example, the author states a central question so broadly that readers and audiences do not understand the central

TABLE 4.3

Problems Typically Found in Central Questions in Qualitative Research

Problems	Poor Example of a Central Question	Better Example of a Central Question
Too general	What is going on here?	What is the process being used by the general education committee at the liberal arts school?
Too focused	How did the committee make a curriculum decision about a course on the environment?	What is the process of the curriculum committee in making decisions about courses?
Too laden with assumptions	How did the curriculum committee address its alienation from the college administration?	What was the role of the college administration in the curriculum committee's deliberations?

phenomenon under study. This situation often occurs when qualitative researchers take too literally the concept of open-ended questions to mean "anything goes."

In the second example, the author focuses the question too much. By asking about specific activities on a committee, the researcher may miss the larger process at work in the committee and lose important information for the research report. In the final example, the researcher starts with the assumption that the committee is "alienated" from the college administration. Although this may be the case, the specification of a *direction* may limit too much what the inquirer can learn from a situation. To open the situation by asking about the "role of the college administration" includes the possibility that the role may be alienating, supportive, or may serve some in-between role.

Subquestions

In addition to a central question, qualitative researchers pose subquestions. These **subquestions** refine the central question into subquestions to be addressed in the research. These subquestions possess the same qualities as central questions (i.e., open ended, emerging, neutral in language, and few in number), but they provide greater specificity to the questions in the study. Preliminary conversations or interviews with your participants can provide useful leads for these subquestions. Writers refer to these subquestions as issue and procedural subquestions (Creswell, 2007; Stake, 1995), as shown in Table 4.4.

Issue Subquestions   **Issue subquestions** are questions that narrow the focus of the central question into specific questions (or issues) the researcher seeks to learn from participants in a study. A script for an issue subquestion is:

> What is (the subquestion issue) for (participants—optional information) at (research site—optional information).

If you state the participants and research site in the central question or purpose statement, you do not need to repeat them in the subquestions. You would state the subquestions immediately after the central question as follows:

> What is self-esteem for high school students? (central question)
>
> What is self-esteem as seen through friends? (subquestion)

TABLE 4.4

Types of Subquestions in Qualitative Research

	Issue Subquestions	Procedural Subquestions
Intent	To subdivide the central question into detailed questions	To subdivide the central question into steps for data collection during the study
Example	*Central Question:*	*Central Question:*
	What does it mean to be a professional teacher?	What is the change process in the revision of a general education curriculum on a college campus?
	Issue Subquestions:	
	What do professional teachers do?	*Procedural Subquestions:*
	What is difficult/easy about being a professional educator?	How did the process unfold?
	When did the teacher first become aware of being a professional?	Who were the people involved?
		What events occurred?
		What was the outcome?

What is self-esteem for the participant's family? (subquestion)

What is self-esteem as experienced in extracurricular activities in school? (subquestion)

As these examples illustrate, the central phenomenon, self-esteem, is divided into three topical areas that the researcher explores.

Procedural Subquestions   As an alternative form of writing subquestions, **procedural subquestions** indicate the steps to be used in analyzing the data in a qualitative study. Researchers use this form of writing subquestions less frequently than issue questions because the procedures for a qualitative study will evolve during a study. To write them, the researcher needs to know what these steps of analysis will be.

However, if the researcher knows the general steps to be taken later in the analysis, procedural subquestions can be written. They provide those reviewing a study with a more precise understanding of the steps than do issue subquestions. A script for writing procedural subquestions is:

To study this central question, the following questions will be addressed in order in this study:

(What question will be answered first?)

(What question will be answered second?)

(What question will be answered third?)

To illustrate this script, assume for a moment that the steps in the process of data analysis will consist of first developing a description of events, followed by the specification of themes and broad dimensions for understanding the phenomenon. Let's use the familiar example of Maria. Maria's research questions might be:

What are students' experiences with weapons in high schools? (central question)

What are the categories of experiences of students? (subquestion)

What process occurs that reflects these experiences? (subquestion)

What propositions or hypotheses reflect the relationship among the categories? (subquestion)

These three subquestions trace a procedure for analyzing the data, from identifying categories to tracing a process that students experience to advancing some hypotheses that test this process. Procedural subquestions help readers visualize the steps to be taken in data analysis, but they do not provide specific material for interview or observation questions.

Distinguishing Qualitative Research Questions from Data Collection Questions

Are the types of questions asked during data collection (e.g., conducting interviews or when observing) the same questions as the subquestions? Yes, the core questions you ask might be the issue subquestions in your study. You would not ask your central question because that is the overall question you seek to answer with your research. Also, you would not limit your data collection questions to only issue subquestions. There are two additional sets of questions that you need to ask, especially in qualitative interviews. Ask the participants about themselves as your opening question. In this way you break the ice and encourage them to answer your questions. Also, when you conclude the interview, you might ask them to suggest individuals that you might visit with to gather additional data.

REEXAMINING THE PARENT INVOLVEMENT AND MOTHERS' TRUST IN PRINCIPALS STUDIES

In both the parent involvement and the mothers' trust in principals studies, the authors use purpose statements and research questions to provide the focus and central direction for the studies. In the quantitative parent involvement study, Deslandes and Bertrand (2005) advanced both the purpose statement and the guiding research question in one succinct paragraph (Paragraph 13). They say:

> To examine how the four psychological constructs influence parent involvement decisions across the three secondary grade levels, we posed the following research question: What are the relative contributions of parents' role construction, self-efficacy, perceptions of teacher invitations, and perceptions of adolescent invitations to predict parent involvement at home and at school in Grades 7, 8, and 9? (p. 166)

Although the authors implied the site to be studied (i.e., secondary schools), the purpose statement clearly conveys the intent of the study. The research question immediately follows the purpose statement and it serves to narrow the broad purpose into a narrower perspective by mentioning the four constructs to be examined. The question also provides more insight about the dependent variable, parent involvement, and the specific grade levels of students to be assessed. We now see in this research question that parent involvement will be measured in two ways, involvement at home and at school, and that the authors are interested in learning (and comparing) parent involvement across seventh, eighth, and ninth grades.

The qualitative mothers' trust in principals study (Shelden et al., 2010) contains a purpose statement and research questions (see Paragraphs 14 and 15). It is of note that they begin with the research question (Paragraph 14) and then pose the purpose under the Method section (in Paragraph 15). This order is typically reversed in qualitative studies with the logic flowing from the broad purpose to the narrow research question. Also, both the purpose statement and the research questions are usually found as the concluding statements in the introduction and not included in the Method section. However their research question is a good open-ended question:

> What are the perspectives of mothers of children with disabilities on trust in school principals? (p. 161)

Their purpose statement that immediately follows is:

> We employed a qualitative research methodology to gain insight into the nature of trust of mothers of children with disabilities in school principals. (p. 161)

This purpose statement has all of the elements of a good purpose statement: a clear central phenomenon (trust), the participants (mothers), and the research site (the schools in which principals are located).

KEY IDEAS IN THE CHAPTER

Distinguish among Purpose Statements, Research Questions, Hypotheses, and Objectives

The primary reason for purpose statements, research hypotheses, and research questions is to signal the major direction or intent of a study. They are the most important elements in a study. A purpose statement is a sentence in an educational study that states the overall direction or objective of the study. Research questions are questions that focus the purpose of the study into specific areas of inquiry. Hypotheses are statements that narrow the purpose statement into specific predictions about the relationship among variables.

Know Why These Statements and Questions Are Important

These statements and questions are the major signposts in a research study. They guide the direction of the data collection and are helpful in understanding the results of the study. Thus, they need to be stated clearly and concisely. If they are vague, the reader is lost throughout the study.

Write Quantitative Purpose Statements, Research Questions, and Hypotheses

To write quantitative purpose statements, research questions, and hypotheses, you need to understand the nature and types of variables. The three primary types of variables are dependent, independent, and intervening. Types of independent variables are measured, control, treatment, and moderating variables. In quantitative research, investigators often test the relationship among variables using theories.

Write Qualitative Purpose Statements and Research Questions

In qualitative research, inquirers seek to explore a central phenomenon and engage in an emerging process of research. These two elements help inform the writing of qualitative purpose statements and research questions. A good qualitative purpose statement includes the central phenomenon, the participants, and the site of the study. Researchers then narrow the purpose statement to two types of qualitative questions: a central question and subquestions. In the central question the researcher asks the most general question that can be asked in a study. This central question is then subdivided into subquestions called issue or procedural subquestions. These questions either subdivide the central question into topics or they indicate the steps used in analyzing and reporting the data.

USEFUL INFORMATION FOR PRODUCERS OF RESEARCH

- ◆ Write a purpose statement and either hypotheses or research questions into your research study.
- ◆ For a quantitative study, know the differences among the types of variables. Be able to identify clearly the independent and dependent variables that you plan to study.
- ◆ Locate and identify a theory to test that will provide an explanation for the relationship among variables in your research questions and hypotheses.
- ◆ Write a purpose statement that includes the major elements advanced in this chapter.
- ◆ Write either hypotheses or research questions, but not both.
- ◆ If you write hypotheses, consider whether your statements are directional or nondirectional. Directional hypotheses are more popular today and reflect a prediction about the expected results of a study resulting from past research.
- ◆ If you write research questions, use the elements advanced in this chapter.

- Consider in your questions whether you are trying to describe a single variable, to relate variables, or to compare groups on a variable.
- For a qualitative study, know the significance of a central phenomenon and be able to identify the phenomenon in your study.
- Write one central question and several subquestions using the elements advanced in this chapter.
- Clearly identify your subquestions as either issue or procedural subquestions and know the difference between the two types.

USEFUL INFORMATION FOR CONSUMERS OF RESEARCH

- Look for a purpose statement at the end of an introduction to a study. Phrases such as "the purpose of" should signal this statement. Alternative phrases might be "the objective of" or "the intent of."
- In a quantitative purpose statement (or hypotheses or questions), the independent variable should be stated in the first position, followed by the dependent variable in the second position. As you examine a study, ask yourself: What outcome is being predicted in this study? What factors are advanced that might explain this outcome?
- Look for hypotheses or research questions at the end of the introductory section of a study.
- An explanation for how and why the variables are related in hypotheses or research questions is called a *theory* or a *theoretical rationale*. This passage should advance researchers' explanations about what they expect to find.
- In a qualitative study, look for the central phenomenon that provides a focus for the inquiry. Authors should state this phenomenon in a few words and it should represent the focus that the inquirer wants to understand.
- Qualitative researchers often pose one central question as the overriding general issue they wish to explore. Then they advance a small number of subquestions that either narrow the focus to specific topics or advance procedural steps to be used in their data analysis.

UNDERSTANDING CONCEPTS AND EVALUATING RESEARCH STUDIES

1. You have just learned how to identify independent and dependent variables in *quantitative* purpose statements, research questions, and hypotheses. For each of the examples below, specify the independent variable(s) (IV) and the dependent variable(s) (DV) by writing the initials above the words:
   a. What is the relation between parental involvement in education and student reading performance?
   b. Our purpose in this study was to isolate the elements of accountability in a learning program and determine if students' knowledge of accountability relates to changes in attitudes toward learning.
   c. Low degrees of mutuality, comprehensiveness, gender sensitivity, and congruence lead to functional mentoring relationships.
2. Show that you can identify the central phenomenon in *qualitative* purpose statements and research questions. In the following examples, place the initials "CP" over the words indicating the central phenomenon.

   a. How are these conceptions of reading played out, or not played out, in the sixth-grade classroom?
   b. In this article, I rely on critical views of culture and power to highlight aspects of sorority life that contribute to the marginalization and potential victimization of women.
   c. What are the major sources of academic change in a community college? What are the major processes through which change occurs?
3. Label each of the following hypotheses as "directional," "nondirectional," or "null."
   a. Students in a supportive environment are more likely to express willingness to seek help from the instructor than are students in a nonsupportive environment.
   b. There is no significant difference between students in a supportive environment and students in a nonsupportive environment in terms of their willingness to seek help from an instructor.

CONDUCTING YOUR RESEARCH

For the educational project you have chosen to design in earlier chapters, write a quantitative purpose statement and research hypotheses. Also, turn the study into a qualitative project and write a qualitative purpose statement and central question.

The Power of Classroom Practice
www.myeducationlab.com

Go to the Topic "Selecting and Defining a Research Topic" in the MyEducationLab (**www.myeducationlab.com**) for your course, where you can:

◆ Find learning outcomes for "Selecting and Defining a Research Topic."
◆ Complete Assignments and Activities that can help you more deeply understand the chapter content.
◆ Apply and practice your understanding of the core skills identified in the chapter with the Building Research Skills exercises.
◆ Check your comprehension of the content covered in the chapter by going to the Study Plan. Here you will be able to take a pretest, receive feedback on your answers, and then access Review, Practice, and Enrichment activities to enhance your understanding. You can then complete a final posttest.

Collecting Quantitative Data

*T*he process of collecting quantitative data consists of more than simply collecting data. You decide on what participants you will study. Then you obtain their permission to be studied. You identify the types of measures that will answer your research question, and you locate instruments to use. Then, you can begin collecting data. This chapter discusses these five steps.

By the end of this chapter, you should be able to:

◆ State the five steps in the process of quantitative data collection.
◆ Identify how to select participants for a study.
◆ Identify the permissions needed for a study.
◆ List different options for collecting information.
◆ Locate, select, and assess an instrument(s) for use in data collection.
◆ Describe procedures for administering quantitative data collection.

Maria decides to study the quantitative research question "Why do students carry weapons in high school?" Maria wonders, "Who can provide this information? Even if I locate some students, will they come forward with information?" Then Maria expresses concern to her graduate advisor about the need to find "a way to obtain this information from students," and she expresses fear that students may not be willing to participate because it is such a volatile topic. Maria digs herself deeper and deeper into complex questions that she needs to sort out so that she can proceed simply and logically through the process of data collection. How does she start?

FIVE STEPS IN THE PROCESS OF DATA COLLECTION

There are five steps in the process of quantitative data collection. This process involves more than simply gathering information; it includes interrelated steps. It involves the steps of determining the participants to study, obtaining permissions needed from several individuals and organizations, considering what types of information to collect from several sources available to the quantitative research, locating and selecting instruments to use that will net useful data for the study, and finally, administering the data collection process to collect data.

WHAT PARTICIPANTS WILL YOU STUDY?

The first step in the process of collecting quantitative data is to identify the people and places you plan to study. This involves determining whether you will study individuals or entire organizations (e.g., schools) or some combination. If you select either individuals or organizations, you need to decide what type of people or organizations you will actually study and how many you will need for your research. These decisions require that you decide on a unit of analysis, the group and individuals you will study, the procedure for selecting these individuals, and assessing the numbers of people needed for your data analysis.

Identify Your Unit of Analysis

Who can supply the information that you will use to answer your quantitative research questions or hypotheses? Some possibilities might be students, teachers, parents, adults, some combination of these individuals, or entire schools. At this early stage in data collection, you must decide at what level (e.g., individual, family, school, school district) the data needs to be gathered. This level is referred to as the **unit of analysis**. In some research studies, educators gather data from multiple levels (e.g., individuals and schools), whereas other studies involve collecting data from only one level (e.g., principals in schools). This decision depends on the questions or hypotheses that you seek to answer. Also, the data for measuring the independent variable may differ from the unit for assessing the dependent variable. For example, in the study of the impact of adolescent aggression on school climate, a researcher would measure the independent variable, adolescent aggression, by collecting data from individuals while measuring the dependent variable, school climate, based on data from entire schools and their overall climates (e.g., whether students and teachers believe the school curriculum supports learning).

If Maria wants to answer the question "Why do students carry weapons in high school?" what unit of analysis will she study? Alternatively, if she wanted to compare answers to the question "Why do students carry weapons in rural high schools and urban high schools?" what two types of unit of analysis will she study?

Specify the Population and Sample

If you select an entire school to study or a small number of individuals, you need to consider what individuals or schools you will study. In some educational situations, you will select individuals for your research based on who volunteers to participate or who is available (e.g., a specific classroom of students). However, those individuals may not be similar (in personal characteristics or performance or attitudes) to all individuals who could be studied.

A more advanced research process is to select individuals or schools who are representative of the entire group of individuals or schools. **Representative** refers to the selection of individuals from a sample of a population such that the individuals selected are typical of the population under study, enabling you to draw conclusions from the sample about the population as a whole. This definition is loaded with terms, and we will sort them so that you can see alternative procedures for deciding what individuals or organizations to study.

A **population** is a group of individuals who have the same characteristic. For example, all teachers would make up the population of teachers, and all high school administrators in a school district would comprise the population of administrators. As these examples illustrate, populations can be small or large. You need to decide what group you would like to study.

In practice, quantitative researchers sample from lists and people available. A **target population** (or the *sampling frame*) is a group of individuals (or a group of organizations) with some common defining characteristic that the researcher can identify and study.

Within this target population, researchers then select a sample for study. A **sample** is a subgroup of the target population that the researcher plans to study for generalizing about the target population. In an ideal situation, you can select a sample of individuals who are representative of the entire population. For instance, as shown in Figure 5.1, you might select a sample of high school teachers (the sample) from the population of all teachers in high schools in one city (the population). Alternatively, you might be able to study only biology teachers in two schools in the city. The first scenario represents rigorous, systematic sampling called *probability sampling* and the second, unsystematic *nonprobability sampling*.

Probabilistic and Nonprobabilistic Sampling

Researchers employ either probability or nonprobability sampling approaches. As shown in Figure 5.2, several types of both approaches are available. Researchers decide which type of sampling to use in their study based on such factors as the amount of rigor they seek for their studies, the characteristics of the target population, and the availability of participants.

In **probability sampling**, the researcher selects individuals from the population who are representative of that population. This is the most rigorous form of sampling in quantitative research because the investigator can claim that the sample is representative of the population and, as such, can make generalizations to the population.

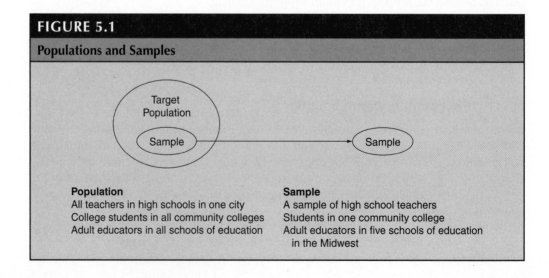

FIGURE 5.1

Populations and Samples

Target Population

Sample

Sample

Population
All teachers in high schools in one city
College students in all community colleges
Adult educators in all schools of education

Sample
A sample of high school teachers
Students in one community college
Adult educators in five schools of education in the Midwest

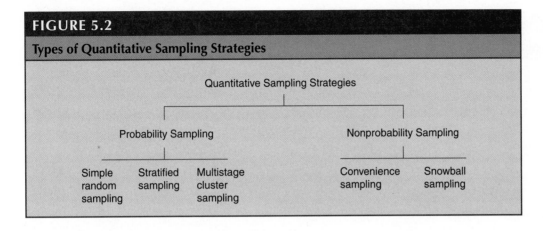

FIGURE 5.2

Types of Quantitative Sampling Strategies

Simple Random Sampling The most popular and rigorous form of probability sampling from a population is simple random sampling. In **simple random sampling**, the researcher selects participants (or units, such as schools) for the sample so that any individual has an equal probability of being selected from the population. The intent of simple random sampling is to choose individuals to be sampled who will be representative of the population. Any bias in the population will be equally distributed among the people chosen. However, equal distribution is not always possible, as was seen during the Vietnam War when officials did not sufficiently turn the drum with names of potential draftees enough times to result in random selection (Wilkinson & The Task Force on Statistical Inference, 1999).

The typical procedure used in simple random sampling is to assign a number to each individual (or site) in the population and then use a random numbers table, available in many statistics books, to select the individuals (or sites) for the sample. For this procedure, you need a list of members in the target population and a number must be assigned to each individual.

An example of a random numbers table is shown in Table 5.1. To use this table, first assign unique numbers to all individuals in the population (say, a population of 100 first graders). Then, starting anywhere in the random numbers table, match the numbers on your list to the numbers in the table. Start at the upper left of Table 5.1 and go down the column. You might choose the first six first graders from the population of 100, having the numbers 52, 31, 44, 84, 71, and 42. This would continue down the column until you have chosen the number of children needed for your sample (later in the "Sample Size" section, we will consider how many first graders you would need).

Systematic Sampling A slight variation of the simple random sampling procedure is to use **systematic sampling**. In this procedure, you choose every nth individual or site in the population until you reach your desired sample size. This procedure is not as precise and rigorous as using the random numbers table, but it may be more convenient because individuals do not have to be numbered and it does not require a random numbers table. To illustrate systematic sampling, assume a school district administrator wants to study parent satisfaction with the schools in the district. Using systematic sampling, the administrator would first study a percentage of the parents (e.g., 20%). If there were 1,000 parents in the school district, the administrator would select 200 (or 20%) for the study. The administrator uses an interval of five (200/1,000, or 1 out of 5) to select parents from the

TABLE 5.1

Excerpt from a Random Numbers Table

52	13	44	91	39	85	22	33	04	29	52	06
31	52	65	63	88	78	21	35	28	22	91	84
44	38	76	99	38	67	60	95	67	68	17	18
84	47	44	04	67	22	89	78	44	84	66	15
71	50	78	48	65	74	21	24	02	23	65	94
42	47	97	81	10	99	40	15	63	77	89	10
03	70	75	49	90	92	62	00	47	90	78	63
31	06	46	39	27	93	81	79	100	94	43	39

Source: Adapted from Kerlinger, 1972, p. 714.

mailing list (or target population list). Therefore, this administrator sends every fifth parent on the list a survey.

Stratified Sampling   Another type of probability sampling is stratified sampling. In **stratified sampling**, researchers divide (stratify) the population on some specific characteristic (e.g., gender) and then, using simple random sampling, sample from each subgroup (stratum) of the population (e.g., females and males). This guarantees that the sample will include specific characteristics that the researcher wants included in the sample.

When do you use stratification? You use stratification when the population reflects an imbalance on a characteristic of a sample. Assume that there are more males than females in a population. A simple random sample from this population would likely result in the selection of more males than females or maybe even no females. In either case, the male views on questions would be the dominant or exclusive view. To correct for this, researchers use stratified sampling. Stratification ensures that the stratum desired (females) will be represented in the sample in proportion to that existence in the population.

Stratification is also used when a simple random sampling procedure would yield fewer participants in a specific category (e.g., females) than you need for rigorous statistical analysis. Having few females in a population, for example, would result in the likelihood of randomly selecting only a few females. This could possibly result in having numbers too small to analyze statistically.

The procedure for selecting a stratified random sample consists of (a) dividing the population by the stratum (e.g., men and women) and (b) sampling within each group in the stratum (e.g., women first and then men) so that the individuals selected are proportional to their representation in the total population. Let's look at an example of how this procedure is applied.

Looking at Figure 5.3, we can see that of the 9,000 Native American children in the state, 3,000 are girls and 6,000 are boys. A researcher decides to choose a sample of 300 from this population of 9,000 children. A simple random sample results in the selection of mostly boys because there are more boys than girls in the population. To make sure that the researcher selects boys in proportion to their representation in the population, she divides the list of 9,000 children into boys and girls.

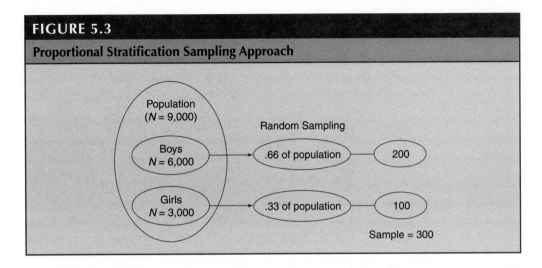

FIGURE 5.3

Proportional Stratification Sampling Approach

Then one third (3,000/9,000) of the sample is chosen to be girls, and two thirds (6,000/9,000), boys. The stratification procedure consists of stratifying by the population into boys and girls and selecting individuals in proportion to their representation in the total population, resulting in 200 boys and 100 girls.

Multistage Cluster Sampling   A fourth form of probability sampling is multistage cluster sampling. In **multistage cluster sampling**, the researcher chooses a sample in two or more stages because either the researchers cannot easily identify the population or the population is extremely large. If this is the case, it can be difficult to obtain a complete list of the members of the population. However, getting a complete list of groups or clusters in the population might be possible (Vogt, 2005). For example, the population of all at-risk students in the United States may be difficult to identify, but a researcher can obtain a list of the at-risk kids in select school districts. Using multistage cluster sampling, the researcher randomly selects school districts in the United States and obtains a list of the at-risk students in each of those school districts. Then the researcher randomly samples within each district. Breaking down the process like this makes it easier to identify groups and locate lists. However, with several stages to this design, it is complex and highly dependent on the characteristics of the population (Babbie, 1998).

It is not always possible to use probability sampling in educational research. Instead, a researcher can use nonprobability sampling. In **nonprobability sampling**, the researcher selects individuals because they are available, convenient, and represent some characteristic the investigator seeks to study. In some situations, you may need to involve participants who volunteer and who agree to be studied. Further, you may not be interested in generalizing findings to a population, but only in describing a small group of participants in a study. It may be appropriate to calculate descriptive statistics on these samples and to compare them with the larger population to make inferences from the sample to the population. Researchers use two popular approaches in nonprobability sampling: convenience and snowball sampling approaches.

Convenience Sampling   In **convenience sampling** the researcher selects participants because they are willing and available to be studied. In this case, the researcher cannot say with confidence that the individuals are representative of the population. However, the sample can provide useful information for answering questions and hypotheses. Let's look at an example of convenience sampling.

> A researcher conducting a study involving Native American students finds that a large percentage of students in one school are Native Americans. The researcher decides to study this group at this one school because they are available and because the researcher has the permission of the principal and can gain consent from the Native American students to participate in the study. This is a convenience sample because the participants are convenient to the researcher and are available for the study.

Snowball Sampling   An alternative to convenience sampling is snowball sampling. In **snowball sampling**, the researcher asks participants to identify others to become members of the sample. For example, you might send surveys to a school superintendent and ask that the superintendent forward copies to the principals of schools in that school district. These principals then become members of the sample. This form of sampling has the advantage of recruiting large numbers of participants for the study. By using this process, however, you give up knowing exactly what individuals will be in your sample. It also eliminates the possibility of identifying individuals who did not return the survey, and those responding may not be representative of the population you seek to study. For example, participants who received the survey (e.g., principals who attended the Monday morning meeting with the superintendent) may not be representative of all individuals in the population (in this case, all principals in the school district).

Sample Size

When selecting participants for a study, it is important to determine the size of the sample you will need. A general rule of thumb is to select as large a sample as possible from the population. The larger the sample, the less the potential error is that the sample will be different from the population. This difference between the sample estimate and the true population score is called **sampling error**. If you were to select one sample after another, the average score of each sample would likely differ from the true average score for the entire population. For example, if we could obtain scores from sixth graders across the country about the importance of student–parent relationships, the average score might be a 30 on a 50-point scale. Of course, we cannot study every sixth grader, so instead we obtain a sample from one school district and get an average score of 35 on the scale. The next time we might obtain a score of 33, and the next time a 36, because our sample will change from one school district to another. This means that our average score is five points, three points, and one point, respectively, away from the "true" population average. This difference between the sample estimate and the true population score is sampling error. Therefore, since you usually cannot know the true population score, it is important to select as large a sample as possible from the population to minimize sampling error.

In some studies, you may have a limited number of participants who are conveniently available to study. In other cases, factors such as access, funding, the overall size of the population, and the number of variables will also influence the size of the samples.

One way to determine the sample size is to select a sufficient number of participants for the statistical procedures you plan to use. This presumes that you have identified the statistic to use in analysis. As a rough estimate, an educational researcher needs:

◆ Approximately 15 participants in each group in an experiment
◆ Approximately 30 participants for a correlational study that relates variables
◆ Approximately 350 individuals for a survey study, but this size will vary depending on several factors

These numbers are estimates based on the size needed for statistical procedures so that the sample is likely to be a good estimate of the characteristics of the population. They do not provide a precise estimate of the sample size available through sample size formulas.

Sample size formulas provide the means for calculating the size of your sample based on several factors. Use of a formula takes the guesswork out of determining the number of individuals to study and provides a precise estimate of your sample size. The formulas take into consideration several factors important in determining sample size, such as confidence in the statistical test and sampling error. Further, you need not calculate the sample size using a formula. With minimal information, you can identify the sample size using tables available to researchers.

Two formulas used are the sampling error formula for surveys (see Fink & Kosekoff, 1985; Fowler, 2009) and a power analysis formula for experiments (Cohen, 1977; Lipsey, 1990; Murphy & Myors, 1998). Appendix B at the end of the text provides factors that you can insert into these formulas to determine the number of participants for your study.

WHAT PERMISSIONS WILL YOU NEED?

After identifying and selecting participants for your study, you next need to obtain their permission to be studied. This permission will ensure that they cooperate in your study and provide data. Besides cooperation, their permission also acknowledges that they understand the purpose of your study and that you will treat them ethically. Federal legislation requires that you guarantee them certain rights and that you request their permission to be involved in your study.

Obtain Different Types of Permissions

In most educational studies, you need to obtain permissions from several individuals and groups before you can gather data. Permissions may be required from:

◆ Institutions or organizations (e.g., school district)
◆ Specific sites (e.g., the secondary school)
◆ A participant or group of participants
◆ Parents of participants (e.g., 10th graders' parents)
◆ The campus on which you conduct the research (i.e., permission from your university or college institutional review board)

Permission is often necessary before you can enter a site and collect data. This approval usually comes from leaders or persons of authority in organizations. Gaining permissions from organizational personnel requires contacting them before the start of a study and obtaining their permission to enter and to study their setting.

The best way to seek permission from the necessary individuals or groups is to ask for it formally in a letter. Include the purpose of the study, the amount of time you will be at the site collecting data, the time required of participants, and how you will use the data or results. Also, state the specific activities you will conduct, the benefits to the organization or individual because of the study, and the provisions you have made to protect the anonymity of study participants. By providing this information, you will show a concern for the potential intrusion of the study into their workplaces and lives and set the stage for realistic expectations on their part.

Obtain Informed Consent

It is important to protect the privacy and confidentiality of individuals who participate in the study. In contrast to early research in education and the social sciences, investigators today are sensitive to the potential harm that participants may experience because of research.

Review Board Approval

In the last 30 years, colleges and universities have required that researchers guarantee to participants that their research will cause minimal risk to participants. In turn, participants consent to participation in research.

In the 1970s, the federal government created legislation to monitor campus-based research because of human abuses in experiments (e.g., Nazi medical experiments, atomic bomb blast tests, and syphilis experiments on African Americans). This legislation mandated that colleges and universities create institutional review boards to approve student and faculty research. An **institutional review board** is a committee made up of faculty members who review and approve research so that the research protects the rights of the participants. The creation of these boards represents the one instance where research done on college and university campuses has been regulated (Howe & Dougherty, 1993).

Process of Obtaining Approval from Review Boards

Institutional review boards implement guidelines developed by the Federal Drug Administration based on three ethical principles: respect for persons (their consent, their right to privacy, and anonymity), beneficence (weighing the benefits of research versus the risks to individuals), and justice (equity for participation in a study). By following the guidelines, researchers guarantee that participants retain their autonomy and judge for themselves what risks are worth taking for the purposes of research (Howe & Dougherty, 1993).

To obtain approval from a campus institutional review board, you are required to summarize the procedures in your research and supply evidence that your research procedures will offer certain protections to participants.

The exact process of gaining approval from an institutional review board varies from campus to campus. However, there are some basic steps that both student and faculty researchers complete when seeking approval. Understanding this process will help you evaluate the ethics of a published study and determine if you are proceeding ethically in your study.

1. *Start by finding out about the review process used by the institutional review board on your campus.*   Identify individuals responsible for reviewing projects, locate the forms required for the review, and become familiar with the overall approval procedure. Campus review boards may have a brochure that describes this process.
2. *Determine what information the review board needs about your project.*   The extent of the review and the concern of the institutional review board will relate to two factors. The first is the level of risk that your participants will likely experience in the study (e.g., psychological, physical, emotional, legal, social, or economic). Is this risk less than minimal—no known risk? Is it minimal—risks encountered in daily life? Is it greater than minimal—risks beyond those ordinarily encountered in daily life? The higher the risk, the more detailed your project description needs to be, and the more closely the institutional review board will scrutinize your project.

    The second factor that affects the extent of the review is whether you are studying a sensitive population considered to be of high risk. These populations include children under the age of 19, who need their own and their parents' consent to participate; mentally incompetent participants, victims, or persons with neurological impairments; pregnant women or fetuses; prisoners; and individuals with AIDS. Also included in this category are studies involving confidential records and/or pathological specimens and HIV testing.

If your study involves a sensitive population, your project will have at least minimal or greater than minimal risk (as opposed to no known risk), and the institutional review board will subsequently scrutinize it closely. Because many educational studies involve children under 19, these studies will require extensive review by the institutional review boards.

3. *Develop an informed consent form for participants to sign before they participate in the study.* Obtain written consent from participants even if your project poses minimal risk to the participants. An exception would be if the return of a questionnaire or instrument implies consent.

An **informed consent form** is a statement that participants sign before they participate in research. This form should state that you will guarantee them certain rights, and that when they sign the form, they are agreeing to be involved in the study and acknowledge the protection of their rights.

Figure 5.4 shows a typical consent form outlining the participants' rights, including their right to withdraw at any time from the study, their voluntary participation in the project, and their right to know the purpose of the study.

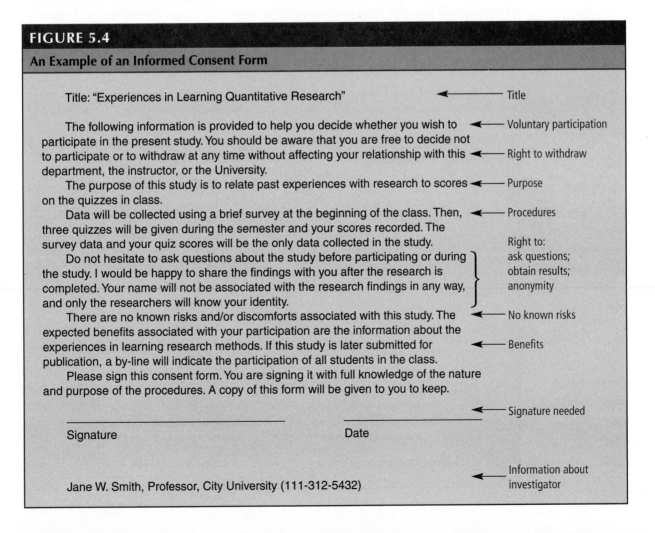

FIGURE 5.4

An Example of an Informed Consent Form

Title: "Experiences in Learning Quantitative Research" ◄——— Title

The following information is provided to help you decide whether you wish to ◄——— Voluntary participation
participate in the present study. You should be aware that you are free to decide not
to participate or to withdraw at any time without affecting your relationship with this ◄——— Right to withdraw
department, the instructor, or the University.

The purpose of this study is to relate past experiences with research to scores ◄——— Purpose
on the quizzes in class.

Data will be collected using a brief survey at the beginning of the class. Then, ◄——— Procedures
three quizzes will be given during the semester and your scores recorded. The
survey data and your quiz scores will be the only data collected in the study.

Do not hesitate to ask questions about the study before participating or during ⎫ Right to:
the study. I would be happy to share the findings with you after the research is ⎬ ask questions;
completed. Your name will not be associated with the research findings in any way, ⎭ obtain results;
and only the researchers will know your identity. anonymity

There are no known risks and/or discomforts associated with this study. The ◄——— No known risks
expected benefits associated with your participation are the information about the
experiences in learning research methods. If this study is later submitted for ◄——— Benefits
publication, a by-line will indicate the participation of all students in the class.

Please sign this consent form. You are signing it with full knowledge of the nature
and purpose of the procedures. A copy of this form will be given to you to keep.

◄——— Signature needed

_____   _____
Signature   Date

◄——— Information about
Jane W. Smith, Professor, City University (111-312-5432)   investigator

You might try writing a sample informed consent form for use in a research project. In your consent form, include the aspects identified in the right column in Figure 5.4 so that it contains the essential information required by a review board.

4. *Submit a description of your proposed study to the institutional review board.* This description includes the purpose of the study, the data collection process, the guarantees for protecting the participants, and a sample consent form.

After you have completed the steps listed above, the review board will evaluate your project and determine whether you have guaranteed the protection of participants. If approved, you can proceed with the study. If denied, you will need to visit with the board representative to determine why it did not approve the study and what you need to change in your project description or procedures to get approval.

WHAT INFORMATION WILL YOU COLLECT?

With the identification of participants and a procedure for gaining permission, you next turn to the specific forms of data that will help you answer your research questions or address your research hypotheses. This step involves identifying the variables in your questions and hypotheses, finding definitions for these variables, and considering types of information that will help you assess these variables, a process outlined in Figure 5.5 using the variable *self-efficacy*.

Specify Variables from Research Questions and Hypotheses

Research questions and hypotheses contain variables. To determine what data need to be collected, you need to identify clearly the variables in your study. This will include

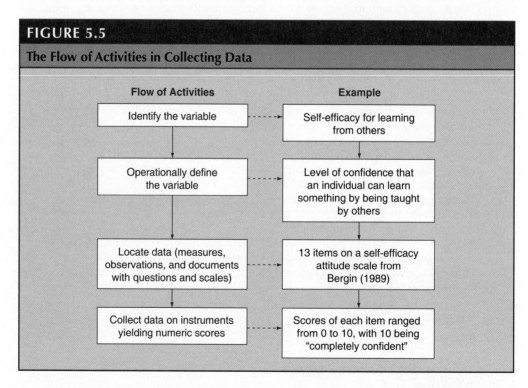

FIGURE 5.5

The Flow of Activities in Collecting Data

independent, dependent, and control variables. A useful strategy is to make a list of the variables so that you can determine what variables are operating in a study.

Operationally Define Each Variable

Many definitions of variables are possible, such as a dictionary definition, but researchers use an operational definition. An **operational definition** is the specification of how you will define and measure the variable in your study. You can find definitions in published research studies on your topic. Sometimes published studies have sections titled "Definition of Terms." Alternatively, you might examine definitions in research summaries such as handbooks or encyclopedias. In some situations, a clear, applied definition suitable for finding a measure is not available, and you will need to construct your own definition. If this is the case, you should test it with other students or individuals knowledgeable about your topic and variable before you use it in your research. A dictionary definition might be used as well, but remember that such a definition often reflects more common usage of a term rather than a research application.

Consider the variable *weapon possession* that Maria needs to define operationally. Write down two or three possible definitions for this variable, such as "a student who has been discovered carrying a knife to school." What other definitions might you use that will help Maria measure the extent to which high school students possess weapons at school? (*Hint:* Think about what happens when a teacher or administrator finds students with weapons in their possession.)

Choose Types of Data and Measures

With operational definitions for your variables, you next need to identify types of data that will measure your variables. Researchers collect data on instruments. An **instrument** is a tool for measuring, observing, or documenting quantitative data. Identified before the researchers collect data, the instrument may be a test, questionnaire, tally sheet, log, observational checklist, inventory, or assessment instrument. Researchers use instruments to measure achievement, assess individual ability, observe behavior, develop a psychological profile of an individual, or interview a person. In quantitative research, four major types of information are gathered, as shown in Table 5.2. Definitions and examples in this table should help you apply your understanding of different forms of quantitative measures.

Performance Measures

You collect **performance measures** to assess an individual's ability to perform on an achievement test, intelligence test, aptitude test, interest inventory, or personality assessment inventory. Participants take tests that measure their achievement (e.g., the Iowa Test of Basic Skills), their intelligence (e.g., Wechsler), or their aptitude (e.g., Stanford–Binet). In addition, you could gather data that measures an individual's career interests or assesses personality traits. These measures are all available through instruments reported in the literature. Through past research, researchers have developed "norms" for these tests (conducted the tests with a number of individuals, averaged their scores, and looked at the differences in their scores) so that they can compare individual scores with typical scores for people who have taken the test. However, one drawback of performance data is that it does not measure individual attitudes, and performance data may be costly, time-consuming to gather, and potentially biased toward specific cultural groups.

TABLE 5.2

Types of Quantitative Data and Measures

Types of Data	Types of Tests, Instruments, or Documents to Collect Data	Definition of the Type of Test, Instruments, or Document	Example of the Specific Tests, Instrument, or Source of Information
Measures of Individual Performance	Achievement test: norm-referenced tests	A test where the individual's grade is a measure of how well he or she did in comparison with a large group of test takers (Vogt, 2005)	Iowa Test of Basic Skills
	Criterion-referenced tests	A test where the individual's grade is a measure of how well he or she did in comparison to a criterion or score	General Educational Development or GED Test Metropolitan Achievement Test Series on Reading
	Intelligence test	A test that measures an individual's intellectual ability	Wechsler Intelligence Scale for Children
	Aptitude test	A test to measure a person's ability to estimate how they will perform at some time in the future or in a different situation	Cognitive ability: Binet–Simon Scale to identify a child's mental level General ability: Stanford–Binet IQ Scale
	Interest inventory	A test that provides information about an individual's interests and helps them make career choices	Strong Interest Inventory
	Personality assessment	A test that helps a person identify and measure human character-istics that help predict or explain behavior over time and across situations (Thorndike, 1997b)	Minnesota Multiphasic Personality Inventory
Measures of Individual Attitude	Affective scale	An instrument that measures positive or negative effect for or against a topic	Attitudes toward Self-Esteem Scale Adaptive Behavior Scales
Observation of Individual Behavior	Behavioral checklist	An instrument used to record observations about individual behavior	Flanders' Interaction Analysis Behavioral Checklist in Reading Vineland Adaptive Behavior Scale
Factual Information	Public documents or school records	Information from public sources that provides data about a sample or population	Census data School grade reports School attendance reports

Attitudinal Measures

Alternatively, you can measure attitudes of individuals, a popular form of quantitative data for surveys, correlational studies, and experiments. Researchers use **attitudinal measures** when they measure feelings toward educational topics (e.g., assessing posi-tive or negative attitudes toward giving students a choice of school to attend). To develop attitudinal measures, researchers often write their own questions or they find an instru-ment to use that measures the attitudes. Regardless of the approach, these measures need to contain unbiased questions (e.g., rather than "Should students carry weapons to schools?", ask, "How do you feel about students carrying weapons to school?") and encourage participants to answer questions honestly. One drawback of attitudinal measures is that they do not provide direct evidence of specific behaviors (e.g., whether or not students actually carry a weapon to school).

Let's examine a research instrument used to gather attitudinal information. Examine the first few questions (out of 74 on the instrument) on the "Student Adaptation to College Questionnaire" available commercially from Western Psychological Services (Baker & Siryk, 1989) in Figure 5.6. This questionnaire begins with personal information questions (e.g., sex, date of birth, current academic standing, and ethnic background) and then asks students to indicate their attitude toward adapting to college on questions using a 9-point scale from "applies very closely to me" to "doesn't apply to me at all." Overall, the questions focus on the quality of the student's adjustment to the college environment (e.g., whether the student fits in well, feels tense, keeps up to date on academic work, makes friends, attends class, is satisfied with social life). To analyze these questions, the researcher groups these questions into four scales (called *subscales*): Academic Adjustment (24 questions), Social Adjustment (20 questions), Emotional Adjustment (15 questions), and Goal Commitment–Institutional Attachment (15 questions). Then the analyst

---

FIGURE 5.6

Example of an Instrument that Measures Attitudes

Source: Partial sample from the *Student Adaptation to College Questionnaire* copyright © 1989 by Western Psychological Services. Reprinted by permission of the publisher, Western Psychological Services, 12031 Wilshire Boulevard, Los Angeles, California, 90025, U.S.A. Not to be reprinted in whole or in part for any additional purpose without the expressed, written permission of the publisher. All rights reserved.

sums the scores to the questions on each scale to identify an individual's score on each scale. Dahmus, Bernardin, and Bernardin (1992) provided a review of these procedures and background about this questionnaire.

Behavioral Observations

To collect data on specific behaviors, you can observe behavior and record scores on a checklist or scoring sheet. **Behavioral observations** are made by selecting an instrument (or using a behavioral protocol) on which to record a behavior, observing individuals for that behavior, and checking points on a scale that reflect the behavior (behavioral checklists). The advantage of this form of data is that you can identify an individual's actual behavior, rather than simply record his or her views or perceptions. However, behaviors may be difficult to score, and gathering them is a time-consuming form of data collection. Further, if more than one observer gathers data for a study, you need to train observers to provide consistent procedures and periodically check that the observers apply consistent scoring.

An example of a behavioral checklist is the Measurement of Inappropriate and Disruptive Interactions (MIDI) developed and used in the Saber-Tooth Project, which studied physical education curriculum changes in one middle school and two comparison schools (Ward, 1999), as shown in Figure 5.7. The investigators used this checklist in a study of four classes in which the teachers provided an instructional unit on lacrosse to eighth-grade students (Ward et al., 1999). During this classroom unit, the researchers observed the students and scored student behaviors using the MIDI scoring sheet in each class portrayed in Figure 5.7.

The legend for this scoring sheet, located at the bottom, lists the codes that observers recorded in each cell. These codes were the first letter of the appropriate word used to describe the context or focus of the lesson in which the behavior occurs (i.e., game, practice, cognitive, instruction, or management/other). The observers also recorded the type of inappropriate behavior during the primary event that involved the most students during the interval (i.e., talking out/noise, inactive, off-task, noncompliance, verbal offense). Finally, observers indicated who was engaged in the disruption (i.e., class, small group, individual) to assess the extent of misbehavior in the class. Numbers at the top of each column on the scoring sheet represent students (e.g., 1, 2, 3, and so forth through 115). Data were collected on-site using this scoring sheet as the instrument, and three observers in the classes recorded their observations (identified by the column numbers) at an interval of 6-second observations. The investigators trained the observers in their scoring procedures so that they would score the behavior consistently. An audiotape recording cued the observers as to when they would mark their observations on the checklist sheet. For example, in the fictitious data shown in Figure 5.7 for student 1, the observer records on the rows:

Context = Game (G)

Inappropriate Behavior = Inactive (I)

Extent of Misbehavior = Individual/s (less than 3 students) (I)

After recording scores for all students, the observers analyzed the differences among students in their disruptive behaviors.

Factual Information

Quantitative, numeric data is also available in public educational records. **Factual information** or personal documents consist of numeric, individual data available in public records. Examples of these types of data include grade reports, school attendance records,

FIGURE 5.7

Example of an Observational Scoring Sheet with Fictitious Data

Social Skills Assessment

Teacher **Alis**   Grade Level **08**   Observer **JC**   Date **2/3**   Content Area **Lacross**   School **School A**

	1	2	3	4	5	6	7	8	9	10	11	12	13	14	15	16	17	18	19	20	21	22	23	24	25
C	G	C	C	I	I	I	G	G	G	G	G	M	M	M	G										
B	I	O	V	I	I	I	I	I	I	T	T	I	I	I	T										
E	I	S	I	I	I	I	S	S	S	S	I	I	I	I	S										

	26	27	28	29	30	31	32	33	34	35	36	37	38	39	40	41	42	43	44	45	46	47	48	49	50
C																									
B																									
E																									

	51	52	53	54	55	56	57	58	59	60	61	62	63	64	65	66	67	68	69	70	71	72	73	74	75
C																									
B																									
E																									

	76	77	78	79	80	81	82	83	84	85	86	87	88	89	90	91	92	93	94	95	96	97	98	99	100
C																									
B																									
E																									

	101	102	103	104	105	106	107	108	109	110	111	112	113	114	115	116	117	118	119	120	121	122	123	124	125
C																									
B																									
E																									

	126	127	128	129	130	131	132	133	134	135	136	137	138	139	140	141	142	143	144	145	146	147	148	149	150
C																									
B																									
E																									

	151	152	153	154	155	156	157	158	159	160	161	162	163	164	165	166	167	168	169	170	171	172	173	174	175
C																									
B																									
E																									

C																									
B																									
E																									

C																									
B																									
E																									

Context Categories	Inappropriate Behaviors	Extent of Misbehavior:
Game:	Talking out/Noise:	Class: (15 or more students)
Practice:	Inactive:	Small Group: (4 or more students up to 15)
Cognitive:	Off-task:	Individual/s (less that 3 students)
Instruction:	Non-compliance:	
Management/Other:	Verbal offense:	

Source: Ward, P., Barrett, T. M., Evans, S. A., Doutis, P., Nguyen, P. T., & Johnson, M. K. (1999). Chapter 5: Curriculum effects in eighth grade lacrosse. *Journal of Teaching in Physical Education, 18,* 428–443. Reprinted with permission of the authors.

student demographic data, and census information. As long as these documents are available in the public domain, researchers can access and use them. Investigators cannot easily access some documents, such as health information about students, because federal regulations protect the privacy of individuals. Also, researchers need to scrutinize the public documents carefully to determine if they represent accurate data. The availability of public documents does not infer that researchers have collected the data carefully, with an eye toward accuracy.

Web-Based Electronic Data Collection

With the use of Web sites and the Internet, electronic data collection in quantitative research is popular. At this time, use of Web sites and the Internet for data collection consists of administering surveys (Solomon, 2001), gathering interview data (Persichitte, Young, & Tharp, 1997), or using existing databases for analysis (e.g., Texas Lotto, U.S. Census Bureau, Louis Harris Pool; Pachnowski, Newman, & Jurczyk, 1997). Survey applications might consist of optically scanning an instrument and placing it on a Web site for participants to complete. Another form is computer-assisted self-interviewing (Babbie, 2003). In this approach, the participant in a study logs on to a computer, downloads a questionnaire from the Internet, completes the questionnaire, and sends the completed questionnaire back to the researcher. Other approaches using electronic questionnaires include voice recognition using the telephone keypad, and computerized self-administered questionnaires (Babbie, 2003). Electronic data collection provides an easy, quick form of data collection. However, use of the Internet may be limited because of (a) limitations involving the use of listservs and obtaining of e-mail addresses, (b) limitations of the technology itself, (c) lack of a population list, and (d) the questionable representativeness of the sample data (Mertler, 2001).

How to Decide What Types to Choose

Confronted by these many options for collecting quantitative data, which one or ones will you use? To select your data sources, ask yourself the following questions:

◆ *What am I trying to learn about participants from my research questions and hypotheses?*   If you are trying to learn about individual behaviors of parents at a student–parent conference meeting, then you could use a behavioral checklist and record observations. If you are trying to measure the attitudes of teachers toward a bond issue, attitudinal questions or an attitudinal instrument will be required.

◆ *What information can you realistically collect?*   Some types of data may not be collectible in a study because individuals are unwilling to supply it. For example, precise data on the frequency of substance abuse in middle schools may be difficult to collect; identifying the number of student suspensions for substance abuse is much more realistic.

◆ *How do the advantages of the data collection compare with its disadvantages?*   In our discussion of each data source, we have talked about the ideal situations for data collection. Given the ease or difficulty of collecting data, each type needs to be assessed.

How would you now advise that Maria collect her data? Assume that she now seeks to answer the general quantitative research question "Why do students carry weapons in high school?" and the following subquestions:

a. "How frequently do students feel weapons are carried into high school?"
b. "What general attitudes do high school students hold toward the possession of weapons in the schools?"
c. "Does participation in extracurricular activities at school influence attitudes of students toward possession of weapons?"
d. "Are student suspensions for possession of weapons on the increase in high schools?"

Before looking at the answers provided, list the type of information that Maria might collect for subquestions a through d.

To answer these subquestions, Maria first needs to locate or develop a questionnaire to send out to a sample of high school students in the school district. Her data collection will consist mainly of attitudinal data. This questionnaire will measure student *attitudes* toward frequency of weapon possession (question a); assess student *attitudes* toward possession of weapons (question b); and gather *factual data* about the students (question c), such as age, level of education, race, gender, and extent of participation in extracurricular activities. To answer question d, she will contact the school officials of several high schools and ask if she can obtain reports on student suspensions—school documents that report quantitative data. In summary, she will collect both attitudinal and factual information.

WHAT INSTRUMENT WILL YOU USE TO COLLECT DATA?

Let's assume that you will collect performance, attitudinal, or observational data. These forms of data collection all involve using an instrument. What instrument will you use to collect your data? Do you find one to use or develop one yourself? If you search for one to use, how will you locate this instrument? Once you find the instrument, what criteria will you use to determine if it is a good instrument to use?

Locate or Develop an Instrument

Three options exist for obtaining an instrument to use: you can develop one yourself, locate one and modify it, or locate one and use it in its entirety. Of these choices, locating one to use (either modifying it or using it in its original form) represents the easiest approach. It is more difficult to develop an instrument than to locate one and modify it for use in a study. **Modifying an instrument** means locating an existing instrument, obtaining permission to change it, and making changes in it to fit your requirements. Typically, authors of the original instrument will ask for a copy of your modified version and the results from your study in exchange for your use of their instrument.

An instrument to measure the variables in your study may not be available in the literature or commercially. If this is the case, you will have to develop your own instrument, which is a long and arduous process. Developing an instrument consists of several steps, such as identifying the purpose of the instrument, reviewing the literature, writing the questions, and testing the questions with individuals similar to those you plan to study. The four phases of development, recommended by Benson and Clark (1983) and shown in Figure 5.8, illustrate the rigorous steps of planning, constructing, evaluating, and checking to see if the questions work (i.e., validating an instrument). In this process, the basic steps consist of reviewing the literature, presenting general questions to a target group, constructing questions for the item pool, and pilot testing the items. The statistical procedures of calculating reliability and item analysis are available in computer software programs.

Search for an Instrument

If you decide to use an existing instrument, the publisher or author will typically charge you a fee for use of the instrument. Finding a good instrument that measures your independent, dependent, and control variables is not easy. In fact, you may need to assemble a new instrument that consists of parts of existing instruments. Whether you search for one instrument or several to use, several strategies can aid in your search:

◆ *Look in published journal articles.* Often authors of journal articles will report instruments and provide a few sample items so that you can see the basic content

---

FIGURE 5.8

Steps in Developing or Constructing an Instrument

Phase I: Planning
    State purpose of test and target groups
    Identify and define domain of test
    Review literature on construct or variable of
       interest
    Give open-ended questions to target group
    Interpret open-ended comments
    Write objectives
    Select item format

Phase II: Construction
    Develop table of specifications
    Hire and train item writers
    Write pool items
    Validate content
    Have judges complete qualitative evaluation
    Develop new or revise items

Phase III: Quantitative Evaluation
    Prepare instrument for first pilot test
    Administer first pilot test
    Debrief subjects
    Calculate reliability
    Run item analysis
    Revise instrument
    Prepare for second pilot test

Phase IV: Validation
    Administer second pilot test
    Run item analysis
    Repeat steps of revision, pilot administration,
       and item analysis
    Begin validation
    Administer for validation data
    Continue validation

Source: Adapted from a flowchart provided by Benson & Clark, 1983.

---

included in the instrument. Examine references in published journal articles that cite specific instruments and contact the authors for inspection copies. Before you use the instrument, seek permission from the author. With limited space in journals, authors are including fewer examples of their items or copies of their instruments.

◆ *Run an ERIC search.* Use the term *instruments* and the topic of the study to search the ERIC system for instruments. Use the online search process of the ERIC database. Use the same search procedure to locate abstracts to articles where the authors mention instruments that they have used in their studies.

◆ *Examine guides to tests and instruments that are available commercially.* Examine the *Mental Measurements Yearbook* (MMY; Impara & Plake, 1999) or the *Tests in Print* (TIP; Murphy, Impara, & Plake, 1999), both of which are available from the Buros Institute of Mental Measurements (**www.unl.edu/buros/**). More than 400 commercial firms develop instruments that are available for sale to individuals and institutions. Published since 1938, these guides contain extensive information about tests and measures available for educational research use. You can locate reviews and descriptions of English-language commercially published tests in the MMY, which is available on CD-ROM databases in many academic libraries.

Criteria for Choosing a Good Instrument

Once you find an instrument, several criteria can be used to assess whether it is a good instrument to use. Ask yourself:

◆ Have authors developed the instrument recently, and can you obtain the most recent version? With knowledge expanding in educational research, instruments over 5 years old might be outdated. To stay current, authors update their instruments periodically, and you need to find the most recent copy of an instrument.

◆ Is the instrument widely cited by other authors? Frequent use by other researchers will provide some indication of its endorsement by others. Use by other researchers may provide some evidence about whether the questions on the instrument provide good and consistent measures.

◆ Are reviews available for the instrument? Look for published reviews about the instrument in the MMY or in journals such as *Measurement and Evaluation in Counseling and Development*. If reviews exist, it means that other researchers have taken the instrument seriously and seek to document its worth.

◆ Is there information about the reliability and validity of scores from past uses of the instrument?

◆ Does the procedure for recording data fit the research questions/hypotheses in your study?

◆ Does the instrument contain accepted scales of measurement?

Because of the importance of the last three criteria—reliability and validity, recording information, and scales of measurement—a discussion will explore these ideas in more depth.

Are Scores on Past Use of the Instrument Reliable and Valid?

You want to select an instrument that reports individual scores that are reliable and valid. **Reliability** means that scores from an instrument are stable and consistent. Scores should be nearly the same when researchers administer the instrument multiple times at different times. Also, scores need to be consistent. When an individual answers certain questions one way, the individual should consistently answer closely related questions in the same way. **Validity** is the development of sound evidence to demonstrate that the test interpretation (of scores about the concept or construct that the test is assumed to measure) matches its proposed use (AERA, APA, NCME, 1999). This definition, in place since 1985, changes the traditional focus on the three-fold types of validity—construct, criterion-referenced, and content—and shifts the emphasis from "types" of validity to the "evidence" and "use" of the test or instrument (Thorndike, 1997b). Thus, validity is seen now as a single unitary concept, rather than three types. Validity is the degree to which all of the evidence points to the intended interpretation of test scores for the proposed purpose. Thus, a focus is on the consequences of using the scores from an instrument (Hubley & Zumbo, 1996; Messick, 1980).

Reliability and validity are bound together in complex ways. These two terms sometimes overlap and at other times are mutually exclusive. Validity can be thought of as the larger, more encompassing term when you assess the choice of an instrument. Reliability is generally easier to understand as it is a measure of consistency. If scores are not reliable, they are not valid; scores need to be stable and consistent first before they can be meaningful. Additionally, the more reliable the scores from an instrument, the more valid the scores may be (however, scores may still not measure the particular construct and may remain invalid). The ideal situation exists when scores are both reliable and valid. In addition, the more reliable the scores from an instrument, the more valid the scores will be. Scores need to be stable and consistent before they can be meaningful.

Reliability   A goal of good research is to have measures or observations that are reliable. Several factors can result in unreliable data, including when:

◆ Questions on instruments are ambiguous and unclear
◆ Procedures of test administration vary and are not standardized
◆ Participants are fatigued, are nervous, misinterpret questions, or guess on tests (Rudner, 1993)

Researchers can use any one or more of five available procedures to examine an instrument's reliability, as shown in Table 5.3. You can distinguish these procedures by the number of times the instrument is administered, the number of versions of the instrument administered by researchers, and the number of individuals who make an assessment of information.

The **test–retest reliability** procedure examines the extent to which scores from one sample are stable over time from one test administration to another. To determine this form of reliability, the researcher administers the test at two different times to the same participants at a sufficient time interval. If the scores are reliable, then they will relate (or will correlate) at a positive, reasonably high level, such as .6. This approach has the advantage of requiring only one form of the instrument; however, an individual's scores on the first administration of the instrument may influence the scores on the second administration. Consider this example:

A researcher measures a stable characteristic, such as creativity, for sixth graders at the beginning of the year. Measured again at the end of the year, the researcher assumes that the scores will be stable during the sixth-grade experience. If scores at the beginning and the end of the year relate, there is evidence for test–retest reliability.

Another approach is **alternative forms reliability**. This involves using two instruments, both measuring the same variables and relating (or correlating) the scores for the same group of individuals to the two instruments. In practice, both instruments need to be similar, such as the same content, same level of difficulty, and same types of scales. Thus, the items for both instruments represent the same universe or population of items. The advantage of this approach is that it allows you to see if the scores from one instrument are equivalent to scores from another instrument, for two instruments intended to measure the same variables. The difficulty, of course, is whether the two instruments are

TABLE 5.3

Types of Reliability

Form of Reliability	Number of Times Instrument Administered	Number of Different Versions of the Instrument	Number of Individuals Who Provide Information
Test–retest reliability	Twice at different time intervals	One version of the instrument	Each participant in the study completes the instrument twice.
Alternate forms reliability	Each instrument administered once	Two different versions of the same concept or variable	Each participant in the study completes each instrument.
Alternate forms and test–retest reliability	Twice at different time intervals	Two different versions of the same concept or variable	Each participant in the study completes each instrument.
Interrater reliability	Instrument administered once	One version of the instrument	More than one individual observes behavior of the participants.
Internal consistency reliability	Instrument administered once	One version of the instrument	Each participant in the study completes the instrument.

equivalent in the first place. Assuming that they are, the researchers relate or correlate the items from the one instrument with its equivalent instrument. Examine this example:

> An instrument with 45 vocabulary items yields scores from first graders. The researcher compares these scores with those from another instrument that also measures a similar set of 45 vocabulary items. Both instruments contain items of approximately equal difficulty. When the researcher finds the items to relate positively, we have confidence in the accuracy or reliability of the scores from the first instrument.

The **alternate forms and test–retest reliability** approach is simply a variety of the two previous types of reliability. In this approach, the researcher administers the test twice *and* uses an alternate form of the test from the first administration to the second. This type of reliability has the advantages of both examining the stability of scores over time as well as having the equivalence of items from the potential universe of items. It also has all of the disadvantages of both test–retest and alternate forms of reliability. Scores may reflect differences in content or difficulty or in changes over time. An example follows:

> The researcher administers the 45 vocabulary items to first graders twice at two different times, and the actual tests are equivalent in content and level of difficulty. The researcher correlates or relates scores of both tests and finds that they correlate positively and highly. The scores to the initial instrument are reliable.

Interrater reliability is a procedure used when making observations of behavior. It involves observations made by two or more individuals of an individual's or several individuals' behavior. The observers record their scores of the behavior and then compare scores to see if their scores are similar or different. Because this method obtains observational scores from two or more individuals, it has the advantage of negating any bias that any one individual might bring to scoring. It has the disadvantages of requiring the researcher to train the observers and requiring the observers to negotiate outcomes and reconcile differences in their observations, something that may not be easy to do. Here is an example:

> Two observers view preschool children at play in their activity center. They observe the spatial skills of the children and record on a checklist the number of times each child builds something in the activity center. After the observations, the observers compare their checklists to determine how close their scores were during the observation. Assuming that their scores were close, they can average their scores and conclude that their assessment demonstrates interrater reliability.

Scores from an instrument are reliable and accurate if an individual's scores are **internally consistent** across the items on the instrument. If someone completes items at the beginning of the instrument one way (e.g., positive about negative effects of tobacco), then they should answer the questions later in the instrument in a similar way (e.g., positive about the health effects of tobacco).

The consistency of responses can be examined in several ways. One way is to split the test in half and relate or correlate the items. This test is called the **Kuder–Richardson split half test (KR-20, KR-21)** and it is used when (a) the items on an instrument are scored right or wrong as categorical scores, (b) the responses are not influenced by speed, and (c) the items measure a common factor. Since the split half test relies on information from only half of the instrument, a modification in this procedure is to use the **Spearman–Brown formula,** which estimates full-length test reliability using all questions on an instrument. This is important because the reliability of an instrument increases as researchers add more items to the instrument. Finally, the **coefficient alpha** is used to test for internal consistency (Cronbach, 1984). If the items are scored as continuous variables (e.g., *strongly agree* to *strongly disagree*), the alpha provides a coefficient to estimate consistency of scores on an instrument. Calculations for the Kuder–Richardson split half, Spearman–Brown prophecy formula, and coefficient alpha are available in Thorndike (1997b).

Validity   In addition to reliability, you should examine whether the scores from the instrument (not the instrument itself) are valid. As a researcher, here are the steps you will likely employ:

◆ Identify an instrument (or test) that you would like to use
◆ Look for evidence of validity by examining prior studies that have reported scores and use of the instrument
◆ Look closely at the purpose for which the instrument was used in these studies
◆ Look as well at how the researchers have interpreted (discussed if the instrument measured what it is intended to measure) the scores in light of their intended use
◆ Evaluate whether the authors provide good evidence that links their interpretation to their use

What types of evidence should researchers seek to establish validity? Impara (2010) provides a useful summary of the AERA, APA, NCME (1999) *Standards,* directs readers to examine closely chapter 1 from the *Standards* on "validity," and then presents an extended list of examples of evidence to document validity. Only a few of the examples will be mentioned here.

The *Standards* mention five categories of evidence as shown in Table 5.4: evidence based on test content, response processes, internal structure, relations to other variables, and the consequences of testing. In the discussion to follow, the word "testing" will be equivalent to "instrument."

Evidence based on test content

Often instruments will be used that measure achievement, assess applicants for credentials, or are used for employment in jobs. The question is whether the scores from the instrument show that the test's content relates to what the test is intended to measure. This idea relates to the traditional idea of content validity. Typically researchers go to a panel of judges or experts and have them identify whether the questions are valid. This form of validity is useful when the possibilities of questions (e.g., achievement tests in science education) are well known and easily identifiable. It is less useful in assessing personality or aptitude scores (e.g., on the Stanford–Binet IQ test), when the universe of questions is less certain.

Evidence based on response processes

Instruments can be evaluated for the fit between the construct being measured and nature of the responses of the individuals completing the instrument or the individuals conducting an observation using the instrument. Do the scores reflect accurate responses of the participants to the actual instrument? Validity evidence can be assembled through interviews of the participants to report what they experienced or were thinking when they completed the instrument. The responses of observers can be compared to determine whether they are responding in a similar way when they observe. The more the response processes fit what the instrument is intended to measure, the better the evidence for validity.

TABLE 5.4			
Sources of Validity Evidence and Examples			
Validity Evidence	**Types of Tests or Instruments to Which Validity Evidence Is Applicable**	**Type of Evidence Sought**	**Examples of Evidence**
Evidence based on test content	Achievement tests, credentialing tests, and employment tests	Evidence of an analysis of the test's content (e.g., themes, wording, format) and the construct it is intended to measure	• Examine logical or empirical evidence (e.g., syllabi, textbooks, teachers' lesson plans) • Have experts in the area judge
Evidence based on response processes	Tests that assess cognitive processes, rate behaviors, and require observations	Evidence of the fit between the construct and how individuals taking the test actually performed	• Interviews with individuals taking tests to report what they experienced/were thinking • Interviews or other data with observers to determine if they are all responding to the same stimulus in the same way
Evidence based on internal structure	Applicable to all tests	Evidence of the relationship among test items, test parts, and the dimensions of the test	• Statistical analysis to determine if factor structure (scales) relates to theory, correlation of items
Evidence based on relations to other variables	Applicable to all tests	Evidence of the relationship of test scores to variables external to the test	• Correlations of scores with tests measuring the same or different constructs (convergent/discriminant validity) • Correlations with scores and some external criterion (e.g., performance assessment—test-criterion validity) • Correlations of tests scores and their prediction of a criterion based on cumulative databases (called meta-analysis—validity generalization)
Evidence based on the consequences of testing	Applicable to all tests	Evidence of the intended and unintended conse-quences of the test	• Benefits of the test for positive treatments for therapy, for placement of workers in suitable jobs, for prevention of unqualified individuals from entering a profession, for improvement of classroom instructional practices, and so forth

Source: Adapted from Impara (2010) and American Educational Research Association, American Psychological Association, and National Council on Measurement in Education (1999).

Evidence based on internal structure

Are the test score interpretations consistent with a conceptual framework for the instrument? This form of validity evidence is gathered by conducting statistical procedures to determine the relationship among test item and test parts. It relates to the traditional notion of construct validity. Through statistical procedures you can:

◆ See if scores to items are related in a way that is expected (e.g., examine the relationship of a question on a "student depression instrument" to see if it relates to the overall scale measuring depression)

◆ Test a theory and see if the scores, as expected, support the theory (e.g., test a theory of depression and see if the evidence or data supports the relationships in the theory)

Evidence based on relations to other variables

This is a large category of evidence that relates to the traditional idea of criterion-related validity (predictive and concurrent). Basically, the researcher looks for evidence of the validity of scores by examining other measures outside of the test. The researcher can look at similar or dissimilar tests to see if the scores can be related positively or negatively. The researcher can see if the scores predict an outside criterion (or test scores) based on many different studies. For example, when the results of a current study showed that boys in middle schools have lower self-esteem than girls, can this prediction hold true when many studies have been assessed? Collecting validity evidence from these many studies provides support for the validation of scores on an instrument.

Evidence based on the consequences of testing

This form of evidence is the new factor that has been introduced into the quantitative validity discussion. Validity evidence can be organized to support both the intended and the unintended consequences of using an instrument. What benefits (or liabilities) have resulted from using the instrument? Researchers can assemble evidence to demonstrate the consequences of testing, such as the enhanced classroom instruction that results as a consequence of testing. Not all of the consequences may be intended; for example, an educational test may be supported on the grounds that it improves student attendance or motivation in classes.

After reviewing the forms of reliability and validity, we can now step back and review what questions you should ask when selecting or evaluating an instrument. A short list of questions, provided in Figure 5.9, should aid in this process.

To practice applying these questions, consider the choice of an instrument by Maria. She finds an instrument titled "Attitudes toward Possession of Weapons in Schools." An author reports this instrument in a published journal article. What might be two forms of

FIGURE 5.9

Validity and Reliability Questions for Selecting/Evaluating a Test or Instrument

When selecting or evaluating an instrument, look for:

Reliability	Validity
1. Did the author check for it?	1. Did the author check for it?
2. If so, what form of reliability was reported?	2. If so, what type of validity was reported?
3. Was an appropriate type used?	3. Was more than one type reported?
4. Were the reliability values (coefficients) reported?	4. Were the values (coefficients) reported?
5. Were they positive, high coefficients?	5. Were they positive, high coefficients?

evidence about reliability and validity she could look for in the author's discussion about this instrument? Write down these forms of reliability and validity.

Do the Instrument's Data Recording Procedures Fit the Research Questions/Hypotheses?

Returning to our question of criteria for assessing a good instrument to use, another criterion was that instruments contain recording procedures that fit the data you need to answer the research questions or hypotheses. Who records the data on the instruments or checklists? Data may be self-reported; that is, the participants provide the information, such as on achievement tests or on attitudinal questionnaires. Alternatively, the researcher may record the data on forms by observing, interviewing, or collecting documents. Having participants supply the data is less time-consuming for the researcher. However, when the researcher records the data, he or she becomes familiar with how the participants respond and hence can control for a higher level of quality of the data.

Are Adequate Scales of Measurement Used?

Another criterion is that the instrument should contain good response options to the questions. Variables can be measured as categories or on a continuous range of scores. Now it is helpful to assess instruments that you might use in research in terms of the adequacy of their scales of measurement. For example, for a study of student attitudes toward the use of wireless laptops in a college classroom, a researcher might ask the question "To what extent does the wireless laptop help you learn in the classroom?" The student might answer this question using a categorical scale such as the following:

_____ To a great extent
_____ Somewhat
_____ To a less extent

The easiest way to think about the types of scales of measurement is to remember that there are two basic types: categorical and continuous scales. Categorical scales have two types: nominal and ordinal scales. Continuous scales (often called *scale scores* in computer data analysis programs) also have two types: interval/quasi-interval and ratio scales. These types of scales are shown in Table 5.5.

Scales of measurement are response options to questions that measure (or observe) variables in categorical or continuous units. It is important to understand scales of measurement to assess the quality of an instrument and to determine the appropriate statistics to use in data analysis.

Nominal Scales   Researchers use **nominal scales** (or categorical scales) to provide response options where participants check one or more categories that describe their traits, attributes, or characteristics. These scales do not have any order. An example of a nominal scale would be gender, divided into the two categories of male and female (either one could be listed first as a response option). Another form of a nominal scale would be a checklist of "yes" or "no" responses. A semantic differential scale, popular in psychological research, is another type of nominal scale. This scale consists of bipolar adjectives that the participant uses to check his or her position. For example, in a psychological study of talented teenagers, researchers were interested in studying the teenagers' emotional responses to their everyday activities (Csikszentmihalyi, Rathunde, Whalen, & Wong, 1993). The researchers used a semantic differential scale for teenagers to record their mood

TABLE 5.5	
Types of Scales Used in Quantitative Research	
Type of Scale	**Examples of Questions Using the Scale**
Nominal scale (uses categories)	How much education have you completed? _____ No college　　_____ Some college _____ Bachelor's degree　_____ Graduate or professional work What is your class rank? _____ Freshman　_____ Sophomore _____ Junior　　_____ Senior
Ordinal scale (uses categories that imply or express rank order)	Has your advisor helped you select courses? _____ Not at all　　　_____ To a small extent _____ To some extent　_____ To a great extent _____ To a very great extent Rank your preference for type of graduate-level instruction from 1 to 4 _____ Activity-based learning _____ Lecture _____ Small-group learning _____ Discussion
Quasi-interval or interval/ratio scale (uses continuous equal intervals)	School is a place where I am thought of as a person who matters. _____ Strongly agree　_____ Agree　　_____ Undecided _____ Disagree　　_____ Strongly disagree Colleges and universities should conduct research to solve economic problems of cities. _____ Strongly agree　_____ Agree　　_____ Undecided _____ Disagree　　_____ Strongly disagree

on several adjectives at certain times of the day. The researchers used a beeping device (p. 52) and the participants were asked to describe their mood as they were beeped, using the following scale:

	very	quite	some	neither	some	quite	very	
alert	0	0	·	—	·	0	0	drowsy

Although the researchers summed scores of teenagers across several questions such as this one, the response scale to each question was nominal or categorical.

Ordinal Scales　Researchers use **ordinal scales** (or ranking scales or categorical scales) to provide response options where participants rank from best or most important to worst or least important some trait, attribute, or characteristic. These scales have an implied intrinsic order. For example, a researcher might record individual performance in a race for each runner from first to last place. Many attitudinal measures imply an ordinal scale because they ask participants to rank order the importance ("highly important" to "of no importance") or the extent ("to a great extent" to "a little extent") of topics. As this example illustrates, the information is categorical in a ranked order.

Interval/Ratio Scales

Another popular scale researchers use is an interval or rating scale. **Interval scales** (or rating scales or continuous scales) provide "continuous" response options to questions with assumed equal distances between options. These scales may have three, four, or more response options. The popular Likert scale ("strongly agree" to "strongly disagree") illustrates a scale with theoretically equal intervals among responses. Although an ordinal scale, such as "highly important" to "of no importance," may seem like an interval scale, we have no guarantee that the intervals are equal, as in the well-tested Likert scale. An achievement test such as the Iowa Test of Basic Skills is assumed to be an interval scale because researchers have substantiated that the response choices are of equal distance from each other.

The popular Likert scale (*strongly agree* to *strongly disagree*) illustrates a scale with theoretically equal intervals among responses. It has become common practice to treat this scale as a rating scale and assume that the equal intervals hold between the response categories (Blaikie, 2003). However, we have no guarantee that we have equal intervals. Hence, often the Likert scale (*strongly agree* to *strongly disagree*) is treated as both ordinal and interval data in educational research (hence the term *quasi-interval* in Table 5.5). How researchers consider this scale (or a similar scale, such as "highly important" to "of no importance") is critical in the choice of statistic to use to analyze the data. Ordinal scales require nonparametric statistical tests whereas interval scales require parametric. Some researchers stress the importance of viewing Likert scales as ordinal data (Jamieson, 2004). Others indicate that the errors for treating the Likert scale results as interval data are minimal (Jaccard & Wan, 1996). In order to consider treating Likert data on an interval scale, researchers should develop multiple categories or choices in their scale, determine whether their data are normally distributed, and establish whether the distance between each value on the scale is equal. If this cannot be done, then you should treat the Likert scale and scales like "extent of importance" or "degree of agreement" as ordinal scales for purposes of data analysis.

Finally, a **ratio scale** (or true zero scale) is a response scale in which participants check a response option with a true zero and equal distances between units. Although educational researchers seldom use this type of scale, examples of it are the height of individuals (e.g., 50 inches, 60 inches) and income levels (from zero dollars to $50,000 in increments of $10,000).

Combined Scales In educational research, quantitative investigators often use a combination of categorical and continuous scales. Of these, interval scales provide the most variation of responses and lend themselves to stronger statistical analysis. The best rule of thumb is that if you do not know in advance what statistical analysis you will use, create an interval or continuous scale. Continuous scales can always be converted into ordinal or nominal scales (Tuckman, 1999), but not vice versa.

 ## Think-Aloud About Finding and Selecting an Instrument

Often I find beginning researchers developing their own instruments rather than taking the time to locate an existing instrument suitable for their study. Unquestionably, developing your own instrument requires knowledge about item or question construction, scale development, format, and length. Although some campuses may have courses that teach this information, most students develop instruments with little feedback from advisors or consultants about how to design the instrument.

Instead of developing your own instrument, I would encourage you to locate or modify an existing instrument. An example can illustrate how you might find this instrument. In Figure 5.6, I showed you an instrument that I had found on students' attitudes toward adaptation to college. How did I find this instrument?

I knew that I wanted to measure the variable "student adjustment to college" because I had formed a general quantitative research question: "What factors influence how freshman students adjust to college?" I began by searching the ERIC database for an instrument using the descriptors of "students" and "college" and "adjustment" in my online key word search. Although I found several good journal articles on the topic, none included a useful instrument. Examining the references in these articles still did not net an instrument that would work.

I turned to two books in our academic library that index available instruments, the Buros Institute of Mental Measurements books, *Tests in Print* and the *Mental Measurements Yearbook*. You may recall from earlier in this chapter that the TIP and MMY publications contain information about commercially available tests and instruments, including attitudinal instruments. Although our library contains book copies of the TIP and MMY, I could have used the CD-ROM version of these books available in our library or visited the Buros Web site at **www.unl.edu/buros/**.

I located the latest book copy of the TIP (Murphy et al., 1999) and looked under the alphabetized listing of tests, searching for any instruments that related to students, especially college students. After trying out several words, I found the Student Adaptation to College Questionnaire (SACQ). Reading through this brief description of the SACQ, I learned basic information about the instrument, such as its purpose, the population for its use (i.e., college freshman), publication date (1989), and scales. This review also contained price information ($89.50 for 25 hand-scorable questionnaires and a manual), the time required to administer it (20 minutes), authors, publishers, and a cross-reference to a review of the instrument to be found in the MMY, 11th edition (Kramer & Conoley, 1992).

Next I was curious about whether scores reported on this instrument were both valid and reliable, so I looked up the instrument in the 11th edition of the MMY (Kramer & Conoley, 1992) and found a review of it by E. Jack Asher, Jr., Professor Emeritus of Psychology, Western Michigan University, Kalamazoo. I also searched the ERIC database and located a review article by Dahmus et al. (1992) reported in the journal *Measurement and Evaluation in Counseling and Development*.

Focusing mainly on the review by Asher, I found that it addressed:

- The purpose of the questionnaire
- The subscales on the questionnaire
- Norms on the questionnaire obtained by the authors by administering it from 1980 through 1984
- Evidence for validity of the scores from the instrument (i.e., criterion-related and construct validity)
- Evidence for reliability of the scores based on coefficients of internal consistency
- The value of the manual, especially the inclusion of potential ethical issues in using the instrument
- The overall value of the instrument for college counselors and research applications
- The limitations of the instrument

After reviewing all of these topics about the questionnaire, Asher concluded by summarizing an overall positive reaction to the instrument. Although somewhat dated

(1989), the instrument has been widely used and positively reviewed. I decided it would be a good instrument to survey college students.

Next I contacted the publisher, Western Psychological Services in Los Angeles, California, for permission to use the instrument and to obtain copies for my study. Using an instrument already developed by someone else, finding one with good validity and reliability scores, and locating a manual for using the instrument led to the early identification of means for collecting my data. You may not be as fortunate in locating an instrument as quickly as I did, but certainly, this process is better than developing numerous versions of your own instrument that might have questionable validity and reliability.

HOW WILL YOU ADMINISTER THE DATA COLLECTION?

The actual process of collecting data differs depending on the data and the instruments or documents you use. However, two aspects are standard across all forms of data and they deserve attention: the use of standard procedures and ethical practices.

Standardization

Performance measures, attitudinal measures, and observations rely on instruments. These instruments may consist of questionnaires that researchers mail to participants or hand out individually to people, surveys often administered in person or over the telephone, and observational checklists that researchers complete. Quantitative investigators also use instruments when they conduct face-to-face interviews with individuals or for a group of individuals.

In all of these cases, it is important to use standard procedures. When procedures vary, you introduce bias into the study and the data for individuals may not be comparable for analysis. Written procedures, as well as other data collectors assisting in the process, help keep you on track. For interviewing using an instrument, you apply the same procedures to each individual. Instructions provided on the interview form will help ensure that you follow a standard process. If others help in interviewing, you will need to train them so that the procedures used by all interviewers are consistent. This training might involve a demonstration interview, followed by a trial interview and a critique of the trial so that all trainees follow the same procedures.

In collecting observational data, training must occur first so that the researchers can collect data using standard procedures. A process similar to the one used in interviewing—demonstration, trial run, and a critique—might be used.

Researchers also collect public documents by obtaining permission to access this information and then taking notes or recording the information in a computer file. Establishing a database of categories of information helps to organize this information. This organization is especially important when you combine data from several sources into one file for analysis (e.g., enrollment data and suspension data for students in high schools).

Ethical Issues

Data collection should be ethical and it should respect individuals and sites. Obtaining permission before starting to collect data is not only a part of the informed consent process but is also an ethical practice. Protecting the anonymity of individuals by assigning numbers to returned instruments and keeping the identity of individuals confidential offers privacy to participants. During data collection, you must view the data as confidential and not share it with other participants or individuals outside of the project. You need to respect the wishes of individuals who choose not to participate in your study. Even when they consent to participate, people may back out or not show up for an observation or interview. Attempts to reschedule may be futile and you may need to select another person for data collection rather than force an individual to participate.

In terms of the research site, you need to recognize that all researchers disrupt the site they are studying, however minimally it might be. Observing in a classroom, for example, may disturb learning by distracting teachers and students, especially when you observe them closely and write down observations about their behavior on checklists. By obtaining permissions and clearly communicating the purpose of the study *before* you collect data, you can lessen the reservations some individuals may have about your presence in their educational setting.

REEXAMINING THE QUANTITATIVE PARENT INVOLVEMENT STUDY

We can turn to the parent involvement study (Deslandes & Bertrand, 2005) to see data collection procedures in action. Examine once again the authors' "Method" section (Paragraphs 14–24). We can assume that the authors had institutional review board consent letters signed from each of the parents they surveyed in Quebec. They may also have had permission from officials at the five public secondary schools they studied to obtain the names of the parents of children attending the schools.

The authors do not indicate in their method discussion the sampling strategy used to select the parents (see Paragraph 14). We do know that they selected schools representative of the general Quebec population and then identified 770 parents of students in seventh, eighth, and ninth grades. This procedure would illustrate multistage sampling. We do not know if the parents represented the entire population of parents or a sample of the parents. We also do not know if the parents were selected randomly or nonrandomly. In terms of the data they reported (see Table 3 and their limitation, Paragraph 46), the actual number of parents representative of each grade level was different, raising a question about whether these differences influenced the results in the study.

The authors then collected data from the parents on several instruments, including the Sharing the Dream! Parent Questionnaire, a questionnaire designed by other authors (see Paragraph 16), and demographic data (Paragraph 23). The questions on the instruments utilized a Likert-type scale that ranged from 1 (*disagree very strongly*) to 6 (*agree very strongly*) (see Paragraph 21, for example). They treated scores on these scales as interval-level scales and used parametric statistics to analyze the data. We do know that the authors selected these instruments to measure the concepts of the model of the parent involvement process. We do not have information about the validity of the scores from past uses of these instruments, although the authors checked for reliability (Cronbach alpha) of questions that would measure each of the factors in the study. We also do not have information about whether the researchers used standard procedures during their data collection or about the potential ethical issues that might have developed in the study.

KEY IDEAS IN THE CHAPTER

State the Five Steps in the Process of Quantitative Data Collection

The process of data collection involves more than simply gathering information; it includes five interrelated steps. It involves the steps of determining the participants to study, obtaining permissions needed from several individuals and organizations, considering what types of information to collect from several sources available to the quantitative research, locating and selecting instruments to use that will net good data for the study, and finally, administering the data collection process to collect data.

Identify How to Select Participants for a Study

The first step is to select participants for the study. This selection involves specifying the population and sample, determining how you will choose the participants, and deciding on an appropriate sample size.

Identify the Permissions Needed for a Study

The second step is to obtain permission from the participants to be involved in your study. Permissions may be needed from leaders of institutions or organizations, individuals at specific sites, participants (and their parents, for minor children), and a campus institutional review board.

List Different Options for Collecting Information

The third step is to decide what type or types of data to collect. This decision begins with specifying the variables in your research questions or hypotheses, defining these variables, and seeking measures that operationalize these definitions. Typical quantitative data consists of measures of performance and attitudes, observations of behavior, and records and documents.

Locate, Select, and Assess an Instrument(s) for Use in Data Collection

The fourth step is to locate, modify, or develop instruments that provide these measures. The easiest procedure is to use an existing instrument or modify one rather than develop your own instrument. Procedures exist for searching for an instrument, and when you find one that may be satisfactory, consider whether scores from past uses of it are reliable and valid, whether the procedure for recording information fits your research questions/hypotheses, and whether the scales will measure either categorical or continuous data.

Describe Procedures for Administering Quantitative Data Collection

The final step involves actually collecting the data. Your procedures need to be standard so that there is a uniform procedure for data collection. Also, as with all phases in research, the data collection process needs to be conducted in a way that is ethical to individuals and to research sites.

USEFUL INFORMATION FOR PRODUCERS OF RESEARCH

- ◆ When collecting data for a study, plan to engage in five steps: selecting participants, obtaining permissions, selecting types of data, identifying instruments, and administering data collection.
- ◆ Identify the population and sample for a study. There are several types of probability and nonprobability sampling. The most rigorous sampling will be simple random sampling. However, the research circumstances may dictate a form of nonprobability sampling.

- ◆ Select as large a sample as possible. Use sampling formulas to be systematic in selecting the size of the sample.
- ◆ Obtain permission to conduct a study. A research study often requires multiple levels of permission, ranging from campus institutional review boards to organizational and site leaders to individual participants. The process of seeking approval from a campus institutional review board may consist of several steps.
- ◆ Consider the provisions that need to be included in a consent form, such as that shown in Figure 5.4.
- ◆ Consider how the research questions or hypotheses will be answered when deciding on what data type(s) to use. Then identify your variables, operationally define them, and select measures (e.g., performance and attitudes, observations of behavior, and factual and personal data) that fit the operational definitions.
- ◆ Decide whether to develop your own instrument or to use or modify an existing instrument for your research. Locating instruments is the easiest choice, and several library references provide good access to them.
- ◆ Consider the types of scales you plan to use on your instruments. These scales will affect the types of statistics to be used in analyzing the data. Make sure they relate to your questions.
- ◆ Before deciding on an instrument to use, make sure that the scores from past uses of it are reliable and valid. There are several forms of reliability and of validity.
- ◆ Determine whether the administration procedure will provide self-reported data or researcher-reported data. This will depend on the type of data to be collected.

USEFUL INFORMATION FOR CONSUMERS OF RESEARCH

- ◆ In evaluating a study, determine if the researcher fully disclosed the data collection. Look in the "Method" section for information about data collection.
- ◆ Look for studies in which researchers use the most rigorous form of sampling—simple random, probabilistic sampling.
- ◆ A rigorous quantitative study often requires multiple types of quantitative data. A research study should provide detailed information about each and all forms of data collected during the investigation.
- ◆ If researchers use instruments in their data collection, they need to report whether the scores from the past use of instruments are both valid and reliable. Look for high, positive coefficients (e.g., .6 or above).

UNDERSTANDING CONCEPTS AND EVALUATING RESEARCH STUDIES

1. Consider the parent involvement study (Deslandes & Bertrand, 2005). In Paragraph 18, the authors mention that they formed a variable (or construct) on parents' role construction that comprised 10 items with an alpha = .72. Explain what type of reliability they may have used and what it means.
2. If the authors of the parent involvement study (Deslandes & Bertrand, 2005) had mentioned the permissions they might have obtained, who would they cite as providing permission for them to conduct the study in the five schools?
3. Assume you seek to measure the variable of parents' role construction (as did the authors in the parent involvement study). Describe the process you would go through to locate an instrument that might measure this variable.

4. Suppose you are assisting Maria with the design of her study. Discuss the five steps of quantitative data collection and identify the decisions that she needs to make to answer her quantitative research questions.

CONDUCTING YOUR RESEARCH

Design a quantitative data collection procedure for a study of your choice. Specify the population and sample, the permissions that you will need, the types of quantitative information you will collect, whether you will develop or locate an instrument, the criteria you will set for your instrument, and the administration procedures that will ensure standardization and ethical practices.

Go to the Topics "Selecting a Sample" and "Selecting Measuring Instruments" in the MyEducationLab (**www.myeducationlab.com**) for your course, where you can:

- Find learning outcomes for "Selecting a Sample" and "Selecting Measuring Instruments."
- Complete Assignments and Activities that can help you more deeply understand the chapter content.
- Apply and practice your understanding of the core skills identified in the chapter with the Building Research Skills exercises.
- Check your comprehension of the content covered in the chapter by going to the Study Plan. Here you will be able to take a pretest, receive feedback on your answers, and then access Review, Practice, and Enrichment activities to enhance your understanding. You can then complete a final posttest.

Analyzing and Interpreting Quantitative Data

*S*tatistics can be challenging. However, calculating statistics is only one step in the process of analyzing data. Analysis also involves preparing your data for analysis, running the analysis, reporting results, and discussing them.

By the end of this chapter, you should be able to:

◆ Identify the steps in the process of analyzing and interpreting quantitative data.
◆ Describe the process of preparing your data for analysis.
◆ Identify the procedures for analyzing your data.
◆ Learn how to report the results of analyzing your data.
◆ Describe how to interpret the results.

Maria has always struggled with math. So when she needs to analyze the data from her questionnaire, she wonders, *Will I be able to analyze my data?* She visits with her introductory statistics professor to learn how to proceed. She expects her professor to talk about what statistics Maria will use. Instead, the professor asks these questions: *How do you plan to organize your data before you analyze it? What questions do you hope to answer with your data analysis? How will you present your results in your paper? How will you structure the interpretation of your results?* Maria now realizes that data analysis consists of several steps.

WHAT ARE THE STEPS IN THE PROCESS OF QUANTITATIVE DATA ANALYSIS?

There are several interrelated steps used in the process of analyzing quantitative data. The first step is to prepare the data for analysis. This involves determining how to assign numeric scores to the data, assessing the types of scores to use, selecting a statistical program, and inputting the data into a program, and then cleaning up the database for analysis. The second step begins the data analysis. Typically you conduct a descriptive analysis of the data reporting measures of central tendency and variation. Then you conduct more sophisticated inferential analysis to test hypotheses and you examine confidence intervals and effect sizes. The next step is to report the results that are found using tables, figures, and a discussion of the key results. Finally, you interpret the results from the data analysis. This consists of summarizing the results, comparing the results with past literature and theories, advancing the limitations of the study, and ending with suggestions for future research.

HOW DO YOU PREPARE THE DATA FOR ANALYSIS?

The first step for you will be to organize data for analysis. **Preparing and organizing data for analysis** in quantitative research consists of scoring the data and creating a codebook, determining the types of scores to use, selecting a computer program, inputting the data into the program for analysis, and clearing the data.

Score the Data

When you collect data on an instrument or a checklist, you will need some system for scoring the data. **Scoring data** means that the researcher assigns a numeric score (or value) to each response category for each question on the instruments used to collect data.

For instance, assume that parents respond to a survey asking them to indicate their attitudes about choice of a school for children in the school district. One question might be:

Please check the appropriate response to this statement:

"Students should be given an opportunity to select a school of their choice."

_____ Strongly agree
_____ Agree
_____ Undecided
_____ Disagree
_____ Strongly disagree

Assume that a parent checks "Agree." What numeric score would you assign to the response so that you will assign the same score to each person who checks "Agree"? To analyze the data, you will need to assign scores to responses such as 5 = strongly agree, 4 = agree, 3 = undecided, 2 = disagree, and 1 = strongly disagree. Based on these assigned numbers, the parent who checks "Agree" would receive a score of 4.

Several guidelines can help in assigning numbers to response options:

◆ For continuous scales (such as interval scales), you should consistently score each question in this scale using the same numbering system. In the above example, you should consistently score a scale such as "Strongly agree" to "Strongly disagree" as a "5" to a "1."

◆ For categorical scales such as "What level do you teach? _____ high school, _____ middle school, _____ elementary," you can arbitrarily assign numbers that make sense, such as 3 = high school, 2 = middle school, and 1 = elementary. A good rule to follow, however, is that the more positive the response or the higher or more advanced the categories of information, the higher the assigned number.

◆ To make scoring easy, you can preassign numbers on the instrument to each response option, such as in this example:

Please respond to this question:

"Fourth graders should be tested for math proficiency."

_____ (5) Strongly agree
_____ (4) Agree
_____ (3) Undecided
_____ (2) Disagree
_____ (1) Strongly disagree

Here you can see that the numbers are already preassigned and you know how to score each response. Sometimes you can have participants fill in circles for responses on "bubble sheets" such as those used to aid in scoring when evaluating teachers in college classrooms. When students darken circles on these sheets, you can optically scan their responses for analysis. If you use a commercially available instrument, the company will often supply scoring manuals to describe how to score the instrument.

◆ One procedure that can aid you in assigning scores to responses is to create a codebook. A **codebook** is a list of variables or questions that indicates how the researcher will code or score responses from instruments or checklists. An example of a codebook is shown in Figure 6.1. Notice that each variable is given a name (i.e., Grade), a brief definition of the variable (i.e., grade level of the student) is given, and numbers are assigned to each response option (i.e., 10 = 10th grade, 11 = 11th grade, 12 = 12th grade).

FIGURE 6.1

Codebook for High School Smoking Project

Variable 1.   ID—identification number assigned to each student, from 1–50

Variable 2.   Gender—sex of the student; 1 = Male, 2 = Female

Variable 3.   Grade—grade level of the student; 10 = 10th grade, 11 = 11th grade, 12 = 12th grade

Variable 4.   Parents—parents' marital status; 1 = married, 2 = divorced, 3 = separated

Variable 5.   Smoke—whether the student smokes or not; 1 = no; 2 = yes

Variable 6.   Chewer—whether student chews tobacco; 1 = no; 2 = yes

Variable 7.   Ability—academic ability based on grade point average last semester; 1 = below 2.0; 2 = 2.0–2.9; 3 = 3.0–3.5; 4 = 3.6–4.0

Variable 8.   Peers—peer group student most closely identifies with at school; 1 = athletes; 2 = singers; 3 = punkers; 4 = other

Variable 9.   Depression—total depression score for all items on an instrument measuring depression; scores from 20 to 100

Determine the Types of Scores to Analyze

Look again at Figure 6.1. Variable 9, Depression, consists of a score based on adding all items on an instrument. Before conducting an analysis of scores, researchers consider what types of scores to use from their instruments. This is important because the type of score will affect how you enter data into a computer file for analysis.

Table 6.1 presents three types of scores for six students: single-item scores, summed scores on a scale, and net or difference scores.

Single-Item Scores

For a research study, you may wish to examine a single-item score. A **single-item score** is an individual score assigned to each question for each participant in your study. These scores provide a detailed analysis of each person's response to each question on an instrument. In one study, researchers asked individuals at a local school district meeting,

---

TABLE 6.1

Types of Scores Used in Quantitative Analysis

	Single-Item Scores*		
	Question 1 Score	Question 2 Score	Question 3 Score
Jane	5	4	3
Jim	4	3	4
John	2	1	2
Jean	4	5	4
Julie	4	3	4
Johanna	5	4	5

	Summed Score or Scale*					
	Question 1	Question 2	Question 3	Question 4	Question 5	Summed Scores
Jane	5	4	3	4	4	20
Jim	4	3	4	4	3	18
John	2	1	2	2	3	10

	Net or Difference Scores		
	Pretest Math Score	Posttest Math Score	Net-Difference Score
Jane	80	85	+5
Jim	76	77	+1
John	65	75	+10
Jean	95	97	+2
Julie	91	94	+3
Johanna	93	95	+2

*Question response scale is 5 = strongly agree; 4 = agree; 3 = undecided; 2 = disagree; and 1 = strongly disagree.

"Will you vote yes or no for the tax levy in the election next Tuesday?" In scoring the data, the researcher would assign a value of 1 to a "no" response and a value of 2 to a "yes" response and have a record of how each individual responded to each question. In Table 6.1, all six participants have individual scores for questions 1, 2, and 3.

Summed Scores

In other cases, we may need to sum responses to all of the questions on the instrument, such as in the response scale scores of Table 6.1. This summing occurs because individual items may not completely capture a participant's perspective. Also, participants may misunderstand a single question or the author may have worded the question so that it biases results. In short, responses to single questions may not be reliable and may not accurately reflect an individual's score. One solution to these problems is to form scales based on responses to single questions. **Summed scores** are the scores of an individual added over several questions that measure the same variable. Researchers add the individual items to compute an overall score for a variable. As shown in Table 6.1, the three participants—Jane, Jim, and John—have provided responses to five questions. The researcher sums scores for each individual to provide a single score for a variable representing all five questions.

Difference Scores

Summed scores for individuals are used to develop an overall test score that can be compared from one time period to another. **Net or difference scores** are scores in a quantitative study that represent a difference or change for each individual. Some gains may be more meaningful than others. A small change in high scores may be more useful than a larger change in small scores. For example, the small gain in moving from 98 to 99 on a 100-point scale may be more meaningful than the large change of going from 46 to 66 on the same scale. In experiments, researchers often gather scores on instruments before the study begins (Time 1) and after it ends (Time 2). The researcher collects these scores on pretests and posttests, which are typical measures collected during experimental research. In Table 6.1, for each of the 6 participants, we see a pretest math score, a summed score over all items on the test before a unit on math is taught. We also see for each participant a posttest math score, a summed score at the end of the unit that represents the overall score on a final test. The net score shows how each participant's performance improved, in all six cases, between the pre- and posttest.

Select a Statistical Program

After scoring the data, researchers select a computer program to analyze their data. Academic researchers generally use statistical programs available as software programs for desktops or laptops, or available on campus computers. The hardest part is deciding which software package to use. Here are some guidelines to follow when selecting a statistical program. (See Leedy & Ormrod, 2001, for additional suggestions.)

◆ Find a program with documentation about how to use the program. Programs often have tutorials so that you can easily learn the key features and practice them using sample data sets. Free tutorials are often available from Web sites.

◆ Ease of use is an important factor when selecting a program. Pull-down menus and easy data entry make a program easy to use.

◆ Look for a program that includes the types of statistics that you will use to answer your research questions and hypotheses.

◆ Make sure that the program can analyze the amount of data in your database. Consider how many participants and the maximum number of variables that you will need in your analysis. A program should adequately accommodate missing data and provide some provisions for handling the situation where some data are missing for a participant. Look for a program that has flexibility for data handling, can read data in many formats (e.g., numbers and letters), and can read files imported from spreadsheets or databases.

◆ Locate a program with the capability to output graphs and tables that you can use in your research reports.

◆ If you need to purchase the software program, weigh the costs of the various programs. Student versions of programs are available (although they may have limited statistical tests) at minimal cost.

◆ Select a program that your campus uses so that you can find assistance to answer questions when they arise. Some programs may provide technical support to help answer questions, but it may be time-consuming and costly.

With these criteria in mind, what are the most frequently used statistical programs available? Web sites contain detailed information about the various statistical analysis computer programs available. Some of the more frequently used programs are:

◆ *Minitab 16* (**www.minitab.com**).   This is an interactive software statistical package available from Minitab Inc., 1829 Pine Hall Rd, State College, PA 16801–3008.

◆ *JMP* (**www.jmp.com**).   This is a popular software program available from SAS Institute, Inc., 100 SAS Campus Drive, Cary, NC 27513–2414.

◆ *SYSTAT* (**www.systat.com**).   This is a comprehensive interactive statistical package available from Systat Software, Inc., 225 W. Washington St., Suite 425, Chicago, IL 60606.

◆ *SAS* (**www.sas.com**).   This is a statistical program with tools as an integral component of the SAS system of products available from SAS Institute, Inc., 100 SAS Campus Drive, Cary, NC 27513–2414.

◆ *Statistical Package for the Social Sciences (SPSS) Student Version 11.0 for Windows and Version 6.0 for Macintosh* (**www.spss.com**).   This is an affordable, professional analysis program for students based on the professional version of the program, available from SPSS Science, Inc., 233 S. Wacker Drive, 11th Floor, Chicago, IL 60606–6307.

There are various online programs useful in simulating statistical concepts for statistical instruction. One example is the Rice Virtual Lab in Statistics found at **http://online statbook.com/rvls.html**. Another is SAS Simulation Studio for JMP (**www.jmp.com**) which harnesses the power of simulation to model and analyze critical operational systems like these in such areas as health care, manufacturing, and transportation. The graphical user interface in SAS Simulation Studio for JMP requires no programming and provides a full set of tools for building, executing, and analyzing results of simulation models.

Input Data

After choosing a statistical program, your next step is to enter the data from your instruments or checklists into the computer program. **Inputting the data** occurs when the researcher transfers the data from the responses on instruments to a computer file for analysis. For those new to this process, this grid is similar to a spreadsheet table used in many popular software packages (e.g., Excel). Table 6.2 shows a small database for 50 high school students participating in a study on tobacco use in schools. You have already seen the variables in this database in the codebook presented in Figure 6.1. A close inspection of Table 6.2 shows that the grid contains cells in rows and columns into which the researcher inputs data for analysis. You see displayed in the first column the number of each participant followed by an ID number assigned to each of the 50 students. In the other columns are variables that the researcher is measuring (i.e., gender, grade, parents, and so forth). Using the codebook, the researcher assigns a number to each response that

TABLE 6.2

Sample Data Grid for Inputting Information

	id	gender	grade	parents	smoke	chewer	ability	peers	depression
1	1.00	1.00	10.00	1.00	1.00	2.00	1.00	2.00	70.00
2	2.00	1.00	11.00	1.00	1.00	2.00	3.00	1.00	75.00
3	3.00	2.00	12.00	2.00	2.00	1.00	2.00	3.00	80.00
4	4.00	1.00	11.00	3.00	2.00	1.00	4.00	2.00	75.00
5	5.00	2.00	10.00	3.00	1.00	1.00	3.00	4.00	60.00
6	6.00	2.00	12.00	2.00	1.00	1.00	2.00	4.00	70.00
7	7.00	2.00	12.00	1.00	1.00	1.00	1.00	3.00	75.00
8	8.00	1.00	11.00	2.00	2.00	1.00	4.00	2.00	78.00
9	9.00	2.00	11.00	2.00	2.00	2.00	3.00	1.00	81.00
10	10.00	2.00	10.00	3.00	1.00	1.00	3.00	2.00	60.00
11	11.00	1.00	11.00	3.00	2.00	1.00	4.00	3.00	75.00
12	12.00	2.00	12.00	2.00	1.00	1.00	2.00	1.00	76.00
13	13.00	1.00	10.00	1.00	2.00	1.00	4.00	4.00	81.00
14	14.00	2.00	10.00	3.00	1.00	1.00	3.00	4.00	76.00
15	15.00	1.00	12.00	2.00	2.00	2.00	3.00	3.00	84.00
16	16.00	2.00	12.00	1.00	1.00	1.00	3.00	3.00	78.00
17	17.00	2.00	11.00	2.00	2.00	1.00	2.00	2.00	80.00
18	18.00	1.00	11.00	3.00	1.00	1.00	1.00	2.00	70.00
19	19.00	2.00	10.00	1.00	2.00	1.00	2.00	1.00	82.00
20	20.00	2.00	11.00	1.00	1.00	1.00	3.00	1.00	70.00
21	21.00	1.00	12.00	1.00	2.00	1.00	4.00	4.00	85.00
22	22.00	1.00	10.00	2.00	2.00	2.00	3.00	2.00	70.00
23	23.00	2.00	11.00	2.00	2.00	1.00	2.00	3.00	75.00
24	24.00	1.00	12.00	1.00	2.00	2.00	3.00	1.00	80.00
25	25.00	2.00	10.00	2.00	2.00	2.00	1.00	2.00	76.00
26	26.00	1.00	11.00	1.00	2.00	1.00	2.00	3.00	82.00
27	27.00	2.00	11.00	2.00	2.00	1.00	4.00	1.00	79.00
28	28.00	1.00	12.00	1.00	2.00	1.00	2.00	2.00	81.00
29	29.00	2.00	12.00	2.00	2.00	1.00	3.00	3.00	75.00
30	30.00	1.00	10.00	2.00	1.00	1.00	3.00	1.00	68.00
31	31.00	2.00	10.00	1.00	1.00	1.00	3.00	2.00	60.00
32	32.00	1.00	12.00	2.00	1.00	2.00	1.00	4.00	61.00
33	33.00	2.00	11.00	1.00	1.00	1.00	1.00	3.00	76.00
34	34.00	1.00	12.00	2.00	1.00	1.00	2.00	2.00	88.00
35	35.00	2.00	12.00	1.00	1.00	1.00	4.00	1.00	70.00
36	36.00	2.00	12.00	2.00	1.00	1.00	4.00	3.00	71.00
37	37.00	2.00	10.00	1.00	1.00	1.00	4.00	4.00	78.00
38	38.00	1.00	10.00	2.00	1.00	1.00	3.00	1.00	69.00
39	39.00	1.00	10.00	1.00	2.00	1.00	3.00	4.00	82.00
40	40.00	1.00	10.00	2.00	2.00	1.00	3.00	4.00	84.00
41	41.00	2.00	12.00	1.00	1.00	1.00	2.00	3.00	75.00
42	42.00	1.00	12.00	3.00	2.00	2.00	2.00	2.00	79.00
43	43.00	2.00	11.00	3.00	1.00	2.00	1.00	1.00	68.00
44	44.00	1.00	12.00	1.00	2.00	2.00	2.00	4.00	88.00
45	45.00	2.00	11.00	2.00	2.00	1.00	3.00	3.00	81.00
46	46.00	1.00	12.00	2.00	2.00	1.00	4.00	2.00	82.00
47	47.00	2.00	11.00	1.00	1.00	1.00	2.00	1.00	70.00
48	48.00	1.00	12.00	1.00	1.00	1.00	4.00	4.00	70.00
49	49.00	2.00	10.00	1.00	1.00	1.00	3.00	3.00	65.00
50	50.00	1.00	11.00	1.00	1.00	1.00	1.00	2.00	57.00

Gender: 1 = male; 2 = female
Grade: 10 = 10th grade; 11 = 11th grade; 12 = 12th grade
Parents: Parent status 1 = married; 2 = divorced; 3 = separated
Smoke: Do you smoke cigarettes? 1 = no; 2 = yes
Chewer: Do you chew tobacco? 1 = no; 2 = yes
Ability (academic, based on grade point average in last semester): 1 = below 2.0; 2 = 2.1–2.9; 3 = 3.0–3.5; 4 = 3.6–4.0
Peers (peer group student most closely identifies with at school): 1 = athletes; 2 = singers; 3 = punkers; 4 = other
Depression = total score on an instrument measuring depression (scores from 20 to 100)

reflects a score on each variable. At the bottom of the sheet is coding information (found in the codebook) that provides an association between the numbers and the responses on the instrument. The names for the variables are short and simple but descriptive (no more than eight characters in SPSS, such as "gender," "smoke," or "chewer").

The actual process of inputting data into this grid (George & Mallery, 2001) to create an SPSS database is as follows:

◆ Enter the data from scores on the instruments in the cells of the grid by selecting a cell and typing the appropriate value. Enter the data by rows for each individual and use the columns for the values of each variable. **Values** are the numbers assigned to response options for a variable (e.g., 1 = male, 2 = female).

◆ Assign an identification number to each participant and place this number in the first column or use the predetermined numbers assigned in column 1 by SPSS (i.e., 001, 002, 003, or 343, 344, 345). Your own numbers may reflect the last three digits in the individual's social security number (e.g., 343, 344, 345) or some other identifying number.

◆ In SPSS, you will see column heads listed as variables: var001, var002, var003, and so forth. Rather than use these headers, replace them with names of your variables (e.g., "var002" could be replaced by "gender").

◆ You can also assign names to both values and variables so that your printout contains these names and provides an easy way to identify your information. You can assign names to your variables, such as "parents," as well as values for this variable, such as "married," "divorced," and "separated."

Clean and Account for Missing Data

After entering data into the computer grid, you need to determine if there are errors in the data or missing data. Errors occur when participants in your study provide scores outside the range for variables or you input wrong numbers into the data grid. Missing data may result when instrument data is lost, individuals skip questions, participants are absent when you collect observational data, or individuals refuse to complete a sensitive question. For ethical reasons, you report how you handled missing data so that readers can accurately interpret the results (George & Mallery, 2001). Because these problems may occur, you need to clean the data and decide how to treat missing data.

Cleaning the Database

Cleaning the data is the process of inspecting the data for scores (or values) that are outside the accepted range. One way to accomplish this is by visually inspecting the data grid. For large databases, a frequency distribution (discussed shortly) will provide the range of scores to detect responses outside of acceptable ranges. For example, participants may provide a "6" for a "strongly agree" to "strongly disagree" scale when there are only five response options. Alternatively, the researcher might type a score for a participant as "3" for gender, when the only legitimate values are "1" for females and "2" for males.

Another procedure is to use SPSS and have the program "sort cases" in ascending order for each variable. This process arranges the values of a variable from the smallest number to the largest, enabling you to easily spot out-of-range or misnumbered cases. Whatever the procedure, a visual inspection of data helps to clean the data and free it from visible errors before you begin the data analysis.

Assessing the Database for Missing Data

You need to examine your database for missing data. Missing data will yield fewer individuals to be included in the data analysis, and because we want as many people included in the analysis as possible, you need to correct as much as possible for missing data. **Missing data** are data missing in the database because participants do not supply it.

How should you handle missing data? The most obvious approach is to have a good instrument that individuals want to complete and are capable of answering so that missing data will not occur. In some research situations, you can contact individuals to determine why they did not respond. When individuals do not respond, something is wrong with your data collection, which may indicate faulty planning in your design.

You can expect, however, that questions will be omitted or some participants will not supply information, for whatever reason. In this case, you have a couple of options:

◆ You can eliminate participants with missing scores from the data analysis and include only those participants for which complete data exist. This practice, in effect, may severely reduce the number of overall participants for data analysis.

◆ You can substitute numbers for missing data in the database for individuals. When the variable is categorical, this means substituting a value, such as "−9," for all missing values in the data grid. When the variable is continuous (i.e., based on an interval scale), the process is more complex. Using SPSS, the researcher can have the computer program substitute a value for each missing score, such as an average number for the question for all study participants. You can substitute up to 15% of the missing data with scores without altering the overall statistical findings (George & Mallery, 2001). More advanced statistical procedures are also available for identifying substitute numbers for missing data (see Gall, Borg, & Gall, 1996).

HOW DO YOU ANALYZE THE DATA?

After you prepare and organize the data, you are ready to analyze it. You analyze the data to address each one of your research questions or hypotheses. Questions or hypotheses in quantitative research require that you:

◆ Describe trends in the data to a single variable or question on your instrument (e.g., "What is the self-esteem of middle school students?"). To answer this question, we need **Descriptive Statistics** that indicate general tendencies in the data (mean, mode, median), the spread of scores (variance, standard deviation, and range), or a comparison of how one score relates to all others (z scores, percentile rank). We might seek to describe any of our variables: independent, dependent, control, or mediating.

◆ Compare two or more groups on the independent variable in terms of the dependent variable (e.g., "How do boys and girls compare in their self-esteem?"). To answer this question, we need **inferential statistics** in which we analyze data from a sample to draw conclusions about an unknown population. We assess whether the differences of groups (their means) or the relationship among variables is much greater or less than what we would expect for the total population, if we could study the entire population.

◆ Relate two or more variables (e.g., "Does self-esteem relate to an optimistic attitude?"). To answer this question, we also use inferential statistics.

◆ Test hypotheses about the differences in the groups or the relationships of variables (e.g., "Boys have higher self-esteem than girls" or "Self-esteem predicts an optimistic attitude among middle school children"). To answer either of these questions, inferential statistics are also used.

Thus, we describe results to a single variable or question or we infer results from a sample to a population. In all quantitative research questions or hypotheses, we study individuals sampled from a population. However, in descriptive questions, we study only a single variable one at a time; in inferential analysis, we analyze multiple variables at the same time. Also from comparing groups or relating variables, we can make predictions about the variables. We can test hypotheses that make predictions comparing groups or relating variables.

Conduct Descriptive Analysis

How do we analyze the data to describe trends? You use **statistics**, the calculations of values based on numbers. Many helpful books provide details about different statistics, their computation, and assumptions (e.g., Abelson, 1995; Gravetter & Wallnau, 2007; Wright, 1997). We focus here on the statistics typically used in educational research.

Choosing a Descriptive Statistics Test

Descriptive statistics will help you summarize the overall trends or tendencies in your data, provide an understanding of how varied your scores might be, and provide insight into where one score stands in comparison with others. These three ideas are the central tendency, variability, and relative standing. Figure 6.2 portrays the statistical procedures that you can use to provide this information.

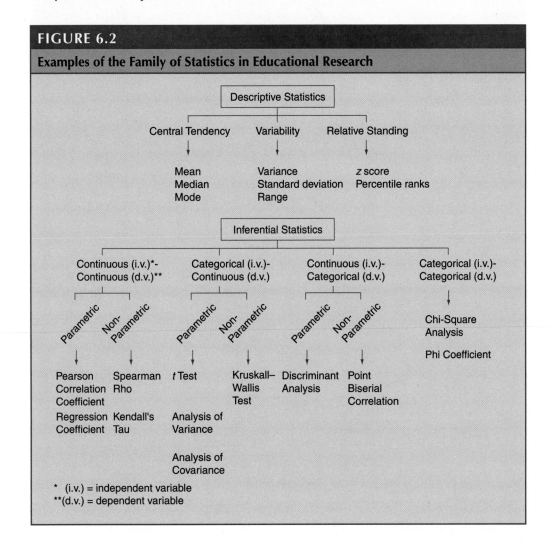

FIGURE 6.2

Examples of the Family of Statistics in Educational Research

Measures of Central Tendency   **Measures of central tendency** are summary numbers that represent a single value in a distribution of scores (Vogt, 2005). They are expressed as an average score (the mean), the middle of a set of scores (the median), or the most frequently occurring score (the mode). In quantitative studies, researchers typically report all three measures. Table 6.3 portrays the differences between the three measures of central tendency for 10 students for whom we have depression scores.

The mean is the most popular statistic used to describe responses of all participants to items on an instrument. A **mean** (*M*) is the total of the scores divided by the number of scores. To calculate the mean, you sum all of the scores and then divide the sum by the number of scores. In Table 6.3, you would divide the sum of 818 by 10 to get a mean of 81.80. In calculating other types of scores for other advanced statistics, the mean plays an important role. Notice that the scores in Table 6.3 are continuous and report a sample of 10 scores for depression. The mean gives us an average for all of the scores.

TABLE 6.3

Descriptive Statistics for Depression Scores

Raw Scores	z Score	Rank
60	−1.57	10.0
64	−1.28	20.0
75	− .49	30.0
76	− .42	50.0
76	− .42	50.0
83	+ .09	60.0
93	+ .81	70.0
94	+ .92	80.0
98	+1.22	90.0
99	+1.24	100.0

Sum = 818

Mode (76)

Median (79.5)

Mean (81.8)

$$\text{Variance } (SD^2) = \sum \frac{(\text{raw score} - M)^2}{N}$$

Variance = 173.96

Standard deviation $(SD) = \sqrt{\text{variance}}$

Standard deviation = 13.18

z score = raw score − mean/SD

Range: minimum = 60; maximum = 99

We may want to know the middle score among all scores. This score is the median. The **median** score divides the scores, rank-ordered from top to bottom, in half. Fifty percent of the scores lie above the median and 50% lie below the median. To calculate this score, the researcher arrays all scores in rank order and then determines what score, the median, is halfway between all of the scores. The median in Table 6.3 is halfway between 76 and 83, giving 79.5. There are five scores above 79.5 and five scores below it. Researchers often report the median score, but the score's usefulness is limited.

However, the mode provides useful information. The **mode** is the score that appears most frequently in a list of scores. It is used when researchers want to know the most common score in an array of scores on a variable. In Table 6.3, the most frequently reported score was 76, and it was a score for 2 people in the sample of 10. Researchers use the mode for reporting variables with categorical variables. Examine Table 6.4. Here is a categorical variable about the peer group affiliation of students. From looking at this table we can see that the "singers" were more numerous than any other group ($N = 14$). The mode would be the "singers" because they are represented more than any other category. Reporting the mean would report meaningless information. If we assigned numbers to each group (athletes = 4, singers = 3, punkers = 2, and other = 1) and calculated a mean score, $137/50 = 2.74$, it would not mean anything because no group is assigned this number. Thus, when we have categorical information, the mode reports meaningful information but the mean does not.

TABLE 6.4

Descriptive Statistics for the Categorical Variable, "Peer Group Affiliation"

		Peer Group Affiliation			
		Frequency	Percent	Valid Percent	Cumulative Percent
Valid	Athletes	12	24.0	24.0	24.0
	Singers	14	28.0	28.0	52.0
	Punkers	13	26.0	26.0	78.0
	Other	11	22.0	22.0	100.0
	Total	50	100.0	100.0	

Measures of Variability   Variability indicates the spread of the scores in a distribution. Range, variance, and standard deviation all indicate the amount of variability in a distribution of scores. This information helps us see how dispersed the responses are to items on an instrument. Variability also plays an important role in many advanced statistical calculations.

We can see how variable the scores are by looking at the range of scores. The **range of scores** is the difference between the highest and the lowest scores to items on an instrument. In Table 6.3, we see that the scores range from a low of 60 to a high of 99, a range of 39 points.

The **variance** indicates the dispersion of scores around the mean. To calculate this score is easy:

◆ Find the difference between the mean and the raw score for each individual.
◆ Square this value for each individual.
◆ Sum these squared scores for all individuals.
◆ Divide by the total number of individuals.

In our example, Table 6.3, the variance equals 173.96. This information, by itself, does not mean much, but it is a useful number when calculating statistics that are more advanced. The square root of the variance, the **standard deviation (SD)**, does provide useful information, and we look at it as an indicator of the dispersion or spread of the scores. In Table 6.3, the standard deviation is 13.90. If the scores had a standard deviation of 7.30, we would say that the variation around the mean is less than if the standard deviation is 13.18.

The meaning of the standard deviation becomes evident when we graph a theoretical distribution of scores, as shown in Figure 6.3. If we collected sample after sample of scores and plotted them on a graph, they would look like a bell-shaped curve as shown in Figure 6.3. This is called a **normal distribution or normal probability curve**. In reality, the actual scores may not simulate the normal distribution (e.g., a distribution of salaries), but if we plotted the means of many samples, a normal curve would result. If, for example, we generated 5,000 random samples and calculated a mean salary for each sample, then plotted these 5,000 means, the distribution would reflect a normal distribution. Looking again at Figure 6.3, the shaded areas indicate the percentage of scores likely to fall within each standard deviation from the mean. For example, 68% of the scores fall between +1 (34%) and −1 (34%) standard deviations from the mean:

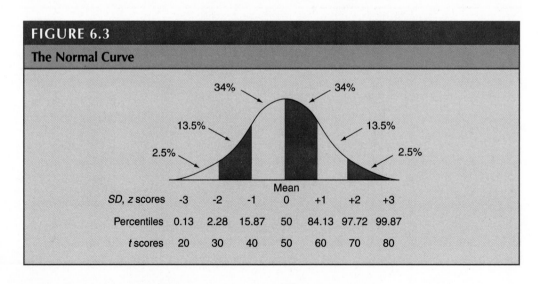

FIGURE 6.3

The Normal Curve

95% between +2 (13.5% + 34%) and −2 (13.5% + 34%). You can also associate percentile scores, *z* scores, and *t* scores with each standard deviation.

Percentiles provide another type of descriptive statistic. **Measures of relative standing** are statistics that describe one score relative to a group of scores. In Figure 6.3, 2.28% of the scores fall more than two standard deviations below the mean, and 97.72% of the scores are below the value two standard deviations above the mean. Knowing where a score falls in this distribution is a key factor in testing hypotheses. Two frequently used statistics are the percentile rank and the *z* score.

A measure of relative standing is the percentile rank. A **percentile rank** of a particular score is the percentage of participants in the distribution with scores at or below a particular score. You use it to determine where in a distribution of scores an individual's score lies in comparison with other scores. In Table 6.3, we see that an individual with a score of 94 is at the 80th percentile, with 20% of the participants having scores above this individual, and 80% of the participants having scores at or below this individual.

Another measure of relative standing is the standard score. A **standard score** is a calculated score that enables a researcher to compare scores from different scales. It involves the transformation of a raw score into a score with relative meaning. A **z score** is a popular form of the standard score, and it has a mean of 0 and a standard deviation of 1. This yields a *z* score, or a standard score that has the advantage of enabling you to compare scores from one instrument to scores from another instrument. Using standardized scores is also central to calculating many statistics. The procedure is to take a score, subtract it from the mean, and divide it by the standard deviation. In Table 6.3, we see that a person with a score of 60 has a *z* score of −1.57, or a score that is more than one and a half standard deviations below the average (or mean).

Conduct Inferential Analysis

Descriptive statistics help you analyze descriptive questions. However, when you compare groups or relate two or more variables, inferential analysis comes into play. The basic idea is to look at scores from a sample and use the results to draw inferences or make predictions about the population. Often you cannot study the entire population because of size and cost, so we instead examine a sample that has been carefully chosen from the population.

When you study this sample and obtain scores, several approaches exist for determining if the sample scores you receive are a good estimate of the population scores (see Vogt, 2005). Ask yourself:

1. Is the sample score (e.g., the mean difference between two groups) probably a *wrong* estimate of the population mean? The procedure you use to examine this question is hypothesis testing. **Hypothesis testing** is a procedure for making decisions about results by comparing an observed value of a sample with a population value to determine if no difference or relationship exists between the values. This is the traditional way to test whether the sample mean is a good estimate of the population mean. It provides a yes–no answer: Either the sample mean is a good estimate or it is not. Because we can never absolutely prove that the sample is a good estimate, we try to establish whether it is a *wrong* estimate.

2. How confident are you that your sample score is right? This is the confidence interval approach. A **confidence interval or interval estimate** is the range of upper and lower statistical values that is consistent with observed data and is likely to contain the actual population mean. In this approach, you determine an interval or range in which your population score would likely fall. In this sense, confidence intervals give us more flexibility than the yes–no options of hypothesis testing.

3. Does the sample score or differences between two groups make practical sense? This is the effect size approach. **Effect size** is a means for identifying the practical strength of the conclusions about group differences or about the relationship among variables in a quantitative study. Effect sizes tell us how different the sample values are and allow us to make a judgment as to whether this is significant based on our knowledge of measures, the participants, and the data collection effort.

The reason we have more than one approach is that recently some researchers have felt that a yes–no hypothesis testing answer to our quantitative questions and hypotheses leads to misinterpretations and errors (Finch, Cumming, & Thomason, 2001). Confidence intervals and effect sizes provide a more practical reading of results. In reporting research today, it is useful to report all three estimates of your population: hypothesis testing, the confidence interval, and the effect size (Wilkinson & Task Force on Statistical Inference, 1999).

Hypothesis Testing

There are five steps in hypothesis testing: (a) identify a null and alternative hypothesis; (b) set the level of significance, or alpha level; (c) collect data; (d) compute the sample statistic; and (e) make a decision about rejecting or failing to reject the null hypothesis.

1. *Identify your null and alternative hypothesis.* The null hypothesis is a prediction about the population and is typically stated using the language of "no difference" (or "no relationship" or "no association"). The alternative hypothesis, however, indicates a difference (or relationship or association), and the direction of this difference may be positive or negative (alternative directional hypotheses) or *either* positive or negative (alternative nondirectional hypotheses).

Returning to the data for high school students in Table 6.2, you may state a null and alternative hypothesis as follows:

Null Hypothesis:
There is no difference between smokers and nonsmokers on depression scores.
Alternative Hypothesis (nondirectional and directional):
There is a difference between smokers and nonsmokers on depression scores.
  (Or, written another way):
Smokers are more depressed than nonsmokers.

2. *Set the level of significance, or alpha level, for rejecting the null hypothesis.* If we were to collect a large number of sample means, and if the null hypothesis is true ("no difference"), the theoretical distribution would approximate a normal or bell-shaped curve, as illustrated in Figure 6.4. In this figure, we see a normal curve illustrating the distribution of sample means of all possible outcomes if the null hypothesis is true. We would expect most of our sample means to fall in the center of the curve if the hypothesis is true, but a small number would fall at the extremes. In other words, we would expect to find that, for any sample of smokers and nonsmokers, their depression scores are similar, but in a small percentage of cases, you might actually find them to be different. As you can see, there are shaded areas at each end of this curve. We would expect there to be an extremely low probability that a score would fall within these areas.

A standard is needed for these low probability areas for precisely marking them on this curve. This is called setting a significance level. A **significance level (or alpha level)** is a probability level that reflects the maximum risk you are willing to take that any observed differences are due to chance. It is typically set at .01 (1 out of 100 times the sample score will be due to chance) or .05 (5 out of 100 times it will be due to chance). This means that 1 out of 100 times (or 5 out of 100 times) an extremely low probability value will actually be observed if the null hypothesis is true. In some situations, it is

FIGURE 6.4

The Normal Curve Distribution of Mean Differences of All Possible Outcomes if the Null Hypothesis Is True

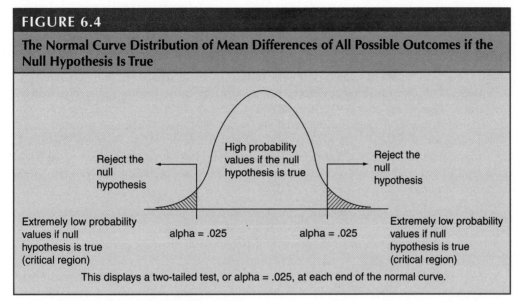

Reject the null hypothesis

High probability values if the null hypothesis is true

Reject the null hypothesis

Extremely low probability values if null hypothesis is true (critical region)

alpha = .025

alpha = .025

Extremely low probability values if null hypothesis is true (critical region)

This displays a two-tailed test, or alpha = .025, at each end of the normal curve.

Source: Adapted from Gravetter & Wallnau, 2007.

important to set the alpha level even stricter than .01 or .05. Assume that a researcher is testing the effects of a drug that has severe side effects. The alpha level might be set at a stricter level for rejection, say .001, if the drug might have damaging side effects for cancer patients rather than a less conservative level of .05 if the drug would have less damaging side effects for individuals with acne.

The area on the normal curve for low probability values if the null hypothesis is true is called the **critical region**. If sample data (i.e., the difference between smokers and nonsmokers on depression) falls into the critical region, the null hypothesis is rejected. This means that instead of "there is no difference" as stated in the null hypothesis, we find the alternative to probably be true: "there is a difference."

Also notice in Figure 6.4 that this critical region marked by a significance level occurs at *both* ends of the normal curve. When the critical region for rejection of the null hypothesis is divided into two areas at the tails of the sampling distribution, we have a **two-tailed test of significance** (Vogt, 2005). However, if we place the region at only one end for rejection of the null hypothesis, we have a **one-tailed test of significance**. You use one-tailed tests when previous research indicates a probable direction (e.g., a directional, alternative hypothesis). In contrast, a two-tailed test of significance is more conservative, or demanding, because the area of rejection at either end of the curve is less than that of a one-tailed test. We say that a one-tailed test has more power, which means that we are more likely to reject the null hypothesis.

3. *Collect data.* You collect data by administering an instrument or recording behaviors on a check sheet for participants. Then, as discussed earlier in this chapter, you code the data and input it into a computer file for analysis.

4. *Compute the sample statistic.* Next, using a computer program, you compute a statistic or p value and determine if it falls inside or outside of the critical region. A **p value** is the probability (p) that a result could have been produced by chance if the null hypothesis were true. After calculating the p value, we compare it with a value in a table located in the back of major statistics books (e.g., Gravetter & Wallnau, 2007) related to the statistical test by finding the value given our significant level (e.g., .01), whether our test is one tailed or two tailed, and the degrees of freedom for our statistical

test (or examine the printout for this value). **Degrees of freedom (df)** used in a statistical test is usually one less than the number of scores. For a sample of scores, $df = n-1$. The degrees of freedom establish the number of scores in a sample that are independent and free to vary because the sample mean places a restriction on sample variability. In a sample of scores, when the value of the mean is known, all scores but one can vary (i.e., be independent of each other and have any values), because one score is restricted by the sample mean (Gravetter & Wallnau, 2007).

The difficult part is determining what statistical test to use. Table 6.5 presents many of the common statistical tests used in educational research. Also, consult Appendix C for common statistical tests, their definition, and examples. Seven questions need to be answered to arrive at the appropriate statistical test (also see Rudestam & Newton, 1992, for similar criteria):

- *Do you plan to compare groups or relate variables in your hypotheses or research questions?*
- *How many independent variables do you have in one research question or hypothesis?*
- *How many dependent variables do you have in one research question or hypothesis?* Typically, researchers use only one dependent variable, or if multiple dependent variables are of interest, each variable is analyzed one by one.
- *Will you be statistically controlling for covariates in your analysis of the research question or hypothesis?*
- *How will your independent variable(s) be measured?* The type of measurement on scale possibilities are categorical (nominal and ordinal) and continuous (interval/ratio) scales.
- *How will your dependent variable(s) be measured?* As with your independent variables, identify whether the dependent variables are categorical or continuous variables.
- *Are the scores on your variables normally distributed; that is, could you assume a normal curve if the scores were plotted on a graph?* Certain statistics have been designed to work best with normally distributed data and others with nonnormally distributed data. (See appendix D for additional information about nonnormal distributions.)

Given these seven questions, what statistical test would you use to study these null hypotheses?

"*There is no difference between smokers and nonsmokers on depression scores.*"

"*There is no difference between smokers and nonsmokers and peer group affiliation.*"

For the first hypothesis, you would select a *t* test, and for the second, the chi-square statistic. Can you identify the decisions that went into selecting both tests based on the seven criteria?

5. *Make a decision about rejecting or failing to reject the null hypothesis.* Let's assume that you have now computed the statistical test for the two hypotheses using the data reported earlier in Table 6.2. Assume that you have used SPSS Version 14.0 and have printouts as shown in Table 6.6. In Table 6.6, you compare smokers and nonsmokers in terms of their scores on depression. The statistical test you computed was a *t*-test analysis and it indicated that the 26 nonsmokers have a mean of 69.77 on the depression scale, whereas the 24 smokers have a mean of 79.79, a difference of 10.02 points between the two groups. The two-tailed significance test indicates a $t = -7.49$ with 48 degrees of freedom, resulting in a two-tailed p value of .00 ($p = .00$). This p value is statistically significant because it is less than alpha = .05. If the p value is less than alpha, you reject the null hypothesis; if it is greater than alpha, you accept the hypothesis. Our overall conclusion, then, is that there *is* a difference between nonsmokers and smokers and their

TABLE 6.5

Statistical Tests and Statistics Frequently Used in Educational Research and Criteria for Choosing the Statistic for Hypothesis Testing

Statistical Test	Type of Hypothesis/ Question	Number of Independent Variables	Number of Dependent Variables	Number of Covariates	Continuous or Categorical Independent Variable	Continuous or Categorical Dependent Variable	Type of Distribution of Scores
t test (independent samples)	Group comparison	1	1	0	Categorical	Continuous	Normal distribution
Analysis of variance	Group comparison	1 or more	1	0	Categorical	Continuous	Normal distribution
Analysis of covariance	Group comparison	1 or more	1	1	Categorical	Continuous	Normal distribution
Multiple analysis of variance	Group comparison	1 or more	2 or more	0	Categorical	Continuous	Normal distribution
Mann–Whitney U test	Group comparison	1	1	0	Categorical	Continuous	Nonnormal distribution
Kruskall–Wallis test	Group comparison	1 or more	1 or more	0	Categorical	Continuous	Nonnormal distribution
Friedman's Chi-square test	Group comparison	2 or more	2 or more	0	Categorical	Continuous	Nonnormal distribution
Chi-square	Category within group comparison	1	1	0	Categorical	Categorical	Nonnormal distribution
Pearson product momen correlation	Relate variables	1	1	0	Continuous	Continuous	Normal distribution
Multiple regression	Relate variables	2 or more	1	0	Continuous	Continuous	Normal distribution
Spearman rank-order correlation	Relate variables	1	1 or more	0	Categorical	Categorical	Nonnormal distribution
Point-biserial correlation	Relate variables	1	1	0	Categorical	Continuous	Nonnormal distribution
Phi coefficient	Relate variables	1	1	0	Categorical	Categorical	Nonnormal distribution

depression, and we reject the null hypothesis (there is no difference) and accept the alternative (there is a difference).

In making this statement, we followed this procedure:

1. Look at the value of the statistical test and its associated p value. You can find this p value on your printout.

TABLE 6.6

t test for Independent Samples for Smoking (Not a smoker, Smoker) on Depression

Variable	Number of Cases	Mean	Standard Deviation	SE of Mean
Depression score				
Nonsmoker	26	69.77	5.33	1.05
Smoker	24	79.79	3.97	.81

Mean difference = −10.02

Leverne's Test for Equality of Variance: $F = 1.26$, Significance = 0.27 ← Test if the variances are equal for the two groups

Variances	t value	df	2-Tail Significance	SE of Difference	95% Confidence Interval	Effect Size
Equal	−7.49	48	.00	1.34	Lower: −12.71 Upper: −7.33	2.154
	↑		↑		↑	↑
	t test statistic		Observed p value		Confidence interval	Effect size

2. Determine if the observed p value is less than or greater than the value obtained from a distribution of scores for the statistic (with certain degrees of freedom and with either a one- or two-tailed test at a significance level). You can determine this table p value by hand by comparing the value of the test statistic with the value in a distribution table for the statistic. Alternatively, you can let the computer program identify the observed p value, and you can interpret whether it is greater or less than your alpha value.

3. Decide to reject or fail to reject the null hypothesis. We need to next decide if our p value is statistically significant to reject or fail to reject the null hypothesis. **Statistical significance** is when p value of the observed scores is less than the predetermined alpha level set by the researcher.

Another example using the chi-square statistic is shown in Table 6.7. This test examines whether nonsmokers and smokers are different in terms of their peer group affiliation. The top table shows cells containing information about the observed count in each cell and an expected count. For example, for athletes, we expected 6.2 individuals to be nonsmokers, and instead we found 8. The Pearson chi-square test = 1.71, with $df = 3$, resulted in a p value (or significance level) of .635. At $p = .05$, .635 is not statistically significant, and our conclusion is to fail to reject the null hypothesis. We conclude that there is no detectable difference between smokers and nonsmokers and peer group affiliation. Although we might have anticipated that the "punkers" group had more smokers than nonsmokers or that the "athletes" group had more nonsmokers than smokers, our statistical test did not find these results to be present.

Potential Errors in Outcomes

In both examples, the t test and the chi-square test, our results might have been in error. Let's consider four possible outcomes that could occur during hypothesis testing. These possibilities are outlined in Table 6.8. The columns in this table represent the two actual states of affairs in the population: There is no difference between smokers and nonsmokers on

TABLE 6.7

Chi-Square Analysis, Smoking by Peer Group Affiliation

Smoke Cigarettes? Peer Group Affiliation Crosstabulation

			Peer Group Affiliation				Total
			athletes	singers	punkers	other	
Smoke Cigarettes?	No	Count	8	6	6	6	26
		Expected Count	6.2	7.3	6.8	5.7	26.0
		Residual	1.8	−1.3	−8	0.3	
	Yes	Count	4	8	7	5	24
		Expected Count	5.8	6.7	6.2	5.3	24.0
		Residual	−1.8	1.3	0.8	−3	
Total		Count	12	14	13	11	50
		Expected Count	12.0	14.0	13.0	11.0	50.0

Chi-square test statistic

	Value	df	Asymptotic Sig. (2-sided)	
Pearson chi-square	1.710	3	.635	← Observed *p* value
Likelihood ratio	1.734	3	.629	
Linear-by-linear	.258	1	.611	
N of valid cases	50			

Symmetric Measures

		Value	Approx. Sig.
Nominal by	Phi	.185	.635
Nominal	Cramer's V	.185	.635
N of valid cases		50	

depression scores (said another way, smokers and nonsmokers are equally depressed), or there really is a difference between smokers and nonsmokers on depression scores. The information in the rows shows the two decisions that researchers make based on actual data they receive: to reject the null hypothesis or to fail to reject the null.

Given these factors, we have four possible outcomes—two possible errors that may occur and two possible positive outcomes in hypothesis testing:

1. The researcher can reject the null hypothesis (i.e., there is a difference) when the population values are truly such that there is no effect. A **Type I error** occurs when the null hypothesis is rejected by the researcher when it is actually true. The probability of this error rate is alpha.

2. The researcher can commit an error by failing to reject the null hypothesis. A **Type II error** occurs when the researcher fails to reject the null hypothesis when an effect actually occurs in the population. The probability of this error rate is called *beta*.

TABLE 6.8		
Possible Outcomes in Hypothesis Testing		
	State of Affairs in the Population	
Decision Made by the Researchers Based on the Statistical Test Value	No Effect: Null True	Effect Exists: Null False
Reject the null hypothesis	**Type I error** (false positive) (probability = alpha)	Correctly rejected: no error (probability = power)
Fail to reject the null hypothesis	Correctly not rejected: no error	**Type II error** (false negative) (probability = beta)

Source: Adapted from Tuckman, 1999; Wright, 1997.

In practical terms, a Type II error is typically considered less of a problem than a Type I error, because failing to reject (finding no difference) is less misleading than rejecting (finding a difference). In educational research, we need to be cautious about saying "there is a difference" when one actually does not exist.

3. The researcher can reject the null hypothesis when it should be rejected because an effect exists. This is a correct decision and, therefore, no error is committed. The **power** in quantitative hypothesis testing is the probability of correctly rejecting a false null hypothesis.

4. The researcher can fail to reject the null hypothesis when it should not be rejected because there was no effect.

Estimating Using Confidence Intervals

In Tables 6.6 and 6.7, we have two inferential statistical tests, with one rejecting the null hypothesis and the other failing to reject the null hypothesis. Although the decision to reject or fail to reject provides useful information, it does not indicate the magnitude of differences in mean scores, especially in the case when the null hypothesis is rejected (as in our *t*-test example). Thus, we turn to confidence intervals to help us decide how large the difference actually might be and to estimate a range of acceptable values.

Confidence intervals provide additional information about our hypothesis test. A confidence interval or interval estimate is the range of upper and lower statistical values that are consistent with observed data and are likely to contain the actual population mean. Because means are only estimates of population values, they can never be precise, and sample means indicate a *point estimate* of the population mean. It is helpful, then, to consider a range of values around the sample mean that it could take given the multiple collection of samples. Researchers set a confidence interval around this mean value of the sample to illustrate the potential range of scores that are likely to occur. Moreover, this occurrence is framed as a percent, such as 95% of the time (95 out of 100), the population value will be within the range of the interval. Moreover, this interval can be identified by upper and lower limits, the values that define the range of the interval.

Turning to Table 6.6 again, the computer program reports a 95% confidence interval for the differences between the means of the two groups. If you draw a large number of samples from the population, 95% of the mean differences would fall between the lower and the upper values reported in the statistics for a *t* test. This conveys that if we could collect a large number of samples of high school students, we might estimate that 95% of the scores for depression would fall between −12.71 and −7.33, around the difference of −10.02 for the mean scores between nonsmokers and smokers (69.77 − 79.79 = −10.02). To know this range provides a more accurate estimate of the population values, and it provides additional information about the results of hypothesis testing.

Determining Effect Size

It is not only important to know whether the statistical test was significant (through p values) and the possible range of acceptable scores (confidence interval), but also to quantify the strength of the difference between two means or two variables. A practical measure of whether means differ is simply to look at the differences and determine whether the difference is meaningful in a practical sense. This is the procedure of calculating effect size. Effect size identifies the strength of the conclusions about group differences or about the relationship among variables in a quantitative study. The calculation of this coefficient differs for statistical tests. For analysis of variance (ANOVA), for example, effect size (eta^2) is measured using the percentage of the variance due to the variable under study. Phi, as used with the chi-square test, is a measure of association of strength. Other measures for effect size for other statistics employ different procedures for calculations, such as omega^2 or Cohen's D (APA, 2010). When examining the mean scores for two groups, however, an effect size of .5 (or one half of an SD) or above is often a standard to use.

We can calculate effect size between groups in our high school smoking example. A researcher, for example, could examine the means in Table 6.6 and see that the mean scores were 10.02 points apart, a sizable difference on a 100-point scale. More precisely, we calculate effect sizes and report them in terms of standard deviation units. For the t-test statistic, the effect size (ES) can be calculated with the equation:

$$ES = Mean_{smokers} - Mean_{nonsmokers} / Standard\ Deviation_{weighted}$$

where the standard deviation$_{weighted}$ can be obtained by averaging the standard deviations for the smokers and nonsmokers, taking into account the size of the groups.

Using this equation, we see in Table 6.6 an effect size reported of 2.154. This means that the average smoker would be over two standard deviations higher than a nonsmoker in terms of depression. This is a large difference, in a practical sense.

Turning to our second illustration, as shown in the chi-square analysis of Table 6.7, we see the effect size phi coefficient with a value of .185 and an approximate significance of .635. Using the phi coefficient is a measure of the strength of the association between two categorical variables (two nominal variables). A value of .185 indicates a weak association, and we have additional evidence that smokers and nonsmokers do not differ in terms of their peer group affiliation.

HOW DO YOU REPORT THE RESULTS?

When researchers conclude the statistical testing, they next turn to representing the results in tables and figures and reporting results in a discussion. You might include these results in a section labeled "Results." Several points might aid in your construction of this section and help you understand the contents of a published results section.

This section should address or respond to each research question or hypothesis. A typical approach is to respond to each question or hypothesis one by one in the order in which they were introduced earlier in the study. In reporting the results, the researcher also stays close to the statistical findings without drawing broader implications or meaning from them. Further, this section includes summaries of the data rather than the raw data (e.g., the actual scores for individuals). A results section includes:

- Tables that summarize statistical information
- Figures (charts, pictures, drawings) that portray variables and their relationships
- Detailed explanations about the statistical results

Tables

Researchers display data in tables that summarize statistical results to research questions or hypotheses. A **table** is a summary of quantitative data organized into rows and columns (see Tables 6.6 and 6.7). Typically, tables for reporting results contain quantitative information, but they might contain text information such as summaries of key studies found in the literature (and incorporated earlier in a study, before the results). One advantage of using tables is that they can summarize a large amount of data in a small amount of space. Below are some guidelines for creating tables.

- Although you can present multiple statistical tests in one table, a general guideline is to present one table for each statistical test. Sometimes, however, you can combine data from different statistical analyses into a single table. For example, all descriptive data to questions (*M, SD,* and range) can be combined into a single table. However, you should present each inferential test in an individual table.
- Readers should be able to grasp easily the meaning of a table. Tables should organize data into rows and columns with simple and clear headings. Also, the title for the table should accurately represent the information contained in the table and be as complete a description as possible.
- It is important to know the level of statistical detail for descriptive and inferential statistics to report in tables. An examination of tables in scholarly journals typically provides models to use for the level of detail required for each type of statistical test. In addition, the *Publication Manual of the American Psychological Association* (APA, 2010) provides examples of the level of detail to be reported in descriptive tables (e.g., *M, SD,* and *N,* or number of participants) and inferential tables (e.g., correlation, ANOVA, and regression). As an additional aid, you might view the typical output for statistical tests using SPSS (e.g., George & Mallery, 2001).
- Authors typically report notes that qualify, explain, or provide additional information in the tables, which can be helpful to readers. Often, these notes include information about the size of the sample reported in the study, the probability values used in hypothesis testing, and the actual significance levels of the statistical test.

Figures

Discerning the difference between tables and figures is not always clear cut. A table includes a summary of quantitative data, whereas a figure presents information in graphs or in visual pictures (APA, 2010). Thus, a **figure** is a summary of quantitative information presented as a chart, graph, or picture that shows relations among scores or variables. Tables are preferred to figures (APA, 2010) because tables convey more information in a simple form.

Figures are suitable for visually presenting information in graphs and pictures in results sections of studies. The *Publication Manual of the American Psychological Association* (APA, 2010) suggests several standards for designing a good figure. A good figure:

- Augments, rather than duplicates, the text
- Conveys only essential facts

◆ Omits visually distracting detail
◆ Is easy to read and understand
◆ Is consistent with and is prepared in the same style as similar figures in the same article
◆ Is carefully planned and prepared (pp. 152–153)

Various types of figures are found in educational research studies:

◆ **Bar charts** depict trends and distributions of data (see the bar chart in Table 6.4).
◆ **Scatterplots** illustrate the comparison of two different scores and how the scores regress or differ from the mean. This information is useful for identifying outliers and upper or lower ceiling effects of scores.
◆ **Line graphs** display the interaction between two variables in an experiment.
◆ **Charts** portray the complex relationships among variables in correlational research designs.

The *Publication Manual of the American Psychological Association* (APA, 2010) provides illustrations of a line graph, a bar graph, a scatterplot, and a correlational chart path model. In all of these examples, the figure caption is placed at the bottom of the figure. This is different from table titles, which are placed at the top of the table.

Present Results

Although tables and figures summarize information from statistical tests, the researcher needs to describe in detail the results of the statistical tests. In a **presentation of results**, the researcher presents detailed information about the specific results of the descriptive and inferential statistical analyses. This process requires explaining the central results of each statistical test and presenting this information using language acceptable to quantitative researchers.

For the results to each statistical test, the investigator summarizes the findings in one or two sentences. These sentences should include sufficient statistics to provide a complete picture of the results. They should also include information necessary for reporting results to each statistical test. What represents "sufficient" information depends on the specific type of test. At a minimum:

◆ Report whether the hypothesis test was significant or not
◆ Provide important information about the statistical test, given the statistics
◆ Include language typically used in reporting statistical results

The information about the statistical test, for example, might include a report on degrees of freedom and sample size for the chi-square statistic, and means and standard deviations for descriptive statistics (APA, 2010).

Figure 6.5 shows examples of results statements for both descriptive and inferential statistics. For descriptive statistics, the means, standard deviations, and the range of scores show useful information about results. For inferential statistics, information such as the alpha level used, the actual p value, the critical region of rejection, the test statistic results, the degrees of freedom, and effect size should be reported. Confidence intervals should also be reported (Wilkinson & Task Force on Statistical Inference, 1999).

HOW DO YOU INTERPRET THE RESULTS?

After reporting and explaining the detailed results, researchers conclude a study by summarizing key findings, developing explanations for results, suggesting limitations in the research, and making recommendations for future inquiries.

FIGURE 6.5

Examples of Results Statements Using an Analysis of Variance Test

Descriptive Statistics

The students who received questions averaged $M = 4.5$ with a $SD = .98$ on math scores.

Inferential Statistics

Standard Statement

The means and standard deviations for each treatment group are presented in Table 2. The analysis of variance revealed a statistically significant difference between the groups, $F(3,8) = 8.98$, $p = 0.0001$.

Effect Size Added

The means and standard deviations for each treatment group are presented in Table 2. The analysis of variance revealed a significant difference among the groups, $F(3,8) = 8.98$, $p < .05$, effect size $= .93$ SD.

Alpha and Actual p Value Indicated

The means and standard deviations for each treatment group are presented in Table 2. At an alpha of .05, the analysis of variance revealed a significant difference among the groups, $F(3,8) = 8.98$, $p = .0001$.

Ideal Model

Mean score   Standard Deviation   Significance Level

The scores varied for the three groups (questions only—$M = 4.5$, $SD = .98$; lecture only—$M = 3.4$, $SD = .88$; in-class discussion—$M = 4.8$, $SD = .90$). At an alpha of .05, the analysis indicated a statistically significant difference among the groups, $F(3,8) = 8.98$, $p = .034$, effect size $= .93$ SD.

Effect size   Results of hypothesis test   Statistical test   Degrees of freedom for F test   Value of test statistic   Probability value of test statistic

---

Summarize the Major Results

In the process of interpreting results, researchers first summarize the major findings and present the broader implications of the research for distinct audiences. A **summary** is a statement that reviews the major conclusions to each of the research questions or hypotheses. This summary is different from the results: It represents general, rather than specific, conclusions. Specific conclusions in the results would include detail about statistical tests, significance levels, and effect sizes. General conclusions state overall whether the hypothesis was rejected or whether the research question was supported or not supported.

The research ends with statements by researchers about positive implications of the study. **Implications** are those suggestions for the importance of the study for different audiences. They elaborate on the significance for audiences presented initially in the statement of the problem. In effect, now that the study has been completed, the researcher is in a position to reflect (and remark) on the importance of the study.

Explain Why the Results Occurred

After this summary, researchers explain why their results turned out the way they did. Often this explanation is based on returning to predictions made from a theory or conceptual framework that guided the development of research questions or hypotheses. In addition, these explanations may include discussing the existing literature and indicating how the results either confirmed or disconfirmed prior studies. Thus, you will frequently find past research studies being presented by authors in this passage. A concluding passage may contrast and compare results with theories or bodies of literature.

Advance Limitations

Researchers also advance limitations or weaknesses of their study that may have affected the results. **Limitations** are potential weaknesses or problems with the study identified by the researcher. These weaknesses are enumerated one by one, and they often relate to inadequate measures of variables, loss or lack of participants, small sample sizes, errors in measurement, and other factors typically related to data collection and analysis. These limitations are useful to other potential researchers who may choose to conduct a similar or replication study. Advancing these limitations provides a useful bridge for recommending future studies. Limitations also help readers judge to what extent the findings can or cannot be generalized to other people and situations.

Suggest Future Research

Researchers next advance future research directions based on the results of the present study. **Future research directions** are suggestions made by the researcher about additional studies that need to be conducted based on the results of the present research. These suggestions are a natural link to the limitations of a study, and they provide useful direction for new researchers and readers who are interested in exploring needed areas of inquiry or applying results to educational practice. These educators often need an "angle" to pursue to add to the existing knowledge, and future research suggestions, typically found at the conclusion of a research study, provide this direction. For those reading a study, future research directions highlight areas that are unknown and provide boundaries for using information from a specific study. Typically, good quantitative studies end with a positive note about the contributions of the research.

REEXAMINING DATA ANALYSIS AND INTERPRETATION IN THE PARENT INVOLVEMENT STUDY

To obtain an overview of the process of quantitative data analysis and interpretation, we can turn once again to the parent involvement study by Deslandes and Bertrand (2005). With some advanced statistics used by the authors, it is easy to focus on statistics and miss the overall picture of analysis and interpretation unfolding in this study.

The authors surveyed 770 parents of secondary-level students attending five public schools in Quebec. These parents completed several instruments. To look closely at the data analysis used by the authors, it is helpful to reflect on the question the authors sought to answer and then examine the statistical analysis they used to obtain answers to the question. The key question can be found in Paragraph 13: "What are the relative contributions of parents' role construction, self-efficacy, perceptions of teacher invitations, and perceptions of adolescent invitations to predict parent involvement at home and at school in Grades 7, 8, and 9?" (p. 166). In this question, "relative contribution" means what independent variables best explain the two outcomes, parent involvement at home and parent involvement at school. Next, let's scan the tables of statistical information the authors presented. Table 1 shows demographic, descriptive statistics (percentages) about the parent participants in the study. Table 2 simply lists the major predictor (independent) variables, the variables controlled in the data analysis, and the two outcome (dependent) variables. This is a helpful table to use to think about the data analysis and the statistical procedures. Table 3 shows descriptive statistics (means, standard deviations) on the four independent variables and the two dependent variables. Tables 4 and 5 show inferential, multiple regression analyses for the independent variables and the demographic control variables for the parent involvement at home and the parent involvement at school dependent variables, respectively. So, from the research question, we know that this study will build toward an understanding of the importance of the four factors in explaining parent involvement. Looking back again at Table 6.5 in this chapter on data analysis, we know that when we have two or more independent variables (four constructs and several control variables in this study) measured with continuous scales (1 = disagree very strongly to 6 = agree very strongly) and one dependent variable (either home or school) measured separately as continuous scales, we will use multiple regression as a statistical procedure. We can look at the two regression tables (Table 4 and Table 5) and see that some of the variables were statistically significant at the $p < .05$, $p < .01$, and $p < .001$ levels (as shown by * markings) as seen in the notes at the bottom of the two tables. Unfortunately, we did not learn about effect sizes in Table 4 or Table 5. But in terms of data analysis, in Table 4 we can see that "parents' perceptions of student invitations in academic domain" strongly predicted parent involvement at home (beta = .44). Then we can read the "Results" section to see the more detailed findings. So our thinking about the major forms of analysis of data in this journal article went from thinking about the research question, exploring the tables, recognizing the major types of statistics and using Table 6.5 in this chapter to assessing why the statistic was chosen and then looking closely at the results presented in the tables as well as in the results discussion.

The Discussion section (starting at Paragraph 32) provides the "interpretation" of the results starting with a general summary of them presented by grade level and for each of the dependent measures, parent involvement at home and parent involvement at school. Note that throughout this discussion, the authors are introducing references to other studies that highlight similar findings (see, e.g., Paragraph 36). Also, the article ends with a discussion of implications for school interventions and for increased parental involvement, and of the importance of teacher–parent contacts. The final section identifies some of the limitations of the study in terms of sampling (Paragraph 46), advances ideas for further research (Paragraph 47), and then ends on a positive note about the final importance of the results of the study (Paragraph 49).

KEY IDEAS IN THE CHAPTER

Identify the Steps in the Process of Analyzing and Interpreting Quantitative Data

The steps in the process of quantitative data analysis and interpretation involve first preparing your numeric data for analysis using statistical programs, conducting the analysis using statistics that report both descriptive and inferential results, representing and reporting the results using tables, figures, and a discussion of each statistical test, and finally interpreting the results by restating the general findings, comparing the findings to past literature, mentioning the potential limitations of the study, and advancing ideas that will extend the research in the future.

Preparing Your Data for Analysis

After collecting numeric scores on instruments or through observations, quantitative researchers need to prepare and organize their data for statistical analysis. This process consists of assigning numeric scores to each response option on instruments (if the instrument does not already include this information); determining whether single-item, net, or difference scores will be used in the analysis; and selecting a computer software program to analyze the data. Next, the investigator enters the data into a computer file by building a data grid consisting of variables and their values.

Analyzing the Data

With the dataset built, the researcher begins the process of analyzing the data to address the research questions or hypotheses. Some questions may call for describing trends in the data, and the researcher uses descriptive analysis such as measures of central tendency, the spread of the scores, and the relative ranking of the scores. Other research questions and hypotheses call for inferential analysis in which the researcher studies a sample and draws inferences from the sample to a population. To conduct inferential analysis, three procedures might be used: (a) Conduct hypothesis testing by using statistical tests and calculating p values that are determined to be significant or nonsignificant, and suggest that the sample mean is or is not a good estimate of the population mean; (b) set a confidence interval to identify a range of scores that is likely to include the population mean; (c) calculate an effect size that examines the strength of the differences and the practical meaning of these differences for group comparisons or relating variables.

Reporting the Results

Whether the analysis consists of descriptive or inferential analysis, or both, the researcher presents results in tables, figures, and a detailed discussion of the results. This detailed discussion involves presenting information about the results of each statistical test and presenting information using language acceptable to quantitative researchers.

Interpreting the Results

Finally, investigators conclude their research by summarizing the detailed results in general statements. They also provide explanations for their findings based on prior predictions made in the literature or in theories, and they contrast their results with past research. It is also important in concluding a study to advance limitations to the research, noting potential weaknesses that might have affected the results. These limitations build directly into suggestions for future research that will improve the weaknesses and further contribute to the literature on a topic.

USEFUL INFORMATION FOR PRODUCERS OF RESEARCH

♦ As you design or plan quantitative research, consider the broad processes of analyzing and interpreting the data as discussed in this chapter, such as preparing and organizing your data, analyzing it descriptively and inferentially, summarizing the results visually and in a discussion, and concluding a study by summarizing and explaining the results. These topics could be headings in your plan for a study or in the final report.

♦ In quantitative research, score your data and then input it into a computer program using a grid.

♦ Choose a computer program that offers a large number of statistical procedures.

♦ Run a descriptive analysis to answer descriptive questions.

♦ Conduct inferential analysis to address your group comparison and relationship questions or hypotheses.

♦ For your inferential analysis, report p values of hypothesis testing, confidence intervals, and effect sizes.

♦ Represent data in tables and figures using the format of the APA style manual.

USEFUL INFORMATION FOR CONSUMERS OF RESEARCH

♦ To best understand the statistics presented in a research report, ask yourself what the research questions were that the investigator sought to answer and look for a discussion of results that match these research questions.

♦ Understand that the selection of statistics by a researcher needs to be based on specific criteria. Examine the data collected to determine if the right decision was made based on the seven factors identified in Table 6.5.

♦ When researchers compare groups, look for not only a report of the statistical test but also information about confidence intervals and effect sizes for interpreting the magnitude of group differences.

UNDERSTANDING CONCEPTS AND EVALUATING RESEARCH STUDIES

1. Assume that you wish to analyze the following hypothesis:

   "There is no significant difference between lectures, small-group discussions, and large-group discussions in terms of math achievement scores for sixth graders."

   Using Table 6.5 as your guide, determine the appropriate statistical test to use to analyze this question. Work with the assumption that your sampling distribution is normal. Answer these questions to determine your statistical test:

   ♦ Is the hypothesis a comparison of groups or the relationship of variables?
   ♦ How many independent variables do you have? Dependent variables?
   ♦ Are there any covariates being controlled?
   ♦ Is the independent variable categorical or continuous?
   ♦ Is the dependent variable categorical or continuous?

2. Five individuals respond to five questions using the Likert scale of 5 (*strongly agree*), 4 (*agree*), 3 (*undecided*), 2 (*disagree*), and 1 (*strongly disagree*). You have input the data into an SPSS database and it looks like this:

    5 5 5 6 4
    3 2 1 3 3
    4 3 1 2
    3 5 8 2 4
    2 1 1 1 1

    Your task is to look over this small database and clean it up. What do you fix?
3. In the parent involvement study (Deslandes & Bertrand, 2005), the authors reported results for parent involvement at home for ninth-grade students. They say that the statistical analysis of the independent variables and the level of parent involvement at home was $F(10, 101) = 6.81$, $p < .001$. Discuss the meaning of this statement. What does F stand for? What is 101? What is 6.81? What does $p < .001$ mean?

CONDUCTING YOUR RESEARCH

For your educational project, design the steps you would take in conducting a quantitative analysis. Discuss how you would score the data, select a statistical program, input the data, and clean and account for missing data. Then describe how you would analyze your data descriptively and inferentially to answer your research questions or hypotheses. Discuss how you would select the appropriate statistic to use. Finally, identify the types of figures and tables you would use and the steps you would use to discuss the results.

PEARSON
myeducationlab
The Power of Classroom Practice
www.myeducationlab.com

Go to the Topics "Descriptive Statistics" and "Inferential Statistics" in the MyEducationLab (**www.myeducationlab.com**) for your course, where you can:

◆ Find learning outcomes for "Descriptive Statistics" and "Inferential Statistics."
◆ Complete Assignments and Activities that can help you more deeply understand the chapter content.
◆ Apply and practice your understanding of the core skills identified in the chapter with the Building Research Skills exercises.
◆ Check your comprehension of the content covered in the chapter by going to the Study Plan. Here you will be able to take a pretest, receive feedback on your answers, and then access Review, Practice, and Enrichment activities to enhance your understanding. You can then complete a final posttest.

Collecting Qualitative Data

*Q*ualitative data collection is more than simply deciding on whether you will observe or interview people. Five steps comprise the process of collecting qualitative data. You need to identify your participants and sites, gain access, determine the types of data to collect, develop data collection forms, and administer the process in an ethical manner.

By the end of this chapter, you should be able to:

◆ Identify the five process steps in collecting qualitative data.
◆ Identify different sampling approaches to selecting participants and sites.
◆ Describe the types of permissions required to gain access to participants and sites.
◆ Recognize the various types of qualitative data you can collect.
◆ Identify the procedures for recording qualitative data.
◆ Recognize the field issues and ethical considerations that need to be anticipated in administering the data collection.

Maria is comfortable talking with students and teachers in her high school. She does not mind asking them open-ended research questions such as "What are your (student and teacher) experiences with students carrying weapons in our high school?" She also knows the challenges involved in obtaining their views. She needs to listen without injecting her own opinions, and she needs to take notes or tape-record what people have to say. This phase requires time, but Maria enjoys talking with people and listening to their ideas. Maria is a natural qualitative researcher.

WHAT ARE THE FIVE PROCESS STEPS IN QUALITATIVE DATA COLLECTION?

There are five interrelated steps in the process of qualitative data collection. These steps should not be seen as linear approaches, but often one step in the process does follow another. The five steps are first to identify participants and sites to be studied and to engage in a sampling strategy that will best help you understand your central phenomenon and the research question you are asking. Second, the next phase is to gain access to these individuals and sites by obtaining permissions. Third, once permissions are in place, you need to consider what types of information will best answer your research questions. Fourth, at the same time, you need to design protocols or instruments for collecting and recording the information. Finally and fifth, you need to administer the data collection with special attention to potential ethical issues that may arise.

Some basic differences between quantitative and qualitative data collection are helpful to know at this point. Based on the general characteristics of qualitative research, qualitative data collection consists of collecting data using forms with general, emerging questions to permit the participant to generate responses; gathering word (text) or image (picture) data; and collecting information from a small number of individuals or sites. Thinking more specifically now,

◆ In *quantitative* research, we systematically identify our participants and sites through random sampling; in *qualitative* research, we identify our participants and sites on purposeful sampling, based on places and people that can best help us understand our central phenomenon.

◆ In both *quantitative* and *qualitative* research, we need permissions to begin our study, but in *qualitative* research, we need greater access to the site because we will typically go to the site and interview people or observe them. This process requires a greater level of participation from the site than does the *quantitative* research process.

◆ In both approaches, we collect data such as interviews, observations, and documents. In *qualitative* research, our approach relies on general interviews or observations so that we do not restrict the views of participants. We will not use someone else's instrument as in quantitative research and gather closed-ended information; we will instead collect data with a few open-ended questions that we design.

◆ In both approaches, we need to record the information supplied by the participants. Rather than using predesigned instruments from someone else or instruments that we design, in qualitative research we will record information on self-designed protocols that help us organize information reported by participants to each question.

◆ Finally, we will administer our procedures of *qualitative* data collection with sensitivity to the challenges and ethical issues of gathering information face-to-face and often in people's homes or workplaces. Studying people in their own environment creates challenges for the qualitative researcher that may not be present in *quantitative* research when investigators mail out anonymous questionnaires or bring individuals into the experimental laboratory.

WHAT ARE THE DIFFERENT SAMPLING APPROACHES FOR SELECTING PARTICIPANTS AND SITES?

In qualitative inquiry, the intent is not to generalize to a population, but to develop an in-depth exploration of a central phenomenon. Thus, to best understand this phenomenon, the qualitative researcher purposefully or intentionally selects individuals and sites. This distinction between quantitative "random sampling" and qualitative "purposeful sampling" is portrayed in Figure 7.1.

In quantitative research, the focus is on random sampling, selecting representative individuals, and then generalizing from these individuals to a population. Often this process results in testing "theories" that explain the population. However, in qualitative research, you select people or sites that can best help you understand the central phenomenon. This understanding emerges through a detailed understanding of the people or site. It can lead to information that allows individuals to "learn" about the phenomenon, or to an understanding that provides voice to individuals who may not be heard otherwise.

Purposeful Sampling

The research term used for qualitative sampling is *purposeful sampling*. In **purposeful sampling**, researchers intentionally select individuals and sites to learn or understand the central phenomenon. The standard used in choosing participants and sites is whether they are "information rich" (Patton, 1990, p. 169). In any given qualitative study, you may decide to study a site (e.g., one college campus), several sites (three small liberal arts campuses), individuals or groups (freshman students), or some combination (two liberal arts campuses and several freshman students on those campuses). Purposeful sampling thus applies to both individuals and sites.

If you conduct your own study and use purposeful sampling, you need to identify your sampling strategy and be able to defend its use. The literature identifies several qualitative sampling strategies (see Miles & Huberman, 1994; Patton, 1990). As seen in Figure 7.2, you have a choice of selecting from one to several sampling strategies that educators frequently use. These strategies are differentiated in terms of whether they are employed before data collection begins or after data collection has started (an approach consistent with an emerging design). Further, each has a different intent, depending on

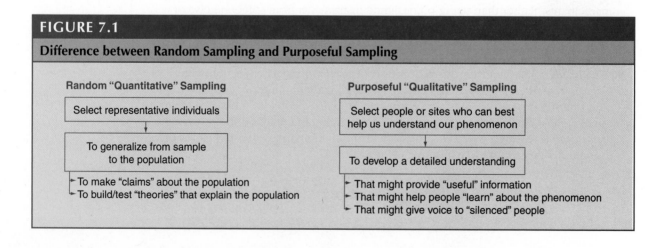

FIGURE 7.1

Difference between Random Sampling and Purposeful Sampling

Random "Quantitative" Sampling

Select representative individuals

To generalize from sample to the population

- To make "claims" about the population
- To build/test "theories" that explain the population

Purposeful "Qualitative" Sampling

Select people or sites who can best help us understand our phenomenon

To develop a detailed understanding

- That might provide "useful" information
- That might help people "learn" about the phenomenon
- That might give voice to "silenced" people

FIGURE 7.2

Types of Purposeful Sampling

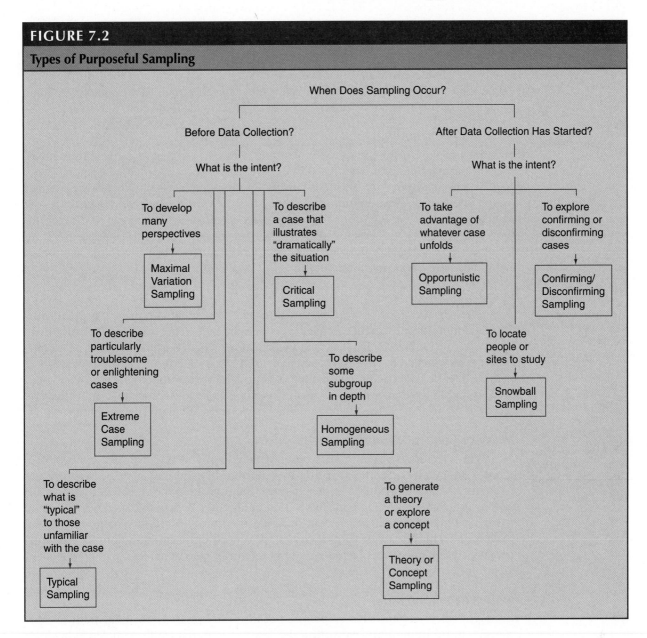

the research problem and questions you would like answered in a study. All strategies apply to sampling a single time or multiple times during a study, and you can use them to sample from individuals, groups, or entire organizations and sites. In some studies, it may be necessary to use several different sampling strategies (e.g., to select teachers in a school and to select different schools to be incorporated into the sample).

Maximal Variation Sampling

One characteristic of qualitative research is to present multiple perspectives of individuals to represent the complexity of our world. Thus, one sampling strategy is to build that complexity into the research when sampling participants or sites. **Maximal variation sampling** is a purposeful sampling strategy in which the researcher samples cases or individuals that differ on some characteristic or trait (e.g., different age groups). This procedure requires that you identify the characteristic and then find sites or individuals that display different dimensions of that characteristic. For example, a researcher might first identify the characteristic of racial composition of high schools, and then purposefully sample three high schools that differ on this characteristic, such as a primarily Hispanic high school, a predominantly white high school, and a racially diverse high school.

Extreme Case Sampling

Sometimes you are more interested in learning about a case that is particularly troublesome or enlightening, or a case that is noticeable for its success or failure (Patton, 1990). **Extreme case sampling** is a form of purposeful sampling in which you study an outlier case or one that displays extreme characteristics. Researchers identify these cases by locating persons or organizations that others have cited for achievements or distinguishing characteristics (e.g., certain elementary schools targeted for federal assistance). An autistic education program in elementary education that has received awards may be an outstanding case to purposefully sample.

Typical Sampling

Some research questions address "What is normal?" or "What is typical?" **Typical sampling** is a form of purposeful sampling in which the researcher studies a person or site that is "typical" to those unfamiliar with the situation. What constitutes typical, of course, is open to interpretation. However, you might ask persons at a research site or even select a typical case by collecting demographic data or survey data about all cases. You could study a typical faculty member at a small liberal arts college because that individual has worked at the institution for 20 years and has embodied the cultural norms of the school.

Theory or Concept Sampling

You might select individuals or sites because they help you understand a concept or a theory. **Theory or concept sampling** is a purposeful sampling strategy in which the researcher samples individuals or sites because they can help the researcher generate or discover a theory or specific concepts within the theory. To use this method, you need a clear understanding of the concept or larger theory expected to emerge during the research. In a study of five sites that have experienced distance education, for example, you have chosen these sites because study of them can help generate a theory of student attitudes toward distance learning.

Homogeneous Sampling

You might select certain sites or people because they possess a similar trait or characteristic. In **homogeneous sampling** the researcher purposefully samples individuals or sites based on membership in a subgroup that has defining characteristics. To use this procedure, you need to identify the characteristics and find individuals or sites that possess it. For example, in a rural community, all parents who have children in school participate in a parent program. You choose members of this parent program to study because they belong to a common subgroup in the community.

Critical Sampling

Sometimes individuals or research sites represent the central phenomenon in dramatic terms (Patton, 1990). The sampling strategy here is to study a **critical sample** because it is an exceptional case and the researcher can learn much about the phenomenon. For example, you study teenage violence in a high school where a student with a gun threatened a teacher. This situation represents a dramatic incident that portrays the extent to which some adolescents may engage in school violence.

Opportunistic Sampling

After data collection begins, you may find that you need to collect new information to best answer your research questions. **Opportunistic sampling** is purposeful sampling undertaken after the research begins, to take advantage of unfolding events that will help answer research questions. In this process, the sample emerges during the inquiry. Researchers need to be cautious about engaging in this form of sampling because it might divert attention away from the original aims of the research. However, it captures the developing or emerging nature of qualitative research nicely and can lead to novel ideas and surprising findings. For example, you begin a study with maximal variation sampling of different pregnant teenagers in high schools. During this process you find a pregnant teenager who plans to bring her baby to school each day. Because a study of this teenager would provide new insights about balancing children and school, you study her activities during her pregnancy at the school and in the months after the birth of her child.

Snowball Sampling

In certain research situations, you may not know the best people to study because of the unfamiliarity of the topic or the complexity of events. As in quantitative research, qualitative snowball sampling is a form of purposeful sampling that typically proceeds after a study begins and occurs when the researcher asks participants to recommend other individuals to be sampled. Researchers may pose this request as a question during an interview or through informal conversations with individuals at a research site.

Confirming and Disconfirming Sampling

A final form of purposeful sampling, also used after studies begin, is to sample individuals or sites to confirm or disconfirm preliminary findings. **Confirming and disconfirming sampling** is a purposeful strategy used during a study to follow up on specific cases to test or explore further specific findings. Although this sampling serves to verify the accuracy of the findings throughout a study, it also represents a sampling procedure used during a study. For example, you find out that academic department chairs support faculty in their development as teachers by serving as mentors. After initially interviewing chairs, you further confirm the mentoring role by sampling and studying chairs that have received praise from faculty as "good" mentors.

Sample Size or Number of Research Sites

The number of people and sites sampled vary from one qualitative study to the next. You might examine some published qualitative studies and see what numbers of sites or participants researchers used. Here are some general guidelines:

◆ It is typical in qualitative research to study a few individuals or a few cases. This is because the overall ability of a researcher to provide an in-depth picture diminishes with the addition of each new individual or site. One objective of qualitative research is to present the complexity of a site or of the information provided by individuals.

◆ In some cases, you might study a single individual or a single site. In other cases, the number may be several, ranging from 1 or 2 to 30 or 40. Because of the need to report details about each individual or site, the larger number of cases can become unwieldy and result in superficial perspectives. Moreover, collecting qualitative data and analyzing it takes considerable time, and the addition of each individual or site only lengthens that time.

Let's look at some specific examples to see how many individuals and sites were used. Qualitative researchers may collect data from single individuals. For example, in the qualitative case study of Basil McGee, a second-year middle school science teacher, Brickhouse and Bodner (1992) explored his beliefs about science and science teaching and how his beliefs shaped classroom instruction. Elsewhere, several individuals participated in a qualitative grounded theory study. The researchers examined 20 parents of children labeled as ADHD (Reid, Hertzog, & Snyder, 1996). More extensive data collection was used in a qualitative ethnographic study of the culture of fraternity life and the exploitation and victimization of women. Rhoads (1995) conducted 12 formal interviews and 18 informal interviews, made observations, and collected numerous documents.

If you were Maria, and you sought to answer the question "What are the students' experiences with carrying weapons in the high school?" what purposeful sampling strategy would you use? Before you look at the answers I provide, write down at least two possibilities on a sheet of paper.

Let's create some options depending on the students that Maria has available to her to study.

◆ One option would be to use *maximal variation sampling* and interview several students who vary in the type of weapon infraction they committed in the school. For instance, one student may have threatened another student. Another student may have actually used a knife in a fight. Another student may have kept a knife in a locker and a teacher discovered it. These three students represent different types of weapon possession in the school, and each will likely provide different views on students having knives in the school.

◆ Another option would be to use *critical sampling.* You might interview a student who actually used a knife during a fight. This is an example of a public use of a weapon, and it represents a dramatic action worthy of study by itself.

Can you think of other approaches to sampling that you might use? Also, how many students would you study and what is the reason for your choice?

WHAT TYPES OF PERMISSIONS WILL BE REQUIRED TO GAIN ACCESS TO PARTICIPANTS AND SITES?

Similar to quantitative research, gaining access to the site or individual(s) in qualitative inquiry involves obtaining permissions at different levels, such as the organization, the site, the individuals, and the campus institutional review boards. Of special importance is negotiating approval with campus review boards and locating individuals at a site who can facilitate the collection of qualitative data.

Seek Institutional Review Board Approval

Researchers applying for permission to study individuals in a qualitative project must go through the approval process of a campus institutional review board. These steps include seeking permission from the board, developing a description of the project, designing an informed consent form, and having the project reviewed. Because *qualitative* data collection consists of lengthy periods of gathering information directly involving people and recording detailed personal views from individuals, you will need to provide a detailed description of your procedures to the institutional review board. This detail is needed because the board may not be familiar with the qualitative approach to educational research and because you will spend time in people's homes, workplaces, or sites in which you gather data.

Several strategies might prove useful when negotiating qualitative research through the institutional review board process:

◆ Determine if individuals reviewing proposals on the review board are familiar with qualitative inquiry. Look for those individuals who have experience in conducting qualitative research. This requires a careful assessment of the membership of the review board.

◆ Develop detailed descriptions of the procedures so that reviewers have a full disclosure of the potential risks to people and sites in the study.

◆ Detail ways you will protect the anonymity of participants. These might be masking names of individuals, assigning pseudonyms to individuals and their organizations, or choosing to withhold descriptors that would lead to the identification of participants and sites.

◆ Discuss the need to respect the research site and to disturb or disrupt it as little as possible. When you gain permission to enter the site, you need to be respectful of property and refrain from introducing issues that may cause participants to question their group or organization. Doing this requires keeping a delicate balance between exploring a phenomenon in depth and respecting individuals and property at the research site.

◆ Detail how the study will provide opportunities to "give back" or reciprocate in some way to those individuals you study (e.g., you might donate services at the site, become an advocate for the needs of those studied, or share with them any monetary rewards you may receive from your study).

◆ Acknowledge that during your prolonged interaction with participants, you may adopt their beliefs and even become an advocate for their ideas.

◆ Specify potential power imbalances that may occur between yourself and the participants, and how your study will address these imbalances. For example, a power imbalance occurs when researchers study their own employers or employees in the workplace. If this is your situation, consider researching sites where you do not have an interest or try to collect data in a way that minimizes a power inequality between yourself and participants (e.g., observing rather than interviewing).

◆ Detail how much time you will spend at the research site. This detail might include the anticipated number of days, the length of each visit, and the times when visits will take place.

◆ Include in the project description a list of the interview questions so reviewers on the institutional board can determine how sensitive the questions may be. Typically, qualitative interview questions are open ended and general, lending support to a noninvasive stance by the researcher.

Gatekeepers

In qualitative research, you often need to seek and obtain permissions from individuals and sites at many levels. Because of the in-depth nature of extensive and multiple interviews with participants, it might be helpful for you to identify and make use of a gatekeeper. A **gatekeeper** is an individual who has an official or unofficial role at the site, provides entrance to a site, helps researchers locate people, and assists in the identification of places to study (Hammersley & Atkinson, 1995). For example, this individual may be a teacher, a principal, a group leader, or the informal leader of a special program, and usually has "insider" status at the site the researchers plan to study. Identifying a gatekeeper at a research site and winning his or her support and trust may take time. You might be required to submit written information about the project to proceed. Such information might include:

- Why their site was chosen for study
- What will be accomplished at the site during the research study (i.e., time and resources required by participants and yourself)
- How much time you will spend at the site
- What potential there is for your presence to be disruptive
- How you will use and report the results
- What the individuals at the site will gain from the study (Bogdan & Biklen, 1998)

Let's look at an example of using a gatekeeper in a qualitative study:

While conducting a qualitative study exploring the behavior of informal student cliques that may display violent behavior, a researcher talks to many high school personnel. Ultimately, the social studies coordinator emerges as a good gatekeeper. She suggests the researcher use the school cafeteria as an important site to see school cliques in action. She also points out specific student leaders of cliques (e.g., the punk group) who might help the researcher understand student behavior.

WHAT TYPES OF QUALITATIVE DATA WILL YOU COLLECT?

Another aspect of qualitative data collection is to identify the types of data that will address your research questions. Thus, it is important to become familiar with your questions and topics, and to review them prior to deciding upon the types of qualitative data that you will collect. In qualitative research you pose general, broad questions to participants and allow them to share their views relatively unconstrained by your perspective. In addition, you collect multiple types of information, and you may add new forms of data during the study to answer your questions. Further, you engage in extensive data collection, spending a great deal of time at the site where people work, play, or engage in the phenomenon you wish to study. At the site, you will gather detailed information to establish the complexity of the central phenomenon.

We can see the varied nature of qualitative forms of data when they are placed into the following categories:

- Observations
- Interviews and questionnaires
- Documents
- Audiovisual materials

Specific examples of types of data in these four categories are shown in Figure 7.3. Variations on data collection in all four areas are emerging continuously. Most recently, videotapes, student classroom portfolios, and the use of e-mails are attracting increasing attention as forms of data. Table 7.1 shows each category of data collection listed, the type of data it yields, and a definition for that type of data. Now let's take a closer look at each of the four categories and their strengths and weaknesses.

Observations

When educators think about qualitative research, they often have in mind the process of collecting observational data in a specific school setting. Unquestionably, observations represent a frequently used form of data collection, with the researcher able to assume different roles in the process (Spradley, 1980).

FIGURE 7.3

A Compendium of Data Collection Approaches in Qualitative Research

Observations

Gather fieldnotes by:

  Conducting an observation as a participant

  Conducting an observation as an observer

  Spending more time as a participant than observer

  Spending more time as an observer than a participant

  First observing as an "outsider," then participating in the setting and observing as an "insider"

Interviews and Questionnaires

Conduct an unstructured, open-ended interview and take interview notes.

Conduct an unstructured, open-ended interview; audiotape the interview and transcribe it.

Conduct a semistructured interview; audiotape the interview and transcribe it.

Conduct focus group interviews; audiotape the interviews and transcribe them.

Collect open-ended responses to an electronic interview or questionnaire.

Gather open-ended responses to questions on a questionnaire.

Documents

Keep a journal during the research study.

Have a participant keep a journal or diary during the research study.

Collect personal letters from participants.

Analyze public documents (e.g., official memos, minutes of meetings, records or archival material).

Analyze school documents (e.g., attendance reports, retention rates, dropout rates, or discipline referrals).

Examine autobiographies and biographies.

Collect or draw maps and seating charts.

Examine portfolios or less formal examples of students' work.

Collect e-mails or electronic data.

Audiovisual Materials

Examine physical trace evidence (e.g., footprints in the snow).

Videotape a social situation of an individual or group.

Examine photographs or videotapes.

Collect sounds (e.g., musical sounds, a child's laughter, or car horns honking).

Examine possessions or ritual objects.

Have participants take photos or videotapes.

Sources: Creswell, 2007; Mills, 2011.

Observation is the process of gathering open-ended, firsthand information by observing people and places at a research site. As a form of data collection, observation has both advantages and disadvantages. Advantages include the opportunity to record information as it occurs in a setting, to study actual behavior, and to study individuals who

TABLE 7.1		
Forms of Qualitative Data Collection		
Forms of Data Collection	**Type of Data**	**Definition of Type of Data**
Observations	Fieldnotes and drawings	Unstructured text data and pictures taken during observations by the researcher
Interviews and questionnaires	Transcriptions of open-ended interviews or open-ended questions on questionnaires	Unstructured text data obtained from transcribing audiotapes of interviews or by transcribing open-ended responses to questions on questionnaires
Documents	Hand-recorded notes about documents or optically scanned documents	Public (e.g., notes from meetings) and private (e.g., journals) records available to the researcher
Audiovisual materials	Pictures, photographs, videotapes, objects, sounds	Audiovisual materials consisting of images or sounds of people or places recorded by the researcher or someone else

have difficulty verbalizing their ideas (e.g., preschool children). Some of the disadvantages of observations are that you will be limited to those sites and situations where you can gain access, and in those sites, you may have difficulty developing rapport with individuals. This can occur if the individuals are unaccustomed to formal research (e.g., a nonuniversity setting). Observing in a setting requires good listening skills and careful attention to visual detail. It also requires management of issues such as the potential deception by people being observed and the initial awkwardness of being an "outsider" without initial personal support in a setting (Hammersley & Atkinson, 1995).

Observational Roles

Despite these potential difficulties, observation continues to be a well-accepted form of qualitative data collection. Using it requires that you adopt a particular role as an observer. No one role is suited for all situations; observational roles vary depending on your comfort at the site, your rapport with participants, and how best you can collect data to understand the central phenomenon. Although many roles exist (see Spradley, 1980), you might consider one of three popular roles.

Role of a Participant Observer   To truly learn about a situation, you can become involved in activities at the research site. This offers excellent opportunities to see experiences from the views of participants. A **participant observer** is an observational role adopted by researchers when they take part in activities in the setting they observe. As a participant, you assume the role of an "inside" observer who actually engages in activities at the study site. At the same time that you are participating in activities, you record information. This role requires seeking permission to participate in activities and assuming a comfortable role as observer in the setting. It is difficult to take notes while participating, and you may need to wait to write down observations until after you have left the research site.

Role of a Nonparticipant Observer   In some situations, you may not be familiar enough with the site and people to participate in the activities. A **nonparticipant observer** is an observer who visits a site and records notes without becoming involved in the activities of the participants. The nonparticipant observer is an "outsider" who sits on the periphery or some advantageous place (e.g., the back of the classroom) to watch and record the phenomenon under study. This role requires less access than the participant role, and gatekeepers and individuals at a research site may be more comfortable with it. However, by not actively participating, you will remove yourself from actual experiences, and the observations you make may not be as concrete as if you had participated in the activities.

Changing Observational Roles   In many observational situations, it is advantageous to shift or change roles, making it difficult to classify your role as strictly participatory or nonparticipatory. A **changing observational role** is one where researchers adapt their role to the situation. For example, you might first enter a site and observe as a nonparticipant, simply needing to "look around" in the early phases of research. Then you slowly become involved as a participant. Sometimes the reverse happens, and a participant becomes a nonparticipant. However, entering a site as a nonparticipant is a frequently used approach. After a short time, when rapport is developed, you switch to being a participant in the setting. Engaging in both roles permits you to be subjectively involved in the setting as well as to see the setting more objectively.

Here is an illustration in which a researcher began as a nonparticipant and changed into a participant during the process of observing:

> One researcher studying the use of wireless laptop computers in a multicultural education methods class spent the first three visits to the class observing from the back row. He sought to learn the process involved in teaching the course, the instructor's interaction with students, and the instructor's overall approach to teaching. Then, on his fourth visit, students began using the laptop computers and the observer became a participant by teaming with a student who used the laptop from her desk to interact with the instructor's Web site.

The Process of Observing

As we just saw in the discussion of different observational roles, the qualitative inquirer engages in a process of observing, regardless of the role. This general process is outlined in the following steps:

1. *Select a site to be observed that can help you best understand the central phenomenon.*   Obtain the required permissions needed to gain access to the site.
2. *Ease into the site slowly by looking around; getting a general sense of the site; and taking limited notes, at least initially.*   Conduct brief observations at first, because you will likely be overwhelmed with all of the activities taking place. This slow entry helps to build rapport with individuals at the site and helps you assimilate the large amount of information.
3. *At the site, identify who or what to observe, when to observe, and how long to observe.*   Gatekeepers can provide guidance as you make these decisions. The practical requirements of the situation, such as the length of a class period or the duration of the activity, will limit your participation.
4. *Determine, initially, your role as an observer.*   Select from the roles of participant or nonparticipant during your first few observations. Consider whether it would be advantageous to change roles during the process to learn best about the individuals or site. Regardless of whether you change roles, consider what role you will use and your reasons for it.
5. *Conduct multiple observations over time to obtain the best understanding of the site and the individuals.*   Engage in broad observation at first, noting the general landscape of activities and events. As you become familiar with the setting, you can begin to

narrow your observations to specific aspects (e.g., a small group of children interacting during reading time). A broad-to-narrow perspective is a useful strategy because of the amount of information available in an observation.

6. *Design some means for recording notes during an observation.* The data recorded during an observation are called *fieldnotes*. **Fieldnotes** are text (words) recorded by the researcher during an observation in a qualitative study. Examine the sample fieldnotes shown in Figure 7.4. In this example, the student-observer engaged in participant observation when the instructor asked the class to spend 20 minutes observing an art object that had been brought into the classroom. This object was not familiar to the students in the class. It was from Indonesia and had a square, bamboo base and a horsehair top. It was probably used for some religious activities. This was a good object to use for an observational activity because it could not be easily recognized or described. The instructor asked students to observe the object and record fieldnotes describing the object and reflecting on their insights, hunches, and themes that emerged during the observation.

As we see in Figure 7.4, one student recorded the senses—touch, sight, sound, and smell—of the object, recording thoughts every 5 minutes or so. Notice that the student's fieldnotes show complete sentences and notations about quotes from other students. The notes in the right column indicate that this student is beginning to reflect on the larger ideas learned from the experiences and to note how other

---

FIGURE 7.4

Sample Fieldnotes from a Student's Observation of an Art Object

$\boxed{\textit{Observational Fieldnotes}}$ —*Art Object in the Classroom*

Setting: Classroom 306
Observer: J
Role of Observer: Observer of object
Time: 4:30 p.m., March 9, 2004
Length of Observation: 20 minutes

<u>*Description of Object*</u>

4:35 p.m <u>*Touch*</u> *J taps on the base. Gritty wood, pieced together unevenly. The object's top feels like a cheap wig. The base was moved and the caning was tight. The wicker feels smooth.*

4:40 <u>*Sight*</u> *The object stands on four pegs that holds a square base. The base is decorated with scalloped carvings. The wood is a light, natural color and sanded smooth and finished. It is in the shape of a pyramid, cropped close at the bottom on the underside.*

4:50 <u>*Sound*</u> *Students comment as they touched the object, "Oh, that's hair?" Is it securely fastened?" A slight rustling is heard from brushing the bristles . . ."*

5:02 *The object <u>smells</u> like roof-dry slate. It is odorless. But it has a musty, dusty scent to the top half, and no one wants to sniff it.*

<u>*Reflective Notes*</u>   *(insights, hunches, themes)*
—*Many students touch the object—most walk up slowly, cautiously.*
—*Several good analogies come to mind.*

—*This object is really hard to describe—perhaps J should use dimensions? But it has several parts.*

—*Pickup on good quotes from the students.*
—*"Sounds" could definitely be one of my themes!*

—*This object seems to change smells the more J am around it—probably a dusty scent fits it best.*

students in the class are reacting to the object. The heading at the top of the field-notes records essential information about the time, place, and activities observed.

7. *Consider what information you will record during an observation.* For example, this information might include portraits of the participants, the physical setting, particular events and activities, and personal reactions (Bogdan & Biklen, 1998). In observing a classroom, for example, you may record activities by the teacher, the students, the interactions between the students and teacher, and the student-to-student conversations.

8. *Record descriptive and reflective fieldnotes.* **Descriptive fieldnotes** record a description of the events, activities, and people (e.g., what happened). **Reflective fieldnotes** record personal thoughts that researchers have that relate to their insights, hunches, or broad ideas or themes that emerge during the observation (e.g., what sense you made of the site, people, and situation).

9. *Make yourself known, but remain unobtrusive.* During the observation, be introduced by someone if you are an "outsider" or new to the setting or people. Be passive, be friendly, and be respectful of the people and site.

10. *After observing, slowly withdraw from the site.* Thank the participants and inform them of the use of the data and the availability of a summary of results when you complete the study.

Figure 7.5 summarizes the steps listed above in a checklist you might use to assess whether you are prepared to conduct an observation. The questions on this checklist represent roughly the order in which you might consider them before, during, and after the observation, but you can check off each question as you complete it.

Interviews

Equally popular to observation in qualitative research is interviewing. A qualitative **interview** occurs when researchers ask one or more participants general, open-ended questions and record their answers. The researcher then transcribes and types the data into a computer file for analysis.

FIGURE 7.5

An Observational Checklist

_____ Did you gain permission to study the site?	_____ Will you develop rapport with individuals at the site?
_____ Do you know your role as an observer?	
_____ Do you have a means for recording fieldnotes, such as an observational protocol?	_____ Will your observations change from broad to narrow?
	_____ Will you take limited notes at first?
_____ Do you know what you will observe first?	_____ Will you take both descriptive as well as reflective notes?
_____ Will you enter and leave the site slowly, so as not to disturb the setting?	
	_____ Will you describe in complete sentences so that you have detailed fieldnotes?
_____ Will you make multiple observations over time?	_____ Did you thank your participants at the site?

In *qualitative* research, you ask **open-ended questions** so that the participants can best voice their experiences unconstrained by any perspectives of the researcher or past research findings. An **open-ended response** to a question allows the participant to create the options for responding. For example, in a qualitative interview of athletes in high schools, you might ask, "How do you balance participation in athletics with your schoolwork?" The athlete then creates a response to this question without being forced into response possibilities. The researcher often audiotapes the conversation and transcribes the information into words for analysis.

Interviews in qualitative research have both advantages and disadvantages. Some advantages are that they provide useful information when you cannot directly observe participants, and they permit participants to describe detailed personal information. Compared to the observer, the interviewer also has better control over the types of information received, because the interviewer can ask specific questions to elicit this information.

Some disadvantages are that interviews provide only information "filtered" through the views of the interviewers (i.e., the researcher summarizes the participants' views in the research report). Also, similar to observations, interview data may be deceptive and provide the perspective the interviewee wants the researcher to hear. Another disadvantage is that the presence of the researcher may affect how the interviewee responds. Interviewee responses also may not be articulate, perceptive, or clear. In addition, equipment issues may be a problem, and you need to organize recording and transcribing equipment (if used) in advance of the interview. Also during the interview, you need to give some attention to the conversation with the participants. This attention may require saying little, handling emotional outbursts, and using icebreakers to encourage individuals to talk. With all of these issues to balance, it is little wonder inexperienced researchers express surprise about the difficulty of conducting interviews.

Types of Interviews and Open-Ended Questions on Questionnaires

Once you decide to collect qualitative interviews, you next consider what form of interviewing will best help you understand the central phenomenon and answer the questions in your study. There are a number of approaches to interviewing and using open-ended questions on questionnaires. Which interview approach to use will ultimately depend on the accessibility of individuals, the cost, and the amount of time available.

One-on-One Interviews   The most time-consuming and costly approach is to conduct individual interviews. A popular approach in educational research, the **one-on-one interview** is a data collection process in which the researcher asks questions to and records answers from only one participant in the study at a time. In a qualitative project, you may use several one-on-one interviews. One-on-one interviews are ideal for interviewing participants who are not hesitant to speak, who are articulate, and who can share ideas comfortably.

Focus Group Interviews   Focus groups can be used to collect shared understanding from several individuals as well as to get views from specific people. A **focus group interview** is the process of collecting data through interviews with a group of people, typically four to six. The researcher asks a small number of general questions and elicits responses from all individuals in the group. Focus groups are advantageous when the interaction among interviewees will likely yield the best information and when interviewees are similar to and cooperative with each other. They are also useful when the time to collect information is limited and individuals are hesitant to provide information (some individuals may be reluctant to provide information in any type of interview).

When conducting a focus group interview, encourage all participants to talk and to take their turns talking. A focus group can be challenging for the interviewer who lacks control over the interview discussion. Also, when focus groups are audiotaped, the transcriptionist may have difficulty discriminating among the voices of individuals in the group. Another problem with conducting focus group interviews is that the researcher often has difficulty taking notes because so much is occurring.

Let's consider an example of a focus group interview procedure:

> High school students, with the sponsorship of a university team of researchers, conducted focus group interviews with other students about the use of tobacco in several high schools (Plano Clark et al., 2001). In several interviews, two student interviewers—one to ask questions and one to record responses—selected six students to interview in a focus group. These focus group interviews lasted one-half hour and the interviewers tape-recorded the interview and took notes during the interview. Because the groups were small, the transcriptionist did not have difficulty transcribing the interview and identifying individual voices. At the beginning of the interview each student said his or her first name.

Telephone Interviews   It may not be possible for you to gather groups of individuals for an interview or to visit one-on-one with single individuals. The participants in a study may be geographically dispersed and unable to come to a central location for an interview. In this situation, you can conduct telephone interviews. Conducting a **telephone interview** is the process of gathering data using the telephone and asking a small number of general questions. A telephone interview requires that the researcher use a telephone adaptor that plugs into both the phone and a tape recorder for a clear recording of the interview. One drawback of this kind of interviewing is that the researcher does not have direct contact with the participant. This causes limited communication that may affect the researcher's ability to understand the interviewee's perceptions of the phenomenon. Also, the process may involve substantial costs for telephone expenses. Let's look at an example of a telephone interview procedure:

> In a study of academic department chairpersons in colleges and universities, Creswell et al. (1990) conducted open-ended telephone interviews lasting 45 minutes each with 200 chairpersons located on campuses in the United States. They first obtained the permission of these chairpersons to participate in an interview through contacting them by letter. They also scheduled a time that would be convenient for the interviewee to participate in a telephone interview. Next, they purchased tape recorders and adaptors to conduct the interviews from office telephones. They asked open-ended questions such as "How did you prepare for your position?" The interviews yielded about 3,000 transcript pages. Analysis of these pages resulted in a report about how chairpersons enhance the professional development of faculty in their departments.

E-Mail Interviews   Another type of interview useful in collecting qualitative data quickly from a geographically dispersed group of people. **E-mail interviews** consist of collecting open-ended data through interviews with individuals using computers and the Internet to do so. If you can obtain e-mail lists or addresses, this form of interviewing provides rapid access to large numbers of people and a detailed, rich text database for qualitative analysis. It can also promote a conversation between yourself as the researcher and the participants, so that through follow-up conversations, you can extend your understanding of the topic or central phenomenon being studied.

However, e-mail interviewing raises complex ethical issues, such as whether you have permission for individuals to participate in your interview, and whether you will protect the privacy of responses. In addition, it may be difficult, under some circumstances, to obtain good lists of e-mail addresses that are current or the names of individuals who will be well suited to answer your questions. For example, how do you locate e-mail addresses for children under the age of 10, who probably do not have such an address? Despite these potential shortcomings, e-mail interviewing as a form of collecting data will probably increase due to expanding technology. Consider this example of an open-ended e-mail survey:

> Four researchers combined resources to develop an e-mail list of faculty who might be teaching courses in mixed methods research (Creswell, Tashakkori, Jensen, & Shapely, 2003). They began with an e-mail list of 31 faculty and sent an open-ended interview to these faculty, inquiring about their teaching practices. They asked, for example, "Have you ever taught a course with a content of mixed methods research?" "Why do you think students enroll in a mixed methods course?" and "What is your general assessment of mixed methods teaching?" After receiving the e-mail survey, the participants answered each question by writing about their experiences, and sent the survey back using the "reply" feature of their e-mail program. This procedure led to a qualitative text database of open-ended responses from a large number of individuals who had experienced mixed methods research.

Open-Ended Questions on Questionnaires   On questionnaires, you may ask some questions that are closed ended and some that are open ended. The advantage of this type of questioning is that your predetermined closed-ended responses can net useful information to support theories and concepts in the literature. The open-ended responses, however, permit you to explore reasons for the closed-ended responses and identify any comments people might have that are beyond the responses to the closed-ended questions. The drawback of this approach is that you will have many responses—some short and some long—to analyze. Also, the responses are detached from the context—the setting in which people work, play, and interact. This means that the responses may not represent a fully developed database with rich detail as is often gathered in qualitative research. To analyze open-ended responses, qualitative researchers look for overlapping themes in the open-ended data and some researchers count the number of themes or the number of times that the participants mention the themes. For example, a researcher might ask a closed-ended question followed by an open-ended question:

> Please tell me the extent of your agreement or disagreement with this statement:
>
> "Student policies governing binge drinking on campus should be more strict."
>
> _____ Do you strongly agree?
>
> _____ Do you agree?
>
> _____ Are you undecided?
>
> _____ Do you disagree?
>
> _____ Do you strongly disagree?
>
> Please explain your response in more detail.

In this example, the researcher started with a closed-ended question and five predetermined response categories and followed it with an open-ended question in which the participants indicate reasons for their responses.

Conducting Interviews

In all of the various forms of interviewing, several general steps are involved in conducting interviews or constructing open-ended questionnaires:

1. *Identify the interviewees.*   Use one of the purposeful sampling strategies discussed earlier in this chapter.

2. *Determine the type of interview you will use.*   Choose the one that will allow you to best learn the participants' views and answer each research question. Consider a telephone interview, a focus group interview, a one-on-one interview, an e-mail interview, a questionnaire, or some combination of these forms.

3. *During the interview, audiotape the questions and responses.*   This will give you an accurate record of the conversation. Use adequate recording procedures, such as lapel microphone equipment (small microphones that are hooked onto a shirt or collar) for one-on-one interviewing, and a suitable directional microphone (one that picks up sounds in all directions) for focus group interviewing. Have an adequate tape recorder and telephone adapter for telephone interviews, and understand thoroughly mail programs for e-mail interviewing.

4. *Take brief notes during the interview.*   Although it is sound practice to audiotape the interview, take notes in the event the tape recorder malfunctions. You record these notes on a form called an *interview protocol,* discussed later in this chapter. Recognize that notes taken during the interview may be incomplete because of the difficulty of asking questions and writing answers at the same time. An abbreviated form for writing notes (e.g., short phrases followed by a dash) may speed up the process.

5. *Locate a quiet, suitable place for conducting the interview.*   If possible, interview at a location free from distractions and choose a physical setting that lends it to audiotaping. This means, for example, that a busy teachers' or faculty lounge may not be the best place for interviewing because of the noise and the interruptions that may occur.

6. *Obtain consent from the interviewee to participate in the study.*   Obtain consent by having interviewees complete an informed consent form when you first arrive. Before starting the interview, convey to the participants the purpose of the study, the time the interview will take to complete, the plans for using the results from the interview, and the availability of a summary of the study when the research is completed.

7. *Have a plan, but be flexible.*   During the interview, stick with the questions, but be flexible enough to follow the conversation of the interviewee. Complete the questions within the time specified (if possible) to respect and be courteous of the participants. Recognize that a key to good interviewing is to be a good listener.

8. *Use probes to obtain additional information.*   **Probes** are subquestions under each question that the researcher asks to elicit more information. Use them to clarify points or to have the interviewee expand on ideas. These probes vary from exploring the content in more depth (elaborating) to asking the interviewee to explain the answer in more detail (clarifying). Table 7.2 shows these two types of probes. The table uses a specific illustration to convey examples of both clarifying and elaborating probes.

9. *Be courteous and professional when the interview is over.* Complete the interview by thanking the participant, assuring him or her of the confidentiality of the responses, and asking if he or she would like a summary of the results of the study.

Figure 7.6 summarizes good interviewing procedures in a checklist adapted from Gay, Mills, and Airasian (2005). The questions on the checklist represent the order in which you might consider them before, during, and after the interview.

Let's return to Maria, who needs to decide what data collection procedure to use. Because she has experience talking with students and fellow teachers, she decides interviewing would be best. She proceeds to conduct five interviews with students and five with teachers in her high school. After obtaining permission from the school district and the principal of her school, she must obtain permission from the students (and their parents or guardians) and the teachers. To select these individuals, she will purposefully sample individuals who can speak from different perspectives (maximal variation sampling). She realizes there are different groups in the school, such as the "athletes," the "singers," the "punkers," the "class officers," and the "cheerleaders." She identifies one

TABLE 7.2

Types of Probes Used in Qualitative Interviewing

	Examples	
	Clarifying Probes	**Elaborating Probes**
A question in the study asks, "What has happened since the event that you have been involved in?" Assume that the interviewee says, "Not much" or simply does not answer.	Probe areas	"Tell me more."
	Comments to other students: "Tell me about discussions you had with other students."	"Could you explain your response more?"
	Role of parents: "Did you talk with your parents?"	"I need more detail."
	Role of news media: "Did you talk with any media personnel?"	"What does 'not much' mean?"

FIGURE 7.6

A Checklist for Interviewing

_____ Who will participate in your interviews?

_____ What types of interviews are best to conduct?

_____ Is the setting for your interview comfortable and quiet?

_____ If you are audiotaping, have you prepared and tested the equipment?

_____ Did you obtain consent from the participants to participate in the interview?

_____ Did you listen more and talk less during the interview?

_____ Did you probe during the interview? (ask to clarify and elaborate)

_____ Did you avoid leading questions and ask open-ended questions?

_____ Did you keep participants focused and ask for concrete details?

_____ Did you withhold judgments and refrain from debating with participants about their views?

_____ Were you courteous and did you thank the participants after concluding the interview?

Source: Adapted from Gay, Mills, & Airasian, 2005.

student from each group, realizing that she will likely obtain diverse perspectives representing complex views on the topic of weapon possession.

Next, she selects five teachers, each representing different subject areas, such as social studies, science, physical education, music, and drama. After that, she develops five open-ended questions, such as "How do weapons come into our school?" and "What types of weapons are in our school?" She needs to schedule interviews, conduct them, record information on audiotapes, take notes, and respect the views and rights of the students and faculty participating in the interviews.

As you read this procedure, what are its strengths and its limitations? List these strengths and weaknesses.

Documents

A valuable source of information in qualitative research can be documents. **Documents** consist of public and private records that qualitative researchers obtain about a site or participants in a study, and they can include newspapers, minutes of meetings, personal journals, and letters. These sources provide valuable information in helping researchers understand central phenomena in qualitative studies. They represent public and private documents. Examples of public documents are minutes from meetings, official memos, records in the public domain, and archival material in libraries. Private documents consist of personal journals and diaries, letters, personal notes, and jottings individuals write to themselves. Materials such as e-mail comments and Web site data illustrate both public and private documents, and they represent a growing data source for qualitative researchers.

Documents represent a good source for text (word) data for a qualitative study. They provide the advantage of being in the language and words of the participants, who have usually given thoughtful attention to them. They are also ready for analysis without the necessary transcription that is required with observational or interview data.

On the negative side, documents are sometimes difficult to locate and obtain. Information may not be available to the public. Information may be located in distant archives, requiring the researcher to travel, which takes time and can be expensive. Further, the documents may be incomplete, inauthentic, or inaccurate. For example, not all minutes from school board meetings are accurate, because board members may not review them for accuracy. In personal documents such as diaries or letters, the handwriting may be hard to read, making it difficult to decipher the information.

Collecting Documents

With so much variation in the types of documents, there are many procedures for collecting them. Here are several useful guidelines for collecting documents in qualitative research:

1. Identify the types of documents that can provide useful information to answer your qualitative research questions.
2. Consider both public (e.g., school board minutes) and private documents (e.g., personal diaries) as sources of information for your research.
3. Once the documents are located, seek permission to use them from the appropriate individuals in charge of the materials.
4. If you ask participants to keep a journal, provide specific instructions about the procedure. These guidelines might include what topics and format to use, the length of journal entries, and the importance of writing their thoughts legibly.
5. Once you have permission to use documents, examine them for accuracy, completeness, and usefulness in answering the research questions in your study.
6. Record information from the documents. This process can take several forms, including taking notes about the documents or, if possible, optically scanning them so a text (or word) file is created for each document. You can easily scan newspaper stories (e.g., on speeches by presidential candidates) to form a qualitative text database.

Collecting personal documents can provide a researcher with a rich source of information. For example, consider a study that used journals prepared by several women:

An important source for learning about women in superintendent positions is for them to keep a personal journal or diary of their experiences. A researcher asked three women superintendents to keep a diary for 6 months and record their reactions to being a woman in their capacity of conducting official meetings comprised primarily of men.

These journals were useful for learning about the working lives of women in educational settings.

Audiovisual Materials

The final type of qualitative data to collect is visual images. **Audiovisual materials** consist of images or sounds that researchers collect to help them understand the central phenomenon under study. Used with increasing frequency in qualitative research, images or visual materials such as photographs, videotapes, digital images, paintings and pictures, and unobtrusive measures (e.g., evidence deduced from a setting, such as physical traces of images such as footsteps in the snow; see Webb's [1966] discussion about unobtrusive measures) are all sources of information for qualitative inquiry. One approach in using photography is the technique of photo elicitation. In this approach, participants are shown pictures (their own or those taken by the researcher) and asked to discuss the contents. These pictures might be personal photographs or albums of historical photographs (see Ziller, 1990).

The advantage of using visual materials is that people easily relate to images because they are so pervasive in our society. Images provide an opportunity for the participants to share directly their perceptions of reality. Images such as videotapes and films, for example, provide extensive data about real life as people visualize it. A potential disadvantage of using images is that they are difficult to analyze because of the rich information (e.g., how do you make sense of all of the aspects apparent in 50 drawings by preservice teachers of what it is like to be a science teacher?). Also, you as a researcher may influence the data collected. In selecting the photo album to examine or requesting that a certain type of drawing be sketched, you may impose your meaning of the phenomenon on participants, rather than obtain the participants' views. When videotaping, you face the issues of what to tape, where to place the camera, and the need to be sensitive with camera-shy individuals.

Collecting Audiovisual Materials

Despite these potential problems, visual material is becoming more popular in qualitative research, especially with recent advances in technology. The steps involved in collecting visual material are similar to the steps involved in collecting documents:

1. Determine what visual material can provide information to answer research questions and how that material might augment existing forms of data, such as interviews and observations.
2. Identify the visual material available and obtain permission to use it. This permission might require asking all students in a classroom, for example, to sign informed consent forms and to have their parents sign them also.
3. Check the accuracy and authenticity of the visual material if you do not record it yourself. One way to check for accuracy is to contact and interview the photographer or the individuals represented in the pictures.
4. Collect the data and organize it. You can optically scan the data for easy storage and retrieval.

To illustrate the use of visual material, look at an example in which the researcher distributed cameras to obtain photographs:

A researcher gives Polaroid cameras to 40 male and 40 female fourth graders in a science unit to record their meaning of the environment. The participants are asked to take pictures of images that represent attempts to preserve the environment in our society. As a result, the researcher obtains 24 pictures from each child that can be used to understand how young people look at the environment. Understandably, photos of squirrels and outside pets dominate the collection of pictures in this database.

WHAT PROCEDURES WILL BE USED TO RECORD DATA?

An essential process in qualitative research is recording data (Lofland & Lofland, 1995). This process involves recording information through research protocols, administering data collection so that you can anticipate potential problems in data collection, and bringing sensitivity to ethical issues that may affect the quality of the data.

Using Protocols

As already discussed, for documents and visual materials, the process of recording information may be informal (taking notes) or formal (optically scanning the material to develop a complete computer text file). For observations and interviews, qualitative inquirers use specially designed protocols. **Data recording protocols** are forms designed and used by qualitative researchers to record information during observations and interviews.

An Interview Protocol

During interviewing, it is important to have some means for structuring the interview and taking careful notes. As already mentioned, audiotaping of interviews provides a detailed record of the interview. As a backup, you need to take notes during the interview and have the questions ready to be asked. An interview protocol serves the purpose of reminding you of the questions and it provides a means for recording notes. An **interview protocol** is a form designed by the researcher that contains instructions for the process of the interview, the questions to be asked, and space to take notes of responses from the interviewee.

Development and Design of an Interview Protocol   To best understand the design and appearance of this form, examine the qualitative interview protocol used during a study of the campus reaction to a gunman who threatened students in a classroom (Asmussen & Creswell, 1995), shown in Figure 7.7. This figure is a reduced version of the actual protocol; in the original protocol, more space was provided between the questions to record answers. Figure 7.7 illustrates the components that you might design into an interview protocol.

◆ It contains a header to record essential information about the interview, statements about the purpose of the study, a reminder that participants need to sign the consent form, and a suggestion to make preliminary tests of the recording equipment. Other information you might include in the header would be the organization or work affiliation of the interviewees; their educational background and position; the number of years they have been in the position; and the date, time, and location of the interview.

◆ Following this header are five brief open-ended questions that allow participants maximum flexibility for responding to the questions. The first question serves the purpose of an icebreaker (sometimes called the "grand tour" question), to relax the interviewees and motivate them to talk. This question should be easy to understand and cause the participants to reflect on experiences that they can easily discuss,

FIGURE 7.7

Sample Interview Protocol

Interview Protocol

Project: University Reaction to a Gunman Incident

Time of Interview:
Date:
Place:
Interviewer:
Interviewee:
Position of Interviewee:

[Describe here the project, telling the interviewee about (a) the purpose of the study, (b) the individuals and sources of data being collected, (c) what will be done with the data to protect the confidentiality of the interviewee, and (d) how long the interview will take.]
[Have the interviewee read and sign the consent form.]
[Turn on the tape recorder and test it.]

Questions:

1. Please describe your role in the incident.

2. What has happened since the event that you have been involved in?

3. What has been the impact on the University community of this incident?

4. What larger ramifications, if any, exist from the incident?

5. Whom should we talk to to find out more about campus reaction to the incident?

(Thank the individuals for their cooperation and participation in this interview. Assure them of the confidentiality of the responses and the potential for future interviews.)

Source: Asmussen & Creswell, 1995.

such as "Please describe your role in the incident." The final question on this particular instrument helps the researcher locate additional people to study.

◆ The core questions, Questions 2 through 4, address major research questions in the study. For those new to qualitative research, you might ask more than four questions, to help elicit more discussion from interviewees and move through awkward moments when no one is talking. However, the more questions you ask, the more you are examining what you seek to learn rather than learning from the participant. There is often a fine line between your questions being too detailed or too general. A pilot test of them on a few participants can usually help you decide which ones to use.

◆ In addition to the five questions, you might use probes to encourage participants to clarify what they are saying and to urge them to elaborate on their ideas.

◆ You provide space between the questions so that the researcher can take short notes about comments made by interviewees. Your notes should be brief and you can develop an abbreviated form for stating them. The style for recording these notes varies from researcher to researcher.

◆ It is helpful for you to memorize the wording and the order of the questions to minimize losing eye contact. Provide appropriate verbal transitions from one question to the next. Recognize that individuals do not always respond directly to the question you ask: when you ask Question 2, for example, they may jump ahead and respond to Question 4.

◆ Closing comments remind you to thank the participants and assure them of the confidentiality of the responses. This section may also include a note to ask the interviewees if they have any questions, and a reminder to discuss the use of the data and the dissemination of information from the study.

An Observational Protocol

You use an observational protocol to record information during an observation, just as in interviewing. This protocol applies to all of the observational roles mentioned earlier. An **observational protocol** is a form designed by the researcher before data collection that is used for taking fieldnotes during an observation. On this form, researchers record a chronology of events, a detailed portrait of an individual or individuals, a picture or map of the setting, or verbatim quotes of individuals. As with interview protocols, the design and development of observational protocols will ensure that you have an organized means for recording and keeping observational fieldnotes.

Development and Design of an Observational Protocol You have already seen a sample observational protocol in Figure 7.4, in which the student took notes about the art object in class. An observational protocol such as that one permits qualitative researchers to record information they see at the observation site. This information is both a description of activities in the setting and a reflection about themes and personal insights noted during the observation. For example, examine again the sample observational protocol shown in Figure 7.4. This sample protocol illustrates the components typically found on a recording form in an observation:

◆ The protocol contains a header where you record information about the time, place, setting, and your observational role.

◆ You write in two columns following the header. These columns divide the page for recording into two types of data: a description of activities and a reflection about themes, quotes, and personal experiences of the researcher.

◆ The exact nature of this description may vary. Figure 7.4 illustrates possible topics for description. For example, you may include a description of the chronological order of events. This description is especially useful if the observer is examining a process or event. You may also describe the individuals, physical setting, events, and activities (Bogdan & Biklen, 1998). You may also sketch a picture of the site to facilitate remembering details of the setting for the final written report.

◆ Reflective notes record your experiences as a researcher, such as your hunches about important results and insights or emerging themes for later analysis.

 Think-Aloud About Observing

I typically ask my graduate students to practice gathering qualitative data by observing a setting. One of my favorite settings is the campus recreational center, where they can watch students learn how to climb the "wall." It is an artificial wall created so that students can learn how to rock climb. At this site, we typically find students who are learning how to climb the wall, and an instructor who is giving climbing lessons. The wall itself is about 50 feet high and has strategically located handholds to assist the climbers. The wall contains several colored banners positioned for climbers to use to scale the wall. The objective is for a student to climb to the top of the wall and then rappel down.

Before the observation, my students always ask what they should observe. Here are the instructions that I give them:

◆ Design an observational protocol using Figure 7.4 as a guide.
◆ Go to the recreational center and to the base of the wall. Find a comfortable place to sit on one of the benches in front of the wall, and then observe for about 10 minutes without recording information. Initially, simply observe and become acclimated to the setting.
◆ After these 10 minutes, start focusing on one activity at the site. It may be a student receiving instructions about how to put on the climbing gear, students actually scaling the wall, or other students waiting their turn to climb.
◆ Start recording descriptive fieldnotes. Consider a chronology of events, portraits of individuals, or a sketch of the site. To provide a creative twist to this exercise, I ask students to describe information about two of the following four senses: sight, sound, touch, or smell.
◆ Also record reflective notes during the observation.
◆ After 30 minutes, the observational period ends, and I ask students to write a brief qualitative passage about what they observed, incorporating both their descriptive and their reflective fieldnotes. This final request combines data collection (observing), data analysis (making sense of their notes), and report writing (trying to compose a brief qualitative research narrative).

WHAT FIELD AND ETHICAL ISSUES NEED TO BE ANTICIPATED?

When collecting data, researchers who engage in qualitative studies typically face issues that they need to resolve. Also, because qualitative research involves going to the research sites of the participants, staying a considerable time, and asking detailed questions, ethical issues are likely to arise that need to be anticipated.

Field Issues

Prior to a study, anticipate potential issues that might arise during data collection. Figure 7.8 lists issues and categorizes them according to the type of data you will be collecting. These issues include access to site problems, observations, interviews, document research, journals, and the use of audiovisual materials.

◆ *Access.*   Anticipate the amount of time it will take to recruit participants to your study and the difficulty of recruitment. Some useful strategies include providing a small financial incentive for individuals to participate. Also, remind participants a day or two before data collection of the exact time and day you will observe or interview them. Stage the data collection so that they will feel comfortable

down how these themes reflect or differ from experiences reported by other researchers in the literature. She also takes the themes back to a few students in a focus group and asks them whether she accurately identifies their experiences.

WHAT ARE THE SIX STEPS IN ANALYZING AND INTERPRETING QUALITATIVE DATA?

Maria has proceeded through the six steps commonly used in analyzing qualitative data. These steps are not always taken in sequence, but they represent preparing and organizing the data for analysis; engaging in an initial exploration of the data through the process of coding it; using the codes to develop a more general picture of the data—descriptions and themes; representing the findings through narratives and visuals; making an interpretation of the meaning of the results by reflecting personally on the impact of the findings and on the literature that might inform the findings; and finally, conducting strategies to validate the accuracy of the findings.

You can visualize the first major steps in this process by examining the "bottom-up" approach to analysis in Figure 8.1. As shown in the figure, qualitative researchers first collect data and then prepare it for data analysis. This analysis initially consists of developing a general sense of the data, and then coding description and themes about the central phenomenon. Let's look at some of the features of this process in more detail.

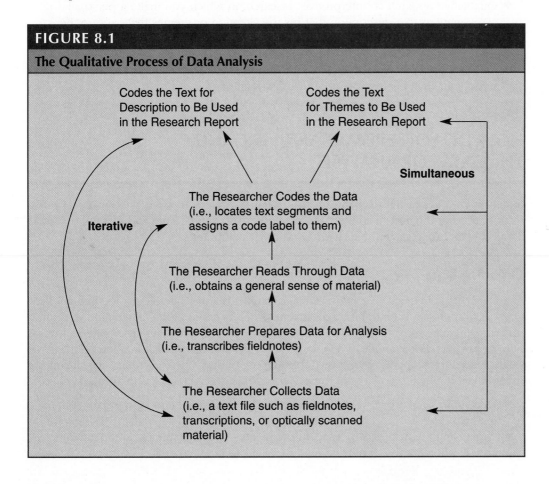

FIGURE 8.1

The Qualitative Process of Data Analysis

Codes the Text for Description to Be Used in the Research Report

Codes the Text for Themes to Be Used in the Research Report

Simultaneous

The Researcher Codes the Data (i.e., locates text segments and assigns a code label to them)

Iterative

The Researcher Reads Through Data (i.e., obtains a general sense of material)

The Researcher Prepares Data for Analysis (i.e., transcribes fieldnotes)

The Researcher Collects Data (i.e., a text file such as fieldnotes, transcriptions, or optically scanned material)

◆ It is inductive in form, going from the particular or the detailed data (e.g., transcriptions or typed notes from interviews) to the general codes and themes. Keeping this in mind helps you understand how qualitative researchers produce broad themes or categories from diverse detailed databases. Although the initial analysis consists of subdividing the data (later we will discuss *coding* the data), the final goal is to generate a larger, consolidated picture (Tesch, 1990).

◆ It involves a simultaneous process of analyzing while you are also collecting data. In qualitative research, the data collection and analysis (and perhaps the report writing) are simultaneous activities. When you are collecting data, you may also be analyzing other information previously collected, looking for major ideas. This procedure differs from traditional approaches in *quantitative* research, in which data collection occurs first, followed by data analysis.

◆ The phases are also iterative, meaning you cycle back and forth between data collection and analysis. In qualitative research, you might collect stories from individuals and return for more information to fill in gaps in their stories as your analysis of their stories proceeds.

◆ Qualitative researchers analyze their data by reading it several times and conducting an analysis each time. Each time you read your database, you develop a deeper understanding about the information supplied by your participants.

◆ There is no single, accepted approach to analyzing qualitative data, although several guidelines exist for this process (see Dey, 1993; Miles & Huberman, 1994). It is an eclectic process.

◆ Qualitative research is "interpretive" research, in which you make a personal assessment as to a description that fits the situation or themes that capture the major categories of information. The interpretation that you make of a transcript, for example, differs from the interpretation that someone else makes. This does not mean that your interpretation is better or more accurate; it simply means that you bring your own perspective to your interpretation.

HOW DO YOU PREPARE AND ORGANIZE THE DATA FOR ANALYSIS?

Initial preparation of the data for analysis requires organizing the vast amount of information, transferring it from spoken or written words to a typed file and making decisions about whether to analyze the data by hand or by computer.

Organize Data

At an early stage in qualitative analysis, you organize data into file folders or computer files. Organization of data is critical in qualitative research because of the large amount of information gathered during a study. The extensive data that an interview yields often surprises new researchers. For example, a 30-minute interview will often result in about 20 pages of single-spaced transcription. With this sizable amount of data, the transcribing and organizing of information requires a system of organization, which could take several forms, such as:

◆ Developing a matrix or a table of sources that can be used to help organize the material

◆ Organizing the materials by type: all interviews, all observations, all documents, and all photographs or other visual materials; as an alternative, you might consider

organizing the materials by participant, site, location, or some combination of these approaches
♦ Keeping duplicate copies of all forms of data

Transcribe Data

During qualitative data collection, you will collect text or words through interviewing participants or by writing fieldnotes during observations. This necessitates a need to convert these words to a computer document for analysis. Alternatively, you might listen to the tapes or read your fieldnotes to begin the process of analysis. When time is short or funds are scarce, you may be able to have only a few interviews or a few observational notes transcribed. The most complete procedure, however, is to have all interviews and all observational notes transcribed. As a general rule of thumb, it takes approximately 4 hours to transcribe 1 hour of tape (Dana Miller, personal communication, April 11, 2000). Hence, the process of transcription is labor intensive and you will need to allow adequate time for it.

Transcription is the process of converting audiotape recordings or fieldnotes into text data. Figure 8.2 lists suggestions for conducting a taped interview from the transcriptionist's point of view. You may use a transcriptionist to type your text files or you can transcribe the information yourself. In either case, for interview data, transcriptionists need special equipment to help create the transcript. This equipment consists of a machine that enables the transcriber to start and stop tape recordings or to play them at a speed so that the transcriber can easily follow them. Here are a few more guidelines to facilitate transcription:

♦ Create 2-inch margins on each side of the text document so that you can jot down notes in the margins during data analysis.
♦ Leave extra space on the page between the interviewer's comments and the interviewee's comments. This enables you to distinguish clearly between speakers during data analysis.
♦ Highlight or mark in some way the questions asked by the interviewer. You will not analyze your questions, but identifying them clearly indicates where one question ends and another begins. Often, you will analyze all answers to a single question.
♦ Use complete, detailed headers that contain information about the interview or observational session. Examine interview and observational protocols to see the type of content to be included in a transcription.
♦ Transcribe all words, and type the word "[*pause*]" to indicate when interviewees take a lengthy break in their comments. These pauses may provide useful information about times when interviewees cannot or will not respond to a question. You can also record other actions occurring during an interview. For example, type "[*laughter*]" when the interviewee laughs, "[*telephone rings*]" to indicate a phone call that interrupts the interview, or "[*inaudible*]" to mark when the transcriptionist cannot determine what is being said. As a general approach, transcribing all words will provide data that captures the details of an interview.

Analyze by Hand or Computer

With the popularity of computers, researchers have a choice about whether to hand analyze data or to use a computer. The **hand analysis of qualitative data** means that researchers read the data, mark it by hand, and divide it into parts. Traditionally, analyzing text data involves using color coding to mark parts of the text or cutting and pasting

FIGURE 8.2

Hints for Transcribing Audiotaped Interviews

Hints for Taped Interviews: The Transcriptionist's View
Donald Callen Freed
Word Processing Center at
Teachers College, University of Nebraska at Lincoln

The following suggestions are a result of several years of experience transcribing research interview tapes. They are offered for your consideration in order that your transcription may be easier and less time consuming. These suggestions were originally developed for persons who have their tapes professionally transcribed, although many are applicable to those who transcribe their own tapes.

1. Please use an external microphone. This places voices closer to the microphone, and away from the noise of the tape recorder itself. If you must use a machine with an internal microphone, place it as close to *both* interviewer and interviewee as possible. High quality tape recorders also ensure better results and reduce background noise, especially if an external microphone is not available. (Most electronic supply shops have external microphones, which are very inexpensive.)
2. For telephone interviews, please use a telephone pick-up device.
3. Please keep the microphone and/or tape recorder away from possible loud-noise interference—electronic devices, the telephone on a desk, coffee cups or glasses that might be set on the same table as the microphone, etc. An important word or phrase can be lost with the interference of one loud noise.
4. Interviewers: Try to induce slower, more distinct speech by speaking calmly yourself. Try asking questions slowly and distinctly, so that the interviewee will respond in a like manner. Practice keeping your voice up all the way to the end of the sentence, using clear diction. Important questions or probes are sometimes lost because the interviewer trails off or speaks less distinctly at the end of the sentence.
5. Use *new, high-quality* tapes and good, well-maintained recording equipment. If you must rely on previously used tapes, make sure they have been used only once or twice. Older tapes often have bleed-over from previous recordings, and are more likely to jam in a machine. In general, transcription equipment works best with 60-minute tapes. Standard-size cassette tapes work much better than micro- or mini-cassettes, and are more easily turned over in an interview.
6. Think clearly about the format you want for your printed transcription. Consider the margin size and the amount of space you want left for comments, double or triple spacing, large margins for coding purposes, etc.

Following these steps can ensure better quality for your research transcriptions, making research easier and your results more accurate. A transcriptionist can only type what he or she can hear. A small amount of forethought and attention to detail on the interviewer's part can result in a better interview tape and transcription.

Source: Adapted from the January 1990 "Words" newsletter, Teachers College Word Processing Center, University of Nebraska-Lincoln, Marlene Starr and Donald C. Freed, editors.

text sentences onto cards. Some qualitative researchers like to hand analyze all of their data. A hand analysis may be preferred when you:

◆ Are analyzing a small database (e.g., fewer than 500 pages of transcripts or field-notes) and can easily keep track of files and locate text passages
◆ Are not comfortable using computers or have not learned a qualitative computer software program
◆ Want to be close to the data and have a hands-on feel for it without the intrusion of a machine
◆ Have time to commit to a hand analysis, since it is a labor-intensive activity to manually sort, organize, and locate words in a text database

For others with a greater interest in technology and with the time to learn a computer program, a computer analysis is ideal. A **computer analysis of qualitative data** means that researchers use a qualitative computer program to facilitate the process of storing, analyzing, sorting, and representing or visualizing the data. With the development of these computer programs, you have a choice as to whether to use hand coding or a computer analysis. You might base your decision on several factors. Use a computer program when you:

◆ Are analyzing a large database (e.g., more than 500 pages of transcripts or field-notes) and need to organize and keep track of extensive information
◆ Are adequately trained in using the program and are comfortable using computers
◆ Have resources to purchase a program or can locate one to use
◆ Need a close inspection of every word and sentence to capture specific quotes or meanings of passages

Use of Qualitative Computer Programs

Qualitative computer programs do not analyze the data for you. However, they do provide several convenient features that facilitate your data analysis. A **qualitative data analysis computer program** is a program that stores data, organizes your data, enables you to assign labels or codes to your data, and facilitates searching through your data and locating specific text or words.

Procedures for Using Software Programs

The general procedures for using a software program are as follows:

1. Convert a word processing file into a text file or import the word processing file directly into the computer program. The word processing file will be a transcribed interview, a set of fieldnotes, or other text, such as a scanned document.
2. Select a computer program to use. This program should have the features of storing data, organizing data, assigning labels or codes, and searching the data.
3. Enter a file into the program and give it a name.
4. Go through the file and mark sentences or paragraphs of ideas that pertain to what the participant is saying in the text.
5. Provide a code label for the blocked text. Continue this process of marking text and providing code labels for the entire text file.
6. After blocking and assigning labels to text, search for all text matching each code, and print out a file of these text passages.
7. Collapse these code labels into a few broad themes, or categories, and include evidence for each category.

Basic Features of Software Programs

Many commercial, qualitative data analysis software programs are available today. A recent review of software programs analyzed their features based on eight major dimensions, as shown in Figure 8.3 (Creswell & Maietta, 2002). Using information from this figure, your basic considerations are to find a program that is easy to use, that will accept both your text files (from transcripts) and your images (from pictures), that allows you to read and review text and categorize it, and that sorts and finds text or image passages easily for your qualitative report. Less frequently, you may be interested in merging analyses compiled by different researchers (such as when a research team analyzes the data) or importing or exporting your analyses to other software programs (such as exporting to SPSS or importing from a spreadsheet).

FIGURE 8.3

Features to Consider When Comparing Qualitative Data Analysis Software

Ease of Integration in Using the Program

    Windows or Macintosh compatible?

    Is it easy to use in getting started?

    Can you easily work through a document?

Type of Data Program Will Accept

    Will it handle text data?

    WIll it handle multimedia (image) data?

Reading and Reviewing Text

    Can it highlight and connect quotations?

    Can it search for specific text passages?

Memo Writing

    Does it have the capability for you to add notes or memos?

    Can you easily access the memos you write?

Categorization

    Can you develop codes?

    Can you easily apply codes to text or images?

    Can you easily display codes?

    Can you easily review and make changes in the codes?

Analysis Inventory and Assessment

    Can you sort for specific codes?

    Can you combine codes in a search?

    Can you develop a concept map with the codes?

    Can you make demographic comparisons with the codes?

Quantitative Data

    Can you import a quantitative database (e.g., SPSS)?

    Can you export a word or image qualitative database to a quantitative program?

Merging Project

    Can more than one researcher analyze the data and merge analyses from these researchers?

Source: Adapted from Creswell & Maietta, 2002.

Specific Programs Available

To choose a software program, you need to examine the specific features available in the program. Visiting Web sites that advertise the program can enable you to assess the various programs available and their features. Mac users can purchase and employ software programs that enable Mac OS to use Windows PC programs. A brief summary of major programs follows:

◆ *Atlas.ti* (**www.atlasti.com**). This Windows PC program enables you to organize your text, graphic, audio, and visual data files, along with your coding, memos, and findings, into a project. Further, you can code, annotate, and compare segments of information. You can rapidly search, retrieve, and browse all data segments and notes relevant to an idea and, importantly, build unique networks that allow you to connect visually selected passages, memos, and codes in a concept map.

◆ *HyperRESEARCH* (**www.researchware.com**). This program is available for both Windows PC and Mac. It is an easy-to-use qualitative software package that enables you to code and retrieve, build theories, and conduct analyses of your data. Now with advanced multimedia capabilities, HyperRESEARCH allows you to work with text, graphics, audio, and video sources, making it a valuable research analysis tool. HyperRESEARCH is a solid code-and-retrieve data analysis program, with additional theory-building features provided by the Hypothesis Tester.

- ◆ *MAXQDA* (**www.maxqda.com**).   This Windows PC program is a powerful tool for text analysis that you can use for grounded theory-oriented "code and retrieve" analysis as well as for more sophisticated text analysis. It enables you to combine both qualitative and quantitative procedures. The program has a simple, easy-to-use interface of four main windows showing imported texts, codes, the coded text segments, and the text itself. A unique feature is that you can weight the codes to give a measure of the significance of a piece of coding. You can easily copy, merge, split, or delete codes. Data matrices can be imported and exported between SPSS, SAS, and other statistical packages. MAXQDA also has mixed methods—quantitative and qualitative—applications.

- ◆ *NVivo* (**www.qsrinternational.com**).   This software program is also for Windows PC. It combines efficient management of nonnumerical, unstructured data with powerful processes of indexing, searching, and theorizing. Designed for researchers making sense of complex data, NVivo offers a complete toolkit for rapid coding, thorough exploration, and rigorous management and analysis. Especially valuable is the ability of the program to create text data matrixes for comparisons. It also provides for visually mapping categories identified in your analysis.

HOW DO YOU EXPLORE AND CODE THE DATA?

After you have organized and transcribed your data and decided whether to hand or computer analyze it, it is time to begin data analysis. This consists of exploring the data and developing codes as first steps in analysis.

Explore the General Sense of the Data

The first step in data analysis is to explore the data. A **preliminary exploratory analysis** in qualitative research consists of exploring the data to obtain a general sense of the data, memoing ideas, thinking about the organization of the data, and considering whether you need more data. For example, Agar (1980) suggested you ". . . read the transcripts in their entirety several times. Immerse yourself in the details, trying to get a sense of the interview as a whole before breaking it into parts" (p. 103). Writing memos in the margins of field-notes or transcripts, or under photographs, helps in this initial process of exploring the data. These memos are short phrases, ideas, concepts, or hunches that occur to you.

Code the Data

The further process of analyzing text (or images) in qualitative research begins when you code the data. Coding is the process of segmenting and labeling text to form descriptions and broad themes in the data. Although there are no set guidelines for coding data, some general procedures exist (see Creswell, 2007; Tesch, 1990).

Using a visual model like the one in Figure 8.4 will help you learn this procedure. The object of the **coding process** is to make sense out of text data, divide it into text or image segments, label the segments with codes, examine codes for overlap and redundancy, and collapse these codes into broad themes. Thus, this is an inductive process of narrowing data into a few themes (J. David Creswell, personal communication, January 1, 2001). Also, in this process you will select specific data to use and disregard other data that do not specifically provide evidence for your themes.

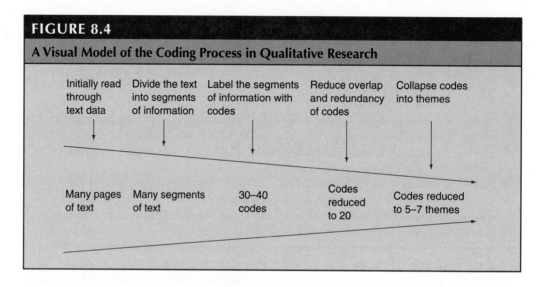

FIGURE 8.4

A Visual Model of the Coding Process in Qualitative Research

Initially read through text data	Divide the text into segments of information	Label the segments of information with codes	Reduce overlap and redundancy of codes	Collapse codes into themes
Many pages of text	Many segments of text	30–40 codes	Codes reduced to 20	Codes reduced to 5–7 themes

Several steps are involved in coding data. Although there is no definite procedure, Tesch (1990) and Creswell (2007) recommend the following steps:

1. Get a sense of the whole. Read all of the transcriptions carefully. Jot down in the margins some ideas as they come to mind.

2. Pick one document (e.g., one interview, one fieldnote). Choose the most interesting, the shortest, or the one on the top of the pile. Go through it, asking the question "What is this person talking about?" Consider the underlying meaning and write it down in the margin in two or three words, drawing a box around it.

3. Begin the process of coding the document. This process involves identifying text segments, placing a bracket around them, and assigning a code word or phrase that accurately describes the meaning of the text segment. Sentences or paragraphs that all relate to a single code are called a **text segment**. **Codes** are labels used to describe a segment of text or an image. Codes can address many different topics, such as those listed here (see also Bogdan & Biklen, 1998):
   - Setting and context (e.g., classroom)
   - Perspectives held by participants (poor learners)
   - Participants' ways of thinking about people and objects (problem children)
   - Processes (disruptions during the class)
   - Activities (student sitting quietly)
   - Strategies (teacher giving time-out)
   - Relationship and social structure (students talking to each other)

   As seen in these examples, you can state codes in the participant's actual words (i.e., a student's perspective about other students, such as "poor learners"), which are called *in vivo* **codes**. They can also be phrased in standard educational terms (a researcher referring to "a classroom") or expressed in your own language (a statement about "students talking to each other"). You do not need to code each sentence or provide multiple codes for each sentence. Instead, use the idea of **lean coding**, in which, the first time through a manuscript, you assign only a few codes. For example, for a 20-page manuscript, you might insert only 10 to 15 codes the first time you analyze it. In this way, you can reduce a smaller number of codes to broad themes rather than work with an unwieldy set of codes.

4. After coding an entire text, make a list of all code words. Group similar codes and look for redundant codes. Your objective is to reduce a list of codes to a smaller,

more manageable number, such as 25 to 30. It is best not to overcode the data because, in the end, you will need to reduce the codes to a small number of themes.

5. Take this list and go back to the data. Try out this preliminary organizing scheme to see whether new codes emerge. Circle specific quotes from participants that support the codes.

6. Reduce the list of codes to get five to seven themes or descriptions of the setting or participants. **Themes** (also called *categories*) are similar codes aggregated together to form a major idea in the database. Identify the five to seven themes by examining codes that the participants discuss most frequently, are unique or surprising, have the most evidence to support them, or are those you might expect to find when studying the phenomenon. The reason for the small number of themes is that it is best to write a qualitative report providing detailed information about a few themes rather than general information about many themes. A **description** is a detailed rendering of people, places, or events in a setting in qualitative research. You might use codes such as "seating arrangements," "teaching approach," or "physical layout of the room" to describe a classroom where instruction takes place.

If you were Maria, what are some likely codes that you might describe about the school in a study of students carrying weapons in school? If you are analyzing data about students carrying weapons, one part of that analysis might be to describe the locations where students carry weapons on the school grounds. You might list a few of these, beginning with "school lockers" or the "parking lot." What others come to mind?

 ## Think-Aloud About Coding a Transcript

In this think-aloud, I will illustrate not only coding a transcript but also developing multiple codes and themes. I will also illustrate the preliminary data analysis process of jotting notes in the margin in a first reading of the data.

Figure 8.5 shows a sample transcript from an interview and the codes that I recorded in the left margin. This transcript resulted from an interview for a project exploring changes in the curriculum in a rural high school (Jones, 1999). Overall, the interviewee talks about changes in the high school from a traditional curriculum to a school based on service-learning in the community. Jones asks questions during the interview and "LU," the interviewee, provides responses. Look over the codes on the left and other ideas recorded in the margins in this figure. I will take you through my thinking as I coded this transcript.

◆ Notice that the margins on the left and right are extra wide so I could jot down my ideas there.

◆ On the left side I inserted codes; on the right side, ideas and emerging themes. These features could have been reversed (e.g., codes on the right), but I prefer this organization.

◆ For codes, I used two or three words as labels. These were the actual words used by the participant, "LU." Sometimes I listed codes as possible alternatives.

◆ I placed boxes around key words that I wanted to use as codes or broad ideas or themes.

◆ By bracketing (drawing a bracket around sentences in the left margin) I identified sentences that seem to "fit together" to describe one idea, my text segments. Notice that I did not bracket all sentences. I did not use all of the data because I needed to reduce it to five to seven themes for my final research report. I asked myself,

FIGURE 8.5

Coding a Page from a Sample Interview Transcript

The Process of Reconstructing Curriculum in a Rural High School Setting

Codes Here		Themes (and Other Ideas) Here
	JJ: One thing, Lucy, that I've heard talked about was the fact that schools reflect the strengths of communities. What do you perceive as strengths of Greenfield as a community and how that relates to schools?	
Close-knit community	LU: Well, I think Greenfield is a fairly close-knit community. I think people are interested in what goes on. And because of that, they have a sense of ownership in the schools. We like to keep track of what our kids are doing and feel a connection to them because of that. The downside of that perhaps is that kids can feel that we are looking TOO close. But most of the time, that is the nurturing environment that we do provide an atmosphere of concern and care. To back up, you said the health of the community itself is	Potential theme: The community Idea: getting a good sense here for the community and its values
Health of community or community values	reflected in schools. A lot of times communities look at schools and say they are not doing this or they aren't doing that, or we're missing something in our schools. I think perhaps we look at the school and see, this is probably a pretty conservative community overall, and look to make sure that what is being talked about in the schools really carries out the community's values. There is a little bit of an idealization I think, perhaps in terms of what we thought of "basic education." [And I think there might be a tendency to hold back a little bit too much because of that idealization of "you know, we learned the basics, the reading, the writing and the arithmetic."] So you know, any change is	A good quote
Change is threatening	threatening. And I think that goes for the community as well as what we see reflected at the school. Sometimes that can get in the way of trying to do different things. I think, again, idealization, older members of the community forget some of the immaturity that they experienced when they were in school and forgetting that kids are kids. So there is a little bit too much of that mental attitude. But for the most part, I think there is a sense of we're all in this together, and concern for the kids.	
	JJ: In terms of looking at leadership strengths in the community, where does Greenfield set in a continuum there with planning process, understanding the need to plan, forward-thinking, visionary people. You talked about that a little bit before.	Potential theme: Leaders
Visionary skills of talented people	LU: I think there are people that have wonderful visionary skills. I would say that the community as a whole would be . . . would not reflect that. I think there are people who are driving the process, but the rest of the community may be lagging behind a little bit. I think we have some incredibly talented people who become frustrated when they try to implement what they see as their . . .	Idea: returns to description of community again

Source: Reprinted with permission of Jean Jones, Ph.D.

"What are they talking about here?" drew a bracket around key sentences that related to a code, and assigned a code label.

◆ On the right, I listed potential themes in the transcript. Also on the right you will see my early jottings (e.g., "getting a good sense here for the community and its values"), and I highlighted a good quote that I might use in my final research report.

The process now, beyond this single page, will be to continue my coding and theme development so that I can construct a description of the community and write about themes relating to this curriculum change in a rural high school setting.

HOW DO YOU USE CODES TO BUILD DESCRIPTION AND THEMES?

From Figure 8.5, you can see that I began thinking about broad themes that emerged from my data. In a qualitative research study, you need to analyze the data to form answers to your research questions. This process involves examining the data in detail to describe what you learned, and developing themes or broad categories of ideas from the data. **Describing and developing themes from the data** consists of answering the major research questions and forming an in-depth understanding of the central phenomenon through description and thematic development. Not all qualitative projects include both description and themes, but all studies include at least themes. Beginning with description, we can explore what it attempts to accomplish, how you might use it, and how it appears in a research report.

Description

Because description is a detailed rendering of people, places, or events in a setting in qualitative research, it is easiest to start the analysis after the initial reading and coding of the data. In some forms of qualitative research design, such as in ethnography or in case studies, the researcher provides a considerable description of the setting. Developing detail is important, and the researcher analyzes data from all sources (e.g., interviews, observations, documents) to build a portrait of individuals or events. To describe an individual, the qualitative analyst might ask, "What is this person like?" For describing a place, the question might be "What is this place like?" or "Where in the school do students go to smoke?"

In providing detailed information, description can transport the reader to a research site or help the reader visualize a person. It takes experience and practice to describe the detail in a setting. For example, examine these two illustrations and note the differences in level of detail.

◆ *Poor example:*   The workers built the education building with three floors.
◆ *Better example:*   As the education building developed, iron beams crossed and connected it together. A giant crane lifted these beams into place with a line secured tightly around each beam. A worker underneath the beam fastened it into place. As we watched, the beam tipped back and forth, leading us to wonder if the crane operator had securely fastened it. One slip and disaster would follow, but the beam landed securely in place.

Another good example is the following passage from a short story by Budnitz (2000). The author was writing about the common process of preparing pancakes.

> He was mixing stuff up in a bowl; flour slopped over the edges and sprinkled on the counter and the floor. I'll have to clean that up, I thought. . . . There was butter bubbling and crackling in the frying pan. . . . He poured in the batter, it was thick and pale yellow; and the hissing butter shut up for a while. . . . There were two large lumpy mounds there, side by side, bubbling inside as if they were alive, turning brown on the edges. He turned them over and I saw the crispy undersides with patterns on them like the moon; and then he pressed them down with the spatula, pressed them flat and the butter sputtered and hissed. (pp. 91–92)

By reading vivid short stories or examining qualitative studies, you can find illustrations where writers used detail to take an ordinary experience (like pancake making) and transport you to the setting so that you can almost feel (or taste) the situation.

Elements of good description can be seen in a passage about a gunman entering a classroom on a college campus (Asmussen & Creswell, 1995). Figure 8.6 reports the events that happened 2 weeks following the gunman incident. The discussion of these events illustrates several features of description that you might include in your own qualitative description or note in a published research report. The labels indicate that:

- The passage starts broadly with the Midwestern city and narrows to the campus, then the classroom, and finally the incident. This broad-to-narrow description helps the reader understand the context or place of the incident and provides a sense of a "real" place where this near-tragedy occurred.
- The authors attempt to use vivid details to create the description. We know, for example, that the rifle was a "Korean War military semiautomatic" and exactly how many "clips" or rounds could be loaded into this weapon.
- The action comes alive in this description with the use of action verbs and movement-oriented modifiers and adjectives. The gunman did not walk out of the building but "hastily departed."
- The authors do not make an interpretation or evaluate the situation—they simply report the "facts" as they heard about them from data sources. Times (e.g., 4:00 p.m.) illustrate detail about the specific occurrence of events.
- The passage includes quotes to provide emphasis and realism in the account. These quotes are short, even one word (e.g., "disturbed"). They may be longer, such as a short phrase or a sentence, but in a brief journal article, writers need to be concerned about space available for the narrative and generally keep the quotes as short as possible.

Themes

In addition to description, the use of themes is another way to analyze qualitative data. Because themes are similar codes aggregated together to form a major idea in the database, they form a core element in qualitative data analysis. Like codes, themes have labels that typically consist of no more than two to four words (e.g., "denial," "campus planning").

Through initial data analyses, you may find 30 to 50 codes. In subsequent analyses, you reduce these codes to five to seven major themes through the process of eliminating redundancies. There are several types of themes, and authors typically identify them as follows:

- *Ordinary themes:* themes that a researcher might expect to find (e.g., "exposure to tobacco at school").

FIGURE 8.6

Elements of Description in a Narrative Passage

The Incident and Response

Description builds from broad to narrow

Situate the reader in the place or context

The incident occurred on the campus of a large public university in a Midwestern city. A decade ago, this city had been designated an "all-American city," but more recently, its normally tranquil environment has been disturbed by an increasing number of assaults and homicides. Some of these violent incidents have involved students at the university.

Provide details

The incident that provoked this study occurred on a Monday in October. A forty-three-year-old graduate student, enrolled in a senior-level actuarial science class, arrived a few minutes before class, armed with a vintage Korean War military semiautomatic rifle loaded with a thirty-round clip of thirty caliber ammunition. He carried another thirty-round clip in his pocket. Twenty of the thirty-four students in the class had already gathered for class, and most of them were quietly reading the student newspaper. The instructor was en route to class.

Detail to create a sense of "being there"

Use of action verbs and vivid modifiers and adjectives

The gunman pointed the rifle at the students, swept it across the room, and pulled the trigger. The gun jammed. Trying to unlock the rifle, he hit the butt of it on the instructor's desk and quickly tried firing it again. Again it did not fire. By this time, most students realized what was happening and dropped to the floor, overturned their desks, and tried to hide behind them. After about twenty seconds, one of the students <u>shoved</u> a desk into the gunman, and students ran past him out into the hall and out of the building. The gunman <u>hastily departed</u> the room and went out of the building to his parked car, which he had left running. He was captured by police within the hour in a nearby small town, where he lived. Although he remains incarcerated at this time, awaiting trial, the motivations for his actions are unknown.

Just describe the "facts," do not interpret situation

Use of quotes or italics to emphasize ideas or "reflective" comments

Campus police and campus administrators were the first to react to the incident. Campus police arrived within three minutes after they had received a telephone call for help. They spent several <u>anxious</u> minutes outside the building interviewing students to obtain an accurate description of the gunman. Campus administrators responded by calling a news conference for 4:00 P.M. the same day, approximately four hours after the incident. The police chief as well as the vice-chancellor of Student Affairs and two students described the incident at the news conference. That same afternoon, the Student Affairs office contacted Student Health and Employee Assistance Program (EAP) counselors and instructed them to be available for any student or staff requesting assistance. The Student Affairs office also arranged for a new location, where this class could meet for the rest of the semester. The Office of Judicial Affairs suspended the gunman from the university. The next day, the incident was discussed by campus administrators at a regularly scheduled campuswide cabinet meeting. Throughout the week, Student Affairs received several calls from students and from a faculty member about "disturbed" students or unsettling student relations. A counselor of the Employee Assistance Program consulted a psychologist with a specialty in dealing with trauma and responding to educational crises. Only one student immediately set up an appointment with the student health counselors. The campus and local newspapers continued to carry stories about the incident.

Source: Asmussen & Creswell, 1995, pp. 576–577.

◆ *Unexpected themes:* themes that are surprises and not expected to surface during a study (e.g., "unenforced school tobacco use policies").

◆ *Hard-to-classify themes:* themes that contain ideas that do not easily fit into one theme or that overlap with several themes (e.g., "students gather in the park").

◆ *Major and minor themes:* themes that represent the major ideas and the minor, secondary ideas in a database. For example, a major theme might be "attempts to quit smoking." Minor themes might be "physical reaction," "peer pressure to continue smoking," or "starts and stops."

It might be helpful to examine themes that emerged during data analysis. Figure 8.7 is a portion of the discussion of the "safety" theme found in the gunman incident study (Asmussen & Creswell, 1995). The marginal annotations mark elements that are included in the theme. You might consider "safety" to be an ordinary theme because we might expect it to occur on campus. Several participants mention this theme, so the authors selected it and used participants' exact wording. The authors analyzed their data for multiple perspectives on this theme of "safety." The term **multiple perspectives** means that you provide several viewpoints from different individuals and sources of data as evidence for a theme. Multiple perspectives are important when conveying the complexity of the phenomenon in qualitative research. In this passage, for example, the authors report the perspectives of:

◆ The chief student affairs officer
◆ University board members

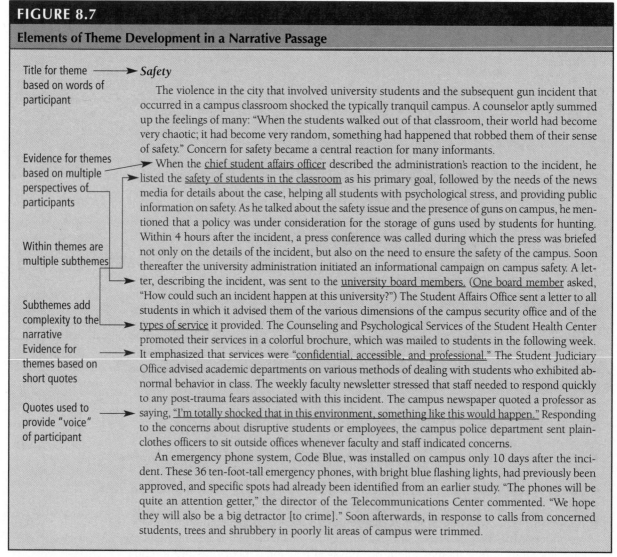

FIGURE 8.7

Elements of Theme Development in a Narrative Passage

Title for theme based on words of participant ⟶ *Safety*

The violence in the city that involved university students and the subsequent gun incident that occurred in a campus classroom shocked the typically tranquil campus. A counselor aptly summed up the feelings of many: "When the students walked out of that classroom, their world had become very chaotic; it had become very random, something had happened that robbed them of their sense of safety." Concern for safety became a central reaction for many informants.

Evidence for themes based on multiple perspectives of participants ⟶ When the <u>chief student affairs officer</u> described the administration's reaction to the incident, he listed the <u>safety of students in the classroom</u> as his primary goal, followed by the needs of the news media for details about the case, helping all students with psychological stress, and providing public information on safety. As he talked about the safety issue and the presence of guns on campus, he mentioned that a policy was under consideration for the storage of guns used by students for hunting.

Within themes are multiple subthemes ⟶ Within 4 hours after the incident, a press conference was called during which the press was briefed not only on the details of the incident, but also on the need to ensure the safety of the campus. Soon thereafter the university administration initiated an informational campaign on campus safety. A letter, describing the incident, was sent to the <u>university board members.</u> (<u>One board member</u> asked, "How could such an incident happen at this university?") The Student Affairs Office sent a letter to all

Subthemes add complexity to the narrative ⟶ students in which it advised them of the various dimensions of the campus security office and of the <u>types of service</u> it provided. The Counseling and Psychological Services of the Student Health Center promoted their services in a colorful brochure, which was mailed to students in the following week.

Evidence for themes based on short quotes ⟶ It emphasized that services were <u>"confidential, accessible, and professional."</u> The Student Judiciary Office advised academic departments on various methods of dealing with students who exhibited abnormal behavior in class. The weekly faculty newsletter stressed that staff needed to respond quickly to any post-trauma fears associated with this incident. The campus newspaper quoted a professor as

Quotes used to provide "voice" of participant ⟶ saying, <u>"I'm totally shocked that in this environment, something like this would happen."</u> Responding to the concerns about disruptive students or employees, the campus police department sent plainclothes officers to sit outside offices whenever faculty and staff indicated concerns.

An emergency phone system, Code Blue, was installed on campus only 10 days after the incident. These 36 ten-foot-tall emergency phones, with bright blue flashing lights, had previously been approved, and specific spots had already been identified from an earlier study. "The phones will be quite an attention getter," the director of the Telecommunications Center commented. "We hope they will also be a big detractor [to crime]." Soon afterwards, in response to calls from concerned students, trees and shrubbery in poorly lit areas of campus were trimmed.

Source: Asmussen & Creswell, 1995, pp. 582–583.

◆ Campus security officers
◆ The counseling and psychological services office
◆ A professor on campus

It is also useful to see that the authors have one major theme and several minor themes subsumed under the major theme. Diagrammed, this thematic development would be:

Major theme: safety

Minor themes (or subthemes): safety of students in the classroom; types of services

Finally, to add realism to this passage, the authors include short quotes from their interviews and newspaper accounts.

This passage does not include one further element of theme development. A realistic presentation of information does not present only one side or the other. In an attempt to capture the complexity of situations, qualitative researchers analyze data for contrary evidence. **Contrary evidence** is information that does not support or confirm the themes and provides contradictory information about a theme. What would this theme be? Had the authors of the gunman case study searched for this evidence, they might have found that some students actually felt "safe" rather than concerned because the gunman left quickly or because they could outnumber the gunman.

One final point to note about developing themes is that you will reach a point where themes are fully developed and new evidence will not provide additional themes. **Saturation** is the point where you have identified the major themes and no new information can add to your list of themes or to the detail for existing themes. When you reach this point is a subjective assessment, but most qualitative researchers realize when it occurs. In the development of the theme of "quit attempts in smoking," the researchers drew on their extensive interviews with high school students. They found evidence through specific examples and quotes to illustrate the theme, and when they returned to the interview transcriptions, no new information surfaced during their reading and rereading of the transcripts. They concluded that they had reached saturation on this theme. A check with participants (see the discussion on validating the accuracy of findings later in this chapter) confirmed that they had adequately specified this theme.

Layering and Interrelating Themes

You will see many qualitative studies that stop at reporting description and themes. However, you can add additional rigor and insight into your study by layering themes or interconnecting them.

Layering Themes

Layering themes builds on the idea of major and minor themes but organizes the themes into layers from basic elementary themes to more sophisticated ones. **Layering the analysis** (also called first- and second-order abstractions) means representing the data using interconnected levels of themes. You subsume minor themes within major themes and include major themes within broader themes. The entire analysis becomes more and more complex as the researcher works *upward* toward broader and broader levels of abstraction. The number of layers may vary from two to four or five, and recognizing these layers will help you understand the use of themes in layered qualitative analysis.

Considering again the gunman incident study (Asmussen & Creswell, 1995), it can be found that layering was used by the authors in this study. Examine Figure 8.8. This figure shows that the authors used four layers, including the database as one layer. The authors

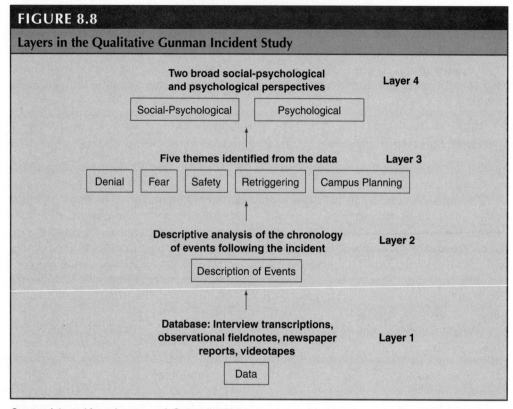

FIGURE 8.8

Layers in the Qualitative Gunman Incident Study

Source: Adapted from Asmussen & Creswell, 1995.

collected data from several sources (Layer 1) and analyzed it to develop a description of events (Layer 2). From this description they then formed five themes (Layer 3) and combined these themes into two broad perspectives (Layer 4). Knowing how layering works will help you see how the authors began with the details and worked their way up to the more general themes in their analysis.

Interrelating Themes

A second thematic analysis approach that interconnects the themes. **Interconnecting themes** means that the researcher connects the themes to display a chronology or sequence of events, such as when qualitative researchers generate a theoretical and conceptual model. For example, look at Figure 8.9. Here we see a sample chart used in a qualitative grounded theory study (Creswell & Brown, 1992). The researchers examined the practices used by 33 academic department chairs to enhance the research of faculty in their college or university units. As shown in the figure, the authors identified numerous themes within each box in the diagram. In addition, arrows show the connection among the boxes. In this sequence, the process of enhancing faculty research performance relates to the type of faculty issue (e.g., getting started with research), the signs that this issue is important (e.g., as identified by the chair), the context of stages of the faculty member's career (e.g., beginning), and the larger institutional context (e.g., good for the department). It also includes the specific strategies employed by the chair (e.g., the chair as a provider), and the outcomes of using that strategy (e.g., too early to tell). In short, this process displays an interconnected set of events or activities in the process of chairs enhancing faculty performances.

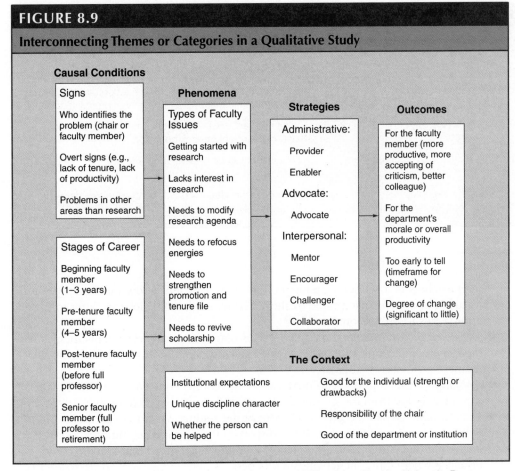

FIGURE 8.9

Interconnecting Themes or Categories in a Qualitative Study

Source: Creswell & Brown, 1992. Reprinted by arrangement with The Johns Hopkins University Press.

HOW DO YOU REPRESENT AND REPORT FINDINGS?

After you code the data, analyze it for description and themes, layer and interconnect themes, and report findings to your research questions. This calls for displaying findings in tables and figures and constructing a narrative to explain what you have found in response to your research questions.

Representing Findings

Qualitative researchers often display their findings visually (Miles & Huberman, 1994) by using figures or pictures that augment the discussion. Different ways to display data are listed here:

◆ *Create a comparison table.*   Create a visual image of the information in the form of a comparison table (see Spradley, 1980) or a matrix, a table that compares groups on one of the themes (e.g., men and women in terms of "safety"; see Miles & Huberman, 1994, for additional examples). In a qualitative study of the meaning of "professionalism," a researcher collected statements from both women and

TABLE 8.1

A Sample Comparison Table Used to Represent Information in a Qualitative Study

Female Statements About "Professionalism"	Male Statements About "Professionalism"
• Helping fellow teachers is part of my day.	• Being concerned about following the coordinator's advice about curriculum shows a high level of professionalism.
• When another teacher asks for advice, I am generally a good listener.	• It is important to be in charge in the classroom and to be aware of student off-task behavior.
• It is important, once I achieve a certain level of experience, that I become a mentor to other teachers, especially new ones.	• I set standards for myself, and try to achieve these goals each year.
• Caring about how other teachers employ high standards in their classroom is a sign of my own professionalism.	• It is necessary that each teacher "pull" his or her weight in this school—a sure sign of professionalism.

men teachers in a school. Statements from these teachers, shown in Table 8.1, are included in a comparison table to show that females and males can differ in their approaches to professionalism.

◆ *Develop a hierarchical tree diagram.* This diagram visually represents themes and their interconnections so that the themes are presented in order from the broad themes to the narrow themes.

◆ *Present figures.* Figures with boxes show the connections among themes (see again Figure 8.9 from the grounded theory study by Creswell & Brown, 1992).

◆ *Draw a map.* Depict the physical layout of the setting. As shown in Figure 8.10, Miller, Creswell, and Olander (1998) displayed the physical setting of a soup kitchen in their study. The authors provided this diagram so that readers could visualize where different activities happened.

◆ *Develop a demographic table.* Describe personal or demographic information for each person or site in the research. In a study of the types of technology used by instructors in college classrooms, the researcher described each instructor and his or her primary delivery style in a demographic table, shown in Table 8.2. The six individuals studied in this qualitative study displayed different personal characteristics as well as diverse approaches to using technology. This table provides readers with various demographic information for each instructor, such as number of years teaching, gender, class level of instruction, instructional approach used in the class, and his or her primary form of technology use.

Reporting Findings

The primary form for representing and reporting findings in qualitative research is a narrative discussion. A **narrative discussion** is a written passage in a qualitative study in which authors summarize, in detail, the findings from their data analysis. There is no set form for this narrative, which can vary widely from one study to another. However, it is helpful to identify some frequently used forms, as shown in Table 8.3. Several of these forms have already been discussed, such as developing description, themes, or interconnecting themes. Others are important, too, especially in advocacy and participatory forms of qualitative inquiry, such as raising questions, challenging assumptions based on evidence supplied by participants, or reflecting on how participants changed (e.g., became

FIGURE 8.10

Sample Diagram of the Physical Layout in a Qualitative Study

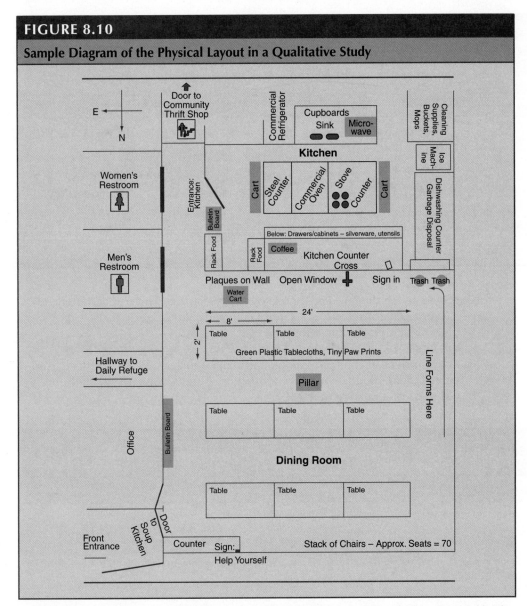

Source: Miller, D. M., Creswell, J. W., & Olander, L. S. (1998). Writing and retelling multiple ethnographic tales of a soup kitchen for the homeless. *Qualitative Inquiry, 4*(4), 475. Copyright © 1998 by Sage Publications. Reprinted by permission of Sage Publications, Inc.

empowered, became advocates, became involved) during the research. Your decision about which form or forms to use depends on the purpose of your research and the type of data you have analyzed for your findings.

Consider also the narrative elements that go into a report of your findings. As you make multiple passes through your database, looking for description and themes, consider these useful hints:

◆ *Include dialogue that provides support for themes.*   For example, in a study about reading disabilities of four middle school students, Kos (1991) provided this

TABLE 8.2

A Sample Demographic Table in a Qualitative Study

Name	Years Teaching	Gender	Class Level of Instruction	Instructional Approach in the Classroom	Primary Form of Technology in the Classroom
Rosa	25	Female	12	Discussion	Internet
Harry	20	Male	11	Critique	Not used
Joan	18	Female	11	Discussion	Web site and Internet
Ray	20	Male	12	Interactive	Web site, Internet, wireless laptops
Jamal	15	Male	11	Discussion	Not used
Yun	36	Male	10	Lecture	Internet

dialogue about the theme "reading-related stress" for a student named Karen. (Kos's comments are labeled "R"; Karen's comments are labeled "K.")

> K: I feel that it's very difficult for me.
>
> R: Mm hmm.
>
> K: And sometimes I can read a book and some books are kind of difficult. And um, my mom said that you have to read or . . . you won't get nowhere.
>
> R: What do you think about that?

TABLE 8.3

Forms of a Narrative Discussion in Qualitative Research

Forms of Narrative Discussion	Examples
A discussion that presents a chronology	The chronology of a teacher's experiences with her special education coordinator leading to her resignation from the school
A discussion that describes events and setting (context)	A description of adolescents reading "teen" magazines
A discussion of themes	A discussion about the theme of the "in-classroom" landscape of a teacher
A discussion of a figure	A figure presenting a model of the process of art therapy with clients
A discussion about layering or interconnecting themes	A discussion about the levels of complexity in a campus response to a gunman incident
A discussion incorporating past literature and research studies	A discussion incorporating past literature of efforts to develop campus plans for avoiding potential violence
A discussion raising further questions that need to be addressed	A discussion that raises questions about the equality and fair treatment of women
A discussion using participants' views to challenge accepted or hidden assumptions	A discussion that probes practices of discrimination in schools
A discussion about how participants are empowered or change	A discussion about how a teacher, by sharing her story, felt empowered

> K: Um, I think, I think it's sad. And um, like mom says, that you, you might be having a night job picking up trash and sweeping.
>
> R: Mm hmm.
>
> K: And you wouldn't have a regular job like my mom and make some money.
>
> R: Mm. But somebody has to pick up the trash.
>
> K: *Yeah, somebody. But I don't know who!* (pp. 885–886)

◆ *State the dialogue in the participants' native language or in the regional or ethnic dialect.* A study that examines the life histories of African American women by Nelson (1990) included examples of *code-switching* of African American dialect to convey the novel metaphors of casual kitchen-table discourse:

> I'm trying to communicate a shoe box full when you only give them (the words) a matchbox. I'm trying to relate the spiritual meaning. (p. 151)

◆ *Use metaphors and analogies.* In reporting on the competition and concerns surfacing during the implementation of distance education in the state of Maine, Epper (1997) wrote metaphorically about how student and citizen support is a "political football" game:

> As the bickering went on, many students stood by watching their education dreams tossed around like a political football. Some were not content to sit on the sidelines. From the islands, valleys, backwoods, and far reaches of the state came letters to the faculty senates, legislators, and newspapers. (p. 566)

◆ *Report quotes from interview data or from observations of individuals.* These quotes can capture feelings, emotions, and ways people talk about their experiences.

◆ *Report multiple perspectives and contrary evidence.* Identify these perspectives based on different individuals, sources of information, or multiple views held by one person.

◆ *Write in vivid detail.* Find good descriptions of an individual, event, or activity.

◆ *Specify tensions and contradictions in individual experiences.* For example, Huber and Whelan (1999) report the personal stories of a female teacher who experiences a lack of support about a special education student in the classroom. They discuss the tension this teacher feels between being in control in her classroom and the out-of-class pressure that she experiences from her school coordinator.

HOW DO YOU INTERPRET FINDINGS?

Interpretation involves making sense of the data, or the "lessons learned," as described by Lincoln and Guba (1985). **Interpretation** in qualitative research means that the researcher steps back and forms some larger meaning about the phenomenon based on personal views, comparisons with past studies, or both. Qualitative research is interpretive research, and you will need to make sense of the findings. You will find this interpretation in a final section of a study under headings such as "Discussion," "Conclusions," "Interpretations," or "Implications." This section includes:

◆ A review of the major findings and how the research questions were answered
◆ Personal reflections of the researcher about the meaning of the data
◆ Personal views compared or contrasted with the literature
◆ Limitations of the study
◆ Suggestions for future research

Summarize Findings

A typical "Discussion" section begins with a general recap of the major findings. Sometimes you will state each individual research question again and provide findings for each question. The overall intent of this passage is to provide readers with an overview of the findings to complement the more detailed results in the description and theme passages.

Convey Personal Reflections

Because qualitative researchers believe that your personal views can never be kept separate from interpretations, personal reflections about the meaning of the data are included in the research study. You base these personal interpretations on hunches, insights, and intuition. Because you may have been to the field and visited personally at great length with individuals, you are in a good position to reflect and remark on the larger meaning of the data. The two examples that follow illustrate the diversity of personal reflections found in qualitative studies.

In the classic ethnography of the "sneaky kid," Wolcott (1983) reflected about the meaning of learning for Brad:

> Learning—in the broad enculturative sense of coming to understand what one needs to know to be competent in the roles one may expect to fulfill in society, rather than in the narrow sense of learning-done-at-school—is an ongoing process in which each human engages throughout a lifetime. (p. 24)

The next example shows how researchers can offer interpretative commentary about new questions that need to be answered. In the discussion by Tierney (1993), who spoke with a 40-year-old African American on a university campus who had AIDS, the researcher left the interview with unanswered questions:

> How do we create understandings across differences so that we are able to acknowledge and honor one another, rather than bring into question one another's legitimacy? It is incumbent on me as the author, then, to present these voices as fully and carefully as possible; at the same time, it is necessary for the reader or methodologist or administrator who does not understand these realities to try to come to terms with them. (p. 27)

Make Comparisons to the Literature

Interpretation may also contain references to the literature and past studies. Similar to quantitative research, the qualitative inquirer interprets the data in view of this past research, showing how the findings may support or contradict prior studies, or both. This interpretation may compare qualitative findings with reported views of a social science concept found in the literature, or it may combine personal views with an educational or social science term or idea. In a qualitative study of sibling interaction between a young man with Down syndrome and his three brothers, the authors Harry, Day, and Quist (1998) concluded with interpretive comments about the inclusion of "Raul" in situations outside of the family setting. They relate their own views to those in the literature:

> We strongly believe, as does much literature on the topic (Hurley-Geffner, 1995; Schnorr, 1990), that the first requirement must be an inclusive and continuous school structure that keeps students with disabilities with their community and family peers from elementary school right through high school. (p. 297)

Offer Limitations and Suggestions for Future Research

Also similar to quantitative research, the qualitative researcher suggests possible limitations or weaknesses of the study and makes recommendations for future research. These limitations may address problems in data collection, unanswered questions by participants, or better selection of purposeful sampling of individuals or sites for the study. Implications for future research may include the use of the findings for practice (e.g., classrooms, schools, or with certain people such as adults or teenagers) or the need for further research (e.g., by gathering more extensive data or by asking additional questions of participants). You might also state implications for decision making, such as planning for new practices (e.g., better campus planning about how to handle violent incidents) or for the audience you identified in the introduction to your study.

HOW DO YOU VALIDATE THE ACCURACY OF YOUR FINDINGS?

Throughout the process of data collection and analysis, you need to make sure that your findings and interpretations are accurate. **Validating findings** means that the researcher determines the accuracy or credibility of the findings through strategies such as member checking or triangulation. Several qualitative researchers have addressed this idea (Creswell & Miller, 2000; Lincoln & Guba, 1985). Qualitative researchers do not typically use the word *bias* in research; they will say that all research is interpretive and that the researcher should be self-reflective about his or her role in the research, how he or she is interpreting the findings, and his or her personal and political history that shapes his or her interpretation (Creswell, 2007). Thus, accuracy or credibility of the findings is of upmost importance. There are varied terms that qualitative researchers use to describe this accuracy or credibility (e.g., see *authenticity* and *trustworthiness* in Lincoln & Guba, 1985), and the strategies used to validate qualitative accounts vary in number (see eight forms in Creswell & Miller, 2000). Our attention here will be on three primary forms typically used by qualitative researchers: triangulation, member checking, and auditing.

- ◆ Qualitative inquirers triangulate among different data sources to enhance the accuracy of a study. **Triangulation** is the process of corroborating evidence from different individuals (e.g., a principal and a student), types of data (e.g., observational fieldnotes and interviews), or methods of data collection (e.g., documents and interviews) in descriptions and themes in qualitative research. The inquirer examines each information source and finds evidence to support a theme. This ensures that the study will be accurate because the information draws on multiple sources of information, individuals, or processes. In this way, it encourages the researcher to develop a report that is both accurate and credible.
- ◆ Researchers also check their findings with participants in the study to determine if their findings are accurate. **Member checking** is a process in which the researcher asks one or more participants in the study to check the accuracy of the account. This check involves taking the findings back to participants and asking them (in writing or in an interview) about the accuracy of the report. You ask participants about many aspects of the study, such as whether the description is complete and realistic, if the themes are accurate to include, and if the interpretations are fair and representative.

◆ Researchers may also ask a person *outside* the project to conduct a thorough review of the study and report back, in writing, the strengths and weaknesses of the project. This is the process of conducting an **external audit**, in which a researcher hires or obtains the services of an individual outside the study to review different aspects of the research. The auditor reviews the project and writes or communicates an evaluation of the study. This audit may occur both during and at the conclusion of a study, and auditors typically ask questions such as those mentioned by Schwandt and Halpern (1988):

• Are the findings grounded in the data?
• Are inferences logical?
• Are the themes appropriate?
• Can inquiry decisions and methodological shifts be justified?
• What is the degree of researcher bias?
• What strategies are used for increasing credibility?

Let's return to Maria, who reflects on whether her own interpretation is "right." You may recall that Maria realizes that the interpretation of her findings includes her own perspectives drawn from personal experiences. As a Latino, she is aware of the marginalization that some of the kids she interviews about weapon possession feel. She realizes, as well, that family support or lack of support plays a prominent role in Latino families, and that her interpretation of themes (e.g., "student alienation" or "right to protect myself") will reflect her own concerns about these issues. How can Maria separate herself from her findings? Of course, the qualitative answer is that any interpretation *must* include the researcher's personal stance. The larger question is whether Maria's report is both accurate and credible to those she studies. Maria can validate her report by convening a small group of students and teachers she interviewed and having them read the narrative of her themes. During this process, the group will openly discuss whether the themes reflect their experiences, and then Maria can make additions or changes to her thematic discussion to report accurately and credibly on student and teacher experiences.

As you think about Maria checking the accuracy of her findings, what other approaches might she use?

REEXAMINING QUALITATIVE DATA ANALYSIS IN THE MOTHERS' TRUST IN PRINCIPALS CASE STUDY

Let's turn to the mothers' trust in principals case study (Shelden et al., 2010) to see the steps of qualitative data analysis and interpretation in action. In terms of preparing the data for analysis, we know from Paragraph 24 that the authors transcribed the semi-structured interviews with the mothers and then entered the text into a computer program (NVivo) for data analysis. They then conducted a "line-by-line" (p. 162) analysis of the transcripts (Paragraph 24) and met as a team to discuss each code and to reach some agreement on the codes. As each case was analyzed, they refined their codes (or categories). From the specific coding, the authors then grouped the codes into themes (see Paragraph 25) and drew a visual picture—called a concept map—of the themes as shown in Figure 1. The "Results" section (see Paragraphs 29–57) reported their findings about the two major themes of principal attributes and principal actions. So their coding built directly into their themes. They represented their findings through a figure (Figure 1) and through a discussion about each theme, employing both specific quotes and subthemes (e.g., personal attributes of principals, accessibility, principals' recognition of the children's disabilities, and so forth). The interpretation in this study is found in the "Discussion" section (Paragraphs 61–69). Here we see a general discussion about the findings (Paragraph 59), a return to the literature and a comparison of findings with that literature (Paragraphs 59–68), and a "Conclusion" section that conveys the implications of the study for school principals, for designing IEP meetings, and for training programs for principals. We do not learn about the limitations of the study or suggestions for future research. However, there is a passage on validity—called confirmability in this study (Paragraph 26). The authors had the participants check the accuracy of their reported findings by viewing a summary of findings and by asking participants (through member checking) to comment on the quotes in the study.

KEY IDEAS IN THE CHAPTER

Six Steps in the Process of Analyzing and Interpreting Qualitative Data

There are six interrelated steps involved in qualitative data analysis and interpretation. Researchers need to prepare and organize the data for analysis. This process involves storing and transcribing the data and deciding on whether the data will be hand or computer analyzed. The next step is to explore the data and to code it. This involves reading through the database and then employing the steps involved in coding. These steps are to identify text segments and then to assign code labels to the segments based on the meaning the researcher sees in the text segment. These codes are then used in forming a description of the central phenomenon or of the context (or setting) of the study. Codes are also grouped together to form broader themes that are used in the study as key findings. From this analysis, the researcher represents the data in the findings through figures, tables, maps, and a detailed discussion of the themes. These representations then inform a broader interpretation of the findings, and these are discussed as general conclusions and compared with existing literature. The conclusion of a study also needs to convey the limitations of the study as well as future research. It is important as well to validate the accuracy of the findings through several strategies such as member checking and triangulation.

Prepare and Organize the Data for Analysis

In a qualitative study, initial data management consists of organizing the data, transcribing interviews and typing fieldnotes, and making the decision to analyze the data by hand or by computer. Several good software programs are available for computer analysis.

Explore and Code the Data

Qualitative researchers conduct a preliminary analysis of the data by reading through it to obtain a general sense of the data. Major analysis of qualitative data consists of coding the data. The process of coding is one of reducing a text or image database to descriptions and themes of people, places, or events. It involves examining the text database line by line, asking oneself what the participant is saying, and then assigning a code label to the text segment.

Coding to Build Description and Themes

Codes are then used to develop descriptions of people and places. They also are used to develop themes that present a broader abstraction than codes. These themes may be layered or organized to tell a story, or they may also be interconnected to portray the complexity of the phenomenon.

Represent and Report Qualitative Findings

Qualitative researchers represent their findings in visual displays that may include figures, diagrams, comparison tables, and demographic tables. They report findings in narrative discussions comprising many forms, such as a chronology, questions, or commentary about any changes that the participants experience.

Interpret the Findings

From this reporting and representing of findings, qualitative researchers make an interpretation of the meaning of the research. This interpretation consists of advancing personal views, making comparisons between the findings and the literature, and suggesting limitations and future research.

Validate the Accuracy of the Findings

To check the accuracy of their research, qualitative inquirers often employ validation procedures such as member checking, triangulation, and auditing. The intent of validation is to have participants, external reviewers, or the data sources themselves provide evidence of the accuracy of the information in the qualitative report.

USEFUL INFORMATION FOR PRODUCERS OF RESEARCH

◆ As you analyze and interpret data, keep in mind that the picture you assemble will be inductive—that is, you will organize and report findings beginning with the details and working up to a general picture.

◆ Realize the extensive time that transcribing takes. If you plan to transcribe your interviews or fieldnotes yourself, use the guidelines recommended in this chapter.

◆ Consider using a computer program if you are analyzing a large database consisting of more than 500 pages of text. A computer analysis of your data has both advantages and disadvantages.

◆ If you decide to use a computer program, weigh the features of the program you plan to purchase. Try out the tutorials and explore the features of programs available from Web sites before you purchase a program.

◆ Recognize that the computer programs do not analyze the data for you; as a researcher and interpreter of the data, you need to actively make meaning of the data and assign codes to text segments.

◆ Take the time to read all of your data to obtain a general sense of it before you conduct a detailed analysis.

◆ When you code your text data, use the steps in the process identified in this chapter. Try not to overcode the material, and remember that the final report will typically include only five to seven themes.

◆ Use the coding model shown in Figure 8.5 for procedures on how to segment text, assign labels, identify themes, and jot down useful ideas on a transcript.

◆ If you code for description, look for vivid detail that will transport a reader into the setting and events in your narrative.

◆ Consider the different types of themes you can identify during coding. Unexpected themes offer surprising findings that spark reader interest, but ordinary, hard-to-classify, and major and minor themes also add complexity to a study.

◆ Design a qualitative study with thematic complexity. Use layering and interconnecting themes as well as a combination of description and themes.

◆ Many possibilities exist for constructing a narrative about the findings. Consider the recommended strategies in this chapter, such as using dialogue, metaphors, analogies, tensions, and contradictions.

◆ To augment your narrative discussion about findings, consider visual displays such as comparison tables, charts with boxes, and descriptive tables.

◆ Include your own views in your interpretation of findings because you can never completely remove yourself from interpretation and personal experiences.

◆ Consider using at least two validation strategies when you conduct qualitative research. The most frequently used strategies are member checking and triangulation.

USEFUL INFORMATION FOR CONSUMERS OF RESEARCH

◆ As you read a qualitative study, remember that the researcher will be presenting information inductively from the narrower themes to the broader themes. Throughout the study, the narrative will likely build from the specific (e.g., database) to the general (e.g., broad themes).

◆ Look to see if an author mentions all of the steps in the data analysis process mentioned in this chapter (e.g., a preliminary reading, the coding, description, thematic development, representation, and interpretation). In well-developed qualitative studies, most of these aspects will be included.

◆ As you look for findings in a study, first examine the research to determine if the authors describe an event or the setting and then search for the themes in their study. Look for the headings as a clue for description and themes.

◆ To see the complexity and make sense of themes, identify multiple perspectives mentioned by different individuals or cited from different sources.

◆ Because qualitative researchers report findings in the form of a narrative discussion, examine qualitative research for these discussions and realize that discussions may take many forms.

◆ Data displays augment the narrative discussion. They should be easy to understand and clearly related to themes or description.

◆ Realize that the "Discussion," "Conclusions," "Interpretations," or "Implications" sections of qualitative research typically include the researcher's personal views. This inclusion acknowledges that all research is biased.

◆ Check if the author uses validation strategies so that you can become confident in the accuracy of the findings.

UNDERSTANDING CONCEPTS AND EVALUATING RESEARCH STUDIES

1. Reexamine the mothers' trust in principals case study (Shelden et al., 2010). The authors did not state limitations in their study or needs for future research. Identify limitations and future research possibilities for this article.

2. Find one page of a transcript of an interview. Using Figure 8.5, code the page by writing code words and brackets around sentences in the left margin. List two or three potential themes in the right-hand margin.

3. Log on to a qualitative computer software program Web site and download a tutorial for one of the programs. Complete the tutorial to learn about the major features of the software program.

4. Locate a qualitative journal article in which the author provides a description of an event, activity, or process. Use the headings to help you locate this description. Then, using the marginal annotations provided in Figure 8.6, identify descriptive features such as (a) the context, (b) broad-to-narrow description, (c) use of action verbs and vivid modifiers, and (d) quotes.

5. Examine a theme in a published journal article. Use the marginal annotations provided in Figure 8.7 to identify (a) the name of the theme, (b) evidence for multiple perspectives on the theme, (c) subthemes, and (d) quotes.

CONDUCTING YOUR RESEARCH

For your educational project, design your qualitative data analysis and interpretation. Include the preparation for analysis and the exploration and coding of data, code both for description and themes, represent findings in figures and discussion, and include the interpretation of your data.

Go to the Topic "Qualitative Research: Data Analysis and Interpretation" in the MyEducationLab (**www.myeducationlab.com**) for your course, where you can:

◆ Find learning outcomes for "Qualitative Research: Data Analysis and Interpretation."

◆ Complete Assignments and Activities that can help you more deeply understand the chapter content.

◆ Apply and practice your understanding of the core skills identified in the chapter with the Building Research Skills exercises.

◆ Check your comprehension of the content covered in the chapter by going to the Study Plan. Here you will be able to take a pretest, receive feedback on your answers, and then access Review, Practice, and Enrichment activities to enhance your understanding. You can then complete a final posttest.

Reporting and Evaluating Research

*R*esearch culminates in a report in different forms. This chapter addresses how to write and compose a research report and how to evaluate the quality of this report. It emphasizes the importance of audience, structuring your report for your audience, writing in a nondiscriminatory, ethical, and scholarly way, and using accepted evaluation criteria to assess the quality of your report.

By the end of this chapter, you should be able to:

◆ Define the purpose of a research report and identify the types.
◆ Identify how to structure your research report.
◆ Identify good sensitive, ethical, and scholarly writing practices.
◆ List criteria for evaluating a research report.

Maria presents her completed research to her school committee and her faculty advisor in her graduate program. She will write her report differently for these two audiences. For the school committee, she will emphasize the results, downplay the methods, and highlight practical implications. For her faculty advisor, Maria will emphasize the research and her careful attention to data collection and analysis to generate thoughtful answers to her research questions. Writing with a focus on audience is central to Maria's approach, as is her emphasis on being sensitive to the students and teachers included in her study. In the end, both the school committee and her advisor will evaluate her research. She now needs to talk over with both of them the criteria they will use to assess the quality of her research.

WHAT IS A RESEARCH REPORT AND WHAT ARE ITS TYPES?

The steps in the process of research end with the development of a written report of your research. A **research report** is a completed study that reports an investigation or exploration of a problem; identifies questions to be addressed; and includes data collected, analyzed, and interpreted by the researcher. It is composed for audiences, varies in length and format, and differs for quantitative and qualitative research.

What Audience Will Receive the Report?

For groups and individuals to understand and potentially use findings from research, you write the research report in a way that is acceptable to the intended audiences. Thus, a cardinal rule for writing is to write for the audience. Unquestionably, different audiences employ varied standards, as shown in Table 9.1.

Rules and procedures in place at colleges and universities govern the criteria used by faculty advisors and committees. Journal reviewers and journal editors employ criteria presented once a year (typically) in their journals and often on the journal's Web page. These criteria set forth, at least in general terms, the standards they use in reviewing a study submitted for publication, the types of research they seek to publish, and guidelines for authors to follow when submitting manuscripts. Policy makers and practicing educators in schools and other educational settings evaluate studies in terms of their

TABLE 9.1

Audiences for Research

Audiences	Standards
Faculty (advisor/committees)	• Standards used in the past in program area • Standards traditionally used by each individual faculty member • Standards used at the college or university
Journal reviewers	• Use of published standards printed typically once for each volume • Separate standards may be published for quantitative and qualitative research • Editor must reconcile differing opinions among reviewers
Policy makers	• Ease of understanding results • Immediate application of results • Clarity and brevity of ideas
Practicing educators in the field	• Relevance of problem or issue being studied • Ease of identifying results • Practical suggestions from a research study
Conference paper reviewer	• Whether the researcher has submitted the proper materials • Whether the proposal fits the conference theme or the priorities for the conference • Whether the project summary is clearly written, organized, and addresses the guidelines for a summary
The researcher	• Standards of the outlet for the study (e.g., faculty, journal, practitioners, conferences) • Standards related to the five elements and the seven phases in the process of research • Standards related to quantitative and qualitative criteria

clarity, simplicity, and utility for practice. Conference paper reviewers often use specific guidelines for reviewing proposals submitted for presentation. In short, researchers need to consider the audience for the study and use both general standards available in the literature and specific standards for quantitative and qualitative research.

Maria needs to consider how she will write her research reports for both her school committee and for her graduate advisor. Look at Maria's notes, shown in Figure 9.1. She considers the interests of each member of the school committee so that she can include some practical implications for each. As for her graduate advisor, she recognizes that he has high standards, has supervised many theses before, and probably has a format in mind for her final thesis report. She also creates a to-do list to remind herself to get the information she needs before she proceeds with this phase of the process.

If you were Maria and needed to write a report as a requirement for your graduate degree, how would you write it? How would you write a report for your school committee? List two or three writing strategies you would use. Then turn to the next sections and read about the types of research reports and their overall structures.

What Are the Types of Research Reports?

Students prepare dissertations and theses as a requirement for their doctoral and master's programs. After completing the dissertation or thesis, researchers often condense it into a journal article for submission to an educational journal. Alternatively, they may present an abbreviated version of the dissertation or thesis at a national, regional, or state conference or to individuals in their school setting. After receiving comments from these audiences and making revisions based on these comments, they might submit the research to a journal for possible publication or file it with a school or school district.

FIGURE 9.1

Maria's Notes About Audiences for Her Report

Notes to myself:

1. *What will be the interests of the people on my school committee?*

   Owen (school administrator and chair) wants data and needs to know how we will use findings

   Ray (finance director) wants "numbers"

   Dana (English teacher) wants "rich" stories

   Deb (social studies teacher) wants good "visuals"

   Carolbel (music teacher) wants it to "sing out" to the public

   Jsabel (parent) wants to know what this means for her 5 kids in school

2. *What will my advisor and faculty at the university want for my graduate research paper?*

   Harry (chair) wants high "scholarly" standards and insightful questions and findings

   Joan (member of committee) wants to see that J know the literature

   Howard (member of committee) wants to know if people in the "field" can use results

3. *What do J need to do now?*
   a. *ask for past reports from school to see how reports have been written*
   b. *obtain from Harry past research studies to study their format*
   c. *learn from Harry about timetable for submitting and receiving approval of my research*

Dissertations and Theses

Dissertations and theses are the doctoral and master's research reports prepared for faculty and graduate committees. The length of a dissertation or thesis can vary, depending on the tradition in a school or department. Faculty advisors and committees may prefer different approaches, which could affect which form is used. The doctoral dissertation might range from the shorter dissertation of 100 pages to more than 400 pages. These dissertations, conducted by doctoral graduate students, are usually longer than master's theses. Master's theses may run from 50 to 100 pages. In general, qualitative studies are much longer than quantitative studies. Qualitative researchers often report many quotes and present multiple perspectives on themes.

The process of preparing a dissertation or thesis involves planning the study (i.e., writing the proposal) and presenting it to an advisor and a faculty committee (see appendix E for strategies for defending a research proposal). After receiving approval to conduct the study, the student completes the study and defends it before a faculty committee.

Dissertation and Thesis Proposals

A **dissertation or thesis proposal** is a plan for a research report, initiated and developed before the research actually begins. We will not discuss proposals for external funding here because other writers have adequately covered them (see Locke, Spirduso, & Silverman, 2007), and they are beyond the scope of this text. Before discussing research proposals, however, it is helpful to distinguish them from research reports.

One essential difference between proposals and reports is that you will write a proposal before conducting the research. In a proposal, the researcher writes about what *will* take place; in the final study, the investigator writes about what *has* taken place. This means that a proposal will likely be written using a future verb tense (i.e., *will*) to describe the action. In a final study, the past verb tense (i.e., *was*) describes what has already occurred. However, when the proposal contains a pilot or preliminary study, you need to describe it as an action that has already occurred.

Another distinction between a proposal and the final study is in the report of results and future research. In a proposal, you have not compiled results, nor have you identified future research needs. Thus, the proposal stops with the methods or procedure. A completed study, however, incorporates results and future research directions because you have already collected and analyzed the data.

To develop a dissertation or thesis, you first create a proposal, which is a formal description of a plan to investigate a research problem. This process begins by considering what topics to include in a plan so that readers can fully understand the project. The next step is to organize and format the plan to be consistent with quantitative or qualitative research. This initial planning process ends with a presentation of your proposal to a committee.

Proposing research is a major step in conducting research for a graduate program. The skills used in writing a proposal are the same skills needed for seeking external funding from public and private funding sources and for writing a plan for conducting a small-scale research study in school districts or other educational settings. Whether educators conduct their own research or evaluate someone else's plan, knowing the importance of a proposal and the elements that go into it is important.

The **purpose of a proposal** is to help an investigator think through all aspects of the study and anticipate problems. A proposal also provides a written document that faculty and advisors can read, evaluate, and critique to improve a study. The research plan or proposal becomes a document to *sell* the study—a written narrative that must convince the faculty of the need, importance, and value of the proposed study. A well-defined proposal:

◆ Facilitates the process of obtaining permissions to study a site or educational setting.

◆ Provides information to gatekeepers and those in authority so that they can determine the likely impact of a study at their site.
◆ Provides criteria to assess the quality of a project. Those evaluating and reviewing a study use these criteria. Knowing the proper elements of a good proposal permits evaluators to examine projects for these elements, and to determine, once you complete a project, whether it fulfills its goals.

Quantitative and Qualitative Dissertation and Thesis Proposals

Figure 9.2 illustrates typical quantitative and qualitative proposal formats for both dissertation and thesis reports. The topics in both formats address the major ideas faculty often seek to know about a project. In the format for a quantitative proposal, most of the plan is included in three major sections: the "Introduction," the "Review of the Literature," and the "Methods." In the format for a qualitative proposal, you will find a less standardized structure. By allowing the study to emerge and to be based on the views of participants, qualitative researchers support a flexible and open format for a proposal. Still, it is important for qualitative researchers to convey enough information to the readers to convince them of the merits of the study.

Recognizing the need for flexibility, recent authors have advanced several formats for a qualitative proposal (e.g., Creswell, 2009; Marshall & Rossman, 2010) to provide guidance for students. Their recommendations, however, are flexible enough to allow a study to emerge and to evolve based on what the researcher learns from participants in the field.

As seen in Figure 9.2, the overall format for a qualitative proposal contains only two major sections: the introduction and the procedure. You will notice that the qualitative proposal format does not contain a separate section on literature review. Instead, you combine the literature with a discussion on the anticipated outcomes of the study,

FIGURE 9.2
Format Quantitative and a Qualitative Proposal

Quantitative Format	Qualitative Format
Title Page	Title Page
Abstract	Abstract
Introduction	Introduction
Statement of the Problem	Statement of the Problem
Purpose and Research Questions or Hypotheses	The Purpose and Research Question
Theoretical Perspective	Delimitations and Limitations
Definition of Terms	Procedure
Delimitations and Limitations of the Study	Qualitative Methodology and Design
Review of the Literature	Research Site and Purposeful Sampling
Methods	Data Analysis Procedures
Study Design	Researcher's Role and Potential Ethical Issues
Procedures, Instruments, Reliability, Validity	Methods of Validation
Data Analysis	Preliminary Findings
Preliminary Results	Anticipated Outcomes of the Study and Tentative
Potential Ethical Issues	Literature Review (Optional)
Time Line, Budget, and Preliminary Chapter Outline	Time Line, Budget, and Preliminary Chapter Outline
References	References
Appendices	Appendices

position it near the end of the proposal, and characterize it as optional. In a qualitative proposal the literature review documents the need to study the problem, but it does not lead to the research questions, as it does in quantitative research. In defending this position to faculty unfamiliar with qualitative research, you would provide this rationale for not including a separate literature review section in your proposal. However, if faculty request that you include a complete literature review in a proposal, it is wise to comply with the request. Still, at the end of the review, you might state that the review is tentative and that it will be developed or completed later, after learning about the participants' views. This stance would be consistent with good qualitative research.

Turning again to Figure 9.2, the qualitative proposal includes a "Procedure" section, in which you present the major characteristics of qualitative research and design as well as information about sampling and data analysis. The final section presents a preliminary investigation of your topic, if you have completed such a study. This preliminary study might include interviews with a couple of individuals or field observations of short duration. The chief advantage of such an approach is to test whether you can collect and analyze data from participants and see if your overall design is workable in the field before receiving approval from your faculty committee.

Journal Articles

You prepare a journal article for readers of scholarly publications as well as for the editor and individuals who review the study. A **journal article** is a polished, shorter research report that you send to an editor of a journal. The editor arranges for two to three reviewers to provide comments about the study. The editor then makes a decision based on the reviewers' comments, which typically falls into one of three categories: accept, revise and resubmit, or reject. Usually, when the reviewers accept the manuscript provisionally, they do so based on their anticipation of successful revisions by the author. If the article is accepted, the editor publishes it in an issue of the journal.

A journal article is much shorter than a thesis or dissertation because of page limitations imposed by publishers and editors of journals. Still, qualitative journal articles are much longer than quantitative articles because of the extensive quotes and the lengthy discussions of descriptions and themes. The format of quantitative and qualitative journal articles varies from one journal to another.

Conference Papers and Proposals

A norm of research is that individuals publicly share their research reports so that information is accessible to the general education community. One way to do this is by presenting a paper at a professional association conference.

A **conference paper** is a research report presented to an audience at a state, regional, national, or international conference typically sponsored by a professional association (e.g., AERA, American Association of Teacher Educators). Developing and presenting a conference paper from a research study helps to publicize the study, provides a research entry for a résumé, helps to advance the work of the author within the educational research community, and builds knowledge among researchers exploring the topic. The audiences for conferences may be researchers, practitioners, or policy makers. Researchers prepare conference papers for audiences who attend the conference as well as for individuals who review and accept the papers for presentation. Typically, the length of a conference paper is about the same as a journal article—about 25 pages plus tables, figures, and appendices.

A **conference proposal** is a brief proposal to present a study at a conference. Typically, these proposals run about three pages long, and reviewers use them to determine whether they will accept the authors' research for presentation at the conference.

A conference proposal needs to conform to the guidelines provided by the conference association.

During or after the completion of a study, the process of presenting a conference paper begins. A researcher sends a proposal to the conference organizers, who have issued a "Call for Proposals" several months in advance of the conference. This call invites researchers to submit proposals about their research for possible presentation at the conference. In response to this call, authors develop a brief proposal about the study and submit it for review. If the proposal is accepted, the author is obligated to attend the conference and present the paper based on the proposal. Following acceptance, the author develops a completed paper, presents it at the conference, and distributes it to conference participants. At the conference, conference organizers often group three or four research papers into a single session and each author has about 15 to 20 minutes to present his or her study. Alternatively, organizers may offer symposia as a format for presenting research papers. This format consists of several research papers from different individuals addressing the same theme.

Sample Guidelines for Proposals

To illustrate the process of developing a proposal for a conference paper, we will examine the AERA "Call for Proposals" that is printed each year in the *Educational Researcher* journal. The format of paper presentations at AERA has changed in recent years to allow for more innovative forms of presentations, such as interactive paper sessions, performances, and town meetings. The most common form of presenting a single research study, called a paper session, requires that an author submit materials by a set deadline. You need to provide a summary about your research that includes:

◆ Objectives or purposes
◆ Perspective(s) or theoretical framework
◆ Methods, techniques, or modes of inquiry
◆ Data sources or evidence
◆ Results and/or conclusions/point of view
◆ Educational or scientific importance of the study (AERA, 1999, p. 33).

You send this summary to a program coordinator for one of AERA's topical divisions or numerous special interest groups (SIGs). To decide what division to send your material to, you might contact the AERA central office (**www.aera.net**). Two to three reviewers who do not know your identity will review your proposal. The review process may take 2 to 3 months, at which time the conference coordinators will inform you as to whether your proposal has been accepted or rejected for presentation.

Report for Policy Makers or School Personnel

A final type of research report is one that you present to practitioners who are in positions of responsibility in education. These individuals may be policy makers in state and federal governments or leaders in schools, such as superintendents, principals, curriculum directors, and teachers. The research report presented to these individuals might follow these guidelines (see Muffo, 1986):

◆ *The timing is most important.*   The topic of the research needs to be timely and provide suggestions for practice. Identify in your research study the suggestions found in the "Implication" section and share these in your research report with practitioners.
◆ *Report specific results from your research.*   You might summarize these results using bullets to highlight the key findings. You should probably not frame the

results in statistical terms in quantitative research or in the many perspectives of qualitative research. Focus on the outcome of the quantitative statistical tests or on the qualitative perspective that most frequently occurred in your database.

◆ *Present the results simply and clearly.*   This means that your report should be short, highlight key findings, and include an abstract that provides an overview of the results. A dramatic graph or a table can bring together many findings.

◆ *Include a one-page executive summary at the beginning of your research report.*   This summary should not dwell on the research or the methods of your study but on the key findings and their implications for practice. You might highlight the problem studied, the question you asked, the data collection, and the major results and implications for practice.

◆ *Obtain clearance from key individuals to present your research.*   You need to have permission from leaders to present and disseminate your research. Share with these individuals the executive summary prior to your presentation or distribution of the report.

Consider Maria's situation. She needs to present her research to the *school committee*. Following the suggestions above, write down the steps Maria should follow to:

1. Make sure that she has approval to present her research
2. Include an executive summary
3. Report specific results simply and clearly
4. Submit the results to the committee in a timely fashion

HOW SHOULD YOU STRUCTURE YOUR REPORT?

A study with a clear structure is easy to understand and easy to read, even though the subject matter may be complex. A nationally known author on the subject of writing, Natalie Goldberg (2000), has stressed the importance of understanding the physical structure of a writing project. The **physical structure of a study** is the underlying organization of topics that forms a structure for a research report. Think about a journal article that you have recently read. Was it difficult or easy to understand? Were you able to read it quickly, or did you labor?

Look at the Physical Structure of Research Reports

Being able to identify the underlying structure of a research report will help you write a study as well as understand one. This is not always easy, but the following four techniques can help:

1. The easiest approach is to examine the different levels of headings used in a study. These headings are road signs used by an author to convey major points in a study. Although some headings are better descriptors of content than others are, examining them helps you identify the structure of a study.
2. Look for the six steps in the research process. All reports, whether quantitative or qualitative, should contain a research problem, literature, a purpose statement and questions or hypotheses, data collection, data analysis and interpretation, and a reporting format.
3. Look for the research questions (or hypotheses) and the answers researchers develop to these questions (or hypotheses). For every question asked, researchers should pose an answer. Start with the introductory passages (i.e., "Introduction")

and then look at the end of the report (i.e., the "Results" or "Discussion") to see how the authors answered the questions.

4. Finally, become familiar with the structures of different types of reports, especially approaches using quantitative and qualitative research.

Design an Appropriate Quantitative Structure

The structure of a quantitative report is shown in Figure 9.3. The body of the paper comprises five major sections. These are the same five sections typically found in published quantitative reports. Knowing this structure will help you read studies and understand where to look for information. For journal articles, the front matter and the back matter sections are limited because of space constraints. For a dissertation or thesis, the researcher includes more front matter to help the reader understand the organization of the study. One front matter section, the abstract, is optional in reports, but, if you write it in a complete form to include all of the elements of an abstract, it helps the reader identify the major parts of a study.

Another part of the body of the paper is the "Method" discussion. This section is likely to vary from one research report to another because of the different procedures authors use for their research designs.

Design an Appropriate Qualitative Structure

For a qualitative dissertation, thesis, and journal article, the structure varies considerably. The standard five-section structure seen in Figure 9.3 may not be appropriate for a qualitative study. For a qualitative report, such as a dissertation or thesis, authors may

---

FIGURE 9.3

The Front, Body, and Back Matter of a Quantitative Study

Front Matter
Title page
Abstract of the study (optional)

Body of the Paper
Introduction
    Statement of the problem
    Purpose statement
    Research questions or hypotheses
    Theoretical or conceptual explanation

Review of the Literature
    Review of the previous research
    Summary of major themes
    How present study will extend literature

Methods
    Sample and site
    Access and permissions
    Instruments and their reliability and validity
    Interventions (if used)
    Procedures of data collection
    Analysis of the data

Results
    Descriptive analysis of all data
    Inferential analysis to address questions/hypotheses
    Tables and figures to display the data

Discussion
    Summary of major results
    Relationship of results to existing studies
    Limitations of the study
    Implications for future research
    Overall significance of the study

Back Matter
References
Appendices (e.g., instruments, key questions)

include six to eight chapters. For example, Miller (1992) conducted a qualitative ethnography case study of the experiences of a first-year president. She included the following 11 chapters:

Chapter 1 Introduction to the Study

Chapter 2 Path to the Presidency

Chapter 3 Early Surprises and Challenges

Chapter 4 Building Relationships

Chapter 5 Presidential Roles

Chapter 6 Providing Vision and Leadership

Chapter 7 Initiating Change

Chapter 8 External Constituents

Chapter 9 Struggles and Difficulties

Chapter 10 The Spouse's Role

Chapter 11 Summary, Conclusions, and Implications

The 11-chapter structure places emphasis on themes that emerged during the study. It does not include a separate chapter on the literature review or the specific procedures of the study.

You can see the flexible structure found in Miller's dissertation also in qualitative journal articles and conference papers. Just as there are multiple perspectives from participants in a study, there are also many variations in how researchers report their findings. Some forms of qualitative reports will emphasize description, whereas others will focus on themes or personal interpretations of findings by the author. This flexible format for reporting undoubtedly makes reading qualitative research difficult for those new to the approach. Although the structures for reporting continue to emerge, knowing several prominent variations will help you begin to see the focus of authors as they report their research.

Consider these alternative forms for writing qualitative research:

◆ A *scientific approach* is similar to a quantitative study in which all or most of the five sections ("Introduction," "Review of the Literature," "Methods," "Results," and "Discussion") are present.

◆ A *storytelling approach* can have varied structure. The author uses literary devices (e.g., metaphors, analogies, plot, climax) and persuasive, creative writing to present the study.

◆ A *thematic approach* includes extensive discussion about the major themes that arise from analyzing a qualitative database. Often, this approach uses extensive quotes and rich details to support the themes. Often these themes are interrelated and incorporated within specific qualitative designs such as grounded theory, ethnographic, or narrative designs.

◆ A *descriptive approach* incorporates a detailed description of people and places to carry the narrative. A study in this mode might convey "a typical day in the life" of an individual.

◆ A *theoretical approach* is when the author either starts with a theory (e.g., a theoretically oriented case study), ends with a theory (e.g., grounded theory), or modifies an existing theory based on views of participants.

◆ An *experimental, alternative,* or *performance approach* may include a report of qualitative research in the form of a poem, a fictional story, a drama, or a highly personalized account, called an *autoethnography* (see Denzin, 1997, or Richardson, 2000). For example, rather than writing a standard research report, the qualitative inquirer develops a play that captures the "unruly, multisited, and emotionally laden" subject matter better than standard writing (Richardson, 2000, p. 934).

Although qualitative reports vary from the traditional theory-scientific approach to the more experimental, it is helpful to look at two broad structural approaches called the scientific and the storytelling approaches. Figures 9.4 and 9.5 present these two approaches. As you can see, the formats differ in the basic topics included and in the headings used to convey the topics. Both differ, as well, from the quantitative structure.

In a **qualitative scientific structure** the researcher includes detailed procedures of inquiry and follows a traditional form for reporting research that includes the introduction, the procedures, the findings, and a discussion. However, a scientific qualitative report does differ from a standard quantitative format. In the qualitative scientific approach, you refer to *procedures* instead of methods, and *findings* instead of results. In addition, Figure 9.4 shows that the format includes a rationale for qualitative research, a description of the site or individuals, and an analysis of themes. You find this structural approach in qualitative designs such as case studies and in grounded theory studies.

Figure 9.5 displays the less recognizable qualitative format, the storytelling structure. A **qualitative storytelling structure** is a flexible approach to writing a qualitative report. The meaning of the study unfolds through descriptions, the author's reflection on the meaning of the data, a larger understanding of the phenomenon, and a return to the author's stance on the topic. Figure 9.5 begins with a description or vignette of an individual and brings the *procedures* into the study at the midpoint. It ends with the meaning of the phenomenon, and presents this meaning in terms of the larger understandings, a comparison with published studies, and the author's own experiences. You find this format in qualitative research designs such as ethnographies and narrative research.

FIGURE 9.4

The Front, Body, and Back Matter of a Scientific Qualitative Structure

Front Matter
Title page
Preface and acknowledgments (optional)
Table of contents (optional)
List of tables (optional)
List of figures (optional)
Abstract of the study (optional)

Body of the Paper
Introduction
    Statement of the problem
    Purpose statement
    Research questions

Procedures
    Rationale for qualitative approach
    Sample and site
    Access and permissions
    Data-gathering strategies
    Data analysis approach

Findings
    Description of site or individuals
    Analysis of themes

Discussion
    Major findings
    Comparison of findings with existing studies
    Limitations
    Implications for future research
    Overall significance of the study

Back Matter
References
Appendices (e.g., figures, interview, or observational
   protocols)

FIGURE 9.5

The Front, Body, and Back Matter of a Qualitative Storytelling Structure

Front Matter
Title page
Preface and acknowledgments (optional)
Table of contents (optional)
List of tables (optional)
List of figures (optional)
Abstract of the study (optional)

Body of the Paper
Specific description of individual of interest in the study
Author's relation or connection to the participant
The data collected during the study
A specific incident to understand the individual's life
The meaning of the incident
Larger understanding of the group of people to which the individual belongs
A comparison of the meaning with published studies
Return to author's personal meaning of the individual and events

Back Matter
References

 ## Think-Aloud About the Structure of a Study

Having discussed the structure of various forms of research reports, I want to return now to an approach for examining the structure of research regardless of these forms. I think of a research report as two parallel railroad tracks. The researcher proceeds ahead on both tracks at the same time. One of the tracks represents the *subject matter* of the study. In every study, the writer addresses a topic and the results unfold about this topic. The second track is the *research* track. This track consists of steps in the process of research and the specific procedures within each step. Knowing that the research exists as well as the subject matter enables me to understand the underlying research process of a published study, to determine what findings I should identify, and to evaluate whether the research is rigorous enough to use in my own study. We need to know that the research track exists so that we can see the author's underlying research procedures at work.

As I examine the structure of a research report:

◆ I use the analogy of two railroad tracks going in the same direction to help visualize the structure of a study.
◆ I look at the study and examine the headings closely to learn about the structure. They are good road signs to help me understand the research.
◆ Realizing that researchers compose all educational studies with six process steps, I search for a research problem, a question, data collection, data analysis, and interpretation.
◆ When reading a study I could give emphasis to both, to learn about the results or findings in a study as well as to *see* the research procedures so that I could critically evaluate the study.

Not all studies are perfect examples of research. Editors of journals make choices about what to publish. Sometimes editors publish an article because the research problem is a timely issue or the issue has not been studied using rigorous procedures. In other cases, the methods are strong, and they cause the editor to accept an article for publication. I am not discouraged if the author only minimally addresses one of the six steps. As a developing researcher, you need to understand both the research and subject matter tracks to comprehend fully the structure of a research report.

HOW DO YOU WRITE IN A SENSITIVE, ETHICAL, AND SCHOLARLY WAY?

In addition to understanding the structure of a study, researchers engage in good writing practices when they compose a research report. They:

◆ Are sensitive to individuals and use language that reduces bias
◆ Use appropriate research terms
◆ Write and report the findings ethically
◆ Employ a point of view consistent with quantitative and qualitative approaches
◆ Balance research and content
◆ Interconnect parts of a study
◆ Advance a concise title

Use Language That Reduces Bias

A research report needs to be sensitive and respectful of people and places. Your study submitted to a dissertation or thesis committee, to a journal, or to a conference will be rejected if you are insensitive to individuals or cultural groups.

The APA has compiled information and developed guidelines about the use of writing strategies for reducing bias in the language of research reports (APA, 2010). These guidelines state using language that avoids demeaning attitudes, including biased assumptions, and awkward constructions that suggest bias because of gender, sexual orientation, racial or ethnic group, disability, or age. One helpful suggestion, developed by Maggio (1991), is to test your written research report for discriminatory language by:

◆ Substituting your own group for groups being discussed
◆ Imagining that you are a member of the group
◆ Revising your material if you feel excluded or offended

Another approach is to spend time studying examples of appropriate language constructions. Determine how these constructions are inclusive and sensitive. You might also examine three guidelines for reducing bias in language recommended in the *APA Style Manual* (APA, 2010):

1. *Describe individuals at an appropriate level of specificity.* This means that you need to use specific terms for persons that are accurate, clear, and free of bias. For example:
  • Be specific:
    Poor: man or woman   Preferred: men and women
    Poor: over 62   Preferred: ages 63–70

2. *Be sensitive to labels for individuals or groups.* This means calling people names they prefer and acknowledging that preferences for names change over time. Writers should not use their own group as the standard against which to judge others. For example:

- Use adjectival forms.

  Poor: the gays   Preferred: gay men

- Put "people" first, followed by a descriptive phrase.

  Poor: schizophrenics   Preferred: people diagnosed with schizophrenia

- Use parallel nouns that do not promote one group as a standard or dominance over another group.

  Poor: man and wife   Preferred: husband and wife

3. *Acknowledge participation of people in a study.* You need to specifically identify participants based on the language they use. For example:

- Use impersonal terms.

  Poor: subjects   Preferred: participants

  Poor: informants   Preferred: participants

- Use nonstereotypical and unbiased adjectives.

  Poor: woman doctor   Preferred: doctor

  Poor: nonaggressive women Preferred: nonaggressive participants

- Use specific cultural identity.

  Poor: American Indians   Preferred: Cherokees

- Put people first, not their disability.

  Poor: mentally ill person   Preferred: person with mental illness

Encode Scholarly Terms into Your Research

As these guidelines for reducing bias suggest, certain terms are preferred over others for referring to participants in a study. Likewise, in the field of research, certain terms need to be included to convey your understanding of research. Others will partly judge your research based on the appropriate use of standard quantitative and qualitative terms. For example, to call the sampling "random" instead of "purposeful" in qualitative research shows your lack of understanding of the basic differences between the two approaches. When you read a research report, you can examine the level of the author's research understanding through the choice of words. The glossary at the end of this text and the key terms (words in bold type) throughout the chapters provide useful words to use in your research report.

Here are some additional ideas that might be helpful in building your vocabulary and using research words:

- As you write your study, consult a dictionary of terms, such as the quantitative dictionary of terms by Vogt (2005) and the qualitative dictionary of terms by Schwandt (2007).
- When writing a research report, encode your writing with the language of research. In this case, **encoding** is the intentional use by an author of specific terms to convey ideas. This practice will enhance the acceptability of your research to graduate committees, publishers, and conference attendees. For example, the terms *compare* and *relate* are good words to use in quantitative research, and the terms *explore* and *discover* are good terms to use in qualitative research.

Use Ethical Reporting and Writing of Research Results

Although much ethical discussion is focused on the data collection process and ethical procedures to use when approaching participants and sites, an equally important aspect of ethical research practices resides in the writing and report phase of inquiry. The central idea of research ethics is that research should be done in a way that honors right or wrong conduct (Kaler & Beres, 2010). **Ethical reporting and writing research** is research that needs to be honestly reported, shared with participants, not previously published, not plagiarized, not influenced by personal interest, and duly credited to authors that make a contribution.

◆ Honest reporting requires that researchers not falsify data to support a hypothesis or research question or omit troublesome results to present a more convincing story. This practice means that researchers should not create artificial data, figures, or tables in their reports, or create or attribute quotes to individuals that are not accurate.

◆ Data sharing means that researchers need to provide copies of their reports to participants. These reports may be in oral or written form and directed toward those participants who helped recruit participants (Brabeck & Brabeck, 2009). The report should be as jargon-free as possible to enable a wide audience to read and understand your report. Also, reports should not sit unpublished and should be shared despite contrary findings. For most audiences, it is necessary as well to make the report convey practical significance. This is especially important when community members are involved directly in the research. For example, as American Indian tribes take over the delivery of services to their members (e.g., day care centers, Head Start, K–12 schools, and tribal colleges and universities), they are reclaiming their right to determine what research will be done and how it will be reported (LaFrance & Crazy Bull, 2009). They challenge whose voice is speaking and the accuracy of the reporting of facts and their interpretation. The knowledge that is shared may be based on that handed down from generations, gained through careful observation from multiple vantage points, and revealed through dreams, visions, and spiritual protocols (Brant-Castellano, 2000). Thus, the sharing of data, and making it available is important for qualified scholars, community members, and professionals. The issue of power dynamics in research situations surfaces when the results are disseminated to a select audience (Ginsberg & Mertens, 2009). To counter this, for example, results might be posted to a Web site for distribution to a wide audience. To make the results available, the APA (2010) style manual recommends that authors keep the raw data for a minimum of five years after publication of the research.

◆ When researchers publish their results, another ethical issue is to refrain from duplicate and piecemeal publication of data. Reports must reflect the independence of separate research efforts. Researchers cannot submit the publication material that has been previously published. Conference papers, unless published in conference proceedings, are not considered to be published material. The key in understanding this is whether the manuscript has been published elsewhere "in substantially similar form or with substantially similar content" (APA, 2010, p. 13).

◆ Plagiarism is the use of someone else's work without giving them credit for the information. Another ethical issue is that researchers should not claim that the words and ideas they use from others are their own; credit needs to be given using quotation marks. Whenever you paraphrase another author, you need to give them credit. A related idea, self-plagiarism, is when researchers present their own previously published work as new scholarship. An acceptable length of duplicated material varies, but the new document needs to constitute an original contribution. When material is duplicated, citations to the other works are needed. Authors might use comments such as "as I have previously discussed . . ." (APA, 2010, p. 16) to signal when the material duplicates other material.

◆ Conducting a research study also raises the potential ethical issue of a conflict of interest. Conflict of interest, such as personal (commercial, economical) interests, leads to bias in a research report. More and more campuses are asking authors to sign forms that indicate that they do not have a conflict of interest in conducting the research. The question of who will profit from the research is an ethical concern that needs to be asked.

◆ For graduate students and faculty, another ethical issue is not giving credit for authorships and not reflecting this credit in the specific order of authorship (APA, 2010). Researchers should take credit for work for which they have actually performed or to which they have substantially contributed. Such contribution may consist of formulating the problem or research questions, designing the methods, gathering or analyzing the data, interpreting the results, or writing a major portion of the paper. Credit for authorship needs to be established early in a project, and it is especially important for graduate students and their advisors to assess authorship credit for publications emanating from student research. Such issues arise because students may need added supervision in conducting their research due to a lack of training or the need for additional analyses. Student-faculty authorship for publications needs to be assessed and reassessed during the evolution of the project. An equally important topic is the order of authorship for publications with the individual providing the greatest contribution listed as the first or senior author. This order should reflect the relative contribution of each author.

Use an Appropriate Point of View

The presence of the researcher in the study varies between quantitative and qualitative research. In *quantitative* research, the investigator is in the background narrating the study—an omniscient third person. For example, the researcher *reports* the results of the study and *explains* their importance. The first-person pronoun *I* is not used, and instead the writer uses the impersonal point of view. This form of writing also includes the use of past tense to create distance between the report and the writer. Use passive constructions sparingly. For example, in a quantitative report, you might find the following passive construction:

> *Passive Construction:*   The results were reported at a significance level of $p = .01$.
>
> *Active Construction:*   The researcher reported results at the significance level of $p = .01$.

Also, a quantitative writer seldom mentions the first names of individuals in a study and also emphasizes objectivity of the results.

In *qualitative* research, however, the researcher is typically present and in the foreground in the narrative report of the study. This is seen in the use of the first-person pronoun *I* (or the collective *we*) and in the personal experiences of the author that are written directly into the report (e.g., the author's difficulty in collecting data, the reflection on themes derived from the data). The author may present sidebars that interpret the personal meaning of themes or personal statements about experiences. The qualitative researcher also seeks to present a persuasive story and often writes in a lively manner using metaphors, similes, analogy, contradictions, and ironies. The study may end with questions that remain unanswered, much like many novels or short stories. Further, qualitative inquirers mention first names of participants (typically using aliases to protect the identity of individuals), and the level of detail, especially in the description, brings the writer and the reader close together.

Balance Your Research and Content

Some researchers feel that their report must demonstrate their knowledge of research more than the content or subject matter of their studies. Other researchers feel just the opposite. Regardless of emphasis, scholarly writing includes a balance between conveying knowledge about research and knowledge about the subject matter of the study (remember the two tracks of the railroad mentioned earlier). When researchers overemphasize methods, they may feel a need to convince faculty, graduate committee members, or journal editors of their knowledge of research methods. However, an underemphasis may indicate that the person lacks skills or knowledge about research. A good research report contains a balance between a discussion about research and the actual content of the study. This balance is in roughly a 50–50 proportion. For example, compare the following two models of a methods discussion about surveying department chairpersons.

> *Poor Model Displaying an Overemphasis on Method:*   In this project, survey random sampling will be used so that each department chair has an equal probability of being selected. Moreover, it is important to use stratification procedures so individuals in the sample are selected in proportion to which they are represented in the population. . . .
>
> *Better Model Displaying Balance:*   In this project, 400 academic chairpersons were randomly sampled so that results could be generalized to the population of academic chairpersons in Research I institutions of higher education ($N = 2,000$ chairs). Moreover, the 400 chairpersons represented both men and women chairs in proportion to which they were represented in the total population (300 males; 100 females).

The good model includes comments by the researcher that not only convey an understanding of adequate survey research methods but also inform the reader about the subject matter (the study of chairpersons) of the actual study.

Interconnect Sections for Consistency

Another writing strategy used in research is to interconnect the sections of your research report so that you provide a consistent discussion to readers. One way to establish this interconnection is by using key concepts as linking devices. **Linking devices** are words or phrases that tie together sections of a research report.

In a quantitative report, stating the *variables* and using their exact name each time you mention them can help connect the parts. Consider the many times that researchers refer to the variables in their studies. The title specifies the variables in a study; they are also included in the purpose statement and research questions. Researchers operationally define them in the method section. When researchers use the exact same terms each time they mention the variables, they provide a useful linkage among parts of a report.

Another linking device in a quantitative study is to *use the same research questions or hypotheses* wherever they appear in the research report. A slight change in wording can throw readers off and convey different meanings in your research. When you introduce research questions or hypotheses early in the study (as they often appear), include the *exact same words* when you return to them in the results of your study.

In a qualitative study, *state the same central phenomenon* each time you introduce it. You may introduce the phenomenon in the title, in the statement of the problem section, in the purpose statement, in the research questions, and in your findings.

In both quantitative and qualitative projects, *repeat the problem* throughout the study. This binds the entire proposal or report together. You present the research problem in the introductory part of a proposal and emphasize its importance during the discussion about research questions or hypotheses. You discuss it again during the data collection and analysis as the investigators provide results to address the problem. It may also appear in the future research section at the end of a study, when you talk about the need for additional research.

Advance a Concise Title

Two components of a scholarly manuscript deserve special attention because they are of major importance: the title and the abstract. Information from the APA (2010) style manual reviews the components of both a good title and an abstract for writing a scholarly paper. The purpose of a **title** is to summarize the major idea of the paper in a concise and clear manner. The title should be no longer than 12 words in length and should avoid superfluous words such as "a study of" or "an investigation of." It should be able to stand alone in clarity and be self-explanatory. This means that all words should be clear to a reader without definition. A concisely stated title will enable a researcher to compress it into a "header" that can be placed on each page of the manuscript, and this "header" will provide key words for use by indexing services for the literature databases (e.g., ERIC) to catalog the article. In addition to these components mentioned in the APA (2010) manual, you might also consider what elements go into a good title from both a quantitative and a qualitative perspective. A good quantitative title would contain:

◆ The major independent and dependent variables in a study, typically listed in order from independent to dependent
◆ The participants in a study
◆ The research site or location for the study

For a qualitative title, the components would be:

◆ The central phenomenon being studied
◆ The participants in the study
◆ The research site or location for the study

HOW DO YOU EVALUATE THE QUALITY OF YOUR RESEARCH?

Both during the process of conducting a study as well as at its conclusion, you need to be mindful of the quality of the research. The improvement of practice, the quality of policy debates, and the advancement of knowledge all call for high-quality educational research. It becomes important, then, to consider the evaluation of research by asking "What criteria should I use?"

Employ Appropriate Standards

Because the quantitative and qualitative approaches to research are different, each merits its own criteria for evaluation. However, both approaches reflect the broader research process (i.e., the six steps in the research process), and some common elements should play into the evaluative criteria as well. Also, the audiences for research, mentioned earlier in this chapter, will employ criteria such as:

◆ Does the research meet the standards for publication?
◆ Will the research be useful in our school?
◆ Will the research advance policy discussions in our region?
◆ Will the research add to our scholarly knowledge about a topic or research problem?
◆ Will the research help address some pressing educational problem?

These are important questions, and the answers will shape how we evaluate a research report. Because of the various audiences involved, we have no single standard for research. Moreover, standards for quantitative and qualitative research differ because the two approaches to research differ.

Quantitative Standards

In a study by Hall, Ward, and Comer (1988), the authors had a panel of judges rate 128 educational *quantitative* articles. The specific shortcomings of these articles, in order of their importance, were:

◆ Lack of validity and reliability in data-gathering procedures
◆ Weaknesses in the research designs
◆ Limitations of the study were not stated
◆ Research design not appropriate for the problem
◆ Inappropriate sampling
◆ Results of analysis not clearly reported
◆ Inappropriate methods used to analyze data
◆ Unclear writing
◆ Assumptions not clearly stated
◆ Data-gathering methods not clearly described

As you can see, quantitative evaluators were most concerned about aspects related to the data collection, the analysis, and the reporting of results of a study—the research design phase of the projects.

   Another perspective on evaluating the quality of quantitative research is available from Tuckman (1999). As shown in Table 9.2, the standards follow the research process with an emphasis on the quality of the hypotheses and variables, the control of extraneous variables, and the importance of the discussion and its implications for research and practice.

Qualitative Standards

Turning to qualitative research, the criteria for a good research report vary depending on your emphasis as a researcher. When we examine current perspectives about

---

TABLE 9.2

Quantitative Criteria for Evaluating Quantitative Research

Research Problem:
- Is it stated?
- Is it clear?
- Is it complete and accurate?
- Does it offer theoretical and practical value?

The Literature Review:
- Is it clear, relevant, recent, based on studies reporting numbers?
- Are the citations and references accurate?

Hypotheses and Variables:
- What are the hypotheses and what types are they?
- Does the study indicate the independent, dependent, intervening moderator, and control variables?
- Were operational definitions given for the variables?
- Were extraneous effects controlled in the study so that bias did not have an effect on the participants, their experiences, or the generalization of the results?
- Were certain variables manipulated?

Design:
- Was the study design identified?
- Were the scores from the measures valid and reliable?
- Were the statistics the right choice?

Findings and Discussion:
- Did the findings fit the problem?
- How significant and important were the findings?
- Did the discussion section report conclusions and were they consistent with the study's results?
- Did the discussion section offer reasonable interpretations of why results did and did not match expectations?
- Did the discussion section suggest reasonable implications about what readers should do with the results?

Source: Adapted from Tuckman, 1999.

---

judging qualitative research, ideas within each of the three themes—philosophy, procedures, and participation/advocacy—combine to form our evaluation criteria. For example, as one interested in the philosophical ideas behind qualitative research, you might draw from perspectives about what constitutes knowledge (e.g., an evolving design) or reality (e.g., subjective experiences). As a procedural researcher, you might emphasize the importance of rigorous data collection (e.g., multiple forms of data) and analysis (e.g., multiple levels of analysis). As a participatory/advocacy writer, you might stress the importance of collaboration (e.g., researcher collaborates on equal terms with participants) and persuasive writing (e.g., does it seem true to participants?).

Let's examine three sets of criteria for evaluating qualitative research developed by three authors within a 6-year time frame. As seen in Table 9.3, the standards reflect both overlap and differences. They all speak to the importance of the participant in the research study, as well as standards set within research communities. Writing persuasively and with respect for participants is also paramount in all three standards. Writing from a point of self-awareness and being sensitive to reciprocity and the impact of the study (e.g., emotionally and intellectually) on readers differs.

TABLE 9.3		
Three Sets of Standards for Evaluating the Quality of Qualitative Research		
Lincoln's (1995) Philosophical Criteria:	**Creswell's (2007) Procedural Criteria**	**Richardson's (2000) Participatory and Advocacy Criteria**
• Standards set in the inquiry community such as guidelines for publication. • Positionality: The "text" should display honesty or authenticity about its own stance and about the position of the author. • Community: All research takes place in, is addressed to, and serves the purposes of the community in which it was carried out. • Voice: Participants' voices must not be silenced, disengaged, or marginalized. • Critical subjectivity: Researchers need to have heightened self-awareness in the research process and create personal and social transformation. • Reciprocity: Reciprocity must exist between the researcher and those being researched. • Sacredness of relationships: The researcher respects the sacredness of the relationships and collaborates on equal terms with participants. • Sharing privileges: The researcher shares rewards with persons whose lives they portray.	• It employs rigorous data collection, which involves multiple forms of data, extensive data, and a long period in the field collecting data. • It is consistent with the philosophical assumptions and characteristics of a qualitative approach to research. These include an evolving design, the presentation of multiple perspectives, the researcher as an instrument of data collection, and the focus on participants' views. • It employs a tradition of inquiry, such as case study, ethnography, grounded theory, or narrative inquiry as a procedural guide for the study. • It starts with a single focus on a central phenomenon rather than a comparison or relationship (as in quantitative research). • It is written persuasively so that the reader experiences *being there*. • Analysis consists of multiple levels of analysis to portray the complexity of the central phenomena. • The narrative engages the reader because of unexpected ideas and believable and realistic information. • It includes strategies to confirm the accuracy of the study.	• Substantive contribution: Does this piece contribute to our understanding of social life? • Aesthetic merit: Does this piece succeed aesthetically? Does the use of practices open up the text and invite interpretive responses? Is the text artistically shaped, satisfying, complex, and not boring? • Reflexivity: How did the author come to write this text? Is there adequate self-awareness and self-exposure for the reader to make judgments about the point of view? • Impact: Does this affect me? Emotionally? Intellectually? Move me to write? Move me to try new research practices? Move me to action? • Expression of a reality: Does this text embody a fleshed out sense of lived experiences? Does it seem "true"?

Source: Lincoln, 1995; Creswell, 2007; Richardson, 2000.

In combination, they all offer philosophical, procedural, and reflexive standards for you to use in evaluating qualitative inquiry.

Evaluate with a Process Approach

Our discussion of evaluation would not be complete without relating evaluation to the steps of the *process of research* addressed in this book. The steps in this process are presented to illustrate complete, rigorous quantitative and qualitative research. Because evaluation will differ depending on whether the study is quantitative or qualitative, Figures 9.6 and 9.7 provide criteria specifically related to the six steps of research. These lists enable you to assess the quality of your own study or to evaluate the quality of a research report.

FIGURE 9.6

Checklist for Evaluating the Process of a Quantitative Study

Title for the Study
_____ Does it reflect the major independent and dependent variables?
_____ Does it express either a comparison among groups or a relationship among variables?
_____ Does it convey the participants and site for the study?

Problem Statement
_____ Does it indicate an educational issue to study?
_____ Has the author provided evidence that this issue is important?
_____ Is there some indication that the author located this issue through a search of past literature or from personal experiences?
_____ Does the research problem fit a quantitative approach?
_____ Are the assumptions of the study consistent with an approach?

Review of the Literature
_____ Are the studies about the independent and dependent variables clearly reviewed?
_____ Does the review end with how the author will extend or expand the current body of literature?
_____ Does the study follow APA style?

Purpose, Hypotheses, and Research Questions
_____ Does the author specify a purpose statement?
_____ Is the purpose statement clear, and does it indicate the variables, their relationship, and the people and site to be studied?
_____ Are either hypotheses or research questions written?
_____ Do these hypotheses or questions indicate the major variables and the participants in a study?
_____ Do the purpose statement and hypotheses or research questions contain the major components that will help a reader understand the study?
_____ Has the author identified a theory or explanation for the hypotheses or questions?

Data Collection
_____ Does the author mention the steps taken to obtain access to people and sites?
_____ Is a rigorous probability sampling strategy used?
_____ Has the author identified good, valid, and reliable instruments to use to measure the variables?
_____ Are the instruments administered so that bias and error are not introduced into the study?

Data Analysis and Results
_____ Are the statistics chosen for analysis consistent with the research questions, hypotheses, variables, and scales of measurement?
_____ Is the unit of analysis appropriate to address the research problem?
_____ Are the data adequately represented in tables and figures?
_____ Do the results answer the research questions and address the research problem?
_____ Are the results substantiated by the evidence?
_____ Are generalizations from the results limited to the population of participants in the study?

Writing
_____ Is the structure of the overall study consistent with the topics addressed in a quantitative study?
_____ Are educational and social science terms carefully defined?
_____ Are variables labeled in a consistent way throughout the study?
_____ Is the study written using extensive references?
_____ Is the study written using an impersonal point of view?
_____ Is the study written appropriately for intended audience(s)?

FIGURE 9.7

Checklist for Evaluating the Process of a Qualitative Study

Title for the Study
_____ Does it reflect the central phenomenon being studied?
_____ Does it reflect the people and site being studied?

Problem Statement
_____ Does it indicate an educational issue to study?
_____ Has the author provided evidence that this issue is important?
_____ Is there some indication that the author located this issue through a search of past literature or from personal experience?
_____ Does the research problem fit a qualitative approach?
_____ Are the assumptions of the study consistent with a qualitative approach?

Review of the Literature
_____ Has the author provided a literature review of the research problem under study?
_____ Has the author signaled that the literature review is preliminary or tentatively based on the findings in the study?
_____ Does the study follow APA style?

Purpose and Research Questions
_____ Does the author specify both a purpose statement and a central research question?
_____ Do the purpose statement and central question indicate the central phenomenon of study and the people and place where the study will occur?
_____ Are subquestions written to narrow the central question to topic areas or foreshadow the steps in data analysis?

Data Collection
_____ Has the author taken steps to obtain access to people and sites?
_____ Has the author chosen a specific purposeful sampling strategy for individuals or sites?
_____ Is the data collection clearly specified and is it extensive?
_____ Is there evidence that the author has used a protocol for recording data?

Data Analysis and Findings
_____ Were appropriate steps taken to analyze the text or visual data into themes, perspectives, or categories?
_____ Was sufficient evidence obtained (including quotes) to support each theme or category?
_____ Were multiple-layer themes or categories derived?
_____ Did the findings answer the research questions?
_____ Were the findings realistic and accurate? Were steps taken to support this conclusion through verification?
_____ Were the findings represented in the themes or categories so that multiple perspectives can be easily seen?
_____ Were the findings represented in narrative discussions or in visuals?

Writing
_____ Was the account written persuasively and convincingly?
_____ Was the overall account consistent with one of the many forms for presenting qualitative research?
_____ Was the account written to include literacy approaches, such as the use of metaphor, surprises, detail, dialogue, and complexity?
_____ Was it written using a personal point of view?
_____ Is the study written appropriately for intended audience(s)?

REEXAMINING THE PARENT INVOLVEMENT AND MOTHERS' TRUST IN PRINCIPALS STUDIES

Let's examine one final time the parent involvement study (Deslandes & Bertrand, 2005) and the mothers' trust in principals case study (Shelden et al., 2010). Both of these studies are actual reports of research found in journal articles. They are aimed at scholarly audiences. As research studies, they address problems or issues, raise questions, and portray the collection of data to answer the questions. Further, as should be apparent, they both reflect the six-step research process introduced in this text. They include a research problem, the use of literature, the collection and analysis of data, interpretation of the meaning of the data, and a format for writing the report. This process constitutes a structure (or organization) for each study. Looking at the headings, you can see this structure. This structure provides a road map to the article and helps you to read, understand, and potentially use the findings. Looking closely at the physical structure of both articles, we see that they are both scientific in structure. This may be due to their publication in the same journal, *The Journal of Educational Research,* and its orientation. In other qualitative articles, we would likely see other alternative forms for the structure of qualitative articles.

Both articles illustrate scholarly writing. The encoding of terms for the quantitative study about parent involvement can be seen in use of words such as "influences" (Paragraph 03) and "measures" (Paragraph 16). In the mothers' trust in principals qualitative study, the encoding appears especially in their discussion about research design (Paragraphs 15 and 16). In the quantitative parent involvement study, the researchers report results in an objective way and they remain largely in the background of the study. They do, however, use the personal pronoun "we" (see Paragraph 24) as they talk about their data collection and discuss the major results (see Paragraph 32). Still, after reading this article, we do not know if the authors had children in the seventh, eighth, or ninth grades or had past experiences with being a parent to adolescents at home or in helping with their schoolwork. We also did not learn how they felt about parent involvement on a personal level. In short, the study is written in a quantitative way, with objective reporting by the authors.

A different approach is used in the mothers' trust in principals qualitative study. In that study, we learn about the personal difficulties the researchers had in recruiting participants (Paragraph 18). Overall, the writing approach for both studies was similar with a key difference in how the results were presented from a more statistical discussion in the quantitative parent involvement study (see Paragraphs 25–43) to a more quote-based thematic discussion in the mothers' trust in principals qualitative study (see Paragraphs 29–57).

KEY IDEAS IN THE CHAPTER

The Purpose of a Research Report and Its Types

A **research report** is a completed study that reports an investigation or exploration of a problem, identifies questions to be addressed, includes the collection and analysis of data, and advances an interpretation of the data. Researchers write their reports with their audiences in mind. The audiences differ for six types of research reports. These reports are dissertations and theses, dissertation and thesis proposals, journal articles, conference papers, conference paper proposals, and policy or school reports. Reports vary in purpose, length, and format.

How to Structure Your Research Report

Researchers also structure these reports differently. A good structure facilitates the reading, understanding, and composing of a research study. The structure of a study can be determined by examining the headings and by looking for the process steps of research. Readers can also search for answers researchers provide to questions (or hypotheses) and become familiar with typical structures used in educational research studies. The structure of a quantitative report follows a standard format: introduction, review of the literature, methods, results, and discussion. A qualitative report can be presented in alternative formats: scientific, storytelling, thematic, descriptive, theoretical, and experimental.

Sensitive, Ethical, and Scholarly Writing Practices

When writing a scholarly study or proposal, use language that will not introduce bias. Language should avoid demeaning attitudes, biased assumptions, and awkward constructions that suggest bias because of gender, sexual orientation, racial or ethnic group, disability, or age. The language of research can be specific, be sensitive to stereotyped labels, and acknowledge participation of people in a study. Incorporate into research reports standard research terms such as those found in glossaries, encode reports with appropriate language, and frame them within either a quantitative or qualitative approach. Address ethical issues when reporting and sharing your research. Research needs to be honestly reported, shared with participants, not previously published, not plagiarized, not influenced by personal interest, and duly credited to authors that make a contribution. The point of view of a study for a quantitative project tends to be the omniscient third-person style of writing. For qualitative research, inquirers express a first-person or collective point of view. In a qualitative study, the writer tends to be more in the foreground than in a quantitative study. Writers need to balance content about their subject matter with good research discussions. The sections of a report need to interrelate so that a proposal or a final study is an integrated set of ideas. Linking devices such as variables, hypotheses or research questions, key concepts or a phenomenon, and the problem of the study interconnect sections in a research report. Titles to studies need to be written in a concise form.

Criteria for Evaluating a Research Report

The criteria for evaluating the quality of a study differ depending on the evaluator. Evaluators may be faculty, journal editors and reviewers, policy makers and practicing educators, and conference paper reviewers. Evaluators look for different characteristics of a good quantitative or qualitative study. Although no set standards exist, several general guidelines are available that researchers might use to evaluate a study. Quantitative evaluators are most concerned about aspects related to data collection, analysis, and the reporting of results. Qualitative researchers are concerned about data collection as well, but also about the persuasiveness of the study and the self-awareness of the researcher.

USEFUL INFORMATION FOR PRODUCERS OF RESEARCH

♦ Write in a way that meets the needs of your audiences.
♦ Design and write your research report following the appropriate structure for the type of report advanced in this chapter.
♦ Write quantitative research to include an introduction, a review of the literature, a method, results, and discussion.

◆ Write qualitative research using either a scientific or storytelling structure. Also consider the other structural variations presented in this chapter.

◆ When you design a proposal for a doctoral dissertation or thesis, consider that the structure will vary depending on whether the proposal is for quantitative or qualitative research.

◆ If you plan a paper for a scholarly conference, follow the guidelines provided by the professional association sponsoring the conference.

◆ Write your report sensitively, following the guidelines for reducing bias advanced by the APA (2010).

◆ To make your research scholarly and easy to read, write your report using research words, advancing a consistent standpoint, and employing consistent style for references and headings.

◆ Write your report ethically and share it with participants in your study.

◆ Interrelate sections of a study. Consider how words can provide linking devices for all parts of a study.

◆ After writing *your project,* evaluate it using the standards for quantitative and qualitative research advanced in this chapter.

USEFUL INFORMATION FOR CONSUMERS OF RESEARCH

◆ To identify how a research report is structured, examine headings, look for the research process steps used in this book, search for results that answer the questions or hypotheses, and become familiar with the varied structures for dissertations, theses, journal articles, proposals, and conference papers.

◆ It is sometimes difficult to identify the structure of a qualitative study because of the variations that exist. Consider looking first for whether the study conforms to a scientific approach or a storytelling approach.

◆ Research reports should be free of language that presents demeaning attitudes, bias, and awkward constructions that suggest bias because of gender, sexual orientation, racial or ethnic group, disability, or age.

◆ This chapter offers separate checklists for evaluating the quality of quantitative and qualitative research. Use these checklists to assess the overall quality of a study.

UNDERSTANDING CONCEPTS AND EVALUATING RESEARCH STUDIES

1. If you were to prepare a research report for your faculty advisor, what three standards might this advisor use to assess the quality of your research?

2. Assume that you come across the following sentences in research reports that biased language. Write an improved, nonbiased version of each sentence.
   a. Teachers under 25 adopt an open learning environment for students.
   b. The at-risk students scored below the average in math.
   c. The homeless used the school shelter at night.

3. Describe why the mothers' trust in principals case study would be categorized as a scientific approach to qualitative research?

4. If you were to develop a research report to be presented to the school district based on the parent involvement study, what topics would you include in a list of bulleted points for your one-page executive summary?

5. Find a journal article and develop an outline of the major elements. Use the four suggestions for identifying the structure advanced in this chapter as a guide.

6. Find a journal article and identify the point of view used by the author. Discuss whether the author uses the first person, the collective, or the omniscient point of view. Provide specific examples to document one or more voices in the study.

7. Change the point of view of the author in the journal article you read for Question 6. Discuss specifically how you would change the words to reflect an alternative point of view.

8. Identify the words in a journal article the author uses to convey a research sense of the study. Also discuss where the author uses these words and how they are either good quantitative or qualitative words.

9. Select either a quantitative or a qualitative study published in an educational journal and critique it. Using the checklist in this chapter (Figure 9.6 or 9.7), discuss the strengths and the weaknesses of the article.

CONDUCTING YOUR RESEARCH

For an educational research study of your choice, provide an outline of the structure of your quantitative or qualitative study. For this type of report, indicate the audience(s) that will receive the report, and discuss writing strategies that you plan to use to make the report acceptable to that audience. List the approaches you will use to enhance the scholarly language of your report if your audience consists of individuals on college and university campuses.

Go to the Topics "Preparing a Research Report" and "Evaluating a Research Report" in the MyEducationLab (**www.myeducationlab.com**) for your course, where you can:

♦ Find learning outcomes for "Preparing a Research Report" and "Evaluating a Research Report."

♦ Complete Assignments and Activities that can help you more deeply understand the chapter content.

♦ Apply and practice your understanding of the core skills identified in the chapter with the Building Research Skills exercises.

♦ Check your comprehension of the content covered in the chapter by going to the Study Plan. Here you will be able to take a pretest, receive feedback on your answers, and then access Review, Practice, and Enrichment activities to enhance your understanding. You can then complete a final posttest.

PART THREE

Research Designs

To understand educational research, you now have the map (the six steps that exist in the process of research) and the different paths you can take (quantitative and qualitative). Now we will explore some distinguishing features along the two paths. These features are the **research designs** you can use to collect, analyze, and interpret data using quantitative and qualitative research. Some of the research designs may be familiar; others may be new, such as how these paths can converge with two designs called mixed methods research and action research.

The discussion of designs will provide a more advanced understanding of educational research on your journey. In each chapter to follow, you will learn about each design: its definition, its historical development, its key characteristics, and the steps and procedures of conducting and evaluating a study. At the end of each chapter is a complete journal article using the design that you can use to apply and check your knowledge about the design.

Chapters 10 through 17 address eight different research designs frequently used in educational research. The first three are quantitative, the next three are qualitative, and the final two combine quantitative and qualitative approaches.

The chapters in Part III are:

- ◆ Chapter 10: Experimental Designs
- ◆ Chapter 11: Correlational Designs
- ◆ Chapter 12: Survey Designs
- ◆ Chapter 13: Grounded Theory Designs
- ◆ Chapter 14: Ethnographic Designs
- ◆ Chapter 15: Narrative Research Designs
- ◆ Chapter 16: Mixed Methods Designs
- ◆ Chapter 17: Action Research Designs

Experimental Designs

*A*n experimental design is the traditional approach to conducting quantitative research. This chapter defines experimental research, identifies when you use it, assesses the key characteristics of it, and advances the steps in conducting and evaluating this design.

By the end of this chapter, you should be able to:

◆ Define experimental research, and describe when to use it, and how it developed.
◆ Identify the key characteristics of experiments.
◆ State the types of experimental designs.
◆ Recognize potential ethical issues in experimental research.
◆ Describe the steps in conducting an experiment.
◆ Evaluate the quality of an experimental study.

Maria decides to conduct an experiment. She studies the question, "Do students who receive in-class instruction about the dangers of weapons in high school have different attitudes toward weapons than do students who do not receive instruction about the dangers?" Using two health classes to participate in her experiment, she gives one class the standard health curriculum, and the other class a standard curriculum plus a series of classes about the dangers of weapons among teenagers. At the end of the semester, she administers a survey measuring attitudes toward weapons in schools. Maria finds that the students who experienced the curriculum plus the classes about the dangers of weapons were more negative toward weapons in schools than the students who had the standard health curriculum.

WHAT IS AN EXPERIMENT, WHEN SHOULD YOU USE IT, AND HOW DID IT DEVELOP?

In an **experiment**, you test an idea (or practice or procedure) to determine whether it influences an outcome or dependent variable. You first decide on an idea with which to "experiment," assign individuals to experience it (and have some individuals experience something different), and then determine whether those who experienced the idea (or practice or procedure) performed better on some outcome than those who did not experience it. In Maria's experiment, she tested whether the special health curriculum changed students' attitudes toward weapons in schools.

When Do You Use an Experiment?

You use an experiment when you want to establish possible cause and effect between your independent and dependent variables. This means that you attempt to control all variables that influence the outcome except for the independent variable. Then, when the independent variable *influences* the dependent variable, we can say the independent variable "caused" or "probably caused" the dependent variable. Because experiments are controlled, they are the best of the quantitative designs to use to establish probable cause and effect. For example, if you compare one group that experiences a lecture and another group that experiences discussion, you control all of the factors that might influence the outcome of "high scores on a quiz." You make sure that personal abilities and test conditions are the same for both groups, and you give both groups the same questions. You control for all variables that might influence the outcome except for the difference in types of instruction (lecture or discussion). You also use an experiment when you have two or more groups to study, as in this lecture versus discussion example.

When Did Experiments Develop?

Experimental research began in the late 19th and early 20th centuries, with psychological experiments. By 1903, Schuyler used experimental and control groups, and his use became so commonplace that he felt no need to provide a rationale for them. Then in 1916, McCall advanced the idea of randomly assigning individuals to groups (Campbell & Stanley, 1963). Authoring a major book in 1925, *How to Conduct an Experiment,* McCall firmly established the procedure of comparing groups. In addition, by 1936, Fisher's book *Statistical Methods for Research Workers* discussed statistical procedures useful in experiments in psychology and agriculture. In this book, Fisher advanced the concept of randomly assigning individuals to groups before starting an experiment. Other developments in statistical procedures at this time (e.g., chi-square goodness of fit and critical values) and the testing of the significance of differences (e.g., Fisher's 1935 *The Design of Experiments*) enhanced experimental research in education. Between 1926 and 1963, five sets of textbooks on statistics had undergone multiple editions (Huberty, 1993).

By 1963, Campbell and Stanley had identified the major types of experimental designs. They specified 15 different types and evaluated each design in terms of potential threats to validity. These designs are still popular today. Then, in 1979, Cook and Campbell elaborated on the types of designs, expanding the discussion about validity threats. By 2002, Shadish, Cook, and Campbell had refined the discussions about the major experimental designs. These books established the basic designs, the notation, the visual representation, the potential threats to designs, and the statistical procedures of educational experiments.

Since the 1980s, experiments have grown in sophistication and complexity, largely because of computers and improved statistical procedures. Researchers now employ multiple independent and dependent variables, compare more than two groups, and study different types of experimental units of analysis, such as entire organizations, groups, and individuals (Boruch, 1998; Neuman, 2000). Procedural refinements represent the latest development in experiments, and a number of "how to" books (e.g., Bausell, 1994) are available for the educational researcher. Also, books that link statistical procedures with experimental design in terms of designing sensitive experiments (e.g., Lipsey, 1990) represent new ideas about strengthening procedures in experimental studies.

WHAT ARE KEY CHARACTERISTICS OF EXPERIMENTS?

Before you consider how to conduct an experiment, you will find it helpful to understand in more depth several key ideas central to experimental research. These ideas are:

- ◆ Random assignment
- ◆ Control over extraneous variables
- ◆ Manipulation of the treatment conditions
- ◆ Outcome measures
- ◆ Group comparisons
- ◆ Threats to validity

To make this discussion as applied as possible, we will use an educational example to illustrate these ideas. A researcher seeks to study ways to encourage adolescents to reduce or stop smoking. A high school has an in-house program to treat individuals caught smoking on school grounds. In this large metropolitan high school, many students smoke, and the smoking infractions each year are numerous. Students caught take a special civics class (all students are required to take civics anyway) in which the teacher introduces a special unit on the health hazards of smoking. In this unit, the teacher discusses health issues, uses images and pictures of the damaged lungs of smokers, and has students write about their experiences as smokers. This instructor offers several civics classes during a semester, and we will refer to this experimental situation as the "civics–smoking experiment."

Random Assignment

As an experimental researcher, you will assign individuals to groups. The most rigorous approach is to randomly assign individuals to the treatments. **Random assignment** is the process of assigning individuals at random to groups or to different groups in an experiment. The random assignment of individuals to groups (or conditions within a group) distinguishes a rigorous, "true" experiment from an adequate, but less-than-rigorous, "quasi-experiment" (to be discussed later in the chapter).

You use random assignment so that any bias in the personal characteristics of individuals in the experiment is distributed equally among the groups. By randomization, you provide *control* for extraneous characteristics of the participants that might influence the outcome (e.g., student ability, attention span, motivation). The experimental term for this process is "equating" the groups. **Equating the groups** means that the researcher randomly assigns individuals to groups and equally distributes any variability of individuals between or among the groups or conditions in the experiment. In practice, personal factors that participants bring to an experiment can never be totally controlled—some bias or error will always affect the outcome of a study. However, by systematically distributing this potential error among groups, the researcher theoretically distributes the bias randomly. In our civics–smoking experiment, the researcher can take the list of offender smokers in the school and randomly assign them to one of two special civics classes.

You should not confuse random assignment with **random selection**. Both are important in quantitative research, but they serve different purposes. Quantitative researchers randomly select a sample from a population. In this way, the sample is representative of the population and you can generalize results obtained during the study to the population.

Experiments often do not include random selection of participants for several reasons. Participants often are individuals who are available to take part in the experiment or who volunteer to participate. Although random selection is important in experiments, it may not be logistically possible. However, the most sophisticated type of experiment involves random assignment.

In the civics–smoking experiment, you may randomly select individuals from the population of offender smokers (especially if there are too many for the special civics classes). However, you will most likely place all of the offenders in the special civics classes, giving you control over random assignment rather than random selection.

Control Over Extraneous Variables

In randomly assigning individuals, we say that we are controlling for extraneous variables that might influence the relationship between the new practice (e.g., discussions on health hazards) and the outcome (e.g., frequency of smoking). **Extraneous factors** are any influences in the selection of participants, the procedures, the statistics, or the design likely to affect the outcome and provide an alternative explanation for our results than what we expected. All experiments have some random error (where the scores do not reflect the "true" scores of the population) that you cannot control, but you can try to control extraneous factors as much as possible. Random assignment is a decision made by the investigator *before* the experiment begins. Other control procedures you can use both before and during the experiment are pretests, covariates, matching of participants, homogeneous samples, and blocking variables.

Pretests and Posttests

To "equate" the characteristics of the groups, experimental researchers may use a pretest. Assume that we are interested in whether the special civics class affects students' attitudes toward smoking. In this experiment, we could measure attitudes before the treatment (i.e., by discussing health hazards) and after, to see if the discussion has an effect on students' attitudes. In this experiment, we need a pretest to measure students' attitudes.

A **pretest** provides a measure on some attribute or characteristic that you assess for participants in an experiment *before* they receive a treatment. After the treatment, you take another reading on the attribute or characteristic. A **posttest** is a measure on some attribute or characteristic that is assessed for participants in an experiment *after* a treatment. In our example, this would be assessing students' attitudes toward smoking at the end of the semester after the experimental treatment. A pretest–posttest comparison of attitudes toward smoking would provide a clearer reading on actual smoking behavior than using the posttest measure alone would.

Pretests have advantages as well as disadvantages. They take time and effort to administer (e.g., students have to fill out an instrument early in the semester). They can also raise the participants' expectations about the outcome (e.g., students might anticipate questions later about their smoking attitudes and inflate or deflate their responses later in the semester). The pretest may influence the experimental treatment (e.g., students may ask questions about the treatment because of the pretest on attitudes toward smoking).

When attitudinal or achievement tests are used as pretests, the scores may also affect post-test scores because participants can anticipate the questions on the posttest based on their experiences with the pretest.

Covariates

Because pretests may affect aspects of the experiment, they are often statistically controlled for by using the procedure of covariance rather than by simply comparing them with post-test scores. **Covariates** are variables that the researcher controls for using statistics and that relate to the dependent variable but that do not relate to the independent variable. The researcher needs to control for these variables, which have the potential to co-vary with the dependent variable. Often, these variables are scores on a pretest, but they might be any variables correlated with the dependent variable. The statistical procedure of analysis of covariance adjusts the scores on the dependent variable to account for the covariance. This procedure becomes another means for equating the groups and controlling for potential influences that might affect the dependent variable.

An illustration related to our civics–smoking example shows how the researcher removes the variance between a covariate and a dependent variable to assess the variance between the independent and dependent variable. Examine Figure 10.1, which portrays two sets of circles. The left side shows two variables, an independent variable and a dependent variable, without a covariate. The darkened area indicates the variability in rates of smoking by type of instruction; the unexplained variability (called error) is shown with a hatch mark. On the right side of Figure 10.1, we introduce a covariate: parents who smoke. Now we can see that the explained variance increases, and the total amount of unexplained variability (error) actually decreases because we explain more variance. By adding a covariate related to parents who smoke, the researcher increases the amount of explained variance in rates of smoking and decreases the unexplained variance. The statistical procedure of covariance removes the variance shared by the covariate and the dependent variable, so that the variance between the independent and dependent variable (plus error) is all that remains. This test allows the researcher to assess accurately the relationship between the treatment and the outcome (i.e., rate of smoking) because of a reduction in the amount of error.

Matching of Participants

Another procedure used for control in an experiment is to match participants on one or more personal characteristics. **Matching** is the process of identifying one or more personal characteristics that influence the outcome and assigning individuals with that characteristic equally to the experimental and control groups. Typically, experimental researchers match on one or two of the following characteristics: gender, pretest scores, or individual abilities.

For example, examine Figure 10.2, which displays matching individuals (say, 10 girls and boys) on gender to the experimental and control groups. Returning to our high school civics–smoking experiment, we might assign the student smokers equally to two special civics classes (assuming that one class receives the treatment and the other does not) based on gender. In this way, our prior knowledge, for example, that boys may smoke more than girls, controls for the potential influence of gender on frequency of smoking. Procedurally, this matching process means assigning the first boy to the control group, the second to the experimental, the third to the control, and so forth. The researcher repeats this process for girls. By using this procedure, we control before the experiment begins for the potential extraneous factor of gender in the experiment.

Homogeneous Samples

Another approach used to make the groups comparable is to choose **homogeneous samples** by selecting people who vary little in their personal characteristics. For example,

FIGURE 10.1

Controlling for Covariate

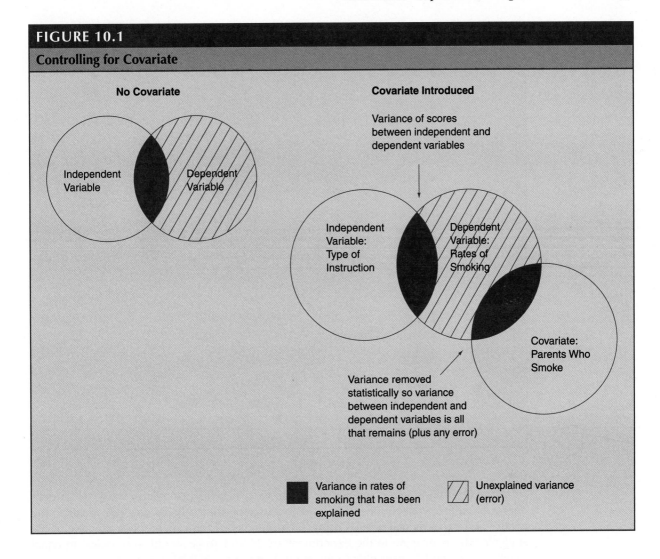

we might assume that the students in the two civics classes (one receives the lecture on "health hazards" and the second does not) are similar in terms of characteristics that students bring to the experiment, such as their academic grade point average, gender, racial group (e.g., Caucasian, African American), or prior abilities in civics. When the experimenter assigns students to the two classes, the more similar they are in personal characteristics or attributes, the more these characteristics or attributes are controlled in the experiment. For example, if all of the smokers assigned to the two civics classes were juniors, then class level would be controlled in the experiment. Unfortunately, this situation is unlikely to occur in our civics–smoking study, and the researcher may need to use other procedures to control for individuals belonging to different grade levels.

Blocking Variables

One such procedure is to "block" for grade level before the experiment begins. A **blocking variable** is a variable the researcher controls before the experiment starts by dividing (or "blocking") the participants into subgroups (or categories) and analyzing the impact of each subgroup on the outcome. The variable (e.g., gender) can be blocked into males and females; similarly, high school grade level can be blocked into four categories: freshmen, sophomores, juniors, and seniors. In this procedure, the researcher forms homogeneous

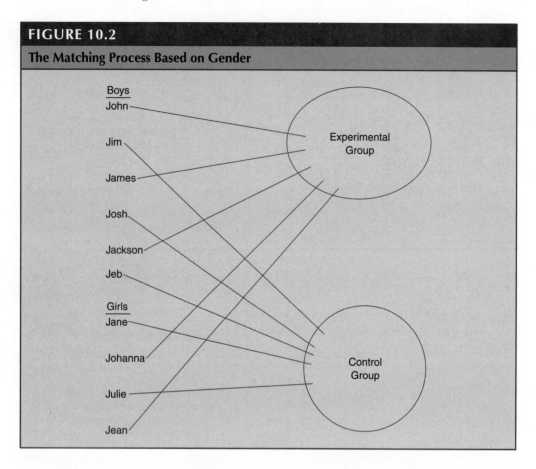

FIGURE 10.2

The Matching Process Based on Gender

subgroups by choosing a characteristic common to all participants in the study (e.g., gender or different age categories). Then the investigator randomly assigns individuals to the control and experimental groups using each category of the variable. For example, if the students who participate in the experiment are 15 and 16 years old, you assign an equal number of 15- and 16-year-olds to the control and experimental groups.

Manipulating Treatment Conditions

Once you select participants, you randomly assign them to either a treatment condition or the experimental group. In **experimental treatment,** the researcher physically intervenes to alter the conditions experienced by the experimental unit (e.g., a reward for good spelling performance or a special type of classroom instruction, such as small-group discussion).

In our high school example, the researcher would manipulate one form of instruction in the special civics class—providing activities on the health hazards of smoking. Specifically, the procedure would be:

Identify a treatment variable: type of classroom instruction in the civics class

Identify the conditions (or levels) of the variable: classroom instruction can be (a) regular topics or (b) topics related to the health hazards of smoking

Manipulate the treatment conditions: provide special activities on health hazards of smoking to one class and withhold them from another class

These procedures introduce several new concepts that we will discuss using specific examples so that you can see how they work.

Treatment Variables

In experiments, you need to focus on the independent variables. These variables influence or affect the dependent variables in a quantitative study. The two major types of independent variables were treatment and measured variables. In experiments, treatment variables are independent variables that the researcher manipulates to determine their effect on the outcome, or dependent variable. Treatment variables are categorical variables measured using categorical scales. For example, treatment independent variables used in educational experiments might be:

◆ Type of instruction (small group, large group)
◆ Type of reading group (phonics readers, whole-language readers)

Conditions

In both of these examples, we have two categories within each treatment variable. In experiments, treatment variables need to have two or more categories, or levels. In an experiment, **levels** are categories of a treatment variable. For example, you might divide type of instruction into (a) standard civics lecture, (b) standard civics lecture plus discussion about health hazards, and (c) standard civics lecture plus discussion about health hazards and slides of damaged lungs. In this example, we have a three-level treatment variable.

Intervening in the Treatment Conditions

The experimental researcher manipulates one or more of the treatment variable conditions. In other words, in an experiment, the researcher physically intervenes (or manipulates with **interventions**) in one or more condition so that individuals experience something different in the experimental conditions than in the control conditions. This means that to conduct an experiment, you need to be able to manipulate at least one condition of an independent variable. It is easy to identify some situations in which you might measure an independent variable and obtain categorical data but not be able to manipulate one of the conditions. As shown in Figure 10.3, the researcher measures three independent variables—age, gender, and type of instruction—but only type of instruction (more specifically, two conditions within it) is manipulated. The treatment variable—type of instruction—is a categorical variable with three conditions (or levels). Some students can receive a lecture—the traditional form of instruction in the class (the control group). Others receive something new, such as a lecture plus the health-hazards discussion (a comparison group) or lecture plus the health-hazards discussion plus slides of lungs damaged by smoking (another comparison group). In summary, experimental researchers manipulate or intervene with one or more conditions of a treatment variable.

Outcome Measures

In all experimental situations, you assess whether a treatment condition influences an outcome or dependent variable, such as a reduced rate of smoking or achievement on tests. In experiments, the **outcome** (or *response, criterion,* or *posttest*) is the dependent variable that is the presumed effect of the treatment variable. It is also the effect predicted in a hypothesis in the cause-and-effect equation. Examples of dependent variables in experiments might be:

◆ Achievement scores on a criterion-referenced test
◆ Test scores on an aptitude test

FIGURE 10.3

The Experimental Manipulation of a Treatment Condition

Independent Variables	*Dependent Variable*

1. Age (cannot manipulate)
2. Gender (cannot manipulate)
3. Types of instruction (can manipulate)
   a. Some receive lecture (control)
   b. Some receive lecture plus health-hazard discussion
      (comparison)
   c. Some receive lecture plus health-hazard discussion
      plus slides of lungs damaged by smoking (experimental)
	Frequency of Smoking

Good outcome measures are sensitive to treatments in that they respond to the smallest amount of intervention. Outcome measures (as well as treatment variables) also need to be valid so that experimental researchers can draw valid inferences from them.

Group Comparisons

In an experiment, you also compare scores for different treatments on an outcome. A **group comparison** is the process of a researcher obtaining scores for individuals or groups on the dependent variable and comparing the means and variance both within the group and between the groups. (See Keppel [1991] for detailed statistical procedures for this process.)

To visualize this process, let's consider some actual data from an experiment by Gettinger (1993), who sought to determine the effects of an error correction procedure on the spelling of third graders. As shown in Figure 10.4, we visualize Gettinger's experiment in three ways.

Gettinger examined whether the error correction procedure related positively to spelling accuracy (Phase 1). She then created three groups of students: Class A, Class B, and Class C. Class A (the control group) received regular spelling practice on 15 words, consisting of workbook exercises, writing sentences containing each word, and studying words on their own. Class B (the comparison group) had the same experience except that they studied a reduced number of words on a list—three sets of five words each. Class C (the experimental group) used an error-and-correction practice procedure consisting of correcting their own tests, noting incorrect words, and writing both the incorrect and correct spelling for each word. As shown in Phase 2, all three groups received the same spelling practice for 6 weeks, then the experimental group received the error correction procedure for 6 weeks, and after a third 6 weeks, all three groups were tested. Phase 3 shows the statistical comparisons made among the three groups on each of the three tests. Class A improved slightly (from 10.3 on Test 1 to 11.1 on Test 3), whereas Class B's scores decreased over the three tests. Class C, the experimental group, improved considerably. *F*-test values showed that the scores varied significantly on Test 2 and Test 3 when the researcher compared the groups. These statistical comparisons took into consideration both the mean scores and the variation between and within each group to arrive at statistical significance at $p < .05$.

Threats to Validity

A final idea in experiments is to design them so that the inferences you draw are true or correct. Threats to drawing these correct inferences need to be addressed in experimental

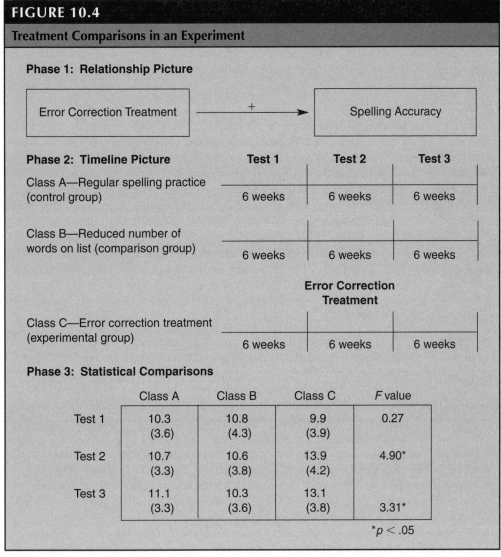

FIGURE 10.4

Treatment Comparisons in an Experiment

Phase 1: Relationship Picture

Error Correction Treatment	$\xrightarrow{\quad + \quad}$	Spelling Accuracy

Phase 2: Timeline Picture

	Test 1	**Test 2**	**Test 3**
Class A—Regular spelling practice (control group)	6 weeks	6 weeks	6 weeks
Class B—Reduced number of words on list (comparison group)	6 weeks	6 weeks	6 weeks
		Error Correction Treatment	
Class C—Error correction treatment (experimental group)	6 weeks	6 weeks	6 weeks

Phase 3: Statistical Comparisons

	Class A	Class B	Class C	*F* value
Test 1	10.3 (3.6)	10.8 (4.3)	9.9 (3.9)	0.27
Test 2	10.7 (3.3)	10.6 (3.8)	13.9 (4.2)	4.90*
Test 3	11.1 (3.3)	10.3 (3.6)	13.1 (3.8)	3.31*

*$p < .05$

Source: Based on Gettinger, 1993.

research. **Threats to validity** refer to specific reasons for why we can be wrong when we make an inference in an experiment because of covariance, causation constructs, or whether the causal relationship holds over variations in persons, setting, treatments, and outcomes (Shadish, Cook, & Campbell, 2002). Four types of validity they discuss are:

◆ Statistical conclusion validity, which refers to the appropriate use of statistics (e.g., violating statistical assumptions, restricted range on a variable, low power) to infer whether the presumed independent and dependent variables covary in the experiment.

◆ Construct validity, which means the validity of inferences about the constructs (or variables) in the study.

◆ Internal validity, which relates to the validity of inferences drawn about the cause and effect relationship between the independent and dependent variables.

◆ External validity, which refers to the validity of the cause-and-effect relationship being generalizable to other persons, settings, treatment variables, and measures.

These threats to validity have evolved over the years from the initial discussions by Campbell and Stanley (1963), to the elaboration of their use by Cook and Campbell (1979), and more recently by Shadish, Cook, and Campbell (2002). The basic ideas are still intact, but more recent discussions have elaborated on the points. Our discussion here will focus on the two primary threats to consider: internal validity and external validity.

Threats to internal validity

A number of threats to drawing appropriate inferences relate to the actual design and procedures used in an experiment. **Threats to internal validity** are problems in drawing correct inferences about whether the covariation (i.e., the variation in one variable contributes to the variation in the other variable) between the presumed treatment variable and the outcome reflects a causal relationship (Shadish, Cook, & Campbell, 2002). Of all of the threats to validity, these are the most severe because they can compromise an otherwise good experiment. The following threats to internal validity and recommended procedures to address them are widely discussed in the literature about experimental designs (see Cook & Campbell, 1979; Reichardt & Mark, 1998; Shadish, Cook, & Campbell, 2002; Tuckman, 1999). To make each potential threat as realistic as possible, we illustrate them using the hypothetical situation of the civics–smoking experiment.

The first category addresses threats *related to participants* in the study and their experiences:

◆ *History:*   Time passes between the beginning of the experiment and the end, and events may occur (e.g., additional discussions about the hazards of smoking besides the treatment lecture) between the pretest and posttest that influence the outcome. In educational experiments, it is impossible to have a tightly controlled environment and monitor all events. However, the researcher can have the control and experimental groups experience the same activities (except for the treatment) during the experiment.

◆ *Maturation:*   Individuals develop or change during the experiment (i.e., become older, wiser, stronger, and more experienced), and these changes may affect their scores between the pretest and posttest. A careful selection of participants who mature or develop in a similar way (e.g., individuals at the same grade level) for both the control and experimental groups helps guard against this problem.

◆ *Regression:*   When researchers select individuals for a group based on extreme scores, they will naturally do better (or worse) on the posttest than the pretest regardless of the treatment. Scores from individuals, over time, regress toward the mean. For example, the selection of heavy smokers for an experiment will probably contribute to lower rates of smoking after treatment because the teens selected started with high rates at the beginning of the experiment. The selection of individuals who do not have extreme scores on entering characteristics (e.g., moderate smokers or average scores on pretests) may help solve this problem.

◆ *Selection:*   "People factors" may introduce threats that influence the outcome, such as selecting individuals who are brighter, more receptive to a treatment, or more familiar with a treatment (e.g., teen smokers ready to quit) for the experimental group. Random selection may partly address this threat.

◆ *Mortality:*   When individuals drop out during the experiment for any number of reasons (e.g., time, interest, money, friends, parents who do not want them participating in an experiment about smoking), drawing conclusions from scores may be difficult. Researchers need to choose a large sample and compare those who drop out with those who remain in the experiment on the outcome measure.

◆ *Interactions with selection:*   Several of the threats mentioned thus far can interact (or relate) with the selection of participants to add additional threats to an experiment. Individuals selected may mature at different rates (e.g., 16-year-old boys and girls may mature at different rates during the study). Historical events may interact with selection because individuals in different groups come from different settings. For instance, vastly different socioeconomic backgrounds of students in the teen smoking experiment may introduce uncontrolled historical factors into the selection of student participants. The selection of participants may also influence the instrument scores, especially when different groups score at different mean positions on a test whose intervals are not equal. If the scale for measuring number of cigarettes is ambiguous (e.g., number of cigarettes per week or per day?), groups are likely to interpret the scale differently.

The next category addresses threats *related to treatments* used in the study:

◆ *Diffusion of treatments:*   When the experimental and control groups can communicate with each other, the control group may learn from the experimental group information about the treatment and create a threat to internal validity. The diffusion of treatments (experimental and nonexperimental) for the control and experimental groups needs to be different. As much as possible, experimental researchers need to keep the two groups separate in an experiment (e.g., have two different civic classes participate in the experiment). This may be difficult when, for example, two civic classes of students in the same grade in the same high school are involved in an experiment about teen smoking.
◆ *Compensatory equalization:*   When only the experimental group receives a treatment, an inequality exists that may threaten the validity of the study. The benefits (i.e., the goods or services believed to be desirable) of the experimental treatment need to be equally distributed among the groups in the study. To counter this problem, researchers use comparison groups (e.g., one group receives the health-hazards lecture, whereas the other receives a handout about the problems of teen smoking) so that all groups receive some benefits during an experiment.
◆ *Compensatory rivalry:*   If you publicly announce assignments to the control and experimental groups, compensatory rivalry may develop between the groups because the control group feels that it is the "underdog." Researchers can try to avoid this threat by attempting to reduce the awareness and expectations of the presumed benefits of the experimental treatment.
◆ *Resentful demoralization:*   When a control group is used, individuals in this group may become resentful and demoralized because they perceive that they receive a less desirable treatment than other groups. One remedy to this threat is for experimental researchers to provide a treatment to this group after the experiment has concluded (e.g., after the experiment, all classes receive the lecture on the health hazards of smoking). Researchers may also provide services equally attractive to the experimental treatment but not directed toward the same outcome as the treatment (e.g., a class discussion about the hazards of teen driving with friends).

The following category addresses threats that typically occur during an experiment and *relate to the procedures* of the study:

◆ *Testing:*   A potential threat to internal validity is that participants may become familiar with the outcome measures and remember responses for later testing. During some experiments, the outcome is measured more than one time, such as in pretests (e.g., repeated measures of number of cigarettes smoked). To remedy this situation, experimental researchers measure the outcome less frequently and use different items on the posttest than those used during earlier testing.

◆ *Instrumentation:* Between the administration of a pretest and a posttest, the instrument may change, introducing a potential threat to the internal validity of the experiment. For example, observers may become more experienced during the time between a pretest and the posttest and change their scoring procedures (e.g., observers change the location to observe teen smoking). Less frequently, the measuring instrument may change so that the scales used on a pretest and a posttest are dissimilar. To correct for this potential problem, you standardize procedures so that you use the same observational scales or instrument throughout the experiment.

Threats to external validity

By ruling out extraneous factors and assuming that the treatment influences an outcome, researchers make claims about the generalizability of the results. **Threats to external validity** are problems that threaten our ability to draw correct inferences from the sample data to other persons, settings, treatment variables, and measures. According to Cook and Campbell (1979), three threats may affect this generalizability:

◆ *Interaction of selection and treatment:* This threat to external validity involves the inability to generalize beyond the groups in the experiment, such as other racial, social, geographical, age, gender, or personality groups. One strategy researchers use to increase generalizability is to make participation in the experiment as convenient as possible for all individuals in a population.

◆ *Interaction of setting and treatment:* This threat to external validity arises from the inability to generalize from the setting where the experiment occurred to another setting. For example, private high schools may be different from public high schools, and the results from our civics experiment on smoking may not apply outside the public high school where the researcher conducts the experiment. This threat may also result from trying to generalize results from one level in an organization to another. For example, you cannot generalize treatment effects you obtain from studying entire school districts to specific high schools. The practical solution to an interaction of setting and treatment is for the researcher to analyze the effect of a treatment for each type of setting.

◆ *Interaction of history and treatment:* This threat to external validity develops when the researcher tries to generalize findings to past and future situations. Experiments may take place at a special time (e.g., at the beginning of the school year) and may not produce similar results if conducted earlier (e.g., students attending school in the summer may be different from students attending school during the regular year) or later (e.g., during semester break). One solution is to replicate the study at a later time rather than trying to generalize results to other times.

In our civics–smoking experiment, the researcher needs to be cautious about generalizing results to other high schools, other students in civics classes, and other situations where discussions about the hazards of smoking take place. The behavior of adolescents who smoke may change due to factors associated with the cost of cigarettes, parental disapproval, and advertising. Because of these factors, it is difficult to generalize the results from our civics experiment to other situations.

WHAT ARE THE TYPES OF EXPERIMENTAL DESIGNS?

Although all experiments have common characteristics, their use and applications vary depending on the type of design used. The most common designs you will find in educational research are:

◆ Between Group Designs
  • True experiments (pre- and posttest, posttest only)
  • Quasi-experiments (pre- and posttest, posttest only)
  • Factorial designs
◆ Within Group or Individual Designs
  • Time series experiments (interrupted, equivalent)
  • Repeated measures experiments
  • Single subject experiments

Being able to identify these types of designs and their major characteristics will help you choose a suitable design for your study or permit a thoughtful evaluation of an experimental design used in a published study.

A basic set of criteria for differentiating among types of experimental designs is shown in Table 10.1. As we discuss each of the designs, keep these criteria in mind to help you distinguish among them. The designs are differentiated by several characteristics, as shown in the first column in Table 10.1:

◆ The random assignment of participants to groups
◆ The number of groups or individuals being compared
◆ The number of interventions used by the researcher

TABLE 10.1

Types of Experimental Designs

	True Experiment	Quasi-Experiment	Factorial	Time Series	Repeated Measures	Single Subject
Random assignment?	Yes	No	May be used	No	No	No
Number of groups/ individuals compared?	Two or more	Two or more	Two or more	One group	One group	One individual studied at a time
Number of interventions used?	One or more interventions	One or more interventions	Two or more interventions	One or more interventions	Two or more interventions	One or more interventions
Number of times the dependent variables measured/ observed?	Once	Once	Once	After each intervention	After each intervention	Multiple points
Controls typically used?	Pretest, matching, blocking, covariates	Pretest, matching, blocking, covariates	Pretest, matching, blocking, covariates	Group becomes its own controls	Covariates	Individuals become their own control

◆ The number of times the dependent variable is measured or observed
◆ The control of extraneous variables

For each design discussed in the following pages, you will be introduced to the major characteristics of the design and its advantages and disadvantages. Among the disadvantages are its potential threats to internal validity—an idea already introduced—but now related specifically to each design. Table 10.2 presents a summary of the internal validity threats for each design.

TABLE 10.2

Threats to Internal Validity in Types of Experimental Designs

	True Experiment	Quasi-Experiment	Factorial	Time Series	Repeated Measures	Single Subject
To Participants:						
History	Controlled	Potential threat	Controlled, if random assignment	May be a threat if short intervals not used	May be a threat if short intervals not used	Potential threat
Maturation	Controlled	Potential threat	Controlled, random assignment	Can be controlled if pattern detected	Controlled	Controlled
Regression	Controlled	Potential threat	Controlled, random assignment	Can be controlled if unusual scores noted	Controlled	Controlled
Selection	Controlled	Potential threat	Controlled, if random assignment	Controlled	Controlled	Controlled
Mortality	Controlled	Potential threat	Controlled, if random assignment	Can be controlled if dropouts noted	Controlled	Controlled
Interaction of selection and maturation, history, and instrumentation	Controlled	Potential threat	Controlled, if random assignment	Controlled	Controlled	Controlled
To Procedures:						
Testing	Potential threat if pre- and posttest used	Potential threat if pre- and posttest used	Potential threat if pre- and posttest used	With repeated measures and observations before (interrupted design), likely to diminish over time	Potential threat if pre- and posttest used	Controlled
Instrumentation	Potential threat if instrument or observational procedures change	Potential threat if instrument or observational procedures change	Potential threat if instrument or observational procedures change	Can be controlled if procedures monitored	Can be controlled if procedures monitored	May be a threat if multiple interventions used

Remember that Maria studied two health classes for her experiment. She gave one class the standard health curriculum and provided the other class the standard curriculum plus a series of classes about the dangers of weapons among teenagers. What type of experimental design should she use? Maria has a between-group design (a quasi-experiment) without random assignment because she uses two intact classes in her experiment. As you read the discussion about a between-group design, see how you would come to this same decision.

Between-Group Designs

The most frequently used designs in education are those where the researcher compares two or more groups. Illustrations throughout this chapter underscore the importance of these designs. We will begin with the most rigorous between-group design available to the educational researcher, the true experiment.

True Experiments

True experiments comprise the most rigorous and strong experimental designs because of equating the groups through random assignment. The procedure for conducting major forms of true experiments and quasi-experiments, viewing them in terms of activities from the beginning of the experiment to the end, is shown in Table 10.3. In **true experiments**, the researcher randomly assigns participants to different conditions of the experimental variable. Individuals in the experimental group receive the experimental treatment, whereas those in the control group do not. After investigators administer the treatment, they compile average (or mean) scores on a posttest. One variation on this design is to obtain pretest as well as posttest measures or observations. When experimenters collect pretest scores, they may compare net scores (the differences between the pre- and posttests). Alternatively, investigators may relate the pretest scores for the control and experimental groups to see if they are statistically similar, and then compare the two posttest group scores. In many experiments, the pretest is a covariate and is statistically controlled by the researcher.

Because you randomly assign individuals to the groups, most of the threats to internal validity do not arise. Randomization or equating of the groups minimizes the possibility of history, maturation, selection, and the interactions between selection and other threats. Treatment threats such as diffusion, rivalry, resentful demoralization, and compensatory equalization are all possibilities in a between-group design because two or more groups exist in the design. When true experiments include only a posttest, it reduces the threats of testing, instrumentation, and regression because you do not use a pretest. If a pretest is used, it introduces all of these factors as possible threats to validity. Instrumentation exists as a potential threat in most experiments, but if researchers use the same or similar instrument for the pre- and posttest or enact standard procedures during the study, you hold instrumentation threats to a minimum.

Quasi-Experiments

In education, many experimental situations occur in which researchers need to use intact groups. This might happen because of the availability of the participants or because the setting prohibits forming artificial groups. **Quasi-experiments** include assignment, but not random assignment of participants to groups. This is because the experimenter cannot artificially create groups for the experiment. For example, studying a new math program may require using existing fourth-grade classes and designating one as the experimental group and one as the control group. Randomly assigning students to the two groups would disrupt classroom learning. Because educators often use intact groups

TABLE 10.3

Types of Between-Group Designs

True Experimental Designs

Pre- and Posttest Design		**Time** →		
Random assignment	Control Group	Pretest	No Treatment	Posttest
Random assignment	Experimental Group	Pretest	Experimental Treatment	Posttest

Posttest-Only Design		**Time** →	
Random assignment	Control Group	No Treatment	Posttest
Random assignment	Experimental Group	Experimental Treatment	Posttest

Quasi-Experimental Designs

Pre- and Posttest Design		**Time** →	
Select Control Group	Pretest	No Treatment	Posttest
Select Experimental Group	Pretest	Experimental Treatment	Posttest

Posttest-Only Design	**Time** →	
Select Control Group	No Treatment	Posttest
Select Experimental Group	Experimental Treatment	Posttest

(schools, colleges, or school districts) in experiments, quasi-experimental designs are frequently used.

Returning to Table 10.3, we can apply the pre- and posttest design approach to a quasi-experimental design. The researcher assigns intact groups the experimental and control treatments, administers a pretest to both groups, conducts experimental treatment activities with the experimental group only, and then administers a posttest to assess the differences between the two groups. A variation on this approach, similar to the true experiment, uses only a posttest in the design.

The quasi-experimental approach introduces considerably more threats to internal validity than the true experiment. Because the investigator does not randomly assign participants to groups, the potential threats of maturation, selection, mortality, and the interaction of selection with other threats are possibilities. Individuals assigned to the two groups may have selection factors that go uncontrolled in the experiment. Because we compare two groups, the treatment threats may also be present. In addition, when the pretest–posttest design is used, additional threats of history, testing, instrumentation, and regression also may occur. While the quasi-experimental design has the advantage of utilizing existing groups in educational settings, it introduces many threats that you need to address in the design of the experiment.

Factorial Designs   In some experimental situations, it is not enough to know the effect of a single treatment on an outcome; several treatments may, in fact, provide a better explanation for the outcome. **Factorial designs** represent a modification of the between-group design in which the researcher studies two or more categorical, independent variables, each examined at two or more levels (Vogt, 2005). The purpose of this design is to study the independent and simultaneous effects of two or more independent treatment variables on an outcome.

For example, in our civics–smoking experiment, the researcher may want to examine more than the effect of the type of instruction (i.e., lecture on health hazards of smoking versus standard lecture) on frequency of smoking. Assume that the experimenter wishes to examine the combined influence of type of instruction and level of depression in students (e.g., high, medium, and low scores on a depression scale) on rates of smoking (as the posttest). Assume further that the investigator has reason to believe that depression is an important factor in rates of teen smoking, but its "interaction" or combination with type of smoking is unknown. The study of this research problem requires a factorial design. Thus, "depression" is a blocking or moderating variable and the researcher makes random assignment of each "block" (high, medium, and low) to each treatment instructional group. This design has the advantage of a high level of control in the experiment. It allows the investigator to examine the combination or interaction of independent variables to better understand the results of the experiment. If only a posttest is used, internal validity threats of testing and instrumentation do not exist. If you randomly assign individuals to groups, you minimize the threats related to participants and their experiences (history, maturation, regression, selection, mortality, and interaction of selection and other factors).

However, with multiple independent variables in a factorial design, the statistical procedures become more complex and the actual results become more difficult to understand. What does it mean, for example, that depression and type of instruction interact to influence smoking rates among teens? Which independent variable is more important and why? As researchers manipulate additional independent variables, more participants are needed in each group for statistical tests, and the interpretation of results becomes more complex. Because of this complexity, factorial designs typically include at most three independent variables manipulated by the researcher.

Let's examine more closely the steps in the process of conducting a factorial design. The researcher identifies a research question that includes two independent variables and one dependent variable, such as "Do rates of smoking vary under different combinations of type of instruction and levels of depression?"

To answer this question, the experimenter identifies the levels of each factor or independent variable:

- ◆ *Factor 1*—types of instruction
  - Level 1—a health-hazards lecture in civics class
  - Level 2—a standard lecture in civics class
- ◆ *Factor 2*—levels of depression
  - Level 1—high
  - Level 2—medium
  - Level 3—low

	TABLE 10.4		
Factorial Design Groups Assigned to Two Conditions			
	Extent of Depression	**Type of Instruction**	**Dependent Variable**
Group 1	Low depression scores	Receives health-hazards lecture	Posttest (scores on instrument measuring smoking)
Group 2	Medium depression scores	Receives health-hazards lecture	Posttest (scores on instrument measuring smoking)
Group 3	High depression scores	Receives health-hazards lecture	Posttest (scores on instrument measuring smoking)
Group 4	Low depression scores	Receives standard lecture	Posttest (scores on instrument measuring smoking)
Group 5	Medium depression scores	Receives standard lecture	Posttest (scores on instrument measuring smoking)
Group 6	High depression scores	Receives standard lecture	Posttest (scores on instrument measuring smoking)

Because you measure two levels of instruction and three levels of depression, the design is called a *two by three* factorial design. It is written as "2 × 3" to indicate the levels involved in each independent variable. With three independent variables, it might be a "2 × 3 × 4" design, with the third variable consisting of four levels.

In the 2 × 3 design, the investigator then assigns participants to six groups so that all groups receive each level on one independent variable (e.g., type of instruction) and each level on the second independent variable (e.g., level of depression). Table 10.4 shows the formation of the six groups and the assignment of participants to each group based on the three levels (i.e., low, medium, and high) of depression and the two levels (i.e., health-hazards lecture, standard lecture) of instruction.

In this process, the researcher creates six groups and assigns student smokers to each group. All students first complete the instrument measuring their level of depression. The researcher scores the instrument and divides the students into low, medium, and high groups based on their depression scores. Further, remember that our study is being conducted in two special civics classes; in one class, the students receive a lecture on the health hazards of smoking, and in the second class, the teacher provides standard lectures on civics topics. Thus, in our factorial design, three groups will receive the health lecture in one civics class and the other three groups will receive the standard lectures in the other civics class. This procedure uses quasi-experimental research in which the investigator uses intact classes for the experiment (two high school civics classes).

At the conclusion of the experiment, the investigator asks all participants to complete a posttest. This posttest will measure the rate of smoking for individuals in the experiment. The means of the posttest scores are organized into six cells to visually portray their differences, as shown in Figure 10.5. A *cell* represents each group in an experiment, and it contains the mean scores for individuals in each group. Once you compute the mean scores, you compare the scores to determine whether they are statistically different. The null hypothesis would be that the means are not different, whereas the alternative would be that they are different.

Let's add one more element into this statistical portrait of scores arrayed in cells as shown in Figure 10.5. Using the parametric statistic of ANOVA, the researcher examines the effect of each independent variable separately and in combination with the dependent

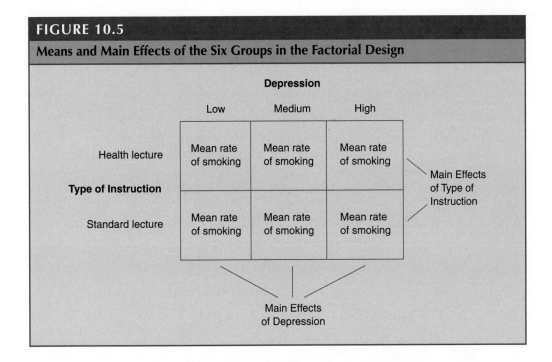

FIGURE 10.5

Means and Main Effects of the Six Groups in the Factorial Design

variable. Using a statistical software program, analysis of variance will produce statistical results for main effects and interaction effects. **Main effects** are the influence of each independent variable (e.g., type of instruction or extent of depression) on the outcome (e.g., the dependent variable, rate of smoking) in an experiment. **Interaction effects** exist when the influence on one independent variable depends on (or co-varies with) the other independent variable in an experiment.

Researchers often graph the main and the interaction effects to help readers visualize them. The graphs in Figure 10.6 portray possible main effects and interaction effects in our hypothetical civics–smoking experiment. Graph (a) displays the results of scores on the posttest (i.e., rate of smoking) and the three factors of depression. The researcher graphs scores for both the groups who receive the health-hazards lecture and the standard lecture in the civics class. As seen in this graph, the extent of smoking for both groups increases with the level of depression. Because the lines are parallel and do not cross, an interaction effect is not present.

However, the results of the experiment could be different, as shown in graphs (b) and (c). In graph (b), the smoking rates for the groups receiving the standard lecture increase as depression increases. Alternatively, smoking rates for students who experience the health-hazards lecture are constant for each level of depression. When these scores are plotted, the lines crossed, showing an interaction effect. In graph (c), the lines again are not parallel, displaying an interaction effect. Typically, in factorial designs, the investigator graphs these trends and explains the meaning of the combination of independent variables.

Within-Group or Individual Designs

In any given experiment, the number of participants may be limited and it may not be possible to involve more than one group. In these cases, researchers study a single group using a **within-group experimental design**. Also, the experimenter might examine

FIGURE 10.6

Graphs of Scores Showing Main Effects and the Interaction Effects

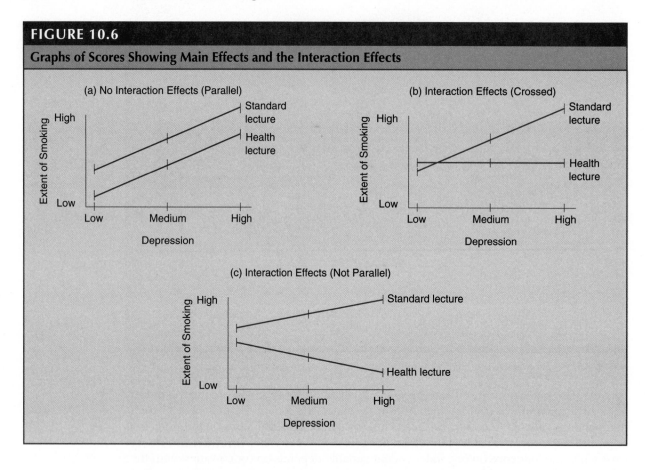

single individuals **(within-individual design)**. This type of design assumes several forms: time series, repeated measures, and single-subject designs.

Time Series

When an experimental researcher has access to only one group and can study them over a period, a time series design is a good experimental approach. A **time series** design consists of studying one group, over time, with multiple pretest and posttest measures or observations made by the researcher. This design does not require access to large numbers of participants, and it requires only one group for the study. It is ideal for examining change in an entire system (e.g., a school district) where it would be difficult to find a control group or system willing to cooperate. However, this design is labor intensive because the researcher needs to gather multiple measures.

These multiple measures are seen in two important variations of this design. As shown in Table 10.5, the first is the **interrupted time series** design. This procedure consists of studying one group, obtaining multiple pretest measures for a period of time, administering an intervention (or interrupting the activities), and then measuring outcomes (or posttests) several times. Data analysis in this example consists of examining difference scores between the pretests and posttests or posttest-only scores and using the pretests as covariates. A variation, also seen in Table 10.5, uses an **equivalent time series** design, in which the investigator alternates a treatment with a posttest measure. The data analysis then consists of comparing posttest measures or plotting them to discern patterns in the data over time.

TABLE 10.5

Time Series Experimental Designs

Interrupted Time Series Design

Select Participants for Group	Pretest Measure or Observation	Pretest Measure or Observation	Pretest Measure or Observation	Intervention	Posttest Measure or Observation	Posttest Measure or Observation	Posttest Measure or Observation

(Time →)

Equivalent Time Series Design

Select Participants for Group	Measure or Observation	Intervention	Measure or Observation	Intervention	Measure or Observation	Intervention	Measure or Observation

(Time →)

The time series design permits significant control over threats to internal validity. The effects of history are not always clear-cut. History effects are minimized by the short time intervals between measures and observations. However, threats to validity may occur because of the overall length of data collection in this design. The maturation of participants may be a problem, although the researcher can estimate changes in maturation by studying them and removing them statistically in the design. To control for statistical regression, researchers can also observe the scores on the pretests and control for unusually high or low scores. Because only one group is studied, the issues of selection and treatment are not relevant, although individuals can choose to drop out of the study. Testing may be a problem, but the repeated measures or observations over time may diminish the effects of testing. When researchers change the instrument during multiple testing administrations, they may also introduce threats to validity.

In our hypothetical experiment in the high school civics class, our examples thus far consist of studying two civics classes (presumably taught by the same instructor). If only *one* class is available, we could use a time series design that would involve collecting multiple measures of smoking behavior among smokers as pretests. Then the teacher would introduce the intervention "health-hazards discussion," followed by multiple measures of smoking behavior on posttests. A plot of this pretest and posttest data would reveal whether the health lecture contributed to reduced smoking among the students in the class.

Repeated Measures

Another experimental design that has the advantage of employing only a single group is a repeated measures design. In a **repeated measures design**, all participants in a single group participate in all experimental treatments, with each group becoming its own control. The researcher compares a group's performance under one experimental treatment with its performance under another experimental treatment. The experimenter decides on multiple treatments (as in factorial designs) but administers each separately to only one group. After each administration, the researcher obtains a measure or observation. The steps in this design are shown in Table 10.6.

TABLE 10.6					
Repeated Measures Design					
Time ———————————————————————————————→					
Select Participants for Group	Measure or Observation	Experimental Treatment #1	Measure or Observation	Experimental Treatment #2	Measure or Observation

After selecting participants, the researcher decides on different experimental treatments to determine the effect of each on one or more outcomes. An outcome measure or observation follows the first experimental treatment, and then a second outcome measure or observation is taken following the second experimental treatment. Variations in outcome measures are then assessed for differences from treatment to treatment.

In terms of threats to internal validity, this design is not affected by threats related to comparing groups (i.e., selection, treatments, regression, mortality, maturation, or interactions with selection). Without use of a pretest, testing and instrumentation are not threats in this design. History is a potential problem in that events may occur during the experiment that raise the potential for extraneous influences to affect the outcome measure. One experimental treatment may influence the next treatment, and researchers need to make the treatments as distinct as possible.

Applying this design to our civics–smoking experiment, assume that the investigator has access to only one civics class and can employ several interventions: a lecture on health hazards, cartoons that depict "bad breath" between couples when one individual smokes, and a handout about the rising cost of a pack of cigarettes. Notice in this example that the three treatments all address teen smoking issues, but they are distinct concerns (i.e., health, relationships, and cost). During the semester, the researcher asks the teacher to introduce each intervention separately, and the investigator measures the rate of smoking after each intervention.

Single-Subject Designs

In your experiment, assume that you seek to learn about the behavior of single individuals rather than groups. You also have an opportunity to observe their behavior over time. In these situations, single-subject experimental designs are ideal. **Single-subject research** (also called N of 1 research, behavior analysis, or within-subjects research) involves the study of single individuals, their observation over a baseline period, and the administration of an intervention. This is followed by another observation after the intervention to determine if the treatment affects the outcome. For example, in one single-subject study, the researcher tested whether elementary students with learning disabilities achieve better if they monitor their own on-task behavior (Kellogg, 1997).

Without random assignment, this design is a quasi-experimental rather than an experimental design. The researcher studies the behaviors of *single* individuals (one or more) rather than a group of subjects, with the subject becoming its own control in the experiment (see Cooper, Heron, & Heward, 1987; Neuman & McCormick, 1995).

The investigator seeks to determine if an intervention impacts the behavior of a participant by observing the individual over a prolonged period of time and recording the behavior before and after the intervention. The researcher assesses whether there is a relationship between the treatment and the target behavior or outcome. The key characteristics of a single-subject study are as follows:

◆ Prior to administering the intervention, the researcher establishes a stable baseline of information about the individual's behavior. A *stable baseline* means that behavior for an individual varies little over several sessions or days. A behavior is stable if (a) variability over time is minimal, and (b) there is no upward or downward trend in performance over time (Poling & Grossett, 1986).

◆ The researcher repeatedly and frequently measures behavior (i.e., the outcome) throughout the experiment based on making observations and recording scores for each individual.

◆ After administering the intervention, the researcher notes the patterns of behavior and plots them on a graph. This pattern may be ascending, descending, flat, or variable. Data are typically analyzed by visually inspecting the data rather than by using statistical analysis. In particular, the researcher notes how the behavior of the individual has changed after the intervention, after withdrawing the intervention, or during multiple interventions.

◆ In a graphic analysis of the data, the single-subject researcher plots behaviors for specific individuals on a graph. On this graph, the vertical axis records percentages or counts of the behavior being studied. Alternatively, the horizontal axis displays the days or sessions in which the observations occur. The plot can show data for several individuals or multiple dependent variables for a single individual.

Single-subject research has the advantage of providing data on single individuals, such as the learning and behaviors of children with disabilities, where a person-by-person analysis is needed. It also controls for many threats to internal validity. Because only one individual is studied at a time, groups are not involved and the threats to selection, treatments, mortality, maturation, regression, and interactions with selection are not relevant. Assuming that observers use the same standard procedures, instrumentation may not be a problem. When multiple treatments are used, the learning from one intervention may affect the second intervention, and history may be an issue since the experiment takes place over time.

A/B Design Because single-subject studies employ different research designs, the best way to understand them is to examine graphs that show the monitoring of behavior and the administration of an intervention. The simplest design is the A/B design. An **A/B design** consists of observing and measuring behavior during a trial period (A), administering an intervention, and observing and measuring the behavior after the intervention (B). This design is shown in Figure 10.7 for a study about elementary children and their achievement in solving math problems. In this study, the researcher observes baseline behavior and then employs an intervention of feedback to the students about their performance in math.

A variation on this design is an *A/B/A,* or a *reversal, design,* in which the researcher establishes a baseline behavior, administers an intervention, and then withdraws the intervention and determines if the behavior returned to the baseline level. Another variation is an *A/B/A withdrawal design.* In this design, researchers may implement one or more treatments. The disadvantage of this type of design is that in some studies, the withdrawing of the intervention may have serious effects on the participants in the study, raising an ethical issue for the researcher. This design may also introduce negative

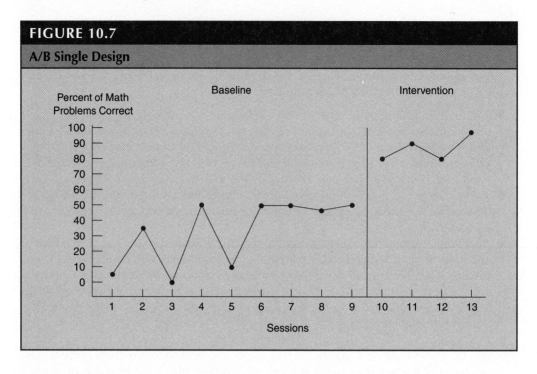

FIGURE 10.7

A/B Single Design

irreversible effects, and it requires numerous sessions or observational periods because of the use of multiple interventions.

Multiple Baseline Design   A frequently used single-subject design is the **multiple baseline design**, as shown in Figure 10.8. In this design, each participant receives an experimental treatment at a different time (hence, multiple baselines exist) so that treatment diffusion will not occur among participants. Researchers choose this design when the treatment (e.g., skill or strategy being taught) cannot be reversed and doing so would be unethical or injurious to participants. In the example shown in Figure 10.8, five individuals participate in the study and the behavior of each is plotted. Variations on this approach could involve different types of behaviors for the participants or behaviors for participants in different settings. The results of this design may be less convincing than the reversal design and it may introduce negative consequences if the treatment is withheld for an extended period.

Alternating Treatments   A final type of single-subject design is the alternating treatment. An **alternating treatment design** is a single-subject design in which the researcher examines the relative effects of two or more interventions and determines which intervention is the more effective treatment on the outcome. As shown in Figure 10.9, four elementary students participated in the experiment on solving math problems. This study had two treatment conditions: practice with feedback from the teacher and practice with a student "coach" in the class. After establishing a baseline of behavior, the researcher implemented the two different experimental treatments and plotted behavior after the treatments. In this type of design, potential problems with threats to internal validity from treatment diffusion may result, but the design permits a test of multiple treatments simultaneously to determine their effect on outcomes.

FIGURE 10.8

Multiple Baseline Single-Subject Design

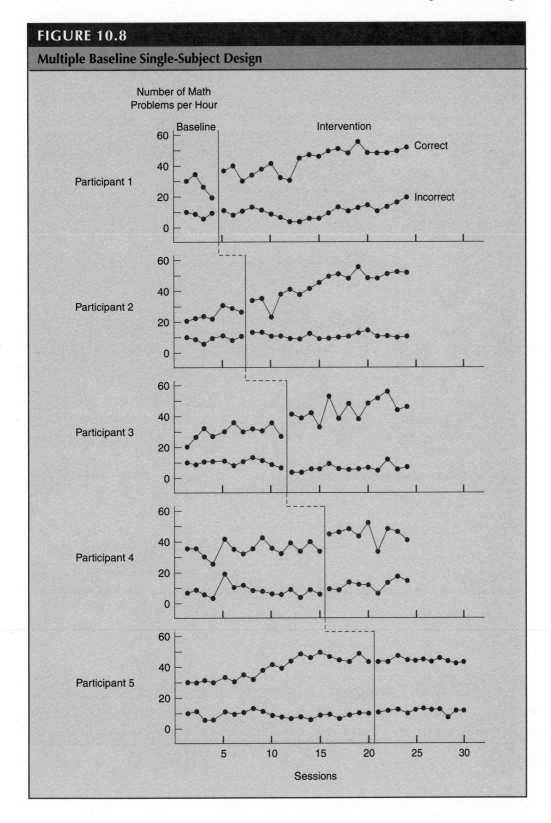

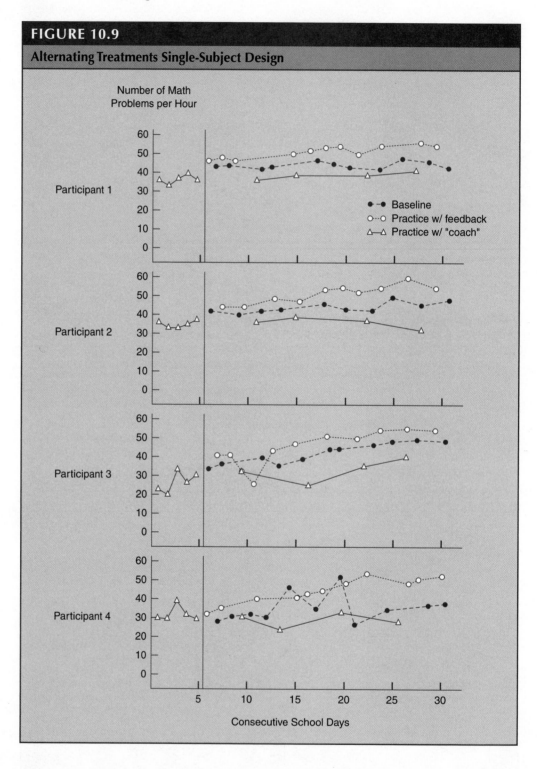

FIGURE 10.9

Alternating Treatments Single-Subject Design

WHAT ARE POTENTIAL ETHICAL ISSUES IN EXPERIMENTAL RESEARCH?

Several excellent discussions of potential ethical issues that arise in experimental research are available in the writing by Shadish, Cook, and Campbell (2002) and in a chapter by Mark and Gamble (2009). These writers address similar issues that relate to the ethics of procedures used in experiments. They are concerned about the ethics of withholding treatments from individuals in control groups when these individuals might be disadvantaged by not receiving the beneficial treatment. In some cases, withholding treatment may be wise, such as if factors exist as a scarcity of resources or if the harmful effects of the treatment may not be known at the time of the experiment. Numerous strategies exist for countering this potential ethical issue, such as giving treatments after the experiment concludes, giving all participants some level of the beneficial treatment, or offering the beneficial treatment to the control group after the experiment concludes. Another ethical concern relates to whether randomized assignments are ethical. There are important claims for the ethics of random assignment, such as a need to understand cause and effect to determine the best course of action and that randomization is preferred to other ways of addressing causality (Mark & Gamble, 2009). On the other hand, individuals may be disadvantaged because randomized experiments are based on the lottery of assignment to groups, no matter what the needs or merits of individuals may be. The case for assignment by need, for example, is the strongest when a treatment has known effectiveness (Shadish, Cook, & Campbell, 2002). Students in a grade school, for example, may be randomly assigned to different math groups despite the proven success of one math curriculum over another. Federal guidelines do exist for determining when a random experiment is justified (Federal Judicial Center, 1981). These stipulate that the study must address an important need, provide the best course of action, not have available equally informative alternatives, offer useful results, and respect the participants' rights. A further ethical concern is that the experiment needs to be concluded and it continues on. The standard for discontinuance is when one treatment condition dramatically produces better results. Additional ethical issues relate to whether the experimental methods will give the best answer to a problem, and the need to consider how high the stakes may be in conducting the experiment (Mark & Gamble, 2009).

What strategies exist for addressing the potential inequity of random assignment? Box 10.1 presents this dilemma:

BOX 10.1   Ethical Dilemma

The Question of Random Assignment

A group of university researchers are conducting a study about the effectiveness of lunchroom vegetables for addressing childhood obesity. The vegetables are grown at the school and prepared by the school chefs for the lunches. Fourth graders are involved in this experiment, and the two classes of fourth graders are assigned to one of two groups. The control group receives a standard portion of vegetables every day for school lunches. The experimental group receives a double portion of

(continued)

BOX 10.1   Continued

---

vegetables at the lunches. At the beginning of the study and at the end, the children are weighed. A parent of a child in the control group calls complaining about the small amount of vegetables her child has received for lunch at school. Hearing about the study at the parent–teacher meeting, this parent wants you to explain why her child was not assigned to the group to get more vegetables each day. How would you justify random assignment? What suggestions would you make to this parent about how you plan on giving the student more vegetables?

WHAT ARE THE STEPS IN CONDUCTING EXPERIMENTAL RESEARCH?

As we have learned about the different types of experimental designs, we have also begun to understand some of the procedures involved in conducting an experiment. Although there is no set procedure for conducting an experiment, it is helpful to understand the general process before you begin.

Step 1. Decide if an Experiment Addresses Your Research Problem

The type of issue studied by experimenters is the need to know whether a new practice influences an outcome. Of all designs in education, it is the best design to use to study cause-and-effect relationships. However, to study these issues, you must be able to control the setting of the experiment as well as manipulate one level of the independent variable. An experiment is not the best choice when the problem calls for generalizing results to a population or when you cannot manipulate the conditions of the experiment.

Step 2. Form Hypotheses to Test Cause-and-Effect Relationships

A hypothesis advances a prediction about outcomes. The experimenter establishes this prediction (in the form of a null or alternative hypothesis) and then collects data to test the hypothesis. Hypotheses are typically used in experimental research more than are research questions, but both can be used. When stating experimental hypotheses, follow these guidelines:

- Independent variables should contain at least one variable with multiple levels, and the researcher needs to manipulate one of the levels. Dependent variables are outcomes, and experimenters often study multiple outcomes (e.g., student learning and attitudes).
- Variables are measured on an instrument or recorded as observations. They need to produce valid and reliable scores. You need to give special attention to choosing measures that will result in scores with high construct validity.

Hypotheses are often based on relationships found in studies by past researchers or contained within theories that are being tested and continually revised. An example of several hypotheses was included in a study about college students' willingness to seek help from faculty:

(a) Students would be more likely to express willingness to seek help from the instructor in the supportive statement condition than in the neutral statement condition; (b) younger students would be less likely to express willingness to seek help from an instructor than would older students, independent of support condition;

and (c) students would be more likely to express willingness to seek help from an instructor when the class size is small than when it is large, independent of support condition. (Perrine, Lisle, & Tucker, 1996, pp. 44–45)

In these hypotheses, the researchers establish predictions about what they will find in their study. They compared two groups: the experimental group, which received supportive statements from the professor, and the control group, which received no supportive statements. The students in both groups then rated the likelihood that they would seek help from the instructor for six academic problems. The first hypothesis directly tests this group comparison. The second and third hypotheses control for the age of the student and the size of the class.

Step 3. Select an Experimental Unit and Identify Study Participants

One of the first steps in conducting an experiment is to decide on your experimental unit. An **experimental unit of analysis** is the smallest unit treated by the researcher during an experiment. When we use the term *treated,* we are referring to the experimental treatment. You may collect data from individuals, but the experimental unit actually treated differs from one experiment to another. The experimental unit receiving a treatment may be a single individual, several individuals, a group, several groups, or an entire organization.

Who will participate in your experiment? Participants in an experimental study are those individuals tested by the researcher to determine if the intervention made a difference in one or more outcomes. Investigators may choose participants because they volunteered or they agreed to be involved. Alternatively, the researcher may select participants who are available in well-defined, intact groups that are easily studied. For example, a study of third-grade reading may require that the researcher use existing classes of third-grade students. Regardless of the participants, investigators must be careful about the ethical issue of not disadvantaging some participants by withholding a beneficial treatment and advantaging others by giving them the treatment.

How many people will you study? In an ideal experiment, the researcher forms at least one control and one experimental group (Bausell, 1994). In many experiments, the size of the overall number of participants (and participants per group) is dictated by practical issues of the number of volunteers who enroll for the study or the individuals available to the researcher. The researcher also uses statistics to analyze the data, and these statistics call for minimum numbers of participants.

How should the participants be chosen? If possible, you should randomly select individuals for the experiment from the study population so that inferences can be made from the results to the population. This selection is accomplished through numbering the individuals in the population and randomly selecting participants using a random numbers table. In practice, this procedure may not always be possible because the population cannot be easily identified or you may not have access to all people in the population. However, because a basic premise of all quantitative research is that the findings will be generalized, random selection enables an investigator to make inferences about the population. When random selection cannot be done, an alternative is to conduct multiple experiments with different participants from the population so that some inference of generalizability or external validity can be made.

How should the individuals be assigned to groups? An optimal situation is to randomly assign the individuals to groups, but this procedure may not always be feasible. Also, to provide added control over extraneous factors, matching, blocking, selecting of homogeneous groups, and the use of covariates are recommended.

Step 4. Select an Experimental Treatment and Introduce It

The key to any experimental design is to set levels of treatment and apply one level to each group, such as one level to an experimental group and another level to a control group. Then the groups are compared on one or more outcomes. Interventions may consist of programs or activities organized by the researcher. In deciding what intervention to use, you might consider several factors:

◆ The experimental researcher should select an intervention of adequate "dosage" (Lipsey, 1998). This means that the intervention must last long enough and be strong enough to actually have an impact on the outcome.

◆ A good intervention is one that has been used by other researchers and it should predict a change in the outcome. The review of the literature and an assessment of past theories as predictions for relationships help researchers locate an intervention that should predict change.

◆ Experimental researchers should choose an intervention that can be implemented with as little intrusion in the setting and on the participants as possible. This means that the researcher needs to respect the school or nonschool setting being studied and gain the cooperation of sponsors at the site and of the participants in the study.

◆ Choose an intervention based on a small pilot test. Select a group of participants in the population and provide the intervention to them. This approach may be a pre-experimental design with a single group (to facilitate ease of implementation) or an intervention of a short duration. It may involve as few as five or six subjects (Bausell, 1994). From this pilot, you can draw conclusions about the potential impact of the intervention for the final experiment.

Step 5. Choose a Type of Experimental Design

One aspect of preparing for the experiment is choosing the design and providing a visual diagram of it. You need to make several decisions based on your experience with experiments, the availability of participants for the study, and your ability to practically control for extraneous influences in the project before choosing a design. The criteria given earlier in Table 10.1 will help lead to the selection of a design.

Step 6. Conduct the Experiment

Conducting the experiment involves procedural steps consistent with the design selected. It may involve:

◆ Administering a pretest, if you plan to use one
◆ Introducing the experimental treatment to the experimental group or relevant groups
◆ Monitoring the process closely so that the threats to internal validity are minimized
◆ Gathering posttest measures (the outcome or dependent variable measures)
◆ Using ethical practices by debriefing the participants by informing them of the purpose and reasons for the experiment, such as asking them what they thought was occurring (Neuman, 2000)

Step 7. Organize and Analyze the Data

Three major activities are required at the conclusion of the experiment: coding the data, analyzing the data, and writing the experimental report. Coding the data means that the researcher needs to take the information from the measures and set up a computer file for data analysis. This procedure begins with cleaning the data to make sure that those who complete the instruments do not enter unusual data in the computer file through keystroke errors or errant mistakes. You can explore the database for these errors by running a descriptive analysis of it using a statistical analysis program and noting variables for which unusual data exist. This descriptive analysis can provide the first review of the outcomes of the study, and scanning the results can provide an understanding of the responses of all participants to the outcome measures. This step becomes the first phase of the data analysis.

After a descriptive analysis of all participants, the researcher begins the analysis of comparing groups in terms of the outcomes. This is the heart of an experimental analysis, and it provides useful information to answer the hypotheses or research questions in the study. The statistic of choice is a group comparison statistic, such as the t test or the family of parametric analysis of variance statistics (e.g., ANOVA, analysis of covariance [ANCOVA]).

Step 8. Develop an Experimental Research Report

The experimental report follows a standard format. In the "Methods" or "Procedures" section of an experiment, the researcher typically includes information about:

◆ Participants and their assignment
◆ The experimental design
◆ The intervention and materials
◆ Control over extraneous variables
◆ Dependent measures or observations

As in a quantitative study, you write this report using standard terms for research (e.g., intervention, control, experimental group, pre- and posttest) and an objective, impartial point of view.

HOW DO YOU EVALUATE EXPERIMENTAL RESEARCH?

The key characteristics and the procedures form a basis for evaluating an experimental study. The following list, adapted from Bausell (1994), presents criteria useful in this evaluation. For a good experiment, here are some criteria:

◆ The experiment has a powerful intervention.
◆ The treatment groups are few in number.
◆ Participants will gain from the intervention.
◆ The researcher derives the number of participants per group in some systematic way.
◆ An adequate number of participants were used in the study.
◆ The researcher uses measures and observations that are valid, reliable, and sensitive.
◆ The researcher controls for extraneous factors that might influence the outcome.
◆ The researcher addresses threats to internal and external validity.

KEY IDEAS IN THE CHAPTER

A Definition of Experimental Research, When to Use It, and How It Developed

Experimental researchers test an idea (or practice or procedure) to determine its effect on an outcome. Researchers decide on an idea with which to "experiment," assign individuals to experience it (and have some individuals experience something different), and then determine whether those who experienced the idea or practice performed better on some outcome than those who did not experience it.

The ideas used in experiments today were mostly in place by the first few decades of the 20th century. The procedures of comparing groups, assigning individuals to treatments, and statistically analyzing group comparisons had been developed by 1940. During the 1960s, the types of experimental designs were identified and the strengths (e.g., control over potential threats) of these designs specified by 1980. Since 1980, computers, improved statistical procedures, and more complex designs have advanced experimental research.

Key Characteristics of Experimental Research

Today, several key characteristics help us understand and read experimental research. Experimental researchers randomly assign participants to groups or other units. They provide control over extraneous variables to isolate the effects of the independent variable on the outcomes. They physically manipulate the treatment conditions for one or more groups. They then measure the outcomes for the groups to determine if the experimental treatment had a different effect than the nonexperimental treatment. This is accomplished by statistically comparing the groups. Overall, they design an experiment to reduce the threats to internal validity and external validity.

Types of Experimental Designs

Various aspects of these characteristics are included in types of experimental designs. There are several types of between-group designs. A "true" experiment involves random assignment of participants to groups or units. This form of an experiment is the most rigorous and controlled of all types. A quasi-experimental design involves the use of an intervention, but not random assignment of participants to groups. A factorial design also involves two or more groups, but the researcher tests for the interaction of two or more independent variables.

Another type of design involves a within-group or within-individual procedure in which a single group or single individuals are studied. A time series design involves studying a single group and collecting typically more than one outcome measure. A repeated measures experiment also involves only one group, but the researcher tests more than one intervention with this group by alternating administrations of the experimental treatment. A single-subject design examines one individual at a time by establishing a baseline of behavior for the individual, administering the intervention, and determining the long-term impact of the intervention on behavior when it is withdrawn.

Ethical Issues in Experimental Research

Ethical issues in conducting experiments relate to withholding the experimental treatment from some individuals who might benefit from receiving it, the disadvantages that might accrue from randomly assigning individuals to groups. This assignment overlooks the potential need of some individuals for beneficial treatment. Ethical issues also arise as to when to conclude an experiment, whether the experiment will provide the best answers to a problem, and considerations about the stakes involved in conducting the experiment.

Steps in Conducting an Experiment

The steps in experimental research involve deciding if an experiment is the best design, forming hypotheses, and selecting the experimental unit and participants to be involved in the experiment. The researchers might randomly assign individuals to groups. They then administer the intervention by conducting the experiment, and they analyze and report results. To evaluate the success of this process, the experimenter assesses the groups, intervention, measures or observations, and extraneous factors and control over threats to validity.

Evaluating an Experiment

A good experiment has a powerful intervention, groups few in number, derived in some systematic way, and where individuals will gain from the experiment. The scores on the measures are both valid and reliable because the researcher has attended to potential threats of validity.

USEFUL INFORMATION FOR PRODUCERS OF RESEARCH

- ◆ When you design an experimental study, use the six characteristics as major features of your "Methods" discussion: random assignment, control over extraneous variables, manipulation of the treatment conditions, outcomes, measures, comparison groups, and threats to validity.
- ◆ Use random assignment of participants to groups whenever possible. This equating of groups removes many potential threats to validity in drawing inferences from scores.
- ◆ When designing and writing an experiment, distinguish between random selection and random assignment in your discussion—they serve two different purposes in research.
- ◆ Consider how you will control for extraneous factors in an experiment. Use pretests, statistically control for covariates, match participants, or select homogeneous samples to better control for characteristics of participants that might influence the relationship between the independent and dependent variables.
- ◆ In designing your study, distinguish in the "Methods" section the treatment variable, your intervention, and the actual treatment condition you manipulate.
- ◆ Also in designing your study, clarify the experimental outcome (the dependent variable) you seek to measure.
- ◆ Select a type of experimental design based on Table 10.1, and identify the potential threats to internal validity that typically relate to this design.
- ◆ In most experimental research, the statistical test of choice is a group comparison statistic, such as the *t* test, ANOVA, or ANCOVA.
- ◆ In planning your experiment, it might be helpful to draw a visual picture of the flow of procedures in your experiment, such as is shown in Table 10.3.
- ◆ When designing and conducting your experiment, follow the eight-step process as a general guide for your procedures.

USEFUL INFORMATION FOR CONSUMERS OF RESEARCH

◆ In reviewing an experimental study, recognize that researchers study different experimental units, such as individuals, groups, or entire organizations.

◆ When you read an experiment, realize that the researcher may not have randomly assigned individuals to groups because of practical limitations in the experimental situation. These experiments, called quasi-experiments, are still valuable, but they do not have the same rigor as true experiments.

◆ Recognize that all types of experiments involve an intervention where the investigator manipulates a treatment variable. Ask yourself as you read an experimental study, "What variable does the researcher physically manipulate?"

◆ Researchers should identify the type of experimental design they use in a research report. If this is unclear, use Table 10.1 and the criteria differentiating the designs as a guide to determine the type they use.

◆ Also useful in determining the type of experimental design in a study is to recognize that there are two broad types: between-group (in which the researcher compares several groups) and within-group (in which the researcher compares only one group or its variation, a within-individual design).

ADDITIONAL RESOURCES YOU MIGHT EXAMINE

For additional detailed discussions about types of experiments and validity issues in experiments (internal, external, construct, statistical conclusion), see:

Campbell, D. T., & Stanley, J. C. (1963). Experimental and quasi-experimental designs for research. In N. L. Gage (Ed.), *Handbook on research in teaching* (pp. 1–80). Chicago: Rand-McNally.

Cook, T. D., & Campbell, D. T. (1979). *Quasi-experimentation: Design and analysis issues for field settings.* Boston: Houghton Mifflin.

Shadish, W. R., Cook, T. D., & Campbell, D. T. (2002). *Experimental and quasi-experimental designs for generalized causal inference.* Boston: Houghton Mifflin.

For resources on experimental designs, see:

Bausell, R. B. (1994). *Conducting meaningful experiments.* Thousand Oaks, CA: Sage.

Boruch, R. F. (1998). Randomized controlled experiments for evaluation and planning. In.

L. Bickman & D. J. Rog (Eds.), Handbook of applied social research methods (pp. 161–191). Thousand Oaks, CA: Sage.

Bickman, L., & Rog, D. J. (2009). (Eds.). *The SAGE Handbook of applied social research methods* (2nd ed.). Thousand Oaks, CA: Sage.

Reichardt, C. S., & Mark, M. M. (1998). Quasi-experimentation. In L. Bickman & D. J. Rog (Eds.), *Handbook of applied social research methods* (pp. 193–228). Thousand Oaks, CA: Sage.

For designing sensitive experiments, power analysis, and statistical procedures, see:

Keppel, G. (1991). *Design and analysis: A researcher's handbook.* Upper Saddle River, NJ: Prentice Hall.

Lipsey, M. W. (1990). *Design sensitivity: Statistical power for experimental research.* Newbury Park, CA: Sage.

The Power of Classroom Practice
www.myeducationlab.com

Go to the Topic "Experimental Research" in the MyEducationLab (**www.myeducationlab.com**) for your course, where you can:

- Find learning outcomes for "Experimental Research."
- Complete Assignments and Activities that can help you more deeply understand the chapter content.
- Apply and practice your understanding of the core skills identified in the chapter with the Building Research Skills exercises.
- Check your comprehension of the content covered in the chapter by going to the Study Plan. Here you will be able to take a pretest, receive feedback on your answers, and then access Review, Practice, and Enrichment activities to enhance your understanding. You can then complete a final posttest.

Example of an Experimental Study

Examine the following published journal article that is an experimental study. Marginal notes indicate the major characteristics of experimental research highlighted in this chapter. The illustrative study is:

Experimental Characteristics in Marginal Annotations

Effects of Classroom Structure on Student Achievement Goal Orientation

Shannon R. Self-Brown
Samuel Mathews, II
University of West Florida

Abstract

The authors assessed how classroom structure influenced student achievement goal orientation for mathematics. Three elementary school classes were assigned randomly to 1 classroom structure condition: token economy, contingency contract, or control. Students in each condition were required to set individual achievement goals on a weekly basis. The authors assessed differences in goal orientation by comparing the number of learning vs. performance goals that students set within and across classroom structure conditions. Results indicated that students in the contingency-contract condition set significantly more learning goals than did students in other classroom structure conditions. No significant differences were found for performance goals across classroom structure conditions. Within classroom structure conditions, students in the contingency-contract group set significantly more learning goals than performance goals, whereas students in the token-economy condition set significantly more performance goals than learning goals.
Key words: classroom structure, goal orientation, mathematics

(01)   Over the last 35 years, considerable research and writings have addressed the relationship between the classroom learning environment and student goal orientation. However, only a paucity of research has focused on establishing a link between the classroom evaluation structure, differences in students' goal orientation, and classroom strategies for the creation of specific goal orientations within the classroom (Ames, 1992c). In this study, we addressed those issues.

(02)   Students' goal orientation has been linked to contrasting patterns that students exhibit when they attend to, interpret, and respond to academic tasks (Dweck & Leggett, 1988). One leading model of goal orientation focuses on two goal orientations—performance goals and learning goals. According to the model, students who set performance goals are focused on demonstrating their abilities to outside observers such as teachers, whereas students who set learning goals seek to increase their competence regardless of the presence of outside observers (Kaplan & Migdley, 1997). Researchers have found consistent patterns of behavior that are related directly to the types of goals that students establish (Dweck, 1986; Nichols, 1984; Schunk, 1990).

(03)   Generally, researchers have concluded that a negative relationship exists between performance goals and productive achievement behaviors (Greene & Miller, 1996; Zimmerman & Martinez-Pons, 1990). Adoption of a performance goal orientation means that ability is evidenced when students do better than others, surpass normative-based standards, or achieve success with little effort (Ames, 1984; Covington, 1984). Consequently, those students often avoid more difficult tasks and exhibit little intrinsic interest in academic activities (Ames, 1992c; Dweck, 1986; Nicholls, 1984). Students with a performance goal orientation can become vulnerable to helplessness, especially when they perform poorly on academic tasks. That result occurs because failure implies that students have low ability and that the amount and quality of effort expended on tasks is irrelevant to the outcome (Ames, 1992c).

In contrast, researchers have consistently found evidence for a positive relationship between learning goals and productive achievement behaviors (Ames & Archer, 1988; Greene & Miller; 1996; Meece, Blumenfeld, & Hoyle, 1988). Students who are focused on learning goals typically prefer challenging activities (Ames & Archer, 1988; Elliot & Dweck, 1988), persist at difficult tasks (Elliot & Dweck; Schunk, 1996), and report high levels of interest and task involvement (Harackiewicz, Barron, & Elliot, 1998; Harackiewicz, Barron, Tauer, Carter, & Elliot, 2000). Those students engage in a mastery-oriented belief system for which effort and outcome covary (Ames, 1992a). For students who are focused on learning goals, failure does not represent a personal deficiency but implies that greater effort or new strategies are required. Such persons will increase their efforts in the face of difficult challenges and seek opportunities that promote learning (Heyman & Dweck, 1992). Overall, researchers have concluded that a learning-goal orientation is associated with more adaptive patterns of behavior, cognition, and affect than is a performance-goal orientation (Ames & Archer, 1988; Dweck & Leggett, 1988; Nicholls, Patashnick, & Nolen, 1985). (04)

In several empirical studies, researchers have established a relationship between the salience of certain goal orientations and changes in individual behavior (Ames, 1984; Elliot & Dweck, 1988; Heyman & Dweck, 1992; Schunk, 1996). Previous laboratory studies have created learning and performance goal conditions by manipulating the instructions provided to children regarding the tasks at hand (Ames, 1984; Elliot & Dweck, 1988). Results from those studies indicate that children who participated in performance goal conditions, in which instructions made salient the external evaluation of skills and/or competitive goals, most often attributed their performance on tasks to ability. Those children also exhibited reactions that were characteristic of a helpless orientation, giving up easily and avoiding challenging tasks. In contrast, children exposed to learning-goal conditions, for which instructions focused on improving individual performance and further developing skills, typically attributed their performance to effort. Those children demonstrated mastery-oriented responses toward tasks by interpreting failures as opportunities to acquire information about how to alter their responses in order to increase their competence. (05)

Schunk (1996) conducted a study in a classroom setting to investigate the influence of achievement goal orientation on the acquisition of fractions (Schunk, 1996). Similar to the laboratory studies, learning and performance goal conditions were established through a distinction in teacher instructions. Results indicated that students in the learning-goal condition had higher motivation and achievement outcomes than did students in the performance-goal condition. The results of that study suggested that varying goal instruction within the classroom can influence students' goal perceptions and achievement-related behavior on academic tasks. (06)

Given that achievement goal orientation is an important predictor of student outcomes in educational settings, researchers must attend to the classroom environment variables that are necessary so that children orient toward a learning-goal orientation versus a performance-goal orientation (Church, Elliot, & Gable, 2001). Researchers have suggested that such variables as the instructional and management practices that teachers use can influence the type of achievement goals that students set (Ames & Ames, 1981; Kaplan & Maehr, 1999; Meece, 1991). One major element of instructional and management practices within a classroom is the structure of classroom evaluation that teachers use in their daily practices. A focus on the type of evaluation, that is, striving for personal improvement or performing to attain a teacher's goal for external reward may be related to students' goal orientation (Ames, 1992c). (07)

Typical evaluation in elementary classrooms compares students against a normative standard, such as that required to pass a course or to receive a reward within a token economy system (Brophy, 1983). Token economy systems provide students with tangible reinforcers and external incentives for meeting normative standards. Although token economy programs have received empirical support for improving student behavior and academic responding in a variety of school subjects, this classroom structure can have paradoxical and detrimental effects when applied with no regard for the varying degrees of students' capabilities (Lepper & Hodell, 1989). For instance, a student who has a learning disability in mathematics will not be motivated by the same amount of tokens to complete mathematics assignments as other students in the same classroom who have average abilities in this subject. In addition. the type of evaluative structure that stems from a token economy tends to increase the perceived importance of ability and public performance in the classroom, which makes performance-goal orientation salient to students (Ames, 1992c). (08)

(09)   To promote a learning-goal orientation, Ames (1992c) suggested a type of classroom structure in which student evaluation is based on personal improvement and progress toward individual goals. The use of contingency contracts as an evaluative tool likely would place emphasis on these variables. Contingency contracting creates an agreement for learning and performing between a student and teacher. Success is based solely on each student's individual performance, according to the goal that he or she sets (Piggott & Heggie, 1986). Contracting allows each student to consider his or her unique needs and competencies when setting goals and places responsibility for learning and performing on the student (Kurvnick, 1993). The use of contingency contracting has been an effective intervention for improving students' academic behavior in a variety of academic subjects (Murphy, 1988). It encourages students to become active participants in their learning with a focus on effortful strategies and a pattern of motivational processes that are associated with adaptive and desirable achievement behaviors (Ames, 1992c). One question that remains, however, is whether an intervention such as contingency contracting will lead to an increase in learning goals relative to performance goals. In this study, we addressed that question.

(10)   We manipulated classroom structures to assess the effects on student goal orientation. Each intact classroom was assigned randomly to either a token-economy classroom structure, contingency-contract classroom structure, or a control classroom structure. We assessed student goal orientation by comparing the number of learning and performance goals that students set according to the classroom-structure condition. On the basis of previous research, we hypothesized that the type of classroom structure would be linked directly to the achievement goals that students set. Our prediction was as follows: (a) The token-economy classroom structure would be related positively to student performance-goal orientation, (b) the contingency contract classroom structure would be related positively to student learning-goal orientation, and (c) the control classroom structure would be unrelated to student goal orientation.

Method

Participants

(11)   Students from three classrooms at a local elementary school participated in this study. Participants included 2 fifth-grade classes and 1 fourth-grade class. Each of the three intact classrooms was randomly assigned to one of the three classroom evaluation structure conditions. Twenty-five 5th-grade students were assigned to the token economy condition, 18 fourth-grade students to the contingency contract condition, and 28 fifth-grade students to the control condition.

Materials

(12)   Materials varied according to the classroom evaluation structure condition. The conditions are described in the following paragraphs.

(13)   *Token economy.* Students in this condition were given a contract that (a) described explicitly how tokens were earned and distributed and (b) listed the back-up reinforcers for which tokens could be exchanged. Students received a contract folder so that the contract could be kept at their desk at all times. Students also received a goals chart that was divided into two sections: token economy goals and individual goals. The token economy goals section listed the student behaviors that could earn tokens and the amount of tokens that each behavior was worth. The individual goals section allowed students to list weekly goals and long-term goals for mathematics. Other materials used for this condition included tokens, which were in the form of play dollars, and back-up reinforcers such as candy, pens, keychains, and computer time cards.

(14)   *Contingency contract.* Students in this condition were given a contingency contract that described the weekly process of meeting with the researcher to set and discuss mathematics goals. Students received a contract folder so that the contract could be kept at their desk at all times. Participants also received a goals chart in which they listed weekly and long-term goals for mathematics. Gold star stickers on the goals chart signified when a goal was met.

(15)   *Control.* Students in this condition received a goals chart identical to the one described in the contingency contract condition. No other materials were used in this condition.

Manipulation
of treatment
conditions

Random
assignment

Outcome
measures

Threats to valid-
ity might have
been discussed

Group
comparisons

Design

In the analysis in this study, we examined the effect of classroom evaluation structure on students' (16)
achievement goals. The independent variable in the analysis was classroom structure, which consisted of three levels: token economy, contingency contract, and control. The dependent variable was goal type (performance or learning goals) that students set for mathematics. We used a two-way analysis of variance (ANOVA) to analyze the data.

Procedure

Each of three intact classrooms was assigned randomly to one of three classroom evaluation struc- (17)
ture conditions: token economy, contingency contract, or control. We applied those classroom evaluation structure conditions to mathematics. The mathematics instruction in each classroom was on grade level. Throughout the study, teachers in the participating classrooms continued to evaluate their students with a traditional grading system that included graded evaluation of mathematics classwork, homework, and weekly tests.

Student participants in each classroom structure condition completed a mathematics goal chart (18)
each week during a one-on-one meeting with the first author. The author assessed goals by defining them as performance goals or learning goals, according to Dweck's (1986) definitions. Further procedures were specific to the classroom structure condition. The treatments are described in the following paragraphs.

Token economy. The first author gave a contract to the students, which she discussed indi- (19)
vidually with each of them. When the student demonstrated an understanding of the terms of the contract, the student and author signed the contract. Reinforcement procedures were written in the contract and explained verbally by the author, as follows:

> For the next six weeks you can earn school dollars for completing your math assignments and/or for making A's or B's on math assignments. For each assignment you complete, you will earn two school dollars. For every A or B you make on a math assignment, your will earn four school dollars. At the end of the five weeks, if you have an A or B average in math and/or have turned in all your math assignments, you will earn ten school dollars. These are the only behaviors for which you can earn school dollars. Your teacher will pay you the dollars you earn on a daily basis following math class.

Tokens were exchanged on a weekly basis when students met with the author. The process was (20)
explained to students as follows: "Once a week you can exchange your school dollars for computer time, pens, markers, keychains, notepads, or candy. You must earn at least ten school dollars in order to purchase an item."

A goals chart also was provided for the students in the token economy condition. At the top of (21)
the goals chart, target behaviors that could earn tokens were identified. Beneath the token economy goals, a section was provided in which students could write their own mathematics goals. During the weekly meeting time that students met with the author, they (a) traded tokens for backup reinforcers, (b) received reminders of the target behaviors that could earn tokens, and (c) wrote individual mathematics goals on the goals chart.

Contingency contract. Students who participated in this condition received a folder with a con- (22)
tract provided by the author. The terms of the contract were presented verbally by the author, as follows:

> Each week we will meet so that you can set goals for math. You will be allowed to set weekly goals and long-term goals. When we meet we will look over the goals you set for the previous week. We will identify the goals you have met and place a gold star beside them on your goals chart form. We will discuss the goals you did not meet and you can decide whether to set those goals again or set new ones.

Contracts were discussed individually with each student, and once the student demonstrated an understanding for the terms of the contract, the student and the author signed the contract.

Students in the contingency contract condition received a goals chart, which was divided into (23)
sections according to the week of the study. Below the weekly sections, a long-term goals section was provided. During the weekly meeting time, the previous week's goals were reviewed. Students received gold stars and positive verbal feedback, contingent on effort when they met a particular goal. Students then set weekly and long-term mathematics goals for the upcoming week.

TABLE 1
Means and Standard Deviations for Learning Goals and Performance Goals,
by Classroom Structure

Classroom structure	Learning goals		Performance goals	
	M	*SD*	*M*	*SD*
Token economy	.75	1.59	4.95	2.15
Contingency contract	14.27	3.98	5.55	3.95
Control	5.36	5.39	5.61	1.96

TABLE 2
Summary of Tukey Post Hoc Test for Classroom Structure-by-Goals Interaction

	Classroom structure results
Token economy	Performance goals > learning goals
Contingency contract	Learning goals > performance goals
Control	Performance goals = learning goals

	Goals results
Learning goals	Token economy < control < contingency contract
Performance goals	Token economy = control = contingency contract

(24)   *Control.* Students in this condition received an individual goals chart identical to the one used in the contingency contract condition. The author met one-on-one with students on a weekly basis so they could write short-term and long-term goals for mathematics on their goals chart. The students did not discuss their goals with the author. Furthermore, the students did not receive verbal feedback or external rewards for achieving their goals from the teacher or author. Thus, this condition simply served as a control for goal setting and time spent with the author.

Results

(25)   We computed an ANOVA by using a two-factor mixed design (classroom structure by goal type) to determine the frequency of learning and performance goals set according to classroom structure condition. Table 1 shows the cell means for learning and performance goals that students set as a function of classroom structure. Results indicated a significant main effect for classroom structure, $F(2, 67) = 36.70$, p <.0001, as well as a significant classroom structure-by-goals interaction, $F(2, 67) = 31.35$, $p <.0001$.

(26)   We computed a Tukey post hoc test to determine the significant differences between classroom structure-by-goals on the ANOVA. A summary of post hoc results are shown in Table 2. In our post hoc analysis, we concluded that students in the contingency contract condition set significantly more learning goals than did students in the other conditions. Students in the control condition set significantly more learning goals than did students in the token-economy group. There were no significant differences between the numbers of performance goals that students set according to classroom structure conditions.

(27)   Within the contingency contract group, students set significantly more learning goals than performance goals. In the control group, there were no significant differences between the number of learning and performance goals that students set. In the token-economy group, students set significantly more performance goals than learning goals.

Discussion

(28)   Results from the goal analyses indicated significant differences within and across classroom structure conditions. Those results were consistent with the theoretical relationship predicted by Ames (1992c) and the hypothesis in this study that the type of classroom evaluation structure would

influence student goal orientation. Students who were in the contingency-contract condition set significantly more learning goals than performance goals and significantly more learning goals than did students in the other classroom structure conditions. Students in the token-economy condition set significantly more performance goals than learning goals. There were no significant differences within the control classroom for the number of learning versus performance goals that students set. However, students in that classroom did set significantly more learning goals than did students in the token-economy condition. There were no significant differences for the amount of performance goals that students set across classroom-structure conditions.

Our results support the idea that a contingency contract classroom structure, in which students were evaluated individually and allowed to determine their own achievement goals, let students to adopt a learning-goal orientation versus a performance-goal orientation. In this classroom structure, student evaluation was focused on individual gains, improvement, and progress. Success was measured by whether students met their individual goals, which creates an environment in which failure is not a threat. If goals were met, then students could derive personal pride and satisfaction from the efforts that they placed toward the goals. If goals were not met, then students could reassess the goal, make the changes needed, or eliminate the goal. A classroom structure that promotes a learning-goal orientation for students has the potential to enhance the quality of students' involvement in learning, increase the likelihood that students will opt for and persevere in learning and challenging activities, and increase the confidence they have in themselves as learners (Ames, 1992b). (29)

In contrast, students in the token-economy classroom structure were rewarded for meeting normative standards and tended to adopt a performance-goal orientation. That is an important finding because token economies have been successful in changing students behavior in classrooms, so teachers may implement this intervention without concern for the special needs of students (McLaughlin, 1981). Students are not motivated by the same amount of tokens for given assignments because of individual differences. Students with lower abilities will likely become frustrated and helpless. According to Boggiano & Katz (1991), children in that type of learning environment typically prefer less challenging activities, work to please the teacher and earn good grades, and depend on others to evaluate their work. As a result, the token-economy classroom evaluation structure makes ability a highly salient dimension of the learning environment and discourages students from setting goals that involve learning and effort. (30)

The number of performance goals that students set did not differ across classroom structure conditions. Students in the contingency-contract and control conditions set similar numbers of performance goals as compared with those in the token-economy condition. That result likely occurred because throughout the study teachers continued to evaluate all students on their schoolwork with a traditional grading system. It would have been ideal if a nontraditional, individually based evaluative system could have been implemented in the contingency-contract condition to assess whether this would have altered the results. (31)

There were limitations to this study. One limitation was that it did not control for teacher expectancies and how these may have influenced students' goal setting. Another potential limitation was that mathematics was the only subject area used for this study. Further studies should include additional academic areas, such as social studies, humanities, and science to investigate whether similar results will ensue. (32)

Control over extraneous variables might have been addressed

This study provides strong evidence that the classroom evaluation structure can influence student achievement goal orientation. Specifically, we demonstrated that in a classroom structure that emphasizes the importance of individual goals and effort, learning goals become more salient to students. That result can lead to many positive effects on elementary student's learning strategies, self-conceptions of ability and competence, and task motivation (Smiley & Dweck, 1994). Students' achievement goal orientation obviously is not contingent on any one variable, but it is comprised of the comprehensive relationship between classroom processes and student experiences. Understanding the influence of classroom evaluation structure on student goal orientation provides a foundation for further research of other potentially related variables. (33)

Notes

Shannon Self-Brown is now in the Department of Psychology at Louisiana State University.

We would like to thank Lucas Ledbetter for assisting in data collection. We would also like to thank the teachers and students at Jim Allen Elementary for participating in the project.

References

Ames, C. (1984). Achievement attribution and self-instructions under competitive and individualistic goal structures. *Journal of Educational Psychology, 76,* 478–487.

Ames, C. (1992a). Achievement goals and the classroom motivational environment. In D. L. Schunk & J. L. Meece (Eds.), *Student perceptions in the classroom* (pp. 327–343). Hillsdale. NJ: Erlbaum.

Ames, C. (1992b). Achievement goals, motivational climate, and motivational processes. In G. C. Roberts (Ed.), *Motivation in sport and exercise.* Champaign, IL: Human Kinetics Books.

Ames, C. (1992c). Classroom: Goals, structures, and student motivation. *Journal of Educational Psychology, 84,* 261–271.

Ames, C., & Ames, R. (1981). Competitive versus individualistic goal structure: The salience of past performance information for causal attributions and affect. *Journal of Educational Psychology, 73,* 411–418.

Ames, C., & Archer, J. (1988). Achievement goals in the classroom: Student learning strategies and motivation processes. *Journal of Educational Psychology, 80,* 260–267.

Boggiano, A. K., & Katz, P. (1991). Maladaptive achievement patterns in students: The role of teachers' controlling strategies, *Journal of Social Issues, 47,* 35–51.

Brophy, J. E. (1983). Conceptualizing student motivation. *Educational Psychologist, 18,* 200–215.

Church, M. A., Elliot, A. J., & Gable, S. L., (2001). Perceptions of classroom environment, achievement goals, and achievement outcomes. *Journal of Educational Psychology, 93,* 43–54.,

Covington, M. C. (1984). The motive for self worth. In R. Ames & C. Ames (Eds.). *Research on motivation in education: Student motivation* (Vol. 1, pp. 77–113). San Diego, CA: Academic Press.

Dweck, C. (1986). Motivational processes affecting learning. *American Psychologist, 41,* 1040–1048.

Dweck, C., & Leggett, E. L. (1988). A social-cognitive approach to motivation and personality. *Psychological Review, 95,* 256–273.

Elliot, E. S. & Dweck, C. S. (1988). Goals: An approach to motivation and achievement. *Journal of Personality & Social Psychology, 54,* 5–12.

Greene, B., & Miller, R. (1996). Influences on achievement: Goals, perceived ability, and cognitive engagement. *Contemporary Educational Psychology, 21,* 181–192.

Harackiewicz, J. M., Barron, K. E., & Elliot, A. (1998). Rethinking achievement goals: When are they adaptive for college students and why? *Educational Psychologist, 33,* 1–21.

Harackiewicz, J. M., Barron, K. E., Tauer, J. M., Carter, S. M., & Elliot, A. J. (2000). Short-term and long-term consequences of achievement goals: Predicting interest and performance over time. *Journal of Educational Psychology, 92,* 316–330.

Heyman, G. D., & Dweck, C. S. (1992). Achievement goals and intrinsic motivation: Their relation and their role in adaptive motivation. *Motivation and Emotion, 16,* 231–247.

Kaplan, A., & Midgley, C. (1997). The effect of achievement goals: Does level of perceived academic competence make a difference? *Contemporary Educational Psychology, 22,* 415–435.

Kaplan, A., & Maehr, M. L. (1999). Achievement goals and student well-being. *Contemporary Educational Psychology, 24,* 330–358.

Kurvnick, K. (1993). Contracting as a motivational teaching tool: An agreement for learning offering simplicity, flexibility, and opportunity. *Journal of College Science Teaching, 22,* 310–311.

Lepper, M. R., & Hodell, M. (1989). Intrinsic motivation in the classroom. In C. Ames & R. Ames (Eds.), *Research on motivation in education* (Vol. 3, pp. 73–105). San Diego, CA: Academic Press.

McLaughlin, T. F. (1981). An analysis of token reinforcement: A control group comparison with special education youth employing measures of clinical significance. *Child Behavior Therapy, 3,* 43–50.

Meece, J. L. (1991). The classroom context and children's motivational goals. In M. Maehr & P. Pintrich (Eds.), *Advances in achievement motivation research* (pp. 261–286). Greenwich, CT: JAI.

Meece, J. L., Blumenfeld, P. C., & Hoyle, R. H. (1988). Students' goal orientation and cognitive engagement in classroom activities. *Journal of Educational Psychology, 80,* 514–523.

Murphy, J. J. (1988). Contingency contracting in schools: A review. *Education and Treatment of Children, 11,* 257–269.

Nicholls, J. (1984). Achievement motivation: Conceptions of ability, subjective experience, task choice, and performance. *Psychological Review, 91,* 328–334.

Nicholls, J. G., Patashnick, M., & Nolen, S. (1985). Adolescents' theories of education. *Journal of Educational Psychology, 77,* 683–692.

Piggott, H. E, & Heggie, D. L. (1986). Interpreting the conflicting results of individual versus group contingencies in classrooms: The targeted behavior as a mediating variable. *Child & Family Behavior Therapy, 7,* 1–15.

Schunk, D. H. (1990). Goal setting and self-efficacy during self-regulated learning. *Educational Psychologist, 25,* 71–86.

Schunk, D. H. (1996). Goals and self-evaluative influences during children's cognitive skill learning. *American Educational Research Journal, 33,* 359–382.

Smiley, P. A., & Dweck, C. S. (1994). Individual differences in achievement goals among young children. *Child Development, 65,* 1723–1743.

Zimmerman, B. J., & Martinez-Pons, M. (1990). Student differences in self-regulated learning: Relating grade, sex, and giftedness to self-efficacy and strategy use. *Journal of Educational Psychology, 82,* 51–59.

11

Correlational Designs

*I*n educational research, your objective may be to relate variables rather than manipulate the independent variable, as in an experiment. If so, your design is correlational research. Although it is not as rigorous as an experiment, you can use it for relating variables or predicting outcomes. This chapter defines correlational research, identifies when you use it, assesses the key characteristics of it, and advances the steps in conducting and evaluating this design.

By the end of this chapter, you should be able to:

◆ Define correlational research, and describe when to use it, and how it developed.
◆ Identify the two types of correlational designs.
◆ Describe the key characteristics of correlational designs.
◆ Identify potential ethical issues in conducting correlational research.
◆ Identify steps in conducting a correlation study.
◆ List the criteria for evaluating a correlational study.

Maria chooses a quantitative correlational design for her graduate school research project. This is her research question: "Is the use of alcohol by students related to suspensions for weapon possession?" In other words, does use of alcohol predict whether a person will receive suspension for possessing weapons in the school? Maria accesses school records for individuals cited for possession of alcohol and the records for weapon possession. She relates these two variables using the correlation statistic. She finds that the two variables are positively related: If a person has been cited for alcohol, he or she is likely to be suspended for weapon possession as well. Maria conducts a correlation research study.

WHAT IS CORRELATIONAL RESEARCH, WHEN DO YOU USE IT, AND HOW DID IT DEVELOP?

Correlational designs provide an opportunity for you to predict scores and explain the relationship among variables. In **correlational research designs**, investigators use the correlation statistical test to describe and measure the degree of association (or relationship) between two or more variables or sets of scores. In this design, the researchers do not attempt to control or manipulate the variables as in an experiment; instead, they relate, using the correlation statistic, two or more scores for each person (e.g., a student motivation and a student achievement score for each individual).

A **correlation** is a statistical test to determine the tendency or pattern for two (or more) variables or two sets of data to vary consistently. In the case of only two variables, this means that two variables share common variance, or they co-vary together. To say that two variables co-vary has a somewhat complicated mathematical basis. **Co-vary** means that we can predict a score on one variable with knowledge about the individual's score on another variable. A simple example might illustrate this point. Assume that scores on a math quiz for fourth-grade students range from 30 to 90. We are interested in whether scores on an in-class exercise in math (one variable) can predict the student's math quiz scores (another variable). If the scores on the exercise do not explain the scores on the math quiz, then we cannot predict anyone's score except to say that it might range from 30 to 90. If the exercise could explain the variance in all of the math quiz scores, then we could predict the math scores perfectly. This situation is seldom achieved; instead, we might find that 40% of the variance in math quiz scores is explained by scores on the exercise. This narrows our prediction on math quiz scores from 30 to 90 to something less, such as 40 to 60. The idea is that as variance increases, we are better able to predict scores from the independent to the dependent variable (Gall, Borg, & Gall, 1996).

The statistic that expresses a correlation statistic as a linear relationship is the **product–moment correlation coefficient**. It is also called the *bivariate correlation, zero-order correlation,* or simply *r,* and it is indicated by an "r" for its notation. The statistic is calculated for two variables (r_{xy}) by multiplying the *z* scores on *X* and *Y* for each case and then dividing by the number of cases minus one (e.g., see the detailed steps in Vockell & Ashner, 1995). The mathematical calculations are illustrated in many introductory statistics books.

When Do You Use Correlational Research?

You use this design when you seek to relate two or more variables to see if they influence each other, such as the relationship between teachers who endorse developmentally appropriate practices and their use of the whole-language approach to reading instruction (Ketner, Smith, & Parnell, 1997). This design allows you to predict an outcome, such as the prediction that ability, quality of schooling, student motivation, and academic coursework influence student achievement (Anderson & Keith, 1997). You also use this design when you know and can apply statistical knowledge based on calculating the correlation statistical test.

How Did Correlational Research Develop?

The history of correlational research draws on the themes of the origin and development of the correlation statistical test and the procedures for using and interpreting the test. Statisticians first developed the procedures for calculating the correlation statistics in the late 19th century (Cowles, 1989). Although British biometricians articulated the basic ideas of "co-relation" during the last half of the 1800s, Karl Pearson presented the familiar correlation formula we know today in a paper before the Royal Society in England in November 1895 (Cowles, 1989). Interestingly, Pearson used illustrations from Darwin's theory of evolution and Sir Francis Galton's ideas on heredity and natural inheritance to advance his ideas about correlation. For example, one idea Pearson explored was to study Galton's idea of the relationship between the left cubit (the distance between the elbow of the bent left arm and the tip of the middle finger) and stature for adult males (Cowles, 1989).

In presenting ideas about correlations, Pearson not only articulated the formula for a correlation, but he also presented concepts familiar to quantitative researchers today, such as the importance of sample size, the value of precise measurement, and the use of unbiased samples. However, Pearson was only one of several British biometricians around the turn of the century who refined and extended ideas about correlations (De Landsheere, 1988). In 1897, Yule (Pearson's student) developed solutions for correlating two, three, and four variables. With Pearson, Yule also advanced the theory of regression and the ability to predict scores using information based on correlating correlation coefficients. By 1904, Spearman published ideas about a correlation matrix to display the coefficients, and he advanced a formula (Spearman's rho) for data that did not fit a normal, bell-shaped distribution.

After the turn of the 20th century, and for almost 50 years, refinements in educational research design centered on experimental procedures rather than correlational designs. However, during this time, Fisher (1935) pioneered significance testing and ANOVA, important statistical ideas for studying the difference between observed and predicted scores in correlational analysis. It was not until 1963 that Campbell and Stanley provided new impetus to correlational research, with their classical treatise on experimental and quasi-experimental designs. In this discussion, they included correlational research as one of the designs, although they saw it as a less rigorous and valid design than experiments. In using correlational research, they encouraged investigators to both recognize and specify the extensive threats to validity inherent in this form of research.

During the 1970s and 1980s, with the advent of computers, improved knowledge about measurement scales, and the need to study complex associations among many variables, quantitative researchers initiated correlational studies. Instead of the physical control available to experimental researchers through techniques such as randomization and matching, correlational researchers sought control through statistical procedures. With computers, they could statistically remove the effects of a large number of variables to examine the relationship among a small set of variables. They could explore the combination of variables (e.g., age, gender, and SAT scores) and an outcome (e.g., college grade point average). From simple regression—the analysis of the variability of a single dependent variable by a single independent variable—the technique of using multiple regression to analyze the collective and separate effects of two or more independent variables on a dependent variable emerged (Pedhazur, 1997). Taking regression to the next step by advancing a theoretical model, collecting data, and estimating the fit of the data to the model led researchers to advanced correlational techniques of path analysis (Kline, 1998). Today, researchers test elaborate models containing many variables (Kline, 1998).

WHAT ARE THE TYPES OF CORRELATIONAL DESIGNS?

Years ago, research method writers specified correlational research as one of the quantitative "designs" (e.g., see Campbell & Stanley, 1963). With the sophisticated applications and explicit procedures of correlations, correlational research can rightfully take its place among our designs in quantitative research. The two primary correlation designs are explanation and prediction.

The Explanatory Design

Various authors refer to explanatory correlational research as "relational" research (Cohen & Manion, 1994, p. 123), "accounting-for-variance studies" (Punch, 1998, p. 78), or "explanatory" research (Fraenkel & Wallen, 2000, p. 360). Because one basic objective of this form of correlational research is to explain the association between or among variables, we will use the term *explanatory research* in this discussion. An **explanatory research design** is a correlational design in which the researcher is interested in the extent to which two variables (or more) co-vary, that is, where changes in one variable are reflected in changes in the other. Explanatory designs consist of a simple association between two variables (e.g., sense of humor and performance in drama) or more than two (e.g., pressure from friends or feelings of isolation that contribute to binge drinking).

When examining a study reported in the literature, how would you identify it as an explanatory correlational study? Look for the following characteristics, which are common in this type of study.

◆ *The investigators correlate two or more variables.* They report the correlation statistical test and mention the use of multiple variables. Readers find these variables specifically mentioned in the purpose statement, the research questions, or the tables reporting the statistical procedures.

◆ *The researchers collect data at one point in time.* Evidence for this procedure will be found in the administration of instruments "in one sitting" to students. In explanatory correlational research, the investigators are not interested in either past or future performance of participants.

◆ *The investigator analyzes all participants as a single group.* Compared to an experiment that involves multiple groups or treatment conditions, the researcher collects scores from only one group and does not divide the group into categories (or factors). Unlike experimental research, all levels of information from the group are used. Rather than divide scores on self-esteem into "high" and "low" categories of scores, as would be done in experimental research, a correlational researcher uses all scores on a continuum, such as from 10 to 90.

◆ *The researcher obtains at least two scores for each individual in the group—one for each variable.* In the method discussion, the correlational investigator will mention how many scores were collected from each participant. For example, for each individual in a study of optimism and appropriate health behaviors, the researcher would collect two scores: an optimism score and a health behavior score.

◆ *The researcher reports the use of the correlation statistical test (or an extension of it) in the data analysis.* This is the basic feature of this type of research. In addition, the researcher includes reports about the strength and the direction of the correlational test to provide additional information.

◆ *Finally, the researcher makes interpretations or draws conclusions from the statistical test results.* It is important to note that the conclusions do not establish a probable cause-and-effect (or causal inference) relationship because the researcher can use only statistical control (e.g., control over variables using statistical procedures) rather than the more rigorous control of physically altering the conditions (i.e., such as in experiments). In correlational research, the investigator "takes the participants as they are," without experimental intervention. Thus, authors of a correlational study often use the phrase "degree of association between two variables"

(Thorndike, 1997a, p. 1107), a connotation that conveys a general co-occurrence between variables rather than probable causality. It also accounts for why correlational writers sometimes refrain from using the terms *independent variable* and *dependent variable* and instead refer to the correlation of two *variables,* a meaning consistent with something less than the independent variable influencing the dependent variable. They also employ the word *relationship* about correlations among variables.

Let's turn to an explanatory correlational study by Anderson and Keith (1997) to illustrate this type of design. Despite gains in achievement test scores, African American, Hispanic, and low-income students typically achieve below the levels of Caucasian, Asian, and high-income students. African American and Hispanic students also drop out of school at higher rates than do their Caucasian peers. To understand the factors that explain academic success of these at-risk students, Anderson and Keith conducted a correlational study. They proposed a model composed of eight variables (family socioeconomic status, ethnicity, gender, ability, quality of schooling, parental involvement, motivation, and academic coursework) and one outcome variable (academic achievement). They studied one group comprised of sophomores in high school who indicated they were of non-Asian minority origin and who had Socioeconomic Status (SES) composite scores within the bottom quartile of the SES range. The data collection involved gathering information during the base year (1980) and 2 years later (1982), but for purposes of analysis, the researchers analyzed data together from both years as if they were collected at one point in time. For all participants ($N = 7,355$), they collected measures on each variable and correlated all variables. They found that each of the variables except parental involvement explained a significant amount of variance in academic achievement.

The Prediction Design

Instead of simply relating variables—two variables at a time or a complex set such as in our last example—in a prediction design, researchers seek to anticipate outcomes by using certain variables as predictors. For example, superintendents and principals need to identify teachers who will be successful in their schools. To select teachers who have a good chance of success, the administrators can identify predictors of success using correlational research. Prediction studies, therefore, are useful because they help anticipate or forecast future behavior.

The purpose of a **prediction research design** is to identify variables that will predict an outcome or criterion. In this form of research, the investigator identifies one or more predictor variable and a criterion (or outcome) variable. A **predictor variable** is a variable used to make a forecast about an outcome in correlational research. In the case of predicting teacher success in a school, the predictor may be "mentoring" during teacher training or "years of experience teaching." In much prediction research, investigators often use more than one predictor variable.

The outcome being predicted in correlational research, however, is called the **criterion variable**. In our example, teacher success is the criterion variable. Although more than one outcome can be predicted, the typical educational study includes only one criterion variable.

To identify a prediction study, look for the following characteristics.

- ◆ *The authors typically include the word* prediction *in the title.* It might also be in the purpose statement or research questions.
- ◆ *The researchers typically measure the predictor variable(s) at one point in time and the criterion variable at a later point in time.* Therefore, you should examine

a study to determine if the researchers build a "time" dimension into the design. For example, the predictor of teacher success, "mentoring," is measured during a student's teacher training program, whereas "success" is measured later, after the students have performed as teachers.

◆ *The authors forecast future performance.* They usually state this intent in the purpose statement or in the research questions. In the justification of the research problem, writers also mention their intent to "predict" some outcome.

A prediction study will report correlations using the correlation statistical test, but it may include advanced statistical procedures. For example, the author may be interested in several predictors that help explain the criterion. Although simple linear regression (explained later) addresses this interest, multiple regression (also addressed later) provides a more complex formula.

Let's view a prediction study to see the procedures the researchers used. Royal and Rossi (1999) were concerned about the problem of teacher isolation and sought to identify the factors that predict a better sense of community for high school teachers. Their study included several predictors and one overall criterion (sense of community). They collected data from three large high schools and gathered several measures. They measured sense of community using an 85-item instrument that included a student-related measure of community, a coworker measure, and a school-related measure. Predictors were time-related variables (e.g., tenure in the school), work arrangements (e.g., mentoring, teaching teams), and school organization variables (e.g., innovation in the school). In this configuration of variables, the researchers assumed that the predictor variables operated earlier in time than the criterion (e.g., after the initiation of innovation, teachers developed a sense of community). The investigators correlated these predictors and the outcome variables and conducted a multiple regression to find that the predictors had different effects on each criterion variable. Overall, school tenure, student interaction, and innovation were the best predictors of the measures of a sense of community in the schools.

WHAT ARE THE KEY CHARACTERISTICS OF CORRELATIONAL DESIGNS?

As suggested by the explanatory and prediction designs, correlation research includes specific characteristics:

◆ Displays of scores (scatterplots and matrices)
◆ Associations between scores (direction, form, and strength)
◆ Multiple variable analysis (partial correlations and multiple regression)

Displays of Scores

If you have two scores, in correlation research you can plot these scores on a graph (or scatterplot) or present them in a table (or correlation matrix).

Scatterplots

Researchers plot scores for two variables on a graph to provide a visual picture of the form of the scores. This allows researchers to identify the type of association among variables and locate extreme scores. Most importantly, this plot can provide useful information about the form of the association—whether the scores are linear (follow a straight line) or curvilinear (follow a U-shaped form). It also indicates the direction of the association (e.g., one score goes up and the other goes up as well) and the degree of the association (whether the relationship is perfect, with a correlation of 1.0, or less than perfect).

A plot helps to assess this association between two scores for participants. A **scatterplot** (or **scatter diagram**) is a pictorial image displayed on a graph of two sets of scores for participants. These scores are typically identified as X and Y, with X values represented on the horizontal axis, and Y values represented on the vertical axis. A single point indicates where the X and Y scores intersect for one individual.

Using scales on the horizontal (abscissa) axis and on the vertical (ordinate) axis, the investigator plots points on a graph for each participant. Examine the scatterplot of scores in Figure 11.1, which shows both a small data set for 10 students and a visual plot of their scores. Assume that the correlation researcher seeks to study whether the use of the Internet by high school students relates to their level of depression. (We can assume that students who use the Internet excessively are also depressed individuals because they are trying to escape and not cope with present situations.) From past research, we would predict this situation to be the case. We measure scores on the use of the Internet by asking the students how many hours per week they spend searching the Internet. We measure individual depression scores on an instrument with proven valid and reliable scores. Assume that there are 15 questions about depression on the instrument with a rating scale from 1 (*strongly disagree*) to 5 (*strongly agree*). This means that the summed scores will range from 15 to 45.

As shown in Figure 11.1, hypothetical scores for 10 students are collected and plotted on the graph. Several aspects about this graph will help you understand it:

◆ The "hours of Internet use" variable is plotted on the X axis, the horizontal axis.
◆ The "depression" variable is plotted on the Y axis, the vertical axis.

FIGURE 11.1

Example of a Scatterplot

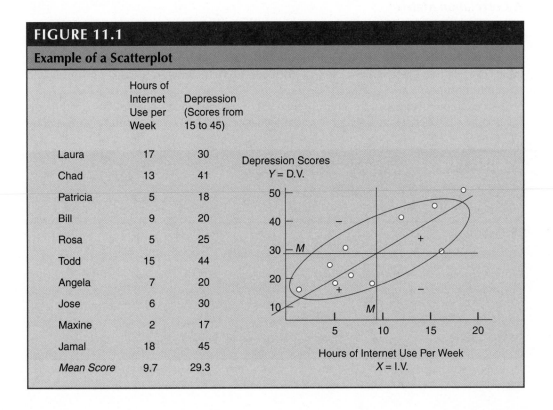

	Hours of Internet Use per Week	Depression (Scores from 15 to 45)
Laura	17	30
Chad	13	41
Patricia	5	18
Bill	9	20
Rosa	5	25
Todd	15	44
Angela	7	20
Jose	6	30
Maxine	2	17
Jamal	18	45
Mean Score	9.7	29.3

◆ Each student in the study has two scores: one for hours per week of Internet use and one for depression.
◆ A mark (or point) on the graph indicates the score for each individual on depression and hours of Internet use each week. There are 10 scores (points) on the graph, one for each participant in the study.

The mean scores (*M*) on each variable are also plotted on the graph. The students used the Internet for an average of 9.7 hours per week, and their average depression score was 29.3. Drawing vertical and horizontal lines on the graph that relate to the mean scores (*M*), we can divide the plot into four quadrants and assign a minus (–) to quadrants where scores are "negative" and a plus (+) to quadrants where the scores are "positive." In our example, to have a depression score below 29.3 (*M*) is positive because that suggests that the students with such a score have less depression. To score above 29.3 (*M*) indicates more severe depression, and this is "negative." Alternatively, to use the Internet less than 9.7 (*M*) hours per week is "positive" (i.e., because students can then spend more time on homework), whereas to spend more time than 9.7 hours is "negative" (i.e., overuse of Internet searching is at the expense of something else). To be both highly depressed (above 29.3 on depression) and to use the Internet frequently (above 9.7 on Internet use) is what we might have predicted based on past literature.

Note three important aspects about the scores on this plot. First, the direction of scores shows that when *X* increases, *Y* increases as well, indicating a positive association. Second, the points on the scatterplot tend to form a straight line. Third, the points would be reasonably close to a straight line if we were to draw a line through all of them. These three ideas relate to direction, form of the association, and the degree of relationship that we can learn from studying this scatterplot. We will use this information later when we discuss the association between scores in correlation research.

A Correlation Matrix

Correlation researchers typically display correlation coefficients in a matrix. A **correlation matrix** presents a visual display of the correlation coefficients for all variables in a study. In this display, we list all variables on both a horizontal row and a vertical column in the table. Correlational researchers present correlation coefficients in a matrix in published research reports.

An example of this can be seen in Table 11.1, which reports coefficients for the correlation of six variables in a study of variables associated with school satisfaction among

TABLE 11.1

Example of a Correlation Matrix

Variables	1	2	3	4	5	6
1. School satisfaction	—					
2. Extracurricular activities	−.33**	—				
3. Friendships	.24*	−.03	—			
4. Self-esteem	−.17	.65**	.24*	—		
5. Pride in school	−.09	−.02	.49**	.16	—	
6. Self-awareness	.29**	−.10	.39**	.03	.22	—

*$p < .05$
**$p < .01$

middle school students. Notice that all six variables are listed in both the horizontal rows and the vertical columns. To simplify the table, the authors assigned numbers to the variables and included only the numbers in the column headings. Coefficients ranging between −.33 and +.65 are reported in cells in the table. We fill only the lower half of the cells because the half of the cells above the diagonal would simply repeat the same information. Finally, the asterisks indicate whether the coefficient statistics are statistically significantly correlated at the $p < .05$ and $p < .01$ levels.

Associations between Scores

After correlation researchers graph scores and produce a correlation matrix, they can then interpret the meaning of the association between scores. This calls for understanding the direction of the association, the form of the distribution, the degree of association, and its strength.

What Is the Direction of the Association?

When examining a graph, it is important to identify if the points intersect, or move in the same or opposite directions. In a **positive correlation** (indicated by a "1" correlation coefficient) the points move in the same direction; that is, when X increases, so does Y or, alternatively, if X decreases, so does Y. In a **negative correlation** (indicated by a "−" correlation coefficient), the points move in the opposite direction; that is, when X increases, Y decreases, and when X decreases, Y increases. If scores on one variable do not relate in any pattern on the other variable, then no linear association exists.

What Is the Form of the Association?

Correlational researchers identify the form of the plotted scores as linear or nonlinear. In the Internet and depression example (Figure 11.1), we found a positive, linear relationship. This type of relationship is only one of several possibilities that might result from actual data. In reality, the relationship might assume any one of the forms shown in Figure 11.2.

Linear Relationship   Part (a) of Figure 11.2 depicts a **positive linear relationship** of scores, where low (or high) scores on one variable relate to low (or high) scores on a second variable. In our example, low scores on depression are associated with low scores on number of hours using the Internet per week.

Part (b) of Figure 11.2 depicts a **negative linear relationship** result, where low scores on one variable relate to high scores on the other variable. Low scores on depression, for example, might be associated with high scores on use of the Internet, suggesting a negative relationship.

Uncorrelated and Nonlinear Relationships   In part (c) of Figure 11.2, we see an **uncorrelated relationship** of scores. In this distribution, the variables are independent of each other. A particular score on one variable does not predict or tell us any information about the possible score on the other variable. In our example, a plot of the scores for depression and the scores for Internet use would be irregular, without any particular pattern.

A **curvilinear distribution** (or nonlinear relationship) shows a U-shaped relationship in scores. This distribution in part (d) of Figure 11.2 shows an increase, plateau, and decline in the Y-axis variable with increasing values of the X-axis variable. The distribution in part (e) of Figure 11.2 indicates a decrease, plateau, and increase in the Y-axis variable, with increasing values of the X-axis variable. For example, it is possible that as Internet use increases, so does depression, up to a point at which the Internet actually becomes a coping mechanism for stress, and depression begins to decrease (as illustrated in part [d]).

FIGURE 11.2

Patterns of Association between Two Variables

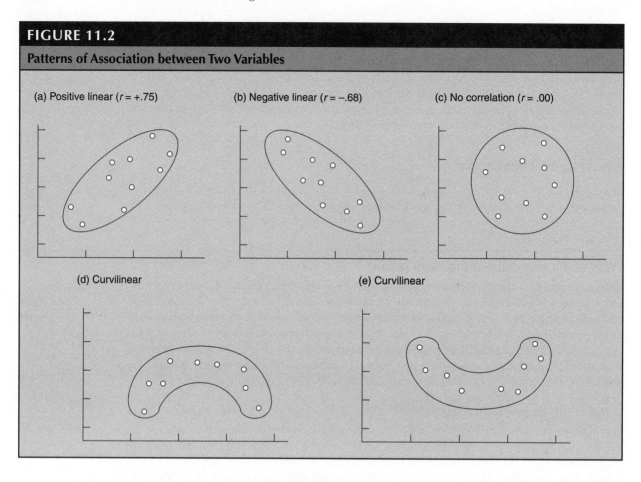

(a) Positive linear (*r* = +.75)

(b) Negative linear (*r* = −.68)

(c) No correlation (*r* = .00)

(d) Curvilinear

(e) Curvilinear

Another example of this form of distribution would be the relationship between anxiety and points scored in a tennis match. With low anxiety initially, a tennis player might score many points, but this may decline as anxiety sets in. As the match progresses, however, anxiety actually helps keep the tennis player alert, and as anxiety builds, performance actually goes up. In short, a plot of anxiety and points scored would show a curvilinear relationship (such as in part [e] of Figure 11.2).

The correlation coefficient is useful for describing and measuring the association between two variables *if the association is linear*. As shown in the patterns of association in Figure 11.2, the association may be curvilinear (or nonlinear). If an *r* is used to estimate a curvilinear association, it would provide an underestimate of the correlation. Therefore, researchers use different statistics than the *r* to calculate the relationship between variables for a curvilinear distribution and for relating ranked data.

Instead of the *r* coefficient, researchers use the **Spearman rho (r_s)** correlation coefficient for nonlinear data and for other types of data measured on categorical (rank-ordered) scales. When you measure one variable on a continuous (interval or ratio) scale and the other is a categorical, dichotomous scale, the correlation statistic should not be the *r* but the **point-biserial correlation**. Assume that a researcher correlates continuous, interval scores on depression with males and females (a dichotomous variable). A point-biserial correlation statistic is used by converting the dichotomous variable (males, females) into numerical scores by assigning males = 1 and females = 2. Using these numbers and the formula for ordinal data, the researcher calculates the point-biserial correlation coefficient that measures the degree and direction of association between males and females on depression.

A variation of this theme of using different types of scales in assessing the association between two variables is the phi coefficient. The **phi coefficient** is used to determine the degree and direction of association when *both* variable measures are dichotomous. In our example, males and females might be correlated with drug usage (no and yes). In this situation, the researcher also converts both dichotomous variables to numeric values (males = 1, females = 2; no to drugs = 1, yes to drugs = 2) and then uses the phi coefficient formula for converted scores.

What Is the Degree and Strength of Association?

Degree of association means that the association between two variables or sets of scores is a correlation coefficient of −1.00 to +1.00, with 0.00 indicating no linear association at all. This association between two sets of scores reflects whether there is a consistent, predictable association between the scores (Gravetter & Wallnau, 2007).

Correlational researchers interpret the magnitude and direction of the correlations. With numbers indicating strength and valence signs indicating direction (+1.00 to −1.00), the statistic provides a measure of the magnitude of the relationship between two variables. Although the correlation measures the degree of relationship, many researchers prefer to square the correlation and use the resulting value to measure the strength of the relationship (Gravetter & Wallnau, 2007). In this procedure, researchers calculate the **coefficient of determination**, which assesses the proportion of variability in one variable that can be determined or explained by a second variable. For example, if you obtain $r = +.70$ (or $-.70$), squaring this value leads to $r^2 = .49$ (or 49%). This means that almost half (49%) of the variability in Y can be determined or explained by X. For example, we might say that parents' education level explains 49% of students' satisfaction with school ($r^2 = .49$).

Other standards for interpreting the strength of the association also exist. General guidelines indicate whether the size of the coefficient provides meaningful information about the strength of association between two variables. One such guide is available in Cohen and Manion (1994). Consider the following interpretations given the following size of coefficients:

◆ *.20–.35:* When correlations range from .20 to .35, there is only a slight relationship; this relationship may be slightly statistically significant for 100 or more participants. This size of a coefficient may be valuable to explore the interconnection of variables but of little value in prediction studies.

◆ *.35–.65:* When correlations are above .35, they are useful for limited prediction. They are the typical values used to identify variable membership in the statistical procedure of factor analysis (the intercorrelation of variables with a scale), and many correlation coefficients for bivariate relationships fall into this area.

◆ *.66–.85:* When correlations fall into this range, good prediction can result from one variable to the other. Coefficients in this range would be considered very good.

◆ *.86 and above:* Correlations in this range are typically achieved for studies of construct validity or test–retest reliability. In fact, researchers want their reliability and validity test correlations to be this high. When two or more variables are related, correlations this high are seldom achieved, and if they result, then two variables actually measure the same underlying trait and should probably be combined in data analysis.

Given a coefficient for the strength of the association between two variables, how do we know if the value is meaningful? One way to find out is to use significance testing. In hypothesis testing, we are selecting a sample and drawing inferences from the sample to the population. For correlational research, the null hypothesis would be that there is no association or relationship among the scores in the population. Testing this hypothesis involves setting a level of significance, calculating the test statistic, examining whether the correlation coefficient value falls into the region of rejection, and rejecting or failing to reject the null hypothesis. In correlational research, the r squared expresses the magnitude of association between the two variables or sets of scores. As such, it represents the effect size—another means of assessing the magnitude of the relationship regardless of hypothesis testing.

Multiple Variable Analysis

In many correlation studies, researchers predict outcomes based on more than one predictor variable. Thus, they need to account for the impact of each variable. Two multiple variable analysis approaches are partial correlations and multiple regression.

Partial Correlations

In many research situations, we study three, four, or five variables as predictors of outcomes. The type of variable called a *mediating* or *intervening variable* "stands between" the independent and dependent variables and influences both of them. This variable is different from a control variable that influences the outcome in an experiment. We use **partial correlations** to determine the amount of variance that an intervening variable explains in *both* the independent and dependent variables.

A picture of two variables followed by the inclusion of a third can help explain partial correlations. Examine Figure 11.3, which shows a bivariate (two variable) correlation on the left-hand side and a partial (three variable) correlation analysis on the right-hand side. Assume that a researcher conducts a study correlating time-on-task with achievement for middle school children. After gathering the scores, our investigator calculates a correlation coefficient with the results of $r = .50$. Figure 11.3 indicates this association as well as the r squared, or the proportion of common shared variance between the two variables. However, the situation is more complicated. Student motivation, a third

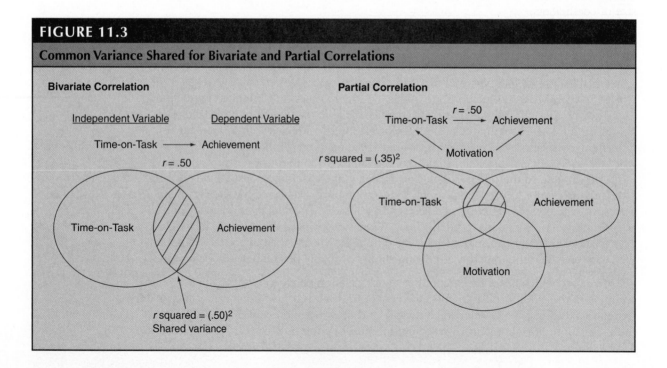

FIGURE 11.3

Common Variance Shared for Bivariate and Partial Correlations

variable, may also influence both the students' time-on-task as well as their achievement in class. The researcher identifies this third variable based on a literature review and a study of past theories that have shown factors likely to influence student achievement. In the design, motivation needs to be removed so that the relationship between time-on-task and achievement can be more clearly determined. A partial correlation statistical analysis is used that removes the shared variance in both time-on-task and achievement by motivation. The mathematical calculations for this coefficient are available in statistics books; it is based on the correlation coefficients among all three variables and their variances. The hatch-marked area indicates this shared variance left after removing the effects of motivation, and the r squared $= (.35)^2$ is now lower than the original correlation of $r = .50$.

Multiple Regression

Correlation researchers use the correlation statistic to predict future scores. To see what impact multiple variables have on an outcome, researchers use regression analysis. We will start with understanding a regression line and then move on to analysis using regression.

A **regression line** is a line of "best fit" for all of the points of scores on the graph. This line comes the closest to all of the points on the plot and it is calculated by drawing a line that minimizes the squared distance of the points from the line. Examine Figure 11.4, which is the same graph used in Figure 11.1, indicating the association between "hours of Internet use per week" and "depression scores" for middle school students. Figure 11.4 now contains additional information: more detail about the regression line. You can see how the line comes close to all of the points on the graph, and we draw it at a diagonal consistent with the positive correlation between Internet use and depression scores.

The calculation of this line holds value for predicting scores on the outcome (i.e., depression) with knowledge about the predictor (i.e., hours of Internet use per week). Based on a mathematical formula, a researcher can calculate an equation that expresses this line:

$$Y \text{(predicted)} = b(X) + a$$

where

  Y = predicted score on depression

  X = actual score on number of hours of Internet use

  b = slope of the regression line (called the unstandardized regression coefficient)

  a = the intercept or a constant, the value of the predicted Y (depression) score
     when $X = 0$.

FIGURE 11.4

Simple Regression Line

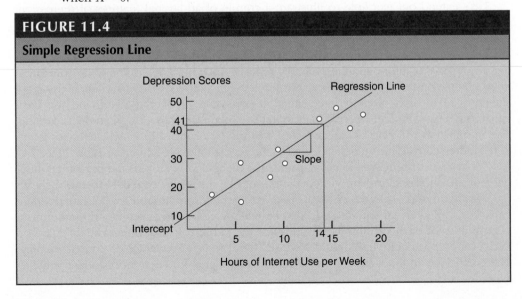

We would expect an individual who uses the Internet 14 hours per week to have a depression score of 41. This score can be estimated by drawing a vertical line from the score for the X-axis variable up to the regression line and over to the Y-axis variable. Alternatively, using the regression formula,

$$\text{If } a = 6, \text{ b} = 2.5, \text{ and } X = 14$$

$$\text{Then } Y(\text{predicted}) = 2.5(14) + 6 = 41$$

Consider a more complicated situation, where multiple independent variables may combine to correlate with a dependent variable. **Multiple regression** (or **multiple correlation**) is a statistical procedure for examining the combined relationship of *multiple* independent variables with a single dependent variable. In regression, the variation in the dependent variable is explained by the variance of each independent variable (the relative importance of each predictor), as well as the combined effect of all independent variables (the proportion of criterion variance explained by all predictors), designated by R^2 (Kline, 1998). Similar to the regression equation mentioned earlier, predicted scores on an outcome can be generated using an equation that is similar to the simple regression equation, but it includes additional predictors. The equation is:

$$Y(\text{predicted}) = b_1(X1) + b_2(X2) + a$$

where

Y = the predicted scores

b_1 = a constant for the slope of $X1$ (b_2, for $X2$)

a = the intercept

Assume that the slope for b_1 = .24 and b_2 = .19 and the intercept is 10.77. The prediction equation for the two independent variables would be:

$$Y(\text{predicted}) = .24\,(X1) + .19\,(X2) + 10.77$$

If we want to predict an individual's score on a quiz, for example, from time-on-task ($X1$) and prior achievement ($X2$), we would substitute their scores on these two measures into the formula. Assume that time-on-task is 10 and prior achievement is 70. The predicted score of this combination of the two independent variables would be:

$$Y(\text{predicted}) = .24\,(10) + .19\,(70) + 10.77$$

Let's extend our example to illustrate a couple of additional features of regression. Suppose that time-on-task, motivation, prior achievement in the subject area, and peer friends are predicted to influence student learning (or achievement) for at-risk high school students. We may want to know how these variables *in combination* predict student learning. Knowing this information is probably more realistic than determining the correlation between time-on-task and achievement; it models the complex world in which high school students live. In short, a complicated situation exists, and we need to determine how each variable individually and in combination helps explain the variation in student learning. This information will help us isolate factors that can be changed in a high school or issues to be addressed with the students. Examine the regression table shown in Table 11.2.

We can calculate regression coefficients for each variable, assess the combined influence of all variables, and provide a picture of the results. A **regression table** shows the overall amount of variance explained in a dependent variable by all independent variables, called R^2 (R squared). It also shows the regression weight—the amount of contribution of each variable controlling for the variance of all other variables, called beta—for each variable. In Table 11.2 we see four predictor variables of student learning. The coefficients in the right column are the beta weights for each independent variable.

TABLE 11.2

Sample Regression Table: Student Learning (Outcome Variable)

Predictor Variables	Beta
Time-on-task	.11
Motivation	.18
Prior achievement	.20*
Peer friend influence	.05

$R = .38$
R squared $= .14$
$*p < .05$
$N = 90$

A **beta weight** is a coefficient indicating the magnitude of prediction for a variable after removing the effects of all other predictors. The coefficient of a beta weight identifies the strength of the relationship of a predictor variable of the outcomes and enables a researcher to compare (in data with a normal distribution) the strength of one predictor variable with the strength of other predictors. Standardized regression coefficients are typically used for such purposes as choosing variables and assessing their relative importance (Bring, 1994). A beta weight is reported in standardized form, a z score standardizes the measures so that all variables can be compared, and is interpreted like a Pearson r, with a value typically from +1.00 to −1.00. Note that regression tables often report a B value (an unstandardized coefficient), but these values, while useful in a prediction formula, do not allow researchers to compare the relative strength of each independent variable as a predictor because the value may be scored in different units. For example, one variable may be scored on a 5-point scale and another one on a 3-point scale.

As seen in Table 11.2, the predictor "prior achievement" explains the most variance, followed by "motivation." Below the table we see the correlation of the combination of variables (the multiple correlation designated by R) of .38 and the proportion of variability explained in the dependent variables by all of the predictors (R^2) of .14. Recall that the value R^2, called the *coefficient of determination,* represents the proportion of variability explained by the independent variables in the dependent variable. In reporting results, correlational researchers should indicate not only the statistical significance of the test, but also the effect size variance, R^2.

Meta-Analysis

In another extension of correlation research, authors integrate the findings of many (primary source) research studies in a **meta-analysis** by evaluating the results of individual studies and deriving an overall numeric index of the magnitude of results. The intent of this research is to summarize the results of many studies.

The process for conducting a meta-analysis follows systematic steps. The researcher locates studies on a single topic and notes the results for all of the studies. Then the researcher calculates an overall result for all of the studies and reports this information. By using this process, the investigator synthesizes the literature, providing a secondary source of primary research reports.

An illustration of a meta-analysis study as well as the difference between a primary and secondary source of information is seen in Figure 11.5. In the top section we see the first page of a *primary source* research report, an investigation by Smetana and Asquith

FIGURE 11.5

Example of a Primary Source (Journal Article) and a Secondary Source (Meta-Analysis)

**Adolescents' and Parents' Conceptions of
Parental Authority and Personal Autonomy**

Judith G. Smetana and Pamela Asquith
University of Rochester

SMETANA, JUDITH G., and ASQUITH, PAMELA. *Adolescents' and Parents' Conceptions of Parental Authority and Personal Autonomy.* CHILD DEVELOPMENT, 1994, 65, 1147–1162. Conceptions of parental authority and ratings of adolescent-parent conflict were assessed in 68 sixth, eighth, and tenth graders and their parents. Boundaries of adolescent personal jurisdiction and conflict over these boundaries were examined. Participants judged the legitimacy of parental authority and rated the frequency and intensity of conflict regarding 24 hypothetical moral, conventional, personal, multifaceted (e.g., containing conventional and personal components), prudential, and friendship issues. Adolescents and parents agreed that parents should retain authority regarding moral and conventional issues. Parents treated multifaceted, friendship, prudential, and personal issues as more contingent on parental authority than did adolescents, based on conventional, prudential, and psychological reasons, whereas adolescents treated these issues as under personal jurisdiction, based on personal concerns. Personal reasoning and judgments increased with age. Multifaceted issues were discussed more than all other issues, but moral and conventional conflicts were more intense than all other conflicts. The findings are discussed in terms of previous research on parental authority and adolescent-parent conflict during adolescence.

◄— The original article as a
primary source of
information
(Smetana & Asquith,
1994)

A meta-analysis
as a secondary
source
of information
(Laursen, Coy, &
Collins, 1998)

Table 2 Parent-Adolescent Conflict Effect Size Estimates for Samples Included in Age Meta-Analyses

| | Effect Size Estimates | | | | | | | | | | | |
| | Early and Mid-adolescence | | | | Mid- and Late Adolescence | | | | Early and Late Adolescence | | | |
Study	n	Total r	Rate r	Affect r	n	Total r	Rate r	Affect r	n	Total r	Rate r	Affect r
Blase (1989)	63	.05	.00	.10	77	.08	.00	.15	52	−.02	.00	−.04
Block (1937)	352	−.56	−.56		440	.33	.33		264	−.82	−.82	
Carlton-Ford & Collins (1988)	40	−.08	−.08		40	.08	.08		40	−.08	−.08	
Connor et al. (1954)					119	.31	.31					
Flannery et al. (1991)	85	.22		.22								
Furman & Buhrmester (1992)	250	−.01	−.01		337	.14	.14		355	−.15	−.15	
Galambos & Almeida (1992)	66	−.09		−.09								
Greene & Grimsley (1990)	72	.13		.13								
Hagan et al. (1992)[a]	138	-.08	−.14	.09								
Inoff-Germain et al. (1988)	60	.00	−.04	.04								
Johnstone (1975)					1,317	−.01	−.01					
Kahlbaugh (1992)	20	.07	.04	.11								
Kahlbaugh et al. (1994)	41	.04	.11	−.04								
Khatri et al. (1993)	171	.29	.29									
Laursen (1993)					685	.00	.00	.00				
Lempers & Clark-Lempers (1992)	799	−.16	−.16		760	.06	.06		619	−.23	−.23	
Noack (1993)					38	.06	.06					
Papini et al. (1989)	193	.00		.00	201	.07		.07	164	−.08		−.08
Rajalu (1991)					365	−.05	−.05					
Schoenleber (1988)	44	−.22	−.22		44	.00	.00		44	−.22	−.22	
Sidhu & Singh (1987)					64	.03	.03					
Smetana (1989)	52	−.16	−.16		50	.19	.19		50	−.32	−.32	
Smetana (1991)	180	.07	.00	.15	158	.16	.16	.16	172	−.08	−.15	.00
Smetana & Asquith (1994)	68	.09	.12	.00								
Smetana et al. (1991)	28	.00	.00	.00								
Wierson et al. (1990)	122	.00	.00	.00								
Wierson & Forehand (1992)	184	.14		.14								

Note: n = participants included in effect size estimates. *r* = effect size estimate. Positive *r* values in contrasts of early adolescence and mid-adolescence, and in contrasts of mid-adolescence and late adolescence indicate greater conflict during mid-adolescence. Positive *r* values in contrasts of early adolescence and late adolescence indicate greater conflict during late adolescence.
[a] The number of participants reported for conflict rate and conflict affect differed; values reported here are averages.

Source: From "Reconsidering Changes in Parent-Child Conflict across Adolescence: A Meta-Analysis," by B. Laursen, K. C. Coy, & W. A. Collins, 1998, *Child Development, 69,* p. 823. Reprinted with permission of S.R.C.D.

(1994). They examine the types of parent authority and ratings of adolescent–parent conflict for 68 sixth, eighth, and tenth graders and their parents.

In the bottom section of Figure 11.5, we see that the original research by Smetana and Asquith (1994) is included as one of 27 studies reported in a *secondary source,* a meta-analysis published by Laursen, Coy, and Collins (1998). The 27 studies shown in the table integrated research examining parent–child conflict changes during early, mid-, and late adolescence. Overall, the authors conclude from the meta-analysis that little support exists for the commonly held view that parent–child conflict rises and then falls across adolescence. Because the primary source research report by Smetana and Asquith (1994) shows only a small positive change in parent–child conflict during early and mid-adolescence, relying on this single study would present false conclusions and meta-analysis is warranted.

POTENTIAL ETHICAL ISSUES IN CONDUCTING CORRELATIONAL RESEARCH

Correlational research is ideal in providing context, in dealing with many variables, and in establishing the total pattern of relationships (Brown & Hedges, 2009). However, ethical issues arise that the educational researcher must consider. These issues relate to data collection, data analysis, and data reporting and presenting. Ethical issues are considered in Brown and Hedges (2009), Lesser and Nordenghaug (2004), and Ramanathan (2006) as well as in some statistics texts. Brown and Hedges (2009) devote an entire section of their chapter to ethical issues in meta-analysis.

In correlational data analysis, it is unethical to not have measured appropriate controls (e.g., age, gender, race, and others). This is especially a problem if controls are omitted that others have pointed out. To help with this problem, use a conceptual model or a theory to guide the selection of variables for measurement. In this way, all possible predictors can be considered. In addition, the study needs sufficient sample size in data collection for adequate power, and to meet the assumptions required of specific statistical tests used in the study.

In terms of data analysis, educational researchers are cautioned about editing data or making up data. For example, researchers breach ethics when they state that they have found cause and effect, or even probable cause and effect, when their results only show patterns of relationships. The failure to analyze and report effect sizes in addition to null hypothesis significance testing can also be considered unethical, since this guideline has been clearly established in the APA manual (APA, 2010). Further, an unusual amount of measurement error (sample results different from population estimates) can cast doubt on the use of analysis in such procedures as factor analysis.

In data reporting and presenting, several additional ethical issues relate to correlational research. Educational researchers should not plagiarize the words of others, fail to report contradictory findings, publish the same evidence many times, and omit negative findings and alternative explanations. At a broader level, the ethics of good scholarship work suggest a willingness to share data with others (especially such as in the high stakes areas of assessment skills for students), publishing one's work in scholarly journals and not letting research reports sit unused in an office drawer, and including key philosophical assumptions about the research in the write-up.

In meta-analysis, Brown and Hedges (2009) point to the ethical concerns of researchers failing to properly abstract and analyze the findings of multiple studies, and how this may lead to erroneous results. They are also concerned about the varying quality of correlational studies used in meta-analyses, and how it is unethical for the researcher to exclude studies because of their small sample sizes and insignificant results.

In the scenario to follow, in Box 11.1, you will be asked to respond to a situation that often arises in correlational research and weigh in on the ethics of the situation:

BOX 11.1 | Ethical Dilemma

Describing Results Inappropriately

A key concept in correlational research is understanding the difference between causation by an independent variable on a dependent variable and an association or a relationship. Because all variables cannot be tightly controlled in a correlational study, the researcher cannot make claims about causation (or probable causation because nothing can be absolutely proved). Instead claims of association or relationship, a lesser standard, can only apply. This impacts how educational researchers write up the results from their correlational studies. It is considered to be an ethical problem when the write-up misconstrues the result to be cause-and-effect. How would you suggest that a researcher rewrite the result "It was found that prior academic success and support systems for freshman students caused (or explained) their high grade point averages in college."?

WHAT ARE THE STEPS IN CONDUCTING A CORRELATIONAL STUDY?

From our discussion about the key characteristics of correlational research, we can begin to see steps emerge that you might use when planning or conducting a study. The following steps illustrate the process of conducting correlational research.

Step 1. Determine If a Correlational Study Best Addresses the Research Problem

A correlational study is used when a need exists to study a problem requiring the identification of the direction and degree of association between two sets of scores. It is useful for identifying the type of association, explaining complex relationships of multiple factors that explain an outcome, and predicting an outcome from one or more predictors. Correlational research does not "prove" a relationship; rather, it indicates an association between two or more variables.

Because you are not comparing groups in a correlational study, you use research questions rather than hypotheses. Sample questions in a correlational study might be:

◆ Is creativity related to IQ test scores for elementary children? (associating two variables)
◆ What factors explain a student teacher's ethical behavior during the student-teaching experience? (exploring a complex relationship)
◆ Does high school class rank predict a college student's grade point average in the first semester of college? (prediction)

Step 2. Identify Individuals to Study

Ideally, you should randomly select the individuals to generalize results to the population, and seek permissions to collect the data from responsible authorities and from the institutional review board. The group needs to be of adequate size for use of the correlational statistic, such as $N = 30$; larger sizes contribute to less error variance and better claims of representativeness. For instance, a researcher might study 100 high school athletes to correlate the extent of their participation in different sports and their use of tobacco. A narrow range of scores from a population may influence the strength of the correlation relationships. For example, if you look at the relationship between height of basketball players and number of baskets in a game, you might find a strong relationship among K–12th graders. But if you are selecting NBA players, this relationship may be significantly weaker.

Step 3. Identify Two or More Measures for Each Individual in the Study

Because the basic idea of correlational research is to compare participants in this single group on two or more characteristics, measures of variables in the research question need to be identified (e.g., literature search of past studies), and instruments that measure the variables need to be obtained. Ideally, these instruments should have proven validity and reliability. You can obtain permissions from publishers or authors to use the instruments. Typically one variable is measured on each instrument, but a single instrument might contain both variables being correlated in the study.

Step 4. Collect Data and Monitor Potential Threats

The next step is to administer the instruments and collect at least two sets of data from each individual. The actual research design is quite simple as a visual presentation. Two data scores are collected for each individual until you obtain scores from each person in the study. This is illustrated with three individuals as follows:

Participants:	Measures or Observations:	
Individual 1	01	02
Individual 2	01	02
Individual 3	01	02

This situation holds for describing the association between two variables or for predicting a single outcome from a single predictor variable. You collect multiple independent variables to understand complex relationships.

A small sample database for 10 college students is shown in Table 11.3. The investigator seeks to explain the variability in first-year grade point averages (GPAs) for these 10 graduate students in education. Assume that our investigator has identified these four predictors in a review of the literature. In past studies, these predictors have positively correlated with achievement in college. The researcher can obtain information for the predictor variables from the college admissions office. The criterion, GPA during the first year, is available from the registrar's office. In this regression study, the researcher seeks to identify which one factor or combination of factors best explains the variance in first-year graduate-student GPAs. A review of this data shows that the scores varied on each variable, with more variation among GRE scores than among recommendation and

TABLE 11.3

Example of Data Collected in a Regression Study

Student	College GPA	GRE Scores (Composite)	Strength of Recommendations (1–10 scale)	Fit to Program (1–10 scale)	First-Semester GPA in Graduate School (4-point scale)
Lindsey	3.5	950	8	6	3.10
Palmira	3.6	1120	9	7	3.60
Benito	3.0	1000	9	8	3.10
Ren	3.8	1250	8	9	3.70
Lucy	3.2	1150	7	7	3.40
Kent	3.5	1000	8	8	3.10
Jason	3.2	900	6	6	3.00
Andrew	3.4	950	7	7	3.10
Dave	3.9	1200	9	9	3.80
Giselle	3.7	1140	8	8	3.70

fit-to-program scores. Also, it appears that higher college GPA and GRE scores are positively related to higher first-semester GPAs.

In this example, because the data were available from admissions offices, the researcher need not be overly concerned about procedures that threaten the validity of the scores. However, a potential for restricted range of scores—little variation in scores—certainly exists. Other factors that might affect the researcher's ability to draw valid inferences from the results are the lack of standard administration procedures, the conditions of the testing situation, and the expectations of participants.

Step 5. Analyze the Data and Represent the Results

The objective in correlational research is to describe the degree of association between two or more variables. The investigator looks for a pattern of responses and uses statistical procedures to determine the strength of the relationship as well as its direction. A statistically significant relationship, if found, does not imply causation (cause and effect) but merely an association between the variables. More rigorous procedures, such as those used in experiments, can provide better control than those used in a correlational study.

The analysis begins with coding the data and transferring it from the instruments into a computer file. Then the researcher needs to determine the appropriate statistic to use. An initial question is whether the data are linearly or curvilinearly related. A scatterplot of the scores (if a bivariate study) can help determine this question. Also, consider whether:

◆ Only one independent variable is being studied (Pearson's correlation coefficient)
◆ A mediating variable explains both the independent and dependent variables and needs to be controlled (partial correlation coefficient)

◆ More than one independent variable needs to be studied to explain the variability in a dependent variable (multiple regression coefficient)

Based on the most appropriate statistical test, the researcher next calculates whether the statistic is significant based on the scores. For example, a p value is obtained in a bivariate study by:

◆ Setting the alpha level
◆ Using the critical values of an r table, available in many statistics books
◆ Using degrees of freedom of $N = 2$ with this table
◆ Calculating the observed r coefficient and comparing it with the r-critical value
◆ Rejecting or failing to reject the null hypothesis at a specific significance level, such as $p < 0.05$

In addition, it is useful to also report effect size (r^2). In correlational analysis, the effect size is the Pearson's correlation coefficient squared. In representing the results, the correlational researcher will present a correlation matrix of all variables as well as a statistical table (for a regression study) reporting the R and R^2 values and the beta weights for each variable.

Step 6. Interpret the Results

The final step in conducting a correlational study is interpreting the meaning of the results. This requires discussing the magnitude and the direction of the results in a correlational study, considering the impact of intervening variables in a partial correlation study, interpreting the regression weights of variables in a regression analysis, and developing a predictive equation for use in a prediction study.

In all of these steps, an overall concern is whether your data support the theory, the hypotheses, or questions. Further, the researcher considers whether the results confirm or disconfirm findings from other studies. Also, a reflection is made about whether some of the threats discussed above may have contributed to erroneous coefficients and the steps that might be taken by future researchers to address these concerns.

HOW DO YOU EVALUATE A CORRELATIONAL STUDY?

To evaluate and assess the quality of a good correlational study, authors consider:

◆ An adequate sample size for hypothesis testing.
◆ The display of correlational results in a matrix or graph.
◆ An interpretation about the direction and magnitude of the association between two (or more) variables.
◆ An assessment of the magnitude of the relationship based on the coefficient of determination, p values, effect size, or the size of the coefficient.
◆ The choice of an appropriate statistic for analysis.
◆ The identification of predictor and the criterion variables.
◆ If a visual model of the relationships is advanced, the researcher indicates the expected direction of the relationships among variables, or the predicted direction based on observed data.
◆ The clear identification of the statistical procedures.

KEY IDEAS IN THE CHAPTER

The Definition, Use, and Development of Correlational Research

In some educational situations, neither the treatment nor the ability to manipulate the conditions are conducive to an experiment. In this case, educators turn to a correlational design. In correlational research, investigators use a correlation statistical technique to describe and measure the degree of association (or relationship) between two or more variables or sets of scores. You use a correlational design to study the relationship between two or more variables or to predict an outcome.

The history of correlational research draws on the themes of the origin and development of the correlation statistical test and the procedures for using and interpreting the statistical test. Statisticians first identified the procedures for calculating the correlation statistics in the late 19th century. In the late 1800s, Karl Pearson developed the familiar correlation formula we use today. With the use of multiple statistical procedures such as factor analysis, reliability estimates, and regression, researchers can test elaborate models of variables using correlational statistical procedures.

Types of Correlational Designs

Although a correlation is a statistic, its use in research has contributed to a specific research design called *correlational research*. This research has taken two primary forms of research design: explanation and prediction. An explanatory correlational design explains or clarifies the degree of association among two or more variables at one point in time. Researchers are interested in whether two variables co-vary, in which a change in one variable is reflected in changes in the other. An example is whether motivation is associated with academic performance. In the second form of design, a prediction design, the investigator identifies variables that will positively predict an outcome or criterion. In this form of research, the researcher uses one or more predictor variables and a criterion (or outcome) variable. A prediction permits us to forecast future performance, such as whether a student's GPA in college can be predicted from his or her high school performance.

Key Characteristics of Correlational Designs

Underlying both of these designs are key characteristics of correlational research. Researchers create displays of scores correlated for participants. These displays are scatterplots, a graphic representation of the data, and correlation matrices, a table that shows the correlation among all the variables. To interpret correlations, researchers examine the positive or negative direction of the correlation of scores, a plot of the distribution of scores to see if they are normally or nonnormally distributed, the degree of association between scores, and the strength of the association of the scores. When more than two variables are correlated, the researcher is interested in controlling for the effects of the third variable, and in examining a prediction equation of multiple variables that explains the outcome.

Ethical Issues in Conducting Correlational Research

Ethical issues arise in many phases of the correlational research process. In data collection, ethics relate to adequate sample size, lack of control, and the inclusion of as many predictors as possible. In data analysis, researchers need a complete statement of findings to include effect size and the use of appropriate statistics. Analysis cannot include making up data. In recording and presenting studies, the write-up should include statements about relationships rather than causation, a willingness to share data, and publishing in scholarly outlets.

Steps in Conducting a Correlational Study

Steps in conducting a correlational study are to use the design for associating variables or making predictions, to identify individuals to study, to specify two or more measures for each individual, to collect data and monitor potential threats to the validity of the scores, to analyze the data using the correlation statistic for either continuous or categorical data, and to interpret the strength and the direction of the results.

Criteria for Evaluating a Correlational Study

Evaluate a correlational study in terms of the strength of its data collection, analysis, and interpretations. These factors include adequate sample size, good presentations in graphs and matrices, clear procedures, and an interpretation about the relationship among variables.

USEFUL INFORMATION FOR PRODUCERS OF RESEARCH

◆ Identify whether you plan to examine the association between or among variables or use correlational research to make predictions about an outcome.
◆ Plot on a graph the association between your variables so that you can determine the direction, form, and strength of the association.
◆ Use appropriate correlational statistics in your design based on whether the data are continuous or categorical and whether the form of the data is linear or nonlinear.
◆ Present a correlation matrix of the Pearson coefficients in your study.

USEFUL INFORMATION FOR CONSUMERS OF RESEARCH

◆ Recognize that a correlation study is not as rigorous as an experiment because the researcher can only control statistically for variables rather than physically manipulate variables. Correlational studies do not "prove" relationships; rather, they indicate an association between or among variables or sets of scores.
◆ Correlational studies are research in which the investigator seeks to explain the association or relationship among variables or to predict outcomes.
◆ Realize that all correlational studies, no matter how advanced the statistics, use a correlation coefficient as their base for analysis. Understanding the intent of this coefficient helps you determine the results in a correlational study.

ADDITIONAL RESOURCES YOU MIGHT EXAMINE

For additional detailed discussions about the correlation statistic and more advanced statistics, see:

Gravetter, F. J., & Wallnau, L. B. (2007). *Statistics for the behavioral sciences* (7th ed.). Belmont, CA: Wadsworth/Thomson Learning.

Salkind, N. J. (2010). *Statistics for people who (think they) hate statistics* (4th ed.). Thousand Oaks, CA: Sage.

For discussions about more advanced correlational procedures, especially regression analysis, see:

Pedhazur, E. J. (1997). *Multiple regression in behavioral research: Explanation and prediction* (3rd ed.). Ft. Worth, TX: Harcourt Brace College Publishers.

For a good discussion about ethical issues in correlational research, consult:

Brown, B. L., & Hedges, D. (2009). Use and misuse of quantitative methods. In D. M. Mertens & P. E. Ginsberg (Eds.), *The handbook of social research ethics* (pp. 373–390). Thousand Oaks, CA: Sage.

Example of a Correlational Study

Examine the following published journal article that is a correlational study. Marginal notes indicate the major characteristics of correlational research highlighted in this chapter. The illustrative study is:

The Influence of Parental Attachment on the College Adjustment of White, Black, and Latina/Hispanic Women: A Cross-Cultural Investigation

Mickey C. Melendez
Nancy Blanco Melendez

Correlational Design Characteristics in Marginal Annotations

Although race and parental attachment are concepts that have been widely researched, few studies have explored how these variables manifest themselves among women or influence their adjustment to college. This study examined how parental attachment effected college adjustment among White, Black, and Latina/Hispanic women attending an urban commuter college. Attachment patterns were measured using the Parental Attachment Questionnaire (Kenny, 1994), and college adjustment was assessed using the Student Adaptation to College Questionnaire (Baker & Siryk, 1989). Results revealed that parental attachment significantly predicted aspects of college adjustment differentially for each racial subgroup. Implications regarding the experiences of diverse groups of female students attending large urban commuter institutions are discussed.

College student adjustment and retention has been a focus of college administrators and student development professionals for decades (Tinto, 2006). Currently, only 55% of all undergraduates who enrolled at 4-year institutions in 1995–1996 with the goal of obtaining a bachelor's degree completed the degree within 6 years at the same institution (Lotkowski, Robbins, & Noeth, 2004). (01)

Moreover, enrollment, retention, and graduation statistics tend to be heavily influenced by demographic variables such as race/ethnicity and gender. Latina/Hispanic and Black students, although demonstrating some improvement in college enrollment and graduation rates in recent decades, are still greatly underrepresented in higher education when compared to White students (Arbona & Nora, 2007). During the 1999–2000 academic year 34% of all Latina/Hispanic and 40% of all Black students enrolled in 4-year colleges as opposed to 46% of all White students (Lotkowski et al., 2004). More recently Whites represented 72% of enrollees at all 4-year colleges nationally, whereas Blacks represented 11% and Latina/Hispanics represented 6% of enrollees nationally (Horn, 2006). (02)

Graduation and retention rates across culture and gender were equally concerning. Among White students, graduation rates were 12% higher than for Latina/Hispanic students and 6% higher than for Black students on average (Horn, 2006). Latina/Hispanic students who attended college reported retention rates of only 34% (Brown, Santiago, & Lopez, 2003). Cross-gender comparisons also revealed that female students tended to graduate at higher rates from college than did their male peers across the board (Horn). Moreover, in 2002–2003 women earned 60% of all associate's degrees, 58% of all bachelor's degrees and 59% of all master's degrees across the nation (Knapp et al., 2005). (03)

Examining the combined impact of gender and culture, U.S. Department of Education (Institute of Educational Sciences, 2004) statistics showed that "among certain minority groups, female representation among bachelor's degree recipients was even higher" (p. 80). For example, Black and Latina/Hispanic females earned 66% and 60% of the degrees conferred, respectively, compared to males of their respective racial/ethnic groups. Comparatively, Asian/Pacific Islander and White females earned a slightly lower proportion (55% and 57%, respectively) of the degrees conferred compared to males of their respective racial/ethnic groups. However, when compared directly to their White female counter parts, non-Asian women of color (i.e., Latina/Hispanic and Black) graduated college in numbers and at rates lower than their White female counterparts (Integrated Post Secondary Education Data System, 2005; National Collegiate Athletic Association, 2007) suggesting that women of color, although out performing their male counterparts, still face serious challenges to their adjustment, retention, and graduation from college compared to their White female peers. (04)

Mickey C. Melendez is Assistant Professor at John Jay College of Criminal Justice, City University of New York.
Nancy Blanco Melendez is a psychologist in independent practice.
Correspondence concerning this article should be addressed to Mickey C. Melendez, Department of Counseling, John Jay College of Criminal Justice, City University of New York, 445 West 59th St., 3149 North Hall, New York, NY 10019; mimelendez@jjay.cuny.edu

(05)   Although compelling, cross-cultural and cross-gender differences in college enrollment and success rates are not new to the college adjustment literature. However, the multifaceted nature of college adjustment and retention for students of color requires closer examination of the various factors involved. Research has identified many variables that influence students' ability to adjust to college life, including such things as finances, health, loneliness, interpersonal skills, difficulty adjusting to change, and development of personal autonomy (Herzog, 2008; Kaczmarek, Matlock, & Franco, 1990; Pascarella & Terenzini, 2005). Research has also identified target groups of students who have the most difficulty adjusting to college life. For example, first generation college students typically experience greater difficulty adjusting to college than do their counterparts who have had family members with college experience as role models (Pascarella, Pierson, Wolniak, & Terenzini, 2004; Pike & Kuh, 2005). Moreover, in the literature college student–athletes (Melendez, 2008, in press; Parham, 1993) and international students (Cemalcilar & Falbo, 2008; Chiu, 1995) have also reported greater difficulty in adjusting to college.

(06)   Adjustment to college is clearly a function of numerous psychological, social, emotional, developmental, and cultural factors (Guiffrida, 2006; Tinto, 2006; Zea, Jarama, & Bianchi, 1995), many of which have yet to be adequately researched in the literature. One factor of particular interest to college counselors and administrators in recent years has been parental attachment. Bowlby (1973) defined attachment as any form of behavior in which a person seeks to attain or maintain proximity to another individual who is perceived to be better able to cope with the world. Attachment to a parent or caregiver is therefore conceptualized as a normative and universal mechanism to assure safety and security from which to explore one's environment. However, although attachment may serve as protective mechanism in infancy and childhood, in the context of adolescent development, separation and individuation, and the adjustment to college, attachment theory presumes a great many challenges for students who may be separating from parents and family for the first time. Challenges typically faced by college students, such as difficulties with romantic relationships, redefining relationships with family and friends, making connections to the college community, coping with alienation, stress, depression, anxiety, and making important career decisions (Herzog, 2008; Melendez, 2008; Pascarella & Terenzini, 2005), may be compounded by separation from family and may require new adaptational resources to overcome (Gloria, Castellanos, Lopez, & Rosales, 2005). Furthermore, external variables, such as relationships with parents and friends, and internal variables, such as self-esteem, are especially helpful when facing the challenges of college (Kenny & Rice, 1995).

(07)   The presumed universality of attachment dynamics has also been called into question, suggesting that cultural/environmental influences may play a larger role in determining normative attachment behaviors than previously theorized. Only recently have the tenets of attachment theory been looked at through a multicultural perspective and the universality of the core assumption been critiqued (LeVine & Miller, 1990; Rothbaum, Weisz, Pott, Miyake, & Morelli, 2000). "Western investigators have been blinded to alternative conceptions of relatedness" (Rothbaum et al., p. 1093), indicating that the dynamics of attachment may be less universal and more culture dependent and specific than originally theorized. Moreover, "if basic assumptions about attachment are not the same for people of different cultures, then it is inevitable that misconceptions about relationships will occur" (Rothbaum et al., p. 1101).

(08)   In light of the research regarding gender, ethnicity, attachment, and college adjustment, the current study more closely examined the potential relationship between attachment patterns and college adjustment among a diverse sample of women (Black, Latina/Hispanic, and White) attending a diverse urban commuter college. Women as a whole have not been adequately studied in the literature, and the current literature has provided little to understanding how women, and especially women of color, are influenced by attachment patterns or how these variables may influence adjustment to college.

Attachment and Adolescent Development

(09)   Attachment theory has emerged as one of the most influential theories of relationships in contemporary psychology. Bowlby's and Ainsworth's renowned contributions in understanding child development have greatly influenced the conceptualization of attachment and development across the lifespan. Attachment theory also looks at the role that powerful affectional relationships play in shaping development throughout the lifespan. The two main premises of attachment theory are that humans are innately programmed to seek closeness to others (and presumably with their parents),

thereby insuring human survival, and that humans develop internal working models of themselves and others. Attachments, formed during infancy and childhood, are believed to serve as a framework for experiencing other relationships throughout the lifespan. The basic framework of attachment theory was established by Bowlby (1969/1982, 1973, 1980) in his classic trilogy on attachment, separation, and loss and was later supplemented by Ainsworth's systematic observations and classification of attachment patterns (Ainsworth, 1989; Ainsworth, Blehar, Waters, & Wall, 1978).

Researchers have supported the idea that adolescents who are securely attached to their parents   (10)
are more likely to experience better adjustment to college, including better social, academic, and emotional adjustment (Bradford & Lyddon, 1993; Holmbeck & Wandrei, 1993; Larose & Boivin, 1998; Mattanah, Hancock, & Brand, 2004; Rice, Fitzgerald, Whaley, & Gibbs, 1995; Schultheiss & Blustein, 1994). This is consistent with developmental theories that focus on the importance of gaining autonomy and independence from family during the college years (Kenny & Donaldson, 1991; Kenny & Perez, 1996). However, "although researchers have focused on the importance of social supports on the college campus, the value of family and extended family attachments among students of color remains largely unexamined" (Kenny & Perez, 1996, p. 527).

Allen and Land (1999) stated that the adolescent stage of human development is   (11)

> characterized by dramatic increases in differentiation of self and other . . . this in turn may allow adolescents to view themselves as distinct from their caregivers to a far greater extent. . . . Views of oneself in attachment relationships can thus become more internally based and less centered around a particular relationship. (p. 320)

This conceptualization of the adolescent period of development has been greatly influenced by values of individualism and autonomy. Traditionally, adolescence has been understood as a period of inevitable stress and conflict, and in order to facilitate growth, detachment from parents is expected. Although this framework may apply to mainstream adolescents, it may not be appropriate when considering people of color, whose value orientation around relationships is likely to be different than the majority culture. Thus, it is unclear if the period of adolescence is marked by the same experience of differentiation for adolescents of color and whether interdependence or independence may be more adaptive for them.

Women, Attachment, and Adjustment. Studies exploring women's psychological development   (12)
found that women are more likely to be affectively close to parents throughout adolescence (Kenny & Donaldson, 1991). However, although research incorporating women's perspectives has increased in the psychology literature, perspectives of women of color are still often overlooked (Ancis, Szymanski, & Ladany, 2008; Buchanan, Fischer, Tokar, & Yoder, 2008; Tomlinson-Clarke, 1998). From an adjustment perspective, women of color present unique challenges to traditionally trained student development and mental health professionals. Women of color tend to seek mental health services more often than do their male counterparts. This can have negative consequences for women of color, as they are more likely to be misunderstood and pathologized. Women of color also tend to be placed along a developmental continuum that denigrates the importance of cultural values and gender roles that have been stereotypically female. Women in general are viewed as too emotional and not logical. Asian women, compared to White women, are viewed as passive and subservient, the "good wife"; Black women as aggressive and sexualized; Latinas as emotional and hysterical" (Chin, 1994, pp. 205–206).

The heterogeneous groups that comprise women of color have woven an ethnocultural and   (13)
racial tapestry in the U.S. These groups encompass those who define themselves as women of color and whose physical characteristics, experiences of oppression, and social status differ from that of women of the White dominant group—differences usually regarded as denoting deficiency and/or inferiority (Comas-Diaz & Greene, 1994). Women of color may share similar experiences, yet are a heterogeneous group of people who are likely to make diverse choices. These choices may be influenced by the specific socialization around relationship values and attachment patterns.

College Adjustment and Retention

Zea et al. (1995) observed that successful adaptation (adjustment) to college was typically defined   (14)
as "remaining in college, enjoying psychological well being, and performing well academically" (p. 511). Similarly, college retention can be defined as a "complex web of events that shape student leaving and persistence" (Tinto, 2006, p. 1).

(15)   Although academic issues are of central importance to newly matriculating students, the ability to adjust to college life and maintain enrollment is affected by a number of nonacademic, socioemotional challenges such as managing romantic relationships and relationships with family and friends, making connections to the college community, coping with alienation, stress, depression, anxiety, and making important career decisions (Melendez, 2008, Tomlinson-Clarke, 1998). In order to meet these challenges, the development of key adaptational resources can be beneficial, including the incorporation of external support structures such as relationships with parents and friends and internal support structures such as self-esteem (Kenny & Rice, 1995).

(16)   Aspects of college adjustment may also differ across racial/ethnic and gender lines. For example, perceived family support has consistently predicted social adjustment and institutional attachment more strongly for ethnic minority student groups than for Whites (Schneider & Ward, 2003). Additionally, parental education was a significant predictor of college adjustment for females but was not significant for males (Toews & Yazedjian, 2007). The level of commitment to completing a college degree and developing an attachment to an institution may also influence students' college adjustment and retention. Students who make clear and purposeful goals are more likely to persist in attaining their academic goals. Many students entering college with unrealistic goals and expectations and actual experiences, therefore increasing their risk of attrition (Gerdes & Mallinckrodt, 1994).

(17)   The differing perspectives of commuter versus residential college students have also been theorized to influence college adjustment in the literature (Pascarella, Duby, & Iverson, 1983; Torres, 2006; Weissberg, Jenkins, & Harburg, 2003). Commuter students (i.e., students living in their own home or with parents) have a very different experience of the college environment than do more traditional students at residential colleges (Torres, 2006), and are more likely to experience conflicting demands amongst family, work, and school environments (Braxton, Hirschy, & McClendon, 2004).

(18)   *Theoretical Models of Retention.* Several theoretical models of student adjustment, retention, and persistence have been developed in the literature to expound upon the multi-dimensional concept of retention. Tinto's (1975, 1987) student integration model was the first to make explicit connections between environmental influences, namely the academic and social systems within the institution and the principals who molded those systems, and student retention (Tinto, 2006). According to Tinto (2006), a major component of the model was "the concept of integration and the patterns of interaction between the student and other members of the institution, especially during the first year of college" (p. 3). Subsequent research exploring student adjustment and persistence in college has since suggested other profound influences such as race/ethnicity (Arbona & Nora, 2007; Gloria et al., 2005; Torres, 2004), connection to family, church, and community (Nora 2001; Torres, 2004), and residential status (i.e., residential versus non-residential commuter two- and four-year colleges; Pascarella et al., 1983; Weissberg et al., 2003; Weissberg & Owen, 2005).

(19)   More contemporary models of retention, such as Nora and Cabrera's (1996) student adjustment model, regarded persistence as a function of the interactions between students and their various college environments (i.e., social spheres and academic realms); precollege characteristics; and experiences with faculty, students, and staff. Their model also incorporated perspectives more salient to the persistence of minority and nontraditional college students such as the influence academic preparedness and separation from the family. Nora's (2003) student/institution engagement model further emphasized the connection (engagement) between the student and the institution. In addition, certain precollege characteristics (i.e., social and academic experiences in high school, finances, and other home and school based influences) along with other pertinent influences such as emotional support (i.e., encouragement and backing of parents, family, and friends) and logistical/environmental hindrances (i.e., family and/or work responsibilities, commuter issues, etc.) were also theorized to influence students' adjustment to college (Arbona & Nora, 2007).

(20)   Accordingly, for students of color the need to stay connected to parents and other salient familial, cultural, and community support networks is essential to their persistence in college (Nora, 2003; Tinto, 2006) and may equal the importance of engagement between the student and the institution during the first critical year of college. Closer examination of the relationship between familial, cultural, and community support and engagement between student and institution during the first year of college is crucial to understanding the persistence formula for students of color (Guiffrida, 2006).

In sum, although much research has been conducted in the area of college adjustment, per-   (21)
sistence, and retention, less is known about the unique factors that influence college adjustment
among diverse groups of students. Relatively few studies on college/academic adjustment have
included and compared ethnically diverse samples. More research is needed in order to determine
if the variables that influence college adjustment differ across racial and ethnic groups rather than
generalizing findings based on samples that do not represent diverse cultural groups.

Moreover, although the role of gender in the adjustment to college has been more extensively   (22)
researched, little is known about the unique experiences of women of color in adjusting to college.
Based on the literature reviewed for the current study, the following hypotheses were proposed:

1. Scores on college adjustment will be influenced by the variables of race and parental college education.
More specifically, White students will report higher college adjustment scores than their non-White peers.
In addition, student who report higher levels of parental education will also report higher scores on college
adjustment

2. Parental attachment will influence scores on college adjustment. More specifically, parental attachment
will serve as a predictor of scores across the four subscales of college adjustment.

3. Race and parental attachment combined will provide the best model for predicting college adjustment.

Method

Procedure

Participants were recruited from a large nonresidential commuter college on the East coast of the   (23)
United States with a high proportion of first generation college students. Initial data collection
included both males and females recruited through undergraduate counseling department courses
and through psychology department subject pools. However, given the focus of the current study
only females were included in the final participant sample. The final sample comprised exclusively
adolescent/young adult females enrolled in their first year of college.

Survey packets were administered in classrooms by the course instructors on behalf of the prin-   (24)
cipal investigator (PI). The survey packets took approximately 30 minutes to complete.

Participants

The final (total) sample of the current study consisted of 95 female college students of which 24   (25)
were White (25% of sample), 27 were Black (29% of sample), and 44 (46% of sample) were Latina/
Hispanic. The students' ages ranged from 17 to 25 years old, with a mean of 18.66 and median of
18 years old ($SD = 1.667$). All of the students had earned between 0 and 19 credits at the time they
participated in this study and had self-identified as full-time students.

Seventeen participants did not complete the survey packets in a satisfactory manner and were,   (26)
therefore, excluded from the final sample. Further examination of these excluded packets revealed
instruments with completely blank pages, nearly blank pages, or pages that were functionally
incomprehensible.

Among the participants in the final sample, 91% were living with a family member, 68% of the   (27)
students' parents' had not completed college, and 31% were born outside of the United States.

Measures

All participants received a packet of questionnaires consisting of a demographics questionnaire, a   (28)
parental attachment questionnaire, and college adjustment measure. Packets were completed inde-   **Multiple variable
pendently and were returned to the researcher.   analysis**

Demographics. Participants completed a short demographics questionnaire assessing their age,   (29)
race/ethnicity, credits completed, current GPA (if any), parental education, current living status,
and parental marital status.

Parental Attachment. The Parental Attachment Questionnaire (PAQ; Kenny, 1987) is 55-item   (30)
self-reported parental relationship questionnaire. Participants respond to the 55 items by choosing the number on a 5-point Likert-type scale from 1 (*not at all*) to 5 (*very much*) that describes
their relationship with and feelings toward their parents. The PAQ comprises three scales derived
through factor analyses: the Affective Quality of Relationships scale (originally called the Affective

Quality of Attachment scale; 27 items; e.g., "Following time spent together, I leave my parents . . . with warm and positive feelings"), the Parents as Facilitators of Independence scale (originally called the Parental Fostering of Autonomy scale; 14 items; e.g., "In general, my parents . . . support my goals and interests"), and the Parents as a Source of Support scale (originally called the Parental Role in Providing Emotional Support scale; 13 items; e.g., "When I have a serious problem or an important decision to make . . . I contact my family if I am not able to resolve the situation after talking it over with my friends"). One additional item of the PAQ did not contribute to any of the scales and assessed the willingness of students to seek out counselors or other advisors in times of stress.

(31)   The PAQ was designed to adapt Ainsworth et al.'s (1978) conceptualization of attachment for use with adolescents and young adults. It was designed to assess perceived parental availability; understanding, acceptance, respect for individuality; facilitation of independence; interest in interaction with parents and affect towards parents during visits or reunion; student help-seeking behavior in situations of stress; satisfaction with help obtained from parents; and adjustment to separation. Participants repond by providing a single rating of parental attachment rather than two separate attachment scores for each parent.

(32)   Kenny (1987) reported full-scale internal consistency reliability of .93 for the male college student sample and .95 for the female college student sample. Cronbach's alpha was calculated for each of the three scales yielding .96 for the Affective Quality of Attachment scale, and .88 for Parental Role in Providing Emotional Support and Parental Fostering of Autonomy scales (Kenny, 1994). The three factor scales are consistent with Ainsworth et al.'s (1978) conceptualization of attachment.

(33)   Kenny and Donaldson (1992) stated that significant relationships have been found between the PAQ Quality of Attachment scale and Cohesion subscale and the of the Moos Family Environment Scale, the PAQ Parental Fostering of Autonomy scale and the FES Expressiveness, Independence and Control subscales, and the PAQ Parental Role in Providing Emotional Support scale and the FES Cohesion and Expressiveness subscales.

(34)   *Adjustment to College.* The Student Adaptation to College Questionnaire (SACQ; Baker & Siryk, 1989) is a 67-item, self-reported appraisal of adaptation to college. The scale can be administered directly to individuals or to groups. Each subscale has items that are responded to on a 9-point scale from *Doesn't apply to me at all to Applies very closely to me.* There are four SACQ subscales. The Academic Adjustment subscale (24 items) measures the student's success in coping with the various educational demands characteristic of the college experience (e.g., "I have been keeping up to date on my academic work"). The Social Adjustment subscale (20 items) measures the student's success in coping with the interpersonal–societal demands inherent in the college experience (e.g., "I am very involved with social activities in college"). The Personal/Emotional Adjustment subscale (15 items) focuses on the student's intra-psychic state during his or her adjustment to college (e.g., "I have been feeling tense or nervous lately"). The Goal Commitment/Institutional Attachment subscale (15 items) measures a student's degree of commitment to educational goals, and the degree of attachment to the particular institution being attended ("I am pleased with my decision to attend this college in particular"). Each of the four subscales generates a separate score and the four subscale scores can be combined to create a total college adjustment score.

(35)   The SACQ has been employed in a variety of studies with a variety of diverse student populations over the past 20 years (Kaczmarek et al., 1990; Melendez, 2006, 2010; Young & Koplow, 1997). Reliability studies report alpha values ranging "from .81 to .90 for the Academic Adjustment subscale, from .83 to .91 for the Social Adjustment subscale, from .77 to .86 for the Personal Emotional Adjustment subscale, from .85 to .91 for the Attachment subscale, and from .92 to .95 for the Full Scale" (Dahmus, Bernardin, & Bernardin, 1992, p. 140). In validity studies reported by Baker and Siryk (1989), academic adjustment was significantly correlated with GPA and membership in an academic honor society.

Results

(36)   Data analysis was conducted in four distinct steps in the current study. Firstly, descriptive statistics and frequencies were calculated for the demographic information for all participants. Secondly, an intercorrelation matrix including all key variables of interest was computed. Thirdly, in order

Multiple variable analysis

to assess the influence of the demographic factors of interest, a 2 × 4 MANOVA (race × parental college education) was computed utilizing the four subscales of the SACQ as dependent variables. Lastly, a series of stepwise multiple regression analyses were calculated to determine the best predictive model of college adjustment among the variables assessed.

Correlational Analyses

Total Group Correlations. Pearson correlation matrices were conducted for the total sample group (37) and for each of the three racial/ethnic subgroups in the study. The variables were age, the three parental attachment subscales, and the four college adjustment subscales. Total group intercorrelations are presented in Table 1.

The three parental attachment scales revealed significant intercorrelations (r ranging from .233 (38) to .622 and p ranging from $< .03$ to $< .001$) for the total group. Furthermore, as expected modest to moderate intercorrelations were revealed among the four college adjustment subscales (r ranging from .338 to .636 and $p < .001$). Other significant correlations were also revealed among key variables of the study. The affective quality scale (PAQ1) was correlated with academic adjustment subscale ($r = .204$, $p < .05$), the personal-emotional adjustment subscale ($r = .267$, $p < .01$), and the institutional attachment subscale ($r = .244$, $p < .02$) of the SACQ. In addition, the parental support scale (PAQ3) was correlated with institutional attachment ($r = .294$, $p < .01$).

Racial/Ethnic Subgroup Correlations. Within all three ethnic subgroups, the parental attach- (39) ment scales revealed moderate to strong intercorrelations, as expected. Moreover, within all three ethnic subgroups the four subscales of the SACQ were also moderately to highly correlated with one another, as expected. This pattern of SACQ subscale intercorrelations, which was consistent with findings from previous studies using this instrument (Baker & Siryk, 1989), was high enough to indicate that the subscales were indeed measuring a common construct but moderate enough to support the conceptualization of the college adjustment construct having different facets as represented by the subscales.

Other significant correlations were also revealed among key variables of the study. For the (40) White student subgroup, there was a moderate correlation between the affective quality scale (PAQ1) and the academic adjustment subscale ($r = .44$, $p < .03$).

For the Black student subgroup, the affective quality scale (PAQ1), significantly correlated with (41) the academic adjustment ($r = .44$, $p < .02$) and personal-emotional adjustment ($r = .52$, $p < .01$) subscales of the SACQ. In addition, the parental independence scale (PAQ2) significantly correlated with personal-emotional adjustment ($r = .49$, $p < .01$). Lastly, the parental support scale (PAQ3) significantly correlated with academic adjustment ($r = .44$, $p < .05$), and personal-emotional adjustment ($r = .52$, $p < .01$).

For the Latina/Hispanic student subgroup, the parental support scale (PAQ3) significantly cor- (42) related with institutional attachment ($r = .40$, $p < .01$).

Associations between scores (beside paragraph 38)

Displays of scores in a matrix (beside Table 1)

TABLE 1
Intercorrelations for the Total Sample

	1	2	3	4	5	6	7	8
1. Age	—							
2. PAQ1	.065	—						
3. PAQ2	.013	.568**	—					
4. PAQ3	−.029	.622**	.233*	—				
5. Acad	.143	.204*	.100	.170	—			
6. Social	−.011	.186	.172	.168	.443**	—		
7. Person	.197	−.267**	.145	.108	.430**	.338**	—	
8. Instit	−.091	.244*	.164	.294**	.520**	.636**	.547**	—

*$p < .05$.

**$p < .01$.

MANOVA Analysis

(43)   A 2 × 4 MANOVA (race × parental college education) revealed no significant main or interaction effects for the independent variables in question across the four SACQ subscales. Therefore hypothesis 1 was not supported.

Regression Analyses

(44)   Findings for the total group revealed that the affective quality scale (PAQ1) significantly predicted personal-emotional adjustment, $\beta = .27$, $t = 2.67$, $F(1, 93) = 7.12$, $p < .01$, accounting for 7% of the variance. In addition, the parental support scale (PAQ3) significantly predicted institutional attachment, $\beta = .29$, $t = 2.97$, $F(1, 93) = 8.82$, $p < .01$, accounting for 9% of the variance.

(45)   Among the three racial/ethnic subgroups, several significant findings were revealed. For the Black student sample the affective quality scale (PAQ1) significantly predicted scores on academic adjustment, $\beta = .44$, $t = 2.46$, $F(1, 25) = 6.04$, $p < .02$, accounting for 19% of the variance. In addition, the affective quality scale (PAQ1) significantly predicted scores on personal-emotional adjustment, $\beta = .52$, $t = 3.01$, $F(1, 25) = 9.1$, $p < .01$, for the Black subgroup accounting for 27% of the variance. For the Latina/Hispanic subgroup, the parental support scale (PAQ3) significantly predicted scores on institutional attachment, $\beta = .41$, $t = 2.79$, $F(1, 39) = 7.78$, $p < .01$, accounting for 17% of the variance. Lastly, for the White student sample, the affective quality scale (PAQ1) significantly predicted scores on academic adjustment, $\beta = .44$, $t = 2.32$, $F(1, 22) = 5.39$, $p < .03$, accounting for 20% of the variance.

Discussion

(46)   The results of the current study further demonstrate the complex nature of adjustment to college and suggest that cultural and familial influences may play a more salient role than previously thought, especially when considering the adjustment to college of women of color. Harrison, Wilson, Pine, Chan, & Buriel (1990) stated that students of color may face discontinuity between their family and college values and expectations. In turn, this discontinuity can make college demands more stressful for them than for their White peers. In addition, for the students in the current study, involvement in college activities, programs, and assistance from college faculty and staff may be limited in comparison to students who live in dormitories on campus. It therefore may be more difficult for them to establish social and cultural networks among peers and to develop relationships with mentors. The establishment of such networks at college has been shown to help students who otherwise feel isolated and alienated from others, and this is especially relevant for students of color (Allen, 1992; Melendez, 2008).

(47)   Conversely, students who live at home with family members may receive support that buffers them from the stressors associated to college, including social, emotional, and academic adjustments that can contribute to students' feelings of isolation, alienation and mistrust (Kenny & Perez, 1996; Melendez, 2008). In such cases, the relationship with parents may be used as an anchor in navigating the world, and parents may be used as support systems to encourage and facilitate the college adjustment experience.

Hypotheses

(48)   In the current study, hypothesis 1 stated that college adjustment would be influenced by race and parental education. This hypothesis was not supported as none of the demographic variables assessed (i.e., race and parental college education) significantly influenced college adjustment. Of particular interest was the lack of significant findings regarding parental college education, especially given that a high percentage (68.4%) of the students had parents who did not complete college in the current study. This was an unexpected finding considering the extant literature regarding the pressures of first generation college students compared to non-first generation college students to achieve, not only for themselves but also for their entire families (Kenny & Perez, 1996; Pascarella et al., 2004; Pike & Kuh, 2005).

(49)   One explanation for the lack of findings may be linked to the sample population. Unlike previous studies, the current study focused exclusively on a commuter college population, thereby excluding students from the benefits and/or hindrances that arise from living in on-campus

residences. Although the benefits or hindrances of commuting to college were not a focus of the current study, they may have minimized the influence of low or no parental college education on college adjustment for the current sample population.

Hypothesis 2 stated that parental attachment would predict college adjustment and hypothesis (50) 3 predicted that race and parental attachment together would create the best model for predicting college adjustment. These hypotheses were partially supported by the correlation and regression analyses.

Correlational Analyses

Correlations were first calculated for the total sample. As stated earlier, correlational analyses (51) revealed that parental attachment was indeed related to college adjustment. The affective quality scale of the PAQ was significantly correlated with academic adjustment, personal–emotional adjustment, and institutional attachment, suggesting that students who scored higher on the affective quality scale, which measures students' perceived parental understanding, sensitivity, availability, and acceptance, were more likely to be managing the academic requirements of college, managing their psychological distress and accompanying somatic concerns, as well as experiencing strong bonds with their college (Baker & Siryk, 1989). Similarly, the parental support scale significantly correlated with institutional attachment, suggesting that students may have felt an increased sense of security in receiving support from family and were thus better able to attach to other systems outside of the family.

Among the three racial/ethnic subgroups the findings were similar. For the White subgroup, (52) affective quality was correlated with academic adjustment indicating that White students who perceived their parents as supportive, understanding, and available may have been better equipped to handle the academic rigors of college.

For the Latina/Hispanic subgroup, parental support correlated with institutional attachment, (53) indicating that Latina/Hispanic students who perceived their parents as offering higher levels of support were better able to bond, or develop feelings of attachment and pride with their college.

For the Black subgroup, there were significant correlations between affective quality and aca- (54) demic and personal–emotional adjustment, suggesting that aspects of students' perceptions of their parents' understanding, acceptance, and availability had an influence on their ability to manage the academic and emotional rigors of college. Moreover, parental independence was correlated with personal–emotional adjustment as well, indicating that students who perceived their parents as fostering higher levels of independence were better able to handle the personal and emotional rigors of college while avoiding distress. Parental support also was correlated with academic and personal–emotional adjustment, indicating that higher perceived parental support may have helped prepare them for the academic and the personal–emotional rigors of college as well as buffer them from possible personal, emotional, and academic challenges experienced in college.

Lastly, among the Black and White students there was a significant correlation between affective (55) quality and academic adjustment. However, this finding was not significant for the Latina/Hispanic group, suggesting that affective quality of parental attachment may have differential affects on academic adjustment across culture.

Regression Analyses

The regression findings of this study, although modest, offered partial support for the hypothesized (56) relations between race, parental attachment, and college adjustment. Findings of the current study showed that aspects of parental attachment were significant predictors of college adjustment for the three racial/ethnic subgroups.

Neither race/ethnicity nor parental attachment reached significance as a predictor of college (57) adjustment for the final sample group. Therefore hypotheses 1 and 2 were not supported. However, race/ethnicity and parental attachment combined did predict aspects of college adjustment, lending partial support to hypothesis 3.

For the Black student subgroup, scores on affective quality predicted scores on academic and (58) personal-emotional adjustment to college. Stated differently, the affective quality of the Black students' relationships with their parents had a meaningful impact on the students' success in coping with educational demands of college, such as keeping up with academic work, as well with their physical and psychological states and the degree to which they experienced general psychological distress and/or somatic problems in college.

(59)   This is consistent with previous findings in the literature (Hinderlie & Kenny, 2002; Pfeil, 2001). Black students who enter college face problems similar to other students who enter college in addition to facing a unique set of challenges associated with being in a college environment where the majority racial and ethnic culture differs from their own (Kenny & Perez, 1996; Tinto, 1987). Black families oftentimes have a strong value of family identification and structure as well as support for and from extended family that includes non-blood or fictive relatives. In turn, traditional theories of college student development that have focused on the importance of establishing autonomy and independence from the family of origin have recently recognized the importance of interdependence rather than separation from family of origin (Chickering & Reisser, 1993; Guiffrida, 2006; Kenny & Perez, 1996).

(60)   Similar to the Black students, affective quality of the parental relationship significantly predicted academic adjustment among the White students as well. In partial support of hypothesis 3, the affective quality of the White students' relationships with their parents had a meaningful impact on the students' success in coping with educational demands, such as keeping up with academic work. The importance of the parental relationship for these students further demonstrates the importance of family relationships in adapting to college.

(61)   Among the Latina/Hispanic subgroup, there was no significant relationship between the affective quality of the parental relationship and college adjustment. Although, the literature has highlighted how important family relationship and affective support is for Latina/Hispanic families, this lack of significant results for scores of affective quality among Latina/Hispanic students was surprising. One explanation might be that the measure of affective quality in the parental relationship used in this study may not have fully captured the feelings and expectations that Latina/Hispanics had toward their parents in the same way that it did for the other two subgroups in this study. Questions on the affective quality scale concerning anxiety, anger, disappointment, warmth and comfort may be less salient to the Latina/Hispanic student population than questions concerning parental understanding, advice, and protection.

(62)   Interestingly, for the Latina/Hispanic subgroup, scores on the parental support scale (PAQ3) of the PAQ were found to significantly predict scores on the institutional attachment subscale of the SACQ. Although unique to the attachment literature, this finding supports the concept of institutional attachment as an imperative influence on students' overall adjustment to, and retention in, college and reinforces previous notions that students making a commitment to completing a degree are more likely to have academic success (Gerdes & Mallinckrodt, 1994). Previous literature on college adjustment of Latina/Hispanic students has also supported this finding. For example, Latina/Hispanic college students who perceive themselves as having support have lower rates of distress as well as greater college adjustment (Solberg, Valdez, & Villarreal, 1994). Support may be serving as a buffer against discrimination or isolation, thereby facilitating the students' commitment and attachment to their college.

Independent and Interdependent Views of Student Persistence and Retention

(63)   Viewed through the conceptual lens of independent and interdependent cultural influence on the self (Markus & Kitayama, 1991), the findings of the current study suggest that the processes of college adjustment and persistence for women of color may need to be reconsidered. According to Tinto (2006):

> Where it was once argued that retention required students to break away from past communities we now know that for some, if not many students, the ability to remain connected to their past communities, family, church, or tribe is essential to their persistence. (p. 4)

(64)   The current findings revealed that a strong attachment to parents was a positive influence on aspects of college adjustment for the participants involved. These findings stood contrary to some earlier models of retention that espoused a more independent/assimilationist notion of breaking away from past associations to become integrated into the fabric of college life (e.g., Tinto, 1975, 1987). However, the current findings were in line with more contemporary and culturally sensitive

theories that espouse more interdependent/collectivist virtues regarding college student retention and persistence (Arbona & Nora, 2007; Guiffrida, 2006; Nora, 2003).

Summary

Findings of the current study partially supported the contention that race and parental attachment would predict college adjustment in a diverse group of female college students. In addition, these finding suggest that parental attachment predicts college adjustment differentially across race/ethnicity and across dimensions of adjustment. Unique to the college adjustment literature, these findings lend further support to the multidimensionality of college adjustment and to the utility of parental attachment as an influence on retention based outcomes.   (65)

In addition, although modest, these findings call into question previous notions of autonomy and independence that were considered imperative aspects of college student persistence and retention in earlier theories (Tinto, 1975, 1987, 2006).   (66)

Implications for Counseling, Programming, and Policy

Psychology has traditionally focused on autonomy, separation, and individuation from parents during the adolescent years and in the transition to college. However, the relationship between parents and their college bound children is extremely important in understanding the adjustment to college. For many students, maintaining strong support within the family and affective quality within the parental relationship positively influences the factors associated with college adjustment. It would be valuable for counselors working with college students to assess the nature of the parent–child relationship within a cultural context in order to help students further develop or maintain relationships with parents and family in general.   (67)

College professionals may also need to consider how institutional practices affect students of color and their relationships with family. The development of culturally sensitive interventions, practices, and policies within the college environment are necessary to facilitate adaptive student development during the college years. When working with diverse populations such as the ones in the current study, relationships with family may need to be more closely considered and policies regarding mental health issues, disciplinary issues, and educational issues, may need to be re-evaluated. For example, providing opportunities for the family of origin to be more present in the lives of students of color through expanded outreach programs may help to ease the adjustment to college for these and other at-risk student populations.   (68)

Moreover, at a conceptual level, the developmental and emotional separation from the family associated with attending college (commuter or residential) may differ across culture. These differences may need to be better incorporated into future recruitment or retention strategies. For example, in Latina/Hispanic families, it is not uncommon for the family to make key decisions regarding education (including what college, what major, and what profession is acceptable) for their children and especially their female children. Furthermore, one of the main reasons Latina/Hispanic students leave high school and college at such high rates is to help their families financially (Sylwester, 2005; Williams, 2002). Therefore, colleges and universities need to be more mindful of interdependent family value systems when addressing rates of retention and graduation among student populations of color.   (69)

Limitations and Future Directions

Findings of the current study have implications for assisting students through the development of programs and strategies that could facilitate college adjustment as well as retention among students with diverse backgrounds. However, the study has limitations and therefore caution must be exercised in generalizing the findings of this study to other groups of students. The current study relied exclusively on self-report measures for its data. In addition, the lack of random sampling coupled with a small sample size may have contributed significantly to bias in the design. Lastly, the inclusion of Black, Latina/Hispanic, and White women exclusively in the sample of the current study also limits the generalizeability of the findings.   (70)

To help offset these limitations, future research should employ larger and more randomized samples to help improve the generalizeability as well as decrease bias in the design. The incorporation   (71) of men into future research designs would also add to the overall scope of the findings and allow for further comparative analysis between genders. In addition, the incorporation of men into future designs would allow for the examination of any interaction effects between gender and race/ethnicity that may exist. It may also be valuable in future research designs to obtain more demographic information regarding socioeconomic status, parental occupation, financial resources in paying for college, language spoken at home, years living in the United States, and social support networks. This information could provide greater clarity regarding the myriad of variables that contribute to students' adjustment to college. Longitudinal research designs would also help to better assess the influence of parental attachment on college adjustment over the course of one's college career. In addition, incorporation of qualitative and phenomenological research designs can help to further illuminate the unique influences of race/ethnicity and parental attachment on college adjustment.

References

Ainsworth, M. (1989). Attachment beyond infancy. *American Psychology, 44,* 709-716.

Ainsworth, M., Blehar, M., Waters, E., & Wall, S. (1978). *Patterns of attachment: A psychological study of the strange situation.* Oxford, England: Lawrence Erlbaum.

Allen, J. P., & Land, D. (1999). Attachment and Adolescence. In J. Cassidy & P. Shaver (Eds.), *Handbook of attachment: Theory, research, and clinical applications* (pp. 319-335). New York: The Guilford Press.

Allen, W. R. (1992). The color of success: African American college student outcomes at predominantly White and historically Black colleges and universities. *Harvard Educational Review, 62,* 26-44.

Ancis, J. R., Szymanski, D. M., & Ladany, N. (2008). Development and psychometric evaluation of Counseling Women Competencies Scale (CWCS). *Counseling Psychologist, 35,* 719-744.

Arbona, C., & Nora, A. (2007). The influence of academic and environmental factors on Hispanic college degree attainment. *Review of Higher Education, 30,* 247-269.

Baker, R. W., & Siryk, B. (1989). *Student Adaptation to College Questionnaire.* Los Angeles: Western Psychological Services.

Bowlby, J. (1973). *Attachment and loss: Vol. 2. Separation.* New York: Basic Books.

Bowlby, J. (1980). *Attachment and loss: Vol. 3. Loss, sadness, and depression.* New York: Basic Books.

Bowlby, J. (1982). *Attachment and loss: Vol. 1. Attachment.* New York: Basic Books. (Original work published in 1969)

Bradford, E., & Lyddon, W. (1993). Current parental attachment: Its relation to perceived psychological distress and relationship satisfaction in college students. *Journal of College Student Development, 34,* 256-260.

Braxton, J. M., Hirschy, A. S., & McClendon, S. A. (2004). *Understanding and reducing college student departure.* San Francisco: Jossey-Bass

Brown, S., Santiago, D., & Lopez, E. (2003). Latinas in higher education. *Change, 35,* 40-46.

Buchanan, T. S., Fischer, A. R., Tokar, D. M., & Yoder J. D. (2008). Testing a culture specific extension of objectification theory regarding African American women's body image. *Counseling Psychologist, 36,* 697-718.

Cemalcilar, Z., & Falbo, T. (2008). A longitudinal study of the adaptation of international students in the United States. *Journal of Cross-Cultural Psychology, 39,* 799-804.

Chickering, A., & Reisser, L. (1993). *Education and identity* (2nd ed.). San Francisco: Jossey-Bass.

Chin, J. L. (1994). Psychodynamic approaches. In L. Comas-Diaz & B. Greene (Eds.), *Women of color: Integrating ethnic and gender identities in psychotherapy* (pp. 194-222). New York: Guilford Press.

Chiu, M. L. (1995). The influence of anticipatory fear on foreign student adjustment: An exploratory study. *International Journal of Intercultural Relations, 19,* 1-44.

Comas-Diaz, L., & Greene, B. (1994). *Women of color: Integrating ethnic and gender identities in psychotherapy.* New York: Guilford Press.

Dahmus, S., Bernardin, J. H., & Bernardin, J. (1992). Student Adaptation to College Questionnaire. *Measurement and Evaluation in Counseling and Development, 25,* 139-142.

Gerdes, H., & Mallinckrodt, B. (1994). Emotional, social, and academic adjustment of college students: A longitudinal study of retention. *Journal of Counseling and Development, 72,* 281-288.

Gloria, A. M., Castellanos, J., Lopez, A. G., & Rosales, R. (2005). An examination of academic nonpersistence decisions of Latina undergraduates. *Hispanic Journal of Behavioral Sciences, 27,* 202-223.

Guiffrida, D. A. (2006). Toward a cultural advancement of Tinto's theory. *Review of Higher Education, 29,* 451-472.

Harrison, A. O., Wilson, M. N., Pine, C. J., Chan S., & Buriel, R. (1990). Family ecologies of ethnic minority children. *Child Development, 61,* 347-362.

Herzog, S. T. (2008). Estimating the influence of financial aid on student retention: A discrete choice propensity score-matching model. Retrieved September 14, 2008, from http://www.aair.org .au/jir/2007Papers/Herzog.pdf

Hinderlie, H. H., & Kenny M. (2002). Attachment, social support, and college adjustment among Black students at predominantly White universities. *Journal of College Student Development, 43,* 327-340.

Holmbeck, G. N., & Wandrei, M. L. (1993). Individual and relationship predictors of adjustment in first year college students. *Journal of Counseling Psychology, 40,* 73-78.

Horn, L. (2006). *Placing college graduation rates in context: How 4-year college graduation rates vary with selectivity and the size of low-income enrollment* (NCES 2007-161). Washington, DC: U.S. Department of Education, National Center for Educational Statistics.

Institute of Educational Sciences. (2004). *Trends in educational equity of girls and women.* Washington, DC: U.S. Department of Education, National Center for Educational Statistics.

Integrated Post Secondary Education Data System. (2005). *Awards conferred by Title IV institutions, by racelethnicity, level of award, and gender: US, academic year 2004–2005.* Washington, DC: U.S. Department of Education, National Center for Educational Statistics.

Kaczmarek, P. G., Matlock, G., & Franco, J. (1990). Assessment of college adjustment in three freshman groups. *Psychological Reports, 66,* 1195-1202.

Kenny, M. (1987). The extent and function of parental attachment among first year college student. *Journal of Youth and Adolescence, 16,* 17-27.

Kenny, M. (1994). Quality and correlates of parental attachment among late adolescents. *Journal of Counseling and Development, 72,* 399-403.

Kenny, M., & Donaldson, G. (1991). Contributions of parental attachment and family structure to the social and psychological functioning of first year college students. *Journal of Counseling Psychology, 38,* 479-486.

Kenny, M., & Donaldson, G. (1992). The relationship of parental attachment and psychological separation to the adjustment of first year college women. *Journal of College Student Development, 33,* 431-438.

Kenny, M., & Perez, V. (1996). Attachment and psychological well-being among racially and ethnically diverse first year college students. *Journal of College Student Development, 37,* 527-535.

Kenny, M., & Rice, K. G. (1995). Attachment to parents in late adolescent college students: Current status, applications, and future considerations. *Counseling Psychologist, 23,* 433-456.

Knapp, L. G., Kelly-Reid, J. E., Whitmore, R. W., Wu, S., Gallego, L., Cong, J., et al. (2005). *Postsecondary institutions in the United States: Fall 2003 and Degrees and other awards conferred: 2002-03* (NCES 2005-154). Washington, DC: U.S. Department of Education, National Center for Education Statistics.

Larose, S., & Boivin, M. (1998). Attachment to parents, social support expectations, and socio-emotional adjustment during the high school-college transition. *Journal of Research on Adolescence, 8,* 1-27.

LeVine, R. A., & Miller, P. M. (1990). Commentary. *Human Development, 33,* 73-80.

Lotkowski, V. A., Robbins, S. B., & Noeth, R. J. (2004). *The role of academic and non-academic factors in improving college retention: ACT policy report.* Iowa City, IA: ACT. Retrieved May 18, 2007, from http://www.act.org/research/policymakers/pdf/college_retention.pdf.

Markus, H. R., & Kitayama, S. (1991). Culture and self: Implications for cognition, emotion, and motivation. *Psychological Review, 98,* 224-253.

Mattanah, J. F., Hancock, G. R., & Brand, B. L. (2004). Parental attachment, separation-individuation, and college student adjustment: A structural equation analysis of mediational effects. *Journal of Counseling Psychology, 51,* 213-225.

Melendez, M. C. (2006). The influence of athletic participation on the college adjustment of freshmen and sophomore student-athletes. *Journal of College Student Retention: Research, Theory and Practice, 8,* 39-55.

Melendez, M. C. (2008). Black football players on a predominantly White college campus: Psychosocial and emotional realities of the Black college athlete experience. *Journal of Black Psychology, 34,* 423-451.

Melendez, M. C. (2010). Psychosocial influences on college adjustment in Division I student–athletes: The role of athletic identity. *Journal of College Student Retention: Research, Theory and Practice, 11,* 345-361.

Miller, P. S., & Kerr, G. A. (2003). The role experimentation of intercollegiate student athletes. *Sport Psychologist, 17,* 196-219.

National Collegiate Athletic Association. (2007). *2007 NCAA graduation rates report.* Retrieved September 25, 2008, from http://www.ncaa.org/grad_rates/.

Nora, A. (2001). The depiction of significant others in Tinto's "Rites of Passage: A reconceptualization of the influence of family and community in the persistence process. *Journal of College Student Retention: Research, Theory, and Practice, 3,* 40-41.

Nora, A. (2003). Access to higher education for Hispanic students: Real or illusory? In J. Castellanos & L. Jones (Eds.), *The majority in the minority: Expanding representation of Latina/o faculty, administration, and students in higher education* (pp. 46-67). Sterling, VA: Stylus.

Nora, A., & Cabrera, A. F. (1996). The role of perceptions of prejudice and discrimination on the adjustment of minority students to college. *Journal of Higher Education, 67,* 119-148.

Parham, W. D. (1993). The intercollegiate athlete: A 1990's profile. *Counseling Psychologist, 21,* 411-429.

Pascarella, E. T., Duby, P. B., & Iverson, B. K. (1983). A test reconceptualization of a theoretical model of college withdrawal in a commuter institution setting. *Sociology of Education, 56,* 88-11.

Pascarella, E. T., Pierson, C. T., Wolniak, G. C., & Terenzini, P. T. (2004). First generation college students: Additional evidence on college experiences and outcomes. *Journal of Higher Education, 75,* 249-284.

Pascarella, E. T., & Terenzini, P. T. (2005). *How college affects students: A third decade of research* (2nd ed.). New York: John Wiley.

Pfeil, L. R. (2001). Parental attachment, attachment style and college adjustment in African-American students. *Dissertation Abstracts International, 61,* 10A.

Pike, G. R., & Kuh, G. D. (2005). First and second generation college students: A comparison of their engagement and intellectual development. *Journal of Higher Education, 76,* 276-300.

Rice, K. G., Fitzgerald, D. P., Whaley, T. J., & Gibbs, C. L. (1995). Cross-sectional and longitudinal examination of attachment, separation–individuation, and college student adjustment. *Journal of Counseling and Development, 73,* 463-474.

Rothbaum, F., Weisz, J., Pott, M., Miyake, K., & Morelli, G. (2000). Attachment and culture: security in the United States and Japan. *American Psychologist, 55,* 1093-1104.

Schneider, M. E., & Ward, D. J. (2003). The role of ethnic identification and perceived social support in Latina's adjustment to college. *Hispanic Journal of Behavioral Sciences, 25,* 539-554.

Schultheiss, D., & Blustein, D. (1994). Role of adolescent-parent relationships in college student development and adjustment. *Journal of Counseling Psychology, 41,* 248-255.

Solberg, V. S., Valdez, J., & Villarreal, P. (1997). Examination of self-efficacy, social support, and stress as predictors of psychological and physical distress among Hispanic college students. *Hispanic Journal of Behavioral Sciences, 19,* 182-201.

Sylwester, M. J. (2005, March 29). Hispanic girls in sport held back by tradition: Family duties keep many from playing high school sports. *USA Today,* p. A.1.

Tinto, V. (1975). Dropouts from higher education: A theoretical synthesis of recent research. *Review of Educational Research, 45,* 89-125.

Tinto, V. (1987). *Leaving college: Rethinking the causes and curses of student attrition.* Chicago: University of Chicago Press.

Tinto, V. (2006). Research and practice of student retention: What next? *Journal of College Student Retention: Theory, Research, and Practice, 8,* 1-19.

Toews, M. L., & Yazedjian, A. (2007). College adjustment among freshmen: Predictors for White and Hispanic male and females. *College Student Journal, 41,* 891-900.

Tomlinson-Clarke, S. (1998). Dimensions of adjustment among college women. *Journal of College Student Development, 39,* 364-372.

Torres, V. (2004). Familial influences on the identity development of Latina first year students. *Journal of College Student Development, 45,* 457-469.

Torres, V. (2006). A mixed method study testing data-model fit of a retention model for Latina/a students at urban universities. *Journal of College Student Development, 47,* 299-318.

Weissberg, N. C., Jenkins, A. H., & Harburg, E. (2003). The incremental variance problem: Enhancing the predictability of academic success in an urban, commuter institution. *Genetic, Social, and General Psychology Monographs, 129,* 153-180.

Weissberg, N. C., & Owen, D. R. (2005). Do psychosocial and study skill factors predict college outcomes? Comment on Robbins et al. (2004). *Psychological Bulletin, 131,* 407-409.

Williams, L. (2002, November 6). Women's sports: Hispanic female athletes are few and far between. *New York Times,* p. C18.

Young, J. W., & Koplow, S. L. (1997). The validity of two questionnaires for predicting minority students' college grades. *The Journal of General Education, 46,* 45-55.

Zea, M. C., Jarama, L., & Bianchi, F. T. (1995). Social support and psychosocial competence: Explaining the adaptation to college of ethnically diverse students. *American Journal of Community Psychology, 23,* 509-531.

Survey Designs

*M*ost people are familiar with surveys. We often receive surveys to record
opinions as voters, to register approval of consumer products, and to measure
opinions about electoral candidates. To many people, survey research is simply a
"survey" instrument, such as a questionnaire or interview. Although we "survey"
people using an instrument in educational research, the instrument is only one
aspect of a broader procedure in survey designs. This chapter defines survey research,
identifies when you use it and how it developed, assesses the key characteristics of it,
and advances the steps in conducting and evaluating this design.

By the end of this chapter, you should be able to:

◆ Define survey research, and describe when to use it, and how it developed.
◆ Describe the types of survey designs.
◆ Identify the key characteristics of survey research.
◆ Describe how to construct and use a mailed questionnaire.
◆ Describe how to design and conduct an interview survey.
◆ Identify potential ethical issues in survey research.
◆ List the steps in conducting survey research.
◆ Identify criteria useful for evaluating survey research.

Maria decides to use survey research for her graduate school research project. Her
research question is "What factors explain why high school students hold positive attitudes toward possessing weapons in school?" By using a survey design to answer this
question, Maria seeks to describe trends in students' thinking. Her approach provides an
economical and efficient means of gathering a large amount of data from many students.
She randomly selects a sample of students, sends them a mailed questionnaire, analyzes
the results, and draws conclusions about the population from her sample. She conducts
survey research.

WHAT IS SURVEY RESEARCH, WHEN DO YOU USE IT, AND HOW DID IT DEVELOP?

With its many applications, survey research is a popular design in education. **Survey research designs** are procedures in quantitative research in which investigators administer a survey to a sample or to the entire population of people to describe the attitudes, opinions, behaviors, or characteristics of the population. In this procedure, survey researchers collect quantitative, numbered data using questionnaires (e.g., mailed questionnaires) or interviews (e.g., one-on-one interviews) and statistically analyze the data to describe trends about responses to questions and to test research questions or hypotheses. They also interpret the meaning of the data by relating results of the statistical test back to past research studies.

Survey designs differ from experimental research in that they do not involve a treatment given to participants by the researcher. Because survey researchers do not experimentally manipulate the conditions, they cannot explain cause and effect as well as experimental researchers can. Instead, survey studies describe trends in the data rather than offer rigorous explanations. Survey research has much in common with correlational designs. Survey researchers often correlate variables, but their focus is directed more toward learning about a population and less on relating variables or predicting outcomes, as is the focus in correlational research.

When Do You Use Survey Research?

You use survey research to describe trends, such as community interests in school bond issues or state or national trends about mandatory student uniform policies. You also use survey research to determine individual opinions about policy issues, such as whether students need a choice of schools to attend. Surveys help identify important beliefs and attitudes of individuals, such as college students' beliefs about what constitutes abusive behaviors in dating relationships. They may be used to follow up with graduates 5, 10, or 15 years after college to learn about their present careers. Surveys provide useful information to evaluate programs in schools, such as the success of a robotics program in science education.

How Did Survey Research Develop?

Surveys have been widely used in education for many years. Early surveys date back to 1817, when Marc Antoine Jullien de Paris designed a 34-page international survey of national education systems (De Landsheere, 1988). In the 1890s, G. Stanley Hall surveyed children, and by 1907, the Pittsburgh Survey examined social problems, including educational issues ranging from educational planning for school buildings to issues of children in classrooms who are slow learners (Bogdan & Biklen, 1998).

During the period from World War I to World War II, the modern survey as we know it began to emerge. Factors that contributed to its development were improvements in sampling techniques and the development of different scales of measurement. Surveys found wide application in many social science fields, including marketing research, journalism, public opinion research, and organizations and charities (Neuman, 2000). By midcentury, efforts were under way to establish standardized questions through surveys at the U.S. Department of Agriculture. Scales improved through the development of the Likert scale (e.g., *strongly agree* to *strongly disagree*). Also, guidelines were written for writing clear questions, standardizing interviewing questions, training interviewers, and checking for consistency among interviewers (Fowler, 2009).

During World War II, surveys examine[...] morale of soldiers, production capacity for w[...] Through these studies, survey researchers reh[...] large-scale assessments, enabling the emergence o[...] American universities after the war. For example, inv[...] centers at Berkeley (Survey Research Center), at the Un[...] ion Research Center), and at the University of Michigan[...] Also, opinion polling organizations, such as Gallup, Roper, a[...] thered the understanding of large-scale data collection. The f[...] vey organizations, combined with the use of computers, the av[...] and storage, and funding from the federal government, helped to e[...] of surveys in education by midcentury (Neuman, 2000).

In recent years, both federal and state governments have funded [...] surveys such as the Youth Risk Behavior Survey developed by the U[...] Disease Control and Prevention (Valois & McKewon, 1998). Electronic sur[...] computer-assisted telephone interviewing (CATI), voice recognition (VR), touc[...] entry (TDE), and other approaches represent innovations in self-administered q[...] naires that make use of the computer and telephone (Babbie, 1998). Individuals[...] increasingly used Web sites and the Internet to collect survey data (Sills & Song, 20[...] Survey researchers can now generate an e-mail survey, place questionnaires in wor[...] processing formats, and create a hypertext file and place surveys on Web sites (Nesbary, 2000). Electronic surveys and communications will probably revolutionize the use and applications of survey research in the future.

WHAT ARE THE TYPES OF SURVEY DESIGNS?

Despite the many applications of surveys today, there are still only two basic types of research surveys: cross sectional and longitudinal. Figure 12.1 shows that each type serves a different purpose. Survey researchers use cross-sectional designs to collect data about current attitudes, opinions, or beliefs. Longitudinal designs are used to study individuals over time.

Cross-Sectional Survey Designs

The most popular form of survey design used in education is a cross-sectional survey design. In a **cross-sectional survey design**, the researcher collects data at one point in time. For example, when middle school children complete a survey about teasing, they are recording data about their present views. This design has the advantage of measuring current attitudes or practices. It also provides information in a short amount of time, such as the time required for administering the survey and collecting the information.

Cross-sectional designs are of several types. A cross-sectional study can *examine current attitudes, beliefs, opinions, or practices*. Attitudes, beliefs, and opinions are ways in which individuals think about issues, whereas practices are their actual behaviors. For example, three authors conducted a survey of the practices of reading teachers in elementary schools (Morrison, Jacobs, & Swinyard, 1999). The purpose of the study was to relate the personal, recreational reading of elementary teachers to their literacy instructional practices. Using a list of elementary teachers nationwide (obtained from a professional mailing list company), the researchers mailed 3,600 questionnaires to a probability sample. Of this sample, 52.3% responded to the four-page questionnaire consisting of

FIGURE 12.1 Types of Cro[...] PART III Research Designs 378

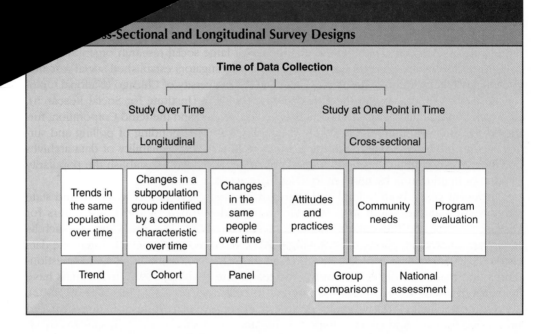

Time of Data Collection

Study Over Time | Study at One Point in Time

Longitudinal | Cross-sectional

| Trends in the same population over time | Changes in a subpopulation group identified by a common characteristic over time | Changes in the same people over time | Attitudes and practices | Community needs | Program evaluation |

| Trend | Cohort | Panel | | Group comparisons | National assessment |

21 questions and several items asking for demographic information such as gender, age, and years of teaching experience. Overall, the authors concluded that teachers who saw themselves as readers were more likely than teachers who did not see themselves as readers to use recommended literacy instructional practices (e.g., "read aloud a picture book to your class," p. 88).

Another cross-sectional design *compares two or more educational groups* in terms of attitudes, beliefs, opinions, or practices. These group comparisons may compare students with students, students with teachers, students with parents, or they may compare other groups within educational and school settings. For example, one study compared 98 rural and urban secondary school teachers from 11 school systems in Georgia and North Carolina in terms of their sources of stress and symptoms of burnout (Abel & Sewell, 1999). This group consisted of 52 rural teachers and 46 urban teachers (a nonprobability sample) who volunteered to participate in the study. The researchers delivered packets that included two instruments, the Sources of Stress Questionnaire and the Maslach Burnout Inventory, to participating school districts. The teachers mailed the instruments back to the researchers. The statistical analysis of the data showed significantly greater self-reported stress for urban teachers than rural teachers because of poor working conditions and poor staff relations.

A cross-sectional design can *measure community needs* of educational services as they relate to programs, courses, school facilities projects, or involvement in the schools or in community planning. For example, community needs of Hispanic, Spanish-monolingual residents in Florida were studied by Batsche, Hernandez, and Montenegro (1999). The authors felt that survey researchers used methods for reaching Hispanic residents that were more appropriate for non-Hispanic residents. To correct this problem, they designed procedures for an assessment interview survey for identifying needs and priorities for human service programs in the Tampa Bay, Florida, area. For example, they used the name "Hispanic" because the survey participants accepted this term. The instrument allowed individuals to identify themselves both by race and ethnicity. To identify the population to study, clubs and organizations were contacted by mail and asked to provide lists of individuals known to be Spanish-monolingual. The researchers first translated the instrument into Spanish and had it reviewed by the local Hispanic community, who translated it back into English to identify discrepancies. The researchers also conducted public meetings to explain the purpose and importance of the needs assessment. Further, the researchers scheduled the times of the interviews to avoid religious events and cultural holidays observed by the Hispanic residents.

Some cross-sectional designs *evaluate a program,* such as a survey that provides useful information to decision makers. In one study, students (and their parents) who had completed a suburban community college enrollment options program responded to surveys evaluating the program (Kiger & Johnson, 1997). This college option provided opportunities for high school students to enroll in the community college. A 23-item survey asked the students and their parents their perceptions, such as whether the program helped "formulate long-term educational goals" (p. 691). An overall positive relationship resulted between student and parent perceptions, although their perceptions differed. Parents wanted the students to use the program as a "hands-on" career identification and planning tool, but students saw the program as an opportunity to "try out" the role of being a college student.

A final type of cross-sectional design is a large-scale assessment of students or teachers, such as a *statewide study or a national survey* involving thousands of participants. For example, the Higher Education Research Institute at the University of California at Los Angeles conducted a faculty survey in 1992–1993 of all operating institutions of higher education, which totaled 2,582 colleges and universities. The four-page instrument assessed many factors about faculty members and resulted in a sample of 29,771 full-time college and university faculty. Dey and Hurtado (1996) analyzed this national data to examine attitudes toward institutional attempts to regulate forms of on-campus speech. They found that the majority of faculty supported the prohibition of "hate speech" on campus but were much less likely to support the right of administrators to ban extreme speakers.

Longitudinal Survey Designs

An alternative to using a cross-sectional design is to collect data over time using a longitudinal survey design. A **longitudinal survey design** involves the survey procedure of collecting data about trends with the same population, changes in a cohort group or subpopulation, or changes in a panel group of the same individuals over time. Thus, in longitudinal designs, the participants may be different or the same people. An example of the study of the same people would be research about high school graduates and their current occupation (e.g., student, food service worker, insurance agent) 1, 2, and 5 years after graduation. Another example of a longitudinal design would be a follow-up with graduates from a program or school to learn their views about their educational experiences. Several types of longitudinal designs are available to the educational researcher, including trend, cohort, and panel designs (Babbie, 1998).

Trend Studies

In some surveys, researchers aim to study changes within some general population over a period of time (Babbie, 1998). This form of longitudinal research is called a trend study. **Trend studies** are longitudinal survey designs that involve identifying a population and examining changes within that population over time. A popular example of this design is the Gallup Poll, which is used during elections to monitor trends in the population of voters from the primary to the final election. Applied to education, this type of study might focus on high school seniors (a population) and study the trends of their attitudes toward dating during the years 2001, 2002, and 2003. In this study, different seniors are studied each year, but they all represent the same population (high school seniors). The researcher can use this data to assess how trends change over time.

Cohort Studies

Rather than studying changing trends in a population, the researcher may be interested in identifying a subgroup in the population, called a *cohort,* that possesses a common defining characteristic. A **cohort study** is a longitudinal survey design in which a researcher identifies a subpopulation based on some specific characteristic and then studies that subpopulation over time. All members of the cohort must have the common characteristic, such as being 18 years old in the year 2001. If age is that characteristic, the researcher studies the group *as the group ages.* For example, a cohort group of 18-year-olds is studied in the year 2001. Five years later (in 2006), a group of 23-year-olds is studied. (They may or may not be the same individuals studied in 2001.) Five years after that (in 2011), a group of 28-year-olds is studied. While the individuals studied each time might be different, they must have been 18 years old in the year 2001 to qualify as representatives of the cohort group.

Panel Studies

A third type of longitudinal survey design is the panel study design. Distinct from both the trend and the cohort study, a **panel study** is a longitudinal survey design in which the researcher examines the same people over time. The high school seniors studied in 1998 will be the same people studied in 2000, 1 year after graduation, and again in 2002, 2 years after graduation. One disadvantage of a panel design is that individuals may be difficult to locate, especially 2 years after graduating from high school. The advantage to this type of study, however, is that the individuals studied will be the same each time, allowing the researcher to determine actual changes in specific individuals. Because of this, the panel study is the most rigorous of the three longitudinal designs.

Let's look at an actual study in which two authors used a longitudinal panel design to examine how adolescents with learning disabilities made the transition from vocational–technical schools to work (Shapiro & Lentz, 1991). The authors surveyed two groups of high school seniors: one with learning disabilities and one without learning disabilities. They were surveyed at graduation and at 6-, 12-, and 24-month intervals after graduation to learn about their occupational and living experiences. The surveys were sent to seniors who graduated in 1986 and 1987. At graduation, both groups held remarkably similar future plans. Only 50% of the individuals with learning disabilities, however, indicated they had specific future plans at graduation. The group with learning disabilities also had lower rates of enrollment in education after high school than the other group did. Further, only about half of all the students studied felt that their training in high school related to their work after graduation.

WHAT ARE THE KEY CHARACTERISTICS OF SURVEY RESEARCH?

Whether a survey design is longitudinal or cross-sectional, there are key characteristics of both that will help you design a survey or read and evaluate a published survey study. Survey researchers engage in the processes of:

◆ Sampling from a population
◆ Collecting data through questionnaires or interviews

◆ Designing instruments for data collection
◆ Obtaining a high response rate

Sampling from a Population

Survey researchers typically select and study a sample from a population and generalize results from the sample to the population. We need to first define three terms: the population, the target population or sampling frame, and the sample. Figure 12.2 shows the differences among these three terms. At the broadest level is the *population,* in which a group of individuals possesses one characteristic that distinguishes them from other groups. For example, we might have a population made up of high school teachers, individuals who all teach in high schools, or school counselors, individuals who occupy counselor positions in all levels of educational schools. At a more specific level, researchers do not always study an entire population, either because they cannot identify the individuals or because they cannot obtain lists of names. (Lists are used when mailing out a questionnaire.) In practical, operational terms, researchers study a *target population* (sometimes called the *sampling frame*). This is the list or record of individuals in a population that a researcher *can* actually obtain. For example, researchers might obtain a list of all secondary high school teachers in one school district. This list constitutes the target population or sampling frame. From the target population, researchers choose a sample. At the most specific level, researchers select a *sample* from the target population. These individuals are the people studied.

The most rigorous form of sampling is to use random sampling by employing a procedure such as using a random numbers table. In this process, the researcher selects a sample representative of the population so that claims or inferences can be drawn from the sample to the population.

In survey research, it is important to select as large a sample as possible so that the sample will exhibit similar characteristics to the target population. Also, in survey studies,

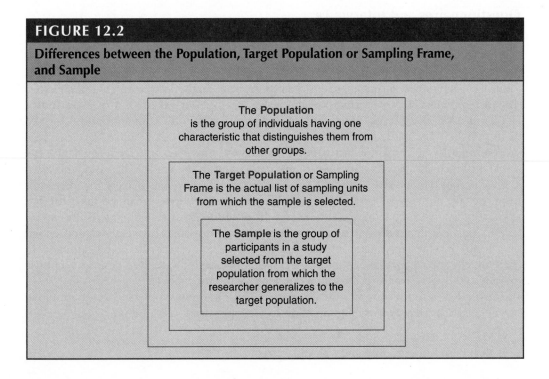

FIGURE 12.2

Differences between the Population, Target Population or Sampling Frame, and Sample

The Population
is the group of individuals having one characteristic that distinguishes them from other groups.

The **Target Population** or Sampling Frame is the actual list of sampling units from which the sample is selected.

The **Sample** is the group of participants in a study selected from the target population from which the researcher generalizes to the target population.

it is sometimes difficult to obtain a good list of the target population. For example, lists of individuals who belong to high school gangs or all left-handed individuals would not be easy to obtain. In many cases, however, the target population can be identified for study, and after several attempts, a good list of individuals for the target population can be compiled. It is also possible in survey research to study the entire population because it is small (e.g., members of literacy councils in a state) and can be easily identified. This type of survey study, sometimes called a *census study,* permits conclusions to be drawn about the entire population. Therefore, random sampling, hypothesis testing, and the use of inferential statistics are not necessary. For this type of study, survey researchers simply report descriptive statistics about the entire population.

When researchers select a sample from a population, however, certain factors may limit a survey researcher's ability to draw valid inference from the sample to the population. Salant and Dillman (1994) identified several factors in good survey research that may compromise drawing these inferences:

◆ *To reduce coverage error, have a good sampling frame list on which to select individuals.* When researchers use a good, complete list, their coverage of the population is adequate and not error prone.
◆ *To reduce sampling error, select as large a sample from the population as possible.* The larger the sample, the more the participants will be representative of the entire population and reflect attitudes, beliefs, practices, and trends of the population. Recognize that all samples selected will be only estimates of population values.
◆ *To reduce measurement error, use a good instrument, with clear, unambiguous questions and response options.* Such instruments will encourage individuals to respond and answer correctly. Later in this chapter, we discuss how to construct a questionnaire to reduce this error.
◆ *To reduce nonresponse error, use rigorous administration procedures to achieve as large a return rate as possible.* Later in this chapter, we discuss these procedures.

Questionnaires and Interviews

Although many different forms of surveys exist, survey researchers typically collect data using two basic forms: questionnaires and interviews. Researchers need to consider the forms and weigh the advantages and disadvantages of each. You can distinguish these forms by examining who completes or records the data on the instrument: the participants (called *respondents* or *interviewees*) or the researcher (see Figure 12.3). A **questionnaire** is a form used in a survey design that participants in a study complete and return to the researcher. The participant chooses answers to questions and supplies basic personal or demographic information. An **interview survey**, however, is a form on which the researcher records answers supplied by the participant in the study. The researcher asks a question from an interview guide, listens for answers or observes behavior, and records responses on the survey. The quantitative interview procedures, discussed here, are not to be confused with qualitative interviewing. In *quantitative survey interviews,* the investigator uses a structured or semistructured interview consisting of mostly closed-ended questions, provides response options to interviewees, and records their responses. In *qualitative survey interviews,* an interviewer asks open-ended questions without response options and listens to and records the comments of the interviewee.

Several different types of questionnaires and interviews are used in quantitative survey research. Here we will highlight the major types used in education:

◆ Mailed questionnaires
◆ Web-based questionnaires

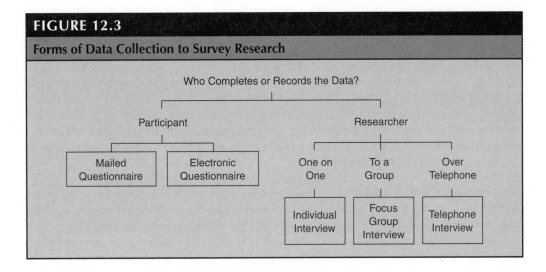

FIGURE 12.3

Forms of Data Collection to Survey Research

- ◆ One-on-one interviews
- ◆ Focus group interviews
- ◆ Telephone interviews

Mailed Questionnaires

A **mailed questionnaire** is a form of data collection in survey research in which the investigator mails a questionnaire to members of the sample. Researchers might develop their own questionnaire, modify an existing one, or use one that they have located in the literature. The process consists of locating or developing a questionnaire, sending it out to the sample of the population, using repeated contacts with the sample to obtain a high response rate, checking for potential bias in responses, and analyzing the data. (These procedures are discussed later in this chapter.)

A mailed questionnaire is a convenient way to reach a geographically dispersed sample of a population. The mail facilitates quick data collection, often in as little time as 6 weeks from the first mailing to the conclusion of data collection. A mailed questionnaire is economical because it involves only duplication and mailing expenses. The disadvantage of mailed questionnaires is that individuals may lack any personal investment in the study and decide not to return the instrument. Also, because the researcher does not have a means for explaining questions, participants may misinterpret items on the survey.

Web-Based Surveys or Questionnaires

With increased use of Web sites and the Internet, Web-based questionnaires are becoming popular. A **Web-based questionnaire** is a survey instrument for collecting data that is available on the computer. Several software programs are available for designing, gathering, and analyzing survey data with sample questions and forms (e.g., see Qualtrix at **http://www.qualtrics.com/survey-software/** or Survey Monkey at **http://www .surveymonkey.com/**).

Educational researchers need to weigh the advantages and disadvantages of using a Web-based survey. On the positive side, such surveys can gather extensive data quickly, employ tested forms and sample questions rather than having to design them, and take advantage of the extensive use of the Web by individuals today, including its use as a site for social networking. However, authors such as Sills and Song (2002) raise important methodological issues that educational survey researchers need to consider. They were concerned about the low response rates from e-mail and Web-based surveys. Contributing to this problem were nonrandom sampling, technological problems, security issues, and problems with Internet junk mail. They note that Internet users often change e-mail addresses. Often surveys are not based on random sampling so that drawing inferences to a general population is difficult. Web-based surveys may be biased toward certain demographic groups that tend to use computers. On the other hand, Web surveys may allow effective and economical surveying of the entire population and thereby skirt around the inference problem. Further, they saw a mixed system of Web-based and mailed surveys as promoting a high response rate.

One-on-One Interviews

One-on-one interviews are a form of survey data collection. In **one-on-one interviewing in survey research**, investigators conduct an interview with an individual in the sample and record responses to closed-ended questions. The process involves developing or locating an instrument and training the interviewer(s) in good interview procedures. This training consists of learning how to provide instructions during the interview, maintaining confidentiality about the interview, asking the exact question on the interview guide, completing the interview within the time allocated, being courteous, and not interjecting personal opinions into the interview. When multiple interviewers are used, researchers train all individuals to use the same procedure so that the mode of administration does not introduce bias into the study.

One-on-one interviews are useful for asking sensitive questions and enabling interviewees to ask questions or provide comments that go beyond the initial questions. Interviews lead to a high response rate because researchers schedule the interviews in advance and sample participants typically feel obligated to complete the interview. However, one-on-one interviews do not protect the anonymity of the participant as questionnaires do. Researchers may also prejudice participant answers, knowingly or unknowingly, through either comments or body language. Also, not all interviewees are comfortable disclosing information about themselves during the interview.

Focus Group Interviews

An alternative to a one-on-one interview is to administer a survey to a focus group. In quantitative **focus group interviews in survey research**, the researcher locates or develops a survey instrument, convenes a small group of people (typically a group of 4 to 6) who can answer the questions, and records their comments on the instrument. For example, this group might consist of parents who evaluate a new math or science curriculum in a school. Alternatively, international students provide views about cultural integration into an American university setting. During processes such as these, researchers ask the group questions on an instrument and record or take notes on the group conversation.

Focus groups provide for interaction among interviewees, collection of extensive data, and participation by all individuals in a group (Krueger, 1994). A disadvantage of focus group interviews is that they require the researcher to find consensus on questions so one score can be marked for all individuals in the group. In addition, some individuals may dominate the conversation, leading to responses that do not reflect the consensus of the group.

Telephone Interviews

In **telephone interview surveys**, the researcher records the participants' comments to questions on instruments over the telephone. The researcher develops or locates an instrument, obtains the telephone numbers of participants in the sample, conducts the telephone calls, and asks the participants to answer questions on the instrument. Telephone interviews allow the researcher easy access to interviewees who are geographically dispersed. However, the researcher cannot see any nonverbal communication on the part of the participant, and people often dislike telephone contacts because of their prior personal experiences with calls from survey firms asking for information.

Assume that you advise Maria on the type of survey data collection she should use to study factors that explain why students hold positive attitudes toward weapon possession in the school. Should she use (a) a mailed questionnaire, (b) an electronic questionnaire, (c) one-on-one interviews, (d) focus group interviews, or (e) telephone interviews? Write down your answer and provide a rationale for your choice, then look at my answer below.

I would advise Maria to consider the sensitive nature of her study and realize that students need to have their anonymity protected. A mailed questionnaire would provide the greatest protection to students, and Maria could say that she will not identify individuals with survey responses in her report. To keep track of students who respond to the survey, she might enclose a postcard with a student identification number on it that the students return separately from their survey.

Instrument Design

Designing good survey instruments is a challenging and complex process. You should first consider whether a survey instrument is available to measure your variables. You might also consider modifying an existing instrument. If neither of these approaches will work, design your own instrument.

When survey researchers design an instrument for data collection, they typically perform the following steps:

1. *They write different types of questions.* These include personal, attitudinal, and behavioral questions; sensitive questions; and closed- and open-ended questions.
2. *They use strategies for good question construction.* This includes using clear language, making sure the answer options do not overlap, and posing questions that are applicable to all participants.
3. *They perform a pilot test of the questions.* This consists of administering the instrument to a small number of individuals and making changes based on their feedback.

Personal, Attitudinal, and Behavioral Questions

Consider the general forms of the types of *content* that questions might take on a survey instrument. There are three popular types. *Background* questions or *demographic* questions assess the personal characteristics of individuals in your sample. These questions can be easy (i.e., gender) or difficult to answer (i.e., level of income). Here are some examples of background questions:

What is your age? _____
How many years of teaching have you completed? (end of school year) _____

A second group of questions relates to obtaining individual *attitudes or opinions* from individuals in your sample. For example, you might ask:

How much do you agree or disagree with this statement:

Most days I am enthusiastic about being a student.
_____ Strongly agree
_____ Agree
_____ Neither agree or disagree

_____ Disagree
_____ Strongly disagree

A third group of questions can solicit information about the actual *behavior* of individuals in the sample. For example:

Did you take a semester off during any of your 4 years of college?
_____ Yes
_____ No

Sensitive Questions

Some surveys contain sensitive questions that must be developed and used with care. Sensitive questions might have to do with:

◆ Drug and alcohol use (e.g., use of cocaine)
◆ Mental health issues (e.g., paranoid behavior)

Depending on your topic, you may decide to use sensitive questions. If the questions are not tactfully stated, individuals may either over- or underrepresent their views, leading to bias in responses. Several strategies can be used to provide good questions (Neuman, 2000). You might include a sensitive question late in the survey, after the individual has "warmed up" by answering neutral questions and has established some rapport with the researcher. Also, initial comments can lead the respondent into the question:

Instead of: Have you ever used marijuana?

You might ask: In past surveys, many men have reported that at some point in their lives they have used marijuana. This could have happened before adolescence, during adolescence, or as an adult. Have you ever smoked marijuana?

Open- and Closed-Ended Questions

Surveys consist mainly of closed-ended questions. In **closed-ended questions in surveys**, the researcher poses a question and provides preset response options for the participant. A closed-ended question might be:

There are many reasons why adults wish to get more education. What is your most important reason for coming to adult basic education classes? (Check one.)
_____ To be able to help my children with their schoolwork
_____ To get a better job
_____ To improve myself
_____ To get a high school equivalency diploma

Here, the author provides a question followed by a limited number of response options. These options need to be mutually exclusive, or distinct from each other, and include the typical responses an individual might provide.

Closed-ended questions such as the example above are practical because all individuals will answer the question using the response options provided. This enables a researcher to conveniently compare responses. They are useful for sensitive questions because participants might feel more comfortable knowing the parameters of response options. Closed-ended questions also provide a means for coding responses or assigning a numeric value and statistically analyzing the data.

At times, however, you may want to probe a little deeper and explore the many possibilities that individuals might create for a question. In this case, open-ended questions are best. **Open-ended questions in a survey** are questions for which researchers do not provide the response options; the participants provide their own responses to questions. For example:

Why are you attending adult education classes?

_____

_____

_____

In an open-ended question, the participant supplies an answer. This question does not constrain individual responses. It is ideal when the researcher does not know the response possibilities and wants to explore the options. Further, open-ended questions allow participants to create responses within their cultural and social experiences instead of the researcher's experiences (Neuman, 2000).

However, open-ended questions have drawbacks of coding and analysis. The researcher needs to categorize the responses into themes, a process that may take considerable time. Open-ended responses require transforming word responses into numbers (e.g., participants mentioned "getting a better job" 15 times).

One further option is the use of **semi-closed-ended questions in a survey**. This type of question has all the advantages of open- and closed-ended questions. The technique is to ask a closed-ended question and then ask for additional responses in an open-ended question. For example:

There are many reasons why adults wish to further their education. What is your most important reason for coming to adult basic education classes? (Check one.)

_____To be able to help my children with their schoolwork

_____To get a better job

_____To improve myself

_____To get a high school equivalency diploma

_____Other (please comment)_____

This question provides the typical response categories to the question, but it also allows respondents to write in answers that may not fit the response choices. While it also provides limited open-ended information to encourage responses, it does not overburden the researcher with information that needs to be coded.

Question Construction

As you select an instrument or develop one of your own, pay attention to the quality of the questions. Using good questions helps participants feel that they understand the question and can provide meaningful answers. Good questions are clear and unambiguous, and they do not confuse the participants. They also show respect for the participant by being sensitive to gender, class, and cultural needs of participants. For example, in the community needs survey mentioned earlier (Batsche et al., 1999), the researchers used the term *Hispanic* out of respect for what the Spanish-monolingual residents preferred to call themselves. By using good questions, you are encouraging the participant to complete the instrument.

When you construct questions for a survey questionnaire or interview, fit the questions to answers, include suitable response options, and do not overlap. These strategies for constructing good questions are identified in Table 12.1. First, read the poor question. Next, determine the problem. Then, read the improved question. When you write questions (or review those provided by others), you might assess them in terms of whether your question is clear, has a clear response, and whether your questions are within the

TABLE 12.1

Common Problems in Item Construction in Survey Designs

Example of a Poor Question	Problem	Example of an Improved Question
Do you support gun control? _____ Yes _____ No _____ Don't know	Unclear question because of vague words	Do you believe that guns do not belong in schools? _____ Yes _____ No _____ Don't know
Do you believe that guns and knives do not belong in schools? _____ Yes _____ No _____ Don't know	Two or more questions (see the conjunction "and")	Do you believe that knives do not belong in schools? _____ Yes _____ No _____ Don't know
Whenever violence occurs in schools, weapons are typically found in school lockers. Do you believe that students should have guns in their lockers? _____ Yes _____ No _____ Don't know	Wordy or lengthy questions	Should students have guns in their lockers? _____ Yes _____ No _____ Don't know
Students should not carry weapons and not have them in their lockers. Do you agree? _____ Strongly agree _____ Agree _____ Undecided _____ Disagree _____ Strongly disagree	Question contains negatives	Should students have guns in their lockers? _____ Yes _____ No _____ Don't know
Should students pack a .45 at school? _____ Yes _____ No _____ Don't know	Question contains jargon	Should students carry a handgun at school? _____ Yes _____ No _____ Don't know
How many times have you seen a student carry a handgun? _____ 0 times _____ 1–2 times _____ 2–3 times _____ More than 3 times	Response categories overlap	How many times have you seen a student carry a handgun? _____ 0 times _____ 1–2 times _____ 3–4 times _____ More than 4 times
To what extent do you feel that handguns are a problem at your school? _____ A great extent _____ Some _____ Not very important _____ Not a problem	Unbalanced response options	To what extent do you feel that handguns are a problem at your school? _____ A great extent _____ Some extent _____ Little extent
To what extent do you feel that handguns are a problem at your school? _____ Very important _____ Important _____ Little importance	Mismatch between the question and the responses	To what extent do you feel that handguns are a problem at your school? _____ A great extent _____ Some extent _____ Little extent

TABLE 12.1

(Continued)

Example of a Poor Question	Problem	Example of an Improved Question
How often have you seen students carry semi-automatic weapons at school? _____ None _____ 1 time _____ 2 times _____ 3 or more times	Respondent does not have understanding to answer question	How often have you seen students carry a rifle at school? _____ None _____ 1 time _____ 2 times _____ 3 or more times
How many students have you seen carrying guns at school? _____ 1 student _____ 2 students _____ 3 students _____ More than 3 students	Not all respondents can answer the question—branching needed	Have you seen students carrying guns at school? _____ Yes _____ No If Yes, how many students? _____ 1 student _____ 2 students _____ 3 students _____ More than 3 students

participants' ability to answer. A review of these potential question construction problems and some solutions will provide guidance for survey development.

◆ *The question is unclear.* This usually occurs because words are vague or imprecise. Identify the unclear or vague words and replace them with words understood by participants in the study.

◆ *There are multiple questions.* Here, the question actually contains two or more questions, called a *double-* or *triple-barreled question.* Reduce the multiple questions to a single question.

◆ *The question is wordy.* When the question is too long, cut out unnecessary words to simplify and shorten the question. Look for excessive use of prepositions (e.g., more than three) or qualifying statements that lengthen the question.

◆ *The question is negatively worded or wordy.* If the question contains one or more negatives, such as "should not," the meaning becomes unclear. Also, reword the question if it leads the participants to one particular stance or another (e.g., using the word "pro-life"). Restate or reword the question to eliminate negative connotations or leading words.

◆ *The question includes jargon.* Jargon may not be familiar to all participants in a study. Eliminate the jargon and use words familiar to all participants.

◆ *There are overlapping responses.* This may lead to confusion when answering a question. Make sure that the response options do not overlap by creating distinct options.

◆ *There are unbalanced response options.* In this case, the responses may be unbalanced in terms of naturally occurring intervals. Response options may start with an "importance" word (e.g., "very important") and end with an "extent" word (e.g., "to a little extent"), rather than a matching adjective (e.g., "not important"). Decide on a single response option and use it consistently for all response categories for a question.

◆ *There is a mismatch between the question and the answers.* The responses may not match the "action" word used in the question. Identify the verb or adjective in the question that will be the basis for the response options and create options using this word. (E.g., if the question says "to what extent," the answer will say "a great extent.")

◆ *The question includes overly technical language.* When this occurs, the respondent may not have the level of understanding needed to respond to the question. Simplify the question so that all individuals will know the meaning of the words and can respond to the question.

◆ *Not all questions are applicable to all participants.* If some participants cannot answer the question, include "branching" or "contingency questions." These questions follow the original question and provide options to include all participants.

Pilot Testing the Questions

After good questions have been developed using principles of question construction, a researcher pilot tests the questions. This helps determine that the individuals in the sample are capable of completing the survey and that they can understand the questions. A **pilot test** of a questionnaire or interview survey is a procedure in which a researcher makes changes in an instrument based on feedback from a small number of individuals who complete and evaluate the instrument. The participants in the pilot test provide written comments directly on the survey, and the researcher modifies or changes the survey to reflect those concerns. Because the pilot group provides feedback on the questionnaire, you exclude them from the final sample for the study.

For example, a survey of 100 middle school students' attitudes toward school might begin with a pilot test of an instrument with 50 questions. In this pilot test, the researcher selects 15 students to complete the instrument. The investigator then asks them to mark any problems on the survey, such as poorly worded questions, responses that do not make sense, or if it takes an excessive amount of time to complete the instrument. Based on student feedback, the researcher then revises the instrument before sending it out to the sample in the study.

Response Rate

Survey researchers seek high response rates from participants in a study so that they can have confidence in generalizing the results to the population under study. When using interviews, the response rate is high because individuals interviewed typically consent to the interview in advance. However, when questionnaires are used, the number of responses returned (through mail or electronically) will vary. In either case, survey researchers place emphasis on obtaining a high response rate to their questionnaire or interview. On the instruments that are returned, the survey researcher is also concerned about whether the returned responses are biased. Even a small return rate may not be biased and be acceptable in survey research. Although response rate is important, bias is a larger concern than return rate because if the returned responses are biased, the database will be inadequate, regardless of the return rate.

Response Rates for Mailed Questionnaires

As mentioned earlier, a high response rate creates a stronger claim in generalizing results from the sample to the population. A **response return rate** is the percentage of questionnaires that participants return to the researcher. Many survey studies in leading educational journals report a response rate of 50% or better. However, this rate will fluctuate depending on proper notification, adequate follow-up procedures, respondent interest in the study, the quality of the instrument, and use of incentives.

Researchers use several strategies to encourage high return rates. One is to *prenotify participants* that they will receive a questionnaire. Individuals receive an introductory letter asking them to participate in the study and telling them that they will receive a survey

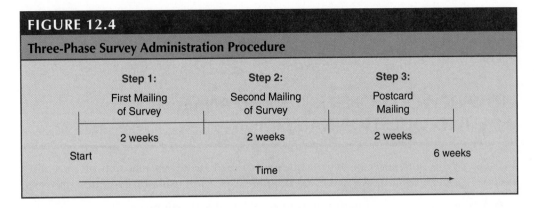

FIGURE 12.4

Three-Phase Survey Administration Procedure

Step 1:	Step 2:	Step 3:
First Mailing of Survey	Second Mailing of Survey	Postcard Mailing
2 weeks	2 weeks	2 weeks

Start

6 weeks

Time

in 2 weeks. Another strategy is to use *good follow-up procedures*. Figure 12.4 shows a three-step procedure that might be used.

1. Mail out the original questionnaire.
2. Follow it 2 weeks later with a second questionnaire to the individuals who have not responded (called *nonrespondents*).
3. After another 2 weeks, send a postcard to the nonrespondents, reminding them to complete the questionnaire.

Although you might take additional steps, this three-step process should help you attain a good return rate. The time for each notification will vary, of course, depending on the study. For most questionnaires mailed within the United States, however, this format should allow the researcher to conclude data collection in 6 weeks.

Another way to encourage a high response rate is to *study a problem of interest* to the population under study. If individuals in the sample are interested in the issue, they will be more apt to complete the survey. Also, *using a brief instrument* usually encourages a high return rate. Typically, a three-page instrument will take less than 15 minutes to complete.

A final strategy is to *consider the use of incentives* to encourage individuals to return the instrument. Studies show mixed results on the impact of incentives, even small ones like giving enough money for a cup of coffee (Babbie, 1998). As a researcher, you need to weigh the costs of incentives against their potential help with returns. In many cases, survey researchers combine many of the strategies mentioned so far—prenotification, follow-up procedures, and clear instrument constructions—with modest incentives to encourage high returns.

Response Bias

What do you do if your response rate is low? You might proceed with your study and report a limitation of a low response rate; extend the time to collect data to gather more responses; or report that your responses, although low, are representative of the sample (and population). This last option is response bias. With a low return rate, the key issue is not necessarily how many people returned an instrument, but whether bias exists in those who *did* return it. **Response bias** occurs in survey research when the responses do not accurately reflect the views of the sample and the population. For example, the individuals who return a questionnaire may be overly negative or positive. Thus, survey researchers monitor their returns to assess whether they display bias. We call this approach wave analysis. **Wave analysis** is a procedure to check for response bias in which investigators group returns by intervals (e.g., each week) and check to see if the answers to a few select questions change from the first week to the final week in a study, indicating response bias. Individuals responding in the final week of survey administration are as close to nonreturns or nonrespondents as possible. However, their responses should be similar (i.e., and not biased) to those returning instruments in the first week. If they differ, researchers report that the potential for bias exists, and the potential that the participants studied may not be representative of the sample and the population.

HOW DO YOU CONSTRUCT AND ANALYZE A MAILED QUESTIONNAIRE?

Because of the popularity of mailed questionnaires for student research projects, they deserve special attention. We will focus on three aspects of using mailed questionnaires:

◆ A cover letter to invite participants to complete the questionnaire
◆ The form and construction of the questionnaire
◆ Statistical procedures typically used to analyze data from a mailed questionnaire

We use a mailed questionnaire from VanHorn-Grassmeyer (1998) as a specific example. VanHorn-Grassmeyer studied 119 individuals new to the field of student affairs (e.g., student activity leaders) in colleges and universities in the central United States and Canada. Her purpose was to explore the perceptions, attitudes, and behaviors of professionals regarding their professional practices. As one aspect of her data collection, she mailed a self-designed questionnaire to the participants. This instrument consisted of five parts:

1. A cover letter
2. Closed-ended questions asking participants about their background (i.e., demographic questions)
3. Closed-ended questions addressing practices or behaviors (e.g., "I claim responsibility when I've made a 'bad call' professionally") and attitudes (e.g., "I benefit from collaborative reflection with colleagues")
4. Open-ended questions permitting respondents to add their perceptions (e.g., "In your opinion, what defines a competent student affairs professional?")
5. Closing instructions thanking the participant for taking part in the study

This cover letter and mailed questionnaire comprised a five-page packet, which can be seen in Figures 12.5 and 12.6 as they were originally reported in VanHorn-Grassmeyer's dissertation.

Inspecting these examples can provide useful ideas for designing your own cover letter and questionnaire.

The Cover Letter

A major component of a mailed questionnaire consists of a cover letter inviting the participant to take part in the study and to complete the instrument. When we inspect the cover letter in Figure 12.5, we find these major elements:

◆ *Importance of participant.*   To encourage individuals to complete the questionnaire, they need to know why they have been sent the instrument. The first few sentences indicate the importance of recipients and the value of their response. It is often helpful to begin a cover letter with this statement, as illustrated in this example.
◆ *Purpose of the study.*   Include a statement indicating, succinctly, the intent or purpose of the study. This statement not only informs the participant about the nature of the study, but it also fulfills an important "informed consent" provision of identifying the purpose of the study for participants.

FIGURE 12.5

Sample Cover Letter

Cover Letter Components	
	July 10, 2004
	Dear Colleague,
Importance of participant	As a relative newcomer to the profession of student affairs, you undoubtedly have ways in which you enhance your practice. Graduate preparation programs, associations, and seasoned professionals must be aware of the strategies that are most useful to you and other professionals in order to help promote professional development, competency, and commitment to the field. Your response to this survey can greatly enhance our understanding.
Purpose of the study	I am conducting this research to explore how professionals new to the field of student affairs enhance their practice. I want to measure the extent to which new professionals use individual and collaborative (that is, in interaction with other professionals) strategies including reflection, and opportunities for development. I will also measure how new professionals view their own skills and knowledge. My population is new professionals in the west-central part of the United States and Canada.
Assurances	Your participation in this research is, of course, voluntary. Your confidentiality and anonymity are assured. Return of the survey to me is your consent for your responses to be compiled with others. Although the survey is coded to allow for follow-up with non-respondents, you will not be individually identified with your questionnaire or responses. Please understand that use of this data will be limited to this research, as authorized by the University of Nebraska at Lincoln, although results may ultimately (and hopefully!) be presented in formats other than the dissertation, such as journal articles or conference presentations. You also have the right to express concerns to me at the number below, my major professor Dr. John
Sponsorship	Creswell at the UNL Department of Educational Psychology address shown above, or the UNL Institutional Review Board.
Completion time Returns	I greatly appreciate your participation in this research. *The survey will take approximately 15–20 minutes to complete.* **Please return the survey within two weeks (by July 25)** in the enclosed, self-addressed, stamped envelope. This will save a follow-up mailing to you.
	If you have been in the field for more than five years, please note as much on survey item #1 and return the entire instrument to me.
	Thank you for your interest and participation in this study. I genuinely appreciate your time.
	Sincerely,
Sponsorship	Kimberly VanHorn-Grassmeyer Associate Director, Student Assistance Center University of Kansas, Lawrence KS 66045 913.864.4064; kgrassmeyer@ukans.edu

Source: Reprinted with permission from Kimberly VanHorn-Grassmeyer, Ph.D.

FIGURE 12.6

Sample Mailed Questionnaire

ENHANCING PRACTICE:
NEW PROFESSIONALS IN STUDENT AFFAIRS

I. DEMOGRAPHICS:

1. Years of employment   ___ a. current Graduate Student   ___ d. more than 5 years
    in Student Affairs: ___ b. 0 up to 2 years   *If d, do not complete remainder of survey.*
                               ___ c. more than 2, up to 5 years   *Return in envelope provided. Thank you.*

2. Graduate program practical experiences *(check any of the following that apply to your experience):*
     ___ a. assistantship in student services (paid training experience)
     ___ b. practica in student services (unpaid training experience)
     ___ c. mentoring relationship with a mid- or senior-level administrator
     ___ d. peer group interactions such as case studies, problem-solving
     ___ e. peer group interactions more social in nature
     ___ f. other out-of-class experience: _____

3. National professional associations in which you are a member *(rank 1-3 in order of importance to you):*
     ___ a. AAHE   ___ d. AERA   ___ g. NASPA
     ___ b. ACPA   ___ e. ASHE   ___ h. NAWE / NAWDAC
     ___ c. ACUHO   ___ f. NACA   ___ i. Other: _____

4. Gender: ___ a. female   ___ b. male

II. PROFESSIONAL PRACTICE:

1. Indicate the amount of institutional funding you received in the past academic year for participation in professional
    development conferences and workshops off-site:
     ___ a. none   ___ c. $101 to $250   ___ e. $501 to $1000
     ___ b. less than $100   ___ d. $251 to $500   ___ f. more than $1000

2. Indicate the amount of personal funds you spent in the past academic year for participation in professional
    development conferences and workshops off-site:
     ___ a. none   ___ c. $101 to $250   ___ e. $501 to $1000
     ___ b. less than $100   ___ d. $251 to $500   ___ f. more than $1000

3. What professional development costs *(full or partial)* does your institution absorb for you?
    (check any of the following that apply):
     ___ a. association membership dues for more than one association
     ___ b. association membership dues for only one association
     ___ c. on-site seminars and workshops
     ___ d. staff retreats
     ___ e. subscriptions to professional journals and newsletters
     ___ f. release time for participation in programmed activities
     ___ g. release time for personal reflection and renewal
     ___ h. release time for courses related to my work
     ___ i. tuition assistance for courses related to my work

4. To what extent do you feel your graduate program prepared you for your work in student affairs?
     ACADEMICALLY: ___ a. not at all   EXPERIENTIALLY: ___ a. not at all
                              ___ b. a little bit   ___ b. a little bit
                              ___ c. fairly well   ___ c. fairly well
                              ___ d. very well   ___ d. very well

Source: Reprinted with permission from Kimberly VanHorn-Grassmeyer, Ph.D.

FIGURE 12.6

(Continued)

Enhancing Practice Survey, p. 2

Using the following 1 - 5 scale, please indicate, by circling the most correct response, the degree to which you agree with the statements listed below:

1	2	3	4	5
strongly disagree	disagree	neutral	agree	strongly agree

1 2 3 4 5   5. I have a strong personal commitment to my professional growth and development.

6. Regarding my professional practice, I value the opinions of my:
1 2 3 4 5   a. colleagues
1 2 3 4 5   b. mentor(s)
1 2 3 4 5   c. graduate program peers

1 2 3 4 5   7. When I reflect on my practice, I know more than I'm really able to describe.

1 2 3 4 5   8. I believe my instincts compare favorably with colleagues I respect.

1 2 3 4 5   9. I have a responsibility to contribute to the development of other student affairs professionals.

1 2 3 4 5   10. My institution expects continued professional development of its staff.

1 2 3 4 5   11. I know that I need to consciously enhance my professional practice.

1 2 3 4 5   12. I like to talk with other professionals about my decision-making and professional practice.

1 2 3 4 5   13. I know most of what I will need to guide my practice.

1 2 3 4 5   14. I feel a sense of connection to the field of Student Affairs.

1 2 3 4 5   15. I have a professional responsibility to continue to learn and develop in my daily work.

1 2 3 4 5   16. I benefit from collaborative reflection with colleagues.

1 2 3 4 5   17. I believe my institution should ensure that I grow as a professional.

1 2 3 4 5   18. I consider myself to be a strong student affairs administrator.

1 2 3 4 5   19. I expect to continue working in student affairs for at least ten years.

20. I receive encouragement for continuing professional growth and development from:
1 2 3 4 5   a. institutional colleagues
1 2 3 4 5   b. my senior student affairs offficer

1 2 3 4 5   21. I still have a lot to learn from experience and practice.

22. I continue to learn a great deal from my:
1 2 3 4 5   a. colleagues
1 2 3 4 5   b. mentor(s)
1 2 3 4 5   c. graduate program peers

1 2 3 4 5   23. I have a sense of self-efficacy and confidence in my work.

FIGURE 12.6

(Continued)

Enhancing Practice Survey, p. 3

1	2	3	4	5
strongly disagree	disagree	neutral	agree	strongly agree

24. I maintain a strong network of or connection to:
1 2 3 4 5   a. professional colleagues
1 2 3 4 5   b. mentor(s)
1 2 3 4 5   c. graduate program peers

1 2 3 4 5   25. I believe my professional development is my responsibility.

1 2 3 4 5   26. I prefer close supervision over my activities at this point in my career.

1 2 3 4 5   27. I have learned about as much as I can of student development theory.

1 2 3 4 5   28. I am able to function autonomously in my professional role.

1 2 3 4 5   29. I have a professional responsibility to promote/advance the student affairs field.

Using the following 1 - 5 scale, please indicate by circling the most correct response, how regularly you practice the activities listed below:

1	2	3	4	5
never	rarely	sometimes	regularly	often

1 2 3 4 5   30. At least one of my institutional job performance measures (e.g., annual review, annual goals) includes an expectation for professional growth and development.

1 2 3 4 5   31. I read professional journals and periodicals to keep current in the field.

1 2 3 4 5   32. I make time for collaborative (with other professionals) reflection.

1 2 3 4 5   33. I claim responsibility when I've made a "bad call" professionally.

1 2 3 4 5   34. I consciously think back to and apply theory as I go about decision-making and professional practice.

1 2 3 4 5   35. I attend conferences even when I'm expected to personally absorb the majority of the cost of attendance.

36. I utilize the expertise of others (listed in a-b-c) to enhance my professional practice:
1 2 3 4 5   a. colleagues
1 2 3 4 5   b. mentor(s)
1 2 3 4 5   c. graduate program peers

1 2 3 4 5   37. After taking action or employing a strategy, I reflect to determine whether it was appropriate, and how I might respond differently next time.

1 2 3 4 5   38. I second-guess my actions in professional situations.

1 2 3 4 5   39. I seek out opportunities to share my professional knowledge and learning with other professionals.
Indicate how you have done so:
___ a. write for publication in professional journals, newsletters, etc.
___ b. present sessions at retreats, workshops and/or conferences
___ c. collaborate with others who seek advice and assistance
___ d. other methods: _____

FIGURE 12.6

(Continued)

Enhancing Practice Survey, p. 4

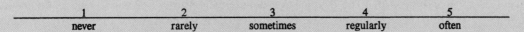

1	2	3	4	5
never	rarely	sometimes	regularly	often

1 2 3 4 5   40. I serve on institution-wide committees, task forces, ad hoc groups, etc.

1 2 3 4 5   41. I seek out opportunities to enhance my professional knowledge and practice.

1 2 3 4 5   42. I attend professional association conferences (regional/state or national).
     For this question only: 1=never, 2=rarely, 3=some years, 4=every year, 5=more than one each year

1 2 3 4 5   43. I feel confident when making particularly difficult professional decisions.

1 2 3 4 5   44. I record my thoughts about professional practice in a journal/diary.

1 2 3 4 5   45. I consciously think back to and apply personal experiences as I go about decision-making and professional practice.

1 2 3 4 5   46. I make time for individual professional reflection.

III. SHORT ANSWER QUESTIONS:
Please respond briefly to the following questions, *using an additional sheet if necessary:*
47. Think back on one of the most difficult professional decisions you've made in your current position, one that involved a situation with others (colleagues, students, supervisees). Please describe how you reached that decision, what factors you considered, who, if anyone, you consulted with beforehand, and whether & how you processed it afterward.

48. In your opinion, what defines a competent student affairs professional? Would you describe yourself in those terms? Why or why not?

THANK YOU FOR YOUR PARTICIPATION AND CANDID RESPONSES.
Please return your survey in the enclosed stamped envelope before July 25.

◆ *Assurances of confidentiality.*   Also, to comply with informed consent and to be ethical, the investigator assures the individual of confidentiality (i.e., not identifying individuals specifically).

◆ *Sponsorship.*   The cover letter includes the advisor's name as well as the institution where VanHorn-Grassmeyer works. In addition, write the letter on letterhead stationery to add additional sponsorship.

◆ *Completion time and returns.*   Add to the letter an estimate of the amount of time the survey will take to be completed and the procedure for returning the instrument to the author.

Overall Questionnaire Construction

Examine Figure 12.6 to see a complete mailed questionnaire. This instrument contains features of good questionnaire construction. It is short and encourages a busy professional to return it. The instrument begins with demographic or personal questions that respondents can easily answer, and in the process of answering them, they become committed to completing the form. For variety, the author used different types of closed-ended questions, from checking the appropriate response (e.g., "years of employment") to an extent of agreement scale ("strongly disagree" to "strongly agree"), to a frequency scale ("never" to "often"). The questionnaire also contains open-ended items to encourage participants to elaborate on their experiences and definitions (e.g., "What defines a competent student affairs professional?"). It also contains a pleasing layout with much "white space" between the questions and the use of one scale (e.g., "strongly disagree" to "strongly agree") for multiple questions so that participants do not repeat responses. It also includes closing instructions thanking the respondent for participating in the study.

Data Analysis of a Research Questionnaire

When researchers compare groups or relate variables, their statistical analysis of questionnaire data extends beyond simple descriptive analysis. Examine the steps identified in Figure 12.7.

These steps describe the process typically used for analyzing mailed questionnaire data. The figure includes reporting response rate and checking for bias in responses. The researcher also descriptively reports aggregate responses to each item on the questionnaire. This process helps to discern general patterns of responses and variation (variance and standard deviation) in results. Typically, researchers using mailed questionnaires also correlate all of the questions and attempt to build scales that reflect multiple questions. As with all instruments, scores need to be reliable and valid, and statistical procedures such as internal consistency checks (e.g., the alpha reliability statistic) and validity (e.g., factor analysis) represent means for making these assessments. Finally, the researcher tests hypotheses or research questions using inferential statistics.

HOW DO YOU DESIGN AND CONDUCT AN INTERVIEW SURVEY?

Instead of a mailed survey, researchers might collect quantitative data using an interview survey instrument. In using this form of data collection, we need to know the stance of the interviewer, recognize the importance of training interviewers (if there is more than

FIGURE 12.7

Checklist for Analyzing Questionnaire Data

_____ Step 1. Identify response rate and response bias.

    _____ Develop table for percent of responses to the survey.

    _____ Develop table for the wave analysis response bias.

_____ Step 2. Descriptively analyze the data to identify general trends.

    _____ Calculate and present a table of descriptive statistics (mean, variance, and range) for each question on the instrument.

    _____ Analyze data to develop a demographic profile of the sample (analyze questions about personal factors).

    _____ Analyze data to provide answers to descriptive questions in the study (if any).

_____ Step 3. Write the report presenting the descriptive results or use advanced statistics.

    _____ Develop scales by combining questions on the instrument (i.e., correlate items using the statistical procedure of factor analysis).

    _____ Check for the reliability of the scores on the scales (i.e., use a coefficient of internal consistency).

    _____ Check for the validity of the scores on scales (or factors) (i.e., use factor analysis).

    _____ Analyze data using inferential statistics to address research questions or hypotheses (i.e., comparing groups, relating variables).

one), and know the general steps in administering this form of data collection. To understand this process, we will use a telephone interview as an example.

Stance of the Interviewer

Researchers often use interview surveys less frequently than mailed questionnaires in educational research. Interview procedures often involve the need for the researcher to establish rapport with and gain the cooperation of the interviewee. Rapport builds through requests for an interview in the cover letter. During an interview, the researcher should remain neutral and should not share opinions (e.g., "I think that budget cutting is a good idea, too"). It is also important to use a positive tone of questioning and to have a neutral appearance.

Training of Interviewers

If more than one interviewer is involved in a research project, each person needs training. This training might consist of a role-playing demonstration by an experienced researcher and a practice interview by the individual researchers who will be conducting the interviews. It is important during this training for interviewers to become familiar with the questions so that they will know if the responses match the questions. Training also covers potential interruptions during interviews or questions interviewees might have about the interview. Problems can arise during an interview, such as when the interviewer:

◆ Does not ask the questions in order (e.g., Question 3 is asked before Question 2)
◆ Intentionally subverts the process because of disinterest in the topic (e.g., the interviewer does not take time to probe on questions)
◆ Brings certain expectations to the interview about how the individuals will answer (e.g., the interviewer prefaces the question with "I think you already know the answer to this . . .")
◆ Dresses or appears inappropriately for the interview (e.g., wears shorts when the interviewee is dressed in a suit)
◆ Is disrespectful by not using names the interviewee wants to be called (e.g., referring to the individual as "Latino" instead of "Hispanic")

Steps in Interviewing

The steps in conducting an interview involve obtaining an interview survey to use and training individual interviewers (if more than one person will be conducting the interviews). Then the researcher gains access to the participants through a formal invitation, such as a cover letter, and establishes a time and place to conduct the interview. During the interview, the survey researcher asks questions, indicates the response options to questions, and records participant answers. The pace of the interview is set to be comfortable for the interviewee. When asking open-ended questions, the interviewer writes down answers to the questions (or tape-records them). The interview ends with the researcher thanking the individual for the interview and telling the participant what the next step will be in the study. After the interview, the researcher may want to write down comments that help explain the data, such as the demeanor of the interviewee or specifics about the situation (e.g., "It was so noisy I could hardly hear at times"). The interviewer might also record any personal feelings about the interview (e.g., "I felt uneasy during this interview and perhaps did not probe as much as I could have").

A Telephone Interview Guide

An example of a telephone interview guide is shown in Figure 12.8. This interview guide was for an interview with 200 academic department chairpersons surveyed to understand how chairpersons assisted faculty in their units (Creswell et al., 1990). Consisting of 25 questions, each interview lasted, on average, about 45 minutes, and all interviews were audiotaped. Six interviewers assisted in the process of data collection, and their training consisted of a demonstration and a practice interview. The researchers constructed this guide to include:

◆ Introductory remarks to help establish rapport and direction for the interview (e.g., the amount of time required)
◆ Clearly marked boxes with instructions for each question in the interview so that each interviewer on the research team would ask the same question
◆ Closed-ended response options for each question, with space between questions permitting the interviewer to write in additional comments
◆ Numbers in parentheses to indicate the column number for coding the response into a data grid of a computer file for statistical analysis

FIGURE 12.8

Sample Telephone Interview Guide

Structured Interview Schedule A

Interviewer's Code Sheet

Pre-Interview Information

    Interviewer's ID _____   (1–2)
    Institutional Code No. _____   (3–5)
    Date of Interview _____   (6–10)
    Discipline Code (Carnegie) for Interviewee _____   (11–12)
    Gender of Interviewee (1) Female _____ (2) Male _____   (13)

[Note to interviewer: Mark # on your tape counter for potentially interesting quotes.]

Interview Information

Interviewer's Introduction

> We appreciate your willingness to be interviewed today. As we indicated earlier, the purpose of our project is to interview department chairs (or their institutional equivalent) who are considered exceptional in assisting faculty on college and university campuses and to identify specific ways in which they enhance the professional growth and development of faculty in their units. This project is being sponsored by the Lilly Endowment and TIAA-CREF, and the information will be used in the preparation of a practical handbook.
>
> The interview should last from 30 to 40 minutes. In our earlier communication with you, we described the nature of our interview questions. Should we go over the question areas at this time? (Pause for response.)

4. How were you selected?   (25)
    (1) National search _____
    (2) Administrative appointment _____
    (3) Elected by faculty _____
    (4) Other _____

5. Please tell me some information about your appointment.

    Do you have a specific length of appointment in calendar years? (Probe: reappointed?)
    (1) Yes, # of years _____
    (2) No _____
    (3) Uncertain _____   (26–27)

    If yes, is this length typical on your campus?
    (1) Yes _____
    (2) No _____
    (3) Uncertain _____   (28)

    Do you serve at the pleasure of faculty in your unit or administrators?
    (1) Faculty _____
    (2) Administrators _____
    (3) Some combination _____   (29)

6. How long do you expect to stay in your current position?
    [Interviewer: Cite reasons where possible.]

    (1) Don't know _____
    (2) Certain number of years _____
    (3) Up to my dean _____
    (4) As long as I want _____
    (5) Up to the faculty _____

WHAT ARE POTENTIAL ETHICAL ISSUES IN SURVEY RESEARCH?

Ethical issues arise in survey research at distinct points in the research process, such as in collecting data, in analyzing results, and in reporting results. Fowler (2009) provides detailed attention to these phases in the survey process and the ethical issues they present. At the outset, it is noted that survey research is often exempt from a detailed review by institutional review boards unless it addresses sensitive topics or involves research with sensitive or minor populations. Survey researchers can use incentives to encourage individuals to participate in a study, but these incentives should not be so large that they become unethical for individual participation. Clearly, good ethical practices dictate that survey researchers do not overstate the benefits of participating and deliver on what benefits are guaranteed.

Ethical responsibility attaches to survey researchers who engage interviewers to go out in the field and gather information. Researchers should not put interviewers at risk for their safety, or put the interviewer in a position of being deceptive, misleading, or inaccurate. Sensible procedures should be used by such interviewers to keep them safe.

The respondent participants need to be kept safe as well. What the researcher learns from the survey respondent should not be shared outside of the research team. Confidentiality of responses should be protected, such as minimizing links between answers and specific participant identifiers. Links between the answers and participants should be made with an ID number that is only known by the researcher or the research team. In analyzing the data, survey researchers should be careful about reporting a small subset of results that will disclose the identity of specific individuals. Also, when the project concludes, the researcher is responsible for the destruction of the survey instruments, keeping in mind that questionnaires and records can be subpoenaed by courts (unless petitions of confidentiality are filed with the courts).

In Box 12.1, we see an ethical dilemma arise in survey research in a large city.

BOX 12.1   Ethical Dilemma

Unsafe Survey Procedures?

A research team hired by the city sought check the authenticity of the homeless count in one large metropolitan city. The intent of the project was to make sure that the city had appropriate resources for the homeless. This research team hired a number of survey researchers. Their task was to be "decoys" and dress up like homeless individuals, go to a designated "project" apartment complex and spend the night standing right near the entrance of a building. When census takers came by, they were to note whether they were being counted. The research team sent these survey researchers out in teams of two. Do you feel that this was a potentially unsafe role for the survey researchers? Was this deceptive survey research practices? What safety precautions would you have taken if you were in charge of this research project?

WHAT ARE THE STEPS IN CONDUCTING SURVEY RESEARCH?

The steps in the process of conducting survey research follow the general process of research. Survey steps, however, address primarily the procedures for collecting data, analyzing data, and writing the final report.

Step 1. Decide if a Survey Is the Best Design to Use

You need to decide whether survey research is the best design to use in the study. Surveys help describe the trends in a population or describe the relationship among variables or compare groups. Instances where surveys are most suitable are to assess trends or characteristics of a population; learn about individual attitudes, opinions, beliefs, and practices; evaluate the success or effectiveness of a program; or identify the needs of a community.

There are several advantages to using surveys. You can administer them in a short time, they are economical as a means of data collection, and they can reach a geographically dispersed population. Further, you can canvass the participants anonymously, without biasing their responses. However, survey data is self-reported information, reporting only what people think rather than what they do. Sometimes the response rates are low and researchers cannot make claims about the representativeness of the results to the population. As mentioned earlier, surveys do not control for many variables that might explain the relationship between the independent and dependent variables, and they do not provide participants flexibility in responding to questions (unless open-ended questions are included).

Step 2. Identify the Research Questions or Hypotheses

You can address both research questions and hypotheses in a survey design. Surveys lend themselves to hypothesis testing because you will be studying a sample to draw inferences to a population. Forms of research questions or hypotheses are those that:

- Describe the characteristics or trends of a population of people, such as the frequency of tobacco use among male high school students
- Compare groups in terms of specific attributes, such as a comparison of teachers and administrators about attitudes toward "in-service" learning days
- Relate two or more variables, such as a survey of teachers to relate "burnout" to number of years of teaching

Step 3. Identify the Population, the Sampling Frame, and the Sample

The process of survey research begins with identifying the population. This step requires defining the population, determining the number of people in it, and assessing whether you can obtain a list of names (i.e., the sampling frame) for the sample. Also, the population may need to be stratified before sampling, so select characteristics of the population (e.g., males and females) are represented in the sample.

Once you have identified the target population and compiled a list of its members, you can select the sample, preferably using random sampling procedures. You will need to identify an adequate sample size, using a sampling error formula.

Step 4. Determine the Survey Design and Data Collection Procedures

The researcher must also determine if the survey study will be cross-sectional or longitudinal. The decision to use a longitudinal or cross-sectional design relates to the nature of the problem studied, access to participants, and the time available to the researchers for data collection. For example, learning about the longitudinal development of adolescent social skills in schools requires following adolescents over time and devoting extensive time to data collection. In contrast, examining parents' attitudes toward discipline in schools requires a cross-sectional study at one point in time to assess attitudes immediately and quickly.

Consider also whether data collection will be based on questionnaires (mailed or electronic) or interviews (individual, focus group, or telephone), and weigh the advantages and disadvantages of each form.

Step 5. Develop or Locate an Instrument

You need an instrument to collect or measure the variables in a study. It is easier to locate an instrument than to develop one. Standards of reliability and construct validity need to be applied to scores from existing instruments before you select them for use. If a study addresses only a few variables, researchers can design their own instruments. A check for the reliability and validity of scores from this instrument during data analysis is most important.

Step 6. Administer the Instrument

This step is perhaps the most time-consuming phase of survey research. It involves seeking and obtaining permission to conduct the survey and using procedures for data gathering, such as training interviewers or preparing questionnaires for mailing. It requires continually following up to obtain a high response rate, checking for response bias if questionnaires are used, and preparing the data for analysis by coding the information from the instruments into a computer file.

Step 7. Analyze the Data to Address the Research Questions or Hypotheses

The data analysis procedures will reflect the types of research questions or hypotheses the researcher plans to address in the study. Analysis consists of noting response rates, checking for response bias, conducting descriptive analysis of all items, and then answering descriptive questions. It might also involve testing hypotheses or research questions using inferential statistics.

Step 8. Write the Report

You should write the survey study using a standard quantitative structure that consists of an introduction, the review of the literature, the methods, the results, and the discussion. Specify in the "Methods" section of the study detailed information about the survey procedures. Include in the "Discussion" section comments about the generalizability of the results to the population.

HOW DO YOU EVALUATE SURVEY RESEARCH?

Whether the research consists of interviews or mailed questionnaires, survey studies need to meet high standards of quality. If you plan to conduct a survey, you need to design and write a "Methods" section in your study that conveys the detailed survey research procedures.

For educators who read and seek to use results from surveys, a checklist of elements to include in a survey design can provide basic information to look for in a published study. The following checklist of quality criteria is based on the key concepts introduced in this chapter and adapted from Fowler (2009) and Neuman (2000). The researcher:

◆ Describes and specifies the target population and the sample.
◆ Identifies how the sample was derived (e.g., random sampling, nonrandom sampling).
◆ Discusses the size of the sample and the means for deriving the sample size.
◆ Uses a type of survey (i.e., longitudinal or cross sectional) that matches the research questions or hypotheses.
◆ Clearly identifies the instruments used in data collection and how they were selected.
◆ Reports information on the reliability and validity of scores from past uses of the questionnaire or interview.
◆ Discusses the procedures for administering the instruments.
◆ Mentions appropriate follow-up procedures to ensure a large return rate and lack of response bias.
◆ Provides an example of the questions on the questionnaire or interview.
◆ Uses data analysis procedures to answer the research questions or hypotheses.
◆ Writes the study in a scholarly way (i.e., follows a standard structure) and identifies potential ethical issues.

KEY IDEAS IN THE CHAPTER

Defining Survey Research, When to Use It, and How It Developed

Although broad in scope, survey research is a form of quantitative research in which the investigator identifies the sample and the population, collects data through question- naires or interviews, and draws conclusions or makes inferences about the population. It is a useful design to use when researchers seek to collect data quickly and economically, study attitudes and opinions, and survey geographically dispersed individuals.

Types of Survey Designs

Surveys are also useful for assessing information at one point in time (a cross-sectional study) or over time (a longitudinal study). Cross-sectional studies are of several types. They can:

◆ examine current attitudes, beliefs, opinions, or practices.
◆ compare two or more educational groups in terms of attitudes, beliefs, opinions, or practices.
◆ assess community needs for educational services.
◆ be used to evaluate programs.
◆ be used statewide or nationally to survey many participants across a large geo- graphic area.

Longitudinal surveys may assess changes over time with trends of a population, changes in a cohort group or subpopulation of a population, or changes in a panel of the same individuals over time.

Key Characteristics of Survey Research

Survey researchers emphasize sample selection of a sample from a population to which they can generalize results; collect data using questionnaires and interviews that vary in forms (e.g., mailed questionnaires, Web-based questionnaires, one-on-one interviews, telephone interviews, and focus group interviews) and weigh the advantages and disadvantages of each; administer well-tested instruments with good questions and scales; and seek a high response rate from participants using procedures that will ensure a high return rate and will not be biased.

Constructing and Using a Mailed Questionnaire

The design of a mailed questionnaire involves several components. It consists of a cover letter to invite participants to complete the questions, and the construction of an instrument that is of appropriate length and that contains an opening beginning with demographic questions, a series of closed-ended questions, and closing statements. The data analysis consists of checking for response rate and bias, descriptive statistics, and inferential statistics to analyze the research hypotheses or questions.

Designing and Conducting an Interview Survey

When interview surveys are used, researchers need to establish rapport and gain the confidence of the interviewee. This often requires training for the interviewee, attending to issues in the process of interviewing, and using an interview guide.

Potential Ethical Issues in Survey Research

Ethical issues in survey research involve engaging in good practices. Often survey research is exempt by institutional review boards. During data collection, attention needs to be given to using appropriate incentives and delivering on benefits guaranteed. The survey data collection procedure cannot put data collectors at risk for their safety. Safety applies to the respondents or participants as well. Confidentiality of their responses needs to be protected, along with minimizing links between data respondents and participants. IDs linked to responses can be an effective means of protecting individual identity. Also, the researcher has an obligation to destroy survey instruments after the conclusion of the study.

Steps in Conducting Survey Research

The steps in conducting a survey consist of determining if a survey design is the best design to use, forming questions or hypotheses, and identifying a population and a sample to study. Then the researcher selects the type of survey to reach this sample or population, collects data to ensure a good rate of response and minimal response bias, and statistically analyzes the data to answer descriptive questions or to address relationship or comparison questions or hypotheses.

Criteria for Evaluating Survey Research

A good survey study includes the identification of the population and the sample, contains an adequate-sized sample systematically derived, employs a cross-sectional or longitudinal design, specifies the instruments (and includes sample questions), determines whether scores from them will likely be reliable and valid, uses appropriate data analysis procedures to answer the questions or hypotheses, and is written acknowledging ethical issues and using a standard structure.

USEFUL INFORMATION FOR PRODUCERS OF RESEARCH

◆ Identify whether your study is cross-sectional or longitudinal. Longitudinal surveys take more time to complete because you are studying individuals over time.

◆ In your research, distinguish between the population, the target population, and your sample. Choose a random sample so that you can generalize to your population. Consider the sources of error that may affect your ability to generalize findings or results to the population.

◆ Specify the type of data collection instrument that you use, such as questionnaires or interviews.

◆ Conduct a pilot test of your questions, whatever your type of data collection instrument, so that it can provide useful information.

◆ Be aware of how you pose sensitive questions to participants. Realize that they may need some introductory comments before you ask participants to respond to sensitive questions.

◆ A number of potential problems arise when you create your own questions. Study Table 12.1 for a list of problems you should avoid when writing your own questions.

◆ A typical high response rate is above 50%, but check for response bias through wave analysis when you use a mailed questionnaire.

◆ Design a mailed questionnaire to include a cover letter, a clear layout of questions, and instructions to the participant. You should keep your instrument as short as possible.

◆ If you conduct an interview, adopt a neutral stance and record responses accurately.

USEFUL INFORMATION FOR CONSUMERS OF RESEARCH

◆ Surveys are used for many purposes in research. When evaluating a study, consider the intent of the author to describe trends, determine attitudes or opinions, describe characteristics of a population, identify practices, evaluate programs, or follow up on individuals over time.

◆ Mailed questionnaires are a popular form of data collection in educational research. However, these instruments need to be carefully designed. Determine whether the researcher used attitudinal, behavioral, or demographic questions in the instrument.

◆ A questionnaire response rate of 50% is considered adequate for most surveys. Examine the response rate of a survey study published in the literature and determine if it reaches this percentage. Also consider whether survey researchers addressed the question of response bias and checked to determine if their responses were biased.

ADDITIONAL RESOURCES YOU MIGHT EXAMINE

Several books provide an excellent introduction to survey research. An introduction to survey research is found in the "toolkit" series on survey research by Arlene Fink (2002).

This nine-volume series by Fink and associates comprehensively addresses all aspects of survey development, from asking questions to writing reports. See:

Fink, A. (2002). *The survey handbook* (2nd ed.). Thousand Oaks, CA: Sage.

Examine the recent survey research book by Dillman (2007) on the use of mail and Internet surveys:

Dillman, D. A. (2007). *Mail and Internet surveys: The tailored design method* (2nd ed.). Hoboken, NJ: Wiley.

Floyd Fowler (2009) has issued a short book on survey research that is popular in introductory survey research courses. He focuses on sampling and design issues, as well as highlighting ethical issues and errors in survey designs. See:

Fowler, F. J. (2009). *Survey research methods* (4th ed.). Los Angeles, CA: Sage.

In a more advanced treatment of survey research, Earl Babbie has authored several books that provide a detailed, technical understanding (Babbie, 1990, 2009). His books broadly assess social research, but they are applicable to education. See:

Babbie, E. (1990). *Survey research methods.* Belmont, CA: Wadsworth.
Babbie, E. (2009). *The practice of social research* (12th ed.). Belmont, CA: Wadsworth.

Go to the Topic "Survey Research" in the MyEducationLab (**www.myeducationlab .com**) for your course, where you can:

- ◆ Find learning outcomes for "Survey Research."
- ◆ Complete Assignments and Activities that can help you more deeply understand the chapter content.
- ◆ Apply and practice your understanding of the core skills identified in the chapter with the Building Research Skills exercises.
- ◆ Check your comprehension of the content covered in the chapter by going to the Study Plan. Here you will be able to take a pretest, receive feedback on your answers, and then access Review, Practice, and Enrichment activities to enhance your understanding. You can then complete a final posttest.

Example of a Survey Study

Examine the following published journal article that is a survey study. Marginal notes indicate the major characteristics of survey research highlighted in this chapter. The illustrative study is:

Literacy as a Leisure Activity: Free-Time Preferences of Older Children and Young Adolescents

Marilyn A. Nippold
Jill K. Duthie
Jennifer Larsen
University of Oregon, Eugene

**Survey Research
Characteristics
in Marginal
Annotations**

Abstract

Purpose

Literacy plays an important role in the development of language in school-age children and adolescents. For example, by reading a variety of books, magazines, and newspapers, students gain exposure to complex vocabulary, and reading becomes a prime opportunity for learning new words. Despite the importance of reading for lexical development, little is known about the pleasure reading habits of today's youth. The first goal of this investigation was to examine the preferences of older children and young adolescents with respect to reading as a leisure-time activity and its relationship to other free-time options that are likely to compete for their attention. The second goal was to examine the amount of time that young people spend reading for pleasure each day and the types of materials they most enjoy reading. The third goal was to determine if preferences for free-time activities and reading materials would evince age- and gender-related differences during the period of development from late childhood through early adolescence (ages 11–15 years). The findings could serve as a reference point for understanding what is reasonable to expect of students during this age range.

Method

The participants were 100 sixth graders (mean age = 11;7 [Years;months]) and 100 ninth graders (mean age = 14;8) attending public schools in western Oregon. Each group contained an equal number of boys and girls, all of whom spoke English as their primary language and were considered to be typical achievers. All participants completed a survey concerning their preferred free-time activities and reading materials. They also reported the average amount of time they spent reading for pleasure each day.

Results

The most popular free-time activities were listening to music/going to concerts, watching television or videos, playing sports, and playing computer or video games. Least preferred activities were cooking, running or walking, writing, and arts and crafts. Reading was moderately popular. The most popular reading materials were magazines, novels, and comics; least popular were plays, technical books, and newspapers. Interest in pleasure reading declined during this age range (11–15 years), and boys were more likely than girls to report that they spent no time reading for pleasure.

Contact author: Marilyn A. Nippold, PhD, Professor, Communication Disorders and Sciences, College of Education, University of Oregon, Eugene, OR 97403. E-mail: nippold@uoregon.edu

Clinical Implications

Given the importance of reading to lexical development in school-age children and adolescents, reading should be promoted as a leisure activity during these years. School-based speech-language pathologists (SLPs), in their role as language consultants, can benefits from understanding the pleasure-reading patterns of today's youth. It is especially important for SLPs to monitor these patterns in students who have language disorders, as it is common for these young people to experience deficits in reading and in lexical development. Fortunately, much can be done in school settings to encourage strong literacy habits in all students if SLPs work collaboratively with teachers, principals, psychologists, librarians, parents, and students. Suggestions are offered for ways to encourage young people to spend more time reading for pleasure.

Key Words: lexical development, literacy, pleasure reading, school-age children, adolescents

(01)   Literacy plays an important role in the development of language during the school-age and adolescent years. Typically developing youth acquire new vocabulary at an impressive rate of 2,000 to 3,000 words per year (Nagy & Scott, 2000; White, Power, & White, 1989), resulting in a working knowledge of at least 40,000 different words by the senior year of high school (Nagy & Herman, 1987). One factor promoting this enormous growth in lexical development is the increased exposure to written language that occurs as children become proficient readers (Miller & Gildea, 1987). Compared to spoken language (e.g., conversations, television shows), written language (e.g., newspapers, novels) contains a greater variety of complex and low-frequency words, and becomes a prime opportunity for learning the meanings of words, particularly after the fifth grade (Cunningham & Stanovich, 1998; Stanovich & Cunningham, 1992). By this time, decoding and fluency skills have improved in most students to the point where reading has become a tool for gaining new knowledge, which includes the learning of words that occur in textbooks for older children and adolescents (Chall, 1983). Increased word knowledge leads to stronger reading comprehension, which, in turn, leads to further lexical expansion (Sternberg & Powell, 1983). Thus, there is an ongoing reciprocal relationship between language and literacy development in youth.

(02)   Learning the meanings of unfamiliar words is a gradual process (Beck & McKeown, 1991) that requires an understanding of subtle nuances and the ability to use those words in different contexts (Nagy & Scott, 2000). A single exposure to an unfamiliar word is unlikely to result in this degree of knowledge, and studies have shown that many new words are learned as a result of having repeated exposure to them while reading (Jenkins, Stein, & Wysocki, 1984; Nagy, Herman, & Anderson, 1985; Schwanenflugel, Stahl, & McFalls, 1997). The mechanisms by which this occurs have been studied in detail. Research has shown that upon exposure to an unfamiliar word, the learner begins to determine its meaning through the use of key metalinguistic strategies—morphological analysis (Anglin, 1993; Nagy, Diakidoy, & Anderson, 1993; White et al., 1989; Wysocki & Jenkins, 1987) and contextual abstraction (Miller & Gildea, 1987; Sternberg, 1987; Sternberg & Powell, 1983). Either or both of these strategies may be used depending on the analyzability of the target word and the quality of context clues surrounding it (Nippold, 2002). For example, consider a child who encounters the word *mineralogy* in a newspaper article about volcanoes. Knowledge of the lexical morpheme *mineral* and the derivational morphemeology can help the learner determine that the word refers to the science of chemicals found in the ground, a conjecture supported by sentences contained in the article, such as, "And when they [the scientists] thought to compare the *mineralogy* of their samples with known Missoula sediments, they were surprised to find that no one had ever examined the clay in detail. . . . Their idea was confirmed when they compared the minerals of the clay and material known to have been ejected by Mount Mazama" (Bolt, p. A9). These strategies offer a viable alternative to less efficient methods of word learning such as the use of a dictionary (Nippold, 1998).

(03)   Nagy and Herman (1987) estimated that children encounter 15,000 to 30,000 unfamiliar words a year from reading only 25 min per day, and argued that up to one half of student vocabulary growth may result from reading. Additionally, Miller and Gildea (1987) reported that students who are avid readers acquire larger vocabularies than those who read less frequently. Indeed, studies have found a consistent link between the amount of time spent reading and word knowledge in both children and adults.

Cunningham and Stanovich (1991) conducted a study to determine if there was a relationship between print exposure, vocabulary, and other skills in fourth- through sixth-grade children (N = 134). Print exposure was measured by a title recognition task (TRT) consisting of a checklist of children's book titles and a series of foils. Additional measures were obtained for vocabulary, verbal fluency, nonverbal problem-solving ability, and general knowledge. Oral vocabulary was measured by a group-administered selection from the Peabody Picture Vocabulary Test—Revised (PPVT-R; Dunn & Dunn, 1981); reading vocabulary was measured by a checklist composed of real words and nonword foils; and verbal fluency was measured by a task in which the children wrote down as many words as they could from four different categories, each in 45 s. Using hierarchical regression analyses to control for age and nonverbal ability, the investigators found that print exposure as measured by the TRT uniquely predicted oral vocabulary, reading vocabulary, verbal fluency, and general knowledge. (04)

Similarly, Stanovich and Cunningham (1992) conducted a study to determine if differences in print exposure were associated with word knowledge in young adults who were college students (N = 300). Participants were administered formal tests of reading vocabulary, oral vocabulary, verbal fluency, reading comprehension, and cognitive ability (nonverbal analogical reasoning). They also were asked to fill out questionnaires that assessed their exposure to print, including their familiarity with authors (Author Recognition Test) and magazines (Magazine Recognition Test). Controlling for reading comprehension and cognitive ability in the participants, hierarchical regression analyses revealed that the level of print exposure uniquely predicted each measure of word knowledge: reading vocabulary, oral vocabulary, and verbal fluency. (05)

West, Stanovich, and Mitchell (1993) also demonstrated a strong relationship between print exposure and word knowledge. Adult participants (N = 217) were selected from an airport lounge on the basis of their observed reading behavior, and were classified as either "readers" or "nonreaders" according to how they spent their waiting time. Each participant was then administered a vocabulary checklist and a series of tasks to measure print exposure (i.e., recognition of authors, magazines, and newspapers) and nonprint exposure (i.e., recognition of television shows, films, and actors). Readers received higher scores on print exposure than nonreaders, but the groups did not differ on nonprint exposure. It was also determined that higher scores on print exposure were significantly related to vocabulary scores, whereas higher scores on nonprint exposure were not. Hierarchical regression analyses indicated that all three measures of print exposure—recognition of authors, magazines, and newspapers—accounted for unique variance in vocabulary while controlling for participant age and amount of education. (06)

This is not to argue that reading is the only source of word learning. Clearly, people can learn new words from other sources such as listening to lectures and news reports, talking with informed individuals, and watching educational television shows (Rice, 1983). Nevertheless, reading is a prime source of word exposure, particularly for complex and low-frequency words, and there is evidence from research that the amount of time spent reading is closely associated with word learning—a relationship that holds during childhood and adulthood (e.g., Cunningham & Stanovich, 1991; Stanovich & Cunningham, 1992; West et al., 1993). This suggests that reading should be promoted, not only as a school-based activity, but as a leisure-time activity as well. (07)

Beyond exposure to new words, reading for pleasure offers additional benefits. Summarizing past research, Worthy, Moorman, and Turner (1999) reported that when children and adolescents engage in voluntary reading about topics that truly interest them, their effort, motivation, and attitudes about reading improve. They also reported that allowing students to read simpler materials such as comics and magazines can improve their basic reading skills (e.g., fluency), leading to increased confidence. This, they suggested, could encourage students to tackle more technical reading materials in school. (08)

Although most speech-language pathologists (SLPs) probably would agree that reading is an important activity that should be promoted in young people, little is known about today's youth and their views concerning the value of reading for pleasure in relation to the multitude of options that exist for spending one's leisure time. Hence, the first goal of the present study was to investigate the preferences of older children and young adolescents with respect to reading as a leisure-time activity and its relationship to other free-time options that are likely to compete for their attention. The second goal was to examine the amount of time that young people spend reading (09) for pleasure each day and the types of materials they most enjoy reading. The third goal was to determine if preferences for free-time activities and reading materials would evince age- and gender-related differences during the period of development from late childhood through early adolescence (ages 11–15 years). The findings could serve as a reference point for understanding what is reasonable to expect of students during this age range.

(10)   This developmental period was of interest because students are beyond the fifth grade, a time when reading has become a primary tool for learning the meanings of new words (Stanovich & Cunningham, 1992). This is also a time when socializing with peers takes on greater importance. In a cross-sectional study, Raffaelli and Duckett (1989) examined the socialization patterns of boys and girls ($N = 401$) during the ages of 10 to 15. They found that, as age increased, students spent greater amounts of time socializing with friends (e.g., talking on the phone and talking in person), a pattern that characterized girls more so than boys. They also found that as age increased, peer interactions made greater contributions to students' personal well-being. At the same time, however, parents remained an important source of information and advice, a finding confirmed by other investigators (e.g., Rawlins, 1992). Given these findings, it is important to examine the literacy habits of children and adolescents during this age range when socialization might be expected to displace solitary activities such as reading, and when differences in the behavior patterns of boys and girls sometimes emerge.

(11)   In public schools today, SLPs frequently work with school-age children and adolescents having language disorders. In an effort to conduct intervention that is relevant and ecologically valid, SLPs increasingly serve as consultants to other school professionals who work with those same students (Whitmire, 2000), such as teachers, psychologists, and librarians. Many students with language disorders experience difficulties in learning to read (Bashir, Wiig, & Abrams, 1987; Catts, Fey, Zhang, & Tomblin, 2001; Catts & Kamhi, 1999; Nippold & Schwarz, 2002; Stothard, Snowling, Bishop, Chipchase, & Kaplan, 1998) and have long-standing deficits in lexical development (Kail, Hale, Leonard, & Nippold, 1984; Kail & Leonard, 1986; McGregor, Newman, Reilly, & Capone, 2002). Students with language disorders who do not enjoy reading are likely to receive less exposure to new vocabulary through text—a situation that can exacerbate their limitations in word knowledge. Given the contribution that reading makes to lexical development, SLPs need to understand the literacy habits of today's youth in order to provide appropriate recommendations in their role as language consultants in public school settings.

Method

Participants

(12)   The participants were 100 sixth-grade children (50 boys, 50 girls) with a mean age of 11;7 (years;months; range = 11;1–12;1) and 100 ninth-grade adolescents (50 boys, 50 girls) with a mean age of 14;8 (range = 14;1–15;7). All participants were enrolled in a public middle school (sixth graders) or high school (ninth graders) located in a lower middle-income neighborhood in western Oregon. According to teacher report, the students represented a range of ability levels and were considered to be typical achievers. None had a known history of language, learning, or cognitive deficits, and none was receiving special education services. More than 90% of the participants were of European American descent, and all reported that English was their primary language spoken at home.

Sampling from a population

(13)   Teachers at each school were asked to volunteer their classes. This request resulted in the recruitment of five sixth-grade English classes and five ninth-grade English classes. A passive consent procedure was employed. The parents of all students enrolled in those 10 classes were provided with a letter informing them of the nature of the study and indicating that it was an optional activity to be carried out during regular school hours. If any parents objected to their son or daughter participating in the study, they were able to communicate that by returning a form letter to the school. No students were pressured to participate, and all were assured that it was a voluntary activity. Students were told that their individual performance would remain confidential. In addition, they were able to indicate their own willingness to participate by signing an assent form on the day of testing. Students who were not participating in the study were allowed to work quietly at their desks or go to the school library during the testing.

The Oregon Department of Education Web site (http://www.ode.state.or.us) reported that (14) 13.8% of the students in this school district live in poverty, as compared to 14.3% for the state as a whole. The Web site also reported the percentage of students who met or exceeded the state benchmarks in reading, based on their performance on the Oregon Statewide Assessment (OSA). In Oregon, this test is administered every year to all students in grades three, five, eight, and ten. The participants in this investigation would have taken the test during their fifth- or eighth-grade year. Although individual student scores were not available, it was reported that, for this district, 75% of the fifth graders met or exceeded the performance standards that year as compared to 79% for the state, and 54% of the eighth graders met or exceeded the standards as compared to 64% for the state. These results suggest that the participants in this investigation were fairly representative of students in Oregon. However, the results also suggest that some of the participants, particularly those in ninth grade, may not have met the performance standards in reading despite the fact that none had been identified as having special needs.

Procedures

All participants were tested in large-group fashion in their classrooms at school by one of the (15) investigators. They were asked to complete a two-page survey, the "Student Questionnaire" (see **High response** Appendix), designed especially for the present study. To ensure that all participants were listening **rate** to the directions and performing the task, the examiner read each question aloud, paused, and allowed time for them to mark their own answers.

The survey required approximately 10 min to complete and consisted of three main questions. (16) Question 1, which asked how students spent their free time, provided a list of activities that were **Collecting data** thought to be of interest to middle-school and high-school students. As a result of investigator **through a ques-** observations of young people and discussions with their parents, it was believed that these activi- **tionnaire design** ties might be good candidates to compete for students' time and attention. In addition to activities **for this study** that are primarily solitary (e.g., reading, writing), the list contained activities that could be carried out either alone or with others (e.g., shopping, media events, sports, games). The category of "other" was also provided to allow students to write in any favorite activities that were not included in the list. Question 2 asked the students to estimate how much time they typically spent each day reading for pleasure outside of the school day, followed by a set of options (e.g., none, 5–10 min, 10–20 min). Question 3 provided a list of common reading materials (e.g., poems, novels, newspapers) and asked the students to indicate which types they enjoyed reading for pleasure. The opportunity to indicate "none of the above" and "other" (write in) was provided to compensate for anything that had been omitted from the list. Upon completion of the testing, all students were rewarded with a ballpoint pen.

Results

Table 1 reports the results of Question 1, free-time activities, showing the percentage of students (17) who selected each item as something they liked to do. For all students combined ($N = 200$), the most popular activities were listening to music/going to concerts (78%), watching television or videos (77%), playing sports (68%), and playing computer or video games (63%). Least popular activities were cooking (32%), running or walking (33%), writing (34%), and arts and crafts (38%). Reading (51%) was a moderately popular activity. For the category of "other," the most popular write-in activity was spending time with friends (e.g., sleepovers, playing with friends, visiting friends' homes, having friends come to visit), especially for girls. Fourteen sixth graders (4 boys, 10 girls) and 11 ninth graders (2 boys, 9 girls) wrote in this activity.

For each activity listed on the questionnaire, the data were analyzed using a 2 × 2 (grade × gen- (18) der) analysis of variance (ANOVA) with Bonferroni corrections for multiple comparisons (adjusted alpha = .003). Effect sizes were computed using the eta coefficient (Meline & Schmitt, 1997) and were interpreted as follows: small = .10–.23; medium = .24–.36; large = .37–.71 (Cohen, 1969, p. 276). For grade, statistically significant main effects were obtained for swimming, $F(1, 196) = 13.25$, $p = .0003$, $\eta = .25$; riding a bicycle or scooter, $F(1, 196) = 20.86$, $p < .0001$, $\eta = .31$; using e-mail $F(1, 196) = 9.90$, $p = .0019$, $\eta = .22$; and reading, $F(1, 196) = 15.70$, $p = .0001$, $\eta = .27$. Effect sizes were small for using e-mail and medium for swimming, riding a bicycle or scooter, and reading. Tukey's studentized range (honestly significant difference [HSD]) test ($p = .05$) indicated that ninth graders showed a stronger preference than sixth graders for e-mail, whereas sixth graders showed a stronger preference than ninth graders for swimming, riding a bicycle or scooter, and reading.

(19)   For gender, statistically significant main effects were obtained for playing computer or video games, $F(1, 196) = 23.14$, $p < .0001$, $\eta = .32$; playing sports, $F(1, 196) = 15.05$, $p = .0001$, $\eta = .27$; talking on the phone, $F(1, 196) = 20.74$, $p < .0001$, $\eta = .31$; using e-mail, $F(1, 196) = 14.03$, $p = .0002$, $\eta = .26$; shopping, $F(1,196) = 83.36$, $p < .0001$, $\eta = .55$; writing, $F(1, 196) = 73.30$, $p < .0001$, $\eta = .52$; and cooking, $F(1, 196) = 9.52$, $p = .0023$, $\eta = .22$. Effect sizes were small for cooking; medium for playing computer or video games, playing sports, talking on the phone, and using e-mail; and large for shopping and writing. Tukey's (HSD) test ($p = .05$) showed that boys preferred playing computer or video games and playing sports, whereas girls preferred talking on the phone, using e-mail, shopping, writing, and cooking. No interactions between grade and gender were statistically significant.

TABLE 1

Percentage of students who responded positively to each item listed under the question, "How do you like to spend your free time?" (standard deviations are reported).

	Grade 6			Grade 9			Grades 6 & 9		
	Boys	Girls	Combined	Boys	Girls	Combined	Boys	Girls	Combined
A. watching TV or videos	88	74	81	74	70	72	81	72	77
	(33)	(44)	(39)	(44)	(46)	(45)	(39)	(45)	(43)
B. playing computer or video games	82	58	70	74	36	55	78	47	63
	(39)	(50)	(46)	(44)	(48)	(50)	(42)	(50)	(49)
C. playing sports	82	56	69	78	54	66	80	55	68
	(39)	(50)	(46)	(42)	(50)	(48)	(40)	(50)	(47)
D. running or walking	32	26	29	30	42	36	31	34	33
	(47)	(44)	(46)	(46)	(50)	(48)	(46)	(48)	(47)
E. swimming	54	64	59	38	30	34	46	47	47
	(50)	(48)	(49)	(49)	(46)	(48)	(50)	(50)	(50)
F. skating	46	42	44	54	22	38	50	32	41
	(50)	(50)	(50)	(50)	(42)	(49)	(50)	(47)	(49)
G. riding a bicycle or scooter	78	70	74	56	32	44	67	51	59
	(42)	(46)	(44)	(50)	(47)	(50)	(47)	(50)	(49)
H. playing cards or board games	64	40	52	36	32	34	50	36	43
	(48)	(49)	(50)	(48)	(47)	(48)	(50)	(48)	(50)
I. talking on the phone	38	64	51	50	84	67	44	74	59
	(49)	(48)	(50)	(51)	(37)	(47)	(50)	(44)	(49)
J. using e-mail	28	42	35	38	74	56	33	58	46
	(45)	(50)	(48)	(49)	(44)	(50)	(47)	(50)	(50)
K. listening to music/going to concerts	68	80	74	74	90	82	71	85	78
	(47)	(40)	(44)	(44)	(30)	(39)	(46)	(36)	(42)
L. shopping/going to the mall	28	72	50	26	90	58	27	81	54
	(45)	(45)	(50)	(44)	(30)	(50)	(45)	(39)	(50)

	Grade 6			Grade 9			Grades 6 & 9		
	Boys	Girls	Combined	Boys	Girls	Combined	Boys	Girls	Combined
M. reading	58	70	64	30	44	37	44	57	51
	(50)	(46)	(48)	(46)	(50)	(49)	(50)	(50)	(50)
N. writing	12	52	32	06	64	35	09	58	34
	(33)	(50)	(47)	(24)	(48)	(48)	(29)	(50)	(47)
O. cooking	22	48	35	22	36	29	22	42	32
	(42)	(50)	(48)	(42)	(48)	(46)	(42)	(50)	(47)
P. arts & crafts	34	54	44	28	36	32	31	45	38
	(48)	(50)	(50)	(45)	(48)	(47)	(46)	(50)	(49)
Q. other (write in)_____	46	40	43	44	44	44	45	42	44
	(50)	(49)	(50)	(50)	(50)	(50)	(50)	(50)	(50)

Table 2 reports the results of Question 2, the amount of time spent reading for pleasure. For each time block, the data were analyzed using a 2×2 (grade $\times$ gender) ANOVA (with Bonferroni corrections; adjusted alpha = .006). Effect sizes were computed using the eta coefficient (Cohen, 1969; Meline & Schmitt, 1997). For grade, no statistically significant main effects were obtained. For gender, the only statistically significant main effect was obtained for "none," $F(1, 196) = 9.29$, $p = .0026$, $\eta = .21$, where boys selected this option more frequently than did girls. The effect size was small. No interactions between grade and gender were statistically significant. (20)

Table 3 reports the results of Question 3, preferred reading materials, showing the percentage of students who said they liked each type of material. For all students combined ($N = 200$), the most popular reading materials were magazines (63%), novels (52%), and comics (41%); least popular were plays (12%), technical books (15%), and newspapers (16%). The category of "other" (27%) was moderately popular. For other, some students wrote in the names of specific books (e.g., *Harry Potter*) or themes (e.g., pets, adventure, science fiction, sports, biographies, mystery, horror) they enjoyed. (21)

For each type of material, the data were analyzed using a 2×2 (grade $\times$ gender) ANOVA (with Bonferroni corrections; adjusted alpha = .005). Effect sizes were computed using the eta coefficient (Cohen, 1969; Meline & Schmitt, 1997). For grade, a statistically significant main effect was obtained only for magazines, $F(1, 196) = 9.95$, $p = .0019$, $\eta = .22$. The effect size was small. Tukey's (HSD) test ($p = .05$) indicated that ninth graders showed a stronger preference than sixth graders for magazines. (22)

For gender, a statistically significant main effect was obtained only for poems, $F(1, 196) = 19.57$, $p < .0001$, $\eta = .30$. The effect size was medium. Tukey's (HSD) test ($p = .05$) indicated that girls showed a stronger preference than boys for poems. No interactions between grade and gender were statistically significant. (23)

Discussion

Given the importance of reading to lexical development in school-age children and adolescents, this study was conducted to investigate the views of young people with respect to reading as a leisure activity in relation to other free-time options that are likely to compete for their attention. Fortunately, the results indicate that reading is at least a moderately popular free-time activity for students in the 11- to 15-year age range. Yet at the same time, the study indicates that many other activities are preferred over reading, such as listening to music/going to concerts, watching television or videos, playing sports, and playing computer or video games. The study also indicates that interest in reading as a free-time activity declines during these years, whereas interest in using e-mail increases, consistent with the trend for young people to spend more time socializing with peers as they transition into adolescence (Raffaelli & Duckett, 1989). (24)

TABLE 2

Percentage of students who selected each option in response to the request, "Please estimate how much time you spend each day, on average, reading for pleasure outside of the school day" (standard deviations are reported).

	Grade 6			Grade 9			Grade 6 & 9		
	Boys	Girls	Combined	Boys	Girls	Combined	Boys	Girls	Combined
A. none	14	02	08	20	06	13	17	04	11
	(35)	(14)	(27)	(40)	(24)	(34)	(38)	(20)	(31)
B. 5–10 minutes	16	10	13	28	22	25	22	16	19
	(37)	(30)	(34)	(45)	(42)	(44)	(42)	(37)	(39)
C. 10–20 minutes	12	14	13	10	14	12	11	14	13
	(33)	(35)	(34)	(30)	(35)	(33)	(31)	(35)	(33)
D. 20–30 minutes	22	28	25	12	22	17	17	25	21
	(42)	(45)	(44)	(33)	(42)	(38)	(38)	(44)	(41)
E. 30–60 minutes	22	28	25	18	18	18	20	23	22
	(42)	(45)	(44)	(39)	(39)	(39)	(40)	(42)	(41)
F. 1–2 hours	12	18	15	06	12	09	09	15	12
	(33)	(39)	(36)	(24)	(33)	(29)	(29)	(36)	(33)
G. 2–3 hours	0	0	0	04	0	02	02	0	01
	(0)	(0)	(0)	(20)	(0)	(14)	(14)	(0)	(10)
H. more than 3 hours	02	0	01	02	06	04	02	03	03
	(14)	(0)	(10)	(14)	(24)	(20)	(14)	(17)	(16)

(25)   Differences between boys and girls also emerged. Boys preferred playing computer or video games and playing sports; girls preferred talking on the phone, using e-mail, shopping, writing, and cooking. Boys were more likely than girls to report that they spent no time reading for pleasure. For all students combined, the most popular reading materials were magazines, novels, and comics; least popular were plays, technical books, and newspapers. Older students showed a stronger preference than younger ones for magazines, and girls showed a stronger preference than boys for poems.

(26)   Reports have indicated that the amount of time that is spent reading predicts word knowledge (e.g., Cunningham & Stanovich, 1991; Stanovich & Cunningham, 1992; West et al., 1993). This is thought to occur because written language exposes learners to large numbers of unfamiliar words, leading them to infer the meanings of those words through metalinguistic strategies—morphological analysis and contextual abstraction (Nippold, 1998). Because word knowledge plays a critical role in academic success and in other intellectual pursuits (Sternberg & Powell, 1983), it is important that school-age children and adolescents spend time reading a variety of materials and that their interest in reading continues into adulthood. Pleasure reading can expose students to new words and allow them to cultivate a positive attitude toward reading as they refine their basic reading skills (e.g., fluency), building confidence in themselves as readers (Worthy et al., 1999).

(27)   This is not to say that other free-time activities are unimportant. For example, in the present study, many participants indicated that they enjoyed socializing with friends through phone calls, e-mail, and personal visits. Because socializing is an activity that offers emotional support and contributes to personal well-being through the lifespan (Raffaelli & Duckett, 1989; Rawlins, 1992), it should be encouraged. In addition, many participants reported that they enjoyed physical activities such as playing sports, swimming, and riding a bicycle or scooter—all of which can benefit one's health. Nonetheless, it is helpful to know where reading fits into the larger picture of free-time options for today's youth, some of whom spend little or no time reading for pleasure.

TABLE 3
Percentage of students who responded positively to each item listed under the question, "What kinds of materials do you like to read for pleasure?" (standard deviations are reported).

	Grade 6			Grade 9			Grades 6 & 9		
	Boys	Girls	Combined	Boys	Girls	Combined	Boys	Girls	Combined
A. poems	14	24	19	08	48	28	11	36	24
	(35)	(43)	(39)	(27)	(50)	(45)	(31)	(48)	(43)
B. short stories	38	40	39	18	44	31	28	42	35
	(49)	(49)	(49)	(39)	(50)	(46)	(45)	(50)	(48)
C. plays	10	16	13	04	16	10	07	16	12
	(30)	(37)	(34)	(20)	(37)	(30)	(26)	(37)	(32)
D. novels	44	64	54	42	56	49	43	60	52
	(50)	(48)	(50)	(50)	(50)	(50)	(50)	(49)	(50)
E. comics	58	38	48	36	32	34	47	35	41
	(50)	(49)	(50)	(48)	(47)	(48)	(50)	(48)	(49)
F. technical books	28	12	20	10	08	09	19	10	15
	(45)	(33)	(40)	(30)	(27)	(29)	(39)	(30)	(35)
G. newspapers	18	06	12	22	16	19	20	11	16
	(39)	(24)	(33)	(42)	(37)	(39)	(40)	(31)	(36)
H. magazines	50	54	52	62	84	73	56	69	63
	(51)	(50)	(50)	(49)	(37)	(45)	(50)	(46)	(49)
I. none of the above	04	04	04	06	02	04	05	03	04
	(20)	(20)	(20)	(24)	(14)	(20)	(22)	(17)	(20)
J. other (write in)_____	36	30	33	14	26	20	25	28	27
	(48)	(46)	(47)	(35)	(44)	(40)	(44)	(45)	(44)

Study Limitations

One limitation of the present study is that it focused only on students who were attending public (28) schools located in lower middle-income neighborhoods in western Oregon. It is possible that different results might have been obtained in schools representing additional socioeconomic levels located in diverse regions of the United States. Another caveat is that the present study focused exclusively on leisure-time reading and did not investigate the amount of time that students spent on other types of reading, such as that required for school assignments. It seems possible that some of the students who reported spending little time reading for pleasure (e.g., ninth graders) may have been spending more time reading for school assignments, particularly if they were college bound. These possibilities should be investigated in future research. In addition, the literacy habits of various subgroups should be examined. This could include, for example, students who have been identified as having language and/or reading disorders, and those who show different levels of reading proficiency (e.g., strong, average, weak).

Implications

In any case, if students are successfully engaging in large amounts of academic reading, there is no (29) reason to be concerned about their exposure to new vocabulary words. However, for those who spend little time reading for pleasure or for school assignments, steps should be taken to promote their interest in reading. School-based SLPs should take note of these patterns, particularly as they occur in children and adolescents with language disorders, as it is common for these young people to experience deficits in reading and in word learning (e.g., Catts & Kamhi, 1999; Kail et al., 1984; Kail & Leonard, 1986; McGregor et al., 2002; Nippold & Schwarz, 2002). In addition, SLPs should note the pleasure-reading habits of struggling readers, as these students also could benefit from increased opportunities to read. As indicated earlier, a certain portion of students in this district (and in many districts in Oregon) failed to meet the state standards in reading as tested by the OSA, data that were obtained from the Oregon Department of Education Web site. Information concerning the literacy habits of students who are struggling to meet state standards can be helpful as SLPs consult with other professionals who may be less familiar with the reciprocal relationship between language and literacy development.

(30)   Fortunately, much can be done in school settings to encourage strong literacy habits in all students as SLPs work collaboratively with teachers, principals, psychologists, librarians, parents, and the students themselves. For example, the activities described below could be spearheaded by the school-based SLP:

◆ *Organize book clubs at school.* High schools and middle schools may offer clubs similar to the successful "Oprah book clubs" that were broadcast on national television. For this activity, books were selected by the television talk show host Oprah Winfrey and read by the general public, followed by interactive discussions on television. Similarly, a ninth-grade book club might vote on a selection of student-recommended books to be read by the club and discussed during their weekly meetings, facilitated by student leaders. For a sixth-grade club, options might include the *Harry Potter* books, which are frequently enjoyed by older children and young adolescents. In addition to their intriguing story lines, these books contain a wealth of low-frequency words used in colorful and imaginative ways, as evidenced in the following passage from *Harry Potter* and the *Goblet of Fire* (Rowling, 2000):

> Slowly, magnificently, the ship rose out of the water, gleaming in the moonlight. It had a strangely skeletal look about it, as though it were a resurrected wreck, and the dim, misty lights shimmering at its portholes looked like ghostly eyes. Finally, with a great sloshing noise, the ship emerged entirely, bobbing on the turbulent water, and began to glide toward the bank. (p. 245)

Book clubs with different themes (e.g., mystery, adventure, animals) and reading levels (e.g., strong, average, weak) could be organized, and reluctant readers could receive academic credit for participating. In organizing these clubs, students should be grouped so that weaker readers are not competing with stronger ones and being subjected to peer ridicule. As appropriate, weaker readers might be asked to lead book clubs for younger students in order to build their own confidence as readers. Alternatively, they might be assigned to book clubs led by mature and supportive adults. For example, a successful book club in an Oregon high school, started by a school librarian, includes senior citizens (e.g., retired teachers) who volunteer their time, helping to engage the students in lively discussions about the books and sharing their unique generational perspectives (Williams, 2003). In working with weaker readers, volunteers will need to understand the students' difficulties and know how to manage them positively. Thus, the SLP may need to train and supervise these volunteers carefully.

◆ *Provide incentives and reward students for reading books and other materials (e.g., magazines, newspapers, plays) at school and at home.* For example, on completing a book, article, or play, a student could earn a ticket to deposit in a special box in the principal's office. At regular intervals, a ticket could be drawn and a desirable prize could be awarded to the lucky ticket holder.

◆ *Provide blocks of class time each day (e.g., 25 min) for "sustained silent reading" (SSR), where all students are required to read a book, magazine, or newspaper of their choice.* Given that many children, as they transition into adolescence, show less interest in reading as a leisure activity, it is beneficial to provide this type of structured opportunity for them to read during the school day. Immediately following each SSR block, students can be requested to spend the next 5 min discussing what they read with a classmate, thereby appealing to the adolescent need for socialization and peer interaction.

◆ *Encourage students to visit the school library and to take books home.* Ensure that the library contains an adequate supply of books for students of differing backgrounds, interests, and levels of reading proficiency. This should include multiple copies of books that have been adapted for weaker readers such as classic novels (e.g., *The Red Badge of Courage, David Copperfield, Treasure Island*) and short biographies of sports heroes and movie stars (PCI Educational Publishing,

2003). Given the findings of the present study, simplified books on sports (e.g., baseball, football, hockey) might be of interest to ninth-grade boys, many of whom indicated enjoyment of sports-related leisure activities but little interest in reading for pleasure. A selection of high-interest books on tape also should be available for students who require additional support when reading.

◆ *Take note of students' preferred reading materials and encourage their use.* Based on the results of the present study, SLPs can expect to find differences in reading preferences based on a student's age or gender. For example, as shown in Table 3, poems were of less interest to ninth-grade boys than to ninth-grade girls, but both boys and girls enjoyed magazines. Given that research has shown that popular magazines can provide exposure to low-frequency words (Cunningham & Stanovich, 1998), magazines should be acceptable for free-time reading.

◆ *Conduct informal surveys of students in the district to determine the names of specific magazines, comics, and books that are currently popular with boys and girls at different grade levels, information that may change rather quickly.* Stocking school libraries and classrooms with these particular materials can help to motivate reluctant readers and generate interest in pleasure reading.

◆ *Explore with students their reasons for rejecting certain types of reading materials.* For example, a ninth-grade boy's dislike for poems may stem from having been forced to read adult-selected works depicting themes that were irrelevant to him (e.g., Emily Dickinson's poems on love). Providing students with a wide range of options depicting themes that interest them, such as horror (e.g., "The Raven" by Edgar Allan Poe, 1884) or adventure (e.g., "Paul Revere's Ride" by Henry Wadsworth Longfellow, 1963), may encourage them to explore this genre.

◆ *Encourage parents to support these efforts by making them aware of the importance of reading and requesting their assistance through parent–teacher organizations designed to secure materials and personnel for the school library.* Additionally, parents can be asked to hold daily sessions at home where they read and discuss with their child or adolescent favorite books, magazines, comic strips, or sections of the newspaper (e.g., sports, movies, television, advice). Contrary to popular myth, as children become adolescents, they continue to enjoy spending time with their parents and other family members (Raffaelli & Duckett, 1989).

For additional information on ways to promote strong literacy habits in school-age children and adolescents, SLPs may wish to consult various Web sites. For example, the International Reading Association (IRA; http://www.reading.org) is an excellent resource for lists of books that are of high interest to adolescents, as judged by students in Grades 7 through 12 attending schools in the United States. This Web site also provides research-based information on how to assist struggling readers, which often includes children and adolescents with language disorders. (31)

It is difficult to overestimate the importance of reading during childhood and adolescence. Yet the present study indicates that as children become adolescents, their interest in reading as a leisure activity may decline as other free-time options compete for their attention. A decline in reading is problematic for students who avoid all other kinds of reading and for those whose language and literacy skills are weak. Fortunately, suggestions such as those offered above can be implemented quite easily, and it is clear that much can be done within school settings to maintain and even expand students' enthusiasm for reading when their individual needs and preferences are considered. Given the intellectual rewards that can accrue from a lifetime of reading, a modest investment in adolescent literacy programs can bring monumental rewards to society. (32)

Acknowledgments

We express sincere gratitude to the children and adolescents who participated in this research project and to the teachers and administrators who granted permission for the project to take place at their schools and who helped to schedule the testing sessions.

References

Anglin, J. M. (1993). Vocabulary development: A morphological analysis. *Monographs of the Society for Research in Child Development, 58*(10), Serial No. 238.

Bashir, A. S., Wiig, E. H., & Abrams, J. C. (1987). Language disorders in childhood and adolescence: Implications for learning and socialization. *Pediatric Annals, 16,* 145–156.

Beck, I., & McKeown, M. (1991). Conditions of vocabulary acquisition. In R. Barr, M. L. Kamil, & P. B. Mosenthal (Eds.), *Handbook of reading research* (Vol. 2, pp. 789–814). White Plains, NY: Longman.

Bolt, G. (2004, March 26). Scientists link valley's clay soil to Mount Mazama ash spew. *The Register-Guard,* pp. A1, A9.

Catts, H. W., Fey, M. E., Zhang, X., & Tomblin, J. B. (2001). Estimating the risk of future reading difficulties in kindergarten children: A research-based model and its clinical implementation. *Language, Speech, and Hearing Services in Schools, 32,* 38–50.

Catts, H. W., & Kamhi, A. G. (1999). *Language and reading disabilities.* Boston: Allyn & Bacon.

Chall, J. S. (1983). *Stages of reading development.* New York: McGraw-Hill.

Cohen, J. (1969). *Statistical power analysis for the behavioral sciences.* New York: Academic Press.

Cunningham, A. E., & Stanovich, K. E. (1991). Tracking the unique effects of print exposure in children: Associations with vocabulary, general knowledge, and spelling. *Journal of Educational Psychology, 83,* 264–274.

Cunningham, A. E., & Stanovich, K. E. (1998, Spring/Summer). What reading does for the mind. *American Educator,* 8–15.

Dunn, L. M., & Dunn, L. M. (1981). *Peabody Picture Vocabulary Test—Revised.* Circle Pines, MN: American Guidance Service.

Jenkins, J. R., Stein, M. L., & Wysocki, K. (1984). Learning vocabulary through reading. *American Educational Research Journal, 21,* 767–787.

Kail, R., Hale, C. A., Leonard, L. B., & Nippold, M. A. (1984). Lexical storage and retrieval in language-impaired children. *Applied Psycholinguistics, 5,* 37–49.

Kail, R., & Leonard, L. (1986). *Word-finding abilities in language-impaired children (ASHA Monograph 25).* Rockville, MD: American Speech-Language-Hearing Association.

Longfellow, H. W. (1963). *Paul Revere's ride.* New York: Crowell.

McGregor, K. K., Newman, R. M., Reilly, R. M., & Capone, N. C. (2002). Semantic representation and naming in children with specific language impairment. *Journal of Speech, Language, and Hearing Research, 45,* 998–1014.

Meline, T., & Schmitt, J. F. (1997). Case studies for evaluating statistical significance in group designs. *American Journal of Speech-Language Pathology, 6*(1), 33–41.

Miller, G. A., & Gildea, P. M. (1987). How children learn words. *Scientific American, 257*(3), 94–99.

Nagy, W., Diakidoy, I., & Anderson, R. (1993). The acquisition of morphology: Learning the contribution of suffixes to the meanings of derivatives. *Journal of Reading Behavior, 25*(2), 155–171.

Nagy, W. E., & Herman, P. A. (1987). Breadth and depth of vocabulary knowledge: Implications for acquisition and instruction. In M. McKeown & M. E. Curtis (Eds.), *The nature of vocabulary acquisition* (pp. 19–36). Hillsdale, NJ: Erlbaum.

Nagy, W. E., Herman, P. A., & Anderson, R. (1985). Learning words from context. *Reading Research Quarterly, 20,* 233–253.

Nagy, W. E., & Scott, J. A. (2000). Vocabulary processes. In M. L. Kamil, P. B. Mosenthal, & R. Barr (Eds.), *Handbook of reading research* (Vol. 3, pp. 269–284). Mahwah, NJ: Erlbaum.

Nippold, M. A. (1998). *Later language development: The school-age and adolescent years* (2nd ed.). Austin, TX: Pro-Ed.

Nippold, M. A. (2002). Lexical learning in school-age children, adolescents, and adults: A process where language and literacy converge. *Journal of Child Language, 29,* 474–478.

Nippold, M. A., & Schwarz, I. E. (2002). Do children recover from specific language impairment? *Advances in Speech-Language Pathology, 4*(1), 41–49.

PCI Educational Publishing. (2003). *Special education & learning differences catalogue: Middle school, high school & adult.* San Antonio, TX.

Poe, E. A. (1884). *The raven.* New York: Harper & Brothers.

Raffaelli, M., & Duckett, E. (1989). "We were just talking . . . ": Conversations in early adolescence. *Journal of Youth and Adolescence, 18,* 567–582.

Rawlins, W. K. (1992). *Friendship matters: Communication, dialectics, and the life course.* New York: DeGruyter.

Rice, M. (1983). The role of television in language acquisition. *Developmental Review, 3,* 211–224.

Rowling, J. K. (2000). *Harry Potter and the goblet of fire.* New York: Scholastic.

Schwanenflugel, P., Stahl, S., & McFalls, E. (1997). Partial word knowledge and vocabulary growth during reading comprehension. *Journal of Literary Research, 29,* 531–553.

Stanovich, K. E., & Cunningham, A. E. (1992). Studying the consequences of literacy within a literate society: The cognitive correlates of print exposure. *Memory & Cognition, 20*(1), 51–68.

Sternberg, R. J. (1987). Most vocabulary is learned from context. In M. G. McKeown & M. E. Curtis (Eds.), *The nature of vocabulary acquisition* (pp. 89–105). Hillsdale, NJ: Erlbaum.

Sternberg, R. J., & Powell, J. S. (1983). Comprehending verbal comprehension. *American Psychologist, 38,* 878–893.

Stothard, S. E., Snowling, M. J., Bishop, D. V. M., Chipchase, B. B., & Kaplan, C. A. (1998). Language-impaired pre-schoolers: A follow-up into adolescence. *Journal of Speech, Language, and Hearing Research, 41,* 407–418.

West, R. F., Stanovich, K. E., & Mitchell, H. R. (1993). Reading in the real world and its correlates. *Reading Research Quarterly, 28,* 35–50.

White, T. G., Power, M. A., & White, S. (1989). Morphological analysis: Implications for teaching and understanding vocabulary growth. *Reading Research Quarterly, 24,* 283–304.

Whitmire, K. (2000). Action: School services. *Language, Speech, and Hearing Services in Schools, 31,* 194–199.

Williams, A. (2003, December 15). Young, old find common ground in the pages of some good books. *The Register-Guard,* pp. B1, B4.

Worthy, J., Moorman, M., & Turner, M. (1999). What Johnny likes to read is hard to find in school. *Reading Research Quarterly, 34*(1), 12–27.

Wysocki, K., & Jenkins, J. R. (1987). Deriving word meanings through morphological generalization. *Reading Research Quarterly, 22,* 66–81.

Appendix.

Student Questionnaire

Please tell us a little about yourself by answering the following questions. There are no "right or wrong" answers. We just want to know more about you and your interests.

1. How do you like to spend your free time?
   Circle all that apply:
   A. watching TV or videos
   B. playing computer or video games
   C. playing sports (e.g., basketball, baseball, football, soccer, etc.)
   D. running or walking
   E. swimming
   F. skating (skate board or roller blades)
   G. riding a bicycle or scooter
   H. playing cards or board games (e.g., Monopoly, chess, checkers, etc.)
   I. talking on the phone with friends or relatives
   J. using e-mail with friends or relatives
   K. listening to music/going to concerts
   L. shopping/going to the mall
   M. reading (e.g., books, magazines, newspapers, etc.)
   N. writing (e.g., diary, poetry, notes to friends, etc.)
   O. cooking
   P. arts & crafts
   Q. other (write in) _____

2. Please estimate how much time you spend each day, on average, reading for pleasure outside of the school day. This includes reading that you **choose** to do. Circle the **one** best answer:
   A. none
   B. 5–10 minutes
   C. 10–20 minutes
   D. 20–30 minutes
   E. 30–60 minutes
   F. 1–2 hours
   G. 2–3 hours
   H. more than 3 hours

3. What kinds of materials do you like to read for pleasure? Circle all that apply:
   A. poems
   B. short stories
   C. plays
   D. novels
   E. comics
   F. technical books (e.g., auto repair, science, history, computers, etc.)
   G. newspapers
   H. magazines
   I. none of the above
   J. other (write in) _____

Grounded Theory Designs

*G*rounded theory enables you to generate a broad theory about your qualitative central phenomenon "grounded" in the data. As a systematic procedure, it appeals to a wide range of educational researchers. This chapter defines grounded theory research, identifies when to use it, assesses the key characteristics of it, examines several ethical issues in this form of inquiry, and advances the steps in conducting and evaluating this design.

By the end of this chapter, you should be able to:

◆ Define grounded theory research, and describe when to use it, and how it developed.
◆ Distinguish among three types of grounded theory designs.
◆ Identify the key characteristics of grounded theory research.
◆ Identify some potential ethical issues in conducting grounded theory research.
◆ Describe the steps in conducting a grounded theory study.
◆ Evaluate the quality of a grounded theory study.

Maria designs a grounded theory study for her school committee and her graduate research project. Her research question is "What is the process involved in apprehending students for weapon possession in their high schools?" To study this question, she plans to explore a process, the process of apprehending students for carrying weapons. Study of this process will help her understand one aspect of carrying weapons in the school. She identifies 10 people to interview: 5 students who were actually caught and 5 teachers or administrators who were involved in the apprehensions. After interviewing these individuals, Maria analyzes the data for themes (or categories). She arranges these categories into a visual model of the process. She develops a theory of the process of "being apprehended" for weapon possession in the hope that this theory will provide an explanation that school officials might use to identify early-warning signs for students who may be prone to possess weapons in high schools. Maria has constructed a grounded theory qualitative study.

WHAT IS GROUNDED THEORY RESEARCH, WHEN SHOULD YOU USE IT, AND HOW DID IT DEVELOP?

A **grounded theory design** is a systematic, qualitative procedure used to generate a theory that explains, at a broad conceptual level, a process, an action, or an interaction about a substantive topic. In grounded theory research, this theory is a "process" theory—it explains an educational process of events, activities, actions, and interactions that occur over time. Also, grounded theorists proceed through systematic procedures of collecting data, identifying categories (used synonymously with themes), connecting these categories, and forming a theory that explains the process.

When Do You Use Grounded Theory?

You use grounded theory when you need a broad theory or explanation of a process. Grounded theory *generates* a theory when existing theories do not address your problem or the participants that you plan to study. Because a theory is "grounded" in the data, it provides a better explanation than a theory borrowed "off the shelf," because it fits the situation, actually works in practice, is sensitive to individuals in a setting, and may represent all of the complexities actually found in the process. For instance, in the study of certain educational populations (e.g., children with attention disorders), existing theories may have little applicability to special populations.

You also use grounded theory when you wish to study some process, such as how students develop as writers (Neff, 1998) or how high-achieving African American and Caucasian women's careers develop (Richie, Fassinger, Linn, & Johnson, 1997). It also is used to explain actions of people, such as the process of participating in an adult education class (Courtney, Jha, & Babchuk, 1994), or an interaction among people, such as the support department chairs provide for faculty researchers (Creswell & Brown, 1992).

For the beginning qualitative researcher, grounded theory offers a step-by-step, systematic procedure for analyzing data. Having this procedure available may be helpful to students when they defend qualitative studies before faculty committees. As a systematic process, grounded theory exhibits the rigor quantitative researchers like to see in an educational study. As part of this process, grounded theory has features that contain a self-correcting nature. Based on analyzing one set of data, the researcher obtains direction from the analysis for the next set of data (Charmaz, 2000). Also, in data analysis, the researcher builds categories systematically from incident to incident and from incident to category. In this way, the researcher stays close to the data at all times in the analysis.

How Did Grounded Theory Develop?

Two sociologists, Barney G. Glaser and the late Anselm L. Strauss, developed grounded theory in the late 1960s. It evolved out of their work at the University of California San Francisco Medical Center with patients who were terminally ill. In studying these patients, Glaser and Strauss recorded and publicized their methods of research. This led to many individuals contacting Glaser and Strauss to learn more about their research methods. In response, Glaser and Strauss developed a pioneering book that expounded in detail on their grounded theory procedures, *The Discovery of Grounded Theory* (1967). This book laid the foundation for the major ideas of grounded theory used today, and it became a procedural guide for numerous dissertations and research reports. In *Discovery*, Glaser and Strauss took the position that the current theory in sociology overly stressed verifying and testing theories rather than discovering the concepts (variables) and hypotheses based on actual field data from participants. A theory discovered during data collection will "fit the situation being researched and will work when put into use" (Glaser & Strauss, 1967, p. 3) better than a theory identified before a study begins.

The ideas in *Discovery* reflected the background of both authors. Glaser trained in quantitative research at Columbia University, with noted researchers who were interested in the inductive development of theory using quantitative and qualitative data. This inductive perspective led him to embrace the importance of generating theory from the perspective of participants in a study. Strauss, however, came to grounded theory from the University of Chicago, with a strong history and tradition in qualitative field research. This background led Strauss to emphasize the importance of field research, that is, going to individuals and listening closely to participants' ideas.

In the years following *Discovery,* both Glaser and Strauss independently authored several books that refined and explained their early methods (Glaser, 1978, 1992; Strauss, 1987). In 1990 and in 1998, Strauss teamed with a community nursing health researcher, Juliet Corbin, to take the techniques and procedures of grounded theory to new levels. They introduced a more prescriptive form of grounded theory, with predetermined categories and with concerns about validity and reliability.

Their systematic approach, although embraced by new qualitative researchers (Charmaz, 2000), provoked a critical response from Glaser (1992), which he detailed in a book to "set researchers using grounded theory on a correct path" (p. 3). Glaser was primarily concerned about how Strauss used preconceived categories and frameworks that did not allow theory to emerge during the process of research. He also took issue with what he saw as an emphasis on simply describing acts rather than actively conceptualizing patterns or connections in the data that would lead to theory.

"So who's got the real grounded theory?" asks Charmaz (2000, p. 513). Her question was more than rhetorical; she answered it by advancing her own approach to grounded theory, the "constructivist" method (Charmaz, 2006). Charmaz felt that both Glaser and Strauss (and Strauss and Corbin) were much too systematic in their procedures. Grounded theorists needed to stress flexible strategies, emphasize the meaning participants ascribe to situations, acknowledge the roles of the researcher and the individuals being researched, and expand philosophically beyond a quantitative orientation to research.

TYPES OF GROUNDED THEORY DESIGNS

We can see that perspectives about conducting grounded theory research have differed depending on the advocate for a particular approach. However, three dominant designs are discernible (Hood, 2007): the systematic procedure allied with Strauss and Corbin (1998) and Corbin and Strauss (2008); the emerging design, associated with Glaser (1992); and the constructivist approach espoused by Charmaz (1990, 2000, 2006).

The Systematic Design

The systematic design for grounded theory is widely used in educational research, and it is associated with the detailed, rigorous procedures that Strauss and Corbin identified in 1990 and elaborated in their second and third editions on techniques and procedures for developing grounded theory (1998). It is much more prescribed than the original conceptualization of grounded theory in 1967 (Glaser & Strauss, 1967). A **systematic design in grounded theory** emphasizes the use of data analysis steps of open, axial, and selective coding, and the development of a logic paradigm or a visual picture of the theory generated. In this definition, three phases of coding exist.

In the first phase, **open coding**, the grounded theorist forms initial categories of information about the phenomenon being studied by segmenting information. The researcher bases categories on all data collected, such as interviews, observations, and researcher's memos or notes. Typically, researchers identify categories and subcategories, as is seen in the grounded theory study by Knapp (1995). She examined the career development of 27 educational trainers in career development. In interviews with these trainers, she learned about their adaptability and resilience. One page from her study, shown in Figure 13.1,

FIGURE 13.1

An Example of Coding Categories in Grounded Theory

	Coding
Categories	*Sources*
Specialization	
definition	1, 2, 5, 6, 7, 10, 12, 13, 14, 15, 16, 17, 18, 19, 20, 21, 25, 26
generalist	1, 5, 7, 10, 12, 14, 15, 16, 19, 21, 23, 24
change agent	13, 17, J
Transferable skills	
previous job experience	CO2, 1, 3, 4, 5, 6, 8, 9, 11, 12, 13, 14, 15, 17, 19, 20, 22, 23, 24, 25, 26
cross training in another department	7, 8, 12, 17, 18, 19, 22, 23, 24, 25
Finding a focus	
entering field serendipitously	5, 6, 8, 9, 10, 11, 13, 15, 16, 19, 20, 22, 23, 24, J, M
occupational fit	2, 3, 4, 5, 6, 7, 8, 10, 11, 12, 13, 14, 15, 16, 17, 18, 19, 20, 21, 22, 23, 25, 26, J
turn down promotions	2, 12, 18, 23
understanding self	3, 6, 16, 17, 18, 19, 21, 22, 23, 24, 25
having a personal mission	3, 14, 16, 17, 18, 19
personally well grounded	2, 6, 13, 14, 19
other centered	CO2, 3, 8, 11, 13, 14, 15, 16, 17, 18, 19, 20, 21, 22, 24
Learning On-the-Job	
wandering around in the dark	CO2, 15, 22, M
trial and error	CO2, 2, 15, 16, 23, 24
gradual development	1, 4, 5, 6, 7, 8, 9, 17, 20, 22
facilitating training	1, 8, 11, 17, 20, 21, 24, 26
keeping current	CO2, 1, 2, 4, 5, 6, 8, 10, 11, 12, 15, 16, 17, 20, 21, 24, 26
learning environment	CO2, 18, 24, 26, F

KEY	
#	Interview
CO#	Pilot
F	Focus groups
J	Journal
M	Memo
O	Observation

Source: Reprinted with permission from Sharon Knapp, Ph.D.

portrays several categories that Knapp identified from her data, such as specialization, transferable skills, finding a focus, and on-the-job learning. In this coding presentation, we find that Knapp also indicates the sources of information that support the categories, such as interviews, focus groups, journals, memos, and observations.

To consider another example of open coding, see Figure 13.2, which displays the coding for a study of 33 academic chairpersons in colleges and universities and their roles in enhancing faculty research (Creswell & Brown, 1992). The authors organized their presentation of open coding differently than Knapp and included broad categories, properties, and dimensionalized examples, and followed the systematic procedures of Strauss and Corbin (1990). The major features of this table are the seven categories of roles: provider, enabler, advocate, mentor, encourager, collaborator, and challenger. However, the authors introduce two new ideas into our understanding of open coding. **Properties** are subcategories in grounded theory of open codes that serve to provide more detail about each category. Each property, in turn, is dimensionalized in grounded theory. A **dimensionalized property** means that the researcher views the property on a continuum and locates, in the data, examples representing extremes on this continuum. For example, the chair, as a provider (category), engages in funding faculty (a property), which consists of possibilities on a continuum of extent of funds ranging from long-term start-up seed money to short-term travel money (dimensionalized property).

In the second phase, **axial coding**, the grounded theorist selects one open coding category, positions it at the center of the process being explored (as the core phenomenon), and then relates other categories to it. These other categories are the causal conditions (factors that influence the core phenomenon), strategies (actions taken in response to the core phenomenon), contextual and intervening conditions (specific and general situational factors that influence the strategies), and consequences (outcomes from using the strategies). This phase involves drawing a diagram, called a **coding paradigm**, which portrays the interrelationship of causal conditions, strategies, contextual and intervening conditions, and consequences.

To illustrate this process, first examine Figure 13.3. In this figure, we see the open coding categories on the left and the axial coding paradigm on the right. A grounded theory researcher identifies one of the open coding categories as the core category that is central to a theory (we review the criteria for selecting this core category later). Then, this core category becomes the centerpoint of the axial coding paradigm. Examining this paradigm, you can see that there are six boxes (or categories) of information:

1. *Causal conditions*—categories of conditions that influence the core category
2. *Context*—the specific conditions that influence the strategies
3. *Core category*—the idea of phenomenon central to the process
4. *Intervening conditions*—the general contextual conditions that influence strategies
5. *Strategies*—the specific actions or interactions that result from the core phenomenon
6. *Consequences*—the outcomes of employing the strategies

In addition, viewing this coding paradigm from left to right, we see that the causal conditions influence the core phenomenon, the core phenomenon and the context and intervening conditions influence the strategies, and the strategies influence the consequences.

The third phase of coding consists of selective coding. In **selective coding** the grounded theorist writes a theory from the interrelationship of the categories in the axial coding model. At a basic level, this theory provides an abstract explanation for the process being studied in the research. It is the process of integrating and refining the theory (Strauss & Corbin, 1998) through such techniques as writing out the story line that interconnects the categories and sorting through personal memos about theoretical ideas (see discussion on memos later in the chapter). In a story line, a researcher might examine

FIGURE 13.2

An Example of Coding Categories in Grounded Theory with Properties and Dimensionalized Properties

Table 1
Open Coding of Chairperson's Role

Broad Categories*	Category	Properties	Dimensionalized Examples	
Administrative role	Provider	With funding	Start-up seed money	Short-term travel
		With nonfinancial aid	Laboratory equipment	Student personnel
	Enabler	With more money	Faculty committees	Long-term sabbatical
		With more visibility	Faculty committees	Administrative assignments
External role	Advocate	For resources	Short-term funds	Long-term facilities
		For interaction	With faculty	With students
		To assist politically	With dean	With faculty
Interpersonal role	Mentor	By role modeling	Time management	Working with others
		By sharing expertise	About research topics	About specific journals
		By reviewing and critiquing	Before manuscript submission	After manuscript submission
	Encourager	By hands off	No pressure	Choice belongs to professor
		By recognition and appreciation	Private communication	Public communication
		By general support	Personal friendship	Professional collegiality
		By task-specific encouragement	Supporting ideas	Encouraging specific book or article
	Collaborator	By jointly setting goals	Informal discussion	Formal performance reviews
		By working together on projects	Writing grant proposals	Writing journal articles
	Challenger	By prodding	Gentle reminder	Direct formal conversation
		By inspiring	Discussing general possibilities	Discussing specific examples
		By evaluating and monitoring	Biweekly conferences	Annual review

Source: Creswell & Brown, 1992.

*Corbin and Strauss (2008) define a category as "a higher-level concept" (p. 159). It is these concepts which analysts group into lower-level concepts according to shared properties. These concepts are sometimes called themes and they enable the researcher to reduce and combine data.

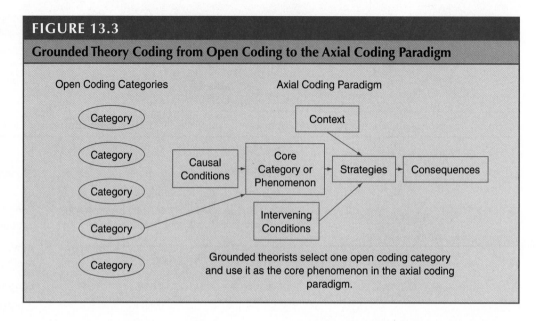

FIGURE 13.3

Grounded Theory Coding from Open Coding to the Axial Coding Paradigm

Grounded theorists select one open coding category and use it as the core phenomenon in the axial coding paradigm.

how certain factors influence the phenomenon leading to the use of specific strategies with certain outcomes.

Use of these three coding procedures means that grounded theorists use set procedures to develop their theory. They rely on analyzing their data for specific types of categories in axial coding and use diagrams to present their theories. A grounded theory study using this approach might end with hypotheses (called *propositions* by Strauss & Corbin, 1998) that make explicit the relationship among categories in the axial coding paradigm.

A study of the process of coping by 11 women who survived childhood sexual abuse illustrates this systematic procedure (Morrow & Smith, 1995). In this study we learn that the women felt threatened, helpless, and powerless, but that they survived and coped by managing their feelings (e.g., avoiding or escaping feelings, not remembering experiences). They also address their feelings of hopelessness and powerlessness using strategies such as seeking control in other areas of their life, reframing abuse to give the illusion of control, or simply rejecting power issues. As an example of the systematic procedure associated with Strauss and Corbin (1990, 1998) and Corbin and Strauss (2008), the authors include the process of open coding, axial coding, and generating a theoretical model. They had clearly identified sections in the study for discussion about each component of axial coding (e.g., causes of feelings and helplessness, the strategies used, and the consequences). A diagram illustrates the "theoretical model" for surviving and coping, and they discuss this diagram as a sequence of steps in the process of coping behavior.

The Emerging Design

Although Glaser participated with Strauss in the book on grounded theory (Glaser & Strauss, 1967), Glaser has since written an extensive critique of the Strauss approach. In this critique, Glaser (1992) felt that Strauss and Corbin (1990) had overly emphasized rules and procedures, a preconceived framework for categories, and theory verification rather than theory generation. (Babchuk [1996, 1997] reviewed the history of the use of grounded theory.) Glaser (1992), however, stressed the importance of letting a theory emerge from the data rather than using specific, preset categories such as we saw in the axial coding paradigm (e.g., causal conditions, content, intervening condition, strategies, and consequences). Moreover, for Glaser, the objective of a grounded theory study was for the author to explain a "basic social process." This explanation involved the constant comparative coding procedures of comparing incident to incident, incident to category, and category to category. The focus was on connecting categories and emerging theory, not on simply describing categories. In the end, the researcher builds a theory and discusses the relationship among categories without reference to a diagram or picture.

The more flexible, less prescribed form of grounded theory research as advanced by Glaser (1992) consists of several major ideas:

1. Grounded theory exists at the most abstract conceptual level rather than the least abstract level as found in visual data presentations such as a coding paradigm.
2. A theory is grounded in the data and it is not forced into categories.
3. A good grounded theory must meet four central criteria: fit, work, relevance, and modifiability. By carefully inducing the theory from a substantive area, it will fit the realities in the eyes of participants, practitioners, and researchers. If a grounded theory works, it will explain the variations in behavior of participants. If it works, it has relevance. The theory should not be "written in stone" (Glaser, 1992, p. 15) and should be modified when new data are present.

Larson's (1997) study portrayed a grounded theory study consistent with Glaser's approach. The goal for Larson was to write a "theory-in-process" (p. 118) for high school social studies teachers' conception of discussion in their classrooms. This example of an emerging design takes the reader through six conceptions that emerged in the data: discussion as recitation, as a teacher-directed conversation, as an open-ended conversation, as posing challenging questions, as guided transfer of knowledge to the world outside the classroom, and as practice of verbal interaction. Larson also identified factors that influenced these conceptions, such as student diversity and lesson objectives.

In this emerging grounded theory approach, Larson's attention was on developing an explanation for discussion in high school social studies classrooms. His procedure was to generate categories by examining the data, refining the categories into fewer and fewer categories, comparing data with emerging categories, and writing a theory of several processes involved in classroom discussions. Larson developed categories but did not present a diagram of his theory.

The Constructivist Design

The constructivist approach has been articulated by Charmaz (1990, 2000, 2006) as a philosophical position. To her, it lies between the more positivist (i.e., more quantitative) stance of Glaser and Strauss and Corbin and postmodern researchers (i.e., those who challenge the importance of methods). Overall, her focus is on the meanings ascribed by participants in a study. She is more interested in the views, values, beliefs, feelings, assumptions, and ideologies of individuals than in gathering facts and describing acts. Charmaz (2000, 2006) suggested that any aspects that obscure experiences, such as complex terms or jargon, diagrams, or conceptual maps, detract from grounded theory and represent an attempt to gain power in their use. Using active codes, such as "recasting life," best captures the experiences of individuals. Moreover, a grounded theory procedure does not minimize the role of the researcher in the process. The researcher makes decisions about the categories throughout the study (Charmaz, 1990). The researcher brings certain questions to the data, along with a "store of sociological concepts" (p. 1165). The researcher also brings values, experiences, and priorities. Any conclusions developed are suggestive, incomplete, and inconclusive.

In applying this approach, a grounded theorist explains the feelings of individuals as they experience a phenomenon or process. The constructivist study mentions the beliefs and values of the researcher and eschews predetermined categories, such as those found in axial coding. The narrative is written to be more explanatory, more discursive, and more probing of the assumptions and meanings for individuals in the study.

Charmaz illustrated the central elements of this approach to grounded theory. In a study of the processes involved in the experiences of 20 men with chronic illnesses (e.g., multiple sclerosis, renal failure, diabetes), Charmaz (1994) explored how and in what way their illnesses precipitated a personal identity dilemma. She contended that chronic illness threatened men's "taken-for-granted" masculine identities. Her findings explored several dilemmas, such as risking activity versus forced passivity, remaining independent versus becoming dependent, maintaining dominance versus becoming subordinate, and preserving a public persona versus acknowledging private feelings. These dilemmas clustered into several processes the men experienced—awakening to death, accommodating uncertainty, defining illness and disability, and preserving self.

Using a constructivist approach to grounded theory, she clearly articulated that her purpose was to understand "what it means to have a disease" (Charmaz, 1994, p. 284). She reported the feelings of the men, using active code labels such as *awakening, accommodating, defining,* and *preserving.* These codes signal basic processes the men were experiencing. Charmaz interrelated their experiences, their conditions, and their consequences in a narrative discussion without the use of diagrams or figures to summarize these processes. She ended with thoughts such as "What are the conditions that shape whether a man will reconstruct a positive identity or sink into depression?" (pp. 283–284), more suggestive and questioning of the data than conclusive.

Choosing Among the Designs

Choosing among the three approaches requires several considerations. As you consider conducting a grounded theory study, you need to weigh how strongly you want to emphasize procedures, use predetermined categories in analysis, position yourself as a researcher, and decide how to end the study, whether it is with tentative questions or hypotheses that are specific.

If you were Maria, seeking to generate a theory of the process of apprehending students for weapon possession, what design would you use? Because Maria is a beginning researcher, the more structured approach of the systematic design would be ideal. With the procedures clearly identified and the axial coding model specified in terms of types of categories to relate, the systematic procedure would be best.

In selecting one of the three approaches, consider that the procedures advanced by Strauss and Corbin (1998) and Corbin and Strauss (2008) may lead to a commitment to a set of analytic categories (Robrecht, 1995) and a lack of conceptual depth (Becker, 1993). Also, in all types, grounded theory has a distinct language that some educators may view as jargon and, hence, in need of careful definition (e.g., constant comparative, open coding, axial coding). One criticism is that these terms are not always clearly defined (Charmaz, 2006), although Corbin and Strauss (2008) provided numerous definitions at the beginning of each chapter of their book. Finally, with the varied approaches to this design and the continual emergence of new perspectives, readers may become confused and not know which procedures would best produce a well-developed theory.

THE KEY CHARACTERISTICS OF GROUNDED THEORY RESEARCH

Grounded theory can incorporate a systematic approach, a flexible emerging design, and the use of active codes to capture the experiences of participants. In the six characteristics that follow, you can find elements of the systematic, emerging, and constructivist approaches. Characteristics that grounded theory researchers use in their designs are:

- Process approach
- Theoretical sampling
- Constant comparative data analysis
- A core category
- Theory generation
- Memos

A Process Approach

Although grounded theorists might explore a single idea (e.g., leadership skills), they more frequently examine a process because the social world that we live in involves people interacting with other people. Grounded theorists generate an understanding of a process related to a substantive topic. A **process in grounded theory research** is a sequence of actions and interactions among people and events pertaining to a topic (Corbin & Strauss, 2008). The educational topic could be AIDS prevention, achievement assessment, or counseling between a school counselor and a student. In all of these topics, researchers can isolate and identify actions and interactions among people. Grounded theorists call these isolated aspects categories. **Categories in grounded theory designs** are themes of basic information identified in the data by the researcher and used to understand a process. A category for the process between a school counselor and student, for example, may be the student's understanding of "success" in the session.

Several types of labels or titles are used for themes or categories. In grounded theory research, a frequently used form is *in vivo* codes. **In vivo codes** are labels for categories (or themes) that are phrased in the exact words of participants, rather than in the words of the researcher or in social science or educational terms. Researchers identify these words by examining passages of transcripts or observational fieldnotes to locate phrases mentioned by participants that capture the intent of a category. For example, rather than use the social science concept "upward mobility," a participant might call this idea "goin' up the ladder." Using in vivo coding, the researcher would use the phrase "goin' up the ladder" to describe the category. Because categories become major headings in research reports, this phrase would be the heading of the discussion about the open coding category "goin' up the ladder."

It is helpful to see how the two ideas of process and categories relate to activities that are typically applied by a grounded theorist. Examine the flow of activities as shown in Figure 13.4.

A researcher begins with a research problem, such as the need to examine how academic chairpersons balance their work and personal lives. The central phenomenon, then, becomes a "balance of work and personal life." To study this central phenomenon, the grounded theorist frames it as a process, such as the "process by which chairs balance their work and personal lives" (alternatively, the process of "imbalance" might be explored). Whatever be the process, it has a sequence of activities, actions and interactions among people. The actions of the chair might include exercising early in

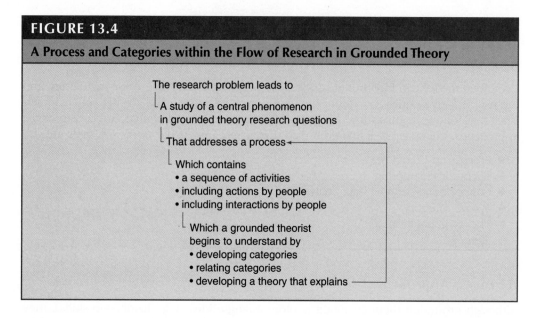

FIGURE 13.4

A Process and Categories within the Flow of Research in Grounded Theory

The research problem leads to

└ A study of a central phenomenon
in grounded theory research questions

└ That addresses a process ←

└ Which contains
• a sequence of activities
• including actions by people
• including interactions by people

└ Which a grounded theorist
begins to understand by
• developing categories
• relating categories
• developing a theory that explains ─

the morning and visiting with faculty later in the morning about stressful situations in the department. Here we have several activities, organized into a sequence, exhibiting actions by people. As the grounded theorist studies chairpersons (e.g., through interviews or observations), an understanding of the process of balancing work and personal life slowly emerges. The researcher categorizes this information, drawing on evidence to support each category. This phase is the open coding phase. Then the researcher starts organizing the categories into a model (axial coding), and interrelating the categories to form a theory that explains the process of balancing work and personal life. In this example, the process emerges from the problem and the need to explore the central phenomenon, and the categories develop from data collection.

As grounded theorists conduct a study, they often use a phrase for the process starting with a gerund word (i.e., *ing* words; as recommended by Charmaz, 2000). As a phrase that appears in titles and purpose statements, it signals the action of the study. Listed below are titles for grounded theory studies in which we can see the use of gerund words, a key category of interest, and the broader topic being explored:

◆ "Educating Every Teacher, Every Year: The Public Schools and Parents of Children with ADHD" (Reid et al., 1996)—the process of educating teachers, the implied category of relations between parents and schools, and the topic of children with ADHD

◆ "'Discovering' Chronic Illness: Using Grounded Theory" (Charmaz, 1990)—the process of patients discovering their illness, the category of chronic illness, and the implied topic of disease

Theoretical Sampling

The data collected by grounded theorists to establish these processes includes many forms of qualitative information. Researchers can collect observations, conversations, interviews, public records, respondents' diaries and journals, and the researcher's own personal reflections (Charmaz, 2000). Many grounded theorists, however, rely heavily on interviewing, perhaps as a way to capture best the experiences of participants in their own words, which is an approach consistent with the constructivist position (Charmaz, 2006; Creswell, 2007).

In the purposeful sampling of individuals to interview or observe, grounded theory espouses a unique perspective that distinguishes it from other qualitative approaches to data collection. Grounded theorists sample theoretically using a procedure involving the simultaneous and sequential collection and analysis of data. **Theoretical sampling** in grounded theory means that the researcher chooses forms of data collection that will yield text and images useful in generating a theory. This means that the sampling is intentional and focused on the generation of a theory. For instance, when a grounded theorist decides to study children's choice of a school, students and their parents are good candidates for interviews because they are actively involved in the process of selecting a school and can speak from firsthand experiences. However, school personnel (e.g., the principal) may have useful information to inform this process, but they would be less central than the students and parents, who are making the choices. In this project, the grounded theorist would begin with students and their parents, who actually make the choice of schools.

Beyond sampling data for its theoretical value, grounded theorists also espouse the idea of using an emerging design. An **emerging design** in grounded theory research is the process in which the researcher collects data, analyzes it immediately rather than waiting until all data are collected, and then bases the decision about what data to collect next on this analysis. The image of a "zigzag" helps us to understand this procedure, as shown in Figure 13.5. As illustrated in this figure, the grounded theorist engages in initial data collection (e.g., the first collection of interview data), analyzes it for preliminary categories, and then looks for clues about what additional data to collect. These clues may be underdeveloped categories, missing information in the sequence of the study process, or new individuals who can provide insight into some aspect of the process. The grounded theorist then returns to the field to gather this additional information. In this procedure, the inquirer refines, develops, and clarifies the meanings of categories for the theory. This process weaves back and forth between data collection and analysis, and it continues until the inquirer reaches saturation of a category. **Saturation** in grounded theory research is a state in which the researcher makes the subjective determination that new data will not provide any new information or insights for the developing categories.

FIGURE 13.5

Zigzag Data Collection and Analysis to Achieve Saturation of Categories

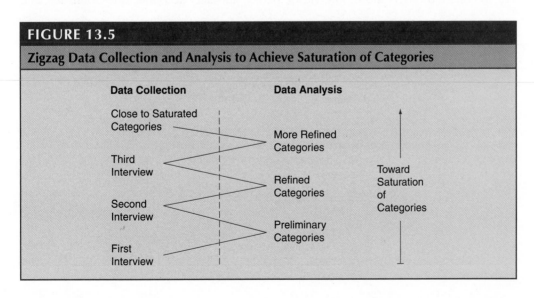

Identifying this process in a published grounded theory study requires close examination of the data collection and analysis process to note whether the researcher seems to be recycling between data collection and data analysis. For example, in a study of the processes of men experiencing chronic illness, Charmaz (1990) carefully documented how she interviewed 7 of the 20 men in her study more than once to refine her emerging categories.

Constant Comparative Data Analysis

In grounded theory research, the inquirer engages in a process of gathering data, sorting it into categories, collecting additional information, and comparing the new information with emerging categories. This process of slowly developing categories of information is the constant comparative procedure. **Constant comparison** is an inductive (from specific to broad) data analysis procedure in grounded theory research of generating and connecting categories by comparing incidents in the data to other incidents, incidents to categories, and categories to other categories. The overall intent is to "ground" the categories in the data. As shown in Figure 13.6, raw data are formed into indicators (Glaser, 1978)—small segments of information that come from different people, different sources, or the same people over time. These indicators are, in turn, grouped into several codes (e.g., Code A, Code B, Code C), and then formed into more abstract categories (e.g., Category I, Category II). Throughout this process, the researcher is constantly comparing indicators to indicators, codes to codes, and categories to categories. This eliminates redundancy and develops evidence for categories. In addition, the grounded theorist compares the emerging scheme with the raw data to ground the categories in the information collected during the study.

In this process, the grounded theorist asks questions of the data. Glaser (1992), for example, suggested that the inquirer ask:

◆ What is the data a study of?
◆ What category or what property of what category does this incident indicate?
◆ What is actually happening in the data?
◆ What is the basic social psychological process or social structural process in the action scene? (p. 51)

In a grounded theory study of becoming an adult student in New Zealand, Cocklin (1996) collected observations, interviews, participant diary accounts, questionnaires, and

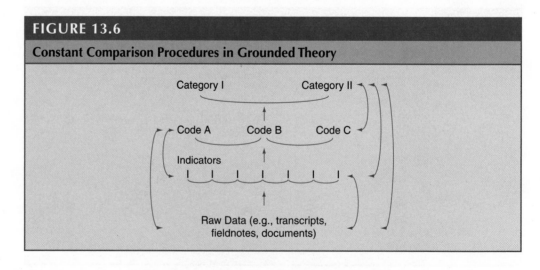

FIGURE 13.6

Constant Comparison Procedures in Grounded Theory

documentary materials from teaching staff in one secondary school. In this study, Cocklin described the process of refining his categories (called themes) by returning to his data repeatedly as themes emerged. He commented:

> While doing this transcription and organization, and as an activity, I undertook at weekends, statutory holidays, and term vacations, I also engaged in a continuous process of reflection and analysis which included placing interpretive comments alongside the transcribed data (see Figure 2). These comments, akin to the derivation of properties and hypotheses, I also subjected to ongoing analysis and development as the year progressed and data emerged. . . . (p. 97)

A Core Category

From among the major categories derived from the data, the grounded theorist selects a core category as the central phenomenon for the theory. After identifying several categories (say, 8 to 10 depending on the size of the database), the researcher selects a **core category** as the basis for writing the theory. (See Figure 13.3 for a visual of this process.) The researcher makes this selection based on several factors, such as its relationship to other categories, its frequency of occurrence, its quick and easy saturation, and its clear implications for development of theory (Glaser, 1978). It is a category that can "process out," in other words, be the center or main theme of the process (Glaser, 1978). Listed here are detailed criteria that Strauss and Corbin (1998) identified for choosing a central (or core) category:

1. It must be central; that is, all other major categories can relate to it.
2. It must appear frequently in the data. This means that within all or almost all cases, there are indicators pointing to that concept.
3. The explanation that evolves by relating the categories is logical and consistent. There is no forcing of data.
4. The name or phrase used to describe the central category should be sufficiently abstract.
5. As the concept is refined, the theory grows in depth and explanatory power.
6. When conditions vary, the explanation still holds, although the way in which a phenomenon is expressed might look somewhat different (p. 147).

We can illustrate a core category by turning to an actual grounded theory study. As shown in Figure 13.7, Mastera (1996) developed a theoretical model of the "stages of forging a curriculum." In this study, she examined three undergraduate colleges from three states in the Midwest that were engaging in the process of changing their general education curricula. Semi-structured interviews with 34 faculty and administrators led to a theory about forging a curriculum. As shown in Figure 13.7, at the center of this theory was the phenomenon (or core category), "stages of forging a curriculum," consisting of several properties: calling for action, selecting the committee, forming the committee, setting the direction, designing the curriculum, and approving the curriculum design and the courses. Mastera's overall model showed how these stages emerged through changes, shaped by institutional context, that led to strategies for leveraging the discourse on the committees and contributed to specific consequences, such as revising the general education curriculum. In this process, Mastera identified early in open coding the importance of her phenomenon or core category, "stages," although "selecting labels that captured this staged process proved to be more elusive" (p. 59).

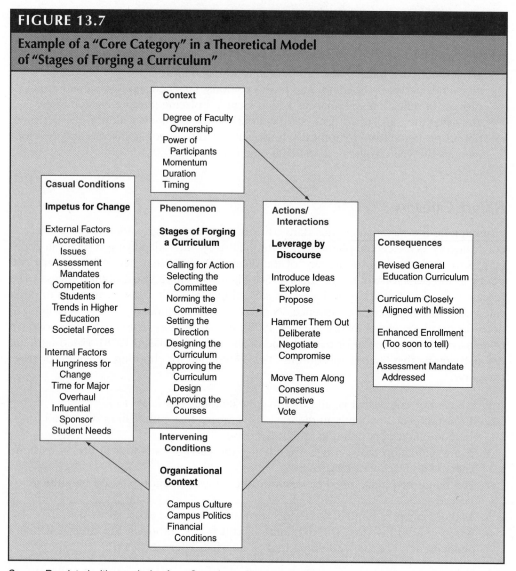

FIGURE 13.7

Example of a "Core Category" in a Theoretical Model of "Stages of Forging a Curriculum"

Source: Reprinted with permission from Georgianne Mastera, Ph.D.

Theory Generation

In identifying a core category and the process categories that explain it, grounded theorists have generated a middle-range theory. The entire procedure leads to generating a theory based on data collected by the researcher. This **theory in grounded theory research** is an abstract explanation or understanding of a process about a substantive topic grounded in the data. Because the theory is close to the data, it does not have wide applicability or scope, such as "grand" theories about human motivation that apply to many people and situations. Nor is it a "minor working hypothesis" (Glaser & Strauss, 1967, p. 33), such as an explanation for students in one school or classroom. Instead, the theory is "middle range" (Charmaz, 2000), drawn from multiple individuals or data sources, which provides an explanation for a substantive topic.

Consider how grounded theorists actually present their theory in three possible ways: as a visual coding paradigm, as a series of propositions (or hypotheses), or as a story written in narrative form.

Theory appears in studies as the visual coding model or coding paradigm discussed earlier in the systematic procedures of Strauss and Corbin (1998). We have viewed several of these coding paradigms already, but a slightly different version is seen in Brown's (1993) model of ethnic minority students' process of community building. As shown in Figure 13.8, Brown explored the process of community building among 23 black and Hispanic freshmen during the first 6 to 10 weeks at a private, predominantly white university in the Midwest. In this study, an inductively developed process of campus community building resulted from the data. The theory or model of this process is shown in Figure 13.8. Based largely on the predetermined, systematic categories of intervening conditions, strategies, causal conditions, and phenomena, Brown developed a picture of the process as the key theoretical description of the process.

Brown's (1993) study also illustrated a visual model and the use of theoretical propositions (or hypotheses) for conveying a theory. **Theoretical propositions** in grounded theory research are statements indicating the relationship among categories, such as in the systematic approach to axial coding that includes causal conditions, the core category or phenomenon, the context, intervening conditions, strategies, and consequences.

FIGURE 13.8

Example of a Theory—A Model of Ethnic Minority Students' Process of Community Building

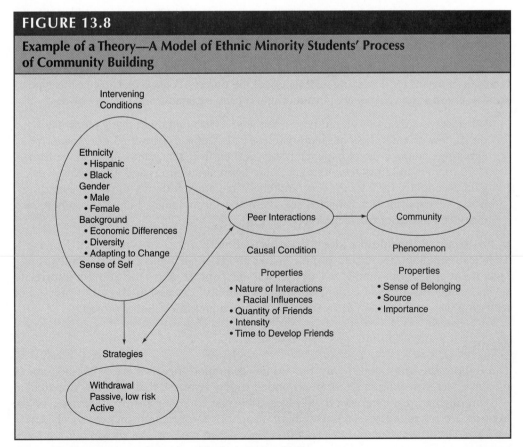

Source: Reprinted with permission from Martha L. Brown, Ph.D.

After presenting her visual model, Brown identified propositions and subpropositions that relate her categories in the model:

1. Peer interactions influence community building among black and Hispanic college freshmen.
2. The more time students spend with peers, the greater their sense of community. The more their free time spent alone, the greater the feelings of loneliness and alienation.
3. The more free time students spend on campus interacting with peers in the residence halls, the greater their sense of community.
4. Active involvement in small groups within the institutional setting (i.e., residence hall floors, freshmen seminar groups, intramural sports teams, clubs) will facilitate feelings of community.

Returning again to Figure 13.8, we can see that Brown is interrelating the causal conditions about interactions and friends in the proposition and subpropositions. In additional propositions in her study, Brown continued to identify relationships that interrelated with other aspects of her model.

Although the "theory" may be easy to identify in a grounded theory study when the author presents it as a visual coding paradigm or as a series of propositions, a discussion written in the form of a story (Strauss & Corbin, 1998) may be less obvious to a reader. In the process of integrating the categories, grounded theorists develop a sense of what the research is all about and start writing a descriptive story about the process. Strauss and Corbin (1998) recommended that the researcher:

> . . . sit down and write a few descriptive sentences about "what seems to be going on here." It may take two, three, or even more starts to be able to articulate one's thoughts concisely. Eventually, the story emerges. (p. 148)

After refinement and reworking, grounded theorists include these stories in their research reports as a means for describing their theory of the process. A good example of this type of passage is a descriptive story about teen drug use cited by Strauss and Corbin (1998):

> What keeps striking us about these interviews is that, although many teens use drugs, few go on to become hard-core users. It seems to be a kind of teenage experimentation, a developmental phase in their lives that marks the passage from child to teen and from teen to adult. They learn about drugs and also themselves, gain acceptance from their peers, and challenge adult authority through using drugs. It is a very specific behavior that sets them apart from family, but, at the same time, makes them one of the teen group. (p. 149)

In this passage, the authors identify a causal condition (i.e., "developmental phase"). They also mention the outcomes (i.e., "marks the passage") and establish context (e.g., "sets them apart from family"). Through this descriptive story, the authors interrelate several categories of axial coding to form a theoretical discussion about the process of teen drug use—a third form for writing theory into a grounded theory project.

Memos

Throughout the grounded theory procedure, grounded theorists create memos about the data. Memo writing is a tool in grounded theory research that provides researchers with an ongoing dialogue with themselves about the emerging theory (Charmaz, 1990). **Memos** are notes the researcher writes throughout the research process to elaborate on ideas about the data and the coded categories. In memos, the researcher explores hunches, ideas, and thoughts, and then takes them apart, always searching for the broader explanations at work in the process. Memos help direct the inquirer toward new sources of data, shape which ideas to develop further, and prevent paralysis from mountains of data. However, grounded theory studies do not often report memoing, or if they do, they do not provide evidence of how it was used (Babchuck, 1997).

We can illustrate memoing in a study about the process of identity loss by individuals with Alzheimer's disease. Orona (1997) discussed how memoing helped her to:

1. Free associate and write whatever thoughts she became aware of
2. Unblock at times when she felt she could not quite describe in words what was occurring in the data
3. Begin conceptualizing by tracking ideas from raw data to coding and into categories

The memos can be short or long, more detailed and related to codes and categories, or broader and more abstract. Here is an illustration of a short, detailed memo written by Charmaz (1994) during her study of patients who were terminally ill, and the "identifying moments" in the hospital when patients developed new insight into themselves.

> It became clear to me that how a particular chronically ill person who was identified by others sometimes became revealed to them in the course of a moment's encounter or interaction. These moments gave the ill individual new reflections of self, often revealing that he (or she) is not the person he felt he was. . . . Negative identifying moments are those shrouded in embarrassment and devaluation. . . . One woman described a demeaning encounter with a social service agency when in the course of a moment, she saw herself as being defined as someone not worth helping. She said, "All I can do is dissolve in tears—there is nothing I can do. I just get immobilized. . . ." (pp. 110–111)

This passage illustrates how a grounded theorist can write a memo, use it in a study, highlight her own reflexive thoughts in a way consistent with qualitative research, and use the memo to highlight categories of information (i.e., "negative identifying moments").

POTENTIAL ETHICAL ISSUES IN GROUNDED THEORY RESEARCH

One way to view grounded theory is that it is an approach or set of approaches to the analysis of data. Consequently, the writings on grounded theory are largely silent on ethical issues in the conduct of research (e.g., privacy, consent, confidentiality, deceit, deception, and harm [Olesen, 2007]). This does not mean that grounded theory is unethical or devoid of ethics, and, when grounded theory emerged during the 1960s, the discussion about ethics in educational research was not widely shared. Still, ethical issues face grounded theorists when they declare the purpose of the study knowing that it will emerge through a grounding in participant views. The central role of interviewing in grounded theory raises questions about power and authority and giving appropriate voice to participants about the process of research. The use of logically building grounded theory from concepts or categories to a theoretical model needs to be documented so that others can recreate similar processes. The idea of using grounded theory to benefit participants looms large just as in other forms of qualitative research.

The following Box 13.1 discusses an ethical issue that arose in the grounded theory study by Creswell and Brown (1992).

BOX 13.1   **Ethical Dilemma**

Walking Off with the Data

The researchers collected qualitative interviews to build a theoretical model of department chair support for faculty in higher education institutions. For a few of these interviews, follow-up campus interviews took place. At these interviews, the researchers were able to visit personally with some of the participants. For the most part the interviews were not on a sensitive topic, but the interviewees on some campuses did talk about the challenges and difficulties they faced with department chairs. During one campus visit, the researchers initiated a casual conversation with an interviewee about the interview. This faculty member asked to see the audiotape. The researchers had a transcription back home. The tape was handed over. This individual then promptly turned and left, taking the audiotape. Should the researchers ethically use the interview from this individual or consider it missing data?

WHAT ARE THE STEPS IN CONDUCTING GROUNDED THEORY RESEARCH?

With the different types of grounded theory procedures—systematic, emerging, and constructivist—researchers might engage in alternative procedures to conduct a grounded theory study. The approach taken here will be the systematic form of inquiry because it consists of easily identifiable steps, is frequently used for grounded theory research, and provides a procedure that beginning researchers will find useful.

Step 1. Decide If a Grounded Theory Design Best Addresses the Research Problem

A grounded theory design is appropriate when you want to develop or modify a theory, explain a process, and develop a general abstraction of the interaction and action of people. As such, it offers a macropicture of educational situations rather than a detailed microanalysis. Because of the generation of an abstract process, it seems suitable for sensitive topics, such as the coping process of women who have been sexually abused (Morrow & Smith, 1995), or any research problem situation in which individuals need their privacy protected. Grounded theory also seems applicable for those individuals who are trained in *quantitative* research but who want to explore a *qualitative* procedure that is rigorous and systematic. For example, in educational fields in which *qualitative* research has made slow inroads, such as educational psychology, inquirers are turning to grounded theory as a useful procedure. (See one of many examples, such as Frontman & Kunkel's [1994] grounded theory study about how counselors construe success with clients.)

Step 2. Identify a Process to Study

Because the intent of grounded theory research is to explain a process, you need to identify early a tentative process to examine in your grounded theory study. This process may change and emerge during your project, but you need to have an idea of the process at this step. This process should naturally follow from the research problem and questions that you seek to answer. It needs to involve people who are acting or interacting with identifiable steps or sequence in their interactions. It is helpful to write down this process early in your plan for a study, such as "What is the process of coping for first-year teachers?" or "What is the process by which faculty develop into productive researchers?"

Step 3. Seek Approval and Access

As with all research studies, you need to obtain approval from the institutional review board. You also need access to individuals who can provide insight into the process that you plan to study. Like other studies, this step involves seeking approval to collect data, appraising individuals of the purpose of your study, and guaranteeing protection of the site and participants as you conduct the inquiry.

If you plan to use the zigzag approach to data collection and analysis, it is difficult to plan and receive prior approval for collecting some data. This approach relies on collecting data, analyzing it, and using this information to determine the next step in data collection. Thus, as you seek permission to conduct a grounded theory study, it is helpful to apprise reviewers of this process and the tentative nature of the data collection procedures at the beginning of the study.

Step 4. Conduct Theoretical Sampling

The key concept in grounded theory data collection is to gather information that can assist in your development of a theory (e.g., individuals who have experienced the process you are studying). Grounded theorists use many forms of data, but many researchers rely on interviews to best capture the experiences of individuals in their own words. A characteristic of grounded theory research, however, is that the inquirer collects data more than once and keeps returning to data sources for more information throughout a study until the categories are saturated and the theory is fully developed. There is no precise time line for this process, and researchers need to make the decision as to when they have fully developed their categories and the theory. One rule of thumb in graduate student research and interviewing is to collect at least 20 to 30 interviews during data collection (Creswell, 2007). This general guideline, of course, may change if you collect multiple sources of data, such as observations, documents, and your own personal memos.

Step 5. Code the Data

The process of coding data occurs during data collection so that you can determine what data to collect next. It typically begins with the identification of open coding categories and using the constant comparative approach for saturation by comparing data with incident and incident with category. A reasonable number of 10 categories may suffice, although this number depends on the extent of your database and the complexity of the process you are exploring. McCaslin (1993), for example, conducted a grounded theory study of the complex question of leadership in rural communities. In exploring "What is leadership?" he identified 50 categories from observing and interviewing individuals participating in educational leadership development programs in six counties.

From open coding, you proceed to axial coding and the development of a coding paradigm. This involves the process identified in Figure 13.3 of selecting a core category from the open coding possibilities and positioning it at the center of the axial coding process as a core category. From here you will likely return to data collection or reanalyze your data to identify causal conditions, intervening and contextual categories, strategies, and consequences to develop the axial coding process. You can assemble this information in the form of a coding paradigm or visual picture of the process in which you indicate with arrows the direction of the process.

Step 6. Use Selective Coding and Develop the Theory

The final process of coding is selective coding, and it involves actually developing your theory. This procedure includes interrelating the categories in the coding paradigm. It may involve refining the axial coding paradigm and presenting it as a model or theory of the process. It may include writing propositions that provide testable ideas for further research. You can present your theory as a series of propositions or subpropositions. This stage may also involve writing a story or a narrative that describes the interrelationships among categories.

Step 7. Validate Your Theory

It is important to determine if your theoretical explanation makes sense to participants and is an accurate rendering of events and their sequence in the process. In grounded theory research, validation is an active part of the process of research (Creswell, 2007). For example, during the constant comparative procedure of open coding, the researcher triangulates data between the information and the emerging categories. The same process of checking data against categories occurs in the axial coding phase. The researcher poses questions that relate the categories, and then returns to the data and looks for evidence, incidents, and events—a process in grounded theory called **discriminant sampling**. After developing a theory, the grounded theorist validates the process by comparing it with existing processes found in the literature. Also, outside reviewers, such as participants in the project who judge the grounded theory using "canons" of good science, may substantiate the theory, including the validity and credibility of the data (Strauss & Corbin, 1998).

Step 8. Write a Grounded Theory Research Report

The structure of your grounded theory report will vary from a flexible structure in the emerging and constructivist design to a more quantitatively oriented structure in the systematic design. Compared with other qualitative designs, such as ethnography and narrative research, the structures of grounded theory studies are scientific and include a problem, methods, discussion, and results. In addition, the point of view of the writer in the systematic approach is sometimes third person and objective in tone. All grounded theory projects, however, end with the theory generated by the researcher reporting his or her abstraction of the process under examination.

HOW DO YOU EVALUATE GROUNDED THEORY RESEARCH?

Criteria for specifically evaluating a grounded theory study are available in Charmaz (2006), Strauss and Corbin (1990, 1998), and in Corbin and Strauss (2008). Charmaz (2006) uses terms such as credibility, originality, resonance, and usefulness. Corbin and Strauss (2008) discuss factors such as how individuals can benefit from the research (i.e., fit, sensitivity, and applicability); the importance of concepts (or categories) and their discussion within a context; the logic, depth, and variation; and the creative, innovative manner in which the researcher says something new.

In a high-quality grounded theory study, some combination of these factors exists, and the author:

◆ Makes explicit the process or action at the heart of the study.
◆ Develops or generates a theory at the end of the study that is grounded in the view of the participants.
◆ Makes certain that a link exists between the data, the generation of categories, and the ultimate theory.
◆ Provides evidence of using memoing and sampling that enables the generation of the theory.
◆ Presents a visual model of the theory.
◆ Provides evidence of the use of one of the types of grounded theory designs, such as the systematic, emerging, or constructivist approaches.

KEY IDEAS IN THE CHAPTER

What Is Grounded Theory, When to Use It, and How It Developed?

A grounded theory design is a set of procedures used to generate systematically a theory that explains, at a broad conceptual level, a process about a substantive topic. You use grounded theory when you seek to generate a theory because one is not available or suitable. It is also useful to study a process, an action, or an interaction. It offers a step-by-step, systematic procedure for the beginning researcher. In using grounded theory, a researcher can stay close to the data at all times in the analysis. This design was developed by sociologists Barney Glaser and Anselm Strauss at the University of California San Francisco in the late 1960s.

Three Types of Grounded Theory Designs

Grounded theory research consists of three types of designs. The systematic procedure of Strauss and Corbin (1998) involved using predetermined categories to interrelate the categories, visual diagrams, and specific propositions or hypotheses to make the connections explicit. The emergent design, consistent with Glaser's (1992) ideas, relied on exploring a basic social process without preset categories. The constructivist approach of Charmaz (2000) focused on subjective meanings by participants, explicit researcher values and beliefs, and suggestive or tentative conclusions.

Key Characteristics of Grounded Theory Research

Despite these differences, six aspects characterize grounded theory. Grounded theorists employ this design to explore a process around a substantive topic. They theoretically sample using a procedure of simultaneous data collection and analysis. Grounded theorists analyze their data for increasing levels of abstraction by using constant comparative procedures and asking questions about their data. During analysis of the data for categories, grounded theorists identify a core category (or central phenomenon) that will "process out" (Strauss, 1987) into a theory. Grounded theorists explore this process to develop a theory. Throughout the grounded theory procedure, grounded theorists write memos to themselves.

Potential Ethical Issues in Grounded Theory Research

Because of the focus of grounded theory on data analysis, not much discussion of ethics has occurred in the grounded theory literature. However, throughout the process of research, grounded theorists may be confronted with ethical challenges ranging from advancing the purpose of the study, to the power and authority issues of interviewing, and on to building a useful chain of evidence from the data to the generation of the theory that will benefit those the study is intended to serve.

Steps in Conducting a Grounded Theory Study

The steps involved in conducting a grounded theory study are to start with the intent to develop a theory, to locate a process (or action or interaction) to study, to obtain necessary approvals, to sample individuals who have experienced the process, to code data into categories or concepts, and to interrelate the categories to form a theory. Next comes validating the theory and writing the grounded theory report.

Evaluating the Quality of a Grounded Theory Study

Several published criteria exist for evaluating the quality of a grounded theory study. A good grounded theory study presents a theory of a process grounded in the views of participants. This theory is developed from the memos written by the researcher, the linking of concepts or categories, the presentation of the theory as a visual model, and the use of systematic, emerging, or constructivist approaches.

USEFUL INFORMATION FOR PRODUCERS OF RESEARCH

- ◆ When planning a grounded theory study, use the steps for conducting a study advanced in this chapter.
- ◆ Consider whether your grounded theory study will be systematic, emergent, or constructivist. Make this decision based on reviewing the arguments for each design type and determining whether you prefer a more flexible or prescribed approach to grounded theory research.
- ◆ The visuals presented in this chapter can be adapted and used to display several processes and to create tables and diagrams, such as the zigzag data collection process and the constant comparative approach.
- ◆ Creating a visual diagram of your theory helps to clearly identify the categories and see their interrelationships.
- ◆ Validate your theory by using constant comparative procedures, triangulating during the research, and by employing member checking with participants in your study.

USEFUL INFORMATION FOR CONSUMERS OF RESEARCH

- ◆ Educators can use the criteria for evaluating a study to assess the quality of a published study.
- ◆ When examining a study to determine if it is a grounded theory project, you might look at the title to determine if the words "grounded theory" are included.

Also, most grounded theory projects clearly include an exploration of a process, and the authors should identify this process in the purpose statement or research questions.

◆ A sign of grounded theory research is that the author employs multiple passes to the field to collect data. A well-refined theory (and categories) consists of saturation and zigzagging back and forth between data collection and analysis to build the categories and theory.

◆ Look for a visual model of the theory. This model is the centerpiece of the grounded theory study and represents the author's attempt to visualize the process under study.

ADDITIONAL RESOURCES YOU MIGHT EXAMINE

Several major books are available to provide the procedures used in grounded theory research. Examine the books by Strauss:

Corbin, J., & Strauss, A. (2008). *Basics of qualitative research: Techniques and procedures for developing grounded theory* (3rd ed.). Thousand Oaks, CA: Sage.

Strauss, A. (1987). *Qualitative analysis for social scientists.* New York: Cambridge University Press.

Examine the books by Glaser:

Glaser, B. G. (1978). *Theoretical sensitivity.* Mill Valley, CA: Sociology Press.

Glaser, B. G. (1992). *Basics of grounded theory analysis.* Mill Valley, CA: Sociology Press.

You might also consult the original book they developed together:

Glaser, B., & Strauss, A. (1967). *The discovery of grounded theory.* Chicago: Aldine.

For a recent perspective on grounded theory from a constructivist perspective, examine the book chapter by Charmaz (2000) and her recent book, Charmaz (2006), and look at her journal articles for applications of her approach. Also, see the edited volume of writings on grounded theory by Bryant and Charmaz (2007).

Bryant, A., & Charmaz, K. (Eds.). (2007). *The SAGE handbook of grounded theory.* Los Angeles: Sage.

Charmaz, K. (1990). "Discovering" chronic illness: Using grounded theory. *Social Science Medicine, 30,* 1161–1172.

Charmaz, K. (1994). Identity dilemmas of chronically ill men. *The Sociological Quarterly, 35,* 269–288.

Charmaz, K. (2000). Grounded theory: Objectivist and constructivist methods. In N. K. Denzin & Y. S. Lincoln (Eds.), *Handbook of qualitative research* (2nd ed., pp. 509–535). Thousand Oaks, CA: Sage.

Charmaz, K. (2006). *Constructing grounded theory.* London: Sage.

Example of a Grounded Theory Study

Examine the following published journal article that is a grounded theory design study. Marginal notes indicate the major characteristics of grounded theory research highlighted in this chapter. The illustrative study is:

Developing a Leadership Identity: A Grounded Theory

**Grounded Theory
Characteristics
in Marginal
Annotations**

Susan R. Komives
Julie E. Owen
Susan D. Longerbeam
Felicia C. Mainella
Laura Osteen

*This grounded theory study on developing a leadership identity revealed a 6-stage developmental pro-
cess. The thirteen diverse students in this study described their leadership identity as moving from a
leader-centric view to one that embraced leadership as a collaborative, relational process. Developing a
leadership identity was connected to the categories of developmental influences, developing self, group
influences, students' changing view of self with others, and students' broadening view of leadership.
A conceptual model illustrating the grounded theory of developing a leadership identity is presented.*

(01)   Burns (1978) observed that despite the large volume of scholarship on the topic, leadership is
not well understood. Recent attempts to classify and make meaning of the evolution of leadership
have been generally successful at organizing theories of leadership into conceptual families (Bass,
1990; Northouse, 2003; Rost, 1993). Numerous books and articles focus on leadership theory, behaviors, effective practices, or on particular populations (e.g., women, youth, ethnic groups), specific
settings (e.g., civic leadership, business leadership, church leadership), and diverse outcomes (e.g.,
satisfaction, effectiveness, social responsibility). Despite the broad scope of this literature, there is
little scholarship about how leadership develops or how a leadership identity develops over time.

The Scholarship of Leadership

(02)   Rost (1993) concluded that most of what has been labeled leadership in the past was essentially
good management. Leadership theories that rely on traits, behaviors, and situations to explain leadership worked well in an industrial era when the predominant goals of leadership were production
and efficiency. However, Rost and other scholars (Allen & Cherrey, 2000; Bennis, 1989; Heifetz,
1994; Wheatley, 1999) noted that society has shifted to a knowledge-based, networked world. Rapid
advancements in technology, increasing globalization, complexity, and interconnectedness reveal the
new postindustrial paradigm of a networked world and call for "new ways of leading, relating, learning, and influencing change" (Allen & Cherrey, p. 1; Rost). Many of these "new ways of leading"
include components of principle-centered leadership such as collaboration, ethical action, moral purposes, and leaders who transform followers into leaders themselves (Burns, 1978; Covey, 1992; Rost).

(03)   The principles involved in postindustrial leadership support a values-centered approach (Chrislip & Larson, 1994; Kouzes & Posner, 2003; Matusak, 1997) and have influenced new pedagogical
leadership models. Scholars who have developed models largely designed for college student leadership development such as the Eisenhower/UCLA ensemble social change model (Higher Education Research Institute, 1996) assert that collaboration among individuals, groups, and communities

Susan R. Komives is Associate Professor, College Student Personnel Program; Julie E. Owen is Coordinator of
Curriculum Development and Academic Partnerships, Maryland Leadership Development Program; each at the
University of Maryland. Susan D. Longerbream is Assistant Professor of Educational Psychology at Northern
Arizona University. Felicia C. Mainella is Assistant Professor of Leadership Studies at Peace College. Laura
Osteen is Director of the LEAD Center at Florida State University. This research was supported by grants from
the American College Personnel Association's Educational Leadership Foundation and the James MacGregor
Burns Academy of Leadership.
*Correspondence concerning this article should be addressed to Susan R. Komives, 3214 Benjamin Building,
University of Maryland, College Park, MD 20742; komives@umd.edu*

is essential for social change to occur. Similarly, the relational leadership model (Komives, Lucas, & McMahon, 1998) defines leadership as "a relational process of people together attempting to accomplish change or make a difference to benefit the common good" (p. 21). This relational leadership model includes elements of inclusiveness, empowerment, ethics, purposefulness, and process orientation. Many leadership educators agree that college students are best informed by learning a postindustrial, relational-values approach to leadership (Higher Education Research Institute; Zimmerman-Oster & Burkhardt, 1999). Although scholarship exists that describes these leadership approaches, none offers a theoretical model of how this kind of relational leadership develops.

Most leadership development scholarship focuses on skill-building or short-term interventions such as retreats or courses, rather than on the process of how leadership capacity or leadership identity is created or changes over time. Although there were conceptual models of leadership development (Brungart, 1996; Velsor & Drath, 2004) at the time of this study there was no known research on how leadership identity was formed. Understanding the process of creating a leadership identity is central to designing leadership programs and teaching leadership. The purpose of this study was to understand the processes a person experiences in creating a leadership identity.

(04)

Process approach

Method

Because the purpose of the study was to understand how a leadership identity develops, a grounded theory methodology was chosen. The intent of a grounded theory is to generate or discover a theory or abstract analytical schema of a phenomenon that relates to a particular situation grounded in the experience and perceptions of the participants (Brown, Stevens, Troiano, & Schneider, 2002; Creswell, 1998; Strauss & Corbin, 1998). The grounded theory in this study reflects the developmental experience of college student participants who had been observed working effectively with others toward shared purposes, that is, who had demonstrated relational leadership (Komives et al., 1998).

(05)

Theory generation

Procedures

Sampling. The study employed the purposeful sampling procedures of intensity sampling to identify "intensity-rich cases that manifest the phenomenon intensely, but not extremely" (Patton, 2002, p. 243). Nominators in professional positions that afforded them the opportunity to observe students interacting in group settings at a large mid-Atlantic research university were invited to nominate students who were exemplars of relational leadership.

(06)

Theoretical sampling

Participants. From the pool of possible participants, we invited 13 students who exhibited the theoretical dimensions of relational leadership to participate in the study. Eight of the participants were White, 1 was Asian American, 3 were African American, and 1 student was African who immigrated to the United States as a child. Eight of the participants were men and 5 were women. There were 2 sophomores, 9 fourth- or fifth-year seniors, and 2 recent graduates. Two participants identified themselves as gay men; others identified themselves as heterosexual or did not identify their sexual orientation. The group was religiously diverse including Muslim, Bahá'í, Jewish, and Christian students, as well as those without active religious affiliations. There was a range of majors from chemistry to speech communications. Students used their own first name or chose their own pseudonym.

(07)

In-Depth Interviews. Each student participated in a series of three interviews with the same interviewer. A research team of five White women conducted the research. A structured interview protocol was designed to ensure continuity across interviewers. After participants gave written informed consent, interviews were tape-recorded and subsequently transcribed. Through constant comparative analysis (Merriam & Associates, 2002; Strauss & Corbin, 1998), the research team modified questions to explore emergent issues. Researchers maintained field notes during each interview.

(08)

Constant comparative data analysis

The three interviews ranged from 1 to 2 hours each. This "three-interview series" followed Seidman's (1991) model focusing on life history, followed by a detailed exploration of the experience, and lastly focusing on "reflection on the meaning" (p. 12). The first interview used a life narrative method (Bruner, 1987; Riessman, 1993) and asked the student to start back in elementary school and reflect on "how you have become the person you are now." This question allowed for the broadest possible story to emerge so researchers could connect various experiences to the emergence of leadership identity. The purpose of the second interview was to identify the students' experiences working with others and to explore their experiences with leadership. The third interview explored how the students' view of leadership changed over time and what influenced that changing view.

(09)

(10)   *Trustworthiness.* The research team ensured the trustworthiness and credibility of the study (Strauss & Corbin, 1998) with multiple procedures. Participants reviewed and responded to transcripts of their interviews (i.e., member checking). Research team members served as peer debriefers for the process. The team sought feedback on the evolving theory and interpretations of the data from diverse colleagues to understand its meaning. Concepts were identified in the data and were examined across the stages of the evolving model. The detail in coding and analysis confirmed saturation in the central category and categories of the theory. Grounded theory does not seek to be generalizable and the degree to which it is transferable is sought through the participant "voices" and the thick descriptions reflected in this study.

No memoing in
data analysis

Data Analysis

(11)   We used open, axial, and selective coding (Strauss & Corbin, 1998) to analyze the data. During open coding, each transcript was analyzed in sentences or groups of sentences reflecting single ideas. These units were given a code to reflect that idea or concept (Strauss & Corbin). The open coding identified 5,922 items that were combined through axial coding into 245 abstract concepts. In selec-

A core category

tive coding the concepts were ultimately organized into one central category or "what the research is all about" (p. 146), in this case, leadership identity along with five categories: (a) essential developmental influences; (b) developing self; (c) group influences; (d) changing view of self with others; and (e) broadening view of leadership. Properties—also known as attributes of a category—were identified for each of these categories. Strauss and Corbin clarified that "whereas properties are the general or specific characteristics or attributes of a category, dimensions represent the location of a property along a continuum or range" (p. 117). Through constant comparative analysis (Merriam & Associates, 2002; Strauss & Corbin), each participant's response was compared and connected to others as categories, properties, and dimensions emerged.

Findings and Emerging Theory

(12)   The experiences and reflections of these students revealed the dynamic process of developing a leadership identity. Students had different experiences, came to new awareness of themselves in a leadership context at different ages, identified a variety of ways these experiences and context had an impact on them, yet they engaged with the process in similar ways leading to credibility in the emergent theory. The theory emerged as the relationships between the concepts combined into an integrated framework that explained the phenomenon of leadership identity (Strauss & Corbin, 1998). The categories interact to create a leadership identity as the central category that developed over six identity stages. Developing self interacted with group influences to shape the student's changing view of self with others. This changing view of self in relation to others shaped the student's broadening view of what leadership is and created a leadership identity. Illustrative quotations from the participants are included in each of the categories to tell the story of this theory.

Developmental Influences

(13)   The essential developmental influences that fostered the development of a leadership identity included adult influences, peer influences, meaningful involvement, and reflective learning. Each of these four properties has dimension, which means they change across the stages of the central category. For example, how adults influenced newer leaders was a different process than with experienced leaders, and meaningful involvement began with an individual joining a variety of organizations but progressed to more in-depth, responsible experiences with one or two core groups.

(14)   *Adult Influences.* Adults played different roles in influencing student movement through the leadership identity development stages. In the family, adults were very important in building confidence and being an early building block of support. Angela noted, "My family is really what built a lot of my character." Adults created safe spaces in classes and organizations where students learned to communicate and relate to peers. On the importance of his scoutmaster, James noted with relief, "When we had moved houses, we didn't move troops" so he still had access to the same scout master who affirmed him. Students explicitly noted the role of school-teachers and the encouragement found in the continuity of those teachers across grades in school.

In the early stages of their leadership identity, adults were particularly influential as role models. (15)
James said,

> Through all this you need that person you look up to, that role model, that figure that you aspire to be like
> or to be. Doesn't have to be a real person, people usually see qualities of what they aspire to be in different
> people, I guess like a hero . . . And [when I was little] I wanted to be like Superman and smart like Batman
> and be in touch with people like Star Trek characters.

Adults were the first to recognize the students' leadership potential. Ed recalled times when he (16)
was encouraged to take leadership roles in groups: "[adults said] 'Oh, you'd be good at that', or
'I really think you should apply for that.'" In the early stages, adults affirmed and sponsored students. They often prompted students initially to get involved in organizations and helped them set
high expectations for themselves. Joey observed: "Positive reinforcement . . . gave me the drive to
get more involved in things." Eventually there was less need for this external affirmation and the
students became self-directed. Ed saw that shift in his motivation and said, "I'm going to go ahead
and do this. I'm going to feel confident in the things I've done in the past, because I don't want to
rely on others to force me forward."

Later, adults continued as models and became actively engaged mentors. Jayme described (17)
watching adults as intentional modeling: "I'm going to learn from other people's experience, and I'll
at least get some information before I jump in there." Students of color, especially, benefited from
the presence of an active adult mentor. Students of color were often apprenticed to an adult and
worked in intensive and intentional ways as an assistant or protégé to that adult. Jayme became the
"protégé" of Miss [Smith]—a highly involved woman at her church. This woman "adopted" her and
took her everywhere including on business and church trips. Jayme observed adult conversation,
manners, and how conflicts were resolved. She drew on those experiences when she subsequently
became the assistant to the dance teacher in her high school and often chose her own behaviors
by asking herself, "What would Miss [Smith] do?"

In college, adults continued as models and mentors, but also become meaning-makers and (18)
even evolved into friends. Ed described how he often thought things through with his advisor:
"We would always talk after any experience. I would go right to [my advisor] and like, 'Okay, this
is what happened, and I'm trying to figure it out.'" Adults were a meaningful part of each stage of
developing students' leadership identity. The dimensions of adult influences ranged from being
affirmers, models, and sponsors in the early stages to being mentors and ultimately to being meaning makers and colleagues or friends.

Peer Influences. Same-aged peers served as friends and older peers served as role models in early (19)
leadership identity stages. Joey emulated an older student who was an officer in his college LGBT
group and observed: "That's kind of cool . . . I could do that." Modeling peers served as a motiva-
tor for involvement as well as a model of leadership. Jimmy admired the SGA president:

> [She] was one of the first people . . . like my role model, like she was . . . this perfect leader. That's what I'm
> going to strive to be, because, you know she takes this group of uninvolved kids, and she makes them do
> so much for the campus. She's so great at like organizing. She's fighting for the students. Like, she has this
> love . . . very selfless like promotion for students in general.

Numerous students cited older peers as the reason they got involved or interested in an organi- (20)
zation in college. These peers served as sponsors and took the student to initial meetings of a
group or encouraged them to join or to run for an office. Peers served as sources of affirmation
and support. For Corey, this peer affirmation was important. He initially described his preference
to be an active member of a group and not the positional leader until he was turned to by peers to
be the formal leader:

> [I] started to realize that in fact that's how I was viewed by my peers. I felt like, okay, well, if my peers have
> put faith in me, faith in the fact that they truly believe that I'm a leader, then I kind of need to take it on. I
> wasn't pressured into it, but I felt like it would be best, that maybe I do have something to offer, so I started
> to embrace it more.

Engaging with peers gained depth and meaning as leadership identity developed. With more (21)
group experience, peers served as followers, teammates, and ultimately as collaborators and peer
meaning-makers.

(22)   *Meaningful Involvement.* Involvement experiences were the training ground where leadership identity evolved. These experiences helped clarify personal values and interests, and helped students experience diverse peers, learn about self, and develop new skills. Early involvements were a way to make friends. Reflecting on his membership on the high school swim team, Joey described his motivation: "It wasn't the athletics event. It was the camaraderie." As they transitioned into new schools and the university, they sought social integration through involvement in sports, band, theater, or service as a source of new friends. Later meaningful involvements showed more complex motivations. Jimmy reported that "SGA was the first kind of goal-oriented group for me . . . I felt like I was working towards something." Other involvements developed values and personal skills. Jayme learned new skills through service: "I've gotten used to just listening like just hearing them talk about their lives."

(23)   Team-based involvements such as sports, theater, and band taught students to do their personal best while concurrently supporting others. From playing sports, Corey said, "I learned it is not just about me" and "your individual achievement helps the team. It doesn't help you shine or stand out, and don't ever put yourself on that pedestal." Marie learned in band that "I'm not trying to beat someone else, but like we're trying to sound good together." Some learned the importance of support from older teammates who established a positive group climate. Ed described his swim team experience as always being "on our feet cheering for each other," and "we cheered more for the kids that were struggling."

(24)   *Reflective Learning.* Structured opportunities for critical reflection, such as journaling and meaningful conversations with others, allowed students to uncover their passions, integrity, and commitment to continual self-assessment and learning. This reflection was initially with a parent or sibling; participants described dinner table conversations, family meetings, and the listening ear of close-age siblings. Over time, they began to process their experiences with other adults and peers. Some students preferred journaling and began to share those journals with others.

(25)   Experiences in which students intentionally learned about leadership, such as trainings, retreats, or classes, provided them with new language and ideas that aided their development. Students used this new leadership language to assess themselves and differentiate experiences. Ed talks about the power of his first undergraduate leadership classes: "We talked about having some kind of lens or framework, or even the language to describe [leadership], it changes not only the way I think about it, but it changes the way I act as a leader in ways that I don't understand . . . in unconscious ways." Becky clearly saw:

> It's a combination of the experiences I've had, the classes and the theories I've learned. I don't think alone any of it would have influenced me as it has. It has really made it spin together to really understand it, because I could come out of class one day and take something that I learned and really implement it in my experience, but because having experienced it I can also talk about it theory-wise. So I think it's definitely that combination.

(26)   Even being a participant in this study supported reflection. Jimmy said, "Now, I feel like having gone through this research study like definitely . . . my interactions are more genuine." As depicted in Figure 1, these developmental influences were the environmental context in which leadership identity developed.

Developing Self

(27)   The category of developing self contains properties with dimensions of personal growth that changed throughout the development of leadership identity. The properties in this category are deepening self-awareness, building self-confidence, establishing interpersonal efficacy, applying new skills, and expanding motivations.

(28)   *Deepening Self-Awareness.* In the early stages of developing their leadership identity, students recalled a highly vague and diffuse sense of self. Attributions from adults, family, and peers helped them identify aspects of themselves that were strengths and aspects that needed attention. Over time they were able to label aspects of their personal identity on their own. For example, Becky said, "I just happen to be a very outspoken, share-my-opinion-kind of person." Joey claimed, "I'm more of an interpersonal person."

When asked about their personal identities, students of color identified race as a critical factor.   (29)
James, an African American student, said, "[the] biggest thing is race"; another African American
student, Ray, described how he was motivated to present "a positive image of a Black male,"
although he tried "not to think about [race] too much." Sammy, an Asian American student, discussed his many identities including the influence of race, ethnicity, and being male, and had come
to see them as assets of diversity that he brought to a group. Both gay students felt being male was
an asset to their leadership; however, Donald worried that sexual orientation could be a barrier to
leadership based on what others might have thought of him.

Gender was a factor in how some approached leadership. After being denied membership   (30)
in a group based upon her gender, Jayme noted, "I decided that I am not going to let anything,
anything at all, push me down." Christine became more activist in her youth after completing
altar server training in her church only to be denied the opportunity to become an altar "boy."
Angela acknowledged that she didn't ever think, "'I can't do [something] because I'm a woman,'"
but acknowledged that "[you] have to succeed to the best of your ability to show that you're not
inferior."

The awareness of majority aspects of the students' identities was largely taken for granted.   (31)
For example, most of the White students did not identify race until asked about it. Donald, a
White male, reflected what many White men in the study shared that: "Race and gender does
sort of make it easier. . . . People sort of expect you to take on a leadership role." Angela did
not think about how being White and heterosexual helped her, although in reflection, said that
it probably did. Ed, however, felt truly transformed and enlightened when he "started to understand my own privilege . . . as a White able-bodied male." Those in later stages of developing their leadership identity were generally more complex in their awareness of their multiple
identities.

Other aspects of self-awareness were the development of personal values and a sense of per-   (32)
sonal integrity that became more important over time. James shared that: "The first time I heard the

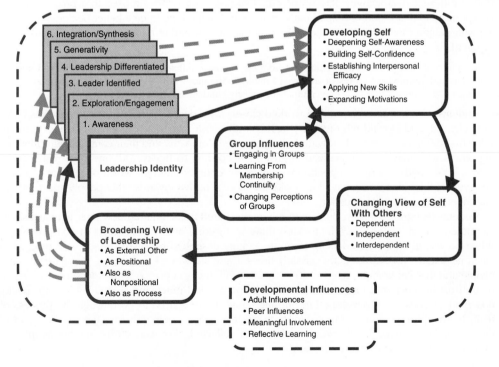

FIGURE 1
Developing a Leadership Identity: Illustrating the Cycle

Theory
generation

word *integrity* was my Dad saying it; and he was like, 'You know when it comes to integrity it is the most important thing because if everything is gone that is all you have.'"

(33)   *Building Self-Confidence.* Most students described feeling special in their families and with other adults. Even when they went through periods of self-doubt and low esteem, they knew they mattered to someone. They sought the support and approval of adults in the early stages of their leadership identity development. For example, James commented, "I always wanted the coach's approval." Building their confidence supported developing a positive self-concept, a sense of themselves. Sammy knew when that happened and shared that: "Things started rolling and I was in a groove . . . I knew what needed to get done." Confidence came with meaningful experience. James said "I can do this because I have done similar things to it." Confidence also came with being able to identify their strengths and weaknesses. Jayme said, "I'm not perfect, but I have something to bring."

(34)   As their confidence built, they were willing to take risks to get more involved and were empowered to take on more active group roles. Jayme reflected, "Eleventh grade was when I started letting myself be open and do what I wanted to do and not think about what other people say." Over time, their growing sense of self-awareness let them take on unpopular issues, stand up for their values, and not need peer affirmation. Ed described antihomophobia programs he did on his residence hall floor as a heterosexual resident assistant, knowing it was the right thing to do so "the alienation doesn't matter as much."

(35)   Once they acknowledged that they were leaders or had leadership potential, they began to incorporate that identity into their sense of self. Corey noted: "Sophomore year in college is when I really started to believe and really identify with being a leader—others had been saying it" and Jimmy noticed that "people showed respect . . . [I] started to think of [my]self this way."

(36)   *Establishing Interpersonal Efficacy.* Participants had numerous experiences that contributed to their efficacy in working with other people. Most students described how they learned to make new friends in the normal transitions from elementary school to middle or junior high school, high school, and on to college. Sammy and Joey, who moved often as children, saw the value of those transitions. Sammy said: "I get to know people a lot quicker because I socialize with everybody."

(37)   Students noted how important it was that they learned to relate to and communicate with people different from themselves. They developed an appreciation of diverse points of view and valued different perspectives. Ray observed: "I've just been really exposed to a broad range of viewpoints and that's kind of helped me to mature and helped me to be a better person in interacting with people too." Ed came to the realization that he first had to understand himself well before he could

> learn to deal with people who are different from me and have different ideals from what I have, I need to understand more what I represent and what I think. So the more work I do about what I value and what biases I have already that I've been culturally or socially conditioned to have, the better.

(38)   Students who felt different or who worked closely with people different from themselves (such as Becky, Ed, and Donald who worked weekly with youth with severe disabilities), later came to value that difference and credit it with the importance of empathy and their commitment to involving others who may be marginalized in groups. According to Becky, "All my work with people with special needs has really opened my eyes to an entirely different world of respect." Donald observed: "I think that [being gay] does make me more sensitive towards other people and what . . . their needs are in a group situation."

(39)   Students recognized that working with others on shared tasks required new inter-personal skills. Ray noted that in leadership: "The trickiest thing was asking one of your peers to do something." When he was in an early leadership position, Sammy described his own struggle with delegation when he stated, "I mean there are certainly times in my life when I feel that . . . I can't trust other people and that I'm going to have to do it myself." With the acceptance of interdependence, developing trust in others became essential. Being a cochair and practicing shared leadership, Becky observed: "I guess it all developed in one big chunk that I started to go through the process of really learning how to build relationships with other people, to help influence them to be a part of the group, and to make the changes [together]." She reflected, "I've gained trust in other people . . . I just took a few years to figure that out."

Each student valued being a self-proclaimed "people-person." They developed an early appreciation of harmonious relationships with others. Few of the participants liked conflict and each had learned to be mediators. Jimmy, for example, described himself as a "smoother" and Joey saw himself as "the connector, the bridge builder." Marie observed: (40)

> I'm just a big believer . . . in the power of personal relationships . . . it's one thing to work with someone in a group or with a campus committee or whatever but if you can get to know that person and they can get to know you outside of that professional or academic experience and have a social bond on top of everything else I think that that personal relationship when you take that into the academic/professional scenario will lead to maybe bigger and better results.

Applying New Skills. Participants worked to develop new skills as they developed their leadership identity. When they first started joining groups, they were conscious they were learning how to work with other people and knew this required new skills. They found developmental opportunities in many experiences; for example, Jimmy spoke about his high school play experience. "The play was the first time I learned how to completely interact with other people." When first serving as positional leaders, they practiced more directive leadership styles and approaches, all with the goal of getting tasks accomplished. Practical skills dominated that stage of their leadership identity. Donald noted he was "a good time framer, practical, an organizer," and Becky developed her public speaking skills. Practicing included learning difficult tasks such as delegation, member motivation, and member recognition. (41)

When they became aware of interdependence, they came to need new skills such as trusting others, and being open to diverse ideas and perspectives. They recognized the need to develop team-building skills and learned how to work alongside others toward common purposes. Becky asserted: "If the group is working together, there needs to be a common set of values, so everyone is working toward the same goal and everyone has the same ideas." Key to the facilitator role was learning to listen actively to others. They knew listening was a learned skill. Jimmy reflected on his awareness of how he was developing this skill with the support of his advisor: (42)

> Sometimes I think I don't realize what I say or what I do can offend other people . . . like . . . for me coming from like a White male background. So working with [an advisor] has really put a spin like I see myself acting differently. Then it comes out in more like not talking, but more listening.

Expanding Motivations. Students' indiscriminant early interests to get involved included personal motivations such as making friends or doing interesting things. Goals were refined as they narrowed their focus to joining or remaining in groups that meant something to them. As they developed personally and gained more experience, they sought a deep sense of commitment to something and knew that passion would be a strong motivation to action. James observed, "I like [having a] passion about things, [but] I didn't know what I was passionate about." Jayme observed that "Every single person needs something bigger than just their everyday life, because then it makes things all worthwhile." As participants' commitments to a change or a passion emerged, they took on a catalyst or a change agent role. (43)

Group Influences

The category of developing self interacted with the category of group influences (see the double arrow in Figure 1). The category of group influences includes the properties of engaging in groups, learning from membership continuity, and changing perceptions of groups. (44)

Engaging in Groups. Students often sought groups for a "sense of place." Ed captured many students' early childhood group experiences when he said, "I had feelings of being an outsider." They sought to find organizations that fit their developing self-image. James observed that "Working at scout camp made me feel like I could do anything." (45)

Students sought a sense of belonging in groups. Donald's college church group was even called "The Welcoming Place." These core groups included identity-based groups such as LGBT organizations or the Black Student Union. As he became more purposeful in his membership, Joey observed he sometimes felt (46)

> the weight of the world on your shoulders . . . you feel like you're alone and there's points where you feel like you need to have a safe space where there's people like you that can identify with you, who are experiencing the same struggle and have the same objectives.

(47)   Participants were also becoming increasingly clear about the conditions under which they would participate in groups and the role of groups in their development. They were developing convictions and narrowing their interests. Donald dropped out of scouts when he feared being "outed" as gay because the group was hostile toward gay students. Ed described dropping out of a sports club because "the more that I learned about myself and who I wanted to be, and what I wanted to do, it just didn't align with kind of their priorities." He shared the painful story of being at dinner with several members of that group who were telling insensitive jokes so he just got up and walked away and never went back to practice again. In reflection, he told us that he wished he had the capacity to tell them why he was upset but he did not know how to say those things then.

(48)   Many kinds of group experiences were critical. Experiences with group projects such as class projects contributed to trust and relationship building when successful and resulted in resentment toward others when not successful. Ed described a bad group experience in a class: "It was a dismal experience. I hated it, and I think some students really hated it since they are the ones that ended up taking on most of the work." Most shared Christine's comment that "[class] group projects are terrible." Conversely, Ray eventually came to learn a lot in group settings: "Everyone has different concerns in the groups that I work with, so that's kind of opened my mind . . . I've been able to understand where people are coming from a lot better."

(49)   We were fascinated by the relationship of a strong group culture to the individual's view of themselves and how that culture influenced developing a leadership identity. Becky described being the chair of a senior honor society committee going into her first meeting with a highly structured agenda and a set of ideas about how the task should be accomplished. The group slowed the process down by affirming that they were all leaders with good ideas and wanted to build a vision together of how the committee should approach its task. The group pulled Becky back from being too directive and supported her in practicing shared leadership. Becky reflected that she actually was very relieved. In a similar way, Jayme described her experience in her work with the local African immigrant community. The group continually reminded her that she and others were there to serve the group, not stand out as leaders themselves. Jayme observed:

> It keeps you grounded, because they'll easily call you out . . . So you don't get too cocky. It doesn't make you think . . . "I'm a leader." They're quick to tell you, . . . "What are you doing? A leader is the one who serves the community. Are you serving us?"

(50)   *Learning From Membership Continuity.* To gain more time and energy to invest in organizations they cared about, students started to narrow down their numerous organizational involvements to a few that were more meaningful. They went deep into these organizations. Corey chose to stay highly involved in his fraternity and reflected on this experience: "[It] . . . just changed my entire life." Students who were committed to a group or organization over time readily gained relational skills such as dealing with conflict, handling transition issues, and sustaining organizations. They increasingly became aware of their responsibility for the development of younger group members. They assumed responsibility and took on positional leadership roles and active member roles. Students often maintained their membership in other groups, while retaining a primary group as their main source of identification; a concept that Marie called her "core group." They eventually became wise senior members and continued their support of their core groups even when less active in the group's leadership. Some sports team experiences were particularly powerful developmental environments, which offered opportunities to develop group spirit, encouraged bonding and morale, and were sustained over time. On some teams, they learned to work with people they might not even like but had to learn to function together. That continuity of being known provided a core group—a safe space—to try on roles and practice processes.

(51)   Students' interaction with others in groups influenced their own self-awareness as well as shaped how they viewed groups and their role with others in groups. Angela, for example, had been used to doing things by herself in most groups but as tasks became more complex in one of her high school organizations, she came to realize she had to depend on others in the group to accomplish their goals. She had learned that working along with others was more productive than working alone. Subsequently, in her first year of college, she was one of several vice presidents of her residence hall association. When the president abruptly resigned, the group of vice presidents decided to share the role as copresidents until a new president was elected some months later.

Changing Perceptions of Groups. Students initially viewed groups as just collections of friends or (52) people they knew. As they began to realize those groups had purposes and objectives, this collection of people began to be seen as an organization with structure and roles. Eventually they saw that those organizations were entities to develop. Becky saw this as a new responsibility in her developing leadership identity: "I really try to . . . make it a better organization . . . [and make] simple changes that maybe in the long run would affect the organization." Organizations were also viewed as communities of people working together. Becky observed that the feeling of "community is necessary to do anything." As they developed in their leadership identity, they had a new sense of how their group was linked to other organizations in a system, and they became interested in how the system worked. Students became aware of those who worked in other groups on campus-wide or community-wide issues, and of those who functioned well in coalitions. These systems views led them to see the contributions of diverse roles of stakeholders in those systems and the complexity of different groups within a system. By gaining a systems-view, Ray even gained a new view of administrators: "Working with administrators [I'm] now . . . able to see where they're coming from . . . I'm a little bit more open-minded about sometimes why they can't get things done."

Changing View of Self With Others

Developing self interacted with group influences to effect how participants changed their view (53) of themselves in relation to other people. In the early stages of engaging in groups, they were *dependent* on others. Even when developing personal efficacy to accomplish their goals, they depended on adults and older peers for sponsorship, affirmation, and support. As students began to be involved in leadership contexts and take on member or leader roles, they engaged in groups from one of two primary pathways: *independent* or *dependent*. On the independent path, students aspired to be the positional leader or had a strong motivation to change something in a group or organization of which they were a part. Others continued to be dependent and preferred to be members or followers in groups. Corey said, "I didn't want to lead, but be part of a team that did." Many functioned on both pathways and clearly saw that they had different roles (independent leader or dependent follower). Whether students entered groups from an independent or dependent position, they shared a leadercentric view of leadership, believing only positional leaders did leadership. Donald said it succinctly, "Leadership is what the leader does." The key transition to a more differentiated view of leadership was facilitated by the awareness that group participants were interdependent with each other. The students continued a consciousness of the interdependence of themselves with others across the final stages of their leadership identity. They believed that leadership came from anywhere in the group and worked to develop their own and their peers' capacity for leadership.

Broadening View of Leadership

Students' changing view of themselves with others influenced their broadening view of leadership (54) and their personal definitions of leadership. The final category concerned participants' construction of leadership and the mental models that framed that construct. In the early stages of leadership identity, the construction of leadership was not yet a personal identity. The initial view of leader was an external adult and it broadened to include an older peer. That view could be stated as: "I am *not* a leader." Leadership then became leader-centric with the belief that a positional leader does leadership. Jayme said,

> When I was a girl, I thought leadership was the person who could boss everyone around, and make them do what they wanted to do. Because you saw all the people around you, those in charge were like, "Do this, do that, do this, do that."

That individual leader takes on responsibility, organizes tasks, and gets things done. Taking on (55) a position meant one was the leader. In their independent or dependent approaches to leadership, students acknowledged they were the leader in some contexts and also knew there were other contexts in which they were not the leader, they were "just" a member or follower. As students recognized they could not do everything themselves as positional leaders and that they valued the diversity of talents and perspectives brought by group members to accomplish goals, they began to engage with others in more meaningful, interdependent ways. This led to differentiation in the concept of leadership acknowledging that leadership could come from those in nonpositional roles (i.e., members) and increasingly was seen as a process among people in the group. Leaders were people facilitating the groups' progress from anywhere in the organization.

(56)   A leadership identity had become a more stable part of self. This led to the view represented by stating: "I can be *a* leader even when not being *the* leader." Evidence for this transition can be seen in Marie commenting: "There is a difference between having a position and being a leader," and in Ed's philosophy that "leadership is more of a fluid thing, it wasn't just rested in one person." From viewing leadership as a process comes the awareness that people can learn to engage in leadership. Sammy summed it up: "You know, everyone has leadership qualities, and everyone can be a leader in some avenue." Ultimately leadership became an integrated part of self-concept.

Leadership Identity

(57)   The central category of this grounded theory was leadership identity and it developed in six stages. Each stage ended with a transition, which signaled leaving that stage and beginning the next stage. The process of developing a leadership identity was informed by the interaction of developing self through group influences that changed one's view of self with others and broadened the view of leadership in the context of the supports of the developmental influences. These stages are briefly described with student voices as illustrations.

(58)   *Awareness*. The first stage was the early recognition that leaders existed. As children, participants were particularly aware of parent figures and of national, historic, or charismatic leaders. Angela said, "I always thought of my mom as a huge leader just because in times of hardship she always was the one that pulled through and seemed to pull everything together, and I think that's a leadership quality." This view of leadership was external to the self and participants did not personally identify as a leader or even differentiate group roles. Becky said, "I would say that my lower school and middle school parts of my life, I was not a leader. I wasn't much, I wasn't really a follower, I was kind of just there."

(59)   *Exploration/Engagement*. The second stage was a time of intentional involvement, experiencing groups, and taking on responsibilities, though not generally in a positional leadership role. They often engaged in a myriad of organizations and activities such as swim teams, church bible study groups, dance, Boy Scouts, student council, and community service, usually for the friendships involved. They liked to belong to groups but their involvement was often unfocused. Ray observed, "I always wanted to be doing things," but, "I wasn't ready for a huge role yet." This was a significant skill development stage, when they were seeking to learn anything they could from their participation in groups, including observing adult and peer models of leadership.

(60)   *Leader Identified*. In this third stage, all participants perceived that groups were comprised of leaders and followers and believed the leaders did leadership—that leaders were responsible for group outcomes. In this leader-centric stage, one was a leader only if one held a leadership position; indeed, one was *the* leader. When Marie became a positional leader as captain of the swim team her junior year in high school, she said to herself, "You are a leader now." Donald saw the responsibility of a leader as "you get a job, and you've got more work than everybody else to make sure everything happened." Students became intentional about their group roles in this stage. Some participants intentionally chose a member role when they joined groups; for example, Christine would "be a member first to see what something is about." As followers, these students might be very active and engaged in the goals of their group, but they still looked to the leader as the person who should be in charge.

(61)   *Leadership Differentiated*. In Stage 4, students differentiated leadership beyond the role of the positional leader and recognized that anyone in the group could do leadership and became aware that leadership was also a process between and among people. Students entered this stage with a new awareness that people in organizations were highly interdependent and that leadership was happening all around them. If they were in a positional leadership role, there was a commitment to engage in a way that invited participation and shared responsibility. They began to view this positional leader role as a facilitator, community builder, and shaper of the group's culture. James realized, "We were actually working together as a group, not under me." When they were

in a member role (i.e., a nonpositional role), there was an awareness of their own influence and the responsibility of every member to engage in leadership together to support the group's goals. James observed, "I like the fact that I can be a leader without a title because I think those are the best types of leaders to have." They affirmed their commitment to the groups' responsibility for its goals—as a "we" thing and not the individual leader doing it all. [Note: The complexity of the data in Stages 3 and 4 led us to identify two phases in each of these stages. An *emerging phase* clarified the ways the student "tried on" the identity early in the stage and the *immersion phase* was the practicing or living with that identity. These phases are discussed further in Komives, Owen, Longerbeam, Mainella, and Osteen (2005).

Generativity. In Stage 5, students became actively committed to larger purposes and to the groups (62) and individuals who sustained them. Students entered this stage and sought to articulate a personal passion for what they did. These passions were explicitly connected to the beliefs and values they identified as important in their lives. Describing her experience in residence hall government, Angela felt rewarded to realize that future "freshmen . . . [were] getting something better because of something we did." Service was seen as a form of leadership activism, a way of making a difference and working toward change. Exploring their interdependence further, they began to accept responsibility for developing others and for regenerating or sustaining organizations. They made a commitment to sponsor, support, mentor and develop others. They recognized that younger group members were in a developmental place that they themselves had experienced. Jimmy saw his responsibility from "having a peer mentor and now turning around and being a peer mentor." They sought to enhance the leadership capacity of newer members so they too could be part of the leadership process, largely to create a leadership pipeline for their groups. Anticipating his graduation, Sammy worked for continuity in the organization so the "person coming after me feels comfortable and can do just as well . . . as I did. . . . My approach to leadership now would have to be a kind of mentoring people."

Integration/Synthesis. Stage 6 was a time of continual, active engagement with leadership as a (63) daily process—as a part of self identity. They were increasing in internal confidence and were striving for congruence and integrity. Ed described this as:

> A conscious shift . . . I feel that I can take ownership and the strengths that I have and the value that I bring to a group of people and have confidence in myself that I can do the things that I could set out to do.

This stage was signaled by many students in the study, but not fully evident in all of them. (64) Those in or approaching this stage were confident that they could work effectively with other people in diverse contexts whether they were the positional leader or as an active group member. Even if they did not own the title of leader, they did have a confident identity of a person who does leadership. They understood organizational complexity and practiced systemic thinking. They were comfortable with contextual uncertainty knowing that because they had internalized leadership into their self-concept they could adapt and contribute to a new, unknown context. Ultimately, they echoed Joey's observation that "I see leadership now as an everyday thing."

A Conceptual Model of the Integration of Categories

The conceptual model in Figure 1 illustrates a cycle of how students engaged in the categories (65) that in turn influenced the development of their leadership identity and how that developed over time. One category, *developmental influences,* defined the supports in the environmental context in which the development of leadership identity was occurring.

As students developed themselves through deepening their self-awareness, building self- (66) confidence, establishing interpersonal efficacy, learning to apply new skills, and expanding their motivations, they changed their perceptions of groups and their role in groups. Similarly, engaging in groups and feedback from group members informed the development of themselves as individuals. This interaction between *developing self* and *group influences* shaped an individual's awareness of who they were in relation to others. Depending on their stage of leadership identity, students saw themselves as dependent on others, independent from others, or interdependent with those around them. Their *changing view of self with others* had a direct bearing on their *broadening view of leadership.* Those who viewed themselves as dependent on others saw leadership as something external to them or as a position someone else held. Those who viewed themselves as independent from others assumed positional leader roles and perceived that the leader does leadership. Those who saw their interdependence with those around them viewed leadership as a relational process and leaders as anyone in the group who was contributing to that process.

(67)   An individual's broadening view of leadership has properties that develop through the six stages of the core category, *leadership identity*. Students remained in a stage of leadership identity for varying lengths of time. Either dissonance with the stage they were in or a new view of themselves and how they related to others in groups eventually led them to a new view of leadership. This new view of leadership signaled a transition to a new stage. These transitions between stages of leadership identity marked a shift in thinking, a very gradual process of letting go of old ways of thinking and acting, and trying on new ways of being. In the new, more complex stage, students repeated the cycle that supported their transition to the next stage of leadership identity. This could be envisioned as a helix where one returns to a category such as *developing self* with a higher level of complexity.

(68)   Each student's story across the stages of developing their leadership identity was unique, yet was reflected in this grounded theory. Even those who did not evidence all six stages are represented in the theory. Donald, for example, was a sophomore in the study who saw himself as the positional leader in most groups he was in. Concurrently, he eloquently described the issues he was wrestling with as he tried to be a good team member for a major group research project in his honors class and knew that his next developmental step was to learn to trust classmates more and be an active leader as a member of the team. His story described his identity in Stage 3, *leader identified,* and he was beginning a transition toward Stage 4.

(69)   We observed that leadership identity is the cumulative confidence in one's ability to intentionally engage with others to accomplish group objectives. Further, a relational leadership identity appears to be a sense of self as one who believes that groups are comprised of interdependent members who do leadership together. This theory is further applied in a leadership identity model (LID) that integrates these categories (Komives, et al., 2005).

Summary of Results

(70)   This grounded theory demonstrated that leadership identity develops through six stages moving from awareness to integration/synthesis. The process within each stage engaged developing self with group influences, which in turn influenced the changing view of self with others from dependence to interdependence and shaped the broadening view of leadership, shifting from an external view of leadership to leadership as a process. Developmental influences facilitated this identity development.

Discussion and Implications

(71)   After developing an awareness of leadership, the students in this study described their shifting leadership identity as moving from a hierarchical, leader-centric view to one that embraced leadership as a collaborative, relational process. Participants' recognition that they function in an interdependent world was an essential part of having a *leadership differentiated* leadership identity. Students in the *generativity* and *integration/synthesis* stages recognized the systemic nature of leadership. The components of this leadership identity theory connect to the observations of many leadership scholars. Margaret Wheatley (1999) described the zeitgeist of the end of the 21st century as an "awareness that we participate in a world of exquisite interconnectedness. We are learning to see systems rather than isolated parts and players" (p. 158). Allen and Cherry (2000) stated that "new ways of leading require the ability to think systemically. One cannot make sense of relationships and connections by looking at a small part of the system" (p. 84).

(72)   This leadership identity theory affirms Wielkiewicz's (2000) operationalization of Allen, Stelzner, and Wielkiewicz's (1998) ecology of leadership model. Wielkiewicz measured two orthogonal dimensions called hierarchical thinking and systemic thinking. Both dimensions were clearly present in the leadership identity stages. Hierarchical thinking was the view of leadership held in *leader identified* and systemic thinking emerged in *leadership differentiated*. This theory extended Wielkiewicz's work by indicating that these appear to be developmental dimensions and that one experiences hierarchical thinking before one develops systemic thinking.

Some leadership scholarship (McCall, Lombardo, & Morrison, 1988) asserted the role of key (73) events and critical incidents in the development of leadership. In McCall et al.'s research, they found key events to include challenging assignments, bosses (good and bad), and hardships as the broad categories that impacted leadership growth. We found that the developmental process for these students does include key events but it is more grounded in the psychosocial dimensions of developing their interdependence, establishing healthy interpersonal relationships, and forging a confident sense of self (Baxter-Magolda, 2001; Chickering & Reisser, 1993; Kegan, 1994).

The students in this study had multiple social identities and factors in *developing self* were (74) central to developing a leadership identity. In research about the multiple identities of college students, Jones (1997) found that students' most salient identity was the one identified with a minority status. On the other hand, students did not usually speak about identities associated with a privileged status; this silence indicated a limitation in their development of the identity associated with a privileged status. This finding is consistent with the development of leadership identity; race, for example, was most salient for the students of color in the study. The leadership identity of women, men who were gay, and students of color connected to those aspects of themselves and led them to view leadership contexts differently, particularly when they anticipated attributions made about them based on those personal dimensions. In organizational settings, they were committed to including all members so that no one would feel excluded or marginalized.

The students in this study had a leadership identity that developed over time. Erikson (1968) (75) asserted that people discover, more than create, their identities, and they do it within a social context. Each person discovers and uncovers their identity through a continual process of observation and reflection. "Identity development is the process of becoming more complex in one's personal and social identities" (McEwen, 2003, p. 205). Identity is often viewed as a global sense of self but it can also refer to a particular dimension of one's identity (McEwen), such as a professional identity, an athlete identity, or as it did in this study, a leadership identity.

Limitations and Implications

This theory has direct implications in both advising individual students and in designing pro- (76) grams to develop the leadership efficacy of students in an organizational context. In this study we identified a number of meaningful factors that work together to facilitate the development of a leadership identity. Komives et al. (2005) described a model integrating the categories with the developmental stages and expanding on practice implications.

It must also be recognized that for this study we examined the identity development process (77) for students who were selected because they exhibited a relational leadership approach to others. Although relational leadership is a broad postindustrial approach, the process for identity development might be different for those who espouse other specific leadership philosophies such as servant leadership. Further, the study reflects the developmental process for students who were involved in organizations that may not be the same for those with little formal group involvement. In addition, more participants of color would have allowed for more saturation in diverse experiences. Although diverse perspectives were incorporated, a more diverse research team might have analyzed the data differently. The transferability of the study is influenced by the methodology, particularly related to the small number of participants from one campus.

The possibilities of research on a new theory such as this one are numerous. For example, more (78) research is needed on environmental interventions that facilitate the key transition from Stage 3 (independence) to the Stage 4 interdependent levels of consciousness (Kegan, 1994). The theory should be tested with students who do not hold extensive organizational involvements as did the students in this study to see if this theory is transferable to the development of their leadership identity; and if so, what the conditions are that facilitate it in non-organizational settings. Further research is needed with those for whom leader-centric approaches are not part of their cultural values in particular, to explore if they experience Stages 3 and 4 differently. As a potential life span model, more research is needed to determine how postcollege adults experience the *integration/ synthesis* stage of leadership identity and whether there are additional stages not reflected in this theory. Leadership identity development could also be explored with noncollege adults. In addition, more research is needed to see if groups or organizations function in ways parallel to the core category and what influences those organizational practices; for example, are group leadership practices dependent on the positional leader's style? Do group structures shape the approaches used?

(79)   The students in this study shared their stories of how they experienced themselves in groups engaging with others that revealed how their leadership identity developed. The theory has implications for working with individuals as they develop their leadership identity and for groups as they learn to work more effectively to enhance the leadership efficacy of group members.

References

Allen, K. E., & Cherrey, C. (2000). *Systemic leadership*. Lanham, MD: University Press of America.

Allen, K. E., Stelzner, S. P., & Wielkiewicz, R. M. (1998). The ecology of leadership: Adapting to the challenges of a changing world. *The Journal of Leadership Studies, 5*(2), 62–82.

Bass, B. M. (1990). *Bass & Stogdill's handbook of leadership* (3rd ed.). New York: Free Press.

Baxter Magolda, M. B. (2001). *Making their own way: Narratives for transforming higher education to promote self-development.* Sterling, VA: Stylus.

Bennis, W. (1989). *On becoming a leader.* Reading, MA: Addison-Wesley.

Brown, S. C., Stevens, R. A., Troiano, P. F., & Schneider, M. K. (2002). Exploring complex phenomena: Grounded theory in student affairs research. *Journal of College Student Development, 43,* 173–183.

Brungardt, C. (1996). The making of leaders: A review of the research in leadership development and education. *Journal of Leadership Studies, 3*(3), 81–95.

Bruner, J. (1987). Life as narrative. *Social Research, 54*(1), 11–32.

Burns, J. M. (1978). *Leadership.* New York: Harper & Row.

Chickering, A. W., & Reisser, L. (1993). *Education and identity* (2nd ed.). San Francisco: Jossey-Bass.

Chrislip, D. D., & Larson, C. E. (1994). *Collaborative leadership.* San Francisco: Jossey-Bass.

Covey, S. R. (1992). *Principle-centered leadership.* New York: Simon & Schuster.

Creswell, J. W. (1998). *Qualitative inquiry and research design: Choosing among five traditions.* Thousand Oaks, CA: Sage.

Erikson, E. (1968). Identity: Youth and crisis. New York: W. W. Norton.

Heifetz, R. (1994). *Leadership without easy answers.* Cambridge, MA: Belknap Press.

Higher Education Research Institute. (1996). *A social change model of leadership development, guidebook III.* Los Angeles: Author.

Jones, S. R. (1997). Voices of identity and difference: A qualitative exploration of the multiple dimensions of identity development in women college students. *Journal of College Student Development, 38,* 376–386.

Kegan, R. (1994). *In over our heads: The mental demands of modern life.* Cambridge, MA: Harvard University Press.

Komives, S. R., Lucas, N., & McMahon, T. R. (1998). *Exploring leadership: For college students who want to make a difference.* San Francisco: Jossey-Bass.

Komives, S. R., Owen, J. E., Longerbeam, S., Mainella, F. C., & Osteen, L. (2005) *Leadership identity development model.* Manuscript submitted for publication.

Kouzes, J., & Posner, B. (2003). *The leadership challenge* (3rd ed.). San Francisco: Jossey-Bass.

Matusak, L. R. (1997). *Finding your voice: Learning to lead anywhere you want to make a difference.* San Francisco: Jossey-Bass.

McCall, M. W., Lombardo, M. M., & Morrison, A. M. (1988). *Lessons of experience.* New York: Free Press.

McEwen, M. K. (2003). New perspectives on identity development. In S. R. Komives & D. B. Woodard, Jr. (Eds.), *Student services: A handbook for the profession* (4th ed., pp. 203–233). San Francisco: Jossey Bass.

Merriam, S. B., & Associates (2002). *Qualitative research in practice.* San Francisco: Jossey-Bass.

Northouse, P. G. (2003). *Leadership: Theory and practice* (3rd ed.). Thousand Oaks, CA: Sage.

Patton, M. Q. (2002). *Qualitative evaluation and research methods* (3rd ed.). Newbury Park, CA: Sage.

Riessman, C. K. (1993). *Narrative analysis.* Newbury Park, CA: Sage.

Rost, J. (1993). *Leadership for the 21st century.* Westport, CT: Praeger.

Seidman, I. E. (1991). *Interviewing as qualitative research: A guide for researchers in education and the social sciences.* New York: Teachers College, Columbia University.

Strauss, A., & Corbin, J. (1998). *Basics of qualitative research* (2nd ed.). Newbury Park, CA: Sage.

Velsor, E. V., & Drath, W. H. (2004). A lifelong developmental perspective on leader development. In C. D. McCauley & E. V. Velsor (Eds.), *The Center for Creative Leadership handbook of leadership development* (pp. 383–414). San Francisco: Jossey-Bass.

Wheatley, M. J. (1999). *Leadership and the new science.* San Francisco: Berrett-Koehler.

Wielkiewicz, R. M. (2000). The Leadership Attitudes and Beliefs Scale: An instrument for evaluating college students' thinking about leadership and organizations. *Journal of College Student Development, 41,* 335–347.

Zimmerman-Oster, K., & Burkhardt, J. C. (1999). *Leadership in the making.* Battle Creek, MI: W. K. Kellogg Foundation.

14

Ethnographic Designs

*T*he term ethnography *literally means "writing about groups of people." Using this qualitative design, you can identify a group of people; study them in their homes or workplaces; note how they behave, think, and talk; and develop a general portrait of the group. This chapter defines ethnographic research, identifies when you use it, assesses the key characteristics of it, reviews key ethical issues, and advances the steps in conducting and evaluating this design.*

By the end of this chapter, you should be able to:

◆ Define ethnographic research, and describe when to use it, and how it developed.
◆ Identify three types of ethnographic designs.
◆ List the key characteristics of ethnographic research.
◆ Identify potential ethical issues in conducting an ethnography.
◆ Describe the steps in conducting an ethnography.
◆ List criteria useful for evaluating an ethnographic research study.

Maria chooses to conduct a qualitative ethnography study for her graduate research project. Her school committee has been meeting throughout the year, and it has set ways in which it operates. As a member of this committee, Maria has a natural vantage point for observing how the committee works. She observes how people act, how they speak, and how they engage in practices such as starting promptly on time. Maria conducts an ethnography. She asks this question: "What are the shared beliefs, values, and attitudes of the school committee on weapon possession in the school?" By answering this question, Maria will gain a deep understanding about how a school committee wrestles with the problem of weapons in the schools.

WHAT IS ETHNOGRAPHIC RESEARCH, WHEN SHOULD YOU USE IT, AND HOW DID IT DEVELOP?

Ethnographic designs are qualitative research procedures for describing, analyzing, and interpreting a culture-sharing group's shared patterns of behavior, beliefs, and language that develop over time. Central to this definition is culture. A **culture** is "everything having to do with human behavior and belief" (LeCompte, Preissle, & Tesch, 1993, p. 5). It can include language, rituals, economic and political structures, life stages, interactions, and communication styles. To understand the patterns of a culture-sharing group, the ethnographer typically spends considerable time "in the field" interviewing, observing, and gathering documents about the group to understand their culture-sharing behaviors, beliefs, and language.

When Do You Conduct an Ethnography?

You conduct an ethnography when the study of a group provides understanding of a larger issue. You also conduct an ethnography when you have a culture-sharing group to study—one that has been together for some time and has developed shared values, beliefs, and language. You capture the "rules" of behavior, such as the informal relationships among teachers who congregate at favorite places to socialize (Pajak & Blasé, 1984). The culture-sharing group may be narrowly framed (e.g., teachers, students, or staff members) or broadly framed (e.g., entire schools and their success, innovation, or violence). The culture-sharing group may be a family, as in the ethnographic study of a 12-year-old child with Down syndrome and his family (Harry et al., 1998). The culture-sharing group may be representative or illustrative of some larger processes, events, or activities (e.g., participating in a graduate program). Fraternity settings are sites where men often exploit and victimize women. In a critical ethnography, Rhoads (1995) studied the culture of one fraternity and its practices that rendered women powerless and marginalized.

Ethnography can provide a detailed day-to-day picture of events, such as the thoughts and activities of a search committee hiring a new principal (Wolcott, 1974, 1994). You conduct an ethnography when you have long-term access to a culture-sharing group so that you can build a detailed record of their behaviors and beliefs over time. You may be a participant in the group or simply an observer, but you gather extensive fieldnotes, interview many people, and collect letters and documents to establish the record of the culture-sharing group.

How Did Ethnographic Research Develop?

Ethnography as practiced in education has been shaped by cultural anthropology, by an emphasis on the issues of writing about culture, and by how ethnographic reports need to be read and understood today. These factors lie at the heart of understanding current practices in ethnography (e.g., Bogdan & Biklen, 1998; Denzin, 1997; LeCompte et al., 1993; Wolcott, 2008).

The roots of educational ethnography lie in cultural anthropology. In the late 19th and early 20th centuries, anthropologists explored "primitive" cultures by visiting other countries and becoming immersed in their societies for extensive periods of time. They refrained from "going native" and identifying too closely with the people they were studying so that they could write an "objective" account of what they saw and heard. At times, these accounts compared distant cultures on other continents with the American way of life. For example, Margaret Mead, a well-known anthropologist, studied child rearing, adolescence, and the influence of culture on personality in Samoa (Mead, 1928).

Observations and interviews became standard procedures for collecting data "in the field." Also, under sociologists at the University of Chicago in the 1920s through the 1950s, research focused on the importance of studying a single case—whether that case was an individual, a group, a neighborhood, or a larger cultural unit. For example, Chicago sociologists conducted qualitative analyses of personal and public documents to construct a view of the life of Polish immigrants (Thomas & Znaniecki, 1927). With an emphasis on city life, they depicted ordinary life in U.S. cities: the Jewish ghetto, the taxi-dance hall, the professional thief, the hobo, and the delinquent (Bogdan & Biklen, 1998). In highlighting the lives of these individuals, they provided "insider" perspectives by reporting detailed accounts of individuals who are often marginalized in our society.

The infant interdisciplinary area of educational anthropology began to crystallize during the 1950s and continued to develop through the 1980s (LeCompte et al., 1993). Jules Henry depicted elementary school classrooms and high schools as tribes with rituals, culture, and social structure, and George and Louise Spindler examined educational decision making, curriculum content, and teaching (LeCompte et al., 1993). Educational anthropologists focused on subculture groups such as:

◆ Career and life histories or role analyses of individuals
◆ Microethnographies of small work and leisure groups within classrooms or schools
◆ Studies of single classrooms abstracted as small societies
◆ Studies of school facilities or school districts that approach these units as discrete communities (LeCompte et al., 1993, p. 14)

In studies such as these, educational ethnographers developed and refined procedures borrowed from anthropology and sociology. From the 1980s to the present, anthropologists and educational anthropologists have identified techniques for focusing on a cultural group, conducting observations, analyzing data, and writing up the research (e.g., Fetterman, 2010; Wolcott, 1992, 1994, 2008).

A watershed event in ethnography, according to Denzin (1997), was the publication of the book *Writing Culture* (Clifford & Marcus, 1986). Ethnographers have been "writing their way out" (Denzin, 1997, p. xvii) of this book ever since. Clifford and Marcus raised two issues that have commanded much attention in ethnography in general and within educational research. The first is the crisis of representation. This crisis consists of a reassessment of how ethnographers interpret the groups they are studying. Denzin argued that we can no longer view the researcher as an objective reporter who makes omniscient pronouncements about the individuals being studied. Instead, the researcher is only one voice among many—individuals such as the reader, the participants, and the gatekeepers—who need to be heard. This has led to a second crisis: legitimacy. No longer do "canons" of validity, reliability, and objectivity of "normal science" represent the standards. Researchers need to evaluate each ethnographic study in terms of flexible standards embedded within the participants' lives; historical and cultural influences; and the interactive forces of race, gender, and class.

Viewed this way, ethnographies need to include perspectives drawn from feminist thought, racial views, sexual orientation, and critical theory, and they need to be sensitive to race, class, and gender. Ethnographies today are now "messy" and find presentation in many forms, such as a performance, poem, play, novel, or a personal narrative (Denzin, 1997).

WHAT ARE THE TYPES OF ETHNOGRAPHIC DESIGNS?

With this development, eclecticism pervades educational ethnographies today. Table 14.1 illustrates the various types of ethnographies. For a researcher new to ethnography, the long list is less important than a focus on primary forms published in educational reports. Unquestionably, ethnographic research does not always fit cleanly into categories, but three forms are apparent:

◆ The realist ethnography
◆ The case study
◆ The critical ethnography

Realist Ethnographies

A realist ethnography is a popular approach used by cultural anthropologists. Characterized by Van Maanen (1988), it reflects a particular stance taken by the researcher toward the individuals being studied. A **realist ethnography** is an objective account of the situation, typically written in the third-person point of view, reporting objectively on the information learned from participants at a field site. In this ethnographic design:

◆ The realist ethnographer narrates the study in a third-person dispassionate voice and reports on observations of participants and their views. The ethnographer does not offer personal reflections in the research report and remains in the background as an omniscient reporter of the "facts."
◆ The researcher reports objective data in a measured style uncontaminated by personal bias, political goals, and judgment. The researcher may provide mundane details of everyday life among the people studied. The ethnographer also uses standard categories for cultural description (e.g., family life, work life, social networks, and status systems).
◆ The ethnographer produces the participants' views through closely edited quotations and has the final word on the interpretation and presentation of the culture (Van Maanen, 1988).

This type of ethnography has a long tradition in cultural anthropology and education. For example, Wolcott (1974, 1994) used a realist approach to ethnography to study the

---

TABLE 14.1

Types of Ethnographies

• Realist ethnography—an objective, scientifically written ethnography	• Critical ethnography—a study of the shared patterns of a marginalized group with the aim of advocacy about issues of power and authority
• Confessional ethnography—a report of the ethnographer's fieldwork experiences	• Feminist ethnography—a study of women and the cultural practices that serve to disempower and oppress them
• Life history—a study of one individual situated within the cultural context of his or her life	
• Autoethnography—a reflective self-examination by an individual set within his or her cultural context	• Postmodern ethnography—an ethnography written to challenge the problems in our society that have emerged from a modern emphasis on progress and marginalizing individuals
• Microethnography—a study focused on a specific aspect of a cultural group and setting	
• Ethnographic case study—a case analysis of a person, event, activity, or process set within a cultural perspective	• Ethnographic novels—a fictional work focused on cultural aspects of a group

Sources: Denzin, 1997; LeCompte et al., 1993; Van Maanan, 1988; Madison, 2005.

activities of a committee appointed to select a principal. This study addressed the process a school selection committee experienced as they interviewed candidates. Wolcott started with Candidate Number 7, and discussed the committee's deliberation for each candidate (except one) until the final individual was identified. Following this description of the interviewing process, Wolcott interpreted the committee's actions in terms of a lack of professional knowledge, their "variety reducing" behavior, and the reluctance of schools to change.

As a realist ethnographer, Wolcott provided an account of committee deliberations as if he were looking in from the outside, reporting the procedures objectively, and including participants' views. The interpretation at the end presented Wolcott's view of the patterns he saw in the selection committee cultural group.

Case Studies

Writers often use the term *case study* in conjunction with ethnography (see LeCompte & Schensul, 1999). A case study is an important type of ethnography, although it differs from an ethnography in several important ways. Case study researchers may focus on a program, event, or activity involving individuals rather than a group per se (Stake, 1995). Also, when case study writers research a group, they may be more interested in describing the activities of the group instead of identifying shared patterns of behavior exhibited by the group. The ethnographer searches for the shared patterns that develop as a group interacts over time. Finally, case study researchers are less likely to identify a cultural theme to examine at the beginning of a study, especially one from anthropology; instead, they focus on an in-depth exploration of the actual "case" (Yin, 2008).

Although some researchers identify "case" as an object of study (Stake, 1995), others consider it to be a procedure of inquiry (e.g., Merriam, 1998). A **case study** is an in-depth exploration of a bounded system (e.g., activity, event, process, or individuals) based on extensive data collection (Creswell, 2007). *Bounded* means that the case is separated out for research in terms of time, place, or some physical boundaries.

It is useful to consider the types of cases that qualitative researchers often study:

◆ The "case" may be a single individual, several individuals separately or in a group, a program, events, or activities (e.g., a teacher, several teachers, or the implementation of a new math program).

◆ The "case" may represent a process consisting of a series of steps (e.g., a college curriculum process) that form a sequence of activities.

◆ As shown in Figure 14.1, a "case" may be selected for study because it is unusual and has merit in and of itself. When the case itself is of interest, it is called an **intrinsic case**. The study of a bilingual school illustrates this form of a case study (Stake, 2000). Alternatively, the focus of a qualitative study may be a specific issue, with a case (or cases) used to illustrate the issue. This type of case is called an **instrumental case**, because it serves the purpose of illuminating a particular issue. For example, the issue of language learning might be studied in a case study of a bilingual school. Case studies may also include multiple cases, called a **collective case study** (Stake, 1995), in which multiple cases are described and compared to provide insight into an issue. A case study researcher might examine several schools to illustrate alternative approaches to school choice for students.

◆ The researcher seeks to develop an in-depth understanding of the case by collecting multiple forms of data (e.g., pictures, scrapbooks, videotapes, and e-mails). Providing this in-depth understanding requires that only a few cases be studied, because for each case examined, the researcher has less time to devote to exploring the depths of any one case.

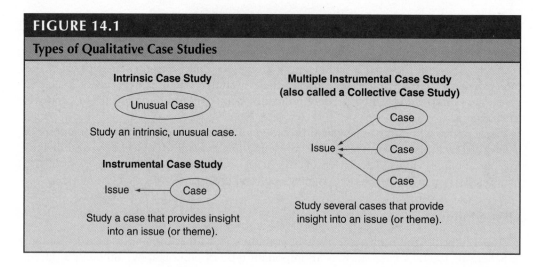

FIGURE 14.1

Types of Qualitative Case Studies

The researcher also locates the "case" or "cases" within their larger context, such as geographical, political, social, or economic settings (e.g., the family constellation consisting of grandparents, siblings, and "adopted" family members).

An example of a case study is the research by Kos (1991) of four middle school students who have reading disabilities. The study examined what factors contributed to the development of reading disabilities in adolescents. The author tutored the four students, observed their reading alone and reading in class, conducted interviews, and gathered school records on each student. All four students, who were between the ages of 13 and 15, were unable to read materials above the third-grade level. After describing each student, the author identified four themes that emerged about each student: reading behavior, negative and frustrating experiences with instruction, anxiety about reading, and histories of reading in kindergarten and first grade. From these individual case analyses, the author then compared the four individuals and found the students to be aware of their deficiencies, to display a connection between reading disability and stress, and to be unable to integrate various reading strategies.

This case study illustrates a study of four bounded systems—specific individuals—and an assessment of patterns of behavior for each individual and for all four students. The researcher focused on the issue of reading disabilities and conducted an in-depth examination of four cases to illustrate this issue. Multiple forms of data were collected, and the analysis consisted of both description and thematic development.

Another example is the case study by Padula and Miller (1999) of four women who had reentered the university as full-time doctoral students. In this case study, the authors questioned the students' decision to return to school, how they described their reentry experiences, and how the graduate experience changed their lives. Through interviewing and observing these women, the researchers found several themes about beliefs that these women held. For example, the women believed that their graduate experiences did not meet their needs, they compared themselves with younger students, and they felt a general need to finish their programs as quickly as possible.

Critical Ethnographies

When Denzin (1997) spoke of the twin crises of representation and legitimation, he was responding to profound changes in our society, such as becoming more multinational, joining a world economy, and changing demographics to include more racial groups. These factors have created a system of power, prestige, privilege, and authority that serves to marginalize individuals of different classes, races, and gender in our society. With roots in German thinking of the 1920s, the historical problems of domination, alienation, and social struggle are now playing out within educational and social science research.

Ethnography now incorporates a "critical" approach (Carspecken, 1995; Carspecken & Apple, 1992; Madison, 2005; Thomas, 1993) to include an advocacy perspective to ethnography. **Critical ethnographies** are a type of ethnographic research in which the author is interested in advocating for the emancipation of groups marginalized in our society (Thomas, 1993). Critical researchers are typically politically minded individuals who seek, through their research, to advocate against inequality and domination (Carspecken & Apple, 1992). For example, critical ethnographers might study schools that provide privileges to certain types of students, create inequitable situations among members of different social classes, and perpetuate boys "speaking up" and girls being silent participants in class.

The major components of a critical ethnography are factors such as a value-laden orientation, empowering people by giving them more authority, challenging the status quo, and a concern about power and control (Madison, 2005). These factors play out in an ethnography in specific procedural characteristics, listed below:

◆ The critical ethnographer studies social issues of power, empowerment, inequality, inequity, dominance, repression, hegemony, and victimization.

◆ Researchers conduct critical ethnographies so that their studies do not further marginalize the individuals being studied. Thus, the inquirers collaborate, actively participate, negotiate the final written report, use care in entering and leaving a site, and reciprocate by giving back to study participants.

◆ The critical ethnographer is self-conscious about his or her interpretation, recognizing that interpretations reflect our own history and culture. Interpretations can be only tentative and are concerned how participants will view them.

◆ Critical researchers position themselves in the text to be reflexive and self-aware of their role, and to be up front in the written research report. This means identifying biases and values; acknowledging views; and distinguishing among textual representations by the author, the participants, and the reader. No longer is the ethnographer an "objective" observer, as in the realist approach.

◆ This nonneutral position for the critical researcher also means that he or she will be an advocate for change to help transform our society so that people are less oppressed and marginalized.

◆ In the end, the critical ethnographic report will be a "messy, multilevel, multi-method" approach to inquiry, full of contradictions, imponderables, and tensions (Denzin, 1997).

The critical ethnographic study of one principal in an "inclusive" elementary school (Keyes, Hanley-Maxwell, & Capper, 1999) illustrated many of these features. The overall purpose was to describe and define the role of administrative leadership in an inclusive school for students with a high incidence of disability classifications (e.g., cognitive, emotional, learning, speech, and language). With the objective of generating a new theory that would empower individuals in the school, the authors began with a framework for empowering leadership: support, facilitation, and possibility.

Based on extensive fieldwork consisting of shadowing the principal (Marta), observing classrooms, conducting individual and focus group interviews, and reviewing weekly announcements, the researchers compiled a picture of Marta's leadership that included a personal belief system of spirituality. Marta's spirituality led him to value personal struggle, espouse the dignity of individuals, merge the professional and the personal, believe that people were doing their best, and emphasize the importance of listening and of dreams. In the end, Keyes et al. (1999) provided a "vision for equity nourished by spiritual beliefs" (p. 233) and posed the concluding questions "School reform for what?" and "Empowering leadership for whom?" (p. 234).

In this ethnography of a school that embraced a critical perspective, the project focused on the issue of empowerment felt by marginalized students and teachers in the school. The principal sought active collaborative participation through a shared dialogue with teachers and students. The researchers advocated for a change and highlighted the tensions that opened up new questions rather than closing down the conversation. Although the authors' views were not made explicit in the text, their interest in change and a new vision for leadership in schools for individuals with disabilities were clear.

WHAT ARE THE KEY CHARACTERISTICS OF ETHNOGRAPHIC RESEARCH?

With the diverse approaches to ethnography identified in the realist, case study, and critical approaches, it is not easy to identify characteristics they have in common. However, for those learning about ethnographies, the following characteristics typically illustrate an ethnographic study:

- ◆ Cultural themes
- ◆ A culture-sharing group
- ◆ Shared patterns of behavior, belief, and language
- ◆ Fieldwork
- ◆ Description, themes, and interpretation
- ◆ Context or setting
- ◆ Researcher reflexivity

Cultural Themes

Ethnographers typically study cultural themes drawn from cultural anthropology. Ethnographers do not venture into the field looking haphazardly for anything they might see. Instead, they are interested in adding to the knowledge about culture and studying specific cultural themes. A **cultural theme** in ethnography is a general position, declared or implied, that is openly approved or promoted in a society or group (see Spradley [1980] for a discussion about cultural themes). As with all qualitative studies, this theme does not serve to narrow the study; instead, it becomes a broad lens that researchers use when they initially enter a field to study a group, and they look for manifestations of it.

What are these cultural themes? They can be found in introductory texts in cultural anthropology. Wolcott (2008) mentioned introductory texts that discuss themes in cultural anthropology, such as those by Kessing (1958), Haviland (1993), or Howard (1996). They can also be found in dictionaries of concepts in cultural anthropology, such as Winthrop's (1991). Another approach is to locate the cultural theme in ethnographic studies in education. Authors announce them in titles or at the beginning of the study. You can see them in purpose statements in ethnographies or in research questions as a "central phenomenon." For example, here are several cultural themes explored by authors:

- ◆ *Persistence* in distance education courses (Garland, 1993)
- ◆ The "coming out" stages of gay *identity development* (Rhoads, 1997)

◆ Development of students' *social skills* in Japan (LeTendre, 1999)
◆ *Enculturation* in an early childhood program among the Maori in New Zealand (Bauermeister, 1998)

A Culture-Sharing Group

Ethnographers learn from studying a culture-sharing group at a single site. Less frequently authors examine single individuals, as in Wolcott's (1974, 1994) single case study of a principal. In the study of a group, ethnographers identify a single site (e.g., an elementary classroom), locate a group within it (e.g., a reading group), and gather data about the group (e.g., observe a reading period). This distinguishes ethnography from other forms of qualitative research (e.g., narrative research) that focus on individuals rather than groups of people. A **culture-sharing group** in ethnography is two or more individuals who have shared behaviors, beliefs, and language. For example, groups were studied in these ethnographies:

◆ 47 students in a distance education course in resource management and environmental subjects (Garland, 1993)
◆ 16 elementary education student teachers (Goodman & Adler, 1985)
◆ 40 college students in an organization who had identified themselves as either gay or bisexual (Rhoads, 1997)

Groups such as these typically possess certain characteristics, which are listed in Table 14.2. A group may vary in size, but the individuals in the group need to meet on a regular basis and interact over a period of time (e.g., more than 2 weeks up to 4 months) to develop shared patterns of behaving, thinking, or talking. The group is often representative of a larger group, such as a reading group within a third-grade classroom.

Often, ethnographers study groups unfamiliar to them to be able to look at them in a "fresh and different way, as if they were exceptional and unique" (LeCompte et al., 1993, p. 3). Individuals sometimes mistake a cultural group with an ethnic group. Ethnic groups are self-identified individuals in a sociopolitical grouping that have a recognized public identity, such as Hispanics, Asian Pacific Islanders, and Arab Americans

---

TABLE 14.2

The Study of a Culture-Sharing Group in a Third-Grade Elementary Classroom

Characteristics of a Culture-Sharing Group	An Example
The group consists of two or more individuals, and it may be small or large.	A small group—two readers in a classroom. A larger group—six to ten readers in a classroom.
The group interacts on a regular basis.	For a period three times a week, the group meets to discuss a reading.
The group has interacted for some time.	Since the beginning of September, the reading group has met three times a week for three periods.
The group is representative of some larger group.	The small reading group is representative of third-grade readers.
The group has adopted some shared patterns of behaving, thinking, or talking.	The group has certain rituals they perform as they begin to read, such as sitting on the floor, opening their book to the assigned page, and waiting to speak until the teacher calls on them to answer a question.

(LeCompte & Schensul, 1999). Using these ethnic labels can cause problems in an ethnography because the labels may not be terms used by the individuals themselves.

Shared Patterns of Behavior, Belief, and Language

Ethnographic researchers look for shared patterns of behavior, beliefs, and language that the culture-sharing group adopts over time. This characteristic has several elements to it. First, the culture-sharing group needs to have adopted shared patterns that the ethnographer can discern. A **shared pattern** in ethnography is a common social interaction that stabilizes as tacit rules and expectations of the group (Spindler & Spindler, 1992). Second, the group shares any one or a combination of behaviors, beliefs, and language.

◆ A **behavior** in an ethnography is an action taken by an individual in a cultural setting. For example, Wolcott (1974, 1994) studied how a principal's selection committee acted as they deliberated about selecting a candidate.

◆ A **belief** in an ethnography is how an individual thinks about or perceives things in a cultural setting. For example, Padula and Miller (1999) found that women doctoral students in psychology shared the concern that they were not able to invest much energy in their families.

◆ **Language** in an ethnography is how an individual talks to others in a cultural setting. In a study of life-history narratives of two African American women, Nelson (1990) analyzed code-switching (changing from Standard English to Black English vernacular). Sara, for example, used the repetitive, parallel clause structure found in Black church tradition when she said, "It is pain, suffering, determination, perseverance" (p. 147).

These shared patterns raise several practical questions that ethnographers need to address in a study. How long does the group need to stay together to "share"? To answer this question, a specific study would have to be examined. Unquestionably, the longer the group is together, the more the individuals will adopt shared behaviors and ways of thinking and the easier it will be for an ethnographer to discern patterns. However, assessment techniques are available for gathering data quickly from a group that may be shared for a short period of time (LeCompte & Schensul, 1999). Fraternity members may form shared beliefs with new pledges quickly or school boards may develop common understandings through "board retreats" that allow an ethnographer to quickly assess patterns.

Another issue is whether the patterns are ideal (what *should* occur), actual (what *did* occur), or projective (what *might have* occurred). As an ethnographer observes or interviews, examples of all three patterns may emerge from the data. An ethnographer visiting a third-grade classroom might observe the reading group to see what did occur, interview the teacher to identify what might have occurred, and consult with the curriculum coordinator as to what the school district hoped should have occurred.

Fieldwork

Ethnographers collect data through spending time at participants' sites where they live, work, or play. To understand best the patterns of a cultural group, an ethnographer spends considerable time with the group. The patterns cannot be easily discerned through questionnaires or brief encounters. Instead, the ethnographer goes "to the field," lives with or frequently visits the people being studied, and slowly learns the cultural ways in which the group behaves or thinks. **Fieldwork** in ethnography means that the researcher gathers data in the setting where the participants are located and where their shared patterns can be studied. This data collection involves the following:

◆ **Emic data** is information supplied by participants in a study. *Emic* often refers to first-order concepts, such as local language and ways of expression used by members in a cultural-sharing group (Schwandt, 2007). In an ethnographic study of a soup kitchen for the homeless, Miller et al. (1998) interviewed and recorded "stories" supplied by Michael, Dan, Sarah, and Robert and used quotes from these individuals to construct their perspectives.

◆ **Etic data** is information representing the ethnographer's interpretation of the participants' perspectives. *Etic* typically refers to second-order concepts, such as the language used by the social scientist or educator to refer to the same phenomena mentioned by the participants (Schwandt, 2007). In the soup kitchen study (Miller et al., 1998), the authors formed themes as their interpretation of participants' data that represented how the soup kitchen worked.

◆ **Negotiation data** consist of information that the participant and the researcher agree to use in a study. Negotiation occurs at different stages in research, such as agreeing to entry procedures for a research site, mutually respecting individuals at the site, and developing a plan for giving back or reciprocating with the individuals. Again in the soup kitchen study (Miller et al., 1998), the authors sought out a gatekeeper to gain entry, helped advocate for the homeless with funding agencies, and participated in serving lunches on a regular basis.

During fieldwork, the ethnographer uses a variety of research techniques to gather data. Table 14.3, which is a composite list from LeCompte and Schensul (1999) and Wolcott (2008), displays mainly qualitative and a few quantitative forms of data collection. Of these possibilities, observation and unstructured interviewing are popular among ethnographers. To see the range of data collection that ethnographers gather in a single study, examine the following forms used by Rhoads (1995) in his ethnographic study of fraternity life:

◆ 12 formal, structured interviews that lasted from 1 to 2 hours
◆ 18 less formal interviews recorded in handwritten notes
◆ Participation in both open fraternity parties and private rituals that were open to only a few outsiders
◆ Ongoing discussions with several key participants who explained the significance of various fraternity practices

TABLE 14.3

Popular Forms of Data Collected by Ethnographers

• Casual conversation	• Tests
• Life history, life-cycle interview	• Content analysis of secondary text or visual material
• Key informant (participant) interview	• Focus group interview
• Semi-structured interview	• Elicitation techniques (e.g., looking at a scrapbook and talking about memories)
• Structured interview	
• Survey	• Audiovisual material (e.g., audio or visual record, such as camera recording)
• Household census, ethnogenealogy	• Spatial mapping (e.g., recording ways data vary across units, such as group and institution)
• Questionnaire (written and/or oral)	
• Projective techniques	• Network analysis (e.g., describing networks in time and space)
• Observations (nonparticipant to participant)	

Sources: Le Compte & Schensul, 1999; Wolcott, 2008.

◆ A review of numerous documents, including the university Greek handbook, minutes from chapter meetings, class papers, and the fraternity liability policy

Description, Themes, and Interpretation

Ethnographic researchers describe and analyze the culture-sharing group and make an interpretation about the patterns seen and heard. During data collection, the ethnographer begins to forge a study. This consists of analyzing the data for a description of both the individuals and sites of the culture-sharing group; analyzing patterns of behavior, beliefs, and language; and reaching some conclusions about the meaning learned from studying the people and the site (Wolcott, 1994).

A **description in ethnography** is a detailed rendering of individuals and scenes to depict what is going on in the culture-sharing group. This description needs to be detailed and thick, and it needs to identify specifics. It serves to place the reader figuratively in the setting, to transport the reader to the actual scene, to make it real. This involves awakening the reader's senses through adjectives, nouns, and verbs that elicit sounds, sights, feelings, and smells. To do this, the researcher must single out some detail to include while excluding others. It means describing events, activities, and places without veering too far from the actual scene of attention and the people whose shared patterns need to be discerned. Passages from ethnographies that "describe" are long and detailed. Sometimes, ethnographers or case study writers provide a description from a general picture to the specific setting in which an event or events take place. For example, examine Figure 14.2, which maps the descriptive passage in the study of a gunman on a university campus (Asmussen & Creswell, 1995). The researchers began with describing the town, then narrowing the description to the campus, and finally focusing on the classroom in which the incident occurred.

In another example, Wolcott (1994) described a candidate for a principal's position who ended up "Mr. Fifth" in the competition:

Committee members were cordial in their greetings and introductions when Mr. Fifth appeared for his interview. He was directed to choose one of the (few)

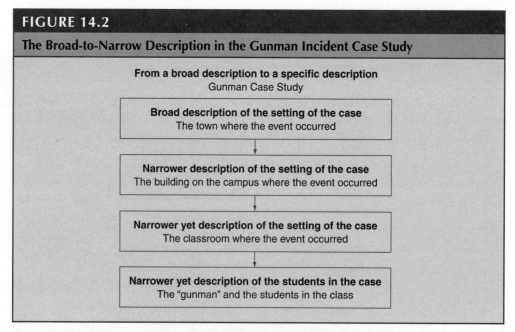

FIGURE 14.2

The Broad-to-Narrow Description in the Gunman Incident Case Study

From a broad description to a specific description
Gunman Case Study

Broad description of the setting of the case
The town where the event occurred

Narrower description of the setting of the case
The building on the campus where the event occurred

Narrower yet description of the setting of the case
The classroom where the event occurred

Narrower yet description of the students in the case
The "gunman" and the students in the class

Source: Adapted from Asmussen & Creswell, 1995.

comfortable chairs in the meeting room, prompting the personnel director to joke, "It won't be this comfortable again." After a folksy prelude, the director of elementary education asked, "What things have you been doing and how have you been involved?" (p. 129)

In this short descriptive passage, Wolcott conveys the feelings of propriety and anxiety, shares the appearance of the room, relates the language of the committee, and provides a sense of the feelings of the committee toward candidates.

The distinction between description and theme analysis is not always clear. Theme analysis moves away from reporting the "facts" to making an interpretation of people and activities. As part of making sense of the information, **thematic data analysis in ethnography** consists of distilling how things work and naming the essential features in themes in the cultural setting. Consistent with the process about describing and developing themes from data, the ethnographer segments the text (or images), codes them, and formulates a small set of nonoverlapping themes. In an ethnography, however, these themes map the shared patterns of behavior, thinking, or talking. The difficulty is in reducing the themes down to a small set and providing adequate evidence for each. The themes are evident in the ethnographies described here:

◆ In an ethnographic study of conflict resolution between "typically developing" children and children with disabilities in an integrated preschool, Malloy and McMurray (1996) found several conflicts related to goals, oppositions, strategies, outcomes, and the teacher's role.

◆ A case study examined student teachers' perspectives toward social studies in elementary-level schools (Goodman & Adler, 1985). Student teachers viewed social studies as a nonsubject, human relations, citizenship indoctrination, school knowledge, an integrative core of the elementary curriculum, and education for social action.

After description and analysis comes interpretation. In **interpretation in ethnography**, the ethnographer draws inferences and forms conclusions about what was learned. This phase of analysis is the most subjective. The researcher relates both the description and the themes back to a larger portrait of what was learned, which often reflects some combination of the researcher making a personal assessment, returning to the literature on the cultural theme, and raising further questions based on the data. It might also include addressing problems that arose during the fieldwork that render the account tentative and hypothetical, at best. In the ethnography of Raul, the 12-year-old child with disabilities, and his brothers, family, and friends (Harry et al., 1998), interpretation consisted of the authors' reflecting on the differences between exclusion in a nonfamily setting and unconditional acceptance in a family.

Context or Setting

Ethnographers present the description, themes, and interpretation within the context or setting of the culture-sharing group. The **context** for an ethnography is the setting, situation, or environment that surrounds the cultural group being studied. It is multilayered and interrelated, consisting of such factors as history, religion, politics, economy, and the environment (Fetterman, 2010). This context may be a physical location such as a description of the school, the state of the building, the color of the classroom walls, or the sounds coming down the hall. It may also be the historical context of individuals in the group, whether they have experienced suppression or domination, or are an emerging people who have arrived excited about their new land. It may be the social condition of the individuals, their longtime reunions to build kinship, their status as a profession, or their earnings and geographic mobility. The economic conditions may also include income levels, working-class or blue-collar background, or the systems of finance that keep the individuals below the poverty level.

Researcher Reflexivity

Ethnographic researchers make interpretations and write their report reflexively. **Reflexivity in ethnography** refers to the researcher being aware of and openly discussing his or her role in the study in a way that honors and respects the site and participants. Because ethnographic research involves a prolonged stay at a site, researchers are concerned about their impact on the site and the people. They negotiate entry with key individuals and plan to leave the site as undisturbed as they found it. As individuals who have a history and a cultural background themselves, they realize that their interpretation is only one possibility, and that their report does not have any privileged authority over other interpretations made by readers, participants, and other researchers. It is important, therefore, for ethnographers to position themselves within their report and identify their standpoint or point of view (Denzin, 1997). They do this by talking about themselves, sharing their experiences, and mentioning how their interpretations shape their discussions about the sites and culture-sharing groups. One researcher, who studied identity development of adolescent females through reading teen magazines (Finders, 1996), documented her role as follows:

> I did not want to be viewed as a teacher or someone in authority. (p. 73)

> I gained their trust slowly and negotiated a relationship that did not fit their established patterns with significant adults. (p. 73)

> On several occasions, a girl would not allow me to see a note that she deemed "too obscene." I did not report such incidents as writing on a restroom wall or faking illness to avoid an exam. (p. 74)

Being reflexive also means that authors' conclusions are often tentative or inconclusive, leading to new questions to answer. The study might end with questions that beg for answers or multiple perspectives or viewpoints for the reader to consider.

ETHICAL ISSUES IN CONDUCTING ETHNOGRAPHIC RESEARCH

Ethical issues in ethnography come up primarily when doing fieldwork because it is there that issues arise in collecting data. As Madison (2005) reminds us, "An ethics of ethnography probes the question, "What are the moral and ethical implications of conducting fieldwork?" (p. 81). These challenges of fieldwork involve negotiating how to get access to the people and sites being studied, how long to stay in the field, whether to tape natural talk or talk that we collect through interviews, and how to interact with participants respectfully (Ryen, 2009). Madison (2005) devotes considerable attention to ethics in ethnography and summarizes several areas of concern. Ethnographers should be open and transparent about gathering data. This means that they need to convey to all individuals involved in a study the purpose of the study, the general impact it will likely have, and the sources of support and funding for the project. Ethnographers also need to study people and places with a respect toward causing them no harm, preserving their dignity, and ensuring privacy. Researchers and participants need to negotiate limits related to these factors. Ethnographers also have a responsibility to the scholarly community. This responsibility entails not deceiving or misrepresenting participants or readers (e.g., fabricate evidence, falsify, plagiarize) or failing to report misconduct. Work in an ethnographic setting should be conducted respectfully so that other researchers might not be barred from entering the site in the future. Ethnographers need to "give back" and provide remuneration to those being studied. This means casting remuneration in terms of what is fair and what the community being studied might require. Another way to compensate is to provide material assistance (e.g., advocating for a group to a funding agency) in a way that reciprocates based on the needs of the participants. Finally, ethnographers need to be aware of the potential negative influence their presentations and publications may have on the population they study.

This last point is illustrated in a specific example in Box 14.1.

BOX 14.1 | Ethical Dilemma

Can We Speak for the Homeless?

We spent six months working in a soup kitchen for the homeless in our city and writing up our ethnographic account (Miller, Creswell, & Olander, 1998). In our write-up of the results, we told the detailed stories of individuals who had come through the soup line. They described their lives and their living conditions and what brought them to the soup kitchen each day for a free meal. Some of these individuals were high on drugs, some were mentally unstable and largely incoherent, and some were clear and articulate. The stories in our final report reproduced their thoughts largely in the language and tone in which we heard them. Later we presented these stories and read some of them to an international conference group of social justice researchers. Many comments from the audience indicated that they felt that we were being unethical in reporting this research. Did we have permission to use the stories? Did we stereotype the individuals by reporting their exact words? Did we, in effect, have a negative influence on the very population we sought to study? How would you have responded to these ethical questions related to the reporting of our research?

WHAT ARE THE STEPS IN CONDUCTING AN ETHNOGRAPHY?

There are probably as many procedures for conducting an ethnography as there are ethnographers. From the early days in cultural anthropology when researchers were "sent" without guidance to remote islands or countries to conduct their ethnography, today we have procedures, albeit general procedures, to guide conduct of an ethnography. A highly structured approach can be found in Spradley (1980), who has advanced a 12-stage "developmental research sequence" for conducting an ethnography. As shown

FIGURE 14.3

Spradley's Developmental Research Sequence

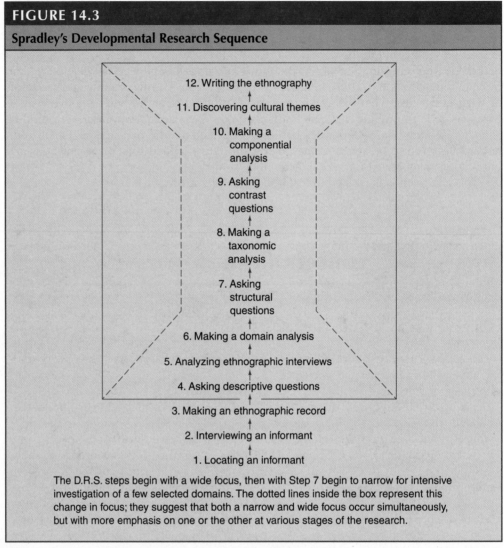

12. Writing the ethnography

11. Discovering cultural themes

10. Making a componential analysis

9. Asking contrast questions

8. Making a taxonomic analysis

7. Asking structural questions

6. Making a domain analysis

5. Analyzing ethnographic interviews

4. Asking descriptive questions

3. Making an ethnographic record

2. Interviewing an informant

1. Locating an informant

The D.R.S. steps begin with a wide focus, then with Step 7 begin to narrow for intensive investigation of a few selected domains. The dotted lines inside the box represent this change in focus; they suggest that both a narrow and wide focus occur simultaneously, but with more emphasis on one or the other at various stages of the research.

Source: From *The Ethnographic Interview* 1st edition by James P. Spradley. Copyright © 1979. Reprinted with permission of Wadsworth, a division of Thomson Learning.

in Figure 14.3, this sequence begins with the researchers locating an informant (today we would call this person a "participant"). Then the ethnographer cycles between collecting data and making analyses of various types, such as a taxonomy or a comparison table to explore relationships among ideas (see Spradley's componential analysis). Other authors besides Spradley have also suggested guidelines, such as Fetterman (2010), LeCompte and Schensul (1999), and Wolcott (2008).

Instead of Spradley's highly structured approach, we will consider a series of steps that represents a general template rather than a definitive procedure for conducting an ethnography. Moreover, the considerations of ethnographers and case study writers differ procedurally, and we will consider both similarities and differences among our three forms of ethnography: realist, case study, and critical. An overview of the steps used in each type of design is shown in Table 14.4.

Step 1. Identify Intent and the Type of Design, and Relate Intent to Your Research Problem

The first and most important steps in conducting research are to identify why you are undertaking a study, which form of design you plan to use, and how your intent relates to your research problem. These factors need to be identified in all three forms of ethnographies and case studies. The intent of your research and the type of problem you seek to study will differ significantly depending on your plan to conduct a realist, case study, or critical ethnography.

For a realist ethnography, the focus is on understanding a culture-sharing group and using the group to develop a deeper understanding of a cultural theme. The culture-sharing group may be an entire school or a single classroom. The themes may include such topics as enculturation, acculturation, socialization, institutionalized education, learning and cognition, and child and adult development (LeCompte et al., 1993).

For a case study, the focus is on developing an in-depth understanding of a case, such as an event, activity, or process. In education, this often includes the study of an individual or several individuals, such as students or teachers. The important consideration is how you will use the case, such as to assess its intrinsic merit, to understand an issue, or to provide information to compare several cases.

In a critical ethnography, the intent changes dramatically from those used in a realist or case study project. A critical ethnographer seeks to address an inequity in society or schools, plans to use the research to advocate and call for changes, and typically identifies a specific issue (e.g., inequality, dominance, oppression, or empowerment) to study.

Step 2. Discuss Approval and Access Considerations

In this step, all three types of designs follow a similar procedure. You need to receive approval from the institutional review board. You also need to identify the type of purposeful sampling that is available and that best answers your research questions. In this process, locate a site for your research and then identify a gatekeeper who can provide access to the site and participants for study. In all research, you need to guarantee provisions for respecting the site and actively design in the study how to reciprocate to the individuals at the site. This means that you will guarantee to disturb the site as little as possible and to follow good ethical practices such as guaranteeing privacy and anonymity, not deceiving individuals, and informing all participants of the purposes of your research.

Step 3. Use Appropriate Data Collection Procedures

We can see from Table 14.4 that the three designs have several common features, with an emphasis on extensive data collection, using multiple procedures for gathering data, and the active involvement of participants in the process.

In a realist ethnography, because you will likely spend considerable time with individuals in the field (e.g., up to 4 months or more), you need to enter the site slowly and as unobtrusively as possible. Building rapport with gatekeepers and key participants is essential for your long-term contacts. In many realist accounts, an emphasis is placed on taking fieldnotes and observing the "cultural scene." Interviews and artifacts such as drawings, relics, and symbols are also important forms of data. Any data that can help you develop an in-depth understanding of the shared patterns of the cultural group would be useful.

For a case study, the intent is to develop an in-depth understanding of a case or an issue, and researchers collect as many types of data as possible to develop this understanding. For example, in the gunman incident (Asmussen & Creswell, 1995),

TABLE 14.4

Procedures for Conducting a Realist Ethnography, a Case Study, and a Critical Ethnography

Procedures	Realist Ethnography	Case Study	Critical Ethnography
Identify your intent, the appropriate design, and how intent relates to your research problem.	The problem relates to a culture-sharing group and how it works. The problem requires detailed description of the daily lives of people. The problem relates to understanding a cultural theme. Identify your cultural theme.	The problem relates to developing an in-depth understanding of a "case" or bounded system. The problem relates to understanding an event, activity, process, or one or more individuals. Identify the type of "case," such as intrinsic, instrumental, or collective.	The problem relates to a need to address inequities in our society or schools. The problem calls for action and advocacy. Identify the "critical" issue (e.g., inequality) that you wish to explore.
Discuss how you plan to receive approval and gain access to study sites and participants.	Receive approval from institutional review board. Locate a research site using purposeful sampling procedures. Identify a gatekeeper to provide access. Guarantee provisions for respecting the site.	Receive approval from institutional review board. Locate a research site using purposeful sampling procedures. Identify how many cases you plan to study. Identify a gatekeeper to provide access. Guarantee provisions for respecting the site.	Receive approval from institutional review board. Locate a research site using purposeful sampling procedures. Identify a gatekeeper to provide access. Guarantee provisions for respecting the site.
Collect appropriate data emphasizing time in the field, multiple sources of information, and collaboration.	Spend extensive time at the site and with the culture-sharing group. Enter the site slowly and build rapport. Plan to reciprocate for data provided. Emphasize observations and record fieldnotes.	Collect extensive data using multiple forms of data collection (observations, interviews, documents, audiovisual materials).	Collaborate with participants by actively involving them in data collection. Collect multiple forms of data that individuals are willing to provide.

the authors provided a table that showed 13 sources of information, including interviews, observations, documents, and audiovisual materials. The provision of a table specifically focused on data collection sources emphasized the extent of data collection.

In a critical ethnography, the data collection is less focused on time in the field or on the extent of data and more on the active collaboration between the researcher and the participants during the study. Because the intent of a critical ethnography is to help bring about change that affects the lives of participants, the participants need to be involved in learning about themselves and steps need to be taken to improve their equity, to provide empowerment, or to lessen their oppression. This collaboration may involve participants in the design of the study, the formulation of research questions, the collection of data, or the analysis of the data collected. It may also include having participants actively write the final research report with you.

Step 4. Analyze and Interpret Data within a Design

In all ethnographic designs, you will engage in the general process of developing a description, analyzing your data for themes, and providing an interpretation of the meaning

TABLE 14.4			
(Continued)			
Procedures	**Realist Ethnography**	**Case Study**	**Critical Ethnography**
Analyze and interpret your data within a design.	Read through data to develop an overall understanding of it. Develop a detailed description of the cultural setting to establish a context for the group being studied. Develop themes about the culture-sharing group. Make interpretations in view of the cultural theme you are studying.	Read through data to develop an overall understanding of it. Describe the case(s) in detail and establish a context for it. Develop issues or themes about the case(s). If more than one case is studied, consider a within-case analysis followed by a cross-case analysis.	Read through data to develop an overall understanding of it. Develop a detailed description of the cultural setting to establish a context for the group being studied. Develop themes that relate to the "critical" issues that are being explored in the ethnography. Identify changes that need to occur, advocate for specific changes, and advance a plan for change.
Write and report your research consistent with your design.	Report it as an objective study. As a researcher, remain in the background in the written report. Keep your biases out. Identify how your exploration of the cultural theme advances knowledge.	Report it based primarily on description of the case, or weigh description, analysis, and interpretation differently or equally. Choose to be objective or subjective in your reporting. Include your biases. Generalize to other cases.	Report it as a call to action to address the "critical" issue that you are studying. Include a specific plan of action for change based on your findings. Discuss how you, as well as those you studied, changed (be reflexive).

of your information. These are typical data analysis and interpretation procedures found in all qualitative studies. However, the different types of ethnographic designs vary in their approach to these procedures.

In a critical ethnography, you need to consider a balance among description, analysis, and interpretation so that each becomes an important element of your analysis. Moreover, you can discuss in your interpretation how you learned about the cultural theme, actively reflect back on what information existed in the literature, and advance how your study added to the understanding of the cultural theme. In a case study, again the analysis follows description, analysis, and interpretation, but the analysis procedures will vary depending on whether you are studying a single case or multiple cases. A typical case study procedure for multiple cases is to first analyze each case separately and then conduct a cross-case analysis (see Stake, 1995) to identify common and different themes among all of the cases.

In a critical ethnography, you shape the description, analysis, and interpretation to focus on the "critical" issue in your study. Specifically, you need to interpret your findings in view of the changes that need to occur and to advocate for improvements in the lives of your participants. Often, critical ethnographers will advance a plan for change with specific steps that need to occur. For example, in a study about improving the conditions for women's ice hockey teams in Canada, Theberge (1997) ended her study with an appeal for action. She calls for "a more fully transformative vision of hockey that would offer empowerment in a setting that rejects violence and the normalization of injury in favor of an ethic of care" (p. 85).

Step 5. Write the Report Consistent with Your Design

A realist ethnography is written as an objective report of information about the culture-sharing group. Your personal views and biases will be kept in the background, and a discussion at the end of the study should indicate how the research contributes to knowledge about the cultural theme based on understanding the shared patterns of behavior, thinking, or language of the culture-sharing group. However, a case study may emphasize the detailed description of the case. You can write entire case studies to focus on description rather than a thematic development, such as Stake's (1995) descriptive case study of "Harper School." Other case studies will balance description with themes, such as the gunman incident case study by Asmussen and Creswell (1995). One additional factor that sets case studies apart from other ethnographic designs is that the author may discuss generalizing the findings to other cases, especially if researchers examine multiple case studies. Although qualitative researchers are reluctant to generalize their findings, the use of multiple case studies provides some ability to identify findings that are common to all cases using cross-case analysis. When this occurs, case study writers may suggest that their findings are generalizable, but they make only modest claims in this direction.

In a critical ethnography, the researchers conclude their reports with the "critical" issue that initiated the study, and discuss how they as well as the participants have changed or benefited from the research. Included within a "call for action" by the critical ethnographer may be a reflection about changes they and the participants have experienced. Undoubtedly, in all forms of research, the investigators change. Critical ethnographers give special emphasis to this, as reflexive, self-conscious researchers.

HOW DO YOU EVALUATE AN ETHNOGRAPHY?

The criteria for evaluating an ethnography begin with applying the standards used in qualitative research. Then, specific factors need to be considered within ethnography properly. In a good ethnography, the researcher:

◆ Identifies a culture-sharing group or case to study.
◆ Focuses on a cultural concept (e.g., power, acculturation) recognizing that this concept may be very broad.
◆ Provides evidence to show how this group has established over time pattern of behavior, language, and beliefs.
◆ Engages in fieldwork and gathers the evidence through multiple sources including observations and interviews.
◆ Shows an analysis of this evidence through a detailed description of the culture-sharing group and the context in which it exists, themes that summarize major ideas about how the group works, and interpretation that suggests how the group illustrates "culture at work."
◆ Portrays the researchers as reflecting on their own role in the study and how their background, gender, and history shape the account that they report.

KEY IDEAS IN THE CHAPTER

Defining Ethnographic Research, Its Use, and Its Development

An ethnography is a useful design for studying groups in education, their behaviors, beliefs, and language, and how they develop shared patterns of interacting over time. Ethnographic research is a qualitative design for describing, analyzing, and interpreting the patterns of a culture-sharing group. *Culture* is a broad term used to encompass all human behavior and beliefs. Typically, it includes a study of language, rituals, structures, life stages, interactions, and communication. Ethnographers visit the "field," collect extensive data through such procedures as observation and interviewing, and write up a cultural portrait of the group within its setting. Thus, ethnographers stress cultural concepts, and they study a group of individuals at a single site. The researcher examines shared patterns of behaviors, beliefs, and language that have developed over time by engaging in fieldwork such as observing and interviewing people where they live and work. The analysis begins with describing and analyzing the culture-sharing group and interpreting their patterns within the context of culture-at-work. Overall, the ethnographer employs a reflexive inquiry style of being self-conscious about the research and the writing and being respectful of participants.

The origins of this approach are found in anthropology, sociology, education, and postmodern, reflexive concerns about interpreting data and writing reports.

Three Types of Ethnographic Designs

These historical factors have led to three types of ethnographies: realist, case studies, and critical studies. A realist account is an objective account of a culture-sharing group. It is written in a third-person point of view, reports on the information learned from participants, and places the researcher in the role of providing the final interpretation and presentation of the culture. Case studies focus on a program, event, or activities and provide a detailed description and analysis of a case based on extensive data collection. A critical ethnography is a type of ethnography in which the researchers advocate for groups marginalized in our society and focus on issues such as power and authority.

Potential Ethical Issues in Ethnographic Research

Ethical issues in ethnography relate to fieldwork concerns. These ethical issues involve such topics as gaining access to the field, staying in the field, gathering data in the field, and the interactions of being in the field of research.

Steps in Conducting an Ethnography

The steps in conducting these ethnographies involve starting with an interest in studying a cultural theme, identifying a bounded site, and examining shared patterns for a group. The researcher poses general research questions to identify shared patterns of behavior, beliefs, or language and also collects extensive fieldwork data. From this data, a general portrait of how the culture-sharing group works is developed through description, analysis, and interpretation. The interpretation and writing are sensitive to the reflexivity of the researcher, and varied forms of writing structures are used.

Conducting an ethnography involves clarifying the intent of the study, selecting an appropriate design, and relating the design to the research problem. Then the researcher needs to seek approval to conduct the study and obtain access to study sites and participants. Once this is accomplished, the ethnographer collects data using multiple sources of information and spends considerable time in the field. After gathering information, the analysis of data consists of describing, analyzing, and interpreting. Some researchers, when conducting a critical ethnography, will identify changes that need to occur and will actively advocate and plan for them. When writing the final research report, ethnographers and case study writers employ practices consistent with their designs, such as being objective or advocative, generalizing findings, and discussing how they and the participants changed during the research process.

Criteria for Evaluating an Ethnography Study

In conducting a good ethnography, a researcher should pay attention to identifying a cultural issue to study, selecting a group to observe or interview over time, and noting shared patterns of behavior, language, and beliefs that the group has developed over time. The account needs to both describe the group and identify themes. Moreover, the researchers need to provide evidence of being reflexive about their role in the study.

USEFUL INFORMATION FOR PRODUCERS OF RESEARCH

◆ Clarify the intent you have for your ethnographic research. Consider whether you plan to develop patterns and a portrait of a culture-sharing group, provide an in-depth description and analysis of a "case," or advocate for an issue based on studying a culture-sharing group.

◆ Recognize that many ethnographies today are written using a critical perspective. Read about these forms of ethnographies by consulting books by Thomas (1993), Carspecken (1995), Denzin (1997), or Madison (2005).

◆ If you conduct a case study, determine whether the issue (instrumental) or the case itself (intrinsic) is of primary interest for addressing your research problem.

◆ When conducting a realist ethnography, identify a cultural theme that you wish to explore. This cultural theme is the central phenomenon of your study.

◆ As you collect data in the field for a realist ethnography, look for shared patterns of behavior, beliefs, or language that develop over time.

◆ Engaging in fieldwork and collecting data involve negotiating relationships with participants and key gatekeepers at research sites. Be respectful of sites and individuals as you conduct your study.

◆ Consider in your ethnography how you will balance description of the culture-sharing group or case, analysis of themes about the group or case, and interpretation of the meaning of the description and analysis. Ideally, you should give them equal weight, but this would depend on the purposes and the research questions you plan to address in your study.

◆ Context is important in ethnographies and case studies. Include it in your description as well as in your themes.

◆ Authors write about how we interpret the "text," or written report, in ethnographic research. Recognize and discuss in your report your own position that affects your interpretation, and acknowledge that multiple interpretations exist in any report, such as those of readers and participants in the study.

◆ Consider the steps in the process of conducting an ethnography and make adjustments in them to reflect the type of design you use. See Table 14.4 as a guide.

USEFUL INFORMATION FOR CONSUMERS OF RESEARCH

◆ To identify the cultural theme in a realist ethnography, look at the purpose statement and the research question for the central phenomenon being examined.

◆ Recognize that the final ethnographic report or case study will vary in structure because of the differences among a realist ethnography, a case study, and a critical ethnography.

◆ Among several factors to use in evaluating an ethnography or case report, especially consider whether the author collects multiple forms of data and spends considerable time in the field gathering information.

◆ The information researchers may report in an ethnography or case study may be insights from examining a portrait of a culture-sharing group, contributions to understanding cultural themes, an in-depth exploration of a case that has not been examined before, or a plan for action to change or remedy inequities in education and in our society.

ADDITIONAL RESOURCES YOU MIGHT EXAMINE

A number of books, listed below, are available to expand your understanding of educational ethnographic research.

Harry Wolcott (1992, 1994, 1995, 2008) has authored several books on ethnography, that, taken as a series, introduce you to all facets of understanding and conducting ethnographic research. His writing style illustrates scholarly approaches and serves as an accessible means for understanding ethnography. His 2008 book is perhaps the best overview of ethnographic practices and ideas available today. Examine Wolcott's books:

Wolcott, H. F. (1992). *Writing up qualitative research*. Newbury Park, CA: Sage.

Wolcott, H. F. (1994). *Transforming qualitative data: Description, analysis, and interpretation*. Thousand Oaks, CA: Sage.

Wolcott, H. F. (1995). *The art of fieldwork*. Walnut Creek, CA: AltaMira.

Wolcott, H. F. (2008). *Ethnography: A way of seeing* (2nd ed.). Walnut Creek, CA: AltaMira.

Margaret LeCompte and Jean Schensul (1999) have authored a "toolkit" of seven short books that provide an excellent introduction to ethnography. See their introductory book as a guide to their toolkit:

LeCompte, M. D., & Schensul, J. J. (1999). *Designing and conducting ethnographic research* (Ethnographer's Toolkit No. 1). Walnut Creek, CA: AltaMira.

Practical step-by-step approaches to educational ethnography can be found in several books. David Fetterman's (2010) book, now in its 3rd edition, is like a travelogue, identifying and discussing the major landmarks every ethnographer encounters. For steps and examples in writing fieldnotes in an ethnography, examine the book by Robert Emerson, Rachel Fretz, and Linda Shaw (1995). For a good understanding of autoethnography, see Muncey (2010), and for an understanding of critical ethnography, see Madison (2005). See:

Fetterman, D. M. (2010). *Ethnography: Step by step* (3rd ed.). Thousand Oaks, CA: Sage.

Emerson, R. M., Fretz, R. I., & Shaw, L. L. (1995). *Writing ethnographic fieldnotes*. Chicago: University of Chicago Press.

Madison, D. S. (2005). *Critical ethnography: Method, ethics, and performance*. Thousand Oaks, CA: Sage.

Muncey, T. (2010). *Creating autoethnographies*. London: Sage.

Finally, books to consult on case study research are Stake's (1995) book on the art of case study research, Yin's (2008) book on case study methods, and Merriam's (1998) introduction to case studies. See:

Stake, R. E. (1995). *The art of case study research.* Thousand Oaks, CA: Sage.
Merriam, S. B. (1998). *Qualitative research and case study applications in education.* San Francisco: Jossey-Bass.
Yin, R. K. (2008). *Case study research* (4th ed.). Thousand Oaks, CA: Sage.

PEARSON
myeducationlab
The Power of Classroom Practice
www.myeducationlab.com

Go to the Topic "Ethnographic Research" in the MyEducationLab (**www.myeducationlab.com**) for your course, where you can:

◆ Find learning outcomes for "Ethnographic Research."
◆ Complete Assignments and Activities that can help you more deeply understand the chapter content.
◆ Apply and practice your understanding of the core skills identified in the chapter with the Building Research Skills exercises.
◆ Check your comprehension of the content covered in the chapter by going to the Study Plan. Here you will be able to take a pretest, receive feedback on your answers, and then access Review, Practice, and Enrichment activities to enhance your understanding. You can then complete a final posttest.

Example of an Ethnographic Study

Examine the following published journal article that uses an ethnographic design. Marginal notes indicate the major characteristics of ethnographic research highlighted in this chapter. The illustrative study is:

Notes on a Country School Tradition: Recitation as an Individual Strategy

Stephen A. Swidler
University of Nebraska-Lincoln

Ethographic Characteristics in Marginal Annotations

This ethnographic case study describes one Nebraska teacher's response to the multiage conditions of this naturally small institution in her use of "recitation" lessons. The form of the country school recitation, with its predictable student-teacher interaction and emphasis on independent work, appears as a sensible practice for curriculum and student management. I investigate the residual form of the recitation in a modern one-teacher school in rural Nebraska as a patterned response to the conditions of smallness. Conservative in its orientation toward knowledge and student learning, the recitation is explored as a functional response to the context of smallness, implicit parental and community expectations, inevitable student transfer to large graded middle and secondary schools, and its symbolic defense of community at a time of rural social and economic decline.

(01)

The one-teacher country school regularly faces the challenge of a wide range of grade levels and academic growth. One response to the multiage conditions of this naturally small institution is a teacher's regular use of "recitation" lessons with individual and small groups of students. This pedagogical device is a common legacy of the one-teacher country school. The old country school recitation conjures up images of children sitting on a hard bench, or standing at attention, orally recounting memorized texts or answers for the teacher while other students prepare quietly and independently for their own impending recitation performances. Accurately memorized and correct-answer recitations were then taken as proxies for learning. While very few would advocate this as an acceptable model of instruction in public schools today, the *form* of the country school recitation, with its predictable student-teacher interaction and emphasis on independent work, nonetheless appears today as a sensible practice for curriculum and student management. Here I investigate ethnographically the residual form of the recitation in a modern one-teacher school in rural Nebraska. I look at this patterned instruction as an established response to the conditions of smallness. I explore how, in its conservative orientation toward knowledge and student learning, the recitation is nonetheless a functional response to the context of smallness, implicit parental and community expectations, and inevitable student transfer to large graded middle and secondary schools.

Cultural theme

Reform and School Size

The research reported here is drawn from the first in a series of comparative case studies designed to examine issues of school size. School size has gained currency in educational reform conversations. Drawing upon decades of research, beginning with Barker and Gump's *Big School, Small School* (1964), and upon articulate practitioner portraits (e.g., Meier, 1995; Snyder, Lieberman, MacDonald, & Goodwin, 1992), contemporary reformers argue strongly that smaller schools are generally better than larger schools for students and their learning. Despite these findings, small school size is no cure-all. Benefits of smallness vary according to social and academic organization and enactment of school purpose. Nevertheless, smallness is thoroughly implicated in robust

(02)

This research is supported by the Annenberg Rural Challenge through *School at the Center,* University of Nebraska-Lincoln. I am grateful to Carol McDaniels, Paul Theobald, Miles Bryant, James O'Hanlon, Jann Pataray-Ching, my QQME research seminar graduate students, and the anonymous reviewers for their comments and feedback on an earlier version. I remain indebted to Eliot Singer for his ongoing ethnographic inspiration.

Correspondence concerning this article should be addressed to Stephen A. Swidler, 118 Henzlik Hall, Center for Curriculum & Instruction, University of Nebraska-Lincoln, Lincoln, NE 68588-0355. (sswidler2@unl.edu)

school improvement (see Lee & Smith, 1997). Consequently, we hear calls for schools to "scale down" (Elmore, 1996), to "restructure" into small, multiage units, and to create "schools within schools" (Darling-Hammond, 1997).

(03)   It is not uncommon to hear some progressive school reformers in the "small schools movement" (see Fine & Somerville, 1998), typically urban, invoke the image of the one-teacher country school as inspiration for their efforts. However, contemporary rural, one-teacher schools continue to be overlooked by educational researchers. Small country schools appear in larger quantitative studies (see Fowler, 1995; Howley, 1989), which ratify what we know from other large, mainstream studies that are not exclusively rural: Smaller is better.[1] Descriptive research of contemporary small, public rural schools, and one-teacher schools in particular, is exceptionally thin.[2] What makes rural one-teachers schools of theoretical import, in relation to larger reform concerns, is that they are *naturally occurring* instances of small-scale schooling. Their size is a function of social and historical circumstance, not of reform intervention. The one-teacher school is a peculiarly, some might claim quintessentially, rural institution that has waned with population decline in rural communities and a hegemony of "economies of scale" ideologies, both contributing to widespread consolidation.

Cultural theme

(04)   The present study was undertaken to look at the practices of some of the remaining one-teacher schools, what might be learned from them, and if or how we might capture a glimpse "of our future in this remaining piece of our past" (Geyer, 1995).

Theoretical Frame and Methodological Concerns

(05)   Since my interests are in Nebraska's remaining one-teacher schools as naturally occurring instances of small scale schooling, I pursue a theoretical and methodological orientation appropriate to study of sociocultural phenomena in natural settings. Ethnographic analysis is best suited to attend holistically to the details and subtleties of such settings, especially when insider perspective is crucial to understanding those settings. While no school is truly "natural" (they are human-made institutions), the rural one-teacher school is, in educational and institutional terms, not a design for change. It is *just so* as a traditional rural institution. I treat it as a mundane cultural setting, where school constituents come together and form and coordinate rights, duties, practices, and shared symbols as a way to "do school" that is small in scale.

(06)   In data collection and analysis, this study takes a more or less mainstream symbolic-interpretive perspective on the school as a cultural setting (Erickson, 1986). The school is thus viewed, in Geertz's (1973a) words, as "an ensemble of texts, themselves ensembles, which the anthropologist strains to read over the shoulders of those to whom they properly belong" (p. 452). In struggling to read over the shoulders of the "natives" in this school, I assume that there is a "historically transmitted pattern of meanings embodied in symbols, a system of inherited conceptions expressed in symbolic form by means of which [people] communicate, perpetuate, and develop their knowledge about and attitudes towards life" (Geertz, 1973b, p. 89). Here, I consider specifically the patterned meaning of the recitation as a central feature of a school. My concerns center on how, as cultural settings, these traditional institutions cohere and connect to their rural circumstance.

Shared patterns of behavior, beliefs, and attitudes

(07)   Consequently, this inquiry employs the ethnographic staples of long-term participant-observation, interviews, and artifact and documentary examination. My data collection has included participant-observation and narrative field-notes from Bighand School[3] for the first 6 months of the 1998-1999 academic year (August-February), at least 2 days/week and in several return visits. I attended monthly school board meetings and conducted in-depth interviews with the teacher, students, school board members, parents, administrators, and community members. I endeavored especially to interview the students, individually and as grade level groups, as most have experienced no other form of schooling and no other teacher in their educational biographies. I conducted follow-up interviews with students, parents, the teacher, and school board members, formally and informally

Fieldwork

Culture-sharing group

---

[1]E.g., the National Educational Longitudinal Study (see Lee, Smith, & Crominger, 1995)
[2]By this I mean systematic qualitative research. Here, perhaps unfairly, I exclude oral history, reminiscence, memoir, autobiography and scores of journalistic accounts. To be sure, there is much to be mined in these, but none of them represents systematic inquiry into living, *contemporary,* one-teacher, public schools.
[3]All names presented here are pseudonyms to guard confidentiality.

(sometime in telephone calls), to verify emergent assertions and to build working hypotheses about "what is going on" at the school. I also reviewed various text-books, curriculum guides, and written school policies as documentary artifacts and symbolic tracings of what the school "means." Much of what I have learned has come from the hundreds of conversations with the teacher and students during the regular school day: in the classroom sitting next to students as they work, in the musty basement during lunch, on the playground in a game of *Andy, Andy Over,* and during dizzying rides on an ancient country school merry-go-round.

Some researcher reflexivity

Nebraska's Remaining One-Teacher Schools

Nebraska continues to have more living one-teacher schools than any other state. From the most recent aggregated, national data we have on one-room schools (DeWalt, 1997; Muse, Hie, Randall, & Jensen, 1998), I estimate that there are roughly 350 one-teacher schools in the U.S. at the time of data collection for this study. (In 1931, there were 143,391 [Leight & Rhienhart, 1992].) For the 1998-1999 school year, Nebraska had 125 one-teacher schools.[4] Calls from various interest groups for their dismantling and consolidation are perennial in Nebraska. However, the one-teacher schools are variants of "Class One" school districts. These districts are K-8 only (i.e., those that have no high school). In the 1998-1999 school year, there were 320 Class One school districts in the state. The one-teacher schools, like all Class Ones, comprise their own districts with their own three-person school boards. They have statutory support to exist; to eliminate entirely the remaining one-teacher schools in the state would require a legislative act on school redistricting. However, rural population decline, ongoing tax struggles, extremely inequitable state aid distribution, and sociopolitical pressure from rural and nonrural school districts, celebrating economies of scale, all contribute to local decisions to close the small, Class One schools.

(08)

The Research Site

Context or setting

(09)

Bighand School is located in the rolling prairie of eastern Nebraska, where corn, soybeans, and winter wheat cover the landscape during the growing season. The school is situated 3 miles from the unincorporated village of Johnville (pop. 170), 7 miles from the town of Sparta (pop. 1,700), and 12 miles from the county seat, Riverview (pop. 6,600). It is literally "in the country," on a dirt state highway. "Not enough rich people live on it to be paved," one parent remarked. It is located on a hill crest and, approaching Bighand School from any direction, one sees an utterly conventional building. Constructed in 1981, the current 30' x 40' building is one story, with white aluminum siding, a storage shed, an old water pump, a detached tornado cellar, two swing sets, and a small merry-go-round. County archives indicate that the school was founded in 1868, a year after Nebraska ceased to be a territory, and remains one of the oldest living schools in the state. Like a great portion of eastern Nebraska and western Iowa, the region in and around Bighand School was homesteaded and settled primarily by German immigrants in the 19th century. The vast majority of the registered voters, as well as all of the students and the teacher at Bighand School, bear German surnames attesting to this historical backdrop. It took the name Bighand sometime in the 1880s, apparently from the name of the farmer whose original homestead property sat next to the school and who served on the school board.[5] In a county that encompasses 19 separate school districts, 9 of which are Class One, Bighand is 1 of the 5 remaining one-teacher schools this year.

Bighand School district encompasses no population centers. Of the residents, most are retired farmers. The land is presently farmed by family farmers or tenant farmers, with a small number of incorporated and consolidated farms. The 1998 school census indicates that there are 66 residents in the Bighand school district and 17 school-age (K-8) children, with 8 of those attending Bighand School. The district has weathered decades of school district reorganization and witnessed neighboring rural districts close and consolidate. Once composed of 10 square miles, Bighand district now includes approximately 25 square miles, some of which is noncontiguous. In the mid-1980s,

(10)
Description

---

[4]Data on Nebraska Schools come from the Nebraska State Department of Education Data Center and from the advocacy Group Class Ones United.

[5]Descendents of Wm. Bighand still own farm property in the district. The name Bighand is the Anglo transliteration of the German "Grossehand."

as part of a state-wide effort to equalize the property taxes, rural landowners were required to declare their association with a school district, and a high school if that district was a Class One. Later in 1990, each Class One school was to formally "affiliate" with one or more high schools or to become a subset of a Class Six, high school only, district. (Bighand is affiliated with 3 high schools.) The current Bighand district configuration is the effect of these land-owners' choices.

(11)   The political and some social boundaries of the community are effectively defined by the school district. Because there are no economic or formal social centers in the district itself, constituents take up shopping and church in the surrounding towns and villages. At least one parent in each of this year's school families is employed in one of these neighboring towns or villages. One parent referred to the school as the "capital" of the community. With no tax advantage in retaining a separate rural school district, and no high school, the preservation of the Bighand district has seemed peculiar to many in the county. In 1981, a regional electric utility's newsletter found it odd yet delightful that while the rest of the state's one-teacher schools were closing and consolidating, Bighand's school board proudly paid $50,000 to replace the deteriorating, 100-year-old building with one that "boasts such amenities as a full basement, fluorescent lighting, a 30-gallon electric hot water heater, an electric cook range, and a new 20-kilowatt electric furnace." A Bighand student, quoted in Riverview's newspaper, said enthusiastically of the new building, "It's bigger, more attractive and it has a drinking fountain and indoor plumbing!"

Bighand Students This Year

(12)   Bighand School has 12 students, spanning kindergarten through eighth grade (see Table 1). Eight of these children resides in the school district.[6] The four whose families do not reside are "option" students. Nebraska statutorily allows "option enrollment," where parents can place their children in any public school in the state as long as they provide transportation, there is room at the selected school, and school desegregation plans for that school are not compromised. Samuel, Christine, and Andrew are from Johnville. Loretta is from Sparta. Though the parents of these students have

TABLE 1
Students at Bighand School, 1998-1999

Grade	Student
K	Haley
K	Andrew*
1st	Samuel*
2nd	Christine*
2nd	Richard
2nd	David
5th	Kimberly
6th	Daisy
6th	Deborah
8th	Mary
8th	Loretta*
8th	Molly

*Children who reside in another district and are "option enrollment" students.

[6]There are nine other eligible students in the district. They attend either a private school in Riverview City, are home schooled, or "optioned" into a neighboring Class One district. One of these nine is Daisy's brother Tom, a seventh grader at Riverview Middle School. His mother transferred him last year from Bighand partly because she said he was restless, "unchallenged" and because he was the only boy his age at a school with five older girls.

different reasons for "optioning" their children into Bighand School, they express a common reservation (all use the terms "fear" or "afraid") toward large, graded schools of the Johnville-Sparta Consolidated School District. They believe that, in a country school, discipline is enforced and children get personal attention from the teacher. Every parent and community member whom I spoke with or interviewed uses the phrase "one-on-one" to describe a major benefit of country schooling. This concern for personal attention, surveillance, and discipline is part of a larger set of values discussed below.

The parents of Bighand's students are mostly skilled laborers and high school educated (see   (13) Table 2). Only Mary and Deborah's parents and Loretta's stepfather have a college education. None of these families considers itself poor. While they never refer to each other as wealthy, I have, though, overheard hushed, reproachful comments as to Loretta's mother's displays of wealth in her clothing, hairstyle, dress, and automobiles. If there is any class consciousness, or resentment, it is buried and ill-defined. (I once heard Loretta call Kimberly "a rich kid," when her own family's income is clearly higher than any other family's in the school.) Finally, 75% of the school is made up of four families: Haley and Molly, Christine and Samuel, David and Kimberly, Mary and Deborah are siblings.

Ruralness and Intimacy at School

The school these children inhabit has a "rural" quality. It is commonly referred to as "the one-room   (14) school north of Johnville." The school board president and secretary farm for a living. The school is deeded on a corner of the board president's farm. Most of the families and the teacher have some substantial connection to agriculture in their family histories. For example, Haley and Molly's father farmed until a decade earlier when he calculated the economic risk was too great and went to work for a prosperous mining company. Daisy's mother "grew up a farm kid" not far from the school. Furthermore, the teacher, parents, school board members, and students make regular and firm distinctions between "country" and "town" schools (small and multigrade vs. large and graded) and imply the inferiority of the latter. Though only one of the school's families currently farms for a living (Deborah and Mary's),[7] the location and social history of its constituents give the school a decidedly "rural" flavor.

TABLE 2
Bighand Parent Occupations and Educational Levels

Student	Parent Occupation		Parent Education ((highest level achieved))	
	Mother	Father	Mother	Father
Haley (K) Molly (8th)	Stay at home	Mining laborer	High School	High School
Andrew (K)	Fast food assistant manager	Small factor laborer	High School	High School
Samuel (1st) Christine (2nd)	Stay at home	Small factory laborer	High School	High School
Richard (2nd)	Factory laborer	out of state (divorced)	High School	unknown
David (2nd) Kimberly (5th)	Seamstress	Power company supervisor	High School	High School
Daisy (6th)	Lumber company clerk	Meat packing laborer (divorced)	High School	High School
Deborah (6th) Mary (8th)	Social worker	Farmer, feed store owner	Undergraduate University	Undergraduate University
Loretta (8th)	Stay at home	Optometrist (stepfather)	High School	Postgraduate

---

[7]Not entirely, though. Their mother works as a social worker and their father owns a feed store in Riverview.

(15)   This rural flavor is accompanied by a peculiar intimacy. Walking into the one-room setting at almost any given time, one will see students preoccupied with preparing for their recitations with the teacher. With its dingy linoleum floor, blond pine book cases, and white painted walls, the school appears quiet and emotionally detached to outsiders like me. Students regularly express an indifference, and sometimes harshness, toward each other in their classroom and playground interactions and in their interviews with me. For instance, Daisy says to me that she "can't stand the younger kids" and snaps to Samuel, "Sit down, be quiet, and stop bothering me" when he squirms in his chair. Mary accuses Kimberly of stealing things from coat pockets and backpacks and calls her "stuck up." Loretta refers to David as a "brat." Defending her brother, Kimberly returns the sentiment and tells that Loretta is "nothing but trouble." And Mrs. Hoffman regularly harangues Richard to "sit down, get to work, or otherwise you will lose your recess," and bluntly tells a crying Deborah that "the older girls pick on you because you sometimes ask for it."

(16)   But the apparent coolness these people hold toward one another belies certain facts. Apart from Richard, a newcomer this year, and Loretta, who option enrolled in the middle of her sixth grade year, Bighand School is the only school these students have attended. Moreover, since she is in her 11th year at the school, Mrs. Hoffman is the only teacher they have known. Consequently, the teacher and students have a protracted familiarity with each other. Molly reports that she and the other older students regard Mrs. Hoffman as a cantankerous "old aunt," and the students frequently call her "Mrs. H." It is an oblique intimacy that Alan Peshkin (1978/1994) describes as knowing, and being known by, others through long-term, mundane interaction characteristic of small and rural communities. At Bighand School, the students know each other through their own everyday interactions, what their brothers and sisters say to them about other students, what they hear from their parents about other students and their families, and so on. When you know someone well, and your school work is centered on working quietly, strenuously, and individually on assignments, sometimes there is not that much to gleefully talk about. And there are some things you want to keep to yourself in such an intimate environment. The people at Bighand School have simply, to paraphrase Lerner and Loewe (1959), grown accustomed to each other's faces. They know each other very well, may not say that they like each other often, but are nonetheless regular parts of each other's lives.

The Teacher

(17)   Mrs. Hoffman is in her 11th year of teaching at Bighand. She returned to teaching not long after the sudden death of her husband. Now in her early sixties, she was originally educated in what was then a normal school in the 1950s. After completing a relatively short course in teacher education, she received a provisional teaching certificate at the age of 18 with the stipulation that she ultimately complete a 2-year teacher certification program. She took up her first teaching job in a country school for 4 years. Like many women of her generation, she left teaching to mary and raise children. Between those early years and her 11-year tenure at Bighand, she has worked as a fraternity house mother, a social service provider, and a seamstress at a retail clothier. She still works part-time at a clothing retailer in Riverview to make ends meet (her salary is less than $19,000). Mrs. Hoffman returned to that same normal school, which had become a 4-year college, to obtain her certification in the early 1980s.

(18)   Mrs. Hoffman calls herself "country schooled." She tells that when she transferred from a small country school to a village high school, with a graduating class of 15, she experienced "culture shock." Culturally and educationally speaking, she has deep roots in country schooling and in the region. For example, she was born and raised in a small town 30 miles south of the school in the same county. She currently lives in Sparta. She went to country schools and recalls vividly a grandmother who taught in country schools ("I learned everything from her"). Before school starts in the mornings, she ordinarily and amicably talks with the school aide (the board president's wife) about mutual friends and acquaintances in the community. She had coursework and practica on country schooling in her early teacher education at the Normal School. The previous board secretary (Molly and Haley's mother) indicated that Mrs. Hoffman was selected from a pool of 30 applicants because the board assumed she understood country children and "schools like these." In Mrs. Hoffman's words, "teaching in a country school is in my blood."

	Themes

A Pedagogical Challenge and Textbooks

A primary challenge Mrs. Hoffman faces is not new to the country school teacher: How to organize curriculum and instruction to accomodate twelve different children, at six different grade levels, that is acceptable to the school board, parents, administrative authorities, and her own sense of a proper education? This challenge involves, at a very basic level, what she sees as the importance of students completing a curricular program, persuading them to attend to their individual work, documenting individual student "progress," disciplining and array of ages, and otherwise helping them "get through" their school work. (19)

Specifically, Mrs. Hoffman is concerned that students are "at grade-level," that they are "keeping up" with, and possibly exceeding, what she determines they may otherwise be doing in a large graded elementary or middle school in town schools like Sparta and Riverview. She is further concerned that the students not get an alien curriculum, but one that feeds into, or is compatible with, what the students will encounter in secondary school and for some who transfer early to middle school (such as Daisy and Kimberly, who will transfer next year to Riverview). (20)

To do this, Mrs. Hoffman organizes her curriculum exclusively around commercially produced, standardized textbook and workbook series. Mrs. Hoffman uses those produced by major textbook publishing companies and is not limited to one company or series. (These include Houghton-Mifflin; Scott/Foresman & Co.; Silver Burdett & Ginn; Holt, Rinehart, & Winston; and Saxon Math.) She communicates with other country school teachers in the county and is informed by the school's contracted administrator (a retired, part-time, off-site principal) and the county superintendent (a part-time, elected official) of the textbooks that neighboring school districts use. However, these inform, not dictate, the choices she makes.[8] (21)

Mrs. Hoffman puts a great deal of faith in these texts for her curricular organization. The specific content of the textbooks is not a major preoccupation for her. In her view, textbooks and workbooks have face validity and represent reliably the grade levels for which they are designed. After all, major textbook producers are established companies and their books are in widespread use. The county superintendent and the principal simply presume the dominant place of these textbooks as curriculum organizers, and they support and approve of Mrs. Hoffman's usage of the books. Their concern is that the books be up to date. They all agree on their importance of using curricular materials comparable to those in surrounding school districts; they speak of "uniformity" or "compatibility" with these districts in describing one goal of Bighand's curriculum. Because these textbooks and workbooks are directed at a generalized and *defacto* national curriculum, their use is a primary way that Mrs. Hoffman and the administrators demonstrate to the school's constituency that they are concerned with students getting a portable education. (22)

Organization of Curriculum and Teaching

The usage of textbooks and, in Mrs. Hoffman's words, the value of "a strict adherence to a fixed curriculum" is, of course, not limited to country schools. But, how textbooks are used and implicated in her teaching practice, as a way of coping with her instructional challenge is particular to a one-teacher school circumstance. For instance, this school is not composed of all second or sixth graders who ostensibly go through the same subject matter at the same time, as might be found in a large and graded school. Rather, there are six different grade levels, and up to three individuals in each of those, not to mention the individual differences within those grades levels. In teacher parlance, excluding kindergarten, Mrs. Hoffman has at least five "preparations" for each subject. (23)

"Classes"

In this school, there is no whole class instruction in any subjects. It is carried out entirely in what are locally called grade-level "classes." At the outset of the school year, I was struck by the almost frenetic pace at which the students cycle through "classes." This involves small groups of students of the same grade level, or individuals, sitting at the teacher's table for short periods of interaction, rarely more than 15 minutes. It is the shared understanding between the teacher and student that (24)

---

[8]She told me she went one summer to an auction at a country school that had closed, where she picked up some textbooks that were "up-to-date."

these "classes" are designed as occasions for the teacher to check student work; briefly introduce a new subject topic (which is invariably the next chapter, lesson, or unit within the presently employed textbook); direct students to the next assignment within the chapter, lesson, or assignment; listen to students read aloud (excerpts from textbook passages or assignment directions); and monitor student work. While these short classes take place, those students who are not "in class" work independently on their assignments at their desks, sometimes at the computer (as a reward for completing all assignments, leaving them with extra time), or with the teacher's aide. At one point, I counted a dizzying 28 classes in one day. Mrs. Hoffman reports to the school board that she has had 30 classes in one day. From my data, the average number is around 23.

(25)   What intrigued me further about these classes is that they echoed old country school "recitations" as described by educational historians (Cuban, 1994; Theobald, 1995). What triggered this connection for me was the "Daily Program" posted in the front of the room (see Table 3). The

TABLE 3
The "Daily Program" Posted in the Front of the Classroom

Begins	Duration	Grade	Recitations In	Tuesday-Thursday Kindergarten
Morning				
8:30	10 min.	All	Opening	
8:40	35 min.	1st-6th	Reading	Reading Readiness
9:15	15 min.	8th	Literature	Free time
9:30	30 min.	1st-8th	Spelling Tests-Friday	Math
10:00	15 min.	All	Recess	
10:17	20 min.	1st-6th	Phonics (Ind. Work)	Phonics
10:20	55 min.	1st-8th	English	Quiet Activity
11:00	15 min.	1st-8th	Writing-Journals	Computer
	30 min.	K-2nd	Computer	Individual Time
11:15	15 min.			Storytime
11:25		All	Wash hands	
11:30	30 min.	All	Lunch	
Afternoon				
12:00	15 min.	1st-2nd	Reading	Rest
12:00	15 min.	5th-8th	Free Reading	
12:15	40 min.	1st-2nd	Math	
12:55	50 min.	5th-8th	Math Tue-Wed Test	Free Quiet Activity
		5th-8th	Computer Time	
1:45	10 min.	All	Recess-P.E.	
2:00	55 min.	1st	Health	Science
2:00		8th	Science Mon and Wed	
			Science Experiments	
2:00	55 min.	All	Social Studies Tue-Thurs (workbooks)	Map Skills
2:00	55 min.	1st-8th	Art-Friday	Kindergarten: Art Thursday
2:55	5 min.	All	Jobs	
3:00		All	Dismiss	

prominent display of the poster, according to the country superintendent, is required by law in Class One schools. It was the heading *Recitations In,* where conceivably the term "subject" might be, that led me to consider whether "classes" were vestiges of the old country school recitation manifest in this modern one-teacher school.

Organization of Classes

In Bighand School, the organization of instruction is the organization of classes. It appears rather straightforward. Students sit in uneven rows facing the blackboard, what is considered the front of the room. Mrs. Hoffman sits in the center of a U-shaped table at the left-hand corner of the front, facing the students. Her table acts as her desk, with teaching materials, grade and plan books, and small piles of student work. It is more significantly, from the students point of view, where classes take place. While she can oversee the entire school from her desk, she is typically preoccupied with classes and record keeping. She relies on students to "discipline themselves" and each other through adherence to long-standing and unwritten rules about "no talking" to each other outside of classes; "no more than two people [walking] on the floor at one time;" and requesting permission to go to the toilet, the library (bookcases in the back of the room), the computer, or to another student for help. These rules, she tells, are so that students can concentrate on their work and be ready for their classes. During classes she is in closer proximity to, and direct interaction with, students around their academic work. She is central in the interaction, leading students through their assignments, having them show that they have done the assigned work, and occasionally checking for evidence of student learning, or "getting what they are supposed to." Her table is understood as a special place for a specific kind of interaction. (26)

There is a generalized pattern to the classes that cuts across subjects or the "recitations in." Mrs. Hoffman usually calls students of a particular grade to class and the students sit in the chairs facing her. Sometimes students will individually approach the table, anticipating their class and stand waiting for her to authorize them to sit down. Once seated at the table, Mrs. Hoffman usually returns the previous day's assignment, quiz, or test that is invariably from a standardized textbook series. She has graded these papers, and students immediately look for their scores on the assignment or test. Mrs. Hoffman has an implied minimal standard of around 85% for passing these assignments, quizzes, or tests. As she returns these, she *always* points out the missed questions or problems, even if it is in a very brief remark (e.g., "You missed a couple. Look them over"). However, Mrs. Hoffman rarely tells students *in class* of the inadequacy of their work. She usually tells them well before class—publicly, in front of the entire school—in order to give the student the chance to correctly complete it. If she determines that the student has failed miserably, Mrs. Hoffman will hold a special class for the individual student for remediation. Otherwise, this opening sequence of the class involves mild praise for successful completion of student work. By doing so, Mrs. Hoffman reinforces her evaluative authority over the students in a close, face-to-face setting. (27)

After this opening sequence, Mrs. Hoffman declares that it is time to proceed to the next chapter, unit, or lesson in the textbook at hand. This sequence involves Mrs. Hoffman directing a student to read aloud the introduction of the new material. In the case of reading, the first classes in the morning, she directs students to the next story in the basal reader. She will ask the students to start the story, and have them read aloud, in round-robin fashion with students alternating paragraphs, until she determines their time is up. She directs students to complete the reading and points out "Comprehension Questions" at the end of the basal story chapter they are to answer in writing. In other subjects, Mrs. Hoffman then directs a student to read the directions for the textbook/workbook assignment, and then asks that student or another to read aloud through the sample exercises. Mrs. Hoffman then directs them to complete the assignment for the following day's class. Mrs. Hoffman writes down in her red plan book the lesson or chapter that is to be completed and the assignment or exercise to be completed. (28)

One Afternoon's Fifth Grade Math Class

To give some sense of the form of this instruction, the following excerpt of the fifth grade math from one afternoon's math classes is presented. Although Kimberly is the only fifth grader, Mrs. Hoffman still refers to Kimberly classes as "the fifth grade." The fifth grade math class took place (29) on what I consider a typical day and a typical series of classes (see Table 4). There are 25 classes on this day, and Kimberly's math class takes place at 1:15 in the afternoon.

(30)   Mathematics classes follow the same pattern described above. Students understand that they are to work quietly and independently on their assignments, hand those assignments in to the teacher, come to class where Mrs. Hoffman informs the students of the acceptability of an assignment or test, be directed to proceed into the next assignment, have students read aloud directions and examples, and then return to one's desk in order to complete and "get through."

(31)   It is important to note that the mathematics curriculum for Bighand School is organized around two separate and very different math textbook series, Scott/Foresman & Co. and Saxon Publishing. Those of Scott/Foresman can be characterized as mainstream mathematics that has some conceptual orientation. Saxon is characterized by isolated skills that recur, or "spiral," within separate lessons or units. The emphasis in Saxon math is on repeated exercise or drill of skills. Mrs. Hoffman added the Saxon series the previous year at the urging of the county superintendent, because he said ambiguously that math was "becoming important." In effect, Bighand students are progressing through two different math programs simultaneously. And even though she has some reservations about Saxon Math, she views it as ultimately helpful in student achievement. Math

TABLE 4
Classes for Wednesday, February 17, 1999

Time	Duration (Minutes)	Subject	Grade/Student
8:36 a.m.	3	Reading	1st grade —Samuel
8:40	8	Reading	2nd grade —Christine alone
8:49	9	Reading	2nd grade —David, Richard
8:59	10	Reading	6th grade
9:10	16	Reading	8th grade
9:37	22	Spelling	2nd grade
10:45	2	English	6th grade
10:47	6	English	1st grade
10:54	5	English	6th grade
11:05	7	English	8th grade
12:05 p.m.	4	Reading	1st grade
12:10	9	Reading	2nd grade —David, Richard
12:21	8	Reading	2nd grade —Christine alone
12:35	7	Reading	2nd grade —David, Richard cont'd
12:47	7	Math	2nd grade
1:01	6	Math	8th grade
1:15	5	Math	5th grade
1:21	2	Math	6th grade
1:25	4	Math	1st grade
1:35	10	Social Studies	2nd grade
2:00	8	Social Studies	6th grade
2:15	7	Social studies	1st grade
2:24	12	Science	8th grade
2:38	8	Science	6th grade
2:48	5	Science	5th grade

classes are thus geared around getting through these two series. These textbooks are not used in complementary fashion around particular mathematical concepts or as thematic resources, but as ends in themselves. This coordinates with her working philosophy of the benefit of quantity or saturation, that more academic work will lead to more learning, or what she off-handedly calls "piling it on."

Fifth grade math begins with Mrs. Hoffman calling Kimberly to the table. Standing about four and a half feet tall, Kimberly has a lanky, rail-thin preadolescent figure, with hands, feet, and a toothy smile that look disproportionately large for her body. When she carries her books or a backpack, it is as if she is towing a third of her own weight. This contrasts with her deep, nasal voice that is eerily reminiscent of her mother's. As Kimberly sits down, Mrs. Hoffman hands her a test she took yesterday and simply starts the class by saying: "Page 253 for tomorrow. And that is more fractions, and you have fractions on your test. Alright?" Kimberly responds, "OK." (32)

After Mrs. Hoffman hands Kimberly the test she completed yesterday, she does not point out Kimberly's grade (a 100). She does notice, however, that Kimberly looks straight for the grade, marked in red at the top of the page. Kimberly cracks a small smile of satisfaction as she sees this. "Page 253" refers to Kimberly's Scott/Foresman math textbook and the exercises on multiplication of fractions for the next day. She merely assumes that Kimberly knows what she needs to do. After sharply admonishing Richard, Mrs. Hoffman moves right on to the Saxon math: (33)

MH: [to Richard] What did I say to do?! I won't say it again. Please! Richard sit down in your seat. I am going to have to write a note to mom if I do not see something happening here very soon. I am going to have to send home a report today. [to Kimberly] Simplifying decimal numbers. What does [your book] say? Go ahead and read that. Mine says the same.

K: [Reading from her textbook, indicated in italics] *When we write numbers, we should write them in the simplest form. When we simplify a number, we change the form of the number, but we do not change the value of the number. We learned how to simplify fractions by reducing. We can often simply. [restarts] We can often simplify decimal fractions as well.*

MH: [correcting] *numbers as well*

K: *numbers as well. We simplify decimal numbers by removing unnecessary zeros. We will explain this by simplifying, twenty* ahh, *twenty-hundredths.*

MH: Right.

K: *The decimal number twenty-hundredths has a 2 in the tenth's place and a 0 in the hundredths' place. The zeros in the hundredths' place mean no hundredths. If we remove the zero from twenty-hundredths, we get two-tenths. The number two-tenths also has a 2 in the tenths place and 'no hundredths.' Thu,*

MH: [correcting] *Thus*

K: *Thus twenty hundredths . . .*

MH: Means "however." *Twenty hundredths equals*

K: *Twenty-hundredths equals two-tenths.*

MH: Even though we say it differently.

K: *That we say that twenty-hundredths simplifies to two-tenths. We can remove zeroes from the front of the whole numbers and from the back of the decimals numbers. We remove zeroes until we come back to a digit that is not a zero or until we come to a decimal point. Below we have simplified* [printed in book as 02.0100, 20.0, and 0.200] *zero 2 and one-hundred, twenty and zero tenths* and *2 thousandths*

MH: *Two-hundred thousandths by removing*

K: *by removing the unnecessary zeros.*

MH: OK. *Simplify each decimal number* in problems A through B. Do you have that?

K: Uh.

MH: Right there (pointing in K's book). These seem to be the same [their books]. OK so what are we going to change this to? Three and

K: Three and two tenths.

MH: [Speaks quietly to herself as she writes down the pages of this assignment in her planbook for documentation of Kimberly's math work.]

MH: Alright. Sixth graders.

(34)   This constitutes a fifth grade math class, "Simplifying Decimal Numbers" on this particular day. Mrs. Hoffman directs Kimberly to read the definitions and description of the Saxon math "lesson." This lesson has no connection to the multiplication of fractions in Kimberly's Scott/Foresman textbook and test. She reads through orally the first of the four sample problems, to the satisfaction of Mrs. Hoffman ("Three and two tenths"). She simply ends by marking in her planbook Kimberly's Saxon math assignment and calls the sixth graders up for their math class. Kimberly returns immediately to her desk and quietly sets to work on her assignment. This class took around 5 minutes.

The Recitation as a Functional Tradition

(35)   The old country school recitation involved the teacher calling upon individual and grade level groups of students (Cuban, 1994; Theobald, 1995). They often stood or sat on a hard bench. This instruction involved little more than the teacher lecturing and students reciting memorized passages or orally answering a series of questions as directed by the teacher's textbook guide (Thayer, 1928). Student learning was determined through the accuracy of the recitation and appropriateness of responses to teacher questions. Students were then introduced to the next topic and their assignment in the textbook. They were expected to work quietly and individually on their preparations for recitations.

(36)   Here in Bighand School, it is possible to see the basic outline of this form of instruction. Most importantly, the textbook is still the unquestioned guide for curricular organization and student progress. Instead of orally quizzing students on whether they can recite a memorized text, or go through question-answer routines, Mrs. Hoffman relies on written performance on lessons and tests for indicators of student learning. Like the old recitation, she uses the class to introduce sequential topics in, and keeps track of student progress through, textbooks. But the oral component involves not memorization or right-answer responses, but supervised or guided reading of printed text that introduces the student(s) to the next topic or lesson. The oral component is front-loaded in Mrs. Hoffman's scheme, to see if students understand what they are supposed to do, not what they have done, as represented in Kimberly' math class.

(37)   What is striking about this form of instruction is its sheer utility and refined functionality for this one-teacher setting, apropos Mrs. Hoffman's goal of getting students through a textbook-based curriculum. It is a convention that helps Mrs. Hoffman organize her work with students and helps them to organize their own work. It requires a good deal of self-discipline on the part of the student. "Doing school" for the students means continually keeping up with one's work, knowing that you will face the teacher regularly, and understanding that neither is a choice. It is traditional in the sense that is presents itself as common sense, or just the way things are done. When I asked Mrs. Hoffman if she had considered organizing her curriculum in ways other than with classes like these, she shrugged her shoulders and looked almost dumbfounded by the question. "I mean," she asked, "what other way can I do it?" It is the most sensible way she can conceive of her instruction.

Tempering Critique

(38)   It is easy for reform-minded educators, urban and rural alike, to criticize this form of pedagogy. It is intellectually conservative, textbook-based, and teacher-controlled. Student interest and intention are epiphenomenal pedagogical concerns. It is possible to claim that it is not academically demanding and does not press students for "higher order thinking." It embodies a concept of knowledge that it is created elsewhere by experts and codified in textbooks, implying a passive theory of student learning. It does not involve any "place-based curriculum" that many rural school reformers claim is the inherent value or potential of rural schools (Theobald & Nachtigal, 1995). The language of curriculum development and reform of the last decade, such as "constructivism," does not emerge in the talk of the teacher, contracted principal, or county superintendent. Students do not interact with each other around their assignments. There are no sustained common projects in which students of varying age levels engage. Academic work is composed entirely of discrete assignments in content areas that have no connection to one another. And, it is easy to name the usage of classes as expedient classroom management rather than some product of Mrs. Hoffman's professional reflection.

(39)   Any analysis of schooling cannot simply avoid possible criticisms such as these, especially as reformers seek to link size to school effectiveness. In seeking to understand the coherence and

sensibility of this kind of practice, I find that there are important things to consider before leaping to a deficit critique. First, I believe this pedagogy is quite consonant with the conservative nature of teaching in public schooling generally, and in graded schools with centralized curricula (e.g., Elmore, Peterson, & McCarthey, 1996). Conservative, textbook-centered instruction is hardly the exclusive possession of small country schools. The traditions of conservative teaching generally would seem to influence Mrs. Hoffman's pedagogy (see Cohen, 1988). More importantly, a culturally sensitive analysis would take into account the larger rural context of the school and Mrs. Hoffman's practice and it to this that I now turn.

Community Values as Context of Pedagogy

Context or setting (40)

The structure of instruction at Bighand School is infused with community values, including respect for and assent to adult authority (i.e., the teacher as manager and academic organizer), independence, hard work, following through, and self-discipline (i.e., completing your work, no matter what you think of it). These values could be described as rural or agricultural, and they are frequently referred to as a "work ethic" by community members and parents. For instance, Mary and Deborah's father, Tom, describes the differences between Bighand School and "town schools" this way:

> Well, I think the work ethic is different, especially in a rural school like this because you're in a farming community and, you know, when you farm, you've got to enjoy the work because there is no money in it. The rewards are not financial. And I think the kids see this, and it helps them for a little bit better work ethic because it makes them realize that you have to do something to earn something. Now, all of the kids in this school do not come from farm families, but they see it.

And when reflecting upon the relationship between his children's experience at Bighand School, farm life, and the values of "following through" and "hard work," Tom avers:

> Well, I mean, they're living in it. They're living in the middle of it. They have come to accept the fact that there are tractors in the spring of the year and it's a very busy time and things are happening very quickly. And they come to realize during the fall, during the harvest season, that the combines are rolling, and you know, at ten, eleven, twelve o'clock at night. The guys across the road are combining. There are trucks on the road all of the time. They know it is another busy time of the year. They've come to realize that this is how they get paid. If they had two very critical times of the year and that sets the basis for their yearly wages. *You got to get the crop in the ground and you've got to get it out* (emphasis added). And I think that concept carries over to the school and [Mrs. Hoffman] understands this.

It is not simply the case that the adult community members, school board, and parents view school as "instilling" these values. For them, the school does do that. But, from a cultural point of view, children's socialization into these values is intertwined with larger community and parental concerns. These include, in ascending order of abstraction, secondary school success, suspicion of youth culture, and symbolic defense of community and a way of life.

(41)

Secondary School Success

From my conversations and interviews with school board members and especially parents, what they want from school seems no different than what most parents want for their children: that school somehow prepare them for life. But more immediately, they are concerned that the school prepare children to cope with life in large, graded middle and secondary schools to which their children will inevitably enroll. There is a pervasive lore in the Bighand community that graduates of the school do very well in secondary school. The families who have students in high school who are graduates of Bighand, and those who have transferred to middle school, regularly indicate that their children are "ahead" and know how to do school work. The county superintendent reports that Bighand students' scores for the Iowa Test of Basis Skills "are well above the median" for Class One schools in the county and that its "students never become an academic problem." The superintendent of Riverview Schools, himself a Class One school graduate, is effusive about the small schools that are affiliated with his district: "The kids from the one-room, Class One schools we get do an outstanding job. We have had no problems with kids from the Class Ones." The superintendent of Sparta-Johnville Schools, who considers Bighand a revenue drain from his district, grudgingly admits that Bighand's graduates are successful high school students. This

(42)

information and these sentiments circulate in the Bighand community. For the adults and parents in the community, one learns to be a good student by the standards of middle and secondary town school organization.

(43)   The habits of self-discipline and following through on one's work learned at Bighand would seem to help one get through middle and secondary school and be a good student. In the large graded middle and secondary, students have little consistent and close contact with their teachers like they do in Bighand and this creates one of the bumpy points of transition for students. For instance, Mary and Deborah's big sister Kayla, a graduate of Bighand and now a sophomore at Riverview High School, says that one of the hardest things in the transition to high school is the lack of regular personal contact with her teachers. She was perplexed about how she had to make appointments with the teachers, sometimes days in advance, about what were for her immediate concerns (e.g., how to complete a particular assignment). Yet, ironically, she was able to cope with this predicament precisely because she felt that she had learned to stick with her work and not give up in frustration. Her mother, Julie, describes how she sees the organization of Bighand school helping Kayla:

> At the school there is more than one grade that the teacher has to work with and so she can't just devote the attention to all of them on an assignment and make sure that they do it. [Students] do have to do some planning and organization and some self-management skills, which again is important when you get older. And, of course, they have to be more self-motivated to complete their work on their own. And they don't . . . well just from being in the public city schools, I know that isn't the way it is. The teacher really organizes your day for you . . . [Kayla] had to be responsible to get her work done and she had to organize what she was going to do and when. She did not get distracted.

Troublesome Youth Culture

(44)   A persistent theme running through my conversations and interviews with parents is their distrust of "youth culture." This distrust seems to grow from a mixture of media images and personal knowledge of kids who have gotten into trouble in and out of school. One evening I had dinner at a Riverview diner with the Bighand Neighborhood Club. It is an informal descendent of the old agricultural extension women's club, now composed of the "young mothers" (those with school-age children and younger). The dominant topic of our conversation was their very real anxiety about the sexualized atmosphere of schools, in the way girls dress and what they sense to be sexual activity among younger and younger girls. They lament what they view as a "lack of basic values," a skyrocketing teenage pregnancy rate, and a fear of loss of control over their own children to a decadent youth culture.

(45)   Schooling at Bighand offers two things to parents who are concerned about this. For one, it offers separation from, and postponement of entry into, the youth culture they see as troublesome. More importantly, they view life at the school, which means life with recitations, as providing their children with a small scale schooling experience that helps them learn to get along with others and the self-discipline to resist a troublesome youth culture and avoid, as Molly's mother said, "leaning toward trouble." That is, the orderly, quiet atmosphere of the school, required of a recitation-based curriculum, and the self-discipline required to succeed in Mrs. Hoffman's system, helps students to cope with the pressures of the youth culture they will inevitably encounter.

(46)   Loretta's mother is clear about what she sees as the "social benefits" of Bighand School. As noted, Loretta transferred in the middle of her sixth grade year, after getting into discipline trouble at the elementary school in Sparta. Nancy was deeply concerned about Loretta's peers as a bad influence and that Loretta was becoming "a bad girl." She was worried about the preoccupations of early adolescent culture and its corrosive values. When I asked Nancy to describe the distinction she saw between Bighand School and Sparta Middle School (from which Loretta transferred) and what kids learn there, she responded emotionally that children at Bighand are:

> much less self-absorbed, I would say, much less preoccupied with how they look. I mean, I can just think of, say the girls here, they probably have chores . . . Where city kids, they go home from school, and they read Teen Magazine or Young Miss and watch a lot of television and are just much more caught up with what's popular rather than just functioning of life. A big difference. And with that I think the country kids are a lot kinder. Just the way, and I'm not trying to make it sound like they're Amish or anything, but I think

they do just live a different life and just have more kindness, and you learn to be kinder and maybe stay out of trouble. And the kids [at Bighand] have to get their work done or else.

Defending Community and a Way of Life

A capacity for students to cope with youth culture and the community's confidence in their sec-   (47)
ondary school success, provided by the curriculum and instruction of Bighand School and epito-
mized by the "class," take on further symbolic meaning in this country school. The late 1990s has
presented rural America, and rural Nebraska in particular, with another farm crisis. Commodity
prices have bottomed out. 1998 in particular saw a widespread and rapid new wave of consolidation of small family farms into bigger farms and bigger agribusiness entities (Drabenstott, 1999).
This economic trend has been underway for some time, but the current rapidity of consolidation is
"producing [social] geographic shifts and dramatically changing agriculture's linkages to local communities" (Drabenstott, 1999, p. 71). Consequently, rural farming communities are experiencing
more intensely a sense of social and economic siege. Bighand's school board members repeatedly
complain that the State continues to add confusing rules and regulations for the school to follow
and that the neighboring school districts, particularly Sparta-Johnville, want them to close down
to appropriate their property tax revenues for school funding. Even their own state senator, who
is understood as a pro-farm/pro-rural politician and well liked in the Bighand community, does
not hide his disdain for small country schools nor his belief in school consolidation. As the school
board secretary said during a school board meeting on a dreary February night, "they want to
make it hard for us to hang on."

There seems to be an air of resignation in the Bighand community that the family farm and the   (48)
small farming community are on the wane, never to recover. In this subtly shared sentiment, only
those big and strong enough can, and ought, to survive. This seems representative of a general
sentiment in the state. Many farmers in the state seem to accept as inevitable the passing of the
family farm and, with it, "a way of life" (Hassebrook, personal communication, April 7, 1999).

Yet, the Bighand community is "hanging on" to its school at a time when it would be just as   (49)
easy for it to close and send its children to the affiliated school districts. Some families in the community already do this precisely because their children will ultimately attend and finish school in
these districts and want them acclimated to the schools. But for those who continue to put their
children at Bighand, this that can be viewed as a way to inculcate some values they hold dear, that
are country, rural or agricultural—the way of life that is under siege and on the wane. These values
appear to be what they want their kids to have as they enter large graded middle and secondary
schools, over which they feel they have no influence or control and is composed of youth culture
of which they are deeply suspicious. Country schooling, in this community and at this school, conceivably symbolizes a defense of the community and a way of life from social and economic siege.

When viewed against these larger sociocultural and economic features, the values of indepen-   (50)
dence, hard work, following through, and self-discipline, take on a deeper hue. Moreover, the primary role of modern recitation instruction of socializing children into these also takes on a deeper
hue. It is easy to criticize school practices when viewed free from culture, history and contemporary politics and economics.

Concluding Thoughts

Interpretation

It has been my goal to offer a more complicated picture of the modern appearance of the recita-   (51)
tion in the form of "classes" at a single one-teacher school. In that they seem consonant with the
old country school recitation and with the general forms of conservative instruction in the U.S., it
is not hard to theorize that a similar version of "classes," as I observed them during the 1998-1999
academic year, are part of a more general phenomenon in small country schools (see Muse et. al,
1998). Serious reform involving country schools must take into consideration the larger cultural
context of rural one-teacher schools generally and the specific communities in which they exist.
Their matrices of community values and desires may lead community members and their educators
to rationally resist changes that they sense may undermine what their schools do for their children
and how they may defend their ways of life.

References

Barker, R., & Gump, P. (1964). *Big school, small school: High school size and student behavior.* Stanford CA: Stanford University Press.

Cohen, D. K. (1988). Teaching practice: Plus ça change . . . In P. W. Jackson (Ed.), *Contributing to educational change: Perspectives on research and practice* (pp. 27–84). Berkeley, CA: McCutcheon.

Cuban, L. (1994). *How teachers taught: Constancy and change in American classrooms.* New York: Teachers College Press.

Darling-Hammond, L. (1997). *The right to learn: A blue-print for creating schools that work.* San Francisco: Jossey-Bass.

DeWalt, M. (1997). *One-room school: Current trend in public and private education* (Research Report). Rock Hill, SC: Winthrop University.

Drabenstott, M. (1999, 1st Quarter). Consolidation in U.S. agriculture: The new rural landscape and public policy. *Federal Reserve Bank of Kansas City Economic Review.*

Elmore, R. F. (1996). Getting down to scale with good educational practice. *Harvard Educational Review, 66*(1), 1–26.

Elmore, R. F., Peterson. P., & McCarthey, S. J. (1996). *Restructuring in the classroom: Teaching, learning, and school organization.* San Francisco: Jossey-Bass.

Erickson, F. (1986). Qualitative methods. In M. C. Wittrock (Ed.), *Handbook of research on teaching* (pp. 119–161). New York: Macmillan.

Fine, M., & Somerville, J. I. (Eds.). (1998). *Small schools, big imaginations: A creative look at urban public schools.* Chicago: Cross City Campaign for Urban School Reform.

Fowler, W. J. (1995). School size and student outcomes. *Advances in Educational Productivity, 5,* 3–36.

Geertz, C. (Ed.). (1973a). *Deep play: Notes on the Balinese cockfight.* New York: Basic Books.

Geertz, C. (Ed). (1973b). Religion as a cultural system. *The interpretation of cultures.* New York: Basic Books.

Geyer, J. (Producer/Director). (1995). *Last of the one-room schools.* Lincoln, NE: Nebraska Educational Television.

Howley, C. (1989). Synthesis of the effects of school and district size: What research says about achievement in small schools and school districts. *Journal of Rural and Small Schools, 4*(1), 2–12.

Lee, V., & Smith, J. B. (1997). High school size: Which works best, and for whom? *Education and Policy Analysis, 19*(3), 205–27.

Lee, V., Smith, J. B., & Croninger, R. G. (1995). Another look at restructuring high schools: More evidence that it improves student achievement, and insight into why. *Issues into restructuring schools.* Madison, WI: Center on Organization and Restructuring of Schools.

Leight, R. L., & Rhienhart, A. D. (1992). Revisiting Americana: One-room school in retrospect. *The Educational Forum, 56*(2), 135–151.

Lerner, A. F., & Loewe, F. (1959). *My Fair Lady* (1956 original Broadway cast recording). New York: Columbia Records.

Meier, D. (1995). *The power of their ideas: Lessons for America from a small school in Harlem.* Boston: Beacon Press.

Muse, I., Hite, S., Randall, V., & Jensen, A. (1998). One-teacher schools in America. *Teacher Educator, 33*(3), 141–149.

Peshkin, A. (1978/1994). *Growing up American: Schooling and the survival of community.* Prospect Heights, IL: Waveland Press.

Snyder, J., Lieberman, A., MacDonald, M. B., & Goodwin, A. L. (1992). *Makers of meaning in a learning-centered school: A case study of Central Park East 1 Elementary School.* New York: National Center for Restructuring Education, School and Teaching.

Thayer, V. (1928). *The passing of the recitation.* Boston: DC Heath.

Theobald, P. (1995). *Call school: Rural education in the Midwest to 1918.* Carbondale, IL: Southern Illinois University Press.

Theobald, P., & Nachtigal. P. (1995). Culture, community, and the promise of rural education. *Phi-Delta-Kappan, 77*(2), 132–35.

Narrative Research Designs

*P*eople live storied lives. They tell stories to share their lives with others and to provide their personal accounts about classrooms, schools, educational issues, and the settings in which they work. When people tell stories to researchers, they feel listened to, and their information brings researchers closer to the actual practice of education. Thus, stories reported in qualitative narrative research enrich the lives of both the researcher and the participant. This chapter defines narrative research, identifies when you use it, assesses the key characteristics of it, and advances the steps in conducting and evaluating this design.

By the end of this chapter, you should be able to:

◆ Describe narrative research, and describe when to use it, and how it developed.
◆ Identify the types of narrative designs.
◆ Describe the key characteristics of narrative designs.
◆ Identify some potential ethical issues in gathering stories.
◆ Understand the steps used in conducting narrative research.
◆ List criteria for evaluating a narrative study.

Maria chooses a narrative design for her research project studying the possession of weapons by high school students. Maria's teacher friend, Millie, has a story to tell about how she encountered a student in the high school who was hiding a weapon in his locker. Maria studies this question: "What is the story of a teacher who found a student hiding a weapon in her high school?" Maria interviews Millie and listens to her stories about her experiences with the student, with other teachers, and with the school principal. The story falls into an easy chronology from the initial incident to the follow-up discussions. To make the story as accurate as possible, Maria collaborates with Millie in writing the story, and she shares the written report as it unfolds. Maria engages in narrative research.

WHAT IS NARRATIVE RESEARCH, WHEN DO YOU USE IT, AND HOW DID IT DEVELOP?

The term *narrative* comes from the verb "to narrate" or "to tell (as a story) in detail" (Ehrlich, Flexner, Carruth, & Hawkins, 1980, p. 442). In **narrative research designs**, researchers describe the lives of individuals, collect and tell stories about people's lives, and write narratives of individual experiences (Connelly & Clandinin, 1990). As a distinct form of qualitative research, a narrative typically focuses on studying a single person, gathering data through the collection of stories, reporting individual experiences, and discussing the meaning of those experiences for the individual. With recent popularity, national research conferences have devoted sessions and papers to it, and educational journals have published stories reported by teachers, students, and other educators. New books are now available from publishers that provide essential information about the process of conducting this form of qualitative inquiry.

When Do You Use Narrative Research?

You use narrative research when you have individuals willing to tell their stories and you want to report their stories. For educators looking for personal experiences in actual school settings, narrative research offers practical, specific insights. By conducting narrative studies, researchers establish a close bond with the participants. This may help reduce a commonly held perception by practitioners in the field that research is distinct from practice and has little direct application. Additionally, for participants in a study, sharing their stories may make them feel that their stories are important and that they are heard. When they tell a story, it helps them understand topics that they need to process (McEwan & Egan, 1995). Telling stories is a natural part of life, and individuals all have stories about their experiences to tell others. In this way, narrative research captures an everyday, normal form of data that is familiar to individuals.

You use narrative research when the stories told to you follow a chronology of events. Narrative research is a literary form of qualitative research with strong ties to literature, and it provides a qualitative approach in which you can write in a persuasive, literary form. It focuses on the microanalytic picture—individual stories—rather than the broader picture of cultural norms, as in ethnography, or abstract theories, as in grounded theory research. As an example of this micropicture, consider the case of Ms. Meyer, who had two children in her fifth- and sixth-grade class write stories about their personal lives. Anthony, a 9-year-old who considered himself an inventor and writer, kept a scientific journal of his discoveries and wrote an expressive piece about his grandmother. Anita, an 11-year-old, wrote about the good times she had in a swimming pool, learning to play kickball, and being able to succeed at something (McCarthey, 1994).

How Did Narrative Research Develop?

Despite substantial interest in narrative research, its methods are still developing, and it is infrequently discussed in the literature (Errante, 2000). This has led to little agreement about its form. The "narrative turn," as Riessman (1993) called it, embraces all of the human sciences, so that this form of research is not the providence of any specific field of study. Writers in literature, history, anthropology, sociology, sociolinguistics, and education all lay claim to narrative and have developed discipline-specific procedures. Like the art and science of portraiture discussed recently in the social sciences, this design involves drawing portraits of individuals and documenting their voices and their visions within a social and cultural context (Lawrence-Lightfoot & Davis, 1997).

However, a comprehensive overview of this design of research in education emerged in 1990. Educators D. Jean Clandinin and Michael Connelly provided the first overview of narrative research for the field of education. In their informative, classic article, "Stories of Experience and Narrative Inquiry," published in the *Educational Researcher* (Connelly & Clandinin, 1990), they cited many social science applications of narrative, elaborated on the process of collecting narrative fieldnotes, and discussed the writing and structure of a narrative study. This article expanded their earlier discussion about narrative within the context of teaching and learning in classrooms (Connelly & Clandinin, 1988). More recently, these two authors expounded their ideas in a book titled *Narrative Inquiry* (Clandinin & Connelly, 2000), which openly espoused "what narrative researchers do" (p. 48).

Within the field of education, several trends influenced the development of narrative research. Cortazzi (1993) suggested three factors. First, there is currently an increased emphasis on teacher reflection. Second, more emphasis is being placed on teachers' knowledge—what they know, how they think, how they develop professionally, and how they make decisions in the classroom. Third, educators seek to bring teachers' voices to the forefront by empowering teachers to talk about their experiences. For example, "Our Own Stories," reported by Meyer (1996), is a collection of stories about teachers sharing their experiences, whether they are sitting in the teachers' lounge at noon or after school. McEwan and Egan (1995) provided collections of stories about educators as teachers and curriculum developers. For women in general, as well as for female teachers, their stories to children, to adolescent girls, and to their own female associates often take on a feminine repertoire to serve their female audiences (Degh, 1995). Hearing these stories has encouraged educational studies using the narrative approach. In fact, within education a special interest group in AERA has been formed to create an ongoing discussion about narrative research.

A growing number of interdisciplinary social scientists outside education have offered procedural guidance for narrative reports as a form of qualitative research (e.g., see the psychologists Lieblich, Tuval-Mashiach, & Zilber, 1998; the sociologist Cortazzi, 1993; and Riessman, 1993). Interdisciplinary efforts at narrative research have also been encouraged by the *Narrative Study of Lives* annual series that began in 1993 (e.g., Josselson & Lieblich, 1993).

WHAT ARE THE TYPES OF NARRATIVE DESIGNS?

Narrative research assumes multiple forms. If you plan to conduct a narrative study, you need to consider what *type* of narrative study to conduct. Narrative research is an overarching category for a variety of research practices (see Casey, 1995/1996), as shown in Figure 15.1. For individuals planning a narrative study, each type of narrative provides a structure for conducting the study and ready references for how to conduct the project that faculty, journal reviewers, and book publishers will recognize. For those reading narrative studies, it is less important to know what *type* of narrative is being used and more important to recognize the essential *characteristics* of the types. The five questions discussed in the following subsections are helpful in determining your type of narrative study.

FIGURE 15.1

Examples of Types of Narrative Research Forms

- Autobiographies
- Biographies
- Life writing
- Personal accounts
- Personal narratives
- Narrative interviews

- Personal documents
- Documents of life
- Life stories and life histories
- Oral histories
- Ethnohistories
- Ethnobiographies

- Autoethnographies
- Ethnopsychologies
- Person-centered ethnographies
- Popular memories
- Latin American *testimonios*
- Polish memoirs

Source: Adapted from Casey, 1995/1996.

Who Writes or Records the Story?

Determining who will write and record the individual's story is a basic distinction in narrative research. A **biography** is a form of narrative study in which the researcher writes and records the experiences of another person's life. Typically, researchers construct biographies from records and archives (Angrosino, 1989), although researchers sometimes use other sources of information, such as interviews and photographs. In an **autobiography**, the individual who is the subject of the study writes the account. Although not a popular approach, you can find reports of autobiographical accounts of teachers as professionals (Connelly & Clandinin, 1990).

How Much of a Life Is Recorded and Presented?

This question introduces a second distinction among narrative studies. In anthropology, numerous examples exist of stories of an individual's entire life. A **life history** is a narrative story of the entire life experiences of a person. Anthropologists, for example, engage in life history research to learn about an individual's life within the context of a culture-sharing group. Often the focus includes turning points or significant events in the life of an individual (Angrosino, 1989). However, in education, narrative studies typically do not involve the account of an entire life but instead focus on an episode or single event in the individual's life. A **personal experience story** is a narrative study of an individual's personal experience found in single or multiple episodes, private situations, or communal folklore (Denzin, 1989). Clandinin and Connelly (2000) broadened the personal experience story to be both personal and social, and conveyed this stance as the essence of the experiences reported about teachers and teaching in schools.

Who Provides the Story?

A third approach for identifying the type of narrative is to examine closely who provides the story. This factor is especially relevant in education, where types of educators or learners have been the focus of many narrative studies. For example, **teachers' stories** are personal accounts by teachers of their own personal classroom experiences. As a popular form of narrative in education, researchers report teachers' stories to capture the lives of teachers as professionals and to examine learning in classrooms (e.g., Connelly & Clandinin, 1988). Other narrative studies focus on students in the classroom. In children's stories, narrative researchers ask the children in classrooms to present orally or in writing their own stories about their learning experiences (e.g., Ollerenshaw, 1998).

Many different individuals in educational settings can provide stories, such as administrators, school board members, custodians, food service workers, and other educational personnel.

Is a Theoretical Lens Being Used?

Another question that shapes the character of a narrative is whether and to what extent the researcher uses a theoretical lens in developing the narrative. A **theoretical lens** in narrative research is a guiding perspective or ideology that provides structure for advocating for groups or individuals in the written report. This lens may be to advocate for Latin Americans using *testimonios,* reporting the stories of women using a feminist lens (e.g., Personal Narratives Group, 1989), or collecting the stories of marginalized individuals. In all of these examples, the narrative researcher provides a voice for seldom-heard individuals in educational research.

Can Narrative Forms Be Combined?

In a narrative, it is possible to have the different elements listed above combined in the study. For example, a narrative study may be biographical because researchers write and report it about a participant in a study. This same study may focus on a personal study of a teacher. It may also address an event in the life of a teacher, such as a dismissal from a school (Huber & Whelan, 1999), resulting in a partial life story, or a personal narrative. In addition, if this individual is a woman, a researcher might use a theoretical lens to examine power and control issues in the school. This could lead to a feminist narrative. The final resulting narrative thus could be a combination of different elements: a biography, a personal story, a teacher's story, and a feminist perspective.

Given the many types of narrative studies, what type of narrative research should Maria conduct? As she gathers stories from Millie about her encounter with the student, (a) does Maria or Millie write the story? (b) Is Maria reporting on an entire life or a specific episode? (c) Who provides the story to Maria? (d) Should Maria advocate for weapon control in the school through her narrative study? Answer each of these questions and think through your rationale for answering them. What would you call Maria's narrative approach as she writes about it in her research study? She would probably use a personal narrative approach. How would you answer each of the questions above to arrive at this approach?

WHAT ARE THE KEY CHARACTERISTICS OF NARRATIVE DESIGNS?

Despite the many forms of narrative inquiry, they share several common characteristics. Before reviewing the key characteristics, we discuss them in general terms and relate them to the qualitative characteristics of research.

As shown in Table 15.1, narrative researchers explore an educational research problem by understanding the experiences of an individual. As in most qualitative research, the literature review plays a minor role, especially in directing the research questions, and the inquirer emphasizes the importance of learning from participants in a setting. This learning occurs through stories told by individuals, such as teachers or students. The stories constitute the data, and the researcher typically gathers it through interviews or informal conversations. These stories, called *field texts* (Clandinin &

TABLE 15.1

The Research Process, Qualitative Characteristics, and Narrative Research Characteristics

The Research Process	Qualitative Characteristics	Narrative Research Characteristics
Identify a research problem	• A qualitative problem requires exploration and understanding.	• Seeks to understand and represent experiences through the stories individual(s) live and tell.
Review the literature	• The qualitative literature plays a minor role. • The qualitative literature justifies the research problem.	• Seeks to minimize the use of literature and focuses on the experiences of the individual(s).
Develop a purpose statement and research questions	• The qualitative purpose statement and research questions are broad and general. • The qualitative purpose statement and research questions seek participants' experiences.	• Seeks to explore the meaning of the individual's experiences as told through a story or stories.
Collect qualitative data	• Qualitative data collection is based on using protocols developed during the study. • Qualitative data collection involves gathering text or image data. • Qualitative data collection involves studying a small number of individuals or sites.	• Seeks to collect field texts that document the individual's story in his or her own words.
Analyze and interpret qualitative data	• Qualitative data analysis consists of text analysis. • Qualitative data analysis consists describing information and of developing themes. • Qualitative interpretations situate findings within larger meanings.	• Seeks to analyze the stories by retelling the individual's story. • Seeks to analyze the stories by identifying themes or categories of information. • Seeks to situate the story within its place or setting. • Seeks to analyze the story for chronological information about the individual's past, present, and future.
Write and evaluate a study	• Qualitative research reports use flexible and emerging structures and evaluation criteria. • Qualitative researchers take a reflexive and biased approach.	• Seeks to collaborate with the participant when writing the research study. • Seeks to write the study in a flexible storytelling mode. • Seeks to evaluate the study based on the depth, accuracy, persuasiveness, and realism of the account.

Connelly, 2000), provide the raw data for researchers to analyze as they retell the story based on narrative elements such as the problem, characters, setting, actions, and resolution (Ollerenshaw & Creswell, 2000). In this process, researchers narrate the story and often identify themes or categories that emerge. Thus, the qualitative data analysis may be both a description of the story and themes that emerge from it. In addition, the researcher often writes into the reconstituted story a chronology of events describing the individual's past, present, and future experiences lodged within specific settings or contexts. Throughout this process of collecting and analyzing data, the researcher collaborates with the participant by checking the story and negotiating the meaning of the database. In addition, the researcher may interweave his or her personal story into the final report.

This brief overview of the process highlights specific characteristics of research often found in narrative reports. As shown in Figure 15.2, seven major characteristics are central to narrative research:

◆ Individual experiences
◆ Chronology of the experiences
◆ Collecting individual stories
◆ Restorying
◆ Coding for themes
◆ Context or setting
◆ Collaborating with participants

Individual Experiences

In narrative research, the inquirer often studies a single individual. Narrative researchers focus on the experiences of one or more individuals. Although less frequent, researchers may study more than one individual (McCarthey, 1994).

In addition to the *study* of an individual, the researcher is most interested in *exploring the experiences* of that individual. For Clandinin and Connelly (2000), these **experiences** in narrative inquiry are both personal, what the individual experiences, and social, the individual interacting with others. This focus on experience draws on the philosophical thoughts of John Dewey, who saw that individual experience was a central lens for

---

FIGURE 15.2

Major Characteristics of Narrative Research

- **Experiences of an individual**—social and personal interactions
- **Chronology of experiences**—past, present, and future experiences
- **Life stories**—first-person, oral accounts of actions obtained through field texts (data)
- **Restorying** (or retelling or developing a metastory) from the field texts
- Coding the field texts for **themes or categories**
- Incorporating the **context or place** into the story or themes
- **Collaboration** between the researcher and the participants in the study, such as negotiating field texts

Source: Adapted from Clandinin & Connelly, 2000; Lieblich et al., 1998; Riessman, 1993.

understanding a person. One aspect of Dewey's thinking was to view experience as continuous (Clandinin & Connelly, 2000), where one experience led to another experience. Thus, narrative researchers focus on understanding individual history or past experiences and how it contributes to present and future experiences.

Chronology of the Experiences

Understanding the individual's past as well as the present and future is another key element in narrative research. Narrative researchers analyze and report a chronology of an individual's experiences. When researchers focus on understanding these experiences, they elicit information about a participant's past, present, and future. **Chronology** in narrative designs means that the researcher analyzes and writes about an individual life using a time sequence or chronology of events. Cortazzi (1993) suggested that the chronology of narrative research emphasizes a sequence, which sets narrative apart from other genres of research. For example, in a study about a teacher's use of computer technology in a high school classroom, the inquirer would include information about the teacher's introduction to computers, current computer use, and future goals and aspirations. The story reported by the researcher would include a discussion about the sequence of events for this teacher.

Collecting Individual Stories

To develop this chronological perspective of individual experiences, the narrative researcher asks the participant to tell a story (or stories) about his or her experiences. Narrative researchers place emphasis on collecting the stories told to them by individuals or gathered from a wide variety of field texts. These accounts might arise during informal group conversations or from one-on-one interviews. A **story in narrative research** is a first-person oral telling or retelling of an individual. Often these stories have a beginning, a middle, and an end. Similar to basic elements found in good novels, these aspects involve a predicament, conflict, or struggle; a protagonist or character; and a sequence with implied causality (a plot) during which the predicament is resolved in some fashion (Carter, 1993). In a more general sense, the story might include the elements typically found in novels, such as time, place, plot, and scene (Connelly & Clandinin, 1990). For those relating to narrative from a literary perspective, the sequence might be the development of the plot as it unfolds, the emergence of a crisis or turning point, and the conclusion or denouement. Narrative researchers hope to capture this story line as they listen to individuals tell their stories.

Narrative researchers collect stories from several data sources. **Field texts** represent information from different sources collected by researchers in a narrative design. Up to this point, our examples have illustrated collecting stories by using discussions, conversations, or interviews between a researcher and one individual. However, the stories might be autobiographical, with the researcher reflecting on his or her story and interweaving that story with those of others. Often the researcher's role in the inquiry process may be central, in which they find themselves in a "nested set of stories" (Clandinin & Connelly, 2000, p. 63). Journals are another form used for collecting stories, as are fieldnotes written by either the researcher or the participant. Letters provide useful data. These letters may be written back and forth between participants, between research collaborators, or between the researchers and participants (Clandinin & Connelly, 2000). Family stories, photographs, and memory boxes—collections of items that trigger our memories—are other forms used for collecting stories in narrative research.

Restorying

After individuals tell a story about their experiences, narrative researchers retell (or restory or remap) the story in their own words. They do this to provide order and sequence to a story that may have been told out of sequence. **Restorying** is the process in which the researcher gathers stories, analyzes them for key elements of the story (e.g., time, place, plot, and scene), and then rewrites the story to place it in a chronological sequence. When individuals tell a story, this sequence is often missing or not logically developed. By restorying, the researcher provides a chronological sequence and a causal link among ideas. There are several ways to restory the narrative.

Examine the transcript, shown in Table 15.2, from a narrative project addressing adolescent smoking behavior (Ollerenshaw & Creswell, 2000). This table displays the process of restorying interview data for a high school student who is attempting to quit smoking. The process involves three stages:

1. The researcher conducts the interview and transcribes the conversation from an audiotape. This transcription is shown in the first column as raw data.
2. Next the narrative researcher retranscribes the raw data by identifying the key elements of the story. This is shown in the second column. The key at the bottom of the table indicates the codes used by the researcher to identify the setting [s], characters [c], actions [a], problem [p], and resolution [r] in the student's transcript.
3. Finally, the narrative researcher restories the student's account by organizing the key codes into a sequence. The sequence presented in this passage is setting, characters, actions, problem, and resolution, although another narrative researcher might report these elements in another order. This restorying begins with the place (McDonald's), the characters (the student), and then the events (behaviors such as "shaky" and "hyper"). The researcher reworks the transcription to identify the elements of the story and restories the elements into a logical sequence of activities.

To clearly identify these elements, the researcher might organize them into a table similar to Table 15.3. This table describes five elements used in restorying (Ollerenshaw, 1998). The setting is the specific situation of the story, illustrated by such factors as time, locale, or year. The researcher may discuss characters in a story as archetypes or portray them through their personalities, behaviors, styles, or patterns. The actions are the movements of the individuals in the story, such as the specific thinking or behaving that occurs during the story. The problem represents the questions or concerns that arise during the story or the phenomena that need to be described or explained. The resolution is the outcome of addressing the problem: the answer to a question or the conclusion reached in the story. It may involve an explanation about what caused the character to change in the story.

The elements of setting, characters, actions, problem, and resolution illustrate only one example of the elements that narrative researchers look for as they restory an individual's experiences. They might also use the elements of the three-dimensional space narrative structure advanced by Clandinin and Connelly (2000). As shown in Table 15.4, the three dimensions of interaction, continuity, and situation create a "metaphorical" (p. 50) inquiry space that defines a narrative study. As researchers construct their story (either their own or someone else's), they would include information about the following:

◆ *Interaction:* the personal interaction based on an individual's feelings, hopes, reactions, and dispositions as well as the social interaction to include other people and their intentions, purposes, assumptions, and points of view

TABLE 15.2

Retranscribing and Restorying a Transcript

Transcription of Audiotape (Raw Data)	Retranscription by the Researcher*	Restory by the Researcher
Well, I know it wasn't the first time but I remember this one most vividly. Almost . . . about a year ago, I had been trying to quit and I hadn't smoked for about, I'd say about a month or more, I think I just didn't want to do it anymore. There was this guy that I liked at McDonald's, but he didn't like me, he liked my best friend. We all worked at McDonald's after school until close. Oh, wow, I had nicotine fits a lot. Sometimes you get shaky. You get really high, you know, just like you need to go get some fresh air. You need to get a cigarette, just like, you know, you just get really hyper and start bouncing off the walls. I calmed down after a little bit, but . . . I was tempted to start again during the month I quit. Uhm, well my friends would be smoking outside by the tree, so it was like you know, you look at it and you're just like, it kind of looks like a cupcake or something good, you know. Just like you want, but then they ask you, "Hey, do you want to drive or something?" Just say, "No." So I'm trying to quit but I can't do it. They understand but then it's just like, "Okay. I gotta go home now" and I get to go to bed. Sometimes I just go back inside the school cause you can't smoke inside there so . . . I might have slipped maybe one or two but I mean I was upset tense. This guy I liked started going out with my best friend and so then I got really upset and started just smoking again just like you know. That's the one that I really remember . . . me and her were best friends no more.	about a year ago, [s] I [c] had been trying to quit and I hadn't smoked for about, I just didn't want to do it anymore [p] was this guy [c], that I liked [a] at McDonald's [s], but he didn't like me, he liked my best friend [c]. I had nicotine fits [a] a lot. You get shaky [a]. You get really high [a] You need to go get some fresh air. You need to get a cigarette [a]. You just get really hyper and start bouncing off the walls [a]. I calmed down after a little bit [a], friends [c] would be smoking outside by the tree [s]. It looks like a cupcake or something good [a]. Hey, do you want to drive or something? [a] "No. I'm trying to quit [a]." I'd go to bed [a]. Sometimes I just go back inside the school [s] cause you can't smoke inside there, [a] I slipped maybe one or two but [a], I was upset, tense [a]. This guy I liked started going out with my best friend [a]. I got really upset and started just smoking again [a]. That's the one that I really remember . . . me and her were best friends no more [r].	• A year ago, I worked at McDonald's and I didn't buy cigarettes for about a month. • I had nicotine fits. • I got shaky. • I got high. • I got hyper. • I started bouncing off the walls. • I needed air. • I went outside. • Friends were smoking by the tree. • I wanted a cigarette because they looked good. • I wanted to drive. • I went inside the school. • I went home to bed. • I calmed down. • The guy I liked from McDonald's started dating my friend. • I got upset and tense. • I slipped one or two cigarettes. • I started smoking again. • We're not friends any more.

*Key to codes in the retranscription: setting [s], characters [c], actions [a], problem [p], and resolution [r].

Source: Adapted from Ollerenshaw & Creswell, 2000.

TABLE 15.3				
Organizing the Story Elements into the Problem Solution Narrative Structure				
Setting	**Characters**	**Actions**	**Problem**	**Resolution**
Context, environment, conditions, place, time, locale, year, and era	Individuals in the story described as archetypes, personalities, their behaviors, style, and patterns	Movements of individuals through the story illustrating the character's thinking or behaviors	Questions to be answered or phenomena to be described or explained	Answers to questions and explanations about what caused the character to change.

Source: Adapted from Ollerenshaw, 1998.

◆ *Continuity:* a consideration of the past that is remembered; the present relating to experiences of an event; and the future, looking forward to possible experiences
◆ *Situation:* information about the context, time, and place within a physical setting, with boundaries and characters' intentions, purposes, and different points of view

Coding for Themes

As with all qualitative inquiry, the data can be segmented into themes. Narrative researchers may code the data of the stories into themes or categories. The identification of themes provides the complexity of a story and adds depth to the insight about understanding individual experiences. As with all qualitative research, the researcher identifies a small number of themes, such as five to seven. Researchers incorporate these themes into the passages about the individual's story or include them as a separate section in a study. Narrative researchers typically present these themes after retelling the story.

TABLE 15.4					
The Three-Dimensional Space Narrative Structure					
Interaction		**Continuity**			**Situation**
Personal	**Social**	**Past**	**Present**	**Future**	**Place**
Look inward to internal conditions, feelings, hopes, aesthetic reactions, moral dispositions.	Look outward to existential conditions in the environment with other people and their intentions, purposes, assumptions, and points of view.	Look backward to remembered stories and experiences from earlier times.	Look at current stories and experiences relating to actions of an event.	Look forward to implied and possible experiences and plot lines.	Look at context, time, and place situated in a physical landscape or in a setting bounded by characters' intentions, purposes, and different points of view.

Source: Adapted from Clandinin & Connelly, 2000.

Context or Setting

Narrative researchers describe in detail the setting or context in which the individual experiences the central phenomenon. In the restorying of the participant's story and the telling of the themes, the narrative researcher includes rich detail about the setting or context of the participant's experiences. The **setting** in narrative research may be friends, family, workplace, home, social organization, or school—the place where a story physically occurs. In some narrative studies, the restoried accounts of an educator may actually begin with a description of the setting or context before the narrative researcher conveys the events or actions of the story. In other cases, information about the setting is woven throughout the story.

Collaborating with Participants

Throughout the process of research, narrative researchers collaborate with the study individuals. **Collaboration** in narrative research means that the inquirer actively involves the participant in the inquiry as it unfolds. This collaboration may include many steps in the research process, from formulating the central phenomenon to deciding which types of field texts will yield helpful information to writing the final restoried story of individual experiences. Collaboration involves negotiating relationships between the researcher and the participant to lessen the potential gap between the narrative told and the narrative reported (Clandinin & Connelly, 2000). It may also include explaining the purpose of the inquiry to the participant, negotiating transitions from gathering data to writing the story, and arranging ways to intermingle with participants in a study (Clandinin & Connelly, 2000). Collaboration often calls for a good working relationship between teachers and researchers, an idealized situation that takes time to develop as a mutually illuminating story between the researcher and the teacher (Elbaz-Luwisch, 1997).

WHAT ARE SOME POTENTIAL ETHICAL ISSUES IN GATHERING STORIES?

When gathering stories, narrative researchers need to be cautious about the stories. Is the story authentic? The participant may "fake the data" (Connelly & Clandinin, 1990, p. 10), providing a Pollyanna story or a story with a typical Hollywood ending, where the good guy or girl always wins. This distortion of the data may occur in any research study, and it presents an issue for narrative researchers in particular because they rely heavily on self-reported information from participants. The collection of multiple field texts, the triangulation of data, and member checking can help ensure that good data are collected.

Participants may not be able to tell the *real* story. This inability may arise when experiences are simply too horrific to report or too raw to recall (e.g., Holocaust victims, disaster victims). It may also occur when individuals fear sanctions against them if they report their story, such as in sexual harassment cases. The real story may also not emerge because individuals simply cannot recall it—the story is buried too deeply in the subconscious. It may also occur because individuals base their stories on events that happened years ago, leading to early memories that may distort events and provide inventions of past actions (Lieblich et al., 1998). Although distortion, fear of reprisal, and inability to tell may plague storytellers, narrative researchers remind us that stories are "truths of our experiences" (Riessman, 1993, p. 22) and that any story told has an element of truth in it.

The telling of the story by the participant also raises the issue of who *owns* the story. In reporting stories of individuals marginalized in our society, narrative researchers run the risk of reporting stories that they do not have permission to tell. At the minimum, narrative inquirers can obtain permission to report stories, and inform individuals of the purposes and use of the stories at the beginning of the project.

Along with the potential problem of ownership is also the issue about whether the participant's *voice is lost* in the final narrative report. For example, when restorying exists, it is possible for the report to reflect the researcher's story and not the participant's story. Using extensive participant quotes and the precise language of the participants, and carefully constructing the time and place for the story, may help to ameliorate this problem. A related issue is whether the researcher *gains* in the study at the expense of the participant. Careful attention to reciprocity or giving back to participants, such as serving as a volunteer in a classroom or providing an award for participating in the study, will maintain gains for both the researcher and the participant. A final issue is whether the story told has long-lasting negative implications for the participant. As discussed in Box 15.1, one strategy is to tell a composite story based on various research experiences.

BOX 15.1 | Ethical Dilemma

When Narrative Researchers Report about Tensions

Ethics spans the entire research process. What happens ethically after the researcher concludes the study? Clandinin (2006) says that responsibilities may not end, and that they may linger and reappear and, "in some sense haunt us . . ." (p. 5). This is especially so when the narratives focus on tensions, and the writer creates "counterstories" that are read by others and create vulnerabilities for individuals, such as teachers, who talk about tension in their schools and classrooms. One strategy for shielding individuals who provide narrative stories is the use of "fictionalized interim research texts" (Clandinin et al., 2010). These texts are composed from multiple field texts based on various research experiences. This composite type of story thus protects individuals who may feel vulnerable to having their stories told. Narrative researchers need to be "awake" to these vulnerabilities when they tell counterstories.

As you consider your narrative research study, assuming that your narrative might create conflict for your participant after the study is completed and shared, what strategies will you use to shield the individual?

WHAT ARE THE STEPS IN CONDUCTING NARRATIVE RESEARCH?

Regardless of the type or form of narrative research, educators who conduct a narrative study proceed through similar steps, as shown in Figure 15.3. Seven major steps comprise the process typically undertaken during a narrative study. A visualization of the process as a circle shows that all steps are interconnected and not necessarily linear.

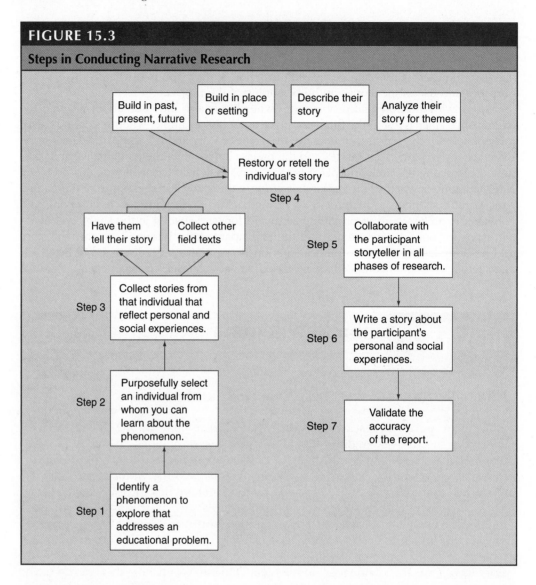

FIGURE 15.3

Steps in Conducting Narrative Research

The use of arrows to show the direction of steps is only a suggestion and is not prescriptive of a process that you might use.

Step 1. Identify a Phenomenon to Explore That Addresses an Educational Problem

As with all research projects, the process begins by focusing on a research problem to study and identifying, in qualitative research, a central phenomenon to explore. Although the phenomenon of interest in narrative is the story (Connelly & Clandinin, 1990), you need to identify an issue or concern. For example, the issue for Huber (1999), in a narrative study of children in a classroom, consisted of stories about the difficulties that she and her student teacher, Shaun, had meeting the diverse needs of students. This included children excluding other children, using hurtful words with each other, and persistently using anger and aggression to solve problems. When exploring issues such as these, you seek to understand the personal or social experiences of an individual or individuals in an educational setting.

Step 2. Purposefully Select an Individual From Whom You Can Learn About the Phenomenon

You next find an individual or individuals who can provide an understanding of the phenomenon. The participant may be someone who is typical or someone who is critical to study because he or she has experienced a specific issue or situation. Other options for sampling are also available. Although many narrative studies examine only a single individual, you may study several individuals in a project, each with a different story that may conflict with or be supportive of each other.

Step 3. Collect the Story From That Individual

Your intent is to collect field texts that will provide the story of an individual's experiences. Perhaps the best way to gather the story is to have the individual tell about his or her experiences, through personal conversations or interviews. You can gather other field texts as well, such as these:

◆ Have the individual record his or her story in a journal or diary.
◆ Observe the individual and record fieldnotes.
◆ Collect letters sent by the individual.
◆ Assemble stories about the individual from family members.
◆ Gather documents such as memos or official correspondence about the individual.
◆ Obtain photographs, memory boxes, and other personal/family/social artifacts.
◆ Record the individual's life experiences (e.g., dance, theater, music, film, art, and literature; Clandinin & Connelly, 2000).

Step 4. Restory or Retell the Individual's Story

Next, review the data that contain the story and retell it. This process includes examining the raw data, identifying elements of a story in them, sequencing or organizing the story elements, and then presenting a retold story that conveys the individual's experiences. You use restorying because the listener and the reader will better understand the story told by the participant if you sequence it into a logical order.

What elements do you identify in the raw data for your story? How do you arrange these elements in *your* story? Narrative researchers differ about the elements to select, although in general you might mention the narrative elements found in a literary analysis of a novel. For example, time, place, plot, and scene are major elements located in stories by researchers (Connelly & Clandinin, 1990). Focusing on the plot, you might identify an abstract of the events or actions, orient the listener, convey the complicating action, evaluate its meaning, and resolve the action (Cortazzi, 1993). Another inquirer might examine the story for setting, characters, actions, problem, and resolution (Ollerenshaw & Creswell, 2000). Although several analytic strategies exist for locating and sequencing a story, all procedures order the story for the reader and listener using literary elements.

Step 5. Collaborate with the Participant–Storyteller

This step is one that interacts with all the other steps in the process. You actively collaborate with the participant during the research process. This collaboration can assume several forms, such as negotiating entry to the site and the participant, working closely with the participant to obtain field texts to capture the individual experiences, and writing and telling the individual's story in the researcher's words.

Step 6. Write a Story About the Participant's Experiences

The major step in the process of research is for the author to write and present the story of the individual's experiences. Although there is no single way to write the narrative report, it is helpful to include several features of narrative. Your restory certainly claims a central place in the narrative report. In addition, you might include an analysis to highlight specific themes that emerged during the story.

Typically, you do not include a specific literature section; instead, you incorporate the literature and research studies about the problem into the final sections of the study. Because readers are often not familiar with narrative, you might write a section about the importance of narrative research and the procedures involved in it so that you can inform readers about narrative research. As with all qualitative research, you are present in the narrative report, and you use the first-person pronoun to refer to yourself.

Step 7. Validate the Accuracy of the Report

You also need to validate the accuracy of your narrative account. When collaboration exists with participants, this validation may occur throughout the project. Several validation practices such as member checking, triangulating among data sources, and searching for disconfirming evidence, are useful to determine the accuracy and credibility of a narrative account.

HOW DO YOU EVALUATE NARRATIVE RESEARCH?

As a form of qualitative research, narrative needs to be consistent with the criteria for a good qualitative study. In addition, there are specific narrative aspects that people reading and evaluating a study might consider. In a high-quality narrative study, the researcher:

- ◆ Keeps the focus on a single individual (or two).
- ◆ Reports the life experiences of individuals as told through their stories.
- ◆ Restories the individual's stories and tells the story using a chronology with a beginning, middle, and end (and possibly not in this order).
- ◆ Describes in some details the context of the story (i.e., the setting, the place where it occurs, the people involved, and so forth).
- ◆ Reports themes (5 to 7) to emerge out of the story.
- ◆ Closely collaborates with the participant providing the story and engages with the participant by having them check the evolving story frequently and examining the final story to see if it accurately reflects the individual's experiences.

KEY IDEAS IN THE CHAPTER

What Is Narrative Research, When Is It Used, and How Did It Develop?

Narrative research has emerged as a popular form of qualitative research. It has become a viable way to study teachers, students, and educators in educational settings. All of these individuals have stories to tell about their experiences. Narrative inquirers describe the lives of individuals, collect and tell stories about people's lives, and write narratives of individual experiences. These qualitative studies focus on identifying the experiences of a single individual or several individuals and understanding their past, present, and future experiences. A researcher uses narrative designs when individuals are willing to provide their stories, when their stories follow a chronology.

The Types of Narrative Designs

Narrative research is an overarching category for a variety of types of narrative studies. These may be such types as autobiographies, biographies, life histories, and personal narratives of teachers or students. The specific type of narrative study depends on who writes or records the story, how much of a life is recorded and presented, who provides the story, and whether a theory is used by the researcher.

The Key Characteristics of Narrative Designs

Narrative researchers collect stories from individuals and retell or restory the participants' stories into a framework such as a chronology of the characters, the setting, the problem, the actions, and a resolution of those actions. In addition, the inquirer may gather field texts and form them into themes or categories and describe, in detail, the setting or context in which the stories are told. Throughout the research process, the researcher emphasizes collaboration between the researcher and the participant.

Potential Ethical Issues in Gathering Stories

Ethical issues may arise at many stages in the process of conducting a narrative study. At the data collection stage, the researcher needs to question whether the story is authentic, determine whether the participants can tell (or recall) the real story, assess who owns the story told, determine if the participant's voice is included in the final story, stage the project so that the participant, not the researcher, gains as a result of the research, and be cognizant of the lasting impact of the story that is told.

Steps in Conducting a Narrative Study

The steps in conducting a narrative study are to identify a problem suited for narrative research and to select one or more participants to study. Researchers then collect stories from the participant about his or her life experiences and retell the story to form a chronology of events that may include the characters, setting, problem, actions, and resolution. Throughout this process, collaboration occurs with the participant, and the story composed by the researcher tells of the participant's life experiences.

Evaluating a Narrative Study

A good narrative study reports the stories of lived experiences of an individual, organizes them into a chronology, situates them within the setting or context, derives several themes that the stories address, and demonstrates a close collaboration in the narrative project between the researcher and the participant.

USEFUL INFORMATION FOR PRODUCERS OF RESEARCH

- ◆ Individuals planning or conducting a narrative study can employ the steps in the process identified in this chapter.
- ◆ Consider the type of narrative design you plan to use. Ask yourself the following questions: Who writes or records the story? How much of a life is recorded and presented? Who provides the story? Is a theoretical lens being used? Can narrative forms be combined?

◆ The three steps used in restorying provide a structure for processing a transcript and developing a retelling of the participant's story.

◆ As you listen to a participant's story, consider some of the potential issues that may arise, such as whether the story is authentic, whether data are distorted, whether individuals can tell the story, and who owns the story.

USEFUL INFORMATION FOR CONSUMERS OF RESEARCH

◆ Consumers can review the steps in the research process in this chapter to determine how narrative inquirers conduct a study.

◆ The evaluation criteria discussed in this chapter can be used to assess the quality of a narrative study.

◆ When narrative researchers conduct an inquiry, they need to report that they have checked the accuracy of their findings. Look for reports about triangulating data, member checking, or providing disconfirming evidence for themes.

◆ The narrative journal article reported in this study provides one example of narrative research. It is used to identify the major characteristics of a narrative study and to model the composition of a narrative study.

ADDITIONAL RESOURCES YOU MIGHT EXAMINE

A major book to consult is the text on narrative inquiry by Clandinin and Connelly (2000). This text captures all aspects of narrative designs from learning to think narratively to constructing a story using the three-dimensional model to the types of field texts that narrative researchers collect. It also includes information about composing a narrative text and using the forms available in dissertations and books. See:

Clandinin, D. J., & Connelly, F. M. (2000). *Narrative inquiry: Experience and story in qualitative research*. San Francisco: Jossey-Bass.

Clandinin (2007) has edited a 24-chapter handbook on narrative research that touches on many aspects of conducting a narrative study. Another useful book in education and teacher education is the book edited by McEwan and Egan (1995). This volume provides helpful examples of specific narrative studies in education. Examine:

Clandinin, D. J. (Ed.) (2007). *Handbook of narrative inquiry: Mapping a methodology*. Thousand Oaks, CA: Sage.
McEwan, H., & Egan, K. (1995). *Narrative in teaching, learning, and research*. New York: Teachers College Press, Columbia University.

Several journals have published excellent overviews of narrative research as applied to the field of education. One article often cited is the Connelly and Clandinin (1990) discussion on "Stories of Experience and Narrative Inquiry" in the *Educational Researcher*. This article is especially good at identifying the procedures used in conducting a narrative study. Another article is by Clandinin (2006), who discusses what happens after the research has been disseminated. An article in the *Educational Researcher* is by Kathy Carter (1993) on "The Place of Story in the Study of Teaching and Teacher Education."

This article presents the pros and cons of studying the stories of teachers, such as the political context of story and the issues of gender, power, ownership, and voice. A third article, by Kathleen Casey (1995/1996), titled "The New Narrative Research in Education," is found in the *Review of Research in Education*. This article addresses the history of narrative research and surveys many topics in narrative research, such as various types (e.g., autobiographical reflections), issues (e.g., plastic identities), and methodological concerns (e.g., nuanced discussions of emotions). See:

Carter, K. (1993). The place of a story in the study of teaching and teacher education. *Educational Researcher, 22*(1), 5–12, 18.

Casey, K. (1995/1996). The new narrative research in education. *Review of Research in Education, 21,* 211–253.

Clandinin, D. J. (2006). *After the research.* Paper presented to the Faculty of Education Graduate Students, University of Alberta, Edmonton, Alberta, Canada.

Connelly, F. M., & Clandinin, D. J. (1990). Stories of experience and narrative inquiry. *Educational Researcher, 19*(5), 2–14.

One entire issue of the journal *Teaching and Teacher Education* (Gudmundsdottir, 1997) addresses "Narrative Perspectives on Teaching and Teacher Education." Including major international writers on narrative research, this volume provides examples of specific narrative studies as well as thoughtful discussions about topics that critique as well as support narrative designs. See:

Gudmundsdottir, S. (1997). Introduction to the theme issue of "narrative perspectives on teaching and teacher education." *Teaching and Teacher Education, 13*(1), 1–3.

Also examine the entire issue of *The Journal of Educational Research* (Kim & Latta, 2009) for a recent discussion about narrative research. It covers timely topics such as narrative inquiry and school reform, ethnic identity, and professional development. See, for example:

Kim, J. H., & Latta, M. M. (2009). Narrative inquiry: Seeking relations as modes of interaction. *Journal of Educational Research, 103*(2), 69–71.

Clandinin, D. J., Murphy, M. S., Huber, J., & Orr, A. M. (2010). Negotiating narrative inquiries: Living in a tension-filled midst. *The Journal of Educational Research, 103,* 81–90.

Outside the field of education, in the social sciences, are several books useful to understanding narrative designs. Riessman (1993) provided thoughtful procedures for analyzing and reporting narratives, Josselson and Lieblich (1993) provided a six-volume series on the study of narrative lives, and Cortazzi (1993) also included systematic approaches to narrative analysis. Examine:

Riessman, C. K. (1993). *Narrative analysis.* Newbury Park, CA: Sage.

Josselson, R., & Lieblich, A. (Eds.). (1993). *The narrative study of lives* (Vol. 1). Thousand Oaks, CA: Sage.

Cortazzi, M. (1993). *Narrative analysis.* London: Falmer Press.

Go to the Topic "Narrative Research" in the MyEducationLab (**www.myeducationlab.com**) for your course, where you can:

◆ Find learning outcomes for "Narrative Research."
◆ Complete Assignments and Activities that can help you more deeply understand the chapter content.
◆ Apply and practice your understanding of the core skills identified in the chapter with the Building Research Skills exercises.
◆ Check your comprehension of the content covered in the chapter by going to the Study Plan. Here you will be able to take a pretest, receive feedback on your answers, and then access Review, Practice, and Enrichment activities to enhance your understanding. You can then complete a final posttest.

Example of a Narrative Study

Examine the following published journal article that is a narrative design study. Marginal notes indicate the major characteristics of narrative research highlighted in this chapter. The illustrative study is:

Living in the Space Between Participant and Researcher as a Narrative Inquirer: Examining Ethnic Identity of Chinese Canadian Students as Conflicting Stories to Live By

Elaine Chan

University of Nebraska–Lincoln

Narrative
Characteristics
in Marginal
Annotations

Abstract

Schooling experiences of 1st-generation Canadians interact with cultural experiences in their immigrant households to shape a sense of ethnic identity both as Canadians and as members of an ethnic community. This long-term, school-based narrative inquiry is an examination of ways in which expectations for academic performance and behavior by teachers and peers at school and immigrant parents at home contributed to shaping the ethnic identity of an immigrant Chinese student as conflicting stories to live by. A narrative approach revealed challenges of supporting immigrant students in North American schools, and contributed to understanding of the nuances of multicultural education.
Key words: narrative inquiry, ethnic identity, curriculum, multicultural education, student experiences

For children, school has enormous implications for their sense of identity as members of society, of their families, and of their ethnic communities. Each individual brings to their school context experiences shaped by their participation in schools, whether in Canada or in their home country, whether positive or negative, enriching or demoralizing. For a child of immigrant parents, tensions between home and school, the interaction of parent and teacher experiences of schooling, and their own experiences of schooling may be felt especially strongly, to the point of being experienced as conflicting stories to live by (Connelly & Clandinin, 1999). These students have their own ideas of how they should be in their school context, shaped by interaction with peers, exposure to popular culture and media, and prior experiences of schooling, schools, and teachers. At the same time, they are evaluated by teachers and supported by parents whose experiences of schooling may be vastly different, by nature of social and political influences as well as personal circumstances of the societies of which their own childhood schools were a part.

(01)

In the present study, I examined the experiences of one Chinese immigrant student, Ai Mei Zhang. I explore her participation in her Canadian middle school curriculum as the interaction of student, teacher, and parent narratives, a story of interwoven lives (Clandinin et al., 2006). I examined ways in which her sense of ethnic identity may be shaped by expectations for her academic performance and her behavior in her school and her home. I focus in particular on ways in which participation in her urban, multicultural school setting may contribute to shaping her sense of affiliation to family members and members of her ethnic and school communities, and contribute to her maternal-language development and maintenance. I also examined ways in which she experienced well-intended school practices and curriculum activities designed to support her academic

(02)
A focus on the experiences of a single individual

Address correspondence to Elaine Chan, Department of Teaching. Learning, and Teacher Education, College of Education and Human Sciences, University of Nebraska–Lincoln, 24 Henzlik Hall, Lincoln, NE 68588-0355. (E-mail: echan2@unl.edu)

Stories collected
from individuals

performance in ways not anticipated by policymakers and educators. I explored these influences as conflicting stories to live by (Connelly & Clandinin, 1999).

(03)   I examined experientially the intersection of school and home influences from the perspective of one middle school student as a long-term, school-based narrative inquirer. I explored features of narrative inquiry, such as the critical role of researcher–participant relationships, and the role of temporal and spatial factors (Clandinin & Connelly, 2000) of the research context in contributing to a nuanced understanding of multicultural education in this diverse school context. The present study is holistic, in that I examined the impact of multiple influences in a connected way as they intersected in the life of one student rather than as examples of ways in which an issue or theme may be experienced by different members of the same ethnic group.

(04)   Given the increasing diversity of the North American population (Statistics Canada. 2008; U.S. Census Bureau, 2002) that is in turn reflected in North American schools (Chan & Ross, 2002; He, Phillion, Chan, & Xu, 2007), addressing the curricular needs of students of minority background and supporting the professional development of teachers who work with them is essential. The present study contributes to existing research in the area of multicultural education and, in particular, curriculum development for diverse student populations, and student experiences of multicultural education.

(05)   To date, research addressing the interaction of culture and curriculum is often presented as an argument for the inclusion of culture in the school curriculum or as documentation for ways in which the inclusion of culture in the curriculum was successful (Ada, 1988; Cummins et al., 2005). There is an abundance of research highlighting the importance of culturally relevant and responsive pedagogy (Gay, 2000; Ladson-Billings, 1995, 2001; Villegas, 1991) and a culturally sensitive curriculum that builds on the experiences and knowledge of immigrant and minority students (Ada; Cummins, 2001; Igoa, 1995; Nieto & Bode, 2008).

(06)   Acknowledging the cultural knowledge of minority students in the classroom has been found to have important implications for their well-being outside of school. For example, Banks (1995) highlighted the inclusion of culture in the curriculum as a means of helping students to develop positive racial attitudes. Rodriguez (1982), Wong-Fillmore (1991), and Kouritzin (1999) presented compelling accounts of ways in which the failure to support the maintenance and development of maternal-language proficiency for students of minority background had dire consequences for their sense of ethnic identity and their sense of belonging in their families and ethnic communities. McCaleb (1994), Cummins (2001), and Wong-Fillmore elaborated on some of the dangers, such as increased dropout rates among immigrant and minority youth as well as increased likelihood of gang involvement, or failing to recognize the cultural communities from which students come.

(07)   Existing research has been invaluable in highlighting the importance of acknowledging the cultural knowledge that immigrant and minority students bring to a school context, and the work of educators as they develop curricula and teach an increasingly diverse student population (Banks, 1995; Cummins, 2001; Moodley, 1995). Research has also accentuated the need to develop ways of learning about the ethnic, linguistic, and religious backgrounds of students to inform curriculum development and policymaking for students of diverse backgrounds. Cochran-Smith (1995), Ladson-Billings (1995, 2001), and Conle (2000) explored the practice of drawing on the cultural knowledge of preservice teachers as a resource for preparing them to teach in culturally diverse classrooms. It is interesting to note that although there is research that has acknowledged the potential difficulties of moving from home to school for students of a minority background, and the difficulties of moving from school back home when minority students have assimilated to the school and societal expectations that differ from those of their home cultures, the day-to-day transition as minority and immigrant students move from home to school and back home again seems to have been overlooked. In the present study, I examine the nuances that one student lives as she makes this transition on a daily basis.

(08)   This work addresses the need for experiential research, focusing specifically on exploring the intersection of home and school influences from the perspective of the students themselves. Presently, there is a surprising lack of research examining ways in which students, in general (Cook-Sather, 2002), and immigrant and minority students, in particular, personally experience their school curriculum and school contexts (He et al., 2007). Bullough's (2007) examination of a Muslim student's response to curriculum and peer interactions in his U.S. school is among the few pieces examining school-curriculum activities from the perspective of a student of ethnic-minority background.

Feuerverger's (2001) ethnographic work exploring tensions that Israeli and Palestinian youth experience in their Israeli-Palestinian school is among few studies documenting and exploring student perspectives of their schooling experiences. Sarroub (2005) and Zine's (2001) accounts of Muslim students in American and Canadian schools, respectively, illustrate the complexities of negotiating a sense of identity among peers in a school context when values in the home differ significantly.

Within the relatively limited body of existing research addressing student experiences of schooling and curriculum presented, I present examples of student experiences thematically to address specific issues, topics, or arguments rather than ways that acknowledge multiple facets and tensions interacting at once to shape the experiences of an individual student. Smith-Hefner (1993), in her ethnographic study of female high school Khmer students, presented examples of Puerto Rican female students whose limited academic success was shaped by cultural and sociohistorical influences in their ethnic communities. Rolon-Dow (2004) examined tensions Puerto Rican students and their teachers experience when values supported in their home and in their ethnic communities seem to conflict with those encouraged in school. Lee's (1994, 1996) ethnographic study focused on ways in which Asian high school students' sense of identity and academic achievement was influenced by self-identified labels and membership in specific peer groups. There does not exist a large body of research examining the experiences of one student in the context of their North American school in a way that presents the stories to illustrate ways in which the interaction of multiple influences and issues of relevance may impact on an immigrant or minority student. (09)

This narrative inquiry is intended to provide a glimpse of the intersection of complex influences shaping the life of an immigrant student. I drew on existing narrative and ethnographic accounts of immigrant and minority students attending North American schools to inform this work. Valdés's (1996) work documenting the experiences of a small number of Latino and Mexican American families in their school and community and Li's (2002) ethnographic study with Chinese families as they supported their children's literacy development provide a glimpse of ways in which transitions between home and school may be challenging, and even overwhelming, due to differences in expectations about the school curriculum and the work of teachers. Carger's (1996) long-term narrative account of a Mexican American family's experiences provides an organizational structure for the present study, in that it is an in-depth account of one family's experiences of supporting their child in school, taking into consideration the intersection of multiple influences shaping the child's education. Ross & Chan's (2008) narrative account of an immigrant student, Raj, and his family's academic, financial, and familial difficulties highlighted the many challenges the family encountered in the process of supporting their children's adaptation to their Canadian school and community. This examination of Ai Mei's experiences contributes to the growing but still limited body of research addressing Chinese students in North American schools (Chan, 2004; Kao, 1995; Kim & Chun, 1994; Lee, 1994, 1996, 2001; Li, 2002, 2005). (10)

Theoretical Framework

Given the focus on experience in contributing to Ai Mei's sense of ethnic identity, I used Dewey's (1938) philosophy of the interconnectedness between experience and education as the theoretical foundation for this study. I examined, in particular, ways in which the many influences in her home, school, and neighborhood life with family members, peers, teachers, administrators, and school curriculum events intersected to contribute to her overall experience or learning of a sense of ethnic identity as an immigrant student in a Canadian school context. Ai Mei's stories are set into the framework of a three-dimensional narrative inquiry space (Clandinin & Connelly, 2000), with Bay Street School as the spatial dimension, the years 2001–2003 as the temporal dimension, and my interactions with Ai Mei, her classmates, her teachers, her parents, and other members of the Bay Street School community as the sociopersonal dimension. The stories are a means of exploring the interaction of influences contributing to Ai Mei's sense of identity; they highlight the extent to which this intersection of narratives may be interpreted as conflicting stories to live by (Connelly & Clandinin, 1999). (11)

Method

I first met Ai Mei when I began observations in her seventh-grade class as a classroom-based participant observer for a research project exploring the ethnic identity of first-generation Canadian students. The focus on examining the intersection of culture and curriculum as experienced by (12)

Chinese Canadian students over the course of their 2 years in middle school was deliberate from the beginning. As I learned about the details of the students' experiences, the complex interaction of factors contributing to Ai Mei's sense of ethnic identity became apparent and merited further analysis.

(13)   Ai Mei's homeroom teacher, William, told me about how she had arrived at Bay Street School from an urban area of Fuchien province in China as a 7-year-old. Although she did not initially speak English at all, she was relatively proficient by the time I met her 4 1/2 years after her arrival. Her English was distinct from that of her native-English-speaking peers by the unusual turns of phrases and unconventional uses of some words, but the animated way in which she spoke about her experiences caught my attention from the beginning. I later appreciated this quality even more as I began to work more closely with her as a research participant. Her dark eyes, partially hidden behind wisps of hair, seemed to flicker and dance as she elaborated on details of interactions with peers and family members, especially when she recounted amusing or troublesome events pertaining to difficulties she had experienced in communicating with others. She also seemed to enjoy telling me about incidents that had occurred at home, at school, or in the community. As I learned about Ai Mei's stories of immigration and settlement, the conflicting influences and expectations of her family members, peers and teachers at school, and members of her ethnic community became more apparent, thus further contributing to my decision to focus on her stories in this study.

Collabora-tion between researcher and participants

Report of a chronology of individual experiences

(14)   As a narrative inquirer, I learned about Ai Mei's stories of experience (Connelly & Clandinin, 1988) using a variety of narrative approaches, including long-term, school-based participant observations, document collection set into the context of ongoing conversational interviews with key participants, and the writing of extensive field notes following each school visit, interview, and interaction with participants (Clandinin & Connelly, 1994, 2000; Clandinin et al., 2006) to explore the interwoven quality of Ai Mei, her teacher, her classmates, and her family members' lives. I observed and interacted with her in the context of regular classroom lessons as I assisted her and her classmates with assignments, accompanied them on field trips, attended their band concerts and performances, and took part in school activities such as Multicultural Night, Curriculum and Hot Dog Night, school assemblies, and festivals. School visits began during the fall of 2001 as Ai Mei and her classmates began seventh grade and continued until June 2003 when they graduated from eighth grade at Bay Street School.

(15)   I conducted interviews as well as ongoing informal conversations with Ai Mei over the course of the 2 years I spent in her homeroom classroom. I also collected documents such as school notices, announcements of community and school events, notices from bulletin boards and classroom walls in the school, agendas and minutes from School Council meetings, and samples of student work. Descriptive field notes, interview transcripts, researcher journals, and theoretical memos written following school visits were computerized and filed into an existing research project archival system. I examined field notes pertaining to Ai Mei's experiences numerous times to identify recurring themes. Her stories were set into the context of field notes written about her classroom teacher, her peers, and her school community since I began research at the school in 2000.

Results

Ai Mei's Stories of Home and School: Conflicting Stories to Live By

(16)   I subsequently present some of Ai Mei's stories of experience to explore challenges and complexities, harmonies and tensions (Clandinin & Connelly, 2002), she lived as she attempted to balance affiliation to her peers while at the same time accommodating for expectations placed on her by her teachers and parents. I explore ways in which parent, teacher, and peer expectations may contribute to shaping her sense of identity, and examine the contribution of narrative methodology in revealing nuances of the intersection of multiple influences in her life.

A description of a setting or context

Bay Street School Context

(17)   Ai Mei's stories were set in the context of Bay Street School, a school known to consist of a diverse student community from the time of its establishment (Cochrane, 1950; Connelly, He, Phillion, Chan, & Xu, 2004), located in an urban Toronto neighborhood where the ethnic composition of residents is known to reflect Canadian immigration and settlement patterns (Connelly, Phillion, & He, 2003).

Accordingly, the student population at the school reflects this diversity. An Every Student Survey administered to students during the 2001–2002 school year (Chan & Ross, 2002) confirmed the ethnic and linguistic diversity of the students. More specifically, 39 countries and 31 languages were represented in the school. This was the context in which Ai Mei's stories played out.

Home Language Conflicting with School Language

I subsequently present the story, "I was trying to hide my identity," as a starting point for examining Ai Mei's experiences of her academic program at Bay Street School.

Development of themes
(18)
The story is retold by the researcher

"I was trying to hide my identity"

Ai Mei: When I first came to Bay Street School, I stayed with the IL (International Language)[1] teacher, Mrs. Lim . . . I stayed with her for the whole week, and she taught me things in English.

Elaine: What did she teach you?

Ai Mei: You know, easy things, like the alphabet, and how to say "Hello." Then I went to Ms. Jenkins' class. I sat with a strange boy.

Elaine: A strange boy?

Ai Mei: Well, he wasn't that strange. My desk was facing his desk, and he did this to me (Ai Mei demonstrates what the boy did), he stuck his tongue out at me. I didn't know what it meant. He had messy orange hair.

Elaine: Did you make any friends?

Ai Mei: No, not for a long time. Some people tried to talk to me but I didn't understand them. Then Chao tried to talk with me in Fujianese and I pretended I didn't understand her. She tried a few times, then gave up. Then one day, my sister said something to me in Fujianese and Chao heard. She looked at me—she was really surprised because she tried to talk with me and I pretended I couldn't understand her. She didn't like me at all.

Elaine: Why did you do that? Why did you pretend you couldn't understand her?

Ai Mei: I don't know. I was trying to hide my identity.

Ai Mei (calling over to Chao): Chao, remember how I didn't talk with you, how I pretended I didn't understand you?

Chao: Yeah, I remember. (Chao scowls at Ai Mei.) I didn't like you for a long time.

Ai Mei: Yeah, a long time.

(Fieldnotes, April, 2003)

When Ai Mei arrived at Bay Street School, new students coming into the school spent a week or two with the respective International Language (IL) teacher prior to placement into a classroom. The new student orientation provided teachers the opportunity to assess the English and maternal-language proficiency of new students, identify potential learning difficulties, and learn about their previous schooling experiences. The orientation also provided students an opportunity to learn about school routines in their home language while being gradually introduced into their age-appropriate classroom.

(19)

Ai Mei's response to the new student orientation, however, was surprising for a number of reasons. From her teachers' perspective, Chao would have seemed like an ideal friend for Ai Mei—both girls were from the same rural province of southern China, grew up speaking Fujianese at home and Mandarin in school, and Chao could help Ai Mei to adapt to Bay Street School because she had arrived two years earlier. However, Ai Mei did not seem to welcome the opportunity to speak with Chao in Fujianese. Her teachers were also likely puzzled that she would try to "hide [her] identity," because, from their perspective, they worked hard to create programs that would acknowledge students' home cultures in a positive way.

(20)

In this context, it is possible that Ai Mei, similar to many students featured in research on immigrant and minority students (Cummins, 2001; Kouritzin, 1999), perceived her affiliation to her family's home language as a hindrance to acceptance by English-speaking peers. She seemed to appreciate learning English from her IL teacher and perhaps felt that her inability to speak in English was an obstacle to forming friendships with English-speaking peers. One day, as we were walking back to her homeroom classroom after art class, she has told me about an incident when

(21)

she felt embarrassed when she attempted to order drinks at a shopping mall and the vendor could not understand her because "[her] English accent was so bad!" Ai Mei may have been attempting to distance herself from those she perceived as non-English-speaking when she said she "tried to hide [her] identity." Wong-Fillmore (1991) elaborated on how a language minority child might abandon the home language when she or he realizes the low status of this language in relation to the English that is used by peers in school. At the same time, in choosing not to respond to her Fujianese-speaking classmate who attempted to befriend her, Ai Mei was giving up the opportunity to make a friend at a time when she did not have the English proficiency to build friendships easily with English-speaking peers.

School Language Conflicting with Home Language

(22) In addition to pressure to achieve a higher level of English proficiency, Ai Mei seemed to be under pressure from her IL Mandarin teacher, Mrs. Lim, to maintain and to develop her Mandarin proficiency. She was in a high level of language within her grade-level Mandarin program,[2] and she was doing well in the class, judging from the grades I saw when she showed me her Mandarin language textbook and workbooks. Her teacher has said that she did well in her assignments and tests, and that she was a strong student in Mandarin. She stated that it was important for Ai Mei to work hard to maintain the advantage she had over her Canadian-born Chinese peers. Mrs. Lim believed that Ai Mei has an easier time learning the characters that many Canadian-born Chinese students have difficulty with, due to her early years of schooling in China before arriving in Canada. She also felt that Ai Mei had an advantage over her Chinese-born peers, in that her schooling prior to leaving China was regular and uninterrupted in a way some of her Chinese-born peers had not experienced.

(23) Maintenance of her Mandarin language proficiency is an achievement her parents support. At the same time, they would like her to maintain fluency in her family's home dialect of Fujianese. For Ai Mei and her parents, maternal language maintenance has important implications for communication within the family. Ai Mei told me about the following mealtime conversation involving her mother and her younger sister, Susan.

> "Susan doesn't speak Fujianese"
> Ai Mei: We were eating supper and my mother said to my sister, "(phrase in Fujianese)." My sister asked me, "What did she say?" so I told her, "She wants to know if you want more vegetables."
> Elaine: Your sister doesn't understand Fujianese?
> Ai Mei: She does but not everything.
> Elaine: What did your mother say? Is she worried that your sister doesn't understand her?
> Ai Mei: She looked at her like this—(Ai Mei showed me how her mother gave her sister a dirty look).
> (Fieldnotes, April, 2003)

(24) From the fieldnote, it seems that Ai Mei's parents were beginning to feel the effects of maternal language loss within the family. Fujianese is not easy to develop and maintain because its use in Canada is not widely supported outside the home, with the exception of exposure to the dialect through other recent immigrants from Fuchien Province. Susan's inability to understand basic vocabulary in her home language likely worried her and Ai Mei's parents, but given the limited resources to support it and limited time to encourage her themselves, they might wonder what can be done. Ai Mei spoke about how her parents reminded her often to speak with her sister in Fujianese. Meanwhile, the sisters had long grown into the habit of speaking to one another in English; communication in their home language of Fujianese would have been stifled at that point due to the lack of ease both felt in using it as well as Susan's limited vocabulary. It might be the case that their parents, as they began to realize the extent of their daughter's maternal language loss, might already be too late to stop it. This pressure to develop and to maintain language proficiency interacted with other factors contributing to Ai Mei's sense of identity and affiliation in her school and in her home and ethnic communities.

Parent Values Conflicting with Peer Values

(25) In addition to pressure to succeed academically, Ai Mei was also under pressure to behave according to the expectations of her peers, teachers, and parents. Through interaction with Ai Mei at Bay

Street School over the course of two full academic years, it became apparent that being included within her peer group was very important to her. Like her peers, Ai Mei was becoming more firmly entrenched into popular movies, music, and fashion trends as she moved into adolescence. These influences were coupled with increasing pressure from peers to scoff at school success and downplay the importance of academic work. During the fall of 2001, there were a number of days when I arrived at Ai Mei's classroom to find her friends trying to console her after a popular and outspoken male classmate, Felix, had made unflattering comments about her appearance. Her homeroom teacher also told me about incidents when she had left school in tears after being excluded from an after school activity that had been planned by classmates. Another day, I overheard Felix mimicking one of the stories from Ai Mei's Mandarin IL text; although he spoke in English, the tone and storyline were along the lines of what might be found in the text. Ai Mei laughed at Felix's attempts and seemed to appreciate that he knew a little about what she did in IL class but I also wondered whether she was embarrassed or annoyed with him.

In addition to concerns about being excluded by her peers and feeling the pull of multiple influences in school to behave in certain ways, Ai Mei also seemed to live the tensions of parental expectations and standards for her behavior and comportment that, at times, conflicted with those of her peers, and ways in which she saw herself. I wrote the following fieldnote after a conversation with Ai Mei in which she complained about her mother's comments about her in relation to her mother's friend during a family outing. (26)

"Dim Sum with her mother's friend"
Ai Mei told me today about going out to dim sum with her mother's friend and her family. She said she was very annoyed at being compared to her mother's friend's daughter who is close in age to Ai Mei but who seems like a perfect daughter in her mother's eyes. Ai Mei told me, "My mother said, 'Look at Ming Ming, so pretty and tall. And so quiet! She helps her mother do the cooking and the cleaning at home.' She said to Ming Ming's mother, 'Look at Ai Mei, 13 years old and so short. And she doesn't help me at home, and she doesn't cook!' She kept comparing us, saying how nice Ming Ming is and how terrible I am." Ai Mei rolled her eyes.
(Fieldnotes, April, 2003)

The interaction between Ai Mei and her mother highlighted the potential for tensions to develop when expressing differences in perspective about the value of certain kinds of behaviors over others. It sounded as if Ai Mei resented that her mother did not think she was quiet or helpful or tall enough when compared with her friend's daughter. Although a generational gap might account for some of the tension about what constituted appropriate behavior and goals for Ai Mei with respect to what she did to contribute to the family, some of this tension might also have been shaped by the very different contexts in which Ai Mei and her mother have spent their childhood. Ai Mei has spent a good portion of her childhood living in different homes in an urban, commercial district of Toronto. Her perception of appropriate behavior and practices has likely been shaped by influences different from what her mother experienced in rural Fuchien province of China where she spent her own childhood. (27)

Teacher Expectations Conflicting with Parent Expectations

Moreover, although Ai Mei's parents and her teachers had in common the goal of academic success for her, tensions surfaced about the time commitment needed to fulfill these school and family responsibilities. Ai Mei seemed to be caught between pressures to help in the family business and teacher expectations for completed homework and thorough preparation for tests and assignments. (28)

Ai Mei's family acquired a dumpling restaurant during the fall of her eighth-grade year, and since then, the whole family had devoted much time and energy toward building a successful business. I knew that Ai Mei's family owned a dumpling restaurant because she had told me about what she did to help. (29)

Ai Mei: There's a door that no one can close but me.
Elaine: What's wrong with it?
Ai Mei: It's stuck, so I have to kick it shut. (She demonstrates as she says this, kicking to one side as she leans over.) Then, we go home, me, my mom, and my dad.

Elaine: How about your sister?
Ai Mei: She goes home a little earlier, with my grandmother and grandfather.
(Fieldnotes, October, 2002)

Each day after school, Ai Mei and her sister, Susan, after spending some time with their friends in the classroom or in the school yard, headed to the dumpling restaurant to spend the evening there helping their parents. Ai Mei's sister, Susan, has told me about how she helped their father by standing outside the restaurant where the family sells vegetables and fruits to watch for people who attempted to take food without paying for it. When I asked her whether this often happened, she nodded gravely.

(30)   The importance of Ai Mei and Susan's participation in the family business could be denied, but Ai Mei's teachers had questioned the time commitment involved. Late in the fall after the family acquired the dumpling restaurant, Ai Mei's teacher, William, noticed that she had begun to come to school looking very tired, and without her homework done. One day while he was meeting with her to discuss the report card that would soon be sent home to her parents, he told her that she could have done better had she submitted all of her homework and done a better job on recent tests. Ai Mei surprised him by bursting into tears. Little by little, William learned that Ai Mei had little opportunity to do her homework or to study because she was helping out at the restaurant during evenings and weekends. By the time the family had closed up the restaurant, traveled home, and eaten supper, it was past 11:00pm or 12:00am, beyond what William thought was appropriate for a 12-year-old. With a sense of professional responsibility to report potentially negligent situations to officials and the support of school board policies guiding his actions, William spoke with his principal about the situation. Both decided it was a borderline case, and with the principal's knowledge, William contacted the Children's Aid Society (CAS) about Ai Mei's family. I wrote the following field note the day William told me about his call to the CAS.

"I called the CAS"
I was helping William straighten up the textbooks, sort student assignments into piles, and organize pens, pencils, and chalk into appropriate places in the classroom. We have gotten into the habit of talking about events of the day as we tidy up the classroom after the students have left for French class toward the end of the day. Today, William said to me, "I called the CAS about Ai Mei. She doesn't do her homework or have time to study because she's up late working in the family restaurant. She's exhausted."
(Fieldnotes, December, 2002)

(31)   The dumpling restaurant was tied to Ai Mei's family's dreams of financial success and family reunification. Ai Mei had spoken about how her parents had sponsored her maternal grandparents to come to Toronto from Fuchien province, and were in the process of trying to bring her paternal grandparents over to join the family as well. The importance of helping her family with their business could not be denied from her parents' perspective and, from what Ai Mei has said about the ways in which she helped the family, it could be assumed that she also recognized the importance of her role as well.

(32)   At the same time, it was beginning to become apparent that assisting her parents in the family business might have diverted her attention away from fulfilling her parents' desire for her to do well in school, in that time spent in the restaurant helping her family was time that she could have otherwise devoted to her school work. Ai Mei was caught between her parents' dreams of financial and business success, her sense of responsibility, as the oldest daughter in the family, to help them achieve this success, her parents' desire for her to perform well academically to secure her own future economic success, and her teacher's professional responsibility to report potentially negligent situations to officials. She lived the tensions of deciding how best to use her time to assist her parents in the family business as well as to perform well academically.

(33)   This situation also needed to be examined in terms of her teacher's professional tensions and ways in which these tensions might have contributed to Ai Mei's sense of identity. Her teacher, William, was aware that the cultural and social narratives guiding his professional practices might have differed from those guiding the practices of the parents of his students, and had expressed a commitment to acknowledging the diversity of his students. The potential for conflict between

teacher, student, and parent perspectives pertaining to Ai Mei's use of time in the evenings and on weekends became apparent when William contacted child-protection officials to report that Ai Mei's time in the family's restaurant in the evenings was contributing to her late arrival at school in the mornings, without her assigned homework completed. He did so with the belief in the importance of protecting Ai Mei's time to ensure that she had adequate time and necessary conditions in her home to complete her school work.

William's call to the CAS, however well intentioned, had the potential to cause difficulties in (34) Ai Mei's family as well as a rift in his own relationship with Ai Mei. In fact, he later told me about how Ai Mei, on realizing that he had reported her parents to the CAS, neither came around after school to spend time in his classroom nor did she tell him about what was happening in her life as she was accustomed to doing up until that time. He felt he had lost her trust and believed that his call to the CAS had been the cause. This example highlights some of the tension William felt as he attempted to balance his professional obligation to report potentially negligent situations to child protection officials and his ideal of the role of teacher as an advocate who supported students in ways they would appreciate.

Learning About Ai Mei's Experiences as a Narrative Inquirer

These stories highlight some of the complexities of the interaction of multiple influences in contributing to Ai Mei's sense of identity. Underlying these accounts of Ai Mei's experiences with her peers, teachers, and parents in the context of school and community-based events are accounts of my interactions with Ai Mei as a narrative inquirer. The narrative inquiry approach used in this study facilitated the identification of the many nuances of living as an immigrant student in a North American school context, and provided a framework in which to ponder these complexities. To begin, the stories of experience documenting Ai Mei's experiences as an immigrant student at Bay Street School were gathered over a long period of time as I spent 2 full school years in her homeroom classroom with her, her teachers, and her peers as a participant observer. During this time, I became a member of the classroom, joining the class for activities such as field trips, special school events, band concerts, and school assemblies. More importantly, however, I was a part of their class during the uneventful days of lessons and regular school activities. It was during these times that I was able to build a relationship with Ai Mei and her peers and teachers. They grew to see me as an additional teacher in the classroom who was able to help them with assignments, act as an adult supervisor during in-school activities or field trips, and as a listening ear when they had disagreements with friends or with teachers.

I learned about the details of Ai Mei's life as she told me about her classmates, her parents, her (36) family's dumpling restaurant, her sister, and family outings. I heard about her perceptions of how she fit into her peer group, her ethnic community, and her family as she told me about specific interactions, such as the family dinner when her sister did not understand what her mother had said in Fujianese, her mother's criticisms of her in comparison with her mother's friend's daughter, or her impressions of the new student orientation that was in place to ease her transition into the school as a new student from China.

As the students came to realize my interest in learning about their school lives, they began to (37) update me on events I had missed between visits, and to fill me in on what they referred to as "gossip" at school. At one point partway through my second year with Ai Mei's homeroom class, I conducted interviews with the students. As I planned the questions and discussed them with William, I remember wondering whether this shift to a more formal kind of interaction with the students would change the relationship we had established. My concern about negatively impacting the relationship turned out to be unfounded. In fact, I was pleased to realize one day when Ai Mei approached me to tell me about a family dinner (see "Susan doesn't speak Fujianese") that the process had opened up further opportunities to learn about the students' lives. Realizing that I was interested in hearing about their interactions at home and in the community with members of their ethnic groups, the students began to tell me more about them. Our existing relationship had provided a foundation such that I could talk with the students about their experiences with family and members of their ethnic communities, and the interviews provided an opportunity for the students to learn, in a more explicit way, about my interest in hearing about out-of-school aspects of their lives. Our relationship was such that they knew they could trust that I would treat their stories and their perceptions of these stories with interest and respect.

(38)   I also saw Ai Mei in the neighborhood with her friends during the after school hours as they moved from house to house visiting one another in the housing project while their parents worked in nearby restaurants and shops, and on weekends as she shopped with her sister and her parents in the stores that lined the commercial area near the school. These brief interactions provided further glimpses of influences interacting in her life to contribute to shaping a sense of identity in ways that would not be possible through formal interviews or a more structured schedule of research observations. In addition, these interactions provided an opportunity for Ai Mei's friends and family to become familiar with my presence and participation in the school.

(39)   Tensions of acting as a researcher with a focus on learning about the experiences of my participants became more apparent as my role as researcher became less clear. As I got to know Ai Mei and her family, I felt the tensions she experienced as she balanced the multiple influences in her life and wanted to advocate for her. I felt a sense of responsibility to Ai Mei, to support her learning and to attempt to ease some of the tensions she experienced as she balanced affiliation to her home and school cultures. I understood a little of the betrayal she felt when her parents were reported to child protection officials, and the fear her parents might have felt. When she told me about how her parents would not be able to attend her eighth-grade graduation because they needed to work, I wanted to be sure to attend and to take photos of her with her sister so that she would have a record of the event. The nature of the researcher-participant relationship in contributing to understanding about the nuances of experiences lived by my student participant heightened my understanding of what the events might mean for her.

(40)   The role of narrative inquiry, and, more specifically, the role of long-term participation in the day to day school life of an immigrant student that was critical to this narrative inquiry, contributed to the researcher-participant relationship I was able to develop with Ai Mei, her peers, and her teachers. Careful attention to the details of life in classrooms (Jackson, 1990) and within the school, and respect for the ongoing negotiation so critical to building a research relationship from initial negotiation of entry into the school research site to negotiation of exit towards the completion of school-based narrative inquiries—features foundational to Clandinin & Connelly's (2000) approach—further contributed to the development of a research relationship based on trust and familiarity with Ai Mei. This trust, in turn, engaged me in careful consideration of the potential implications of telling and retelling Ai Mei's stories, and what they might mean for her, as well as other immigrant and minority students who may struggle with similar challenges of balancing tensions of affiliation to home and school cultures in a North American school context. It was also through this commitment to examining these tensions narratively from multiple perspectives of others in Ai Mei's school, as well as in relation to temporal, spatial, and sociopersonal dimensions at play in her school, that enabled me to see some of the nuances and complexities of the conflicting influences in Ai Mei's life. In the process of examining Ai Mei's experiences narratively, I also became a participant, in that my experiences and interpretations of Ai Mei's stories were continually being examined and reflected on as I shared my interpretations with Ai Mei in an ongoing process to better understand the stories she told.

(41)   This relationship, in turn, was critical to my learning about the complexities of Ai Mei's experiences. In this way, this long-term, school-based narrative inquiry approach contributes not only to knowledge about the experiences of my participants as I focus on examining nuances of the research phenomenon at hand but it also raises awareness about the intricacies, and the impact, of the work of researchers in the lives of our participants.

Discussion

Conflicting Student, Teacher, and Parent Stories to Live By: Implications for Practice, Research, and Theory

(42)   This examination of the intersection of home, school, and ethnic community influences in Ai Mei's life provided a glimpse of the challenges immigrant or minority students might encounter as they negotiate a sense of ethnic identity. More specifically, examining Ai Mei's stories reveals ways in which immigrant and minority students may be pulled in many directions, with some of these influences experienced as conflicting stories to live by as teacher, peer, and parent expectations intersect on a school landscape. The stories highlight the potential for conflict when immigrant

students have values shaped by interaction with family and members of their ethnic community as well as values shaped by interaction with peers, teachers, and other members of their North American school communities.

As Ai Mei grows up, she needs to determine which aspects of her home and school communities she incorporates into her own set of values. The age-old tension between children and their parents as children move toward adulthood and make decisions pertaining to their education and the kind of life they see themselves leading is exacerbated by differences in perspective that are influenced by differences in culture between their new host society that the children are navigating and the landscape that their immigrant parents experienced as children in their home countries. This tension is further complicated by struggles that their parents have endured in the immigration process as they settle into new countries. Ai Mei's stories revealed the extent to which ideas for innovative curricula and the good intentions of teachers, administrators, researchers, and policymakers may unfold in unexpected ways. Learning about Ai Mei's conflicting stories to live by highlighted the importance of examining ways in which curriculum and school events may contribute to shaping the ethnic identity of immigrant and minority students in ways much more complex than anticipated by their teachers, their parents, and even the students themselves. (43)

This knowledge, in turn, informs the work of teachers and administrators as they attempt to meet the needs of their increasingly diverse student populations. Teachers need to learn to meet the academic and social needs of their immigrant and minority students in a school context with sometimes little knowledge about the cultures and education systems from which they are coming. In this way, knowledge gained from this study has implications for teachers working in diverse school contexts, professional development for in-service and pre-service educators, and decision making pertaining to the development of curriculum policies for multicultural school contexts. Examining Ai Mei's experiences of the intersection of home and school influences informs the development and implementation of programs designed to facilitate the adaptation of immigrant students in North American schools. Ai Mei's stories of experience may be referred to as an example of a life-based literary narrative (Phillion & He, 2004), and contribute to the body of student lore introduced by Schubert and Ayers (1992) and recognized by Jackson (1992) in Pinar, Reynolds, Slattery, and Taubman's book, *Understanding Curriculum* (1995). Attention to the narratives of students and their families is a reminder not to lose sight of the diversity in student populations and highlights the need for attention to issues of social justice and equity in education. Not only does this research address the dearth of research focused specifically on students' experiences from their perspective, but it also contributes to understanding of the experiences of immigrant and minority students to provide insights into the experiences of a group about which educators and policymakers involved in developing and implementing school curriculum are desperately in need of better understanding. (44)

Conclusion

Teachers and administrators with whom I shared this piece appreciated the acknowledgment of the challenges they encounter in their work with their students. William, as a beginning teacher, recognized the need for further attention to prepare teachers for diverse classrooms and felt that stories such as those presented in this article contributed to raising awareness of difficulties teachers may encounter; he recognized the potential of the stories as a forum to generate discussion among teachers and administrators. His administrators spoke of the challenges inherent to meeting the needs of their student population, and referred to the tensions of needing to abide by existing policies even as they lived the difficulties of implementing some of the policies with their students and teachers. (45)

Exploring the multitude of influences shaping student participation in school curriculum using a narrative inquiry approach to examining student experiences is also a means of acknowledging the complexity of schooling and teacher preparation (Cochran Smith, 2006), and the need for guidance about how best to develop curriculum and pedagogy for students of minority background, and the challenges associated with working with diverse student populations. Given the increasingly diverse North American context, is it essential that educators and policymakers are well informed about the students for whom educational practices and policies are developed. (46)

Notes

1. Students at Bay Street School chose from IL classes in Cantonese or Mandarin Chinese, Vietnamese, Arabic, Swahili/Black History, or Spanish that were integrated into their regular school day.

2. The Mandarin texts used in the IL program were based on a multigrade format in which each grade level was in turn divided into six levels of difficulty ranging from beginner to advanced to accommodate for differences in language proficiency among students in the same grade level.

References

Ada, A. F. (1988). The Pajaro Valley experience: Working with Spanish-speaking parents to develop children's reading and writing skills in the home through the use of children's literature. In T. Skutnabb-Kangas & J. Cummins (Eds.), *Minority education: From shame to struggle* (pp. 223–237). Clevedon, UK: Multilingual Matters.

Banks, J. A. (1995). Multicultural education: Its effects on students' racial and gender role attitudes. In J. A. Banks & C. A. McGee Banks (Eds.), *Handbook of research on multicultural education* (pp. 617–627). Toronto, Canada: Prentice Hall International.

Bullough, R. V. Jr. (2007). Ali: Becoming a student—A life history. In D. Thiessen & A. Cook-Sather (Eds.), *International handbook of student experience in elementary and secondary school* (pp. 493–516). Dordecht, The Netherlands: Springer.

Carger, C. (1996). *Of borders and dreams: Mexican-American experience of urban education.* New York: Teachers College Press.

Chan, E. (2004). *Narratives of ethnic identity: Experiences of first generation Chinese Canadian students.* Unpublished doctoral dissertation, University of Toronto, Ontario, Canada.

Chan, E., & Ross, V. (2002). *ESL Survey Report. Sponsored by the ESL Work-group in collaboration with the OISE/UT Narrative and Diversity Research Team.* Toronto, Canada: Centre for Teacher Development, Ontario Institute for Studies in Education, University of Toronto, Ontario, Canada.

Clandinin, D. J., & Connelly, F. M. (1994). Personal experience methods. In N. K. Denzin & Y. S. Lincoln (Eds.), *Handbook of qualitative research in the social sciences* (pp. 413–427). Thousand Oaks, CA: Sage.

Clandinin, D. J., & Connelly, F. M. (2000). *Narrative inquiry: Experience and story in qualitative research.* San Francisco: Jossey-Bass.

Clandinin, D. J., & Connelly, F. M. (2002, October). Intersecting narratives: Cultural harmonies and tensions in inner-city urban Canadian schools. Proposal submitted to the Social Sciences and Humanities Research Council of Canada.

Clandinin, D. J., Huber, J., Huber, M., Murphy, M. S., Murray Orr, A., Pearce, M., et al. (2006). *Composing diverse identities: Narrative inquiries into the interwoven lives of children and teachers.* New York: Routledge.

Cochrane, M. (Ed.). (1950). *Centennial story: Board of education for the city of Toronto: 1850–1950.* Toronto, Canada: Thomas Nelson.

Cochran-Smith, M. (1995). Uncertain allies: Understanding the boundaries of race and teaching. *Harvard Educational Review, 65,* 541–570.

Cochran-Smith, M. (2006). Thirty editorials later: Signing off as editor. *Journal of Teacher Education, 57*(2), 95–101.

Conle, C. (2000). The asset of cultural pluralism: an account of cross-cultural learning in pre-service teacher education. *Teaching and Teacher Education, 16,* 365–387.

Connelly, F. M., & Clandinin, D. J. (1988). *Teachers as curriculum planners: Narratives of experience.* New York: Teachers College Press.

Connelly, F. M., & Clandinin, D. J. (1999). Stories to live by: Teacher identities on a changing professional knowledge landscape. In F. M. Connelly & D. J. Clandinin (Eds.), *Shaping a professional identity: Stories of educational practice* (pp. 114–132). London, Canada: Althouse Press.

Connelly, F. M., He, M. F., Phillion, J., Chan, E., & Xu, S. (2004). Bay Street Community School: Where you belong. *Orbit, 34*(3), 39–42.

Connelly, F. M., Phillion, J., & He, M. F. (2003). An exploration of narrative inquiry into multiculturalism in education: Reflecting on two decades of research in an inner-city Canadian community school. *Curriculum Inquiry, 33,* 363–384.

Cook-Sather, A. (2002) Authorizing students' perspectives: toward trust, dialogue, and change in education. *Educational Researcher, 31*(4), 3–14.

Cummins, J. (2001). *Negotiating identities: Education for empowerment in a diverse society* (2nd ed.). Ontario, CA: CABE (California Association for Bilingual Education).

Cummins, J., Bismilla, V., Chow, P., Cohen, S., Giampapa, F., Leoni, L., et al. (2005). Affirming identity in multilingual classrooms. *Educational Leadership, 63*(1), 38–43.

Dewey, J. (1938). *Experience and education.* New York: Simon & Schuster.

Feuerverger, G. (2001). *Oasis of dreams: Teaching and learning peace in a Jewish-Palestinian village in Israel.* New York: Routledge.

Gay, G. (2000). *Culturally responsive teaching: Theory, research, & practice.* New York: Teachers College Press.

He, M. F., Phillion, J., Chan, E., & Xu, S. (2007). Chapter 15— Immigrant students' experience of curriculum. In F. M. Connelly, M. F. He, & J. Phillion (Eds.), *Handbook of curriculum and instruction* (pp. 219–239). Thousand Oaks, CA: Sage.

Igoa, C. (1995). *The inner world of the immigrant child.* New York: St. Martin's Press.

Jackson, P. (1990). *Life in classrooms.* New York: Teachers College Press.

Jackson, P. (1992). Conceptions of curriculum specialists. In P. Jackson (Ed.), *Handbook of research on curriculum* (pp. 3–40). New York: Peter Lang.

Kao, G. (1995). Asian Americans as model minorities? A look at their academic performance. *American Journal of Education, 103,* 121–159.

Kim, U., & Chun, M. J. B. (1994). The educational 'success' of Asian Americans: An indigenous perspective. *Journal of Applied Developmental Psychology, 15,* 329–339.

Kouritzin, S. G. (1999). *Face(t)s of first language loss.* Mahwah, NJ: Erlbaum.

Ladson-Billings, G. (1995). Multicultural teacher education: Research, practice, and policy. In J. A. Banks & C. A. McGee Banks (Eds.), *Handbook of research on multicultural education* (pp. 747–759). Toronto, Canada: Prentice Hall International.

Ladson-Billings, G. (2001). *Crossing over to Canaan: The journey of new teachers in diverse classrooms.* San Francisco: Jossey-Bass.

Lee, S. J. (1994). Behind the model-minority stereotype: Voices of high and low-achieving Asian American students. *Anthropology & Education Quarterly, 25,* 413–429.

Lee, S. J. (1996). *Unraveling the "model minority" stereotype: Listening to Asian American youth.* New York: Teachers College Press.

Lee, S. J. (2001). More than "model minority" or "delinquents": A look at Hmong American high school students. *Harvard Educational Review, 71,* 505–528.

Li, G. (2002). "East is East, West is West"? Home literacy, culture, and schooling. In J. L. Kincheloe & J. A. Jipson (Eds.), *Rethinking childhood book series* (Vol. 28). New York: Peter Lang.

Li, G. (2005). *Culturally contested pedagogy: Battles of literacy and schooling between mainstream teachers and Asian immigrant parents.* Albany, NY: SUNY Press.

McCaleb, S. P. (1994). *Building communities of learners: A collaboration among teachers, students, families and community.* New York: St. Martin's Press.

Moodley, K. A. (1995). Multicultural education in Canada: Historical development and current status. In J. A. Banks & C. A. McGee Banks (Eds.), *Handbook of research on multicultural education* (pp. 801–820). Toronto, Canada: Prentice Hall International.

Nieto, S., & Bode, P. (2008). *Affirming diversity: The sociopolitical context of multicultural education* (5th ed.). New York: Longman.

Phillion, J., & He, M. F. (2004). Using life based literary narratives in multicultural teacher education. *Multicultural Perspectives, 6*(2), 3–9.

Pinar, W. F., Reynolds, W. M., Slattery, P., & Taubman, P. M. (1995). *Understanding curriculum: An introduction to the study of historical and contemporary curriculum discourses.* New York: Peter Lang.

Rodriguez, R. (1982). *Hunger of memory: The education of Richard Rodriguez.* Boston: David R. Godine.

Rolon-Dow, R. (2004). Seduced by images: Identity and schooling in the lives of Puerto Rican girls. *Anthropology & Education Quarterly, 35,* 8–29.

Ross, V., & Chan, E. (2008). Multicultural education: Raj's story using a curricular conceptual lens of the particular. *Teaching and Teacher Education, 24,* 1705–1716.

Sarroub, L. K. (2005). *All-American Yemeni girls: Being Muslim in a public school.* Philadelphia: University of Pennsylvania Press.

Schubert, W., & Ayers, W. (Eds.) *Teacher lore: Learning from our own experience.* New York: Longman.

Smith-Hefner, N. (1993). Education, gender, and generational conflict among Khmer refugees. *Anthropology & Education Quarterly, 24,* 135–158.

Statistics Canada. (2008). *Canada's ethnocultural mosaic, 2006 census.* Retrieved July 1, 2008, from http://www12.statcan.ca/english/census06/analysis/ethnicorigin/pdf/97-562-XIE2006001.pdf

U.S. Census Bureau. (2002). *United States Census 2000.* Washington, D.C.: U.S. Government Printing Office.

Valdés, G. (1996). *Con respeto: Bridging the distances between culturally diverse families and schools. An ethnographic portrait.* New York: Teachers College Press.

Villegas, A. M. (1991). *Culturally responsive pedagogy for the 1990's and beyond.* Princeton, NJ: Educational Testing Service.

Wong-Fillmore, L. (1991). When learning a second language means losing the first. *Early Childhood Research Quarterly, 6,* 323–346.

Zine, J. (2001). Muslim youth in Canadian schools: Education and the politics of religious identity. *Anthropology & Education Quarterly, 32,* 399–423.

Author Note

Elaine Chan is an assistant professor of Diversity and Curriculum Studies in the Department of Teaching, Learning, and Teacher Education at the College of Education and Human Sciences, the University of Nebraska–Lincoln. Her research and teaching interests are in the areas of: narrative inquiry, culture and curriculum; multicultural education; ethnic identity of first-generation North Americans; student experiences of schooling; and educational equity policies. She has taught and conducted long-term classroom-based research in Canadian, Japanese, and American schools. She is currently co-authoring a book on engaging ELL students in arts education with Margaret Macintyre Latta.

Mixed Methods Designs

*I*f you have access to both quantitative and qualitative data, you can use both forms of data to understand your research problem and answer your research question. With qualitative research now accepted by educational researchers, and with quantitative research long established as an approach, mixed methods research has become popular as the newest development in research methods and in approaches to "mixing" quantitative and qualitative research. This chapter defines mixed methods research, identifies when research problems merit its use, assesses the key characteristics of it, highlights ethical issues that may arise when using it, and advances the steps in conducting and evaluating this design.

By the end of this chapter, you should be able to:

◆ Define mixed methods research, and describe when to use it, and how it developed.

◆ Identify the types of mixed methods designs.

◆ Describe the key characteristics of mixed methods research.

◆ Identify some potential ethical issues in mixed methods research.

◆ Understand the steps used in conducting mixed methods research.

◆ List criteria for evaluating a mixed methods study.

Maria chooses to collect both quantitative and qualitative data. She decides to conduct a survey and then use follow-up interviews with a few students to explain the results of the survey. She views this research in two phases. For the first, quantitative phase, her research question is "What factors influence student attitudes toward weapon possession?" Later, in the follow-up, qualitative phase, her question is "When students mention 'peers' as a factor influencing student attitudes, what do they mean?" In this study, Maria collects quantitative survey data and then follows up with qualitative interview data to help explain the initial quantitative results. Maria conducts a study using mixed methods research.

WHAT IS MIXED METHODS RESEARCH, WHEN IS IT USED, AND HOW DID IT DEVELOP?

A **mixed methods research design** is a procedure for collecting, analyzing, and "mixing" both quantitative and qualitative methods in a single study or a series of studies to understand a research problem (Creswell & Plano Clark, 2011). The basic assumption is that the uses of both quantitative and qualitative methods, in combination, provide a better understanding of the research problem and question than either method by itself.

If you use this design, you need to understand *both* quantitative and qualitative research. This makes this type of design an advanced methods procedures. The procedures are time-consuming, requiring extensive data collection and analysis, and such time requirements may require that you participate in a research team when using it. Also, mixed methods research is not simply collecting two distinct "strands" of research—qualitative and quantitative. It consists of merging, integrating, linking, or embedding the two "strands." In short, the data are "mixed" in a mixed methods study.

When Do You Conduct a Mixed Methods Study?

There are several reasons for using a mixed methods design to conduct a study. In general, you conduct a mixed methods study when you have both quantitative and qualitative data and both types of data, together, provide a better understanding of your research problem than either type by itself. Mixed methods research is a good design to use if you seek to build on the strengths of both quantitative and qualitative data. Quantitative data, such as scores on instruments, yield specific numbers that can be statistically analyzed, can produce results to assess the frequency and magnitude of trends, and can provide useful information if you need to describe trends about a large number of people. However, qualitative data, such as open-ended interviews that provide actual words of people in the study, offer many different perspectives on the study topic and provide a complex picture of the situation. When one combines quantitative and qualitative data, "we have a very powerful mix" (Miles & Huberman, 1994, p. 42). For example, by assessing both outcomes of a study (i.e., quantitative) as well as the process (i.e., qualitative), we can develop "a complex" picture of social phenomenon (Greene & Caracelli, 1997, p. 7).

You also conduct a mixed methods study when one type of research (qualitative or quantitative) is not enough to address the research problem or answer the research questions. More data is needed to extend, elaborate on, or explain the first database. For example, you may want to first explore the data qualitatively to develop an instrument or to identify variables to test in a later quantitative study. You engage in a mixed methods study when you want to follow up a quantitative study with a qualitative one to obtain more detailed, specific information than can be gained from the results of statistical tests.

You use mixed methods when you want to provide an alternative perspective in a study. An example of this would be an experimental study in which the experiment yields useful information about outcomes, but the additional collection of qualitative data develops a more in-depth understanding of how the experimental intervention actually worked. Another example would be when a policymaker wants both the "numbers" and the "stories" about an issue. These different sources of information provide both a condensed understanding of a problem as well as the detail. On a practical level, you use mixed methods research for studies in graduate programs in which qualitative research has yet to be fully accepted and in which quantitative approaches are the norm.

Although individuals in these programs may recognize the value of qualitative research, a mixed methods study is more acceptable than a "pure" qualitative study because there is still a component of quantitative research in the study. Also on a practical level, mixed methods studies are increasingly being published in the scholarly literature. Graduate students use mixed methods research in order to learn and experience this form of research design so that they are well-informed about the latest research approaches.

How Did Mixed Methods Research Develop?

The historical development of mixed methods research has been outlined elsewhere (e.g., Creswell & Plano Clark, 2011; Tashakkori & Teddlie, 1998), and this review builds on these earlier discussions. We can trace this evolution through several phases.

Mixing Forms of Quantitative Data

Since the 1930s, educational and social science investigators were collecting multiple methods of data (Sieber, 1973). In 1959, Campbell and Fiske introduced the multitrait, multimethod approach, stimulating interest in employing multiple methods in a single study. Campbell and Fiske's interest was not in mixed methods research; rather, they sought to develop valid psychological traits by collecting multiple forms of quantitative data. To develop these traits, they suggested a process whereby researchers would collect multiple measures of multiple traits and assess each measure by at least two methods. When they correlated scores and placed them into a matrix, a multimethod, multitrait matrix resulted. An investigator could determine if the trait was valid by examining this matrix and assessing whether the measures of the trait correlated higher with each other than they did with measures of different traits involving separate methods. Evidence from these correlations provided useful information about different forms of validity. At a broader level, the use of multiple methods to measure a trait encouraged other researchers to collect more than one type of data, even if this data was only quantitative, such as peer judgment scores and word association tests.

Combining Quantitative and Qualitative Data

Soon others were collecting multiple forms of data, but now it consisted of quantitative and qualitative data. By 1973, Sieber suggested the combination of in-depth case studies with surveys, creating a "new style of research" and the "integration" of research techniques within a single study (p. 1337). A few years later, Jick (1979) used the combination of surveys, semistructured interviews, observations, and archival materials to provide a "rich and comprehensive picture" (p. 606) of anxiety and job insecurity during organizational mergers.

Jick's (1979) study was more than an examination of mergers; his article used the merger study to illustrate the procedure of triangulating data. *Triangulation,* a term drawn from naval military science, is the process where sailors use multiple reference points to locate an object's exact position at sea (Jick, 1979). Applied to research, it meant that investigators could improve their inquiries by collecting and converging (or integrating) different kinds of data bearing on the same phenomenon. The three points to the triangle are the two sources of the data and the phenomenon. This improvement in inquiries would come from blending the strengths of one type of method and neutralizing the weaknesses of the other. For example, in a study of middle school principal leadership, a researcher can augment qualitative observations of behavior with a quantitative survey in order to provide a more complete understanding of leadership. To converge data in a single study continues to be an attractive approach to mixed methods research today.

Questioning the Integration of Worldviews and Methods

Further developments on procedures, however, had to wait for several years. The issue arose as to whether quantitative and qualitative research could be combined because each approach drew on different philosophical assumptions. This debate was more than tension between those who embraced traditional quantitative research and those who advocated for qualitative inquiry. The issue was whether a researcher who used certain methods also needed to use a specific worldview—the "compatibility" (Tashakkori & Teddlie, 1998) between worldviews and methods. Worldviews are the broad philosophical assumptions researchers use when they conduct studies. Although some researchers may not recognize it, they make assumptions about knowledge (e.g., math scores exist to demonstrate achievement for seventh graders) and how it can be obtained (e.g., we can measure math ability using standardized achievement tests). Those who argued for "incompatibility" said that quantitative methods (e.g., student scores on an instrument) belonged to one worldview (e.g., an attempt to measure, objectively, student achievement), whereas qualitative methods (e.g., an observation of students) apply to another worldview (e.g., the researcher assesses reality subjectively through his or her lens). The logic of this argument led to the conclusion that mixed methods research was untenable because a single worldview did not exist for the inquiry.

The worldview–method argument—called the paradigm debate—played out for several years, during the late 1980s and early 1990s, especially at national conferences such as the American Evaluation Association's annual meetings (Reichardt & Rallis, 1994). But it has largely diminished because of several factors. Some said that those who argued for the incompatibility of worldviews and methods created a false dichotomy (Reichardt & Cook, 1979) that does not hold under close inspection. For example, there is an "objective" reality (e.g., the classroom). But under close inspection there is also a "subjective" reality (e.g., we see different things as we look at a classroom). Some methods are more closely associated with one worldview than the other, but to categorize them as "belonging" to one worldview more than another creates an unrealistic situation.

Others contended that mixed methods research has its own philosophical worldview: pragmatism. The pragmatists, for example, believe philosophically in using procedures that "work" for a particular research problem under study and that you should use many methods when understanding a research problem (e.g., see discussion by Tashakkori & Teddlie, 1998). In addition, the dialectical position, embraced by Greene and Caracelli (1997), recommends that researchers report the multiple worldviews they hold—thus honoring worldviews as important—and also collect both quantitative and qualitative data. Other philosophies have emerged as a foundation for mixed methods research, such as the transformative research perspective advancing the need for addressing issues of social justice for underrepresented groups (Mertens, 2009).

Developing Procedures for Mixed Methods Studies

Another factor that quieted the debate was the increased interest in the procedural aspects of conducting mixed methods research. Authors explored the "purposes" of mixed methods research, identified alternative designs to use, and specified a notation system and visual models for these designs.

The idea of triangulation had already introduced one purpose for mixing methods—to integrate multiple databases to understand a phenomenon and research problem (Rossman & Wilson, 1985). Other reasons soon emerged. You could collect quantitative and qualitative data separately in two phases so that data from one source could enhance, elaborate, or complement data from the other source (Greene, Caracelli, & Graham, 1989). In more complicated designs, the data collection could extend from two to three phases (e.g., see Miles & Huberman, 1994) or be collected from multiple levels in an organization, such as the district, school, teacher, and student (e.g., see Tashak-kori & Teddlie, 1998; Teddlie & Tashakkori, 2009). You could also embed data, with one form of data becoming less important in a design emphasizing the other form of data (Creswell, 2009).

Central to this thinking about different models or designs has been the visualization of procedures and the use of a notation system designed by Morse (1991). This system, shown in Figure 16.1, is a way to portray the procedures in mixed methods designs. Shorthand labels for quantitative (quan) and qualitative (qual) simplify the terms.

Figure 16.1 also portrays two sample designs. As shown in Study #1, a researcher places an emphasis on both quantitative and qualitative data and integrates or combines the data in the study. In Study #2, the investigator emphasizes quantitative data in the first phase of a study, followed by a minor emphasis on qualitative data in the second phase of the study. Later in this chapter we consider names for these designs and explore several variations of them.

Advocating for a Distinct Design

With emerging procedures, a notation system, and specific designs, the discussion has turned to viewing mixed methods research as a separate and distinct design. To experiments, surveys, grounded theory, and others, we now add mixed methods research or we incorporate this form of research into these designs. Advocates for mixed methods research have written entire chapters and books on its use in the social and health sciences (Creswell, 2009; Creswell & Plano Clark, 2011; Greene, 2007; Tashakkori & Teddlie, 1998, 2011). In addition, refinements continue in the process of data analysis in mixed methods research (Caracelli & Greene, 1993), the use of computer programs for merging quantitative statistical programs with text analysis programs (Bazeley, 2000, 2010), and the identification and discussion of numerous mixed methods studies reported in the scholarly literature (e.g., Creswell & Plano Clark, 2011; Greene et al., 1989).

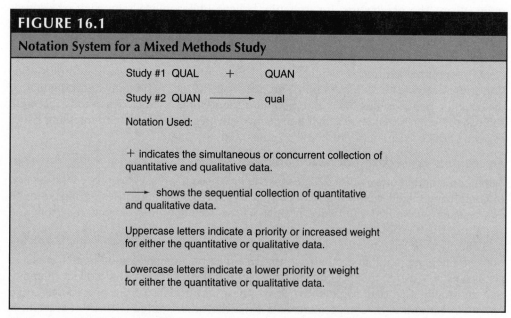

FIGURE 16.1
Notation System for a Mixed Methods Study

Study #1 QUAL   +   QUAN

Study #2 QUAN ⟶ qual

Notation Used:

+ indicates the simultaneous or concurrent collection of quantitative and qualitative data.

⟶ shows the sequential collection of quantitative and qualitative data.

Uppercase letters indicate a priority or increased weight for either the quantitative or qualitative data.

Lowercase letters indicate a lower priority or weight for either the quantitative or qualitative data.

Source: Adapted from Morse, 1991.

Reflective Period

In the last 5 to 7 years, mixed methods has entered a new historical period in its evolution. This reflective period is characterized by two major themes: a current assessment or mapping of the field and the emergence of constructive criticisms that have challenged the nature of mixed methods research. The mapping of the field consists of establishing priorities for research in mixed methods (Tashakkori & Teddlie, 2003), identifying the domains of inquiry (Greene, 2007), and summarizing topics being addressed so that emerging and experienced scholars can add to the ongoing discussions (Creswell, 2011). The challenges that have arisen in the last few years have come from scholars around the world and range from more basic concerns about a definition and language for mixed methods, to philosophical issues of "mixing" paradigm and the dominant discourse in the field, to the applied issues of the types of designs and the claims being advanced by mixed methods scholars (Creswell, in press). These controversies signal a healthy development for mixed methods research. For example, the controversial discussion by Freshwater (2007) asks for a greater openness to new ideas in mixed methods and to challenge accepting key ideas without reservation.

WHAT ARE THE TYPES OF MIXED METHODS DESIGNS?

Although work has begun on identifying types of mixed methods designs, many models and approaches have been advanced in the literature. (To review the possibilities, see the discussions by Creswell & Plano Clark, 2011). The strategy authors have taken is to review published studies and classify them by type of design.

Before examining the types of designs, it might be helpful to reflect on useful strategies for identifying a mixed methods study reported in the published literature. One strategy is to ask the following questions to help you identify a study as mixed methods research:

◆ *Is there evidence in the title?* Look at the title to determine if it includes words such as *quantitative and qualitative, mixed methods,* or other related terms to signify the collection of both quantitative and qualitative data. Related terms might be *integrated, combined, triangulation, multimethod,* or *mixed methodology* (Tashakkori & Teddlie, 1998).

◆ *Is there evidence in the data collection section?* Examine the "Methods" or "Procedure" section where the author addresses data collection and identify if researchers discuss forms of quantitative data (i.e., numbers reported) and qualitative data (i.e., words or images) as part of the data collection.

◆ *Is there evidence in the purpose statement or the research questions?* Examine the abstract or the introduction of the study to identify the purpose or research questions. Do these statements indicate that the researcher intends to collect both quantitative and qualitative data during the study?

Having identified the study as mixed methods, next determine the type of mixed methods design the author is using. You might ask the following questions:

1. *What priority or weight does the researcher give to the quantitative and qualitative data collection?* Priority or weight means that one form of data is given more attention or emphasis in the study; however, quantitative and qualitative data are sometimes treated equally.

2. *What is the sequence of collecting the quantitative and qualitative data?*   Determine whether the qualitative data (or quantitative data) comes first and second in the data collection or whether they are collected concurrently.
3. *How does the researcher actually analyze the data?*   Determine if the researchers combine the data in one analysis or keep the analyses separate.
4. *Where in the study does the researcher "mix" the data?*   The two forms of data might be combined, linked, or mixed during data collection, between data collection and data analysis, during data analysis, or in the interpretation of a study.

Using these four questions, you can locate and identify most mixed methods designs commonly used in educational research. Figure 16.2 illustrates six mixed methods designs, with the first four as the basic designs in use today and the last two as complex designs that are becoming increasingly popular (Creswell & Plano Clark, 2011). The designs are:

◆ the convergent parallel design
◆ the explanatory sequential design
◆ the exploratory sequential design
◆ the embedded design
◆ the transformative design
◆ the multiphase design

The Convergent Parallel Design

The purpose of a **convergent (or parallel or concurrent) mixed methods design** is to simultaneously collect both quantitative and qualitative data, merge the data, and use the results to understand a research problem. A basic rationale for this design is that one data collection form supplies strengths to offset the weaknesses of the other form, and that a more complete understanding of a research problem results from collecting both quantitative and qualitative data. For example, quantitative scores on an instrument from many individuals provide strengths to offset the weaknesses of qualitative documents from a few people. Alternatively, qualitative, in-depth observation of a few people offers strength to quantitative data that does not adequately provide detailed information about the context in which individuals provide information (e.g., the setting).

How does the process of a convergent study work? The researcher gathers both quantitative and qualitative data, analyzes both datasets separately, compares the results from the analysis of both datasets, and makes an interpretation as to whether the results support or contradict each other. The direct comparison of the two datasets by the researcher provides a "convergence" of data sources. As shown in Figure 16.2, in this design:

◆ *The mixed methods researcher often gives equal priority to both quantitative and qualitative data (see QUAN and QUAL).*   The researcher values both quantitative and qualitative data and sees them as approximately equal sources of information in the study. For example, interview data are as important as the scores gathered on an instrument.
◆ *The mixed methods researcher collects both the quantitative and qualitative data concurrently or simultaneously during the study.*   Qualitative documents about what the students learn in preschool are reviewed, for example, at the same time that the researcher collects quantitative observations on student behavior using a checklist.
◆ *The mixed methods researcher compares the results from quantitative and qualitative analyses to determine if the two databases yield similar or dissimilar results.*

FIGURE 16.2

Types of Mixed Methods Designs

Convergent Parallel Design

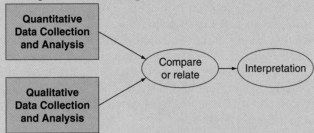

Explanatory Sequential Design

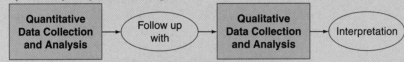

Exploratory Sequential Design

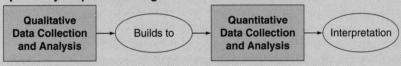

Embedded Design

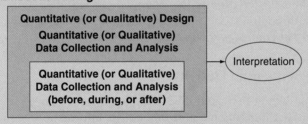

Transformative Design

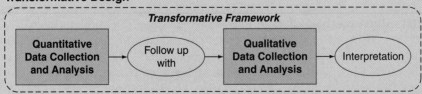

Multiphase Design

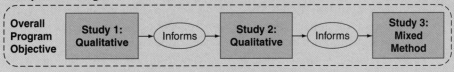

This comparison may occur in several ways. The most popular approach is to describe the quantitative and qualitative results side by side in a discussion section of a study. For example, the researcher would first present the quantitative statistical results and then provide qualitative quotes to either confirm or disconfirm the statistical results. Another approach is to actually merge the quantitative and qualitative data in a single table. For each major topic in the study, the researcher could array the quantitative results and the qualitative themes in columns that match each topic. A third approach is to transform one of the datasets so that they can be directly compared with the other dataset. For instance, qualitative themes identified during interviews are "quantified" and given a score as to their frequency. These scores are then compared with scores from instruments measuring variables that address the same ideas as the themes.

The strength of this design is that it combines the advantages of each form of data; that is, quantitative data provide for generalizability, whereas qualitative data offer information about the context or setting. This design enables a researcher to gather information that uses the best features of both quantitative and qualitative data collection. One difficulty with this design is how to merge the two forms of data, and, when this is done, to determine how to assess results that diverge.

In a convergent mixed methods study, Lee and Greene (2007) examined the relationship between graduate students' placement test scores for English as a second language on a daylong, process-oriented writing assessment and assessment of first-semester academic performance. This outcome was assessed through GPA and both quantitative questionnaires and qualitative interviews with faculty members and students. Thus, this study reported both quantitative and qualitative data. The design was described as a "complementarity" mixed methods study (Lee & Greene, 2007, p. 369) and it illustrated the researchers approach to converge the quantitative and qualitative data. Each data source was collected independently and then analyzed separately. The authors integrated the quantitative and qualitative data during data analysis, and they represent this combination in two ways: through a scatterplot that includes both extreme scores and quotes and through a table that compares scores with quotes.

The Explanatory Sequential Design

Instead of collecting data at the same time and merging the results, a mixed methods researcher might collect quantitative and qualitative information sequentially in two phases, with one form of data collection following and informing the other. This design, also shown in Figure 16.2, is an explanatory mixed methods design; perhaps the most popular form of mixed methods design in educational research. An **explanatory sequential mixed methods design** (also called a two-phase model; Creswell & Plano Clark, 2011) consists of first collecting quantitative data and then collecting qualitative data to help explain or elaborate on the quantitative results. The rationale for this approach is that the quantitative data and results provide a general picture of the research problem; more analysis, specifically through qualitative data collection, is needed to refine, extend, or explain the general picture. Referring back to Figure 16.2, you can see that in this design,

◆ *The mixed methods researcher places a priority on quantitative data (QUAN) collection and analysis.*   This is done by introducing it first in the study and having it represent a major aspect of data collection. A small qualitative (qual) component typically follows in the second phase of the research.

◆ *The mixed methods researcher collects quantitative data first in the sequence.*   This is followed by the secondary qualitative data collection. Researchers often present these studies in two phases, with each phase clearly identified in headings in the report.

◆ *The mixed methods researcher uses the qualitative data to refine the results from the quantitative data.*   This refinement results in exploring a few typical cases, probing a key result in more detail, or following up with outlier or extreme cases.

This design has the advantage of clearly identified quantitative and qualitative parts, an advantage for readers as well as for those designing and conducting the study. Unlike the convergent design, the researcher does not have to converge or integrate two different forms of data. This design also captures the best of both quantitative and qualitative data—to obtain quantitative results from a population in the first phase, and then refine or elaborate these findings through an in-depth qualitative exploration in the second phase. The difficulty in using this design, however, is that the researcher needs to determine what aspect of the quantitative results to follow up on. This follow-up means deciding on the participants to sample in the second qualitative phase as well as the questions to ask in this follow-up phase that builds on the initial quantitative phase. Also, this design is labor intensive, and it requires both expertise and time to collect both quantitative and qualitative data.

A two-phase project by Ivankova and Stick (2007) is a good example of an explanatory design. Their research examined factors contributing to students' persistence in a distributed (on-line) doctoral program in educational leadership in higher education. They called their study a "sequential explanatory study" (Ivankova & Stick, 2007, p. 93). They first gathered quantitative survey data from 278 current and former students and then followed up with four qualitative case study respondents to explore the survey responses in more detail. This project illustrates rigorous quantitative methods using good sampling and sophisticated data analysis as well as persuasive qualitative case study procedures that show the development of themes for each case and a cross-case comparison. They present a good figure of their mixed methods procedures showing the quantitative and the qualitative phases, following by summarizing both results. By studying four specific cases as a follow-up, they were able to gain greater insight into the important predictors of student persistence.

The Exploratory Sequential Design

Rather than first analyzing or collecting *quantitative data* as is done in the explanatory design, the mixed methods researcher begins with *qualitative data* and then collects quantitative information. The purpose of an **exploratory sequential mixed methods design** involves the procedure of first gathering qualitative data to explore a phenomenon, and then collecting quantitative data to explain relationships found in the qualitative data. A popular application of this design is to explore a phenomenon, identify themes, design an instrument, and subsequently test it. Researchers use this design when existing instruments, variables, and measures may not be known or available for the population under study. Again refer to Figure 16.2. In this design,

◆ *The mixed methods researcher emphasizes the qualitative data (QUAL) more than the quantitative data (quan).*   This emphasis may occur through presenting the overarching question as an open-ended question or discussing the qualitative results in more detail than the quantitative results.

◆ *The mixed methods researcher has a sequence to data collection that involves first collecting qualitative data followed by quantitative data.*   Typically in these designs, the researcher presents the study in two phases, with the first phase involving qualitative data collection (e.g., interviews, observations) with a small number of individuals, followed by quantitative data collection (e.g., a survey) with a large, randomly selected number of participants.

◆ *The mixed methods researcher plans on the quantitative data to build on or explain the initial qualitative findings.* The intent of the researcher is for the quantitative data results to refine and extend the qualitative findings by testing out an instrument or survey developed using the qualitative findings or by testing a typology or classification that developed from the qualitative findings. In both cases, the initial qualitative exploration leads to detailed, generalizable results through the second quantitative phase.

One advantage of this approach is that it allows the researcher to identify measures actually grounded in the data obtained from study participants. The researcher can initially explore views by listening to participants rather than approach a topic with a predetermined set of variables. However, it has the disadvantage of requiring extensive data collection as well as the time required for this process is long. The testing of an instrument adds considerably to the length of time this design requires to be implemented. It also asks researchers to make decisions about the most appropriate qualitative data (e.g., quotes, codes, themes) to use in the follow-up quantitative phase of the study.

In the exploratory sequential mixed methods design by Meijer, Verloop, and Beijaard (2001), the authors studied language teachers' practical knowledge about teaching reading comprehension to 16- to 18-year-old students. They first conducted a qualitative study of teachers' practical knowledge from 13 teachers about reading comprehension by collecting semistructured interviews and concept-mapping assignments. They then used information from this qualitative phase to identify six categories of teachers' knowledge. They also used the teachers' expressions from the qualitative data to form Likert-type items and scales for the follow-up questionnaire. Thus, the second phase of their study consisted of developing and testing an instrument based on their qualitative data. Sixty-nine teachers completed the questionnaire and the results were used to assess the teachers' shared practical knowledge about teaching reading comprehension and the variations that existed among the teachers. A significant element of this study is that the reader learns about the detailed process of designing and developing an instrument based on initial qualitative data.

The Embedded Design

A second form of mixed methods design is similar to both the parallel and the sequential design, with some important differences. The purpose of the **embedded design** is to collect quantitative and qualitative data simultaneously or sequentially, but to have one form of data play a supportive role to the other form of data. The reason for collecting the second form of data is that it augments or supports the primary form of data. The supportive data may be either qualitative or quantitative, but most examples in the literature support adding qualitative data into a quantitative design. For example, during a quantitative experiment, the researcher may collect qualitative data to examine how participants in the treatment condition are experiencing the intervention. Also, the researcher may collect qualitative data either before or after the experiment to help support the experimental study. Collecting data before the experiment can help to design an intervention that is tailored to the participants. Collecting data after the experiment can help to explain and follow up on the quantitative outcome results. As another example, during a correlational study, the researcher may gather secondary qualitative data to help understand the reasons for the correlational results. In some embedded designs, the procedures are sequential, with the secondary form of data gathered before the experiment (or the correlational study) begins (e.g., to help determine the best means for recruiting participants) or after it concludes (e.g., to follow up and help explain the results).

How does the process of an embedded study work? The researcher collects both quantitative and qualitative data during a single study (e.g., an experiment or a correlational study), the two datasets are analyzed separately, and they address different research questions. For example, the quantitative data will address whether the intervention had an impact on the outcomes, whereas the qualitative data will assess how the participants experienced the intervention. As shown in Figure 16.2, in this design:

◆ *The mixed methods researcher gives priority to the major form of data collection (e.g., often QUAN) and secondary status to the supportive form (e.g., often qual) of data collection.* The secondary form is used in the mixed methods study to support and provide additional information to the primary form.
◆ *The mixed methods researcher collects both the quantitative and qualitative data simultaneously or sequentially.* Both forms of data are collected during the study at roughly the same time or in sequence. It is important to understand and describe the purpose for which the secondary data is being collected.
◆ *The mixed methods researcher uses the secondary form of data to augment or provide additional sources of information not provided by the primary source of data.* The augmentation is to gather information that typically addresses a different question than asked for by the primary form of data. For example, the collection of qualitative data during an experiment may be to understand the "process" the participants are going through, whereas the quantitative data assesses the impact of the treatment on the outcomes.

The strength of this design is that it combines the advantages of both quantitative and qualitative data. Quantitative data are more effective at recording outcomes of the experiment than identifying through qualitative data how individuals are experiencing the process. It also provides a type of mixed methods design in which the researcher can collect qualitative data, but the overall design still emphasizes quantitative approaches. In some fields new to qualitative research, this role of qualitative data helps to legitimize the use of such forms of data. One challenge in using this design is to be clear about the intent of the secondary database. In addition, the two databases may not be easily compared because the data address different research questions. There is also the possibility that introducing qualitative data collection during an experiment (or correlational study) will influence the outcomes. Strategies need to be put into place to minimize this effect (e.g., collecting qualitative data at the end of the experiment, having participants complete journals of their experience that are turned in after the experiment). Further, like the convergent design, the simultaneous data collection of quantitative and qualitative data may be labor intensive for a single researcher.

Harrison's (2007) correlational study of an undergraduate mentoring program in teacher education illustrates the embedded mixed methods design. Using quantitative longitudinal analysis, she followed 18 undergraduates in a leadership program over 2 years as they learned how to forge mentor–mentee relationships in an undergraduate teacher education program. Harrison collected quantitative data on an instrument, the Working Alliance Inventory (WAI), during six administrations over a 2-year period. This quantitative information represented the major source of information during her study, and her correlation model suggested that a number of factors (e.g., number of times the mentors–mentees met) would influence the building of positive relationships. She also collected limited data in the form of three qualitative focus group interviews with the students. She plotted the longitudinal trends in relationship building using the WAI scores over time, and then used the secondary data, the focus group information, to help her understand why some mentor–mentees forged closer relationships, plateaued, or formed more distant relationships over time. Her study was a good example in education of an embedded design with a major quantitative correlational component and a smaller, supportive qualitative focus group element.

The Transformative Design

At a more complex level than the four previous designs, we have the transformative mixed methods design. The intent of the **transformative mixed methods design** is to use one of the four designs (convergent, explanatory, exploratory, or embedded), but to encase the design within a transformative framework or lens (Creswell & Plano Clark, 2011). This framework provides an orienting lens for the mixed methods design. It informs the overall purpose of the study, the research questions, the data collection, and the outcome of the study. The intent of the framework is to address a social issue for a marginalized or underrepresented population and engage in research that brings about change. Thus, strength of this design is that it is value-based and ideological (Greene, 2007). The typical frameworks found in mixed methods are feminist, racial, ethnic, disability, and gay or lesbian perspectives. A challenge in using this design is that we are still learning about how to best integrate the framework into a mixed methods study.

A diagram of the procedures is found in Figure 16.2. For purposes of discussion, this figure shows the use of a transformative lens within an explanatory sequential design (i.e., quantitative data collection followed by qualitative data collection). In this design:

◆ *The mixed methods researcher uses either a convergent, explanatory, exploratory, or embedded design.*   The basic designs provide the cornerstone for the transformative design, but the transformative design goes beyond simply the use of the basic design.

◆ *The mixed methods researcher uses an overall orienting lens in the study as a transformative framework. This framework may be a feminist perspective, a racial or ethnic perspective, or some other perspective.*   It is this framework that shapes many aspects of the mixed methods design, such as the framing of the title, the questions, the methods, and the conclusions. The framework basically addresses an issue for an underrepresented group and presents research intended to bring about change for that group.

◆ *The mixed methods researcher calls for change that will address the social issue faced by the group under study.*   A strong key to a good transformative mixed methods study is whether the research calls for reform or changes at the end of the study. This call may be an explicit request for change or steps that will be required to bring about change.

In a sequential explanatory mixed methods study by Buck, Cook, Quigley, Eastwood, and Lucas (2009), the authors used a feminist lens to study 89 African American girls' personal orientations toward science learning. The study begins with a theoretical framework about the writings of feminist researchers in science education and what it means to be a girl in science as well as an African American girl in science. In this sequential design, a quantitative first phase study of the girls' attitudes toward science was collected on an inventory to provide descriptive results. This was followed by a qualitative second phase consisting of focus group interviews and themes related to girls' definition of science, the importance with science, and their experiences and success in school science. As a final step, the authors linked the qualitative themes to categories. In the conclusion of the article, the authors call for reforming the instructional strategies in science for girls to be positively connected to science, and they comment how their study has "illustrated the use of a feminist lens in a study in which specific myths have been dispelled and recommendations for change made." (p. 408)

Multiphase Design

Like the transformative design, the multiphase design is a complex design that builds on the basic convergent, explanatory, exploratory, and embedded designs. **Multiphase mixed methods designs** occur when researchers or a team of researchers examine a problem or topic through a series of phases or separate studies. The groups of phases or studies are considered to be a mixed methods design and the intent of the design is to address a set of incremental research questions that all advance one programmatic research objective (Creswell & Plano Clark, 2011). The phases or studies may employ a combination of concurrent or sequential designs and this form of design is popular in large-scale health research and in evaluation research. The strength of this design lies in the use of multiple projects to best understand an overall program objective. Challenges include forming a research team that can work comfortably together given diverse method orientations, making sure that the phases or studies link together, and having all of the studies provide insight into an overall project objective. As shown in Figure 16.2, the major elements of this design are:

◆ *The mixed methods researchers use either a convergent, explanatory, exploratory, or embedded design in multiple phases or projects in the study.* The multiphase design builds on the basic mixed methods designs and adds to these designs multiple phases or projects conducted over time. Any one phase may have a combination of concurrent and sequential mixed methods designs. In addition, this form of research is most amenable to large-scale funded investigations.

◆ *The mixed methods researchers need to clearly identify projects or phases that help address a larger program objective. These researchers also need experience in large-scale research.* Teams might be composed of individuals with quantitative, qualitative, and mixed methods research skills.

◆ *The mixed methods researchers need to interrelate the different phases or projects so that they tie together to address a common research objective.* Typically, one phase or project leads to another and, in this sense, the phases or projects build on (or inform) each other throughout the study.

In a multiphase mixed methods study, Nastasi et al. (2007) provide a program development research study of culture-specific definitions of mental health constructs (e.g., stressors, competencies) for adolescents in Sri Lanka. This study was part of the Sri Lanka Mental Health Promotion Project. In the beginning of the article we are introduced to twelve different phases in the research project that form formative research, instrument development, program development, and evaluation research. At these different phases, the researchers engaged in combinations of quantitative and qualitative research, some presented as concurrent and some as sequential. A table in their article showed how they combined the qualitative and quantitative data in each phase (e.g., in the final evaluation phase they combined qualitative and quantitative results based on an experimental design and post-intervention interviews). In this study, they used the basic mixed methods designs in different phases, conducted research toward the program objective of establishing culturally relevant understanding of mental health, and engaged in this large-scale investigation over several years involving at least six primary researchers.

When Maria starts with a survey and follows it up with an interview in her mixed methods study, what type of design did she use? What would be the possible priority and sequence for her design? What would be the reason for using this type of design?

WHAT ARE THE KEY CHARACTERISTICS OF MIXED METHODS DESIGNS?

Mixed methods designs can be distinguished from other types of designs in several ways. In reviewing the following six characteristics, consider incorporating them into your plan for a study if you intend to conduct a mixed methods study. Also, look for them in a mixed methods study you might be reviewing or reading. They are:

◆ Provide a rationale for the design
◆ Include collecting quantitative and qualitative data
◆ Consider priority
◆ Consider sequence
◆ Match the data analysis to a design
◆ Diagram the procedures

Provide a Rationale for the Design

Readers and those who review mixed methods studies need to know why you are mixing methods. Mixed methods researchers include a justification or rationale for the use of both quantitative and qualitative data. One justification is that collecting quantitative data in a second phase is important to test the qualitative explorations of the first phase of the study (i.e., exploratory design).

Alternatively, a reason for conducting a mixed methods study might be that you seek to explain in more detail through qualitative research the initial quantitative statistical results (i.e., explanatory design) or one form of data plays a supporting role to the other database (i.e., embedded design). Another justification results from combining the "best" of both quantitative and qualitative research (i.e., convergent design). Quantitative provides the opportunity to gather data from a large number of people and generalize results, whereas qualitative permits an in-depth exploration of a few individuals. Whatever the rationale, mention this rationale early in a study, such as in the introduction.

Include Collecting Quantitative and Qualitative Data

In any mixed methods study, you should clearly indicate that you are collecting both quantitative and qualitative data. Methods of data collection are typically associated with either numbers or numeric data and words or text and image data. Mixed methods researchers collect both quantitative and qualitative data.

A broader picture of data forms is shown in Table 16.1. In this table, the columns illustrate both methods and data. In practice, mixed methods researchers use different methods to collect different forms of data. In a mixed methods study, researchers include specific forms of both quantitative and qualitative data and incorporate this discussion into the methods or procedure section of the study.

Consider Priority

Mixed methods researchers often advance a priority for the collection of quantitative and qualitative data. Three options are available to the researcher for prioritizing data:

◆ Quantitative and qualitative data are of equal weight.
◆ Quantitative data is of greater weight than qualitative data.
◆ Qualitative data is of greater weight than quantitative data.

TABLE 16.1			
Quantitative and Qualitative Methods of Data Collection and Types of Data			
Quantitative Research		**Qualitative Research**	
Methods of Data Collection	**Data**	**Methods of Data Collection**	**Data**
Instruments (e.g., questionnaire, closed-ended interview, closed-ended observation)	Numeric scores	Open-ended interviews	Text data from transcribed interviews
Documents (e.g., census, attendance records)	Numeric scores	Open-ended questions on questionnaires	Text data transcribed from questionnaires
		Open-ended observations	Fieldnotes (text) from researcher's notes
		Documents (e.g., private or public)	Text data optically scanned from diaries, journals, letters, or official documents
		Visual materials	Image data from pictures, photography, or audiotapes

Priority means that in a mixed methods design, the researcher places more emphasis on one type of data than on other types of data in the research and the written report. This emphasis may result from personal experience with data collection, the need to understand one form of data before proceeding to the next, or the audience reading the research. Whatever the reason, in examining a mixed methods study for priority, ask the following questions:

◆ What do you emphasize more in the purpose statement—exploration or prediction of outcomes?
◆ Which data collection process—quantitative or qualitative—do you give the most attention to (e.g., number of pages in a report) in the "Methods" and "Results" sections?
◆ Which data collection process do you examine in the most depth (e.g., detailed statistical analysis or multiple-layered thematic analysis)?

Consider Sequence

Mixed methods researchers advance the **sequence** of data collection using concurrent or sequential approaches or some combination. Again, several options exist for the sequencing of data collection:

◆ You collect both quantitative and qualitative data at the same time.
◆ You collect quantitative data first, followed by qualitative data.
◆ You collect qualitative data first, followed by quantitative data.
◆ You collect both quantitative and qualitative at the same time as well as in sequence.

If the purpose of the study is to explain quantitative results further with qualitative data (i.e., explanatory design) or to develop an instrument from qualitative data (i.e., exploratory design), the procedures should clearly indicate this sequence. The data collection procedures are independent of each other and typically presented as phases. If the intent of the study is to converge the findings (i.e., convergent design), then the data are collected at the same time, and the researcher is explicit about this process. This process involves two data collection efforts that proceed simultaneously and are related to each other. Some mixed methods studies involve both the concurrent and the sequential processes of data collection.

Match the Data Analysis to a Design

One of the most difficult challenges for the mixed methods researcher is how to analyze data collected from qualitative and quantitative research. This is more than simply being able to link or intersect data and numbers, although this connection does present some challenges. Several authors have begun the discussion about data analysis in mixed methods research (Bazeley, 2010). To examine options for data analysis, reflect back on the type of design and the options for analysis within each design. An overview of these options for the four primary mixed methods designs is presented in Table 16.2. This list is not comprehensive and should not limit the creative potential of a mixed methods researcher; it is largely to focus the discussion and present typical analytic procedures discussed by writers and illustrated in mixed methods studies.

Convergent Design Analysis

Of all of the designs, this analysis is perhaps the most difficult and controversial. The standard approach seems to converge or compare in some way quantitative data (e.g., scores) and qualitative data (e.g., text). One way is to provide a discussion—in a side-by-side analysis—about the themes emerging from the data and how they support or refute the statistical analysis. In a study conducted about controversial art on college campuses (e.g., a painting or novel), the researcher might collect questionnaires from campus constituents as well as interview data from administrators, faculty, and students. The researcher might then compare the two sources of data to determine if the interviews supported the questionnaire results.

Another approach is to combine the qualitative and quantitative data to arrive at new variables or new themes for further testing or exploration. In the controversial art case, the interview data and questionnaires' scores combine to produce a new variable, such as the sensitivity of campus constituents to some forms of art. This variable becomes information for further exploration.

Some mixed methods researchers quantify qualitative data to compare the data directly with statistical results. For instance, you could reduce interview data from campus personnel to themes and make counts of the occurrences of each theme. You could compare the frequency of these themes with the descriptive statistics about information from scales. Alternatively, the researcher might analyze the questionnaires, develop themes (or scales) that reflect issues surrounding campus art, and compare the themes to those generated by campus personnel during the qualitative interviews.

A final approach is to directly compare the quantitative results and the qualitative findings in a table, a joint display. This was one of the analytic procedures used by Lee and Greene (2007) in which they arrayed quotes that showed both convergent and divergent findings from their quantitative data.

TABLE 16.2

Basic Mixed Methods Designs and Data Analysis/Interpretation Procedures

Basic Type of Mixed Methods Designs	Examples of Analytic and Interpretive Procedures
Convergent (QUAN and QUAL data collected simultaneously)	• *Quantifying qualitative data:* Qualitative data are coded, codes are assigned numbers, and the number of times codes appear are recorded as numeric data. Quantitative data are descriptively analyzed for frequency of occurrence. The two datasets are compared. • *Qualifying quantitative data:* Quantitative data from questionnaires are factor analyzed. These factors then become themes that are compared with themes analyzed from qualitative data. • *Comparing results:* The results from qualitative data collection are directly compared with results from quantitative data collection. Statistical trends are supported by qualitative themes or vice versa. • *Consolidating data:* Qualitative data and quantitative data are combined to form new variables. Original quantitative variables are compared with qualitative themes to form new quantitative variables. (Caracelli & Greene, 1993) A variation on this is to develop a joint display that consolidates the data into one table showing how the quantitative results are compared with the qualitative findings (see Lee & Greene, 2007).
Explanatory (QUAN followed by qual)	• *Following up on outliers or extreme cases:* Gather quantitative data and identify outlier or residual cases. Collect qualitative data to explore the characteristics of these cases. (Caracelli & Greene, 1993) • *Explaining results:* Conduct a quantitative survey to identify how two or more groups compare on a variable. Follow up with qualitative interviews to explore the reasons why these differences were found. • *Developing a typology:* Conduct a quantitative survey and develop factors through a factor analysis. Use these factors as a typology to identify themes in qualitative data, such as observations or interviews. (Caracelli & Greene, 1993) • *Examining multilevels:* Conduct a survey at the student level. Gather qualitative data through interviews at the class level. Survey the entire school at the school level. Collect qualitative data at the district level. Information from each level builds to the next level. (Tashakkori & Teddlie, 1998)
Exploratory (QUAL followed by quan)	• *Locating an instrument:* Collect qualitative data and identify themes. Use these themes as a basis for locating instruments that use concepts parallel to the qualitative themes. • *Developing an instrument:* Obtain themes and specific statements from individuals that support the themes. In the next phase, use these themes and statements to create scales and items as a questionnaire. Alternatively, look for existing instruments that can be modified to fit the themes and statements found in the qualitative exploratory phase of the study. After developing the instrument, test it out with a sample of a population. • *Forming categorical data:* Site-level characteristics (e.g., different ethnic groups) gathered in an ethnography in the first phase of a study become a categorical variable in a second phase correlational or regression study. (Caracelli & Greene, 1993) • *Using extreme qualitative cases:* Qualitative data cases that are extreme in a comparative analysis are followed in a second phase by quantitative surveys. (Caracelli & Greene, 1993)
Embedded Design (QUAN or QUAL embedded within QUAN or QUAL)	• *Embedding quantitative or qualitative data:* Quantitative or qualitative data can be embedded as a secondary data source and analyzed separately. • *Analyzing the data at different stages in the research:* The primary database may be analyzed, and the results compared with the secondary database, or the secondary database may be collected and analyzed prior to or after the primary database.

Explanatory Design Analysis

Because you collect data in distinct phases, the analysis of an explanatory design is easier to see and conduct than in a convergent design. A popular approach is to collect quantitative data and look for extreme cases to follow up in a qualitative phase. In a mixed methods study about the transition of adults from school to work, Blustein et al. (1997) first conducted a quantitative correlational analysis of transition measures (i.e., job satisfaction and congruence) and then employed the results to provide an "in-depth and focused approach to analyze the corresponding qualitative narratives" (p. 373). Specifically, they identified individuals with high and low scores (i.e., extreme cases) on the dependent measures and then conducted a qualitative, thematic analysis using interviews with these individuals.

Alternatively, within an explanatory design, the researcher might seek to explain the results in more depth in a qualitative phase of the study. This was the approach taken by Houtz (1995) in her study of attitudes and achievement of seventh- and eigth-grade science students. She first gathered survey data and found that her data on achievement and attitude were contradictory. Accordingly, in a follow-up qualitative phase, she interviewed science teachers, the school principal, and the university consultant.

Less frequently seen within the explanatory design is typology development through quantitative data collection and the use of this typology as a framework for identifying themes in a qualitative database. If Houtz (1995) had actually looked for themes based on her statistical results, she would have used this approach. The application of this approach would have been to study children's attitudes, teachers' attitudes, and organizational characteristics that support views toward science in a school. In this project, the survey of children might be followed by teacher interviews, and then by census or document data from organizational school records.

Exploratory Design Analysis

In this design, the substantial qualitative data collection becomes a means for developing or locating quantitative instruments; forming categorical information for later quantitative data collection; or developing generalizations from a few initial qualitative cases. Perhaps the most popular use is to generate an instrument well grounded in the qualitative data from participants in a study. In the case of a researcher who studied first-year teachers in reservation-based, Native American elementary schools, the existing instruments were not sensitive enough to identify the cultural factors that affected this first-year experience. Thus, the researcher first conducted interviews with first-year teachers, identified themes and supporting statements, and developed an instrument to measure broadly the experiences of first-year teachers. As an alternative to this approach, the researcher might have identified the themes and located an instrument using the library resources.

In addition, you might combine categories of information from an exploratory qualitative data collection with continuous data in a statistical analysis. In the preceding example, the researcher would categorize experiences of the first-year teachers into their stages of development, such as "initiation," "apprentice," and "recruit," and use this categorization in a correlation or regression analysis. Unusual or extreme-case individuals in these categories might serve as the basis for extensive analysis across a population. In this follow-up, the survey researcher might study Native American first-year teachers who saw themselves as in the "initiation" phase of development.

Embedded Design Analysis

In the embedded design analysis, the analyses of the quantitative and qualitative data are kept separate because the two datasets often reflect different questions. Thus, in an experiment, the outcome analysis is conducted for the quantitative data and the process qualitative data is analyzed for themes. In an embedded design for a correlational study (see Harrison, 2007), the analyses also proceed independently of each other. In both the experimental and the correlational examples, results of the two databases can be interpreted together—how one reinforces the other or complements the other. When a sequential design is used with the embedded design, researchers will use one form of analysis (e.g., qualitative data collected and analyzed before an experiment) to inform the quantitative phase or qualitative phase of the study.

Diagram the Procedures

Mixed methods researchers often provide a **visualization** or diagram of their design depicting the procedures. A visualization is a figure like the examples of Figure 16.2 that indicates the process of data collection. It consists of labeling the quantitative and qualitative data, indicating the sequence of activities (using arrows or plus signs), and emphasizing the priority (using lowercase or uppercase letters). By including this visualization, the researcher helps readers identify the sequence of data collection, an important aid when collecting multiple forms of data. The notation system by Morse (1991), described in Figure 16.1, can be useful in developing this visualization.

WHAT ARE SOME POTENTIAL ETHICAL ISSUES IN MIXED METHODS RESEARCH?

Substantive discussions about the ethical issues that arise in mixed methods research have not been undertaken, but the conversation is certainly beginning with the Mertens, Holmes, and Harris (2009) discussion about transformative research and ethics. Thus, these authors suggest that the transformative approach is a site of multiple interpretive practices and ethical considerations occur at multiple points in the research process. The sampling in a mixed methods transformative design needs to consider the dangers of grouping all participants together in a general category that may stereotype them. The data collection should not further marginalize groups of participants, and the data decisions need to benefit involving community members and be aware of the cultural issues involved. The data findings need to be linked to social action.

Since mixed methods research combines quantitative and qualitative research, ethical considerations need to attend to typical ethical issues that surface in both forms of inquiry. Quantitative issues relate to obtaining permissions, protecting anonymity of respondents, not disrupting sites, and communicating the purposes for the study. In qualitative research, these issues relate to conveying the purpose of the study, avoiding deceptive practices, respecting vulnerable populations, being aware of potential power issues in data collection, respecting indigenous cultures, not disclosing sensitive information, and masking the identities of participants. In mixed methods basic designs, some ethical issues may arise that are unique to each type of design:

◆ In a convergent design, the quantitative and qualitative sample sizes may be different. Care needs to be taken to not minimize the importance of a sample because of its size.

◆ In an explanatory design, researchers may use a large quantitative database for the initial phase of the research. In order to follow up on these individuals with qualitative interviews, there needs to be an identifier linked to the quantitative database.

Some individuals may not want their quantitative data released. Using names without permission constitutes an ethical mixed methods issue.

◆ In an embedded design, conducting initial qualitative interviews to build an intervention before an experiment may be helpful in designing the intervention. However, using the initial interview data to place participants into a control group where they do not receive a beneficial treatment presents an ethical issue.

Box 16.1 suggests another issue that may arise during a multiphase mixed methods design.

BOX 16.1 | Ethical Dilemma

When Mixed Methods Researchers Do Not Seek Ongoing Permission in a Multiphase Project

An educational researcher has a funded project to study the oral traditions of language use among the Cherokee Indian Nation. This researcher decides to collect both quantitative data in the form of surveys and qualitative data in several focus groups with members of the Cherokee tribe. The survey and the focus groups will occur over several years, and when the researcher first designed the project, permissions were sought from tribal leaders about when the data could be collected and how it was to be used (for research purposes). As the project unfolds, the researcher begins to take some findings into his college classroom on the topic of American Indians and use the data in talking about the needs of tribes today. This raises the question: Is this practice ethical? How might this researcher/teacher obtain permission to use the data for classroom purposes? The Cherokee Nation now wants a certain percentage of the monies raised to fund the project because the researcher has allegedly been unethical. Should they be given some of these monies?

WHAT ARE THE STEPS IN CONDUCTING A MIXED METHODS STUDY?

Now that you have a basic understanding of mixed methods research, we can turn to specific steps typically undertaken by researchers when they use this design. These steps are not lockstep procedures; they provide a general guide to help you get started. See Figure 16.3 for an overview of this process.

Step 1. Determine If a Mixed Methods Study Is Feasible

The first step in the process is to assess the feasibility of using this design. You need skills in gathering both quantitative and qualitative data, time to collect extensive information, and a working knowledge of the different types of designs. Also important is whether

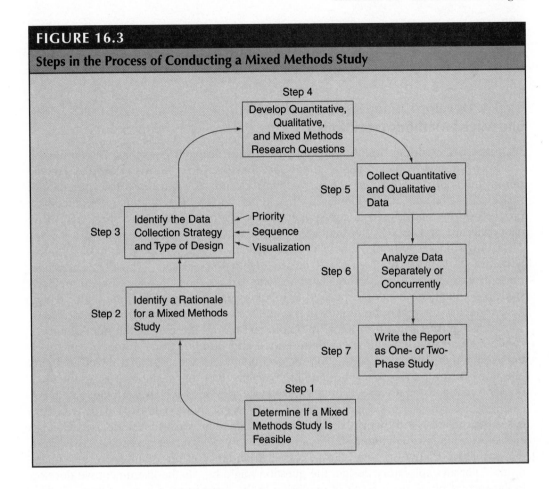

FIGURE 16.3

Steps in the Process of Conducting a Mixed Methods Study

audiences such as graduate committees, publishers, other researchers, and practitioners in educational settings will appreciate the complexity of your mixed methods study.

Step 2. Identify a Rationale for Mixing Methods

Assuming that a study is feasible, you need to consider why you are collecting both quantitative and qualitative data. The rationale for the four designs should provide a good starting point. Be explicit in this rationale, and include it early in your research plan or report. See the reasons for conducting mixed methods studies advanced earlier in this chapter.

Step 3. Identify a Data Collection Strategy

Identifying your rationale for the study will lead to planning your procedures for collecting data. You need to know:

◆ The priority you will give to quantitative and qualitative data
◆ The sequence of your data collection, if you do not plan to collect the data concurrently
◆ The specific forms of quantitative data (e.g., attendance records) and qualitative data (e.g., pictures) you will collect

Once you have made these decisions, create a diagram of the procedures. Use the notation system in Figure 16.1 and the models shown in Figure 16.2 to help you create this diagram.

Step 4. Develop Quantitative, Qualitative, and Mixed Methods Questions

With the specific design in mind, next develop your research questions. Depending on the type of design, you can identify these questions prior to a study or they may emerge during the study. For instance, in a two-phase design, the questions for your second phase cannot be specifically identified early in the study—they will emerge as the study progresses. Alternatively, for a convergent design, you can present the questions before data collection and specify them in detail.

If you can identify both quantitative and qualitative questions, pose both sets of questions (for institutional review boards, create tentative questions). Typically, researchers present both exploratory questions and analytic-variable questions in a mixed methods study. Quantitative questions specify the relationship among independent and dependent variables. They may be written in the null form but are typically written to convey an alternative directional form (e.g., the more mentoring, the greater the publications of faculty). Qualitative questions are open ended and nondirectional in nature and seek to describe the phenomenon. In addition, you might consider posing a mixed methods question. Most researchers are not familiar with this type of question. It is essentially a question that is to be answered by the mixed methods research design being used. For example, in a convergent design, the mixed methods question could be "Do the two databases (quantitative and qualitative) converge and present consistent findings or diverge and show contradictory findings?" For an explanatory design, we might ask, "How does the qualitative follow-up data help us to better understand the quantitative first phase results?" For an exploratory design, the question might be, "Is the instrument we develop in the second phase (as a result of exploring in the first phase) a better instrument than those available to measure the variables?" For an embedded design, the question might be: "How do the qualitative findings provide support and enhanced understanding for the quantitative results?" For a transformative design, the question might be: "How can the social issue be better addressed using results from both quantitative and qualitative findings?" A multiphase design would have a combination of these questions introduced in different phases or projects in the line of inquiry.

Step 5. Collect Quantitative and Qualitative Data

Collecting data in a mixed methods study follows rigorous quantitative procedures and persuasive qualitative procedures. For a mixed methods study, the sequence in which you collect the data will depend on the type of design. However, in all designs, this phase of the research will be lengthy and requires good organization of the information. Statistical programs and text analysis programs can provide useful systems for storing, managing, and recording the data.

Step 6. Analyze Data Separately, Concurrently, or Both

The data analysis will also relate to the specific type of mixed methods design you are using. You can analyze quantitative data separately from qualitative data, as in the explanatory and exploratory designs, or integrate the data analysis, as in the convergent design. Specific techniques have emerged for data analysis, as discussed in Table 16.2.

Step 7. Write the Report as a One- or Two-Phase Study or a Multiple-Phase Study

The final step in a mixed methods study is to write a scholarly report of the project. Some variations are seen in the writing structure of mixed methods studies, as outlined here:

◆ *The report is written in two phases.* The report contains one section to specify the problem and the literature. Then, the sections of data collection, analysis, and interpretation, two phases—one quantitative and one qualitative—are used for each section.

◆ *The report integrates the quantitative and qualitative phases of the study in each section.* The problem statement, for example, contains a need to explore (qualitative) and to predict or explain outcomes (quantitative). The research questions are posed as both quantitative and qualitative questions, and the data collection is in one section displaying an integration of quantitative and qualitative forms. The data analysis is an attempt to converge the two databases, and you form the results and interpretation into information that sheds light on the research problem. This structure results in a convergent design.

HOW DO YOU EVALUATE A MIXED METHODS STUDY?

As a form of qualitative and quantitative research, mixed methods research needs to be consistent criteria for a good qualitative and quantitative study. In addition, there are specific aspects that people reading, evaluating, and conducting a study might consider. In a high-quality mixed methods study, the researcher (Plano Clark & Creswell, 2010):

◆ Describes that mixed methods is the best approach to answer the research questions because neither qualitative nor quantitative is adequate as an approach.
◆ Incorporates both qualitative and quantitative data collection and analysis.
◆ Explicitly combines or mixes the two datasets.
◆ Uses rigorous quantitative and persuasive qualitative procedures of data collection and analysis.
◆ Frames the study within one of the mixed methods research designs.
◆ Provides a diagram of the procedures to clarify the timing, priority, and mixing within the study.
◆ Signals to the reader that the study is using mixed methods (e.g., in the title, purpose statement, and methods sections) to indicate their awareness of this research design.

KEY IDEAS IN THE CHAPTER

Mixed Methods Research, Its Use, and Its Development

With a better understanding of qualitative research and the advantages of collecting both quantitative and qualitative data, mixed methods research designs are becoming popular in education. From initial multimethod quantitative studies, designs have emerged that incorporate quantitative data (e.g., scores from instruments, scores from observations, and census data) and qualitative data (e.g., open-ended interviews, observations, documents, and visual materials). Today, writers talk about a separate design in education—the mixed methods design—in which investigators collect and analyze at least one quantitative method of data and one qualitative method of data, with attention to sequence and priority. A mixed methods design involves the collection, analysis, and "mixing" of both quantitative and qualitative data to best understand a research problem.

Types of Mixed Methods Designs

Four basic types of mixed methods designs exist. The convergent design includes the collection of both quantitative and qualitative data simultaneously, with the purpose of merging or integrating the data. The explanatory design begins with quantitative data collection and analysis followed by qualitative data collection and analysis. In this way, the researcher follows up on quantitative findings with qualitative explorations. The exploratory design reverses the data collection procedure. The mixed methods researcher first gathers qualitative data and then builds on the analysis of it using quantitative data. The embedded design includes collecting a primary form of data and then a secondary form of data that plays a supportive role in the study. Both forms of data are often collected simultaneously. In addition, more complex mixed methods designs are becoming more frequently used in this form of inquiry. The transformative design employs the use of a theoretical framework (e.g., feminist research) as an orienting lens for the entire study. The specific mixed methods designs within this framework can be any of the four basic designs or combinations of them. The multiphase design is a mixed methods project conducted over time using multiple phases or projects that build on each other. Any combination of the four basic mixed methods designs can be used.

Key Characteristics of Mixed Methods Research

A major characteristic of mixed methods designs is a need to justify or provide a rationale for mixing methods. Researchers also collect both quantitative and qualitative data and provide a priority to one form of the data or the other, and they often sequence collecting both forms of data. Data analysis needs to relate to the type of design, and this analysis may involve such data analysis approaches as transforming data, following up or explaining outlier or extreme cases, or using qualitative themes to develop a quantitative instrument.

Potential Ethical Issues in Mixed Methods Research

Ethical issues are becoming part of the conversation for mixed methods research. The most discussion has been written about ethical issues in using a transformative design, and these issues focus on respecting individuals and underrepresented groups. Ethics in mixed methods does need to relate to important issues arising in both quantitative and qualitative research. Moreover, they can relate to mixed methods designs because different types of design raise specific ethical issues that need to be anticipated by the researcher.

Steps Used in Conducting Mixed Methods Research

The steps in conducting a mixed methods design involve assessing the feasibility of the study and presenting a rationale for mixing methods. They also involve making decisions about the priority and sequence of the analysis and developing research questions for the study. Researchers then collect both quantitative and qualitative data and analyze them together or separately (or both), depending on the design. The final research report may present the study as one phase or as two phases, based on the research design chosen for the project.

Evaluating a Mixed Methods Study

Evaluating a mixed methods study means using mixed methods when it is appropriate, collecting both qualitative and quantitative data, and integrating or combining the two forms of data. The methods used for the qualitative and quantitative procedures need to be rigorous and persuasive. Part of this detail requires framing the study within one of the designs, and presenting a diagram of the procedures. Finally, throughout the project, researchers should use appropriate terms and language of mixed methods research.

USEFUL INFORMATION FOR PRODUCERS OF RESEARCH

◆ When presenting your mixed methods research to others, discuss your design as a distinct design in educational research.

◆ In the design of a mixed methods study, identify the advantages that will accrue from collecting both quantitative and qualitative data. Let these advantages point you toward the most appropriate design (e.g., convergent, explanatory, exploratory, embedded, transformative, multiphase) to study your research problem. In this chapter, the advantages of each design are specified.

◆ Of the designs, recognize that it is easier to conduct a sequential explanatory or exploratory design than a convergent design. With a convergent design, you need to merge both quantitative and qualitative databases (e.g., numbers and text) and possibly collect additional data if the two databases are in conflict.

◆ Recognize that in selecting a mixed methods design you have taken on a challenging project. Mixed methods research involves extensive data collection and data analysis. Weigh the trade-off between drawbacks of time and resources and the advantages of collecting both quantitative and qualitative data to understand your research problem.

◆ Use the two factors, priority and sequence, to help you decide what mixed methods research design is appropriate for your study.

◆ To best present the procedures in your mixed methods design, create a diagram that portrays the steps in the process. Use the guidelines about notation introduced in this chapter to help you design this visual.

USEFUL INFORMATION FOR CONSUMERS OF RESEARCH

◆ Because researchers have only recently identified mixed methods as a specific design in educational research, authors of studies may not label their research as mixed methods (although this is becoming more frequent). You might identify a mixed methods study by determining whether the researcher collects both quantitative and qualitative data to examine a research problem.

◆ When reading a mixed methods study, look for a diagram of the procedures to help you understand the flow of activities in the mixed methods research. If such a visual is not present, you may want to sketch out the sequence of activities, including the time sequence for collecting quantitative and qualitative data, how they were analyzed, and the intent for using both forms of data.

◆ Because both quantitative and qualitative data are being collected, you might judge a mixed methods study on the basis of both quantitative and qualitative criteria. Look in journals reporting mixed methods studies for criteria for assessing mixed methods studies.

◆ To locate useful information from mixed methods studies, look for the detailed picture that emerges from qualitative research and the generalizable results that emerge from quantitative research. This combined impact—the detail and the general—can help you best understand a research problem in education.

ADDITIONAL RESOURCES YOU MIGHT EXAMINE

There are many excellent journal articles and book chapters on mixed methods research, but in recent years many books on mixed methods have also been published. Here are some recent books organized in alphabetical order:

Creswell, J. W. (2007). *Research design: Quantitative, qualitative, and mixed method approaches* (3rd ed.). Thousand Oaks, CA: Sage.

Creswell, J. W., & Plano Clark, V. L. (2011). *Designing and conducting mixed methods research* (2nd ed.). Thousand Oaks, CA: Sage.

Greene, J. C. (2007). *Mixed methods in social inquiry.* San Francisco: John Wiley & Sons.

Morse, J. M., & Niehaus, L. (2009). *Mixed method design: Principles and procedures.* Walnut Creek, CA: Left Coast Press.

Plano Clark, V. L., & Creswell, J. W. (2008). *The mixed methods reader.* Thousand Oaks, CA: Sage.

Tashakkori, A., & Teddlie, C. (Eds.). (2011). *Handbook of mixed methods in social and behavioral research.* (2nd ed.). Thousand Oaks, CA: Sage.

Teddlie, C., & Tashakkori, A. (2009). *Foundations of mixed methods research: Integrating quantitative and qualitative approaches in the social and behavioral sciences.* Thousand Oaks, CA: Sage.

PEARSON
myeducationlab
The Power of Classroom Practice
www.myeducationlab.com

Go to the Topic "Mixed Methods Research" in the MyEducationLab (**www.myeducationlab.com**) for your course, where you can:

◆ Find learning outcomes for "Mixed Methods Research."

◆ Complete Assignments and Activities that can help you more deeply understand the chapter content.

◆ Apply and practice your understanding of the core skills identified in the chapter with the Building Research Skills exercises.

◆ Check your comprehension of the content covered in the chapter by going to the Study Plan. Here you will be able to take a pretest, receive feedback on your answers, and then access Review, Practice, and Enrichment activities to enhance your understanding. You can then complete a final posttest.

Example of a Mixed Methods Study

Examine the following published journal article that is a mixed methods design study. Marginal notes indicate the major characteristics of a mixed methods research highlighted in this chapter. The illustrative study is:

Individual Differences and Intervention Flaws

A Sequential Explanatory Study of College Students' Copy-and-Paste Note Taking

L. Brent Igo
Clemson University, South Carolina
Kenneth A. Kiewra
Roger Bruning
University of Nebraska–Lincoln

Mixed Methods
Characteristics
in Marginal
Annotations

In this study, qualitative themes and quantitative findings from previous research were used to justify the exploration of four experimental, note-taking conditions and the impact of those conditions on student learning from Web-based text. However, puzzling results obtained from dependent measures of student learning were quite inconsistent with the previous research. With no adequate theoretical explanation for these results, a follow-up explanations phase of qualitative investigation was conducted. Analyses of interview data indicated that certain experimental conditions imposed upon students an unexpected distraction. Furthermore, quantitizing students' note-taking documents showed that many students in this study used a more effective note-taking strategy than did students in a similar condition in previous research.

Key words: Internet learning; note taking; cognitive processes; sequential explanatory

In research addressing cognitive approaches to learning, experiments typically are conducted and subsequent statistical results are used to discuss support or lack of support for predetermined, theoretical hypotheses. Mixed methods research might offer cognitive researchers a path toward deeper understanding of their experimental results, however. The primary purpose of this article is to present the findings of an in-depth study of college students' Web-based note taking. As shall be seen, an experiment yielded some results that were not hypothesized and other results that were, in fact, contradictory to previous research. A qualitative follow-up phase of study provided data that allowed us to make sense of the puzzling experimental results. Thus, secondarily, this study illustrates the value of the sequential explanatory mixed method design in cognitive research. (01)

The Preference to Paste

Most students seem to prefer copying and pasting their notes to typing their notes while they gather text information online. Studies have shown that roughly 80% of general education high school students (Igo, Bruning, McCrudden, & Kauffman, 2003), as well as 80% of middle school students with learning disabilities (Igo, Riccomini, Bruning, & Pope, 2006), will choose copy and paste if the option is offered. Why students prefer to paste their Web-based notes seems to differ among students, however. Whereas high school students' tendency to paste their notes might be a function of diminished motivation, middle school students with learning disabilities report that pasting reduces anxiety associated with monitoring spelling and grammar during note taking. (02)

Not all students share this preference for copy and paste, however. In one particular study, high school students in advanced placement courses overwhelmingly preferred to type their notes from Web-based sources (Igo et al., 2003). Similarly, middle school students with learning disabilities, but with higher spelling and grammar achievement, seemed to prefer writing notes to copying and (03)

Authors' Note: Please address correspondence to L. Brent Igo, Clemson University, Educational Foundations, 407b Tillman Hall, Box 340705, Clemson, SC 29634-0705; e-mail: ligo@clemson.edu.

pasting notes (Igo et al., 2006). But to date, little research has addressed how learning is affected by the use of copy and paste while students read and note Web-based text. In this report, we first synthesize the limited copy-and-paste note-taking literature. Next, we present a cognitive learning study driven by this research question: How do different copy-and-paste note-taking interventions affect college students' learning of Web-based text ideas? The first two words in this question indicate that a mixed methods approach is warranted, with *do* indicating the need for an experiment and *how* indicating the need for a qualitative follow-up. Thus, in this sequential explanatory mixed methods study (Creswell & Plano Clark, 2007), a cognitive experiment was followed by interview and document analyses intended to help explain results obtained in the experiment. As shall be seen, this study exemplifies the need for the follow-up explanations model in educational research when cognitive experiments yield puzzling results.

How Copying and Pasting Notes Affects Learning From Text

(04)   Despite its apparent appeal to most students, there is an educational problem associated with copy-and-paste note taking. Students' initial learning of text ideas suffers (Igo et al., 2003, 2006), as do students' abilities to transfer text information later (Katayama, Shambaugh, & Doctor, 2005). One explanation for this negative effect on learning is that many students take copy-and-paste notes in a decidedly mindless way—selecting and pasting large amounts of text at any given time with little evaluation of which text ideas are critical to their notes. Upon testing of the information they have noted, then, those students tend to recall little, if any, of the information in their notes. This behavior and subsequent impact on initial learning was documented in studies that examined copy-and-paste note taking with high school students (Igo, Kiewra, & Bruning, 2004) and college students (Igo, Bruning, & McCrudden, 2005b; Katayama et al., 2005), alike.

(05)   Other students (albeit far fewer, based on the extant research) are more selective while taking copy-and-paste notes. They evaluate which text ideas are essential to their notes and paste smaller amounts of text, and consequently, they learn more (Igo et al., 2005b). For example, in a study by Igo et al., students who pasted fewer words per cell of a note-taking chart remembered more ideas from Web-based text, and students who pasted more words per cell (most students) remembered successively fewer ideas. In short, there seems to be an upside and downside to students' default copy-and-paste note-taking strategies; some students are selective and learn more, but most students are not selective and learn little.

(06)   Research also suggests that students can be prompted to be more selective in their pasting and think more deeply about text as they take notes (Igo et al., 2005b). Subsequently, they can achieve dramatic improvements in learning, as described by levels-of-processing theory (Craik & Lockhart, 1972). For example, a computer program that restricts the amount of text students may paste into their notes (an electronic chart that limits the content of each cell to 7 words) has been shown to increase students' text-pasting selectivity and prompt students to engage in evaluative and metacognitive processes while reading and taking notes.

(07)   But there seems to be both benefits and drawbacks to students' restricted copy-and-paste note taking. A study by Igo, Bruning, and McCrudden (2005a) showed that under the 7-word restricted copy-and-paste conditions, roughly one third of students were compelled to make minor modifications to their notes—to tinker or fine-tune. The authors concluded that this behavior led students' attention away from the meaning of the text, focusing it instead on certain note characteristics. Ultimately, learning decreased; students who modified their notes recalled fewer facts and inferred fewer relationships from text than students who did not make modifications. In short, a 7-word level of restriction from previous research, although beneficial to most students, might be too restrictive for others.

(08)   The key to learning through the copy-and-paste note-taking process, then, seems to be selectivity in one's pasting decisions (and the requisite mental processes), whether such selectivity is simply the note taker's personal approach or strategically imposed by a computer note-taking program. A similar theme is found in related text-learning literature. For example, the extent to which students learn text ideas through the underlining or the paper-and-pencil note-taking processes is related to how selective students are and how deeply they process text during the activities (Anderson & Armbruster, 1984; Blanchard, 1985; Hidi & Anderson, 1986; Johnson, 1988; Marxen, 1996; Mayer, 2002; McAndrew, 1983; Peterson, 1992; Rickards & August, 1975; Rinehart & Thomas, 1993; Slotte & Lonka, 1999).

To date, however, relatively little is known about how students use copy and paste to take notes from Web-based text. The research synthesized above leaves important questions unanswered. First, only one study has deeply explored students' unrestricted copy-and-paste note taking. How might another population of students approach unrestricted copy-and-paste note taking? Also, previous research has tested only the learning effects of a 7-word copy-and-paste restriction. What effects do different levels of copy-and-paste note-taking restriction have on learning from Web-based text, and how are those effects manifested? This study seeks to answer these questions. (09)

The purpose of this sequential explanatory mixed methods study (Collins, Onwuegbuzie, & Sutton, 2006; Creswell & Plano Clark, 2007; Greene 2006; Tashakkori & Teddlie, 1998) is to explore the impact of different levels of copy-and-paste note-taking restriction on learning from Web-based text. In the quantitative, first phase of this study, college students took notes in one of four experimentally imposed copy-and-paste conditions and then were tested for the learning of facts, concepts, and relationships among text ideas they noted. The experimental findings and previous research then guided the data-gathering and analysis stages of a qualitative phase of study in which two kinds of data were collected and analyzed (student notes and interviews) to help explain and extend the findings from the experiment. (10)

No diagram of procedures but good use of mixed methods terms

Quantitative and qualitative data were collected

Rationale for the design

Quantitative Phase

The quantitative phase of this study addresses how different levels of copy-and-paste note-taking restriction affect learning from Web-based text. Whereas previous research has investigated the impact of a 7-word restricted copy-and-paste condition on learning, the present study investigates differing levels of restriction. (11)

In true pragmatist, mixed methods fashion (Tashakkori & Teddlie, 1998), two other levels of copy-and-paste restriction were created for exploration based on learning theory and qualitative themes from previous studies. First, previous research indicates that when students attempt to learn prose, making more difficult decisions (which might require analysis of text) yields better learning of the prose material than making less difficult decisions (which might require only recall of text; see, e.g., Benton, Glover, Monkowski, & Shaughnessy, 1983). As such, the superior learning effect of restricted copy and paste over unrestricted copy and paste in previous research might have been due to the increased difficulty required to make 7-word pasting decisions (where fewer words must be selected) over unrestricted pasting decisions (where any number of words can be pasted). If so, perhaps other levels of pasting restriction might affect the difficulty of note-taking decisions and, in turn, affect learning. (12)

Qualitative evidence helps determine which levels of restriction should be tested. Participant interviews and an analysis of notes stemming from the Igo et al. (2005b) study suggest that the 7-word restriction be doubled and tripled to create two new experimental groups that differ in how much restriction is imposed upon students' copy-and-paste capabilities (14- and 21-word restrictions). Simplistically enough, students who created 7-word restricted copy-and-paste notes stated that they believed they would have been able to "do a better job" if they had twice as many words with which to work. This is not to say, however, that they would have encoded twice as many ideas with a 14-word restriction, but it is possible that they may have encoded as many or even more. Thus, interview data provide a justification for doubling the allowed number of words. (13)

The last piece of evidence that justifies different copy-and-paste restrictions stems from the performances of certain unrestricted pasters in the Igo et al. (2005b) study. Some students in the unrestricted copy-and-paste group were highly selective in their copy-and-paste decisions, choosing to paste approximately 21 words per cell in their note-taking charts (where the average unrestricted paster chose 42 words per cell). They exhibited this preference fairly consistently, and they performed better on each of the three tests (fact, concept, skill) than other members of the unrestricted group who chose to paste more words. (14)

Thus, qualitative interview data suggest that students believed 14 words would have allowed them the flexibility to more efficiently construct notes. Furthermore, an analysis of notes coupled with test performances suggests that students who restrict themselves to 21 words per cell in their charts learn more than students who do not restrict their own pasting. The quantitative phase of this study tests how four note-taking conditions affect learning from Web-based text: the new (15)

14-word and 21-word restricted copy and paste and the former 7-word and unrestricted copy and paste (which were retained for purposes of replication and comparison to the new conditions).

Hypothesis and Prediction

(16)
Priority given
to quantitative
research

The restriction hypothesis was created based on previous research and levels-of-processing theory (Craik & Lockhart, 1972). The restriction hypothesis postulates that more learning will occur when students are assigned to restricted copy-and-paste conditions because restricted pasting leads to deeper mental processing of the text. As such, this hypothesis predicts that students assigned to the 7-word, 14-word, and 21-word copy-and-paste conditions will perform better on tests assessing (a) cued recall of facts, (b) recognition of concepts, and (c) inferences regarding relationships among text ideas than students in the unrestricted copy-and-paste condition.

Method

(17) Ninety-three students from a large Southeastern university volunteered to participate to receive extra credit in their introductory educational psychology class or in a psychology class. Students who participated (a) were judged to have minimal background knowledge of the experimental content (based on a pretest score of the content), (b) ranged from sophomore to senior standing at the university (juniors > seniors > sophomores), (c) had self-reported grade point averages ranging from 2.6 to 4.0, and (d) had an average Scholastic Aptitude Test score of 1,240 (self-reported). Participants were assigned randomly to one of four conditions in which the copy-and-paste feature of a note-taking tool was either restricted to 7, 14, or 21 words or was unrestricted. Students drew slips of paper from a box, with the slips numbered 1 through 4 and corresponding to the experimental conditions. Twenty-two students were assigned to the unrestricted group, 24 to each of the 21-word and 14-word restricted groups, and 23 to the 7-word restricted copy-and-paste group. Of the participants, 23 were men and 70 were women. Among the sample, 8 students reported being African American, 3 Asian, 2 Latino, and the rest Caucasian.

Materials

(18) For purposes of across-study comparison, materials were identical to the Igo et al. (2005a, 2005b) studies. Students took notes from a text passage was that was 1,796-words long. The text described three learning theories (behavioral, social, and constructivist) and was presented on a single, continuous Web page (HTML document) and accessed through Microsoft Internet Explorer. Describing each learning theory along parallel lines, the text identified each theory's (a) definition, (b) view of the importance of the environment, (c) view of the importance of mental activity, (d) key assumptions, (e) impact on curriculum, (f) impact on instruction, (g) impact on assessment, and (h) criticism.

(19)   The note-taking tool used was an electronic matrix (or chart) fit with the text's structure. It contained three columns corresponding to the three text topics and 11 rows corresponding to the 11 text categories. The three columns were labeled from left to right as *behavioral theory, social theory,* and *constructivist theory.* The eleven rows were labeled *definition, environment, mental activity, key assumptions 1-4, impact on curriculum, impact on instruction, impact on assessment,* and *criticism.* Thus, at the outset, the tool presented students with 33 blank cells, 11 for each learning theory, with cues directing students to find information intersecting topics and categories. The tool itself could be minimized, maximized, or reduced in the same way as other computer programs. The students could choose to have the tool appear on the screen as they engaged in copy-and-paste decisions with the text, or they could expand the text to cover the screen and hide the chart.

(20)   Students' ability to enter information into the tool by typing was disabled. Thus, students were obliged to copy and paste information into the tool (under either restricted conditions or an unrestricted condition). Students could paste words that appeared together in the text or combine words from disparate areas of the text, as long as the total number of words pasted per cell did not exceed their level of restriction (if one was indeed assigned). They also were permitted to change or delete part or all of their selections as they saw fit.

Three tests assessed recall of facts, concept recognition, and relational inferences. In the facts test, students filled in a cued paper chart (analogous to the online note-taking chart) with all, or any part of, the information they could remember reading or pasting into their notes. The columns and rows were labeled in the same way the note-taking chart was labeled; the cells were blank. The test was scored by awarding 1 point per idea recalled and placed in the correct, cued cell corresponding to an idea from the text, whether the idea was originally noted or not. There were 33 possible points. Two raters scored the quiz, blind to experimental conditions, with a clearly acceptable level of interrater reliability (Cohen's $K = .87$).   (21)

A 13-item multiple-choice concept test ($\alpha = .64$) required students to recognize novel examples of information presented in the text (e.g., "How would a teacher who subscribes to social learning theory use praise during instruction."). One point was awarded for each correct response.   (22)

Relational inferences were measured with a single essay test item requiring students to compare and contrast ideas presented in the text. Students were asked, "Describe how each theory's views of the importance of the environment and the importance of mental activity are related." These descriptions were scored using a rubric that included eight idea units. A total of eight points were possible—one for each idea. Maximum points were given if a student's complete answer described the opposite relationship of each theory's emphases on the environment and mental activity, as well each theory's position on the importance of the environment and mental activity (e.g., behavioral theory places a greater emphasis on the environment and tends to discount mental activity, whereas constructivist theory is just the opposite). Two scorers rated the essays based on the rubric, blind to experimental conditions, with a clearly acceptable level of interrater reliability (Cohen's $K = .83$).   (23)

Procedure

The experiment occurred over two days. On Day 1 (in four separate sessions), students met in a university computer lab and were assigned randomly to one of the four experimental groups. Next, they were given an overview of the note-taking task and completed informed consent forms. In the overview, the students were informed that the experiment was going to be conducted on two separate days. The primary researcher told the students that on Day 1 they were going to read and take notes over material that would later be covered in their course and that on Day 2 (two days later) they would be given tests of facts, concepts, and relationships. They then read a brief two-paragraph statement describing the note-taking chart and a written explanation of the version of the chart they were supposed to use (7-, 14-, or 21-word restriction or unrestricted). Next, participants logged on to their computers and created user names and passwords (which permitted their notes to be saved and printed). The students were instructed by the primary researcher to take notes using the cues provided in the chart—for example, *definition* and *criticism*—(which they also read in the two-paragraph statement), to read and take notes at a pace that was comfortable to them, and to take as much time as they needed to complete their notes. Students then read, completed their notes, and saved their notes on the computers. All students completed the note-taking task in approximately 42 to 51 minutes. Students were not forced to conform to identical time on task because the researchers wanted to most closely approximate typical student behaviors, as prompted by the different versions of the note-taking tool.   (24)

On Day 2 (two days later), participants took the three tests. The fact test was administered first because it contained the fewest retrieval cues (i.e., hints about what the students were supposed to have learned), ensuring that students' recall of the text ideas was not prompted by the other tests, which contained additional cues. The relational test then was administered, as it contained the second fewest retrieval cues. Finally, the concept test, which contained the most cues, was administered last. Each test was collected before the next test was given.   (25)

Results

A multivariate analysis of variance (MANOVA) and three separate analyses of variance (ANOVAs) were conducted to evaluate the effects of the copy-and-paste restrictions on student performances on the (a) fact test, (b) relational test, and (c) concept test. Table 1 displays a summary of the means and standard deviations for each of the three tests.   (26)
Match data analysis to design

TABLE 1
Means and Standard Deviations for Experimental Groups

	Unrestricted	21-Word Restricted	14-Word Restricted	7-Word Restricted
Fact test				
M	4.77	2.63	2.00	4.87
SD	3.79	2.44	1.84	3.84
Relational test				
M	2.73	1.00	0.54	2.39
SD	2.41	1.45	0.88	2.21
Concepts test				
M	8.05	6.96	6.67	7.87
SD	2.88	2.42	2.44	2.32

Multivariate Analysis of Variance

(27)   A one-way MANOVA was conducted to determine the effect of the copy-and-paste conditions on student learning, as measured by the three tests. Significant differences were obtained, Wilk's $\Lambda = .76$, $F(9, 211) = 2.80$, $p < .005$. The relationship between copy-and-paste condition and test performance was moderate, as assessed by multivariate η^2 based on Wilk's Λ, accounting for 8.9% of the variance in performance. ANOVAs were conducted on each of the three tests to follow up the MANOVA.

Fact Test ANOVA

(28)   The purpose of the fact test was to measure the learning of facts from the Web-based text. The ANOVA for the main effect of copy-and-paste conditions on cued recall of facts was significant, $F(3, 89) = 5.33$, $MSE = 50.36$, $p < .005$. The strength of the relationship between level of copy-and-paste restriction and cued recall was strong as assessed by η^2, with level of restriction accounting for 15.2% of the variance in cued recall.

(29)   Although the performances of the four copy-and-paste groups had significantly different standard deviations (based on Levene's test), an error bar analysis revealed that the differences were acceptable. Nonetheless, Dunnet's *C* was the procedure used in followup post hoc comparisons because it does not assume equal variances and is a more conservative basis for comparison. Dunnet's *C* indicated that the unrestricted copy-and-paste group and the 7-word restriction group each recalled significantly more text ideas than did those in the 14-word restricted copy-and-paste group.

Relational Inferences ANOVA

(30)   The purpose of the essay test was to measure student ability to compare the three theoretical viewpoints from the text. A one-way ANOVA for the main effect of copy-and-paste restriction on relational learning was significant, $F(3, 89) = 7.8$, $MSE = 25.923$, $p < .001$. The strength of the relationship between level of copy-and-paste restriction and relational inferences was strong as assessed by η^2, with level of restriction accounting for 20.8% of the variance in relational inferences.

(31)   As was the case on the cued recall measure, the variances in performance on the relational inferences measure were significantly different among the four copy-and-paste groups (as assessed by Levene's test). Another error bar analysis, however, again showed that the differences were acceptable. As a conservative precautionary measure, Dunnet's *C* was again the procedure used in post hoc comparisons. The unrestricted copy-and-paste group made more relational inferences than the 21-word and 14-word restricted groups. Also, the 7-word restricted group made more relational inferences than the 14-word group.

Conceptual Recognition ANOVA

(32)   The purpose of the multiple-choice test was to measure student ability to recognize novel examples of the concepts that were in the text. The ANOVA for this conceptual test was not significant, $F(3, 89) = 1.66$, $MSE = 44.026$, $p = .181$. Although the analysis indicated that there were no

significant differences among group performances, the groups' performances nonetheless differed in ways analogous to the performances on the cued fact and essay tests. That is, the performances of the groups varied in ways similar to the other tests: the 14- and 21-word groups performed worse than the 7-word and unrestricted groups.

Need for Follow-up Explanations

The results of this experiment do not support the restriction hypothesis. Based on previous research, this hypothesis predicted that the restricted copy-and-paste groups would learn more than the unrestricted group. Instead, the results indicate that the unrestricted copy-and-paste group actually outperformed two of the other groups and performed similarly to the 7-word group. (33)

Although two of the groups (7-word and unrestricted) seemed to have learned more than the other two (14- and 21-word), the higher performances were not made by the groups that one might assume would do better in light of previous research (Igo et al., 2005b). The most restricted group and least restricted group, oddly, performed the best. The middle-restricted groups performed the worst. This finding is somewhat puzzling, as in previous research the 7-word group learned significantly more than the unrestricted group. Why did this happen? (34)

A preliminary analysis of notes revealed that all participants completed the note-taking chart and that all participants conformed to their copy-and-paste assignment. That is, all cells were filled in each note chart, and each student filled the cells with an appropriate number of words as per experimental condition. In addition to containing the correct amount of text, the cells also contained information appropriately addressing the note-taking cues. These characteristics of the notes, however, provide no insight into our experimental findings. (35)

In particular, the answers to two questions seem critical to understanding our results. The first question is, Why did students in the unrestricted pasting group perform as well as those in the 7-word restricted pasting group? A clear and definitive answer to this question is beyond the scope of the experimental findings. More data are needed to resolve the contradictory findings. The second unanswered question is, Why did the 14- and 21-word pasting groups perform worse than the 7-word and unrestricted pasting groups? Students seemingly were able to learn with an unrestricted tool and a highly restrictive tool (7-word), but learning was impeded somehow by a tool that was only moderately restrictive (14- and 21-word). This question, too, is elusive—unanswerable in light of the experimental results alone. Again, more data are needed to determine why there were discrepancies in learning. Together the two questions posed above can be categorized under the same qualitative question: How did the different note-taking conditions affect students during the experiment? The aim of the follow-up component of this study is to provide an explanation to this question. (36)

Sequence of quantitative research followed by qualitative research

Qualitative Phase

In cases where experimental inquiry does not provide enough description of a phenomenon, researchers can use qualitative follow-up procedures to aid understanding (Creswell, 2003; Creswell & Plano Clark, 2007; Tashakkori & Teddlie, 1998). Two types of qualitative data were used to address the unanswered questions above. Note-taking documents were collected and analyzed to address why the unrestricted pasting groups and the restricted pasting groups performed comparably. Interview data were collected and analyzed to address why the 14- and 21-word pasting groups learned less than the 7-word and unrestricted pasting groups. (37)

Following the data analyses, which are described below, a researcher outside of the present study performed an external audit of the qualitative analyses and general inferences made from the findings. She was chosen to perform the audit because she had adequate knowledge of both qualitative analysis techniques and cognitive research. In her oral report to the primary researcher, she communicated that the themes were justified by the data and that our inferences stemming from those themes (and from the quantitative data) were logical. (38)

Note-Taking Data Collection and Analysis

After the experiments, the students' notes were printed and analyzed. The notes were checked for both content and text length. Content was checked by comparing each set of notes with a master (39)

TABLE 2
Quantitized Note Documents From the Experiment

	Unrestricted $n = 22$	21-Word Restricted $n = 24$	14-Word Restricted $n = 24$	7-Word Restricted $n = 23$
Mean words per cell	24.42	15.08	10.54	6.87
Range	16.23–52.44	12.82–19.40	8.75–13.79	6.54–6.94

set of notes that contained the correct ideas in each cell. Text length was measured by calculating an average number of words used per cell in each student's note chart.

(40) As mentioned earlier, each student's notes were appropriately constructed in terms of both word count (as per experimental condition) and appropriateness of ideas (where the cued cells contained the correct information). However, within each group there were discrepancies in word count (see range in Table 2). Although no members of the restricted groups (7, 14, or 21) exceeded their words-per-cell limits (as the assigned version of the tool would not permit it), some did use fewer words per cell than their imposed limits (which the tool did permit). Certain students within each experimental group pasted fewer words than other students did.

(41) For example, students in the 14-word group chose to paste an average of about 11 words per cell. Across students within that group, word pasting ranged from about 9 words to just under 14 words per cell. So whereas some students pasted fewer words than their version of the tool permitted, other students chose to paste as many as their imposed limit would allow. Similarly, although the average words per cell of students restricted to the 21-word group was 15, some students pasted only 13, and other students pasted more than 19 words per cell. In short, within each pasting restriction group, student preferences in how much text to paste varied.

(42) This variance in word count per cell was, of course, also evident among students in the unrestricted pasting group. Although the average number of words per cell pasted by the unrestricted group was 24, certain students in the unrestricted group chose to paste an average of 16 words per cell, and still other students pasted more words—as many as 52. Again, students' preferences in how much text to paste varied among members of the unrestricted group.

(43) Interestingly, the notes taken by students in the unrestricted group in this study differed from the notes taken by unrestricted students in previous research (Igo et al., 2005b). In the present experiment, members of the unrestricted group pasted an average of 24 words per cell of their note-taking charts. However, the average number of words pasted by the unrestricted group in previous research was 42 per cell, despite use of the same materials and procedures.

(44) This discrepancy in apparent selectivity regarding how much text to paste had a bearing on test performance in the previous research (Igo et al., 2005b). Consistently, the students who pasted the fewest words remembered the most, and the students who pasted the most words remember the least of what they had read or noted. But in that study, relatively few unrestricted students were highly selective. In the present study, many were.

(45) When one considers that students in the present study were, overall, much more selective in what they pasted than were students in the previous research (choosing on average 24 words rather than 42) and that choosing fewer words has positive consequences for learning and recall, a plausible answer to the first qualitative subquestion emerges. Why did the unrestricted and 7-word restricted pasting groups perform similarly, when in the previous research they did not? Because in the present study, more of the unrestricted pasters imposed a self-restriction, were highly selective, chose to paste fewer words, and benefited from that strategic approach.

Interview Data Collection and Analysis

(46) Two to three days after the tests were graded and the statistical analyses were completed (approximately five to six days after tests were administered), interviews were conducted with 12 participants. The interviewees were students from two different educational psychology classes, and they were chosen at random to participate. Five students were unable to meet for the interviews, at

which time 5 other participants were chosen at random. Three participants represented each of the four experimental groups (7-, 14-, 21-word pasting and unrestricted pasting).

This part of the investigation began with a priori assumptios regarding students' note-taking behaviors and the effects those behaviors have on learning. The assumptions were based on a study by Igo et al. (2005a), which documented that note-taking decisions and note-modifying decisions affect learning differently. In that study, students who took copy-and-paste notes (making only note-taking decisions) learned more than students who took copy-and-paste notes and frequently distracted themselves by making minor note changes (note-taking decisions plus note-modifying decisions). Consequently, an interview protocol was designed to prompt students for a description of the processes they used to take their notes: (47)

◆ Describe how you decided what information to include in your notes.
◆ (Student is given his or her printed notes.) Are there any cells that you remember filling in, and could you describe how you decided which information would be placed in that/those cell/cells?
◆ How often, if at all, did you change your notes once you filled in a cell, and how did your notes change?
◆ If you did change your notes, what were your reasons for doing so?

Additional questions were asked to further prompt answers from interviewees who at first gave brief or nondescript answers to one or more of the questions. The interviews were conducted individually by the primary researcher, were audiotaped, and lasted from 5 to 10 minutes, in general.

Verbatim transcriptions were made of the audiotaped interviews, and then an analysis of the interview data was conducted. First, the transcriptions were read and then reread. Next, descriptive, meaningful statements made by each participant were extracted. A pre-determined set of coding schemes—based on note taking versus note modification—then was used to sort the statements into three categories: two addressing a student's tendency to change or not change the notes and one addressing note taking with note modification (see Table 3). (48)

Following the prescriptions of Miles and Huberman (1994), an effects matrix was constructed to serve three purposes: organization of the interview data, explanation of effects, and drawing conclusions. Several themes emerged from the matrix once the data were organized—themes that plausibly answer the question, Why did the 14- and 21-word pasting groups perform worse on the tests? (49)

Organization of the Interview Data

The interview data were sorted and then compared and contrasted. Two researchers, blind to experimental condition, sorted the statements into the categories with a high degree of agreement (Cohen's $K = .97$). First, the statements made by the participants were sorted into categories indicative of (50)

TABLE 3
Coded Categories Used to Sort Interview Statements

	No Note Changes	Note Changes
Note taking	Student kept the original note selections. Student selected an idea from the text and placed the idea in the appropriate cell of the chart.	Student did not keep the original note selection. Student selected an idea from the text, placed the idea in the appropriate cell of the chart, and then later deleted that idea from the cell, replacing it with an entirely new idea.
Note modification	By definition, students who did not change their notes also did not modify their notes.	Student selected an idea from the text, placed the idea in the appropriate cell of the chart, and then modified that idea within the cell by deleting certain words or by combining disparate areas of the text.

note-taking changes or no note-taking changes. The statements then were cross-sorted into the categories *note taking* and *note modification* (see Table 3).

(51)   *Note taking* involved choosing ideas from the text while the text was being read or reread. This included the student's decisions that led to the original selection of ideas in the pasting groups (the first words chosen to be pasted into each cell). Note-taking decisions also included choices made while reading or rereading the text that led to alterations in one's notes—where an entire original idea was replaced with a new idea. A student described making such decisions this way: "Sometimes I would get farther along [in the reading] and go back and paste a different part [of the text] instead." In each case, a decision regarding note construction was made while students read the text, and the pasted product was either entered into an empty cell or was used to replace an idea already in the cell.

(52)   *Note modification* involved decisions that were made while students read or reread their notes that led them to modify the contents of a cell. That is, modification involved decisions made after students had entered information into their notes, then examined their notes, and finally altered the contents of a cell. For example, one participant explained, "I wasn't sure what the best parts were, or how many words I had [selected] so I would read what I already had [in the cell] and take some parts out." Hence, note-modifying decisions focused on noted ideas, whereas note-taking decisions focused on text ideas that may or may not have been noted. Table 4 shows the number of interviewees per experimental group who described note taking and note modification.

TABLE 4
Effects Matrix for Coded Interview Statements

	Number of Interviewees per Group Who Described Note Taking	Number of Interviewees per Group Who Described Note Modification	Themes	Exemplar Quotes
Number of interviewees who described making no note changes	3 unrestricted pasters	None	1. Unrestricted pasters were likely to engage in note taking and not change their notes after entering information into the cells.	"While I was reading I would think about the [cues in the matrix] and when the part of the reading was done I would summarize the paragraph."
				"I just put in the [sentence] that I thought fit the category best."
Numbers of interviewees who described making note changes	Two 7-word pasters One 21-word paster	Three 14-word pasters Two 14-word pasters One 7-word paster	2. 7-, 14-, and 21-word paster were likely to change their notes.	"I always had to fix the things I put in my notes . . . I usually [pasted] too much."
			3. 7-word pasters were likely to replace whole ideas with other ideas.	"A lot of times I'd find something better [for my notes] the more I read."
			4. 14- and 21-word pasters tended to modify their notes within the cells of the chart.	"In some cells, there were things that didn't need to be in there. . . . I would take them out."
			5. 14- and 21-word pasters counted the number of words they were using several times and found it difficult to count while scrolling through the cells.	"It was frustrating to narrow things down to the right number of words because I had to scroll-up while I counted."

Note: Three members of each group were interviewed.

Explanation of Themes

Based on the interview data, five note-taking themes are evident (see Table 4). These themes are manifest in the note-taking decisions made by the experimental participants, which differed from group to group. Unrestricted pasters made similar decisions, 14- and 21-word pasters made similar decisions, and 7-word pasters made decisions somewhat different from the other groups. Each of the note-taking themes is now distinguished and discussed.

(53)

Match the data analysis to the design

The first theme in the effects matrix concerns students who took notes without making any subsequent changes to their notes. That is, they decided what information to note while they read the text and then they noted it without second-guessing their decisions.

(54)

As can be seen in Table 4, unrestricted pasters who were interviewed described that they were likely to take notes and not change them. In fact, all three participants from this group who were interviewed described their note-taking process this way. For example, an unrestricted paster described her choices saying, "I just put in the [sentence] that I thought fit the category best . . . I didn't want to change what I had . . . I just went with my instinct about it." Apparently, the unrestricted paste condition allowed students to make a decision about which information to note and then move to the next set of cues in the note-taking tool. As such, these students saw no need to change their notes and were perhaps able to focus their mental efforts on the text ideas. Clearly, such focus could have resulted in their relatively high test performance (as compared to the 14- and 21-word groups).

(55)

The second note-taking theme concerns note taking coupled with making note changes. Students displaying this theme were likely to insert information into their charts and then change the information before finally saving their notes. The 7-, 14-, and 21-word pasters were likely to change their notes. Nine participants from these three groups were interviewed, and 8 of them described making frequent changes in their charts while taking notes. For example, one participant assigned to the 14-word paste condition said, "I always had to fix the things I put in my notes . . . Some of the things that seemed right were too long. . . . I usually [copied] too much . . . [and] had to get rid of some of it." On a similar note, a 7-word paster described filling a note-taking cell this way: "I usually pasted the first thing that sounded like it was supposed to go in there . . . but then other things would come along, too . . . so I changed the things I put in [the cell]."

(56)

Each restricted copy-and-paste condition, then, seemed to prompt students to evaluate their notes as well as the text ideas. Recall that unrestricted pasters described only evaluation of the text, not note evaluation. Still, the performances of the restricted pasting groups differed, with 7-word pasters outperforming the 14- and 21-word pasters. So although the second theme distinguishes the unrestricted pasters from the restricted pasters, it does little to explain the performance differences among the restricted groups. The next three note-taking themes help to explain our experimental results by distinguishing the 7-word pasters from the 14- and 21-word pasters.

(57)

The third theme concerns making note changes without minor alterations within cells. When students changed their notes this way, they did so because they encountered new, perhaps better, ideas in the text. That is, they changed their notes when, while reading further in the text, a different piece of information was deemed more representative of the cues in the note-taking chart. This theme relates solely to the 7-word pasters. In fact, of the three 7-word pasters interviewed, two described making changes based on further reading in the text. "A lot of times I would find something better [for my notes] the more I read," was how one participant described how she chose to change her selections. In the 7-word paste condition, then, students may have been prompted to be critical of their selections but only when the text presented them with additional information worthy of being noted. This theme is supported by Igo et al. (2005a). Of 34 students assigned to the 7-word pasting group in their study, 21 changed their notes in Theme 3 fashion—a proportion consistent with the 2 of 3 interviewees from the present study.

(58)

Finally, the fourth and fifth themes further distinguish the three restricted pasting groups, and they relate to the note-taking decisions made by participants assigned to the 14- and 21-word paste conditions. The fourth theme concerns note modifications, or making minor note alterations within the cells were of the chart. When a participant modified notes in some way, it was done in a fine-tuning, where the note cells were reread, examined, and then changed by deleting certain pieces of information from the cells.

(59)

(60)   The 14- and 21-word pasting groups tended to modify their notes—the distracting behavior mentioned earlier in this report (Igo et al., 2005a). Consider the similarities between these two descriptions made by a 14-word paster and a 21-word paster: "In some cells, I had things that didn't need to be there. . . . I took them out" and "I usually took a couple of sentences that sounded good and then put them in [the cell] and trimmed them down to 14 words."

(61)   Whereas the 7-word group made changes based on new information in the text, the 14- and 21-word paste groups made changes based on the information that was already in the notes. They may, at some level, have moved their attention away from the actual text meaning, focusing instead on certain qualities of their notes.

(62)   The fifth and last theme suggested by the interview data follows from the fourth theme, as it more specifically addresses the note modification of the 14- and 21-word pasters. Whereas all experimental groups were mindful of the text ideas they were pasting into their notes, the 14- and 21-word groups were, in addition, particularly mindful of the number of words they were using. In fact, the interviewees described actually counting the number of words they were pasting in each cell. For example, one participant said, "I didn't really need 14 words but I still counted how many words I was using to make sure it wasn't going to get cut off." This statement refers to how the restricted copy-and-paste tool functions, and it needs some qualification: When a student first pasted information into the chart (in any paste condition), the tool would accept an unlimited number of words in the cell. However, when the student then left that cell and returned to the text, the tool would, by default, save only the initial 7, 14, or 21 words from the pasted segment. The remainder of the text would be cut off.

(63)   Another practical, yet distracting, phenomenon described by the 14- and 21-word groups was their tendency to use the scrolling feature of the note-taking tool. This feature works the same way as the scrolling feature of any word-processing or Internet program. When an electronic document is too long to fit on the screen at one time, a button on the side of the window allows the user to scroll down a page—as if pulling down a window shade—exposing the text on the lower part of the document. In the note-taking tool, each cell of the chart is in fact a separate window with its own scroll button. Students who put large amounts of text into a cell would not be able to view the entire contents of the cell without using the scrolling feature. Interviewees from the 14- and 21-word groups described using this feature with some frequency while making changes to their notes. For instance, one student said, "It was frustrating to narrow things down to the right number of words because I had to scroll-up while I counted."

(64)   Although the 7-word pasters also made changes to their notes, they did not describe counting words or using the scroll button. This is perhaps because the size of the note-taking cells allowed for 7 words to be viewed in each cell without scrolling (provided they were not excessively long words).

(65)   It seems that participants in the 14- and 21-word groups chose to paste more than the allowed number of words (temporarily) in each cell and then made decisions about which parts of the text should stay and which other parts should be removed, all the while keeping count of how many words they were using and scrolling through the cells. Clearly, this is a task more different than selecting consecutive words from the text, pasting them, and then proceeding onward, as described by the unrestricted and 7-word pasters.

(66)   Thus, the second unanswered question from the experiment seems to have a practical answer, in light of cognitive psychology: Why did the 14- and 21-word pasting groups perform worse than the other pasting groups on the tests? Because the versions of the tool they were using prompted them to engage in different note-taking activities than did the unrestricted or 7-word paste tools. In addition to guiding them through the note-taking process (based on the cues and organization of the chart), the 14- and 21-word versions of the tool imposed a distraction from the meaning of the text. As students began to modify their note-taking choices, they were forced to move attention away from the meaning of the text and focus instead on the physical characteristics of their notes (the number of words they had in each cell). Given the limited nature of human attention and the dependence of attention on learning, then, it makes sense that they would learn less than the other note-taking groups who did not experience the same distraction.

Drawing Conclusions, Data Mixing, and Instructional Impact

(67)   Although copy-and-paste note taking is still a relatively unexplored research area, this study, along with previous studies by Igo and colleagues (2003, 2004, 2005a, 2005b, 2006), helps illuminate how

copy-and-paste note taking affects learning from Web-based text. The extent to which students encode (or learn) ideas through the pasting process seems related to the subsets of behaviors in which they engage, the selectivity with which they paste, and the kinds of mental processes requisite for those behaviors and such selectivity.

In a previous study (Igo et al., 2005b), unrestricted pasters were, in general, not at all selective in what they chose to paste into their notes. Whereas the bulk of those students learned little from Web-based text, there were certain students who were more selective in their pasting and who learned considerably more. The present study, however, extends the previous findings, showing that among a different population of students, default copy-and-paste strategies can be much more productive. Unrestricted students in the present experiment performed as well on dependent measures of learning as did students in a condition designed to prompt deeper thinking (7-word paste). The follow-up component of this study then explained how those students approached learning in the supposed disadvantaged condition—strategically and selectively. Thus, we can conclude that students' personal approaches to copy-and-paste note taking vary considerably in terms of effectiveness, with the type of approach relating to how much is learned from Web-based text. (68)

Similarly, previous research indicated that restricting students' pasting capability to 7 words can positively affect learning for many students (Igo et al., 2003, 2005b), but it also can impose a minor distraction (Igo et al., 2005a). The present study extends this theme. Students assigned to the 14- and 21-word restricted condition performed poorly on the dependent measures of learning. The qualitative follow-up then showed how those conditions affected learning. Students described the imposition of severe distractions that were, in fact, quite antithetical to learning. (69)

In essence, the key to learning while taking copy-and-paste notes is to approach the task selectively while maintaining one's focus on the meaning in the text and not on the characteristics of one's notes. As such, student learning through the copy-and-paste note-taking process realistically might be influenced by simple teacher-given instructions. Although a restrictive note-taking tool is not currently available to teachers for use in classrooms, students could follow certain guidelines that would simulate the benefits of a restrictive tool. When students take notes from the Web, prompting them to be more selective in their pasting might produce similar gains in learning. For example, a teacher might prompt students to copy and paste main ideas from paragraphs in lieu of pasting entire paragraphs. Or students could be instructed to identify the sentences most valuable to a set of notes. In each case, the directions might function as prompts for productive monitoring. (70)

Contribution to Mixed Methods Literature

This study evinces the value of the follow-up explanations model in experimental, cognitive research. Consider, for example, the American Psychological Association's requirement that researchers report effect sizes related to their experimental findings. An effect size suggesting that treatment conditions explain 15% of the variance between groups in an experiment would be considered a strong effect size (Green, Salkind, & Akey, 2000). But from a practical standpoint, such as that of a teacher who wants to know as much as possible about student learning, the remaining 85% of the variance might be of great interest. The follow-up explanations model can help researchers fill this need. (71)

For instance, the experimental phase of this study indicated effect sizes of roughly 21%, 15%, and 9%. These measures perhaps indicate the extent to which the copy-and-paste conditions influenced learning outcomes. But the qualitative phase provided evidence of varying ways in which students behaved within those conditions and how the treatments influenced students' behaviors. This level of understanding would not have been possible without a mixed methods approach to research. Whereas the experiment provided evidence solely of learning differences among students assigned to the four conditions, the qualitative phase clarified the impact of two important factors related to those differences. First, interview data revealed design flaws antithetical to learning (that were present in two of the experimental conditions) and that reduced certain students' capacity to learn during the experiment. Second, analyses of students' note documents showed that the effectiveness of students' personal strategies can vary between samples of a population (as the present study and past research sampled the population of college students, with more effective strategies being employed in the present study). (72)

(73)   In short, given only the experimental findings, we merely could have concluded that (a) two of the treatments yielded better learning than the other two and (b) particular aspects of the present study were inconsistent with previous research. But given the mixing of qualitative and quantitative data, we can explain why we obtained these results. As exemplified by this study, the collection and analysis of qualitative data relevant to the goals of a cognitive experiment can illuminate important nuances that might otherwise remain hidden.

Limitations

(74)   In the present study, sampling participants from a different population than that of the previous studies yielded unexpected results. The findings of this study may only generalize to the type of student who participated. The few studies that have addressed copy-and-paste note taking have produced results that are in some ways consistent and yet in other ways inconsistent.

(75)   Another limitation of this study is its use of a single text. This might raise a serious question of generalizability of the findings. Consider that texts differ in their complexity and density of ideas, as well as in readability, grade level, and content. Future research should include multiple texts to ensure that present findings can truly affect instruction and learning.

Future Research

(76)   Given the present and previous research, at least two avenues of future research are pertinent. First, future research should explore the use of instructions to students regarding how they should approach copy-and-paste notes. Finally, the present and previous copy-and-paste studies have failed to address the complete benefits of note taking. Until now, studies have addressed only the encoding function of note taking, neglecting to address the external storage function (where notes are studied). This leaves several important questions unanswered. For example, does a level of copy-and-paste restriction perhaps boost initial encoding but then result in an inferior set of notes from which to study? It is possible that a student who pastes large amounts of information, and then performs poorly on measures of initial encoding, might in fact have produced a more complete set of notes and might then be at an advantage when study time is allowed? On the other hand, a student might have only produced a more lengthy set of notes, whereas a restricted paster may have created a more concise record from which to study. In any event, many topics related to copy-and-paste note taking remain unexplored.

References

Anderson, T. H., & Armbruster, B. B. (1984). Studying. In P. D. Pearson (Ed.), *Handbook of reading research* (pp. 657–679). New York: Longman.

Benton, S. L., Glover, J. A., Monkowski, P. C., & Shaughnessy, M. (1983). Decision difficulty and recall of prose. *Journal of Educational Psychology, 75,* 727–742.

Blanchard, J. S. (1985). What to tell students about underlining . . . and why. *Journal of Reading, 29,* 199–203.

Collins, K., Onwuegbuzie, A., & Sutton, I. (2006). A model incorporating the rationale and purpose for conducting mixed methods research in special education and beyond. *Learning Disabilities: A Contemporary Journal, 4*(1), 67–100.

Craik, F., & Lockhart, R. (1972). Levels of processing: A framework for memory research. *Journal of Verbal Learning and Verbal Behavior, 11,* 671–684,

Creswell, J. W. (2003). *Research design: Qualitative, quantitative, and mixed methods approaches* (2nd ed.). Thousand Oaks, CA: Sage.

Creswell, J. W., & Plano Clark, V. L. (2007). *Designing and conducting mixed methods research.* Thousand Oaks, CA: Sage.

Green, S. B., Salkind, N. J., & Akey, T. M. (2000). *Using SPSS for Windows: Analyzing and understanding data* (2nd ed.). Upper Saddle River, NJ: Prentice Hall.

Greene, J. C. (2006). Toward a methodology of mixed methods social inquiry. *Research in the Schools, 13*(1), 93–99.

Hidi, S., & Anderson, V. (1986). Producing written summaries: Task demands, cognitive operations, and implications for instruction. *Review of Educational Research, 56,* 473–493.

Igo, L. B., Bruning, R., & McCrudden, M. T. (2005a). Encoding disruption associated with copy and paste note taking. In L. M. Pytlik-Zillig, M. Bodvarsson, & R. Bruning (Eds.), *Technology-based education: Bringing researchers and practitioners together* (pp. 107–119), Greenwich, CT: Information Age.

Igo, L. B., Bruning, R., & McCrudden, M. T. (2005b). Exploring differences in students' copy and paste decision-making and processing: A mixed-method study. *Journal of Educational Psychology, 97*(1), 103–116.

Igo, L. B., Bruning, R., McCrudden, M. T., & Kauffman, D. F. (2003). InfoGather: Six experiments toward the development of an online, data-gathering tool. In R. Bruning, C. A. Horn, & L. M. Pytlik-Zillig (Eds.), *Web-based learning: What do we know? Where do we go?* (pp. 57–77) Greenwich, CT: Information Age.

Igo, B., Kiewra, K., & Bruning, R. (2004, April). *Further explorations in online, copy and paste note taking: Mixed methods evidence for how levels of restriction affect encoding.* Paper presented at the annual conference of the American Educational Research Association, San Diego, CA.

Igo, L. B., Riccomini, P. J., Bruning, R., & Pope G. (2006). How should middle school students with LD take Web-based notes:

A mixed methods study. *Learning Disability Quarterly, 29*(2), 112–121.

Johnson, L. L. (1988). Effects of underlining textbook sentences on passage and sentence recall. *Reading Research and Instruction, 28,* 18–32.

Katayama, A. D., Shambaugh, R. N., Edmonds, T., & Doctor, T. (2005). Promoting knowledge transfer with electronic note taking. *Teaching of Psychology, 32,* 129–131.

Marxen, D. E. (1996). Why reading and underlining a passage is a less effective strategy than simply rereading the passage. *Reading Improvement, 33,* 88–96.

Mayer, R. R. (2002). *The promise of educational psychology: Volume 2. Teaching for meaningful learning.* Columbus, OH: Merrill Prentice Hall.

McAndrew, D. A. (1983). Underlining and note taking: Some suggestions from research. *Journal of Reading, 27,* 103–108.

Miles, M. B., & Huberman, A. M. (1994). *Qualitative data analysis.* Thousand Oaks, CA: Sage.

Peterson, S. E. (1992). The cognitive functions of underlining as a study technique. *Reading Research and Instruction, 31,* 49–56.

Rickards, J. P., & August, G. J. (1975). Generative underlining strategies in prose recall. *Journal of Educational Psychology, 67,* 860–865.

Rinehart, S. D., & Thomas, K. A. (1993). Summarization ability and text recall by novice studies. *Reading Research and Instruction, 32,* 24–32.

Slotte, V., & Lonka, K. (1999). Review and process effects of spontaneous note taking on text comprehension. *Contemporary Educational Psychology, 24,* 1–20.

Tashakkori, A., & Teddlie, C. (1998). *Mixed methodology: Combining qualitative and quantitative approaches.* Thousand Oaks, CA: Sage.

Action Research Designs

*O**f all of the research designs, action research is the most applied, practical design. Action researchers explore a practical problem with an aim toward developing a solution to a problem. This chapter defines action research, identifies when you use it, assesses the key characteristics of it, and advances the steps in conducting and evaluating this design.*

By the end of this chapter, you should be able to:

◆ Define action research, and describe when to use it, and how it developed.

◆ Identify the types of action research designs.

◆ Describe the key characteristics of action research.

◆ Anticipate potential ethical issues in action research.

◆ Identify the steps in conducting an action research study.

◆ List the criteria for evaluating an action research report.

Maria chooses to conduct an action research study. Her school committee especially likes this approach because Maria will develop a practical solution to the problem of students carrying weapons in school. She asks this research question: "What steps can our school take to encourage students to be more concerned about the possession of weapons in the school?" Maria collects information from her students by asking them to complete a brief questionnaire (quantitative data) and by having them keep and write in a journal (qualitative data) for a couple of months about their experiences with other students who carry weapons to school. Maria also holds conversations with fellow teachers and obtains their reaction to the problem. From this data, Maria compiles a list of possible solutions and rank orders them based on how individuals rated them. She presents this list to her school committee, and they choose which solutions they can realistically implement. Maria has conducted an action research study.

WHAT IS ACTION RESEARCH, WHEN DO YOU USE IT, AND HOW DID IT DEVELOP?

Action research has an applied focus. Similar to mixed methods research, action research uses data collection based on either quantitative or qualitative methods or both. However, it differs in that action research addresses a specific, practical issue and seeks to obtain solutions to a problem. Thus, **action research designs** are systematic procedures done by teachers (or other individuals in an educational setting) to gather information about, and subsequently improve, the ways their particular educational setting operates, their teaching, and their student learning (Mills, 2011). Educators aim to improve the practice of education by studying issues or problems they face. Educators reflect about these problems, collect and analyze data, and implement changes based on their findings. In some cases, researchers address a local, practical problem, such as a classroom issue for a teacher. In other situations, researchers seek to empower, transform, and emancipate individuals from situations that constrain their self-development and self-determination.

When Do You Use Action Research?

You use action research when you have a specific educational problem to solve. This problem may be assessing the difficulties faced by part-time faculty (Watters, Christensen, Arcodia, Ryan, & Weeks, 1998), ascertaining whether problem-based learning is superior to the traditional lecture (Dods, 1997), or discovering how literacy in writing emerges for first-grade students (Ceprano & Garan, 1998). Action research provides an opportunity for educators to reflect on their own practices. Within the scope of a school, action research offers a means for staff development, for teachers' development as professionals, and for addressing schoolwide problems (Allen & Calhoun, 1998). In fact, the scope of action research provides a means for teachers or educators in the schools to improve their practices of taking *action* and to do so by participating in research.

How Did Action Research Develop?

Three stages mark the development of action research. The first stage consisted of the identification of a process for addressing societal issues. The second stage turned toward practice and the need to involve practitioners, such as teachers, in the solution to their own problems. The third and most recent phase represented the participatory, emancipatory, or community action research approach in which groups assume responsibility for their own emancipation and change.

The social-psychologist Kurt Lewin coined the term "action research" in the 1930s (Mills, 2011). Lewin felt that social conditions in the 1940s—such as the shortage of meat, the need for aerial reconnaissance during World War II, and the improvement of intercultural group relations after the war—might be enhanced through the process of group discussions (Kemmis, 1994). These group processes consisted of four steps: planning, acting, observing, and reflecting. By focusing on group processes and identifying phases of action, Lewin's approach introduced many of the modern ideas of action research: a process of steps, participation, the democratic impulse of involvement, and the contribution to social change (Kemmis, 1994). Spreading from the social sector to education, Lewin's ideas were adopted at the Horace-Mann-Lincoln Institute at Teachers College, Columbia University, and in England at the Tavistock Institute.

This spread of action research slowed during the mid- to late 1950s. The growing gulf between theory and practice, the emphasis on research development in regional educational laboratories, and the use of experiments and systematic research all contributed to this decline. Then, in the 1970s, action research projects in Great Britain, the United States, and Australia reemerged. For example, the Fort Teaching project in England focused on teachers studying their own practices. The Classroom Action Research Network at the Cambridge Institute of Education in Great Britain addressed practical issues between teachers and students. Team-based inquiry between researchers and the schools emerged at Columbia University in the United States. The emancipation of individuals in education based on the German writings of Habermas became the focus of inquiry by the Australian Stephen Kemmis and his colleague (Kemmis & McTaggart, 2005).

Having teachers study their own classroom problems and issues has emerged as an important direction for school renewal today. As shown in Figure 17.1, the movement toward action research has evolved from the in-service days of the 1970s to the site-based plans for staff development during the 1980s, to the present emphasis on educators reflecting on their own practices (Schmuck, 1997). Reasons cited today for the importance of action research reinforce these trends. Action research:

◆ Encourages change in the schools
◆ Fosters a democratic (i.e., involvement of many individuals) approach to education
◆ Empowers individuals through collaboration on projects
◆ Positions teachers and other educators as learners who seek to narrow the gap between practice and their vision of education
◆ Encourages educators to reflect on their practices
◆ Promotes a process of testing new ideas (Mills, 2011)

Although action research has gained support in education, it is not without critics, who are reluctant to view it as a legitimate form of inquiry (Stringer, 2007). Some view it as an informal process of research, conducted by teachers and other educators who are not formal academic researchers. The practical aspect of action research also suggests

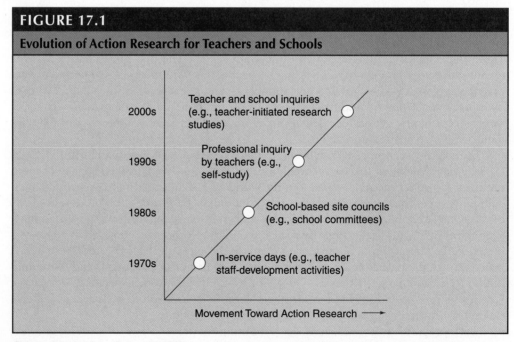

FIGURE 17.1

Evolution of Action Research for Teachers and Schools

Source: Adapted from Schmuck, 1997.

an applied orientation to this form of inquiry with a less-than-scientific approach. Action researchers typically report results of their studies not to scholarly journals in education, but to online journals, Web sites, or local school groups. The methods are adapted and changed in response to the practitioners' objectives to understand a practical problem. Hence, the design may not have the rigor and systematic approach found in other designs.

Despite these concerns, action research fulfills an important role for the teacher–researcher and school-based teams formed to study local school issues. It also provides a design that encourages collaboration among school and community participants and researchers to help transform schools and educational practices.

WHAT ARE THE TYPES OF ACTION RESEARCH DESIGNS?

Action research means different things to different people. A review of the major writers in education, however, shows that the following two basic research designs are typically discussed (Mills, 2011):

◆ Practical action research
◆ Participatory action research

As you read about these two forms of action research, the overview of their differences shown in Figure 17.2 will help you distinguish between their major features.

Practical Action Research

Teachers seek to research problems in their own classrooms so that they can improve their students' learning and their own professional performance. Teams composed of teachers, students, counselors, and administrators engage in action research to address common issues such as escalating violence in schools. In these situations, educators seek to enhance the practice of education through the systematic study of a local problem.

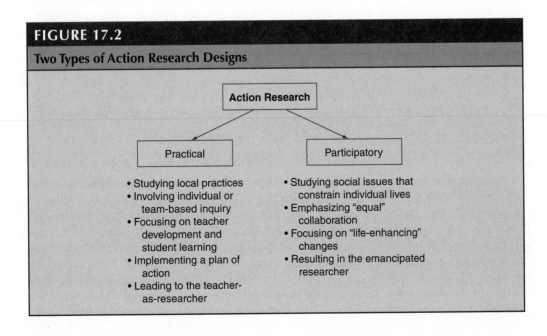

FIGURE 17.2

Two Types of Action Research Designs

Action Research

Practical
- Studying local practices
- Involving individual or team-based inquiry
- Focusing on teacher development and student learning
- Implementing a plan of action
- Leading to the teacher-as-researcher

Participatory
- Studying social issues that constrain individual lives
- Emphasizing "equal" collaboration
- Focusing on "life-enhancing" changes
- Resulting in the emancipated researcher

This form of action research is called **practical action research**, and its purpose is to research a specific school situation with a view toward improving practice (Schmuck, 1997). Practical action research involves a small-scale research project, narrowly focuses on a specific problem or issue, and is undertaken by individual teachers or teams within a school or school district. Examples of practical action research studies include these:

◆ An elementary teacher studies the disruptive behavior of a child in her classroom.
◆ A team composed of students, teachers, and parents studies the results of implementing a new math program in the junior high.
◆ A community college instructor studies his professional development using technology in teaching.

In all of these examples, action research seeks to improve specific, local issues. It calls for educators to involve teachers in research to study concerns in their own schools or classrooms and to implement site-based councils or committees in schools to enhance research as an integral part of daily classes and education. In this spirit, educators can test their own theories and explanations about learning, examine the effects of their practices on students, and explore the impact of approaches on parents, colleagues, and administrators within their schools.

A drawback of this approach is that although teachers seek to improve their classroom practices, they have little time to engage in their own research. Although teachers may be good at what they do and familiar with teaching kids in classes, they may need assistance in becoming researchers. To this end, they can participate in graduate classes, which will help them renew or develop the requisite skills for inquiry required in an action research project.

To understand practical action research, we need to review its major ideas or principles. As identified by Mills (2011), the following principles focus on assumptions about the role of teachers as learners, as reflective practitioners, and as individuals engaging in small-scale research projects:

◆ Teacher–researchers have decision-making authority to study an educational practice as part of their own ongoing professional development.
◆ Teacher–researchers are committed to continued professional development and school improvement, a core assumption for any teacher who decides to engage in action research.
◆ Teacher–researchers want to reflect on their practices. They reflect so that they can improve their practices. They do this individually or in school-based teams composed of students, teachers, and administrators.
◆ Teacher–researchers use a systematic approach for reflecting on their practices, meaning that they use identifiable procedures to study their own problems rather than using a random, anything-goes design.
◆ Teacher–researchers will choose an area of focus, determine data collection techniques, analyze and interpret data, and develop action plans.

This final point refers to the process of research. The books about practical action research advance detailed steps that teachers and other educators might use to conduct a study. Mills (2011), for example, discusses several of these models, then advances his own and uses it as the framework for chapters in his book. He calls his model the *dialectic action research spiral*. This model, shown in Figure 17.3, provides teachers with a four-step guide for their action research project. Mills emphasizes that it is a model for teachers to use to study themselves, not a process of conducting research *on* teachers. It is a "spiral" because it includes four stages where investigators cycle back and forth between data collection and a focus, and data collection and analysis and interpretation.

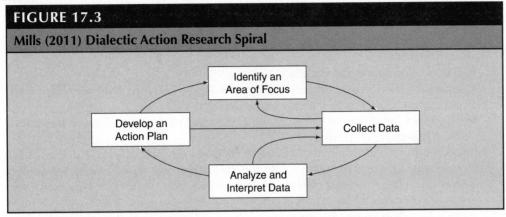

FIGURE 17.3

Mills (2011) Dialectic Action Research Spiral

Source: Mills (2011), p. 19. Reprinted by permission of Pearson Education/Allyn & Bacon.

In this procedure, the teacher–researcher identifies an area of focus. This process involves defining this area, doing reconnaissance (self-reflection and description), reviewing the literature, and writing an action research plan to guide the research. Then the teacher–researcher collects data by gathering multiple sources of data (quantitative and qualitative) and by using a variety of inquiry tools, such as interviews, questionnaires, or attitude scales. Data collection also consists of attending to issues of validity, reliability, and ethics, such as provisions for informed consent from participants.

The action researcher follows this phase with analysis and interpretation. The process includes identifying themes; coding surveys, interviews, and questionnaires; asking key questions; doing an organizational review; engaging in concept mapping (i.e., visualizing the relationship of ideas); analyzing antecedents and consequences; and displaying findings. Interpretation involves extending the analysis by raising questions, connecting findings to personal experiences, seeking the advice of critical friends, and contextualizing the findings in literature and theory.

In the final stage, the teacher–researcher finally completes an action plan. This plan includes a summary of findings, recommended actions, and the identification of individuals responsible for action and those who need to be consulted and informed. The plan also indicates who will monitor and collect the data, the time line for data collection, and the resources needed to carry out the action.

Overall, this process emphasizes practical action research centered around studying a local problem, engaging in inquiry by an individual teacher (teacher-as-researcher) or a team, and focusing on teacher development. A review of an actual study can illustrate this practical approach to action research.

Hughes (1999) was a fourth-grade teacher in a small country-suburban K–8 district school. She began by describing her class and the problem of not having in-class support for high-ability students in her room. The gifted students were pulled out of her classroom daily during math instruction to work on special science projects. In view of this, she wondered whether she was meeting the needs of these high-ability students, and she initiated an action research study. Here are the steps she took:

1. She first reviewed the published literature on her issue (e.g., pull-out programs, inclusion of gifted in the classroom, and the needs of the gifted).
2. In addition, she interviewed colleagues from her school and neighboring elementary schools for their perspectives.

3. From the literature review and her interviews, she identified four themes—school reform, enrichment versus acceleration, pull-out versus in-class, and new educational strategies—and developed a flowchart listing the factors that surfaced for each theme, such as:
   ◆ school reform-movement ideas
   ◆ equity for all—every child receives what he or she needs to grow and learn, and not every child receives the exact same instruction
   ◆ excellence for all where every child is challenged to the limit of his or her abilities (Hughes, 1999, p. 284).

4. Based on this information, she refined her original research questions and collected both quantitative and qualitative data through parent telephone interviews, student surveys, teacher conferences with students about their work portfolios, and classroom observations by six different teachers for each question. She placed this information in a chart so that her team members could help her analyze the data.

5. She enlisted six other elementary teachers from her building to create a team to help with the process of data analysis.

6. The team first skimmed the data to obtain a clear picture of it and then sorted all of the data under four themes about how to incorporate gifted children into the class (in-class flexible groups, differentiated instruction, enrichment, and acceleration).

7. She turned these themes into four major activities for the teacher to try in her classroom.

8. Next she put the findings into an *action plan,* resulting in specific activities (e.g., continue to self-evaluate and find ways to incorporate differentiated instruction and assessment in the classroom).

9. She shared her findings with others, to "make a difference on a larger scale" (Hughes, 1999, p. 295). This included sharing her study with other fourth-grade teachers, her principal, and a district committee.

10. The study ended with Hughes reflecting on future questions that she needed answered, such as "Which is better, pull-out programs, in-class programs, or a combination?"

These 10 steps illustrated a good practical action research study in which a teacher collaborated to study a local problem, developed as a professional, used a systematic approach to inquiry (e.g., gathering and analyzing data), and implemented a plan of action.

Participatory Action Research

Participatory action research (PAR) has a long history in social inquiry involving communities, industries and corporations, and other organizations outside of education (e.g., Kemmis & McTaggart, 2005). Rather than focus on individual teachers solving immediate classroom problems or schools addressing internal issues, PAR has a social and community orientation and an emphasis on research that contributes to emancipation or change in our society. Drawing on the work of the Brazilian Paulo Freire, the German critical theorist Jurgen Habermas, and more recently Australians Stephen Kemmis and Ernest Stringer, this approach has emerged as an action-oriented, advocacy means of inquiry. Often PAR includes qualitative data collection, but it may also involve quantitative data collection.

Individuals refer to participatory action research by different names, such as *participatory research, critical action research,* or *classroom action research* (Kemmis & McTaggart, 2005, pp. 560–561). To acknowledge the collaborative nature of this type of inquiry, this chapter uses the term *participatory action research.*

The purpose of **participatory action research** is to improve the quality of people's organizations, communities, and family lives (Stringer, 2007). Although espousing many of the ideas of teacher and school-based practical action research, it differs by incorporating an emancipatory aim of improving and empowering individuals and organizations in education (and other) settings. Applied to education, the focus is on improving and empowering individuals in schools, systems of education, and school communities. PAR also has a distinct ideological foundation that shapes the direction of the process of inquiry; the type of issue that commands attention of the action researcher; the procedures of research, especially data collection; and the intent and outcomes of the inquiry.

For example, participatory action researchers study issues that relate to a need to address social problems that constrain and repress the lives of students and educators. For example, consider these issues that address social, economic, political, and class problems in our society that may be the focus of a PAR study:

◆ Tests that label and stereotype students
◆ Texts that omit important historical persons or events of cultural and ethnic groups
◆ Assessments that serve to confirm student failure rather than learning
◆ K–12 classroom interactions that silence or quiet the voices of minority students

In addition to studying these sensitive issues, the participatory action researcher also engages in a process of research that promotes egalitarian and democratic aims. Participatory action researchers strive for an open, broad-based involvement of participants in their studies by collaborating in decisions as consensual partners and engaging participants as equals to ensure their well-being. For example, in their inquiries, researchers emphasize the importance of establishing contacts, identifying stakeholder groups, locating key people, negotiating the researcher's role, and building a preliminary picture of the field context of the study (Stringer, 2007). The social values of liberation and life-enhancing changes are also important, and action researchers seek to bring about a new vision for schools, community agencies, youth clubs, and ethnic groups within schools.

Kemmis and McTaggert (2005) summarized six central features of PAR:

1. *PAR is a social process in which the researcher deliberately explores the relationship between the individual and other people.* The objective is to understand how social interaction forms and re-forms individuals. Applied to education, participatory action researchers might explore teachers working together in teams.
2. *This form of inquiry is participatory.* This means that individuals conduct studies *on* themselves. During this process, people examine how their own understandings, skills, values, and present knowledge both frame and constrain their actions. Teachers, for example, would study themselves to gain a better understanding of their practices and how this knowledge shapes (and constrains) their work with students.
3. *This form of research is practical and collaborative.* It is collaborative because it is inquiry completed *with* others. It is practical because researchers typically explore acts of communication, the production of knowledge, and the structure of social organization to reduce irrational, unproductive, unjust, or unsatisfying interactions. Teachers, for example, might collaborate with other teachers to reduce the levels of bureaucracy in a school that might inhibit classroom innovations.
4. *PAR is emancipatory in that it helps unshackle people from the constraints of irrational and unjust structures that limit self-development and self-determination.* The intent of a study, for example, might be to change the bureaucratic procedures for teachers in schools so that they can better facilitate student learning.
5. *PAR is critical in that it aims to help people recover and release themselves from the constraints embedded in social media (e.g., their language, their modes of work, their social relationships of power).* For instance, teachers may be constrained by a subservient role in the school district so that they do not feel empowered in their classrooms.

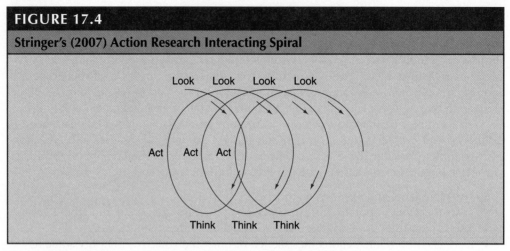

FIGURE 17.4

Stringer's (2007) Action Research Interacting Spiral

Source: Stringer (2007), p. 9. Reprinted by permission of Sage Publications, Inc.

6. *PAR is reflexive (e.g., recursive or dialectical) and focused on bringing about change in practices.* This occurs through spirals of reflection and action. When teachers reflect on their roles in schools, they will try one action and then another, always returning to the central question of what they learned and accomplished because of their actions.

A spiral of looking, thinking, and action best reflects the action research process. This process, called the interacting spiral by Stringer (2007), is shown in Figure 17.4. This model contains three phases: look, think, and act. The spiral of this model conveys that action research is not neat, orderly, and linear, but is a process of repeating and revising procedures and interpretations.

Let's examine more closely the components of the action research process for looking, thinking, and acting. The detailed analysis of the three phases is shown in Figure 17.5.

FIGURE 17.5

Steps in Stringer's (2007) Action Research Model

Look: Building the Picture	Think: Interpreting and Analyzing	Act: Resolving Problems
Purpose: To assist stakeholding groups in building a picture	Purpose: To distill the information gathered, identify elements of people's experiences, and enable the participants to understand the way the issue affects their lives and activities	Purpose: To plan and implement practical solutions to problems

Process:
  Gather information
  Record information
  Extend understanding
  Organizing meetings
  Communicating
	Process:
	  Frameworks
	  Categorizing and coding
	  Analyzing key experiences
	  Enriching analysis using frameworks
	  Writing reports collaboratively
	  Presentations and performance
		Process:
		  Planning
		  Implementing
		  Reviewing
		  Evaluating

Source: Adapted from Stringer (2007), pp. 63, 124, 144.

In this model, Stringer (2007) placed emphasis on the importance of "looking" to build a picture to help stakeholders understand issues they are experiencing. The "look" phase consists of collecting data (e.g., through interviews, observation, and documents), recording and analyzing the information, and constructing and reporting to stakeholders about the issue. The "think" phase then moves into interpreting the issues in greater depth and identifying priorities for action. In the final phase, the researcher identifies the "act" phase: devising practical solutions to the problems. This involves devising a plan and setting direction, such as objectives, tasks, and persons to carry out the objectives and secure needed resources. It also means implementing the plan, encouraging people to carry it out, and evaluating it in terms of its effect and achievements.

Let's examine a PAR study to see this process at work. Stanulis and Jeffers (1995) studied the mentoring relationship among a fifth-grade classroom teacher (Lynn), her student teacher (Shawna), and a university coordinator (Randi). Called critical action research, the authors described Lynn's mentoring of Shawna. Randi, as the coordinator of field experiences and a university mentor, worked with Lynn to compile data to assess the mentoring of her student teacher. They collected three sets of data to explore this mentoring:

◆ Five videotaped conferences were recorded between the student and the classroom teachers every other week during a 10-week period.
◆ Weekly personal journal entries of the classroom teacher and the student teacher were reviewed.
◆ The university coordinator conducted five interviews with the classroom and the student teachers using the method of individual stimulated recall, a procedure of viewing the videotapes and answering interview questions (e.g., "Was there a point in the conference that you chose not to say something?").

Based on this data, the university coordinator and the classroom teacher identified four themes: (a) the process in which the student teacher gained the students' respect, (b) how the student teacher learned about the children as a learning community (e.g., their family backgrounds, their interests), (c) the mentoring relationship between the student teacher and the classroom teacher, and (d) ideas learned from action research.

Consistent with participatory action research, the authors mentioned that the student teacher brought to the classroom issues of knowledge and authority. The mentoring teacher viewed authority, embedded within the structure of the student-teaching experience, as shifting and changing during the course of the experience. The mentoring began as a springboard where the teacher told and shared how to teach the children and shifted to the mentor teacher serving as someone to listen and help clarify the students' ideas. The semester ended with the student teacher and mentor teacher viewing each other as colleagues, sharing ideas, and, in the process, loosening the constraints of teacher authority lodged within a student-teaching experience. They changed and transformed the mentoring relationship during this work together—a result consistent with PAR. Also, in the student teacher–teacher conferences, the opportunity to reflect on each individual's approach to teaching provided collaboration and reflection before action. Each individual learned about themselves and became sensitive to changes in the teacher–student relationship.

As you think back on Maria's action research project where she addresses the question "What steps can our school take to encourage students to be more concerned about the possession of weapons in the school?" should she use practical action research or PAR as her action research approach? Please provide three reasons for your choice.

WHAT ARE THE KEY CHARACTERISTICS OF ACTION RESEARCH?

Despite differences between practical action research and PAR, both types of designs have common characteristics found in action research. Understanding these characteristics will help you better design your own study or read, evaluate, and use an action research study published in the literature. These characteristics are:

◆ A practical focus
◆ The educator–researcher's own practices
◆ Collaboration
◆ A dynamic process
◆ A plan of action
◆ Sharing research

A Practical Focus

The aim of action research is to address an actual problem in an educational setting. Thus, action researchers study **practical issues** that will have immediate benefits for education. These issues may be a concern of a single teacher in a classroom or a problem involving many educators in a building. It may be a school–community issue, an issue with a school policy or structure that constrains individual freedom and action, or a concern of individuals in towns and cities. Action researchers do not undertake this form of research to advance knowledge for knowledge's sake, but to solve an immediate, applied problem.

The Teacher–Researcher's Own Practices

When action researchers engage in a study, they are interested in examining their own practices rather than studying someone else's practices. In this sense, action researchers engage in **participatory or self-reflective research** in which they turn the lens on their own educational classroom, school, or practices. As they study their own situation, they reflect on what they have learned—a form of self-development—as well as what they can do to improve their educational practices. Action researchers deliberately experiment with their own practices, monitor the actions and circumstances in which they occur, and then retrospectively reconstruct an interpretation of the action as a basis for future action. In this reflection, action researchers weigh different solutions to their problems and learn from testing ideas. Action research has been called "a spiral of self-reflection" (Kemmis, 1994, p. 46).

Collaboration

Action researchers **collaborate with others**, often involving coparticipants in the research (Schmuck, 2009). These coparticipants may be individuals within a school or outside personnel such as university researchers or professional association groups. This does not mean that outsiders should co-opt practitioners by gathering data that serve only their needs. So that this co-opting will not occur, outsiders need to negotiate their entry to a site with participants and be sensitive to the involvement of participants in the project (Stringer, 2007). It involves establishing acceptable and cooperative relationships, communicating in a manner that is sincere and appropriate, and including all individuals, groups, and issues. As shown in Figure 17.6, many individuals and groups may participate in an action research project. Individuals may review results of findings with the researcher, help collect data, or assist in the presentation of the final report. Many aspects of the research process are open

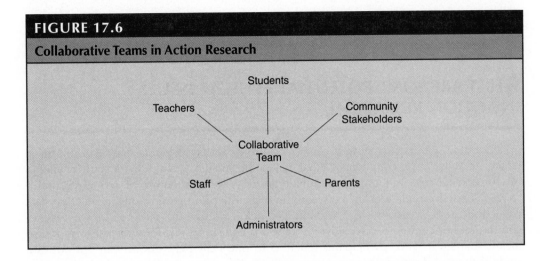

FIGURE 17.6

Collaborative Teams in Action Research

to collaboration in action research. During this collaboration, roles may vary and may be negotiated, but the concept of interacting is central to understanding one's practices.

A Dynamic Process

Action researchers engage in a **dynamic process** involving iterations of activities, such as a "spiral" of activities. The key idea is that the researcher "spirals" back and forth between reflection about a problem, data collection, and action. A school-based team, for example, may try several actions after reflecting on the best time for high school classes to begin. Reflecting, collecting data, trying a solution, and spiraling back to reflection are all part of the process of action research. The process does not follow a linear pattern or a causal sequence from problem to action.

A Plan of Action

The next step is to identify a **plan of action**. At some point in the process, the action researcher formulates an action plan in response to the problem. This plan may be simply presenting the data to important stakeholders, establishing a pilot program, starting several competing programs, or implementing an ongoing research agenda to explore new practices (Stringer, 2007). It may be a formal written plan or an informal discussion about how to proceed, and it may engage a few individuals (e.g., students in a classroom) or involve an entire community (e.g., in a participatory research study).

Sharing Research

Unlike traditional research that investigators report in journal and book publications, action researchers report their research to educators, who can then immediately use the results. Action researchers often engage in **sharing reports** with local school, community, and educational personnel. Although action researchers publish in scholarly journals, they are typically more interested in sharing the information locally with individuals who can promote change or enact plans within their classroom or building. Action researchers share results with teachers, the building principal, school district personnel, and parent associations (e.g., Hughes, 1999). In addition, online journals (both with and without standards for inclusion), Web sites, and discussion blogs provide opportunities for action researchers to publicize their studies (see Mills, 2011). Innovative forums also exist for performance texts where the researchers perform what they have learned through action research (see Denzin, 1997). These performances might be a play, a poem, a reading of text, slides, or music.

WHAT ARE SOME POTENTIAL ETHICAL ISSUES IN ACTION RESEARCH?

Collaborating with participants, a central feature of action research, may lead to ethical issues. As Mills (2011) comments, "What makes the subject of ethics particularly challenging for teacher researchers is the intimate and open-ended nature of action research." (p. 29). This close relationship between the researcher and participants means that data collection cannot be coercive. It should also acknowledge the dual role of the teacher and the researcher and the sensitivity it takes to engage in this form of research. It also means that students or participants (such as in one's own classroom) can opt out of a study if they so desire without being penalized. These are special ethical concerns that arise in action research. Following in a similar manner, Brydon-Miller (2009) wrote about ethics and action research and advocated that researchers should adopt "covenantal ethics" established on the basis of caring relationships among community research partners and a shared commitment to social justice (p. 244). This commitment entails open and transparent participation, respect for people's knowledge, democratic and nonhierarchical practices, and positive and sustainable social change among the action research community. Thus, the research needs to be in the best interest of those facing the problem or issue being addressed in the action research project. Some of the ethical needs in collaborating with community participants are to continually renegotiate the purpose of the study, to consider how the results will be used, and to involve participants in as many phases of the process of research as possible. In addition, as Box 17.1 indicates, the initiation of the process through the consent process form may present an ethical problem.

BOX 17.1 | Ethical Dilemma

When the Consent Form May Mislead Participants

Newkirk (1996) has written about one ethical challenge in conducting action research. He focused his attention on the use of the consent form completed by participants before the study begins. He referred to this form as an "act of seduction" (p. 3). The consent form, he maintained, may aid the researcher by providing an all-too-brief and vague description of the project, and convey an impression of the solicitousness of the researcher. The form also heightens the sense of importance of the study and encourages the participants to divulge deeply felt beliefs and cherished experiences. Newkirk goes on to make important recommendations in regards to these ethical issues. He says that the consent process should acknowledge the potential for negative interpretations made during the study, and that participants should have a role in making interpretations of the study results. Could you provide several suggestions about practical steps a researcher might take when using the consent form in action research in order to address these ethical issues?

WHAT ARE THE STEPS IN CONDUCTING AN ACTION RESEARCH STUDY?

In the steps that follow, remember that action research is a dynamic, flexible process and that no blueprint exists for how to proceed. However, several steps in the process can illustrate a general approach for your use.

Step 1. Determine if Action Research Is the Best Design to Use

Action research is an applied form of inquiry and it is useful in many situations. You might use it to address a problem, typically one in your work situation or community. It requires that you have the time to collect and analyze data and to experiment with different options for solving the problem. To help with the process of reflection, you ideally need collaborators with whom to share findings and who can potentially serve as coresearchers on the project. Action research also requires a broad understanding of the many types of quantitative and qualitative data collection to gather information to devise a plan of action.

Step 2. Identify a Problem to Study

The most important factor in action research is that you need to solve a practical problem. This problem may be one that you face in your own practice or in your community (Kemmis & Wilkinson, 1998). After reflection, you write down the problem or phrase it as a question to answer.

The research problem is only one place that you might begin your study. In addition to starting with solving a problem, you might enter action research at other points (Schmuck, 1997). Action researchers may begin with identifying an area of focus, collecting data, analyzing and interpreting data, or developing an action plan (Mills, 2011).

Step 3. Locate Resources to Help Address the Problem

Explore several resources to help study the problem. Literature and existing data may help you formulate a plan of action. You may need to review the literature and determine what others have learned about solving the issue. Asking colleagues for advice helps initiate a study. Teaming with university personnel or knowledgeable people in the community provides a resource base for an action research project. Individuals who have conducted action research projects can also help you during your research study.

Step 4. Identify Information You Will Need

Plan a strategy for gathering data. This means that you need to decide who can provide data, how many people you will study, what individuals to access, and the rapport and support you can expect to obtain from them. You may need to file a proposal for data collection with the institutional review board if you plan to use the research for your graduate research project.

Another consideration is what type of data you need to collect. Your choices are to collect quantitative or qualitative data, or both. It is helpful to understand the possibilities

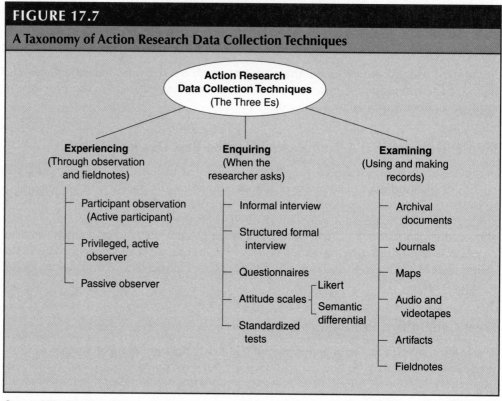

FIGURE 17.7

A Taxonomy of Action Research Data Collection Techniques

Source: Mills (2011), p. 89.

that exist for both forms of data. Mills (2011), for example, has organized quantitative and qualitative sources, as shown in Figure 17.7, into three dimensions:

- ◆ *Experiencing*—observing and taking fieldnotes
- ◆ *Enquiring*—asking people for information
- ◆ *Examining*—using and making records

The choice of data sources depends on the questions, time and resources, availability of individuals, and sources of information. In general, the more sources used and the more triangulation among them, the more you will be able to understand the problem and develop viable action plans (Sagor, 2005). It is probably wise to limit data collection in your first action research study so that you have a manageable amount of information to analyze.

Step 5. Implement the Data Collection

Implementing data collection takes time, especially if you gather multiple sources of information. In addition, your participants may have limited time to complete instruments or engage in interviews. Keeping an accurate record of the information collected, organizing it into data files for numeric or theme analysis, and examining the quality of the information are important data collection steps.

Step 6. Analyze the Data

You may decide to analyze the data yourself or enlist the help of other educators or data analysts. You might show your results to others to find out how they would interpret the findings. In most situations, descriptive statistics will suffice for your action research data analysis, although you may want to compare some group data or relate several variables. The major idea is to keep the data analysis manageable so that you can identify useful information in formulating a plan of action.

Step 7. Develop a Plan for Action

A plan may be an informal statement about the implementation of a new educational practice. It might be a plan to reflect on alternative approaches to addressing the problem or to share what you have learned with others, such as teachers, individuals in district offices, or other schools and communities. You might formally write out this plan or present it as an outline. You can develop it yourself or collaborate with school personnel in writing it. The important point is that you now have a strategy for trying out some ideas to help solve your problem.

Step 8. Implement the Plan and Reflect

In many action research projects, you will implement your plan of action to see if it makes a difference. This involves trying out a potential solution to your problem and monitoring whether it has impact. To determine this difference, you might consult your original objectives or the research question that you sought to answer in the action research project.

You also need to reflect on what you have learned from implementing your plan and sharing it with others. You may need to share it broadly with school colleagues, school committees, university researchers, or policy makers. In some cases, you will not achieve an adequate solution, and you will need to try out another idea and see if it makes a difference. In this way, one action research project often leads to another.

HOW DO YOU EVALUATE AN ACTION RESEARCH STUDY?

To evaluate an action research study, consider using the following criteria to assess its quality. These criteria are applicable to both practical action research and PAR (see Kemmis & Wilkinson, 1998; Mills, 2011). In a high-quality action research study, the author:

◆ Focuses on an issue in practice or an issue in the local community.
◆ Collects multiple sources of data (often quantitative and qualitative) to help address the problem.
◆ Collaborates with others during the study to find the best solutions.
◆ Shows respect for all collaborators so they are equal partners in the action research process.
◆ Advances a plan of action for trying to solve the problem.
◆ Reflects on his/her own development as a professional.
◆ Helps to enhance the lives of participants by solving a problem, empowering them, changing them, or providing them with new understandings.
◆ Develops a plan recommending changes to practice.
◆ Reports the research in a way that is understandable and useful to audiences, including other professionals.

KEY IDEAS IN THE CHAPTER

Definition of Action Research, Its Use, and Its Development

The purpose of action research is to improve the practice of education, with researchers studying their own problems or issues in a school or educational setting. Educators engage in reflection about these problems, collect and analyze data, and implement changes or a plan of action based on their findings. In some cases, the research solves a local, practical problem, such as a classroom issue for a teacher. In other situations, the research seeks ideological aims, such as to empower, transform, and emancipate individuals and communities.

Action research developed in the 1930s with citizen group processes. After a short time, it resurfaced in the 1970s with projects in Great Britain, the United States, and Australia. These projects focused on teachers studying their own practices, educators working with schools, and researchers helping individuals emancipate themselves from social issues in educational settings. Today, action research has grown in importance as a means for enhancing school renewal, promoting teacher development, and testing new ideas.

Types of Action Research Designs

Action research is an informal process of research in which educators engage in a study of their own practices. Individual teachers, teams within a school or district, or school–community inquiry groups undertake this form of research. Two types of action research designs exist. The first design, practical action research, is an approach that involves educators examining a school situation with a view toward improving practice. Rather than a focus on individual teachers solving immediate classroom problems or schools addressing internal issues, the second design, PAR (or critical action research), has a social and community orientation and places emphasis on research that contributes to emancipation or change in our society. The PAR approach seeks to improve the quality of organizations, community, and family lives. It espouses an objective of improving and empowering individuals and organizations in educational settings. Both the practical and the participatory forms of action research have basic principles and models for conducting research.

Key Characteristics of Action Research

Action researchers use a process of inquiry, regardless of design. The teacher or educator becomes the researcher. As the researcher, the practitioner becomes self-reflective about the process. Action researchers often engage others collaboratively in the process as coparticipants and enact a dynamic model of inquiry involving iterations of activities, cycling back and forth between identifying a problem, trying a solution, reflecting on information learned, and applying new solutions. During this process, they use a plan of action to guide the use of a new practice. They base this plan on what they learned about the research problem, and they share it with others, such as in informal reports to colleagues, school officials, school boards, and community members.

Potential Ethical Issues in Action Research

Ethical issues are central to conducting action research that involves participants in a substantial way. The action researcher needs to conduct the inquiry in a way that respects the care of the participants, involves them collaboratively in all phases of the research, and is sensitive to obtaining consent and advancing the purpose of the study when all of the phases may not be initially known. It is also important for participants to have the option to withdraw from the study.

Steps in Conducting an Action Research Study

Action researchers begin with a practical problem that they face or someone in a community might face. They help locate resources and information to address the problem, and they engage in data collection that might involve both quantitative and qualitative forms of data. They analyze the data, often done collaboratively with participants, and develop and implement a plan of action.

Evaluating an Action Research Study

Evaluation of an action research study is based on assessing whether it addresses a practical issue, involves the collection of multiple sources of data, proceeds with collaboration and respect for participants, advances a plan of action and, in the end, reflects both the researcher's and the participants' growth toward improved changes to practice.

USEFUL INFORMATION FOR PRODUCERS OF RESEARCH

◆ Design an action research project that matches your time and resources.
◆ Recognize that the process of conducting an action research study is like a spiral with phases that repeat, such as looking, thinking, and acting, as in the Stringer (2007) model.
◆ Remember that in action research, you will be the participant in your own research project. You are not studying someone else; instead, you are examining your own practices.
◆ It is useful to collaborate with others in action research. Consider university personnel, other colleagues, or individuals familiar with this form of research. They may have insight or be able to draw conclusions that you cannot draw.
◆ Collect data and analyze it so that it will be understandable to the applied audience for action research studies in your school, district, or other educational unit.
◆ Consider the full array of data collection types for your action research, such as quantitative and qualitative data.
◆ Construct a plan of action that you can realistically carry out in your school or educational setting.

USEFUL INFORMATION FOR CONSUMERS OF RESEARCH

◆ Recognize the differences between practical action research and PAR. The former has the intent of addressing a practical problem in education, whereas the latter has a social or community orientation and emphasizes emancipation or change in our society.
◆ Action researchers study their own situation and attempt to develop solutions to practical (or community) problems. When you review a study, identify the intent of the researcher and look for how the study addresses some issue in which the researcher is involved.
◆ Action research studies are applied and the results should be action oriented and easy to understand.
◆ Evaluate whether the action research study made a difference or changed the situation presented in the research problem.

ADDITIONAL RESOURCES YOU MIGHT EXAMINE

A number of useful books can help expand your understanding of action research:

Geoffrey Mills (2011) authored an excellent guide for the teacher–researcher who seeks to engage in action research. Mills provided a good discussion of both practical and critical action research perspectives and reviewed the primary process models available for conducting this form of inquiry. His discussion includes a chapter on ethical issues, a chapter on developing action plans after the action research has concluded, and a chapter on criteria for evaluating a good action research study. See:

Mills, G. E. (2011). *Action research: A guide for the teacher researcher* (4th ed.). Boston, MA: Pearson.

Sagor (2005) has authored a "practical" action research guide to help teachers become action researchers. This guide provides a useful, readable approach to practical action research with a focus on teachers collaborating with other teachers. It takes the reader through the many aspects of action research. Examine:

Sagor, R. (2005). *The action research guidebook: A four-step process for educators and school teams.* Thousand Oaks: Corwin Press.

Another book on practical action research by Schmuck (2009) provides 27 school-based cases and reviews on educational action research. These cases and reviews show that educational action research is participatory, reciprocal, and democratic. They illustrate living examples of both proactive and responsive action research. See:

Schmuck, R. A. (Ed.). (2009). *Practical action research: A collection of articles* (2nd ed.). Thousand Oaks, CA: Corwin Press.

Turning to participatory action research, Stringer's (2007) book provides an excellent guide to the principles of community-based action research (e.g., relationships, communication, participation, and inclusion) as well as how to negotiate entry to a research site. An entire chapter addresses writing formal reports, theses, and dissertations. This is an invaluable guide to students who plan to undertake their own action research studies within a critical, emancipatory, and participatory framework. Examine:

Stringer, E. T. (2007). *Action research* (3rd ed.). Thousand Oaks, CA: Sage.

Another participatory perspective is available in the works by Kemmis (e.g., Kemmis & McTaggart, 2005). Atweh, Kemmis, and Weeks (1998) have edited a book of readings about PAR in education. This book offers numerous examples of action research projects based on Participatory Action Research for the Advancement of Practice in Education and Teaching at the Queensland University of Technology in Australia. Especially valuable in this volume is the chapter by Kemmis and Wilkinson (1998), which advances the central features of participatory action research and its interface with the study of practice in education. A major statement about participatory action research can also be found in the *SAGE Handbook of Qualitative Research* (Denzin & Lincoln, 2005). See:

Kemmis, S., & McTaggart, R. (1988). *The action research planner.* Geelong, Victoria, Australia: Deakin University Press.

Kemmis, S., & Wilkinson, M. (1998). Participatory action research and the study of practice. In B. Atweh, S. Kemmis, & P. Weeks (Eds.), *Action research in practice: Partnerships for social justice in education* (pp. 21–36). London and New York: Routledge.

Kemmis, S., & McTaggart, R. (2005). Participatory action research. In N. K. Denzin & Y. S. Lincoln (Eds.), *Sage handbook of qualitative research* (3rd ed., pp. 559–603). Thousand Oaks, CA: Sage.

PEARSON
myeducationlab
The Power of Classroom Practice
www.myeducationlab.com

Go to the Topic "Action Research" in the MyEducationLab (**www.myeducationlab .com**) for your course, where you can:

◆ Find learning outcomes for "Action Research."
◆ Complete Assignments and Activities that can help you more deeply understand the chapter content.
◆ Apply and practice your understanding of the core skills identified in the chapter with the Building Research Skills exercises.
◆ Check your comprehension of the content covered in the chapter by going to the Study Plan. Here you will be able to take a pretest, receive feedback on your answers, and then access Review, Practice, and Enrichment activities to enhance your understanding. You can then complete a final posttest.

Example of an Action Research Study

Examine the following published journal article that is an action research design study. Marginal notes indicate the major characteristics of action research highlighted in this chapter. The illustrative study is:

The Internet and Student Research: Teaching Critical Evaluation Skills

Delilah Heil

To use the internet effectively, students need to be taught critical-evaluation skills that they can apply to each web site they use for research. The action research report discussed in this article exemplifies the collaborative teamwork involved in creating a critical-evaluation unit for Internet sites to be used with middle school students.

(01)   Results of the unit show that giving students background information on the Internet and showing Internet site examples to change their previous perceptions increased their understanding of the research tool. Teaching students about ways to evaluate Internet sites gave the students the information they needed to make more informed decisions about how they use the Internet.

Introduction

(02)

A practical focus

The school year has begun and research projects are underway, but the library shelves are quiet and unused. A quick survey of the computer area shows once again that the students are using the Internet as their first source to locate information. As I watch this scene day after day, I ask these questions: Why do students find the Internet so appealing? Do students know the credibility of sites on the Internet? Do students know how to evaluate sites before using them? Would a unit on how to critically evaluate Internet sites increase the information literacy of the students? I decided to do action research to answer these questions.

Literature Review

(03)   Information literacy is defined as "a set of abilities requiring individuals to recognize when information is needed and have the ability to locate, evaluate, and use effectively the information needed" (Association of College and Research Libraries, 2000, p. 2). An important part of information literacy is the ability to evaluate Internet sources critically and to decide if each source is unbiased, accurate, and written by a qualified person who has specific knowledge on the topic. This ability is crucial to being a good user of resources and to research. However, many Internet users do not realize that "quality control does not exist on the Internet . . . there is a cesspool of waste" (Herring, 2001, Reasons section, para. 3).

(04)   Internet users "have developed an infatuation with information; any information is good information—the more of it, the better, as long as it is easy to obtain" (Scott & O'Sullivan, 2000, Value of Learning section, para. 6). Students usually choose less reliable commercial sites over educational or government sites for their research even though only one fourth of the commercial sites are suitable for academic purposes (Haycock, 2000). Students avoid more reliable databases and library materials because these sources take more time and involve more steps with fewer results (O'Sullivan & Scott, 2000).

(05)   The results of a questionnaire study (O'Sullivan & Scott, 2000) about students' preferred use of materials indicated that the majority of the students chose the Internet to conduct research, citing ease of use, speed of use, and the convenience of finding infinite information quickly as the top reasons for their choice. Almost 63% of the students cited the information's depth and variety as being a benefit of the Internet. Only 10% noted downfalls to the Internet, such as bias or inaccurate information. Students' responses also showed that they do not view information on the Internet critically.

Watson's research (2001) focused on the grade level at which students would be most receptive to learning Internet critical evaluation skills. The research showed that middle school students are the prime targets for information literacy skill training because they are still actively experimenting with the Internet and have reached a developmental stage where they can better comprehend the reliability of information. (06)

These studies indicate a strong need for information literacy instruction on the quality of the material presented on the Internet. Teacher-librarians must teach students that although there is a large quantity of information available on the Internet, the quality of the sites is extremely important when using the Internet as a research tool. (07)

Collaboration Aspects

Collaboration is an important factor in anything teacher-librarians do, but it is particularly important when doing action research. The easiest way to begin collaboration is to publicize what the project entails and see if anyone is interested. Many of the school's teachers were attending an in-school summer workshop with me at the time I publicized the project. The computer teacher commented that the topic fit into her eighth-grade computer class. She was looking for materials to use along with the required text-book lessons and felt that this unit would cover her needs and benefit students. She became a collaborative teaching partner. (08)

Collaboration with others

While discussing the requirements for the research, we decided to use only research topics that were relevant and necessary to the eighth-grade curriculum. Students are required to do so much research for classes that having them work on topics we chose simply to fulfill our needs seemed wasteful. We asked the eighth-grade teachers attending the workshop what research projects they were planning to assign. The geography teacher wanted to assign a research project but could not work lab time into the schedule because all the labs had scheduled classes during her class time. Our research project met her needs, so we became a collaborative team. The final project that each student created would have to meet the requirements of that student's teachers. The collaborative team then decided how to best set up the final project. (09)

The educator–researcher's own practices

Other people soon collaborated with us. Former students at the workshop who were teacher helpers heard of our plans. Learning that we needed Internet sites that would make the problem areas clearer to the students, they volunteered to create the teaching models. Using our notes and worksheets, they put their technology expertise to work developing two legitimate-looking sites. (10)

Research Site and Subject Description

The school district is located in a small, rural Midwest community that is in the low to middle socioeconomic group, discerned by the fact that 47% of the students are eligible for free or reduced-price lunches. The school serves 391 students with the following ethnic backgrounds: 98% Caucasian, 2% Native American. Of the total eighth-grade class, 50% of the students participated. These 14 students (8 female and 6 male) were all of Caucasian descent. (11)

Pre-Unit Data Collection Description and Analysis

Students completed a pre-unit survey to determine their Internet use habits, their research habits, and their knowledge of the Internet and critical evaluation skills. Table 1 lists the Internet use statements, the research statements, and the students' responses. The Internet and research use responses showed that about 75% of the students used the Internet for games and for socialization activities such as e-mail. All of the students used the Internet for research projects. The research statement responses showed that 71% of students used the Internet first for research and that 85% of the students either do not choose to or do not know how to critically evaluate the Internet sites. (12)

The two students who responded yes to the critical evaluation statement were interviewed further to determine their understanding of critical evaluation. When asked what is involved in critical evaluation of sites, one student responded that looking at the site to see if some of the information matches what is already known and seeing that the site contains the information that is being researched shows critical evaluation skills. The other student responded that checking out the pictures and graphs to see if they contain good information and the site's professional appearance is a method to critically evaluate a site. (13)

TABLE 1
Internet and Research Use

Internet Use	Yes	No
Do you use the Internet for pleasure activities such as games?	10	4
Do you use the Internet for e-mail?	12	2
Do you use Internet chat rooms?	8	6
Do you use the Internet to research homework projects?	14	0
Do you use online databases provided by local libraries?	5	9

Research Use			
When you are assigned research, which do you use first?		Books 4	Internet 10
Do you critically evaluate a site before choosing it as a research source?	Yes 2	No 6	Don't Know 6

(14)   Do students have adequate perceptions of the Internet? To find out, students were presented statements pertaining to the Internet and asked to rate the statements using a Likert Scale. Table 2 lists the statements and the responses. The responses indicated that 85% of the students had not formed strong opinions about the cost of publishing materials on the Internet. Forty-two percent of the students had not formed a strong opinion or agreed that information on the Internet is reliable. Ninety-two percent of the students either did not have a strong opinion or agreed that one must have approval before publishing on the Internet. This data presented strong indications that students do not have a good understanding of the Internet.

(15)   Students also responded to open-ended questions on the survey. The overwhelming response to the question, "What attracts you to the Internet for research?" was that the Internet provides fast access to information on any topic. When asked, "What do you consider to be reasons for not using the Internet?" the responses varied. A few students responded that there were no reasons; others suggested that the unwanted pop-ups and inappropriate sites were reasons to avoid using the Internet.

(16)   Finally, students completed a worksheet to determine how they select Internet sites. They had to locate one reliable Internet site on the Korean War and then respond to two questions: "In the search list, what number in the list was the site that you chose to use and why?" Six of the 14

TABLE 2
Internet Perceptions

Statement About Internet	Strongly Agree	Agree	Neither Agree nor Disagree	Disagree	Strongly Disagree
All the information found on the Internet is reliable.	1	1	4	4	4
It is costly to publish materials on the Internet.	0	1	12	1	0
A person must get approval before publishing to the Internet.	1	6	6	0	1

students selected the first site and cited the reason for their choice as, "because the first hits in a search are always the best ones." The other 8 students picked from various sections of the list and cited good charts, graphs, information, and that the sites "looked official" as reasons for their choices.

Our survey reflected results similar to other researchers' data. It also showed that students would benefit from a unit on how to evaluate Internet sites. (17)

The Internet Site Critical Evaluation Unit

The unit involved six critical steps and a great deal of practice and review of the steps. The following is a description of each step as well as observations to students' reactions throughout the process. (18)

A plan for action

Step 1: Get the Students' Attention and Provide Motivation

The collected data showed that students believe the Internet is a reliable source of information, so their perception had to change before they would understand the importance of evaluating sites. To get their attention, we showed them sites that presented information that was contrary to what they had learned. We selected two sites that said the earth is flat. (19)

Students agreed that the earth is not flat and realized that everything on the Internet is not accurate. This led students to question the credentials of Internet site creators. Understanding that anyone can post any information to the Internet offered an opportunity to address some of the other misconceptions that became apparent during data collection. (20)

We discussed with the students what elements, such as logos and emblems, they thought made a site look credible. We also mentioned the fact that experts who understand how search engines work can cause a site to register in the top 10 hits of a search even if it is not the most applicable. Students began to question how they could determine if a site contains reliable information. (21)

Step 2: Overview of Critical Evaluation Process and Terminology

Using a PowerPoint presentation, we reviewed information and introduced new information, and we gave the students an Internet Evaluation Checklist that showed the essential steps so that they were not distracted by having to take notes. (22)

Step 3: Applying the Process to the Model Internet Sites

Using the Internet Evaluation Checklist, the teaching team guided students through the first model web site. We also reviewed and gave oral quizzes on the step-by-step processes that students had to memorize. Next, the students evaluated the second site on their own, allowing them to work through the process and to find the fun areas embedded in the site. Although these fun areas were also evaluated, they served to lighten the tension and frustration the students were experiencing in their first attempts to critically evaluate Internet sites. During this process the teaching team was deluged with questions showing that the students were attempting to think through and make meaning of the process for themselves. We then reviewed the site and their findings. (23)

Step 4: Group Work

Evaluating Internet sites is hard, time consuming, and often frustrating for beginners. The teaching team divided students into groups of two. The paired students became peer-evaluation partners who worked through the site-evaluation process together and learned from each other. The teaching team changed the group dynamics after two site evaluations. (24)

Sharing research

Before starting the evaluation process for each web site, the teaching team gave a specific teaching prompt such as, "You need to know about both sides of the cloning issue for your research. Would this site be a good choice?" Such a question was extremely important where bias could factor into the decision to use or reject a web site. After each group completed one web site evaluation checklist, the entire class reviewed the process and the findings of each group. Students demonstrated where they looked to find information and discussed their decision-making process for using or rejecting a site. (25)

(26)   Initially, students were frustrated with the process as could be seen from their journal entries and from their in-class comments. They wanted everything they were looking for to be easy to find. They questioned why sites were not all created the same, and why there were no required areas on web sites that would make looking up information easier. After gathering all the information, the students also had great difficulty analyzing all the data and making their own judgment on the sites—a critical part of the process.

(27)   As students continued to evaluate more sites, the teaching team saw a glimmer of understanding as many of the students delved deeper into web sites, questioning more of what they found. We also noticed, however, that if a site had information that students wanted, they chose to ignore clear signals that the site was inappropriate for research.

Step 5: Introducing Students to Databases on the Internet

(28)   The teaching team also made students aware that not all material on the Internet is unreliable and discussed the databases purchased by libraries and institutions that are credible for research purposes. We talked to the students about the purpose of databases and the evaluation process that goes into these publications. The information in the students' journals suggested that they found databases to be more difficult to use than a search engine on the Internet but easier than looking up magazines in the *Reader's Guide to Periodical Literature.*

(29)   The students questioned why we did not tell them about the usefulness of the databases earlier. We responded that they were so engrossed in the Internet that they would not have given something that seemed harder to use a second glance; many of the students agreed that our assumption was right. They also agreed that learning how difficult it is to really evaluate information on the Internet made the Internet less appealing for research.

Step 6: Applying the Unit to Real Research

(30)   The teaching team gave each student a geography research topic along with the rubrics listing the requirements for both the geography class and the computer class. Students could use library resources, Internet resources, or their geography textbook to complete their research project; however, they had to evaluate at least five Internet sites and find two credible sites to include in the research project. To use an Internet site in their paper they had to critically evaluate it and explain why they chose the site as being usable for research purposes.

(31)   Initially, students still questioned their abilities to critically evaluate sites. Their journals and class discussion showed that they were frustrated when the teaching team did not have an answer key for the site they selected to use. Later, the majority of students applied much time and effort and asked many questions about sites they wanted to use. They questioned themselves and the teachers more when they found a site that had the information they were looking for but that had questionable evaluation areas. This process showed that they knew what they found was probably not quality material, but they desperately wanted someone to say that it was acceptable to use so they would have their sources.

Post-Unit Data Collection Description and Analysis

(32)   When compared with the pre-unit survey, the post-unit student responses for what draws students to the Internet was the same. The students' Internet perceptions, however, had changed to be more realistic and better informed. Responses to the essay questions gave the greatest insight to the change in perception. Students no longer found a great deal of information to be the most valuable part of the Internet. In fact, the two most popular disadvantages they listed to using the Internet were too much information and too much evaluation required of the information.

(33)   Students were also asked to rank a predetermined list of resource materials in an attempt to find out where the Internet was now ranked. The list included general Internet, subscription databases on the Internet, magazines in the library, encyclopedias, and library books. In the pre-unit survey, 71% of the students selected the Internet as their first choice. Then, 75% of the students selected subscription databases on the Internet and encyclopedias as the top choices, followed by library books and magazines in the library, and last, the general Internet.

Conclusion

The Internet site critical-evaluation unit that was designed to help students understand critical-evaluation skills was challenging for the teachers as well as the students. Both the teaching team and the students grappled with the fact that although there are many clues that one can use to evaluate an Internet site, there are no clear-cut answers. (34)

The action research process helped me to answer my initial questions. Why do students find the Internet so appealing? Collected data showed that students generally find the Internet appealing because of the large amount of information that the medium contains. Do students know the credibility of sites on the Internet? Survey results showed that students do not have adequate background knowledge of the Internet and how it functions to understand the credibility of sites found on the Internet, and students do not know how to critically evaluate sites. Would a unit on critically evaluating Internet sites benefit students? Results of the unit showed that giving students background information on the Internet and showing Internet site examples to change their previous perceptions increased their understanding of the research tool. Teaching students about ways to evaluate Internet sites gave the students the information they needed to make more informed decisions about how they use the Internet. (35)

The process does not end here for me. As a teacher-researcher, I followed up with this group to gather further data on how they are applying the knowledge they gained from this unit. As a teacher-librarian, I find it vital to provide the information contained in this unit to all students across multiple grade levels so that Internet users can make more informed decisions about their choices. (36)

A dynamic process

Update

This Internet site critical-evaluation project has been replicated several times since writing this article, and the results have not varied significantly from the results of the initial project. Other teachers are also emphasizing the need to critically evaluate web sites. Over this time I have observed the positive long-term results of the unit, finding that—with a strong emphasis and reminders—as research projects arise in the students' lives, exposure to this information does change the way students perceive and use the Internet. (37)

References

Association of College & Research Libraries. (2000). *Information literacy competency standards for higher education.* Retrieved April 15, 2002, from www.ala.org/acrl/ilintro.html

Haycock, K. (2000). Web literacy [Electronic version]. *Teacher Librarian, 27*(5), 34.

Herring, M. Y. (2001). Why the Internet can't replace the library [Electronic version]. *The Education Digest, 67*(1), 46–49.

O'Sullivan, M., & Scott, T. (2000). Teaching Internet information literacy: A collaborative approach (part II) [Electronic version]. *Multimedia Schools, 7*(3), 34–37.

Scott, T. J. & O'Sullivan, M. (2000). The Internet and information literacy: Taking the first step toward technology education in the social studies [Electronic version]. *The Social Studies, 91*(3), 121–126.

Watson, J. (2001). Snapshots of a teen Internet user [Electronic version]. *Educational Media and Technology Yearbook, 26,* 115–124.

Feature articles in *TL* are blind refereed by members of the advisory board. This article was submitted November 2003 and updated and accepted June 2005.

APPENDICES

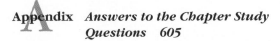

Answers to the Chapter Study Questions

Chapter 1

1. Three advantages you might identify are that research contributes to knowledge, that it helps with practice, and that it provides information to policy makers. Three disadvantages might be that results are vague, are contradictory, and may be based on inaccurate data.

2. If I were Maria, I would first clearly identify the issue that needed to be studied by visiting with a member or two of the committee. Second, I would go to the university library and begin to locate studies on the issue. Third, I would write down the central question that I would like answered.

3. If the parent involvement study was qualitative instead of quantitative, the authors would have sought the views of the parents on the question of their involvement with their adolescents in school and at home. They may have asked the parents open-ended questions and explored their different perspectives. Instead, the authors chose to test whether four factors would help explain parental involvement. If the mothers' trust in school principals study was quantitative rather than qualitative, the authors would have set up an experiment to test whether one group of mothers (e.g., those who were more vocal in their concerns about school) differed from another group of mothers (e.g., those who voiced few concerns about the school) in terms of their responses to the principals. The authors might also have surveyed mothers to determine their trends in views toward principals. But, as a qualitative study, the authors were interested in exploring the mothers' attitudes toward principals and identifying themes in their responses.

Chapter 2

1. The parent involvement study (Deslandes & Bertrand, 2005) narrative hook is fair. It is a reference to another article in which the author makes the case for the importance of parent involvement. It points to the many studies that have documented parent involvement as a problem worth studying. It is, in short, a literature-based hook, but it would be of more interest to academics and other researchers than to educational personnel in the schools or to parents. It lacks emotion and numbers to back up the stance. The mothers' trust in school principals (Shelden et al., 2010) is better. It addresses a topic that many readers can relate to. However, it does not use numeric information to indicate how pervasive the issue of parent participation might be. It also does not cause a particular emotional or attitudinal response in the reader.

2. The problem in the parent involvement study discusses the importance of learning how the four constructs influence parent involvement. *Explaining* the relationship among variables is a key element in quantitative research. In the mothers' trust study, however, the authors seek to develop an *understanding* of mothers' attitudes toward principals. Explanation is a central characteristic of quantitative research, whereas understanding is a characteristic of qualitative research.

3. The parent involvement study contributes to knowledge by helping to fill a void in the existing literature. The mothers' trust in school principals study contributes to knowledge by studying a problem that also fills a void (i.e., we do not know the elements of mothers' trust and need a study to learn about it).

4. In the parent involvement study, a justification based on personal experience would require that the researchers talk about their personal experiences with adolescents, with parenting, and with the schools of their children (if they have them). In the mothers' trust in school principals study, the authors might have talked about whether they were mothers, and whether they had experienced issues of trust with the schools or with school officials.

5. If we compare the introductions to the two studies, the authors of both studies cite extensive literature to document the importance of the problem of study. In the qualitative mothers' trust study, this might appear to be an excessive use of the literature up front in a study that would tend to close down the discussion rather than open it up. However, the literature review at the beginning of this qualitative study does a nice job of narrowing the topic down from the broad issue of parent involvement in schools to the issue of mothers and their trust of principals.

6. Answers will vary.

Chapter 3

1. The key terms would be *teens, high schools,* and *pregnancies*. I would need to see if these terms are those used in the ERIC system or use the *Thesaurus* to see what terms would be appropriate to use when running my ERIC search.

2. I would first examine recent articles, say, those articles published in the last 2 to 3 years. Because they are all journal articles, they represent a good place to start. I may not be familiar with the quality or stature of the journals, but they all seem like national, review-based journals. This leaves me with scanning the titles. Some titles seem to convey content broader than others. I would begin with the broader articles first (e.g., "Violence-related attitudes and behaviors of high school students" rather than "Response of African American adolescents . . .").

3. The reference might look might look like this:

    Kingery, P. M., Coggeshall, M. B., & Alford, A. A. (1998). Violence at school: Recent evidence from four national surveys. *Psychology in the Schools, 35*(3), 247–258.

Chapter 4

1a. Independent variable = parental involvement; dependent variable = student reading performance.

1b. Independent variable = students' knowledge of accountability; dependent variable = changes in attitudes toward learning.

1c. Independent variables = mutuality, comprehensiveness, gender sensitivity, congruence; dependent variable = functional mentoring relationships.

2a. Central phenomenon = conceptions of reading.

2b. Central phenomenon = aspects of sorority life.

2c. Central phenomenon = academic change (sources and processes).

3a. Directional hypothesis

3b. Null hypothesis

Chapter 5

1. Cronbach's alpha is a measure of reliability and, more specifically, internal consistency. A coefficient of .93 is a high coefficient; .6 is an acceptable level for determining whether the scale has internal consistency. With a .72 reliability coefficient, the reliability is satisfactory for the scores.

2. Permissions should have been obtained from (a) the administrator in the school district responsible for permitting researchers to enter schools and conduct research, (b) possibly the building principal, (c) the teachers in the classrooms of the parents' students, and (d) the campus institutional review board at the authors' institution.

3. Steps in locating this instrument: (a) Run an ERIC search and examine the references netted in this search. (b) Next look in the Buros Institute indices, TIP, or MYY, to see if there are any instruments that measure this variable. (c) Look for published research journal articles that contain this variable. See if the authors cite an instrument that they may have used to measure the variable. (d) Ask your advisor or a specialist in the field who may have studied this variable. Find out if this person knows of an instrument that you might use.

4. Maria needs to make these decisions: Whom will she study? She needs to decide whether she will study students in high schools, teachers, administrators, or other personnel. She also needs to determine how she will select these individuals. A random sampling procedure would be ideal. Also, she needs to identify how many individuals she needs for her sample using the rough guide in the section on "Sample Size." Next, based on the questions she plans to answer, she needs to determine what kinds of data she will collect. For example, she may collect attitudinal data or public school document data. With this decision, she will next look for instruments to use in collecting this information and perhaps conduct a search of the literature for existing instruments. These instruments need to be of high quality, reliable, and valid. The procedure for data collection needs to fit the individuals who will provide the data, and the scales need to conform to standard types of interval, ordinal, or nominal scales. Finally, with an instrument identified, she will collect data using standardized procedures for all participants and ethical practices.

Chapter 6

1. Is the hypothesis a comparison of groups or the relationship of variables? It is a comparison of three groups.

   How many independent variables do you have? Dependent variables? One independent variable with three groups; one dependent variable, math scores.

   Are there any covariates being controlled? No.

   Is the independent variable categorical or continuous? Categorical.

   Is the dependent variable categorical or continuous? Continuous.

   Statistical test of choice: Analysis of variance (ANOVA).

2. You fix the responses that are out of range (e.g., 6 and 8).

3. In this statement:

   What does F stand for? ANOVA, the statistical test.

   What is (1, 110)? The degrees of freedom.

   What is 6.81? The calculated value using the ANOVA formula.

   What does p = .001 mean? The p value or the significance level of the calculated value; the groups differ statistically at the alpha level of .001.

Chapter 7

1. The purposeful sampling snowballing strategy involved three approaches: to distribute district-level material through administrators, to hand out material through school personnel, and to have mothers refer other mothers. The approach of distributing materials through administrators resulted in few responses because it did not protect the identities of the mothers. Consequently, the researchers asked school principals and various school personnel to assist in recruiting participants.

2. Ethical issues might have developed in how the interviews were collected and whether the researchers might have created a power imbalance by their role as researchers versus mothers in this study. Also, issues might arise in how the results would be used from this study. Did the results have a negative impact on some principals? Did the authors use the results to point out problems in the schools (as opposed to opening a dialogue about constructive change) or to coerce the principals? The authors should certainly have mentioned the issue of the use of the results of this study in a sensitive project such as this one.

3. When a study topic is sensitive (e.g., mothers' trust in school administrators), the best approach is to collect one-on-one interview data in which the interviewee can feel free to express their views. Observations in the school would not necessarily yield perspectives of mothers. The researchers might have collected additional information through having the mothers journal about their experiences, or collecting notes written to the school by mothers about their children. Additional insight might have been gained from visiting (through interviews) with other members of the families, such as fathers or siblings of the children.

Chapter 8

1. Some limitations in this study would be that only mothers were interviewed, and that the researchers did not have information about how different school contexts or settings might have influenced the mothers' views toward principals. Also, children with disabilities vary considerably in their needs, and these were not factored into the study. Future research might involve entire families, might develop specific types of modeling mothers needed by the principals, and the specific steps in coaching for teachers and administrators that would encourage the mothers' participation.

2. Responses will vary to this question. Look for multiple code words in the left margin and two or three themes in the right margin of the transcript.

3. Responses will vary to this question. Students could provide feedback on their experiences in using the software tutorial.

4. Answers will vary for this description. Look for answers related to context, broad-to-narrow description, use of action verbs, vivid modifiers, and quotes.

5. Answers will vary for this description. Look for the name of the theme, evidence for multiple perspectives on the theme, subthemes, and quotes.

Chapter 9

1. The standards might be those (a) used by the advisor in assessing past students in the program, (b) held personally by the advisor, and (c) used by the college or university.

2. Correct the discriminatory language:

   a. **Poor** (level of specificity problem): Teachers under 25 adopt an open learning environment for students.

      Improved: Teachers in their first 2 years out of teacher education adopt an open learning environment for students.

   b. **Poor** (insensitive to labels): The at-risk students scored below the average in math.

      Improved: The students who have been identified as at risk scored below the average in math.

   c. **Poor** (fails to acknowledge participation of individuals with specific cultural identification): The homeless used the school shelter at night.

      Improved: The adults who do not have a permanent residence used the school shelter at night.

3. It was more of a quantitative approach. It had a structure much like a quantitative study, especially in the introduction with the extensive use of literature.

4. The bulleted points that I would include would address the key results for each of the four research questions. I might pose each question and then provide the results to the question in nonstatistical terms. I would strongly emphasize the results and the implications of the study.

5–9. Answers will vary.

Determine Size Using Sample Size Tables

In the process of collecting data, researchers need to determine the number of participants to use in their studies. Several options are available. They can make an educated guess as to how many people are needed, such as 10% of the population. They can ask as many people to participate as possible within the resources and time that both researchers and participants can provide. They can select a number that satisfies different types of statistical procedures, such as approximately 30 scores for each variable in a correlational analysis.

A more rigorous approach than any of these is to systematically identify the number of participants based on sample size tables available in published texts. To understand these tables, you need to understand the fundamentals of the formulas used. Two formulas will be explained here: the sampling error formula and the power analysis formula.

This discussion about the two formulas builds on earlier comments about the importance of systematically calculating sample size using formulas in quantitative research. This importance was introduced in chapter 5 in the "Sample Size" section and reinforced in chapter 10 on experimental designs under "Step 3. Select an Experimental Unit and Identify Study Participants." It was also mentioned in chapter 11 on correlational designs, although sample size is often dictated by the required size for making assumptions about normality of the distribution of scores. (See chapter 11 discussion about size in correlation studies in "Step 2. Identify Individuals to Study.") However, a sampling error formula may be used when the intent of the correlational study is to generalize from a sample to a population. Using a formula was also encouraged again in chapter 12 on survey designs in "Step 3. Identify the Population, the Sampling Frame, and the Sample." Here

we will explore the calculations involved in the sample size formulas and present tables that simplify the process of making the calculations.

SAMPLING ERROR FORMULA

A sampling error formula is often used in survey or correlational research (see Fink & Kosekoff, 1985; Fowler, 2008) when investigators seek to generalize results from a sample to a population. A **sampling error formula** is a calculation for determining size of a sample based on the chance (or proportion) that the sample will be evenly divided on a question, sampling error, and a confidence interval.

The formula is based on the proportion of the sample that will have the desired characteristic that you are trying to estimate. For example, when parents are polled to determine whether they would vote "yes" or "no" on a school bond issue, there is a 50/50 chance that they will vote "yes." Selecting a proportion of 50/50 means that the population will be evenly split, and this proportion yields the largest size for your sample.

The sampling error formula is also based on stating the amount of sampling error you are willing to tolerate. Recall that sampling error (stated as a percent, such as from 4% of the time) is the difference between your sample mean and the true population mean. This error results because samples are randomly selected from the population and may not represent the true characteristics of the population (see chapter 5). Finally, the formula also includes identifying a confidence interval, such as a 95%

TABLE B.1

Fowler's (1988, p. 42) Sample Size Table: Confidence Ranges for Variability Due to Sampling*

Sample Size	Percentage of Sample with Characteristic				
	5/95	10/90	20/80	30/70	50/50
35	7	10	14	15	17
50	6	8	11	13	14
75	5	7	9	11	12
100	4	6	8	9	10
200	3	4	6	6	7
300	3	3	5	5	6
500	2	3	4	4	4
1000	1	2	3	3	3
1500	1	2	2	2	2

Note: Chances are 95 in 100 that the real population figure lies in the range defined by +/− number indicated in table, given percentage of sample reporting characteristics and number of sample cases on which the percentage is based.

* This table describes variability due to sampling. Errors due to nonresponse or reporting errors are not reflected in this table. In addition, this table assumes simple random sample. Estimates may be subject to more variability than this table indicates due to the sample design or the influence of interviewers on the answers they obtained; stratification might reduce the sampling errors below those indicated here.

Source: Fowler, F. J. *Survey Research Methods,* p. 41. Copyright © 2009. Reprinted by permission of Sage Publications, Inc.

confidence interval. Recall that a confidence interval indicates the upper and lower values that are likely to contain the actual population mean (see chapter 6).

Understanding these three factors helps you interpret a sample size formula table, such as Table B.1 by Fowler (1988, p. 42). The first row in this table shows the percentage of the sample with the desired characteristic, ranging from 5/95 (small chance) to 50/50 (equally split chance). To maximally divide the sample, researchers typically select 50/50 as the proportion of the sample with the characteristic they are trying to estimate. In terms of the confidence interval, this table reports only a 95% confidence interval (default), which means that 95 out of 100 times the sample mean will fall within the upper and lower limits, or range, of the population mean. This is a rigorous standard to use. In the columns under the heading "Percentage of Sample with Characteristic," we see values, such as 17, 14, and 12, under the 50/50 column. These values are the amount of sampling error we are willing to tolerate. Typically, researchers set a small error that they are willing to tolerate, such as 4% or 6%. This means that only 4% or 6% of the time the sample mean will differ from the true

population mean. Finally, in the left column we see the sample size recommendation that you would use as a guide to the minimum sample size for the sample in your study.

Let's apply information from this table to a study to see how it works. Assume that you need to determine the size of your sample in a study of Native American students in a school district. You want to survey students in high schools in a large metropolitan district to determine if students plan to enroll in advanced placement courses ("yes" they plan to enroll, "no" they do not plan to enroll). The procedure needs to be as rigorous as possible, so you decide to use Fowler's (1988) table to calculate the sample size for your study.

A given in Fowler's (1988) table is that you will use a rigorous confidence interval standard—a 95% confidence interval (95 out of 100 times your sample value will fall within the range of the population mean). You assume that students have a 50/50 chance of participating in these courses. Based on this information, you select the column 50/50. Further, you want a low error rate—a small percentage of the time your sample mean will differ from the population mean. You select an error of 4% (4 out of 100 times).

To identify the appropriate sample size you need in your study, you look at the last column (50/50), go down the column to "4" (4%), and then look across the row and find that the ideal sample size is 500 Native American students. This number, based on the sample size formula, will ensure that 95 out of 100 times (95% confidence interval) your sample mean will have an equal chance (50/50 split) of differentiating among the students 96% of the time (or an error of 4%).

POWER ANALYSIS FORMULA

In many experiments, the size of the overall number of participants (and participants per group) is dictated by practical issues related to the number of volunteers who enroll for the study or the individuals who are available to the researcher. Researchers can also use statistics to analyze the data, and these statistics call for minimum numbers of participants for each group when group comparisons are made.

A rigorous, systematic approach is to use a power analysis. A **power analysis** is a means of identifying appropriate sample size for group comparisons by taking into consideration the level of statistical significance (alpha), the amount of power desired in a study, and the effect size. By determining these three factors, you can look up the adequate size for each comparison group in an experiment and use tables available in published texts (e.g., Lipsey, 1990). The process works this way as shown in Table B.2:

◆ First identify the statistical level of significance to use in testing your group comparison hypothesis, typically set at $p = .05$ or $p = .01$. (See chapter 6 discussions on hypothesis testing.)

◆ Next identify the power needed to reject the hypothesis when it is false, typically set at .80. (See chapter 6 discussions on types of outcomes of hypothesis testing.)

◆ Determine the effect size, which is the expected difference in the means between the control and experimental groups expressed in standard deviation units. This effect size is often based on expectations drawn from past research and is typically set at .5 for much educational research (Murphy & Myors, 1998). (See chapter 6.)

◆ Go to a table for calculating the size of the sample given these parameters, and identify the size of each group in the experiment. This size becomes

TABLE B.2

Lipsey's (1990, p. 137) Sample Size Table: Approximate Sample Size per Experimental Group Needed to Attain Various Criterion Levels of Power for a Range of Effect Sizes at Alpha = .05

Effect Size	Power Criterion		
	.80	.90	.95
.10	1570	2100	2600
.20	395	525	650
.30	175	235	290
.40	100	130	165
.50	65	85	105
.60	45	60	75
.70	35	45	55
.80	25	35	45
.90	20	30	35
1.00	20	25	30

Source: Lipsey, M. W. *Design Sensitivity: Statistical Power for Experimental Research,* p. 137. Copyright © 1990 by Sage Publications. Reprinted by permission of Sage Publications, Inc.

the number of participants you need for each group in your sample. The approximate sample size per experimental group with an alpha set at .05 is given in Table B.2 (Lipsey, 1990, p. 137).

Let's take an example to apply the power formula and Lipsey's table. Assume that elementary education children identified as gifted in a school district are assigned to one of two groups. One group receives an enrichment program (the experimental group), and the other group receives traditional instruction (the control group). At the end of the semester both groups are tested for creativity. How many gifted students are needed for both the experimental and control groups? We might use the number of students available and equally assign them to groups. Although such an experiment could be made, we want a sufficient number of students in our groups so that we can be confident in our hypothesis test of no differences between the control and experimental groups.

In other words, we need an experiment with sufficient size to have power (see Table 6.8 on possible outcomes in hypothesis testing). We turn to Lipsey's (1990) power analysis table for assistance in determining the appropriate sample size for our experimental and control groups. This table will indicate the size needed given a confidence level, the amount of power desired, and the effect size. Examining Lipsey's table, we find that the significance level for the table is set at an alpha = .05.

We use a rigorous standard for power, such as .80 (80% of the time we will reject the null when it is false), and select the column ".80." Then we look at the column for effect size and choose ".50" as the standard for differences in the means (in standard deviation units) that we will expect between the two groups. Using this information, and going down the column of .80 to the row .50, we find that 65 students are needed for each of our two groups, the experimental and control groups, in our study of gifted children.

Commonly Used Statistics in Educational Research

Statistics Name	Symbol	Use	Example Application
t test	*t*	To test for a difference between 2 groups in terms of 1 dependent variable	Compare boys and girls on time spent reading
Analysis of variance (ANOVA)	*F*	To test for a difference among 2 or more groups in terms of 1 dependent variable	Compare four groups (freshman, sophomores, juniors, and seniors) on time spent studying
Chi square	χ	To test for a difference among groups in terms of a categorical dependent variable	Compare men and women in terms of their political party affiliation (democrat, republican, independent)
Pearson correlation	*R*	To test for a relationship between two variables	Determine whether time spent studying is related to grade point average
Multiple regression	*R*	To determine the degree to which 2 or more independent variables are related to (or predict) 1 dependent variable	Determine whether grade point average, SAT score, and depression combined predict retention in the first year of college

Source: Adapted from Plano Clark, V. L., & Creswell, J. W. (2010).

Nonnormal Distribution

We cannot collect sample after sample of individuals to study (e.g., collect their depression scores), but we can plot the scores of our sample and see what shape the distribution of their scores might be. On the one hand, they may reflect a normal curve. On the other hand, they may not be normal. Examine Figure D.1. Here we see a **nonnormal distribution** of scores in which the actual shape of a frequency distribution of scores may be negatively skewed to the right, positively skewed to the left, concentrated around the mean (negative kurtosis), or resemble a flat picture (positive kurtosis). In a **skewed distribution**, the scores tend to pile up toward one end of the scale and then taper off slowly at the other end (Gravetter & Wallnau, 2000). In a **kurtosis distribution**, the scores pile up at the middle or spread out to the sides. Most distributions are not normal and will exhibit some skewness or kurtosis. Whether the distribution of scores from your sample are normal or nonnormal is one factor that determines what statistical test you will use to analyze your comparative or relationship questions or hypotheses.

FIGURE D.1

Skewness and Kurtosis

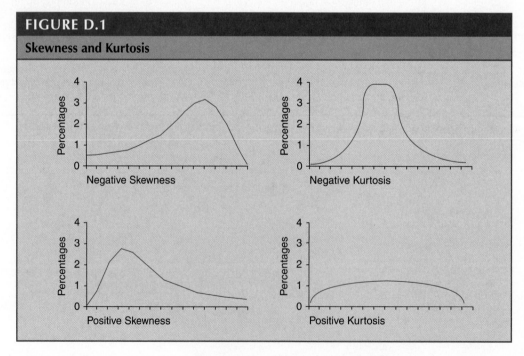

Strategies for Defending a Research Proposal

In doctoral programs and in many master's programs, students are required to complete a formal research study as part of their requirements for graduation. This requirement is included in programs so students can demonstrate their knowledge and application of research. As a first step in preparing the formal research study, a student develops a proposal or plan for the study. The proposal is distributed to the student's faculty. Then, a short time later, the student presents the proposal to the faculty in a meeting called a *proposal defense*. The intent of this meeting is for faculty to have a chance to react and provide constructive comments about the study before the student begins the project. It also serves to provide an opportunity for the student to carefully review the entire project, practice giving an oral presentation of research, and improve the study based on faculty feedback.

The proposal defense meeting varies in length. A typical meeting might last about 1 hour. During this meeting, the student presents an overview of the study, and faculty ask questions that arose when they read the proposal. Some defense meetings are open to all faculty and students, whereas others are closed to all participants except for the student's faculty committee. To best prepare for this meeting and to leave with productive ideas, several strategies are identified here that students might use before, during, and after the meeting.

PRIOR TO THE MEETING

◆ Look over the composition of your committee. Do you have individuals who can assist you in all phases of your research? Can you substitute faculty on your committee to obtain needed faculty resources at this point in your program? An ideal committee consists of a statistician or research methodologist who can help with the technical aspects of a study, an editor who can help you shape your writing, a content specialist who knows the literature about your topic, and a supporter who can give positive feedback throughout the process.

◆ Talk with your advisor about the degree of formality required during the meeting. A formal meeting consists of a brief, organized presentation by the student followed by faculty questions. It may also include a slide presentation to present the proposal for the research study. An informal meeting may be a discussion or conversation about your proposed project without the use of a slide presentation or an organized, formal presentation.

◆ If possible, attend proposal defenses held by other students so that you can gain some experience with the procedures of this meeting.

◆ Visit with your faculty committee members before the meeting to gauge their feedback. They will likely have suggestions for improving the study before the defense meeting.

◆ Consider how you will build rapport with your faculty committee prior to the meeting and during your program. Rapport might be established informally through social interaction or formally through collaboration on projects or by serving as a teacher's assistant.

◆ Discuss with your advisor her or his role during the meeting. Advisors assume different roles, such as advocate, supporter, arbitrator, and adversary. The better you understand his or her role, the better you can anticipate how your advisor will respond during a defense meeting.

◆ Anticipate questions that faculty will ask during a proposal meeting. Sample questions during a meeting for a *quantitative* proposal might be:

Research design questions:
◆ Is the problem trivial?
◆ What is the research question being addressed?
◆ Is the theory a good predictor to use?
◆ Is the study internally valid?

Data collection and analysis questions:
◆ Are the methods detailed?
◆ Is the best data collection approach used?
◆ Was the most appropriate statistic chosen?
◆ Are the constructs valid?
◆ Do items on the instrument need refinement?
◆ Was a good instrument chosen to be used in the study?

◆ Sample questions during a meeting for a *qualitative* study will likely range from research design to the legitimacy of the design as compared with quantitative research.

Design questions:
◆ Why did you choose a qualitative study (instead of a quantitative study)?
◆ What is the type of design you are using (e.g., ethnography, grounded theory)?
◆ Is the study valid?

Quantitative-type questions that require knowledge about qualitative research:
◆ How can you generalize from this study?
◆ Are your variables measurable and valid?
◆ Do you plan to use theory in this study?
◆ Why did you conduct a brief literature review?

Legitimacy questions:
◆ Are there journals that will publish this type of research?
◆ Is this type of research rigorous enough?
◆ Will your involvement in the study influence the findings?

DURING THE MEETING

◆ Keep your presentation brief—15 minutes or less.
◆ Be open, negotiable, and responsive to faculty questions.
◆ Restate questions in your own words to indicate that you have correctly heard them.
◆ Be willing to admit that you have not considered the question being raised.
◆ Have your advisor intercede if the questions become unfair or unrelated to your topic.
◆ Listen for constructive suggestions for improving your project. Keep notes of these suggestions or have your advisor take notes for you so that later there will not be any question about changes needed.

AFTER THE MEETING

◆ Review the events of the meeting with your advisor.
◆ Note suggestions that need to be made to improve or change your study. Negotiate with your advisor about what committee suggestions need to be implemented and what suggestions need to be revisited with members of the committee.
◆ Visit with faculty on your committee, if needed, to clarify their suggestions for improvement.
◆ Talk with your advisor about the next step in the process—what chapters you should begin to write and when.

Glossary

A/B designs are single-subject studies in experimental research that consist of observing and measuring behavior during a trial period (A), administering an intervention, and observing and measuring the behavior after the intervention (B).

abstracts are summaries of the major aspects of a study or article, conveyed in a concise way (for this purpose, often no more than 350 words) and inclusive of specific components that describe the study.

action research designs are systematic procedures used by teachers (or other individuals in an educational setting) to gather quantitative, qualitative (or both) data about—and subsequently improve—the ways their particular setting operates, how they teach, and how well their students learn (Mills, 2011).

adding to knowledge means that educators undertake research for it to contribute to existing information about issues.

alternate forms and test–retest reliability is an approach to reliability in which the researcher administers the test twice and also uses an alternate form of the test from the first administration to the second.

alternating treatment designs are a type of single-subject design in which the researcher examines the relative effects of two or more interventions and determines which intervention is the more effective treatment on the outcome.

alternative forms reliability involves using two instruments, both measuring the same variables and relating (or correlating) the scores for the same group of individuals to the two instruments.

analyzing and interpreting the data indicates that researchers analyze the data; represent it in tables, figures, and pictures; and explain it to come up with answers to research questions and statements asked in the research.

attitudinal measures seek to assess affect or feelings toward educational topics (e.g., assessing positive or negative attitudes toward giving students a choice of school to attend).

audience consists of individuals who will read and potentially use information provided in a research study. Audiences will vary depending on the nature of the study, but several often considered by educators include researchers, practitioners, policy makers, and individuals participating in the studies.

audiovisual materials consist of images or sounds that are collected by the qualitative researcher to help understand the central phenomenon under study. Photographs, videotapes, digital images, paintings and pictures, and physical traces of images (e.g., footsteps in the snow) are all sources of information for qualitative inquiry.

autobiography is a narrative account written and recorded by the individual who is the subject of the study.

axial coding is when the grounded theorist selects one open-coding category, positions it at the center of the process being explored (as the core phenomenon), and then relates other categories to it.

bar charts depict trends and distributions of data.

behavior in ethnography is an action taken by an individual in a cultural setting.

behavioral observations consist of selecting an instrument to record a behavior, observing individuals for that behavior, and checking points on a scale that reflect the behavior (e.g., behavioral checklists).

belief in ethnography is how an individual thinks about or perceives things in a cultural setting.

beta weights are coefficients indicating the magnitude of prediction for a variable after removing the effects of all other predictors.

between-group designs are those in which the researcher compares results between different groups in terms of outcome scores.

biography is a form of narrative study in which the researcher writes and records the experiences of another person's life.

blocking variable is a variable in an experiment that the researcher controls before the experiment starts by dividing (or "blocking") the participants into subgroups (or categories) and analyzing the impact of each subgroup on the outcome.

case study is a variation of an ethnography in that the researcher provides an in-depth exploration of a bounded system (e.g., an activity, an event, a process, or an individual) based on extensive data collection (Creswell, 2007).

categories in grounded theory designs are themes of basic information identified in the data by the researcher and used to understand a process.

central phenomenon is an issue or process explored in qualitative research.

central question is the overarching question being asked in a qualitative study. It is the attempt by the researcher to ask the most general question that can be addressed in a study.

changing observational role is one in which researchers adapt their role to the situation, such as entering a site and observing as a nonparticipant and then later becoming a participant.

charts portray the complex relationships among variables in correlational research designs.

children's stories in educational research are narrative studies in which children in classrooms are asked to present orally, or in writing, their own stories about their learnings.

chronology in narrative designs means that the researcher analyzes and writes about an individual's life using a time sequence or chronology of events.

cleaning the data is the process of visually inspecting the data for scores (or values) that are outside the accepted range of scores.

closed-ended questions in surveys consist of questions posed by the researcher in which the participant responds to preset response options.

codebooks are lists of variables or questions that indicate how the researcher will code or score responses from instruments or checklists.

codes are labels used to describe a segment of text or an image.

coding paradigm is a diagram that portrays the interrelationship of causal conditions, strategies, contextual and intervening conditions, and consequences in grounded theory research.

coding process is a qualitative research process in which the researcher makes sense out of text data, divides it into text or image segments, labels the segments, examines codes for overlap and redundancy, and collapses these codes into themes.

coefficient alpha is a measure of the internal consistency of items on an instrument when the items are scored as continuous variables (e.g., *strongly agree* to *strongly disagree*).

coefficient of determination assesses the proportion of variability in one variable that can be determined or explained by a second variable.

cohort studies are longitudinal survey designs in which a researcher identifies a subpopulation, based on some specific characteristic, and studies that subpopulation over time.

collaborate with others is a task often central to action research, and it involves actively participating with others in research. These coparticipants may be "inside" individuals in a school or "outside" personnel, such as university researchers or professional association groups.

collaboration in narrative research means that the inquirer actively involves the participant in the inquiry as it unfolds. This collaboration may include many steps in the research process, from formulating the central phenomena to be examined, to the types of field texts that will yield helpful information, to the final written "restoried" rendition of the individual's experiences by the researcher.

collecting data means identifying and selecting individuals for a study, obtaining their permission to be studied, and gathering information by administering instruments through asking people questions or observing their behaviors.

collective case studies are case studies in which multiple cases are described and compared to provide insight into an issue.

comparison question addresses how two or more groups differ in terms of one or more outcome variables. A comparison question is typically used in an experiment, and the researcher provides some intervention to one group and withholds it from the second group.

compensatory equalization is a potential threat to internal validity when only the experimental group receives a treatment and an inequality exists that may affect the experiment.

compensatory rivalry is a potential threat to internal validity when rivalry develops between the groups because the control group feels that it is the "underdog."

computer analysis of qualitative data means that researchers use a qualitative computer program to facilitate the process of storing, analyzing, and making sense of the data.

conference papers are research reports presented to an audience at a state, regional, national, or international conference typically sponsored by professional associations (e.g., AERA, American Association of Teacher Educators).

conference proposals are short summaries of a study, typically about three pages, that reviewers use to determine whether research studies should be presented at conferences.

confidence intervals are the range of upper and lower sample statistical values that are consistent with observed data and are likely to contain the actual population mean.

confirming and disconfirming sampling is a purposeful strategy used during a qualitative study to follow up on specific cases to test out or explore further specific findings.

confounding variables (sometimes called *spurious variables*) are attributes or characteristics that the researcher cannot directly measure because their effects cannot be easily separated from other variables, even though they may influence the relationship between the independent and the dependent variable.

constant comparison is an inductive (from specific to broad) data analysis procedure in grounded theory research of generating and connecting categories by comparing incidents in the data to other incidents, incidents to categories, and categories to other categories.

construct is an attribute or characteristic expressed in an abstract, general way, whereas a variable is an attribute or characteristic stated in a specific, applied way.

construct validity is a determination of the significance, meaning, purpose, and use of scores from an instrument.

content validity is the extent to which the questions on the instrument and the scores from these questions are representative of all the possible questions that could be asked about the content or skills.

context in ethnography is the setting, situation, or environment that surrounds the cultural-sharing group being studied.

contrary evidence is information that does not support or confirm the themes and provides contradictory evidence for a theme.

control variable is a variable that the researcher does not want to measure directly but is important to consider and "neutralize" because it potentially influences the dependent variable. Typically, control variables are personal, demographic attributes or characteristics.

convergent mixed methods design consists of simultaneously collecting both quantitative and qualitative data, merging the data, and using the results to best understand a research problem.

convenience sampling is a quantitative sampling procedure in which the researcher selects participants because they are willing and available to be studied.

core category in grounded theory research is the central category around which the theory is written.

correlation is defined as a statistical test to determine the tendency or pattern for two (or more) variables or two sets of data to vary consistently.

correlation matrix is a visual display of the correlation coefficients for all variables in a study.

correlational research designs are quantitative designs in which investigators use a correlation statistical technique to describe and measure the degree of association (or relationship) between two or more variables or sets of scores.

covariates are variables that the researcher controls for using statistics and that relate to the dependent variable but do not relate to the independent variable.

co-vary means that a score can be predicted on one variable with knowledge about the individual's score on another variable.

criterion variable is the outcome variable being predicted in correlational research.

criterion-related validity refers to whether scores from an instrument are a good predictor of some outcome (or criterion) they are expected to predict.

critical ethnographies are a type of ethnographic research in which the author has an interest in advocating for the emancipation of groups marginalized in our society (Thomas, 1993).

critical region is the area on the normal curve for low probability values if the null hypothesis is true.

critical sampling is a qualitative purposeful sampling strategy in which the researcher selects an exceptionally vivid case for learning about a phenomenon.

cross-sectional survey design is a design in which the researcher collects data at one point in time.

cultural theme in ethnography is a general position, declared or implied, that is opened, approved, or promoted in a society or group (Spradley, 1980).

culture is "everything having to do with human behavior and belief" (LeCompte, Preissle, & Tesch, 1993, p. 5). It can include language, rituals, economic and political structures, life stages, interactions, and communication styles.

culture-sharing group in ethnography is two or more individuals that have shared behaviors, beliefs, and language.

curvilinear or nonlinear relationship is a U-shaped distribution in scores on a graph.

data recording protocols are forms designed and used by qualitative researchers to record information during observations and interviews.

deficiency in the evidence refer to a situation in which the past literature or practical experiences of the researchers do not adequately address the research problem. In the "Statement of the Problem" the researcher summarizes the ways the literature or experiences are deficient.

degree of association means the association between two variables or sets of scores with a correlation coefficient of −1.00 to +1.00, with .00 indicating no linear association at all.

degrees of freedom (*df*) indicate to the researcher how much data was used to calculate a particular statistic; usually one less than the number of scores.

dependent variable is an attribute or characteristic that is influenced by the independent variable. Dependent variables are dependent or influenced by independent variables.

describing and developing themes from the data in qualitative research consists of answering the major research questions and developing an in-depth understanding of the central phenomenon.

description in ethnography is a detailed rendering of individuals and scenes to depict what is going on in the culture-sharing group.

descriptive fieldnotes record a description of the events, activities, and people (e.g., what happened).

descriptive question identifies participants' responses to a single variable or question in quantitative research.

descriptive statistics present information that helps a researcher describe responses to each question in a database as well as determine overall trends and the distribution of the data.

dictionaries and glossaries contain terms with which researchers must be familiar when studying a particular topic.

diffusion of treatments is a potential threat to internal validity when the experimental and control groups can communicate with each other and the control group may learn from the experimental group information about the treatment.

dimensionalized properties are when the grounded theory researcher views the property on a continuum and locates, in the data, examples representing extremes on this continuum.

directional alternative hypothesis predict a certain direction for the relationship between the independent variable and the dependent variable. This prediction is typically based on prior research conducted by the investigator or reported by others in the literature.

discriminant sampling in grounded theory is when the researcher poses questions that relate the categories and then returns to the data and looks for evidence, incidents, and events to develop a theory.

dissertation or thesis proposals are plans for a research report, initiated and developed prior to the actual conduct of research.

dissertations and theses are the doctoral and master's research reports prepared by students for faculty and graduate committees.

documents consist of public and private records that qualitative researchers can obtain about a site or participants in a study, such as newspapers, minutes of meetings, personal journals, or diaries.

DOI (digital object identifier) System provides a means of identification for managing information on digital networks (see http://www.doi.org/). A DOI is a unique alphanumeric string assigned by a registration agency to identify content and provide a persistent link to its location on the Internet.

dynamic process in action research involves iterations of activities, such as a "spiral" of activities. The key idea is that the researcher "spirals" back and forth between reflection about a problem and data collection and action.

educational topic is the broad subject matter area that a researcher wishes to address in a study.

effect size is a means for identifying the strength of the conclusions about group differences or about the relationship among variables in a quantitative study. The calculation of this coefficient differs for statistical tests (e.g., R^2, eta^2, omega^2, phi, Cohen's D; APA, 2010).

electronic questionnaire is a survey instrument for collecting data that is available on the computer.

e-mail interviews consist of collecting open-ended data through interviews from individuals using the technology of Web sites or the Internet.

embedded mixed design in mixed methods research consists of presenting a study with a primary data source of quantitative or qualitative data, and a secondary data source of qualitative or quantitative data that plays a supportive auxiliary role in the study. Examples would include a quantitative experiment with a supportive qualitative data component or a correlational study with a smaller qualitative component to help explain the quantitative correlational results.

emerging design in grounded theory research is the process in which the researcher collects data, immediately analyzes it rather than waiting until all data are collected, and then bases the decision about what data to collect next on this analysis. The image of a "zigzag" helps explain this procedure.

emerging process indicates that the intent or purpose of a qualitative study and the questions asked by the researcher may change during the process of inquiry based on feedback or participants' views.

emic data is information supplied by participants in a study. It often refers to first-order concepts such as local language, concepts, and ways of expression used by members in a cultural-sharing group (Schwandt, 2007).

encoding is the intentional use, by an author, of specific terms to convey ideas, such as using research terms.

encyclopedias provide information about a lot of broad topics and are a good starting place for someone who knows little about a certain topic.

end-of-text references are references listed at the end of a research report.

equating the groups means that the researcher randomly assigns individuals to groups equally and equally distributes any variability of individuals between or among the groups or conditions in the experiment.

equivalent time series design is an experimental design in which the investigator alternates a treatment with a posttest measure. The data analysis then consists of comparing posttest measures or plotting them to discern patterns, over time, in the data.

ERIC database is a database of educational information that contains information about journal articles and documents addressing educational topics, broadly construed.

ethical issues in qualitative research include issues such as informing participants of the purpose of the study, refraining from deceptive practices, sharing information with participants (including your role as a researcher), being respectful of the research site, reciprocity, using ethical interview practices, maintaining confidentiality, and collaborating with participants.

ethical reporting and writing research involves research that is honestly reported, shared with participants, not previously published, not plagiarized, not influenced by personal interest, and duly credited to authors who make a contribution.

ethnographic designs are qualitative procedures for describing, analyzing, and interpreting a cultural group's shared patterns of behavior, beliefs, and language that develop over time.

etic data is information representing the ethnographer's interpretation of the participant's perspective. *Etic* typically refers to second-order concepts such as the language used by the social scientist or educator to refer to the same phenomena mentioned by the participants (Schwandt, 2007).

evaluating research involves making an assessment of the quality of a study using standards advanced by individuals in education.

experiences in narrative research are both personal, what the individual experiences, and social, the individual's interacting with others (Clandinin & Connelly, 2000).

experimental group is a group in an experiment that receives the treatment (e.g., the activity or procedure) that the researcher would like to test.

experimental treatment is when the researcher physically intervenes to alter the conditions experienced by the experimental unit.

experimental unit of analysis is the smallest unit treated by the researcher during an experiment.

experiments are used by researchers to test activities, practices, or procedures to determine whether they influence an outcome or dependent variable.

explanatory sequential mixed methods design (also called a *two-phase model;* Creswell & Plano Clark, 2011) consists of first, collecting quantitative data, and then collecting qualitative data to help explain or elaborate on the quantitative results.

explanatory research design is a type of correlational research in which the researcher is interested in the extent to which two variables (or more) co-vary, where variance or change in one variable is reflected in variance or change in the other.

exploratory sequential mixed methods design consists of first, gathering qualitative data to explore a phenomenon, and then collecting quantitative data to test relationships found in the qualitative data.

external audit in qualitative research is when a researcher hires or obtains the services of an individual outside the study to review many aspects of the research. This auditor reviews the project and writes or communicates an evaluation of the study.

extraneous factors are any influences in the selection of participants, procedures, statistics, or design likely to affect the outcome and provide an alternative explanation for the results than what was expected.

extreme case sampling is a form of purposeful sampling in which the researcher studies an outlier case or one that displays extreme characteristics.

factorial designs represent a modification of the between-group design in which the researcher studies two or more categorical, independent variables, each examined at two or more levels (Vogt, 2005).

factual information or personal documents consist of numeric data in public records of individuals. This data can include grade reports, school attendance records, student demographic data, and census information.

field texts represent information from different sources collected by researchers in a narrative design.

fieldnotes are text (or words) recorded by the researcher during an observation in a qualitative study.

fieldwork in ethnography means that the researcher gathers data in the setting where the participants are located and where their shared patterns can be studied.

figures are summaries of quantitative information presented as a chart, graph, or picture that shows relations among scores or variables.

focus group interviews in survey research involve the researcher locating or developing a survey instrument, convening a small group of people—typically a group of four to six people—who can answer the questions asked on the instrument, and recording their comments about the questions on the instrument.

future research directions are suggestions made by the researcher about additional studies that need to be conducted based on the results of the present research.

gatekeepers are individuals who have an official or unofficial role at the site, provide entrance to a site, help researchers locate people, and assist in the identification of places to study.

grounded theory designs are systematic, qualitative procedures that researchers use to generate a theory that explains, at a broad conceptual level, a process, action, or interaction about a substantive topic.

group comparison is an analytic process in experiments of obtaining scores for individuals or groups on the dependent variable and making comparisons of their means and variance both within the group and between the groups.

hand analysis of qualitative data means that researchers read the data and mark it by hand and divide the data into parts. Traditionally, hand analyzing of text data involves color coding parts of the text or cutting and pasting sentences onto cards.

handbooks are concise reference books on a specific topic.

history is a potential threat to internal validity in an experiment in which time passes between the beginning of the experiment and the end, and events may occur during that time that affect the outcome of the experiment.

homogeneous samples are individuals in an experiment who vary little in their personal characteristics.

homogeneous sampling is a purposeful sampling strategy in which the researcher samples individuals or sites based on membership in a subgroup with defining characteristics.

hypotheses are declarative statements in quantitative research in which the investigator makes a prediction or a conjecture about the outcomes of a relationship.

hypothesis testing is a procedure for making decisions about results by comparing an observed value with a population value to determine if no difference or relationship exists between the values.

identifying a research problem consists of specifying an issue to study, developing a justification for studying it, and suggesting the importance of the study for select audiences that will read the report.

implications in a study are those suggestions for the importance of the study for different audiences. They elaborate on the significance for audiences presented initially in the statement of the problem.

in vivo codes are labels for categories (or themes) that are phrased in the exact words of participants rather than in the words of the researcher or in social science or educational terms.

independent variable is an attribute or characteristic that influences or affects an outcome or dependent variable.

inferential statistics enable a researcher to draw conclusions, inferences, or generalizations from a sample to a population of participants.

informed consent form is a statement that participants sign before they participate in research. This form includes language that will guarantee them certain rights. When they sign the form, they agree to be involved in the study and acknowledge that their rights are protected.

inputting the data means that the researcher transfers the data from the responses on instruments to a computer file for analysis.

institutional review board is a committee of faculty who reviews and approves research so that the rights of humans are protected.

instrumental case is a type of qualitative case study in which the researcher studies a particular issue and finds one or more cases that illuminates the issue.

instrumentation is a potential threat to validity in an experiment when the instrument changes during a pretest and a posttest.

instruments are tools for measuring, observing, or documenting quantitative data. Researchers identify these instruments before they collect data, and they may include a test, a questionnaire, a tally sheet, a log, an observational checklist, an inventory, or an assessment instrument.

interaction effects exist when the influence on one independent variable depends on (or co-varies with) the other independent variable in an experiment.

interaction of history and treatment is a threat to external validity in an experiment that arises when the researcher tries to generalize findings to past and future situations.

interaction of selection and treatment is a threat to external validity in an experiment that involves the inability to generalize beyond the groups in the experiment, such as to other racial, social, geographical, age, gender, or personality groups.

interaction of setting and treatment is a threat to external validity in an experiment that arises from the inability to generalize from one setting, where the experiment occurred, to another setting.

interactions with selection may pose a potential threat to internal validity in an experiment. Threats may interact with selection of participants, such as individuals selected may mature at different rates (e.g., 16-year-old boys and girls may mature at different rates during the study), historical events may interact with selection because individuals in different groups come from different settings, or the selection of participants may also influence the instrument scores, especially when different groups score at different mean positions on a test whose intervals are not equal.

interconnecting themes means that the researcher connects the themes to display a chronology or sequence of events, such as when qualitative researchers generate a theoretical and conceptual model or report stories of individuals.

internally consistent means that scores from an instrument are reliable and accurate if they are consistent across the items on the instrument.

interpretation in ethnography is the process in qualitative ethnographic research in which the inquirer assesses how, overall, the culture-sharing group works.

interpretation in qualitative research means that the researcher steps back and forms some larger meaning about the phenomenon based on personal views, comparisons with past studies, or both.

interrater reliability means that two or more individuals observe an individual's behavior and record scores, and then the scores of the observers are compared to determine whether they are similar.

interrupted time series design consists of experimental procedures for studying one group, obtaining multiple pretest measures, administering an intervention (or interrupting the activities), and then measuring outcomes (or posttests) several times.

interval (or rating) scales provide "continuous" response options to questions that have presumably equal distances between options.

intervening variable is an attribute or characteristic that "stands between" the independent and dependent variables and exercises an influence on the dependent variable apart from the independent variable. Intervening variables transmit (or mediate) the effects of the independent variable on the dependent variable.

interventions (or manipulations) in an experiment are ways a researcher physically intervenes with one or more conditions so that individuals experience something different in the experimental conditions than what is experienced in the control conditions.

interview protocol is a form designed by the researcher that contains instructions for the process of the interview, the questions to be asked, and space to take notes on responses from the interviewee.

interview surveys are forms on which the researcher records answers supplied by the participant in the study. The researcher asks a question from an interview guide, listens for answers or observes behavior, and records responses on the survey.

interviews occur when researchers ask one or more participants general, open-ended questions and record their answers.

intrinsic case is a type of qualitative case study in which the researcher studies the case itself because it is of exceptional interest.

issue subquestions are questions that narrow the focus of the central question into specific topics the researcher seeks to learn from participants in a qualitative study.

journal articles are polished, short research reports that have been sent to an editor of a journal, accepted for inclusion, and published in a volume of the journal.

justifying a research problem means that the researcher presents reasons for the importance of studying the issue or concern.

Kuder–Richardson split half test (KR-20, KR-21) is a formula for calculating reliability of scores when (a) items on an instrument are scored right or wrong as categorical scores,

(b) the responses are not influenced by speed, and (c) the items measure a common factor.

kurtosis distribution is a distribution of scores that pile up at the middle or spread out to the sides.

language in ethnography is how an individual talks to others in a cultural setting.

layering the analysis (also called *first-* and *second-order abstractions*) in qualitative research means representing the data using interconnected levels of themes.

lean coding is the assignment of only a few codes the first time a researcher goes through a manuscript.

levels in an experiment are categories of a treatment variable.

levels of headings in a scholarly study and literature review provide logical subdivisions of the text.

life history is a narrative study of an individual's entire life experiences.

limitations are potential weaknesses or problems in quantitative research that are identified by the researcher. In quantitative research, these weaknesses are enumerated one by one, and they often relate to inadequate measures of variables, loss or lack of participants, small sample sizes, errors in measurement, and other factors typically related to data collection and analysis.

line graphs display the interaction between two variables in an experiment.

linking devices in writing are words or phrases that tie together sections of a research report.

literature map is a figure or drawing that displays the research literature (e.g., studies, essays, books, chapters, and summaries) on a topic.

literature review is a written summary of articles, books, and other documents that describe the past and current state of knowledge about a topic.

longitudinal survey design is a design in which the researcher collects data about trends with the same population, changes in a cohort group or subpopulation, or changes in a panel group of the same individuals over time.

mailed questionnaires are forms of data collection in survey research in which the investigator mails a questionnaire to members of the sample.

main effects are the influence of each independent variable (e.g., type of instruction or extent of depression) on the outcome (e.g., the dependent variable, rate of smoking) in an experiment.

matching is the process of identifying one or more personal characteristics that influence the outcome and assigning individuals to the experimental and control groups equally matched on that characteristic.

maturation is a potential threat to internal validity in an experiment in which individuals develop or change during the experiment (i.e., become older, wiser, stronger, and more experienced). These changes may affect their scores between the pretest and the posttest.

maximal variation sampling is a purposeful sampling strategy in which the researcher samples cases or individuals who differ on some characteristic.

mean (*M*) is the total of the scores divided by the number of scores.

measured variable is an independent variable that is measured or observed by the researcher and consists of a range of continuous or categorical scores for variables.

measurement means that the researcher records information from individuals by asking them to answer questions on an instrument (e.g., a student completes questions on a survey asking about self-esteem) or by observing an individual and recording scores on an instrument (e.g., a researcher watches a student playing basketball).

measures of central tendency are summary numbers that represent a single value in a distribution of scores (Vogt, 2005).

measures of relative standing are statistics that describe one score relative to a group of scores. Two frequently used statistics are the z score and the percentile rank.

measures of variability indicate the spread of the scores in a distribution. Variance, standard deviation, and range all indicate the amount of variability in a distribution of scores.

median is the term given to the score that divides the scores, rank-ordered from top to bottom, in half.

member checking is a qualitative process during which the researcher asks one or more participants in the study to check the accuracy of the account.

memos are notes the researcher writes throughout the research process to elaborate on ideas about the data and the coded categories.

meta-analysis is a type of research report in which the author integrates the findings of many (primary source) research studies.

missing data is information that is not supplied by participants to specific questions or items. This is because information may be lost, individuals may skip questions, participants may be absent when observational data is collected, or persons may actually refuse to complete a sensitive question.

mixed methods research designs are procedures for collecting, analyzing, and "mixing" both quantitative and qualitative methods in a single study or a series of studies to understand a research problem.

mode is the term given to the score that appears most frequently in a list of scores.

moderating variables are new variables constructed by the researcher by taking one variable times another to determine the joint impact of both variables together.

modifying an instrument means locating an existing instrument, obtaining permission to change it, and making changes in it to fit the participants.

mortality is a potential threat to internal validity in an experiment when individuals drop out during the experiment for any number of reasons (e.g., time, interest, money, friends, or parents who do not want them to participate).

multiphase mixed methods designs occur when researchers or a team of researchers examine a problem or topic through a series of phases or separate studies.

multiple baseline designs are single-subject studies in experimental research consisting of procedures in which the participant receives an experimental treatment at a different time (hence, multiple baselines exist) so that treatment diffusion will not occur among participants.

multiple perspectives in qualitative research refer to evidence for a theme that is based on several viewpoints from different individuals and sources of data.

multiple regression (or multiple correlation) is a statistical procedure for examining the combined relationship of multiple independent variables on a single dependent variable.

multistage cluster sampling is a quantitative sampling procedure in which the researcher chooses a sample in two or more stages because the populations cannot be easily identified or they are extremely large.

narrative discussion is a written passage in a qualitative study in which authors summarize, in detail, the findings from their data analysis.

narrative hooks are the first sentences in a research report that draw readers into a study, cause readers to pay attention, elicit an emotional or attitudinal response from readers, and encourage readers to continue reading.

narrative research designs are qualitative procedures in which researchers describe the lives of individuals, collect and tell stories about these individuals' lives, and write narratives about their experiences (Connelly & Clandinin, 1990).

negative correlations (indicated by a "−" correlation coefficient) are when the points move in the opposite direction—when X increases, Y decreases and when X decreases, Y increases.

negative linear relationship results when low scores (or high scores) on one variable relate to high scores (or low scores) on the other variable.

negotiation data consists of information that the participant and the researcher agree to use in a study.

net or difference scores are scores in a quantitative study in which the researcher develops a score that represents a difference or change for each individual.

nominal (or categorical) scales provide response options where participants check one or more categories that describe their traits, attributes, or characteristics.

nondirectional alternative hypothesis predict a difference between groups on the dependent variable but do not indicate the direction of this prediction (e.g., positive or negative).

nonnormal distributions of scores result in frequency distributions that may be negatively skewed to the right, positively skewed to the left, concentrated around the mean (negative kurtosis), or resemble a flat picture (positive kurtosis).

nonparticipant observer is an observational role adopted by researchers when they visit a site and record notes without becoming involved in the activities of the participants.

nonprobability sampling is a quantitative sampling procedure in which the researcher chooses participants because they are available, convenient, and represent some characteristic the investigator seeks to study.

normal distribution or normal probability curve is a distribution of scores by participants that can be represented by a graph that approximates a bell-shaped curve.

null hypotheses make predictions that there will be no statistically significant difference between the independent variable and the dependent variable.

observation is the process of gathering firsthand information by observing people and places at a research site.

observational protocol is a form designed by the researcher, before data collection, that is used for taking fieldnotes during an observation.

one-on-one interviewing in survey research consists of investigators conducting an interview with an individual in the sample and recording responses to questions.

one-on-one interviews are the data collection processes in which the researcher asks questions to and records answers from only one participant in the study at a time.

one-tailed tests of significance are when the region for rejection of the null hypothesis is placed only at one end of the distribution.

open coding is the process used by the grounded theorist to form initial categories of information about the phenomenon being studied.

open-ended questions in surveys consist of questions posed by the researcher in which the participant provides his or her own responses to questions.

open-ended responses to a question allow the participant to create the options for responding.

operational definitions are the specification of how variables will be defined and measured (or assessed) in a study.

opportunistic sampling is purposeful sampling undertaken after the research begins, to take advantage of unfolding events.

ordinal (or ranking) scales are response options in which participants rank order from best, or most important, to worst, or least important, some trait, attribute, or characteristic.

outcomes (or *responses, criteria,* or *posttests*) are the dependent variables in an experiment that are the presumed effect of the treatment variables. They are also the effects predicted in a hypothesis in the cause-and-effect equation.

panel studies are longitudinal survey designs in which a researcher examines the same people over time.

partial correlations are used to determine the amount of variance that an intervening variable explains in both the independent and dependent variables.

participant observer is an observational role adopted by researchers in which they take part in activities in the setting they observe.

participatory action research (PAR) is a design in action research aimed at improving the quality of people's organization, community, and family lives (Stringer, 2007). Although espousing many of the ideas of teacher- and school-based practical action research, it differs by incorporating an emancipatory aim of improving and empowering individuals and organizations in educational (and other) settings.

participatory or self-reflective research means that the researchers are self-reflective and study their own classrooms, schools, or practices.

percentile rank of a particular score is the percentage of participants in the distribution with scores at or below a particular score.

performance measures assess an individual's ability to perform on an achievement test, an intelligence test, an aptitude test, an interest inventory, or a personality assessment inventory.

personal documents in quantitative research consist of numeric, individual data available in public records such as grade reports or school attendance records.

personal experience story is a narrative study of an individual's personal experience found in single or multiple episodes, private situations, or communal folklore (Denzin, 1989).

phi coefficient is the correlation statistic used to determine the degree and direction of association when *both* variables being related are dichotomous measures.

physical structure of a study is the underlying organization of topics that form a structure for a research report.

pilot test of a questionnaire or interview survey is a procedure in which a researcher makes changes in an instrument based on feedback from a small number of individuals who complete and evaluate the instrument.

plagiarism is using someone else's work without giving them credit for the information.

plan of action in action research is where the researcher formulates an action plan in response to a problem. This plan may be presenting the data to important stakeholders, establishing a pilot program, starting several competing programs, or implementing an ongoing research agenda to explore new practices (Stringer, 2007).

point-biserial correlation is the correlation statistic used when one variable is measured as an interval or ratio scale and the other has two different values (a dichotomous scale).

population is a group of individuals who comprise the same characteristics. For example, all teachers would make up the population of teachers, and all high school administrators in a school district would make up the population of administrators.

positive correlations (indicated by a "+" correlation coefficient) are when the points move in the same direction—when X increases, so does Y, or alternatively, if X decreases, so does Y.

positive linear relationship means that low (or high) scores on one variable relate to low (or high) scores on a second variable.

posttest in an experiment measures some attribute or characteristic that is assessed for participants after a treatment.

power in quantitative hypothesis testing is the probability of correctly rejecting a false null hypothesis.

power analysis is a means of identifying appropriate sample size for group comparisons by taking into consideration the level of statistical significance (alpha), the amount of power desired in a study, and the effect size.

practical action research is a design in action research in which educators study a specific school situation with a view toward improving practice (Schmuck, 1997). This form of action research focuses on a small-scale research project, narrowly focused on a specific problem or issue and undertaken by individual teachers or teams within a school or school district.

practical issues are often the focus of action research. These issues are concerns or problems that teachers or other school officials have in their educational setting.

practical research problems are those that arise from the setting and activities of educators.

prediction research design is a type of correlational research in which the researcher identifies variables that will positively predict an outcome or criterion.

predictor variable is the variable the researcher uses to make a forecast about an outcome in correlational research.

preliminary exploratory analysis in qualitative research consists of obtaining a general sense of the data, memoing ideas, thinking about the organization of the data, and considering whether more data are needed.

preparing and organizing data for analysis in quantitative research consists of assembling all data, transforming it into numeric scores, creating a data file for computer or hand tabulation, and selecting a computer program to use in performing statistical tests on the data.

presentation of results in quantitative research is where the investigator presents detailed information about the specific results of the descriptive and inferential statistical analyses.

pretest in an experiment measures some attribute or characteristic that is assessed for participants before they receive a treatment.

primary source literature is literature reported by the individual or individuals who actually conducted the research or who originated the ideas.

probability sampling is a quantitative sampling procedure in which the researcher selects individuals from the population so that each person has an equal probability of being selected from the population.

probable causation means that researchers attempt to establish a likely cause-and-effect relationship between variables, rather than *prove* the relationship.

probes are subquestions under each question that the researcher asks to elicit more information. These probes vary from exploring the content in more depth (elaborating) to asking the interviewee to explain his or her answer in more detail (clarifying).

procedural subquestions indicate the steps in analyzing the data to be used in a qualitative study. This form of writing subquestions is less frequently used than issue questions.

process in grounded theory research is a sequence of actions and interactions among people and events pertaining to a topic (Strauss & Corbin, 1998).

process of research consists of a series of six steps used by researchers when they conduct a study. They are identifying a research problem, reviewing the literature, specifying a purpose and research questions or hypotheses, collecting data, analyzing and interpreting the data, and reporting and evaluating research.

product–moment correlation coefficient is called the *bivariate correlation,* the *zero-order correlation,* or simply the *Pearson r,* and it is indicated by an *"r"* for its notation. The statistic is calculated for two variables (r_{xy}) by multiplying the z scores on X and Y for each case and then dividing by the number of cases minus 1 (e.g., see the detailed steps in Vockell & Asher, 1995).

properties are subcategories in grounded theory of open codes that serve to provide more detail about each category.

purpose for research consists of identifying the major intent or objective for a study and narrowing it into specific research questions or hypotheses.

purpose statement is a declarative statement that advances the overall direction or focus of a study. Researchers describe the purpose in one or more succinctly formed sentences. It is used both in quantitative and qualitative research, and it is typically found in the introduction or beginning section of research.

purpose statement in qualitative research indicates the need to explore or understand the central phenomenon with specific individuals at a certain research site.

purposeful sampling is a qualitative sampling procedure in which researchers intentionally select individuals and sites to learn or understand the central phenomenon.

purposes of a proposal are to help an investigator think through all aspects of the study and anticipate problems.

***p* values** are the probability (*p*) that a result could have been produced by chance if the null hypothesis were really true.

qualitative data analysis computer programs are programs that store and organize qualitative data (i.e., text, such as transcribed interviews or typed fieldnotes) and facilitate the process of analyzing data.

qualitative research is an inquiry approach useful for exploring and understanding a central phenomenon. To learn about this phenomenon, the inquirer asks participants broad, general questions, collects the detailed views of participants in the form of words or images, and analyzes the information for description and themes. From this data, the researcher interprets the meaning of the information, drawing on personal reflections and past research. The final structure of the final report is flexible, and it displays the researcher's biases and thoughts.

qualitative research questions are open-ended, general questions that the researcher would like answered during the study.

qualitative scientific structure of a research report includes detailed procedures of inquiry and follows a traditional form for reporting research to include the introduction, the procedures, the findings, and a discussion.

qualitative storytelling structure is a flexible approach to writing a qualitative report. The meaning of the study unfolds through descriptions, an author's reflection on the meaning of the data, a larger understanding of the phenomenon, and a return to the author's stance on the topic.

quantitative purpose statement identifies the variables, their relationship, and the participants and site for research.

quantitative research is an inquiry approach useful for describing trends and explaining the relationship among variables found in the literature. To conduct this inquiry, the investigator specifies narrow questions, locates or develops instruments to gather data to answer the questions, and analyzes numbers from the instruments, using statistics. From the results of these analyses, the researcher interprets the data using prior predictions and research studies. The final report, presented in a standard format, displays researcher objectivity and lack of bias.

quasi-experiments are experimental situations in which the researcher assigns, but not randomly, participants to groups because the experimenter cannot artificially create groups for the experiment.

questionnaires are forms used in a survey design that participants in a study complete and return to the researcher. Participants mark answers to questions and supply basic, personal, or demographic information about themselves.

random assignment is the process of assigning individuals at random to groups or to different conditions of a group in an experiment. It is a characteristic of a true experiment in research.

random selection is the process of selecting individuals so each individual has an equal chance of being selected.

range of scores is the difference between the highest and the lowest scores for items on an instrument.

ratio (or true zero) scale is a response scale in which participants check a response option with a true zero and equal distances between units.

realist ethnography is a type of ethnographic design in which the researcher provides an objective account of the situation, typically written in the third-person point of view, reporting on the information learned from participants at a field site.

reflective fieldnotes record personal thoughts that researchers have that relate to their insights, hunches, or broad ideas or themes that emerge during an observation.

reflexivity means that the researchers reflect on their own biases, values, and assumptions and actively write them into their research.

reflexivity in ethnography means that the researcher is aware of and openly discusses his or her role in a study in a way that honors and respects the site and the people being studied.

regression is a potential threat to internal validity in an experiment in which the researchers select individuals for a group based on extreme scores, and because they will naturally do better (or worse) on a posttest than on the pretest regardless of the treatment, they will threaten the validity of the outcomes.

regression line in correlation research is a line of "best fit" for all of the points of scores on a graph. This line comes the closest to all of the points on the plot and it is calculated by drawing a line that minimizes the squared distance of the points from the line.

regression tables show the overall amount of variance explained in a dependent variable by all independent variables, called R^2 (R squared).

relationship questions seek to answer the degree and magnitude of the relationship between two or more variables. These questions often relate different types of variables in a study, such as independent variables to independent variables or dependent variables to control variables.

reliability means that individual scores from an instrument should be nearly the same or stable on repeated administrations of the instrument and that they should be free from sources of measurement error and consistent.

repeated measures design is an experimental design in which all participants in a single group participate in all experimental treatments. Each group becomes its own control. The researcher compares a group's performance under one experimental treatment with their performance under another experimental treatment.

reporting research involves deciding on audiences, structuring the report in a format acceptable to these audiences, and then writing the report in a manner that is sensitive to all readers.

representative refers to the selection of individuals from a sample of a population such that the individuals selected are typical of the population under study, enabling the researcher to draw conclusions from the sample about the population as a whole.

research is a cyclical process of steps that typically begins with identifying a research problem or issue of a study. It then involves reviewing the literature, specifying a purpose for the study, collecting and analyzing data, and forming an interpretation of the information. This process culminates in a report, disseminated to audiences, that is evaluated and used in the educational community.

research designs are procedures for collecting, analyzing, and reporting research in quantitative and qualitative research.

research objective is a statement of intent for the study that declares specific goals that the investigator plans to achieve in a study.

research problems are the educational issues, controversies, or concerns studied by researchers.

research questions are interrogative statements that narrow the purpose statement to specific questions that researchers seek to answer in their studies.

research report is a study that reports an investigation or exploration of a problem; identifies questions to be addressed; and includes data collected, analyzed, and interpreted by the researcher.

research-based research problems are problems that need further research because a gap in the research exists or because the research needs to be extended into other areas.

resentful demoralization is a potential threat to internal validity when a control group is used and individuals in this group feel resentful and demoralized because they perceive that they receive a less desirable treatment than other groups.

response bias occurs in survey research when the responses do not accurately reflect the views of the sample and the population.

response return rate is the percentage of questionnaires that are returned from the participants to the researcher.

restorying is the process in which the researcher gathers stories, analyzes them for key elements of the story (e.g., time, place, plot, and scene), and then rewrites the story to place it in a chronological sequence.

reviewing the literature means locating summaries, books, journals, and indexed publications on a topic; selectively choosing which literature is relevant; and then writing a report that summarizes that literature.

reviews and syntheses provide summaries on various topics.

sample is a subgroup of the target population that the researcher plans to study for the purpose of making generalizations about the target population.

sample size formulas provide formulas, based on several parameters, that can be used to calculate the size of the sample.

sampling error is the difference between the sample estimate and the true population score.

sampling error formula is for determining the size of a sample based on the chance (or proportion) that the sample will be evenly divided on a question, sampling error, and a confidence interval.

saturation in qualitative research is a state in which the researcher makes the subjective determination that new data will not provide any new information or insights for the developing categories.

scales of measurement are response options to questions that measure (or observe) variables in nominal, ordinal, or interval/ratio units.

scatterplot (or scatter diagram) is a pictorial image of two sets of scores for participants on a graph.

scoring means that the researcher assigns a numeric score (or value) to each response category for each question on the instruments used to collect data.

secondary source literature summarizes primary sources, and it does not represent material published by the original researchers or the creators of the idea.

selection is a potential threat to internal validity in an experiment in which "people factors" may introduce threats that influence the outcome, such as selecting individuals who are brighter, more receptive to a treatment, or more familiar with a treatment.

selective coding is the process in which the grounded theorist writes a theory based on the interrelationship of the categories in the axial coding model.

semi-closed-ended questions in a survey consist of questions that include both closed-ended and open-ended questions.

sequence in mixed methods designs means that the researcher collects data using concurrent or sequential procedures.

setting in narrative research may be friends, family, workplace, home, social organization, or school—the place in which a story physically occurs.

shared pattern in ethnography is a common social interaction that stabilizes, as tacit, rules and expectations of the group (Spindler & Spindler, 1992).

sharing reports in action research means that the inquirer shares the action research study locally with individuals who can promote change or enact plans within their classroom or building. Action researchers share results with teachers, the building principal, school district personnel, and parent associations (e.g., Hughes, 1999).

significance (or alpha) level is a probability level that reflects the maximum risk you are willing to take that any observed differences are due to chance. It is called the *alpha level* and is typically set at .01 (1 out of 100 times the sample statistic fall will be due to chance) or .05 (5 out of 100 times it will be due to chance).

simple random sampling is a quantitative sampling procedure in which the researcher selects participants (or units, such as schools) for the sample so that any sample of size N has an equal probability of being selected from the population. The intent of simple random sampling is to choose units to be sampled that will be representative of the population.

single-item scores are individual scores to each question for each participant in your study.

single-subject research (also called *N = 1 research, behavior analysis,* or *within-subjects research*) involves the study of single individuals, their observation over a baseline period, and the administration of an intervention. This is followed by another observation after the intervention to determine if the treatment affects the outcome.

skewed distribution is a distribution of scores that tends to pile up toward one end of the scale and taper off slowly at the other end (Gravetter & Wallnau, 2007).

snowball sampling is a sampling procedure in which the researcher asks participants to identify other participants to become members of the sample.

Spearman–Brown formula is a formula for calculating the reliability of scores using all questions on an instrument.

Because the split half test relies on information from only half of the test, a modification in this procedure is to use this formula to estimate full-length test reliability.

Spearman rho (rs) is the correlation statistic used for nonlinear data when the data are measured on ordinal scales (rank-ordered scales).

standard deviation (SD) is the square root of the variance.

standard scores are calculated scores that enable a researcher to compare scores from different scales.

statement of the problem is a section in a research report that contains the topic of the study, the research problem within this topic, a justification for the problem based on past research and practice, deficiencies or shortcomings of past research or practical knowledge, and the importance of addressing the problem for diverse audiences.

statistical indexes report trends that are useful for research.

statistical significance is when the observed values (e.g., before and after a treatment in an experiment, the difference between mean scores for two or more groups or the relationship between two variables) provide a statistical value (p value) that exceeds the predetermined alpha level set by the researcher.

statistics are the numbers derived from formulas to measure aspects of a set of data.

story in narrative research is a first-person oral telling or retelling of events related to the personal or social experiences of an individual. Often these stories have a beginning, middle, and an end.

stratified sampling is a quantitative sampling procedure in which researchers stratify the population on some specific characteristic (e.g., gender) and then sample, using simple random sampling, from each stratum of the population.

study-by-study review of the literature is a detailed summary of each study grouped under a broad theme.

style manuals provide a structure for citing references, labeling headings, and constructing tables and figures for a scholarly research report.

subquestions in qualitative research refine the central question into subtopics or indicate the processes to be used in research. These subquestions contain the same elements as in central questions (e.g., they are open ended, emerging, neutral in language, and few in number), but they provide greater specificity to the questions in the study. They are of two types: issue and procedural subquestions.

summaries provide overviews of the literature and research on timely issues in education.

summed scores are scores of an individual added over several questions that measure the same variable.

survey research designs are procedures in quantitative research in which investigators administer a survey or questionnaire to a sample or to the entire population of people to describe the attitudes, opinions, behaviors, or characteristics of the population.

systematic design in grounded theory emphasizes the use of data analysis steps of open, axial, and selective coding, and the development of a logic paradigm or a visual picture of the theory generated.

systematic sampling is a quantitative sampling procedure in which the researcher chooses every "*n*th" individual or site in the population until the desired sample size is achieved.

tables are summaries of quantitative data organized into rows and columns.

target population (sometimes called the *sampling frame*) is a group of individuals with some common defining characteristic that the researcher can identify with a list or set of names.

teachers' stories are narrative research, personal accounts by teachers of their own classroom experiences.

telephone interview surveys are interviews in which the researcher records comments by participants to questions on instruments over the telephone.

telephone interviews are used to gather data using the telephone and asking a small number of general questions.

testing is a potential threat to validity in an experiment when participants become familiar with the outcome measures and remember responses for later testing.

test–retest reliability examines the extent to which scores from one sample are stable over time from one test administration to another.

text segments are sentences or paragraphs that all relate to a single code in qualitative research.

thematic data analysis in ethnography consists of distilling how things work and naming the essential features in these in the cultural setting.

thematic review of the literature includes a theme and supporting literature found by the researcher to document the theme.

themes in qualitative research are similar codes aggregated together to form a major idea in the database.

theoretical lens in narrative research is a guiding perspective or ideology that provides a structure for advocating for groups or individuals and writing the report.

theoretical propositions in grounded theory research are statements indicating the relationship among categories, such as in the systematic approach to axial coding that includes causal conditions, the core category or phenomenon, the context, intervening conditions, strategies, and consequences.

theoretical sampling in grounded theory means that the researcher chooses forms of data collection that will yield text and images useful in generating a theory.

theory or concept sampling is a purposeful sampling strategy in which individuals or sites are sampled because they can help the researcher generate or discover a theory or specific concept within the theory.

theory in grounded theory research is an abstract explanation or understanding of a process about a substantive topic "grounded" in the data. The theory is "middle-range" (Charmaz, 2000), drawn from multiple individuals or data sources that provide an explanation for a substantive topic.

theory in quantitative research explains and predicts the relationship between independent and dependent variables. They are called the *outcome, effect, criterion,* or *consequence variables.*

threats to external validity are problems that threaten our ability to draw correct inferences from the sample data to other persons, settings, treatment variables, and measures (Shadish, Cook, & Campbell, 2002).

threats to internal validity are problems in drawing correct inferences about whether the covariation (i.e., the variation in one variable contributes to the variation in the other) between the presumed treatment variable and the outcome reflect a causal relationship (Shadish, Cook, & Campbell, 2002).

threats to validity refer to specific reasons for why we can be wrong when we make an inference in an experiment because of covariance, causation constructs, or whether the causal relationship holds over variations in persons, setting, treatments, and outcomes (Shadish, Cook, & Campbell, 2002).

time series is an experimental design consisting of studying one group, over time, with multiple pretest and posttest measures or observations made by the researcher.

title summarizes the major idea of the paper in a concise and clear manner. It should be no longer than 12 words in length and should avoid superfluous words such as "a study of" or "an investigation of."

transcription is the process of converting audiotape recordings or fieldnotes into text data.

transformative mixed methods design uses one of the four designs (convergence, explanatory, exploratory, or embedded), but encases the design within a transformative framework or lens.

treatment variable is an independent variable that the researcher manipulates to determine the effect it will have on an outcome. It is always a categorically scored variable measuring two or more groups or levels.

trend studies are longitudinal survey designs that involve identifying a population and examining changes within that population over time.

triangulation is the process of corroborating evidence from different individuals (e.g., a principal and a student), types of data (e.g., observational fieldnotes and interviews), or methods of data collection (e.g., documents and interviews) in descriptions and themes in qualitative research.

true experiments are experimental situations in which the researcher randomly assigns participants to different conditions (or levels) of the experimental variable.

two-tailed tests of significance are when the critical region for rejection of the null hypothesis is divided into two areas at the ends of the sampling distribution (Vogt, 2005).

type I error occurs when the null hypothesis is rejected by the researcher when it is actually true. The probability of this error rate is called "alpha."

type II error occurs when the researcher fails to reject the null hypothesis when an effect actually occurs in the population. The probability of this error rate is called "beta."

typical sampling is a form of purposeful sampling in which the researcher studies a person or site that is "typical" to those unfamiliar with the situation.

uncorrelated relationship of scores means that the scores in the distribution are independent of each other.

unit of analysis refers to the unit (e.g., individual, family, school, school district) the researcher uses to gather the data.

URL is used to map digital information on the Internet. A URL contains several components: a protocol, a host name, the path to the document, and the specific file name.

validating findings in qualitative research means that the researcher determines the accuracy or credibility of the findings through strategies such as member checking or triangulation.

validity is the development of sound evidence to demonstrate that the intended test interpretation (of the concept or construct that the test is assumed to measure) matches the proposed purpose of the test. This evidence is based on test content, responses processes, internal structure, relations to other variables, and the consequences of testing.

values are scores assigned to response options for questions.

variable is a characteristic or attribute of an individual or an organization that (a) can be measured or observed by the researcher and that (b) varies among individuals or organizations studied.

variable measured in categories are variables measured by the researcher as a small number of groups or categories.

variable measured as continuous are variables measured by the researcher on a point along a continuum of scores, from low to high.

variance means that scores will assume different values depending on the type of variable being measured.

visualization in mixed methods research consists of a figure or drawing displaying the procedures of a study.

wave analysis is a survey research procedure to check for response bias in which investigators group returns by intervals (e.g., by week) and check to see if the answers to a few select questions change from the first week to the final week in a study.

within-group experimental design is an experiment design in which the researcher studies only one group of individuals, such as time series or repeated measure designs.

within-individual design is an experimental design in which the researcher studies single individuals, such as single-subject designs.

within-text references are references cited in a brief format within the body of the text to provide credit to authors.

z scores have a mean of 0 and a standard deviation of 1 and enable the researcher to compare scores from one instrument to scores from another instrument.

References

Abel, M., & Sewell, J. (1999). Stress and burnout in rural and urban secondary school teachers. *Journal of Educational Research, 92,* 287–293.

Abelson, R. P. (1995). *Statistics as principled argument.* Hillsdale, NJ: Erlbaum.

Agar, M. H. (1980). *The professional stranger: An informal introduction to ethnography.* San Diego, CA: Academic Press.

Alkin, M. C. (Ed.). (1992). *Encyclopedia of educational research* (6th ed.). New York: Macmillan.

Allen, L., & Calhoun, E. F. (1998). Schoolwide action research: Findings from six years of study. *Phi Delta Kappan, 79*(9), 706–710.

American Anthropological Association. (1998). *Code of ethics of the American Anthropological Association.* Arlington, VA: Author.

American Educational Research Association. (1999). American Educational Research Association 2000 Annual Meeting call for proposals. *Educational Research, 28,* 33.

American Educational Research Association, American Psychological Association, National Council on Measurement in Education. (1999). *Standards for educational and psychological testing.* Washington, DC: American Educational Research Association.

American Psychological Association. (1927–). *Psychological abstracts.* Washington, DC: Author.

American Psychological Association. (2010). *Publication manual of the American Psychological Association* (6th ed.). Washington, DC: Author.

American Psychological Association. (2003). *Ethical principles of psychologists and code of conduct.* Washington, DC: Author.

Anderson, E. S., & Keith, T. Z. (1997). A longitudinal test of a model of academic success for at-risk high school students. *Journal of Educational Research, 90,* 259–266.

Angrosino, M. V. (1989). *Documents of interaction: Biography, autobiography, and life history in social science perspective.* Gainesville: University of Florida Press.

Annual review of psychology. (1950–). Stanford, CA: Annual Reviews.

Asmussen, K. J., & Creswell, J. W. (1995). Campus response to a student gunman. *Journal of Higher Education, 66,* 575–591.

Babbie, E. (1990). *Survey research methods.* Belmont, CA: Wadsworth.

Babbie, E. (1998). *The practice of social research* (8th ed.). Belmont, CA: Wadsworth.

Babbie, E. (2003). *The practice of social research* (9th ed.). Belmont, CA: Wadsworth.

Babbie, E. (2009). *The practice of social research* (12th ed.). Belmont, CA: Wadsworth.

Babchuk, W. A. (1996). *Glaser or Strauss?: Grounded theory and adult education.* Paper presented at the Midwest Research-to-Practice Conference in Adult, Continuing and Community Education, University of Nebraska–Lincoln.

Babchuk, W. A. (1997). *The rediscovery of grounded theory: Strategies for qualitative research in adult education.* Unpublished doctoral dissertation, University of Nebraska–Lincoln.

Baker, R. W., & Siryk, B. (1989). *Student adaptation to college questionnaire (SACQ).* Los Angeles: Western Psychological Services.

Banks, J. A., & Banks, C. A. (1995). *Handbook of research on multicultural education.* New York: Macmillan.

Barzun, J., & Graff, H. G. (1985). *The modern researcher* (4th ed.). New York: Harcourt Brace & World.

Batsche, C., Hernandez, M., & Montenegro, M. C. (1999). Community needs assessment with Hispanic, Spanish-monolingual residents. *Evaluation and Program Planning, 22,* 13–20.

Bauermeister, M. L. (1998). *The child of the mist: Enculturation in a New Zealand Kohanga Reo.* Unpublished doctoral dissertation, University of Nebraska–Lincoln.

Bausell, R. B. (1994). *Conducting meaningful experiments.* Thousand Oaks, CA: Sage.

Bazeley, P. (2000). *Mixed methods data analysis using NUD*IST/Nvivo with table based software and/or a statistics program.* Paper presented at the American Educational Research Association Annual Meeting, New Orleans, LA.

Bazeley, P. (2010). Computer-assisted integration of mixed methods data sources and analysis. In A. Tashakkori & C. Teddlie (Eds.), *SAGE handbook of mixed methods in social and behavioral research* (2nd ed.). Thousand Oaks, CA: Sage.

Becker, P. H. (1993). Common pitfalls in published grounded theory research. *Qualitative Health Research, 3,* 254–260.

Benson, J., & Clark, F. (1983). A guide for instrument development and validation. *The American Journal of Occupational Therapy, 36,* 790–801.

Bickman, L., & Rog, D. J. (2009). (Eds.). *SAGE handbook of applied social research methods* (2nd ed.). Thousand Oaks, CA: Sage.

Blaikie, N. (2003). *Analysing quantitative data: From description to explanation.* London: Sage.

Bluestein, D. L., Phillips, S. D., Jobin-David, K., Finkelberg, S. L., & Roarke, A. E. (1997). A theory-building investigation of the school-to-work transition. *The Counseling Psychologist, 25,* 364–402.

Bogdan, R. C., & Biklen, S. K. (1998). *Qualitative research for education: An introduction to theory and methods* (3rd ed.). Boston: Allyn & Bacon.

Boruch, R. F. (1998). Randomized controlled experiments for evaluation and planning. In L. Bickman & D. J. Rog (Eds.), *Handbook of applied social research methods* (pp. 161–191). Thousand Oaks, CA: Sage.

Brant-Castellano, M. (2000). Updating aboriginal traditions of knowledge. In G. J. Sefa Dei, B. L. Hall, & D. Goldin-Rosenberg (Eds.), *Indigenous knowledge in global contexts: Multiple readings of our work* (pp. 21–36). Toronto, Ontario, Canada: University of Toronto Press.

Brabeck, M. M., & Brabeck, K. M. (2009). Feminist perspectives on research ethics. In D. M. Mertens & P. E. Ginsburg (Eds.), *The handbook of social research ethics* (pp. 39–53). Thousand Oaks, CA: Sage.

Brickhouse, N., & Bodner, G. M. (1992). The beginning science teacher: Classroom narratives of convictions and constraints. *Journal of Research in Science Teaching, 29,* 471–485.

Bring, J. (1994). How to standardize regression coefficients. *The American Statistician, 48*(3), 209–213.

Brown, B. L., & Hedges, D. (2009). Use and misuse of quantitative methods: Data collection, calculation, and presentation. In D. M. Mertens & P. E. Ginsberg (Eds.), *The handbook of social research ethics* (pp. 373–385). Los Angeles, CA: Sage.

Brown, M. L. (1993). *Ethnic minority student's process of community building on a predominantly white campus*. Unpublished doctoral dissertation, University of Nebraska–Lincoln.

Brown, R. (1998). *Theory about the process of community-building in distance learning courses*. Unpublished dissertation proposal, University of Nebraska–Lincoln.

Brown, B. L., & Hedges, D. (2009). Use and misuse of quantitative methods. In D. M. Mertens & P. E. Ginsberg (Eds.), *The handbook of social research ethics* (pp. 373–390). Thousand Oaks, CA: Sage.

Brown, S. P., Parham, T. A., & Yonker, R. (1996). Influence of a cross-cultural training course on racial identity attitudes of white women and men: Preliminary perspectives. *Journal of Counseling & Development, 74*(5), 510–516.

Bryant, A., & Charmaz, K. (Eds.). (2007). *The SAGE handbook of grounded theory*. Los Angeles, CA: Sage.

Buck, G., Cook, K., Quigley, C., Eastwood, J., & Lucas, Y. (2009). Profiles of urban, low SES, African American girls' attitudes toward science. *Journal of Mixed Methods Research, 3*(4), 386–410.

Budnitz, J. (2000). Flush. In M. Cunningham, P. Houston, & G. Saunders (Eds.), *Prize stories 2000*. New York: Random House.

Brydon-Miller, M. (2009). Covenantal ethics and action research. In D. M. Mertens & P. E. Ginsberg (Eds.), *The handbook of social research ethics* (pp. 243–258). Los Angeles, CA: Sage.

Campbell, D. T., & Fiske, D. W. (1959). Convergent and discriminant validation by the multitrait–multimethod matrix. *Psychological Bulletin, 56*, 81–105.

Campbell, D. T., & Stanley, J. C. (1963). Experimental and quasi-experimental designs for research. In N. L. Gage (Ed.), *Handbook on research in teaching* (pp. 1–80). Chicago: Rand-McNally.

Campbell, W. G., Ballou, S. V., & Slade, C. (1990). *Form and style: Theses, reports, and term papers* (8th ed.). Boston: Houghton Mifflin.

Caracelli, V. J., & Greene, J. C. (1993). Data analysis strategies for mixed-method evaluation designs. *Educational Evaluation and Policy Analysis, 15*(2), 195–207.

Carspecken, P. F. (1995). *Critical ethnography in educational research: A theoretical and practical guide*. London: Routledge.

Carspecken, P. F., & Apple, M. (1992). Critical qualitative research: Theory, methodology, and practice. In M. D. LeCompte, W. L. Millroy, & J. Preissle (Eds.), *The handbook of qualitative research in education* (pp. 507–553). San Diego: Academic Press.

Carter, K. (1993). The place of a story in the study of teaching and teacher education. *Educational Researcher, 22*(1), 5–12, 18.

Casey, K. (1995/1996). The new narrative research in education. *Review of Research in Education, 21*, 211–253.

Ceprano, M. A., & Garan, E. M. (1998). Emerging voices in a university pen-pal project: Layers of discovery in action research. *Reading Research and Instruction, 38*(1), 31–56.

Chan, E. (2010). Living in the space between participant and researcher as a narrative inquirer: Examining ethnic identity of Chinese Canadian students as conflicting stories to live by. *Journal of Educational Research, 103*, 113–122.

Charmaz, K. (1990). "Discovering" chronic illness: Using grounded theory. *Social Science Medicine, 30*, 1161–1172.

Charmaz, K. (1994). Identity dilemmas of chronically ill men. *Sociological Quarterly, 35*, 269–288.

Charmaz, K. (2000). Grounded theory: Objectivist and constructivist methods. In N. K. Denzin & Y. S. Lincoln (Eds.), *Handbook of qualitative research* (2nd ed., pp. 509–535). Thousand Oaks, CA: Sage.

Charmaz, K. (2006). *Constructing grounded theory*. London: Sage.

Clandinin, D. J. (2006). *After the research*. Paper presented to the Faculty of Education Graduate Students, University of Alberta, Edmonton, Alberta, Canada.

Clandinin, D. J. (Ed.) (2007). *Handbook of narrative inquiry: Mapping a methodology*. Thousand Oaks, CA: Sage.

Clandinin, D. J., & Connelly, F. M. (2000). *Narrative inquiry: Experience and story in qualitative research*. San Francisco: Jossey-Bass.

Clandinin, D. J., Murphy, M. S., Huber, J., & Orr, A. M. (2010). Negotiating narrative inquiries: Living in a tension-filled midst. *Journal of Educational Research, 103*, 81–90.

Clifford, J., & Marcus, G. E. (Eds.). (1986). *Writing culture*. Berkeley: University of California Press.

Cocklin, B. (1996). Applying qualitative research to adult education: Reflections upon analytic processes. *Studies in the Education of Adults, 28*, 88–116.

Cohen, J. (1977). *Statistical power analysis for the behavioral sciences* (rev. ed.). New York: Academic Press.

Cohen, L., & Manion, L. (1994). *Research methods in education* (4th ed.). London and New York: Routledge.

Congressional Information Service. (1973–). *American statistics index*. Washington, DC: Author.

Connelly, F. M., & Clandinin, D. J. (1988). *Teachers as curriculum planners: Narratives of experience*. New York: Teachers College Press.

Connelly, F. M., & Clandinin, D. J. (1990). Stories of experience and narrative inquiry. *Educational Researcher, 19*(5), 2–14.

Connelly, F. M., Dukacz, A. S., & Quinlan, F. (1980). *Curriculum planning for the classroom*. Toronto, Canada: OISE Press.

Cook, T. D., & Campbell, D. T. (1979). *Quasi-experimentation: Design and analysis issues for field settings*. Boston: Houghton Mifflin.

Cooper, H. (1984). *The integrated research review: A systematic approach*. Beverly Hills, CA: Sage.

Cooper, H. M., & Lindsay, J. J. (1998). Research synthesis and meta-analysis. In L. Bickman & D. J. Rog (Eds.), *Handbook of applied social research methods* (pp. 315–337). Thousand Oaks, CA: Sage.

Cooper, J. O., Heron, T. E., & Heward, W. L. (1987). *Applied behavior analysis*. Columbus, OH: Merrill/Prentice Hall.

Corbin, J., & Strauss, A. (2008). *Basics of qualitative research: Techniques and procedures for developing grounded theory* (3rd ed.). Thousand Oaks, CA: Sage.

Cortazzi, M. (1993). *Narrative analysis*. London: Falmer Press.

Courtney, S., Jha, L. R., & Babchuk, W. A. (1994). Like school?: A grounded theory of life in an ABE/GED classroom. *Adult Basic Education, 4*, 172–195.

Cowles, M. (1989). *Statistics in psychology: A historical perspective*. Hillsdale, NJ: Erlbaum.

Creswell, J. W. (1999). Mixed-method research: Introduction and application. In G. J. Cizek (Ed.), *Handbook of educational policy* (pp. 455–472). San Diego: Academic Press.

Creswell, J. W. (2007). *Qualitative inquiry and research design: Choosing among five approaches* (2nd ed.). Thousand Oaks, CA: Sage.

Creswell, J. W. (2009). *Research design: Qualitative, quantitative, and mixed methods approaches* (3rd ed.). Thousand Oaks, CA: Sage.

Creswell, J. W. (2011). Mapping the developing landscape of mixed methods research. In A. Tashakkori & C. Teddlie (Eds.), *SAGE handbook of mixed methods in social and behavioral research* (2nd ed., pp. 45–68). Thousand Oaks, CA: Sage.

Creswell, J. W. (in press). Controversies in mixed methods research. In N. Denzin & Y.S. Lincoln (Eds.), *SAGE handbook of qualitative research* (4th ed.). Thousand Oaks, CA: Sage.

Creswell, J. W., & Brown, M. L. (1992). How chairpersons enhance faculty research: A grounded theory study. *The Review of Higher Education, 16*(1), 41–62.

Creswell, J. W., & Maietta, R. C. (2002). Qualitative research. In D. C. Miller & N. J. Salkind (Eds.), *Handbook of social research* (pp. 143–184). Thousand Oaks, CA: Sage.

Creswell, J. W., & Miller, D. M. (2000). Determining validity in qualitative inquiry. *Theory into Practice, XXXIX*(3), 124–130.

Creswell, J. W., & Plano Clark, V. L. (2011). *Designing and conducting mixed methods research* (2nd ed.). Thousand Oaks, CA: Sage.

Creswell, J. W., Tashakkori, A., Jensen, K., & Shapley, K. (2003). Teaching mixed methods research: Practice, dilemmas and challenges. In A. Tashakkori & C. Teddlie (Eds.), *Handbook of mixed methods in the behavioral and social sciences*. Thousand Oaks, CA: Sage.

Creswell, J. W., Wheeler, D. W., Seagren, A. T., Egly, N. J., & Beyer, K. D. (1990). *The academic chairperson's handbook*. Lincoln and London: University of Nebraska Press.

Cronbach, L. J. (1984). *Essentials of psychological testing* (4th ed.). New York: Harper & Row.

Csikszentmihalyi, M., Rathunde, K., Whalen, S., & Wong, M. (1993). *Talented teenagers: The roots of success and failure*. New York: Cambridge University Press.

Dahmus, S., Bernardin, H. J., & Bernardin, K. (1992). Test review: Student adaptation to college questionnaire. *Measurement and Evaluation in Counseling and Development, 25*, 139–142.

Davis, T. C., Arnold, C., Nandy, I., Bocchini, J. A., Gottlief, A., George, R., et al. (1997). Tobacco use among male high school athletes. *Journal of Adolescent Health, 21*, 97–101.

De Landsheere, G. (1988). History of educational research. In J. P. Keeves (Ed.), *Educational research, methodology, and measurement: An international handbook* (pp. 9–16). Oxford: Pergamon Press.

Degh, L. (1995). *Narratives in society: A performer-centered study of narration*. Helsinki, Norway: Suomalainen Tiedeakatemia, Academia Scientiarum Fennica.

Denzin, N. (1989). *Interpretative biography*. Newbury Park, CA: Sage.

Denzin, N. K. (1997). *Interpretive ethnography: Ethnographic practices for the 21st century*. Thousand Oaks, CA: Sage.

Denzin, N. K., & Lincoln, Y. S. (Eds.). (2005). *The SAGE handbook of qualitative research* (3rd ed.). Thousand Oaks, CA: Sage.

Department of Health, Education, and Welfare. (1978). *The Belmont Report: Ethical principles and guidelines for the protection of human subjects of research*. Washington, DC: Government Printing Office.

Deslandes, R., & Bertrand, R. (2005). Motivation of parent involvement in secondary-level schooling. *Journal of Educational Research, 98*(33), 164–175.

Dey, E. L., & Hurtado, S. (1996). Faculty attitudes toward regulating speech on college campuses. *The Review of Higher Education, 20*, 15–32.

Dey, I. (1993). *Qualitative data analysis: A user-friendly guide for social scientists*. London: Routledge.

Dillman, D. A. (2007). *Mail and internet surveys (electronic resource): The tailored design method*. Hoboken, NJ: Wiley.

Dods, R. F. (1997). An action research study of the effectiveness of problem-based learning in promoting the acquisition and retention of knowledge. *Journal for the Education of the Gifted, 20*(4), 423–437.

Educational Resources Information Center (U.S.). (1966–). *Resources in education*. Washington, DC: Author.

Educational Resources Information Center (U.S.). (1969–). *Current index to journals in education*. New York: Macmillan.

Educational Resources Information Center (U.S.). (1991). *ERIC directory of education-related information centers*. Washington, DC: Author.

Ehrlich, E., Flexner, S. B., Carruth, G., & Hawkins, J. M. (1980). *Oxford American dictionary*. New York and Oxford: Oxford University Press.

Elbaz-Luwisch, F. (1997). Narrative research: Political issues and implications. *Teaching and Teacher Education, 13*(1), 75–83.

Emerson, R. M., Fretz, R. I., & Shaw, L. L. (1995). *Writing ethnographic fieldnotes*. Chicago: University of Chicago Press.

Epper, R. M. (1997). Coordination and competition in postsecondary distance education. *Journal of Higher Education, 68*(5), 551–587.

Errante, A. (2000). But sometimes you're not part of the story: Oral histories and ways of remembering and telling. *Educational Researcher, 29*, 16–27.

Federal Judicial Center (1981). *Experimentation in the law* (Report of the Federal Judicial Center Advisory Committee on Experimentation in the Law). Washington, DC: Government Printing Office.

Fetterman, D. M. (2010). *Ethnography: Step by step* (3rd ed.). Thousand Oaks, CA: Sage.

Finch, S., Cumming, G., & Thomason, N. (2001). Reporting of statistical inference in the *Journal of Applied Psychology*: Little evidence of reform. *Educational and Psychological Measurement, 61*(1), 181–210.

Finders, M. J. (1996). Queens and teen zines: Early adolescent females reading their way toward adulthood. *Anthropology and Education Quarterly, 27*, 71–89.

Fink, A. (2002). *The survey handbook* (2nd ed.). Thousand Oaks, CA: Sage.

Fink, A., & Kosekoff, J. (1985). *How to conduct surveys: A step-by-step guide*. Newbury Park, CA: Sage.

Fisher, R. A. (1935). *The design of experiments*. London: Oliver & Boyd.

Fowler, F. J. (2009). *Survey research methods* (4th ed.). Los Angeles, CA: Sage.

Fraenkel, J. R., & Wallen, N. E. (2000). *How to design and evaluate research in education* (4th ed.). Boston: McGraw-Hill.

Freshwater, D. (2007). Reading mixed methods research: Contexts for criticism. *Journal of Mixed Methods Research, 1*(2), 134–145.

Frontman, K. C., & Kunkel, M. A. (1994). A grounded theory of counselors' construal of success in the initial session. *Journal of Counseling Psychology, 41*, 492–499.

Gall, M. D., Borg, W. R., & Gall, J. P. (1996). *Educational research* (6th ed.). White Plains, NY: Longman.

Garland, M. (1993). Ethnography penetrates the "I didn't have time" rationale to elucidate higher order reasons for distance education withdrawal. *Research in Distance Education, 5*, 6–10.

Gay, L. R., Mills, G. E., & Airasian, P. (2005). *Educational research: Competencies for analysis and application* (8th ed.). Upper Saddle River, NJ: Merrill/Prentice Hall.

George, D., & Mallery, P. (2001). *SPSS for Windows: Step by step. A simple guide and reference 10.0 update*. Boston: Allyn & Bacon.

Gettinger, M. (1993). Effects of error correction on third graders' spelling. *Journal of Educational Research, 87*, 39–45.

Ginsberg, P. E., & Mertens, D. M. (2009). Frontiers in social research ethics: Fertile ground for evolution. In D. M. Mertens & P. E. Ginsburg (Eds.), *The handbook of social research ethics* (pp. 580–613). Los Angeles, CA: Sage.

Glaser, B. G. (1978). *Theoretical sensitivity*. Mill Valley, CA: Sociology Press.

Glaser, B. G. (1992). *Basics of grounded theory analysis*. Mill Valley, CA: Sociology Press.

Glaser, B., & Strauss, A. (1967). *The discovery of grounded theory*. Chicago: Aldine.

Glesne, C., & Peshkin, A. (1992). *Becoming qualitative researchers: An introduction*. White Plains, NY: Longman.

Goldberg, N. (2000). *Thunder and lightning: Cracking open the writer's craft*. New York: Bantam Books.

Goodman, J., & Adler, S. (1985). Becoming an elementary social studies teacher: A study of perspectives. *Theory and Research in Social Education, 15*, 1–20.

Gravetter, F. J., & Wallnau, L. B. (2007). *Statistics for the behavioral sciences* (7th ed.). Belmont, CA: Thomson Learning.

Greene, J. C. (2007). *Mixed methods in social inquiry*. San Francisco: John Wiley & Sons.

Greene, J. C., & Caracelli, V. J. (Eds.). (1997). *Advances in mixed-method evaluation: The challenges and benefits of integrating diverse paradigms* (New Directions for Evaluation, No. 74). San Francisco: Jossey-Bass.

Greene, J. C., Caracelli, V. J., & Graham, W. F. (1989). Toward a conceptual framework for mixed-method evaluation designs. *Educational Evaluation and Policy Analysis, 11*(3), 255–274.

Gudmundsdottir, S. (1997). Introduction to the theme issue of "narrative perspectives on teaching and teacher education." *Teaching and Teacher Education, 13*(1), 1–3.

Hall, B. W., Ward, A. W., & Comer, C. B. (1988). Published educational research: An empirical study of its quality. *Journal of Educational Research, 81*, 182–189.

Hammersley, M., & Atkinson, P. (1995). *Ethnography: Principles in practice* (2nd ed.). New York: Routledge.

Harrison, A. (2007). *Relationship-building in an undergraduate leadership program in teacher education*. Unpublished doctoral dissertation, University of Nebraska–Lincoln.

Harry, B., Day, M., & Quist, F. (1998). "He can't really play": An ethnographic study of sibling acceptance and interaction. *Journal for the Association of the Severely Handicapped (JASH), 23*(4), 289–299.

Hatch, J. A. (2002). *Doing qualitative research in education settings.* Albany: State University of New York Press.

Haviland, W. A. (1993). *Cultural anthropology* (7th ed.). Forth Worth, TX: Harcourt Brace.

Heil, D. (2005). The Internet and student research: Teaching critical evaluation skills. *Teacher Librarian, 33*(2), 26–29.

Hesse-Bieber, S. N., & Leavy, P. (2006). *The practice of qualitative research.* Thousand Oaks, CA: Sage.

Hood, J. C. (2007). Orthodoxy vs. power: The defining traits of grounded theory. In A. Bryant & K. Charmaz (Eds.), *The SAGE handbook of grounded theory* (pp. 151–164). Los Angeles, CA: Sage.

Houston, W. R., Haberman, M., & Sikula, J. P. (1990). *Handbook of research on teacher education.* New York: Macmillan.

Houtz, L. (1995). Instructional strategy change and the attitude and achievement of seventh- and eighth-grade science students. *Journal of Research in Science Teaching, 32*(6), 629–648.

Hovater, S. E. (2000). *Preparing culturally responsive teachers through preservice teaching programs.* Unpublished manuscript, University of Nebraska–Lincoln.

Howard, M. C. (1996). *Contemporary cultural anthropology* (5th ed.). New York: HarperCollins College Publishers.

Howe, K. R., & Dougherty, K. C. (1993). Ethics, institutional review boards, and the changing face of educational research. *Educational Researcher, 22,* 16–21.

Huber, J. (1999). Listening to children on the landscape. In F. M. Connelly & D. J. Clandinin (Eds.), *Shaping a professional identity: Stories of educational practice* (pp. 9–19). New York and London: Teachers College Press.

Huber, J., & Whelan, K. (1999). A marginal story as a place of possibility: Negotiating self on the professional knowledge landscape. *Teaching and Teacher Education, 15,* 381–396.

Huberty, C. J. (1993). Historical origins of statistical testing practices: The treatment of Fisher versus Neyman-Pearson views in textbooks. *Journal of Experimental Education, 61,* 317–333.

Hubley, A. M., & Zumbo, B. D. (1996). A dialectic on validity: Where we have been and where we are going. *Journal of General Psychology, 123,* 207–215.

Hughes, L. (1999). Action research and practical inquiry: How can I meet the needs of the high-ability student within my regular educational classroom? *Journal for the Education of the Gifted, 22,* 282–297.

Husen, T., & Postlethwaite, T. N. (Eds.). (1994). *The international encyclopedia of education* (2nd ed.). Tarrytown, NY: Elsevier Science.

Igo, L. B., Kiewra, K. A., & Bruning, R. (2008). Individual differences and intervention flaws: A sequential explanatory study of college students' copy-and-paste note taking. *Journal of Mixed Methods Research, 2*(2), 149–168.

Impara, J. C. (2010). Assessing the validity of test scores. A paper presented at the Buros Center for Testing Conference on Monitoring Assessment Quality in the Age of Accountability, April 9–10, 2010, Lincoln, NE.

Impara, J. C., & Plake, B. S. (Eds.). (1999). *The thirteenth mental measurements yearbook.* Lincoln: Buros Institute of Mental Measurements, University of Nebraska–Lincoln.

Institute for Scientific Information. (1969–). *Social sciences citation index.* Philadelphia: Author.

Institute for Scientific Information. (1989–). *Social sciences citation index* (Compact disc ed.). Philadelphia: Author.

Ivankova, N. V., & Stick, S. L. (2007). Students' persistence in a Distributed Doctoral Program in Educational Leadership in Higher Education: A mixed methods study. *Research in Higher Education, 48*(1), 93–135.

Jaccard, J., & Wan, C. K. (1996). *Lisrel approaches to interaction effects in multiple regression.* Thousand Oaks, CA: Sage.

Jamieson, S. (2004). Likert scales: How to (ab)use them. *Medical Education, 38,* 1212–1218.

Jeffries, R. B. (1993). To go or not to go: Rural African-American students' perspective about their education. *Journal of Negro Education, 62*(4), 427–432.

Jick, T. D. (1979). Mixing qualitative and quantitative methods: Triangulation in action. *Administrative Science Quarterly, 24,* 602–611.

Joint Committee on Standards for Educational Evaluation. (1995). *Program evaluation standards.* Kalamazoo: Evaluation Center, Western Michigan University.

Jones, J. (1999). *The process of structuring a community-based curriculum in a rural school setting: A grounded theory study.* Unpublished doctoral dissertation, University of Nebraska–Lincoln.

Josselson, R., & Lieblich, A. (Eds.). (1993). *The narrative study of lives* (Vol. 1). Thousand Oaks, CA: Sage.

Kaler, A., & Beres, M. (2010). *Essentials of field relationships.* Walnut Creek, CA: Left Coast Press.

Keeves, J. P. (Ed.). (1988). *Educational research, methodology, and measurement: An international handbook.* Oxford: Pergamon.

Kellogg, J. M. (1997). A study of the effectiveness of self-monitoring as a learning strategy for increasing on-task behavior. Unpublished master's thesis, Western Illinois University, Macomb.

Kemmis, S. (1994). Action research. In T. Husen & T. N. Postlethwaite (Eds.), *International encyclopedia of education* (2nd ed., pp. 42–49). Oxford and New York: Pergamon and Elsevier Science.

Kemmis, S., & McTaggart, R. (1988). *The action research planner.* Geelong, Victoria, Australia: Deakin University Press.

Kemmis, S., & McTaggart, R. (2005). Participatory action research. In N. K. Denzin & Y. S. Lincoln (Eds.), *SAGE Handbook of qualitative research* (3rd ed., pp. 559–603). Thousand Oaks, CA: Sage.

Kemmis, S., & Wilkinson, M. (1998). Participatory action research and the study of practice. In B. Atweh, S. Kemmis, & P. Weeks (Eds.), *Action research in practice: Partnerships for social justice in education* (pp. 21–36). London and New York: Routledge.

Keppel, G. (1991). *Design and analysis: A researcher's handbook.* Upper Saddle River, NJ: Prentice Hall.

Kerlinger, F. N. (1972). *Behavioral research: A conceptual approach.* New York: Holt, Rinehart and Winston.

Kessing, F. (1958). *Cultural anthropology: The science of custom.* New York: Rinehart and Company.

Kester, V. M. (1994). Factors that affect African-American students' bonding to middle school. *The Elementary School Journal, 95*(1), 63–73.

Ketner, C. S., Smith, K. E., & Parnell, M. K. (1997). Relationship between teacher theoretical orientation to reading and endorsement of developmentally appropriate practice. *Journal of Educational Research, 90,* 212–220.

Keyes, M. W., Hanley-Maxwell, C., & Capper, C. A. (1999). "Spirituality? It's the core of my leadership": Empowering leadership in an inclusive elementary school. *Educational Administration Quarterly, 35,* 203–237.

Kiger, D. M., & Johnson, J. A. (1997). Marketing the perceptions of a community college's postsecondary enrollment options program. *Community College Journal of Research and Practice, 21,* 687–693.

Kim, J. H., & Latta, M. M. (2009). Narrative inquiry: Seeking relations as modes of interaction. *Journal of Educational Research, 103*(2), 69–71.

Kline, R. B. (1998). *Principles and practice of structural equation modeling.* New York: Guilford Press.

Knapp, S. (1995). *Reframing paradox: A grounded theory of career development in HRD.* Unpublished doctoral dissertation, University of Nebraska–Lincoln.

Komives, S. R., Owen, J. E., Longerbeam, S. D., Mainella, F. C., & Osteen, L. (2005). Developing leadership identity: A grounded theory. *Journal of College Student Development, 46*(6), 593–611.

Kos, R. (1991). Persistence of reading disabilities: The voices of four middle school students. *American Educational Research Journal, 28*(4), 875–895.

Kramer, J. J., & Conoley, J. C. (Eds.). (1992). *The eleventh mental measurements yearbook.* Lincoln: Buros Institute of Mental Measurements, University of Nebraska–Lincoln.

Krueger, R. A. (1994). *Focus groups: A practical guide for applied research* (2nd ed.). Thousand Oaks, CA: Sage.

Larson, B. W. (1997). Social studies teachers' conceptions of discussion: A grounded theory study. *Theory and Research in Social Education, 25,* 114–146.

LaFrance, J., & Crazy Bull, C. (2009). Researching ourselves back to life: Taking control of the research agenda in Indian country. In D. M. Mertens & P. E. Ginsberg (Eds.), *The handbook of social research ethics* (pp. 135–149). Thousand Oaks, CA: Sage.

Laursen, B., Coy, K. C., & Collins, W. A. (1998). Reconsidering changes in parent–child conflict across adolescence. *Child Development, 69*(3), 817–832.

Lawrence-Lightfoot, S., & Davis, J. H. (1997). *The art and science of portraiture.* San Francisco: Jossey-Bass.

LeCompte, M. D., Millroy, W. L., & Preissle, J. (1992). *The handbook of qualitative research in education.* San Diego: Academic Press.

LeCompte, M. D., Preissle, J., & Tesch, R. (1993). *Ethnography and qualitative design in educational research* (2nd ed.). San Diego: Academic Press.

LeCompte, M. D., & Schensul, J. J. (1999). *Designing and conducting ethnographic research* (Ethnographer's Toolkit, No. 1). Walnut Creek, CA: AltaMira.

Lee, Y. J., & Greene, J. (2007). The predictive validity of an ESL Placement Test: A mixed methods approach. *Journal of Mixed Methods Research 1*(4), 366–389.

Leedy, P. D., & Ormrod, J. E. (2001). *Practical research: Planning and design* (7th ed.). Upper Saddle River, NJ: Prentice Hall.

Lesser, L. M., & Nordenhaug, E. (2004). Ethical statistics and statistical ethics: Making an interdisciplinary module. *Journal of Statistics Education, 12*(3). www.amstat.org/publications/jse/v12n3/lesser.

LeTendre, G. K. (1999). Community-building activities in Japanese schools: Alternative paradigms of the democratic school. *Comparative Education Review, 43,* 283–310.

Libutti, P. O., & Blandy, S. G. (1995). *Teaching information retrieval and evaluation skills to education students and practitioners: A casebook of applications.* Chicago: Association of College and Research Libraries.

Lieblich, A., Tuval-Mashiach, R., & Zilber, T. (1998). *Narrative research: Reading, analysis, and interpretation.* Thousand Oaks, CA: Sage.

Lincoln, Y. S. (1995). Emerging criteria for quality in qualitative and interpretive research. *Qualitative Inquiry, 1,* 275–289.

Lincoln, Y. S. (2009). Ethical practices in qualitative research. In D.M. Mertens & P. E. Ginsberg (Eds.), *The handbook of social research ethics* (pp. 150–169). Los Angeles, CA: Sage.

Lincoln, Y. S., & Guba, E. G. (1985). *Naturalistic inquiry.* Newbury Park, CA: Sage.

Lincoln Public Schools. (ND). *Guidelines for conducting external research in the Lincoln public schools.* Retrieved November 21, 2006, from http://misc.lps.org.

Lipsey, M. W. (1990). *Design sensitivity: Statistical power for experimental research.* Newbury Park, CA: Sage.

Lipsey, M. W. (1998). Design sensitivity: Statistical power for applied experimental research. In L. Bickman & D. J. Rog (Eds.), *Handbook of applied social research methods* (pp. 39–68). Thousand Oaks, CA: Sage.

Locke, L. F., Spirduso, W. W., & Silverman, S. J. (2007). *Proposals that work: A guide for planning dissertations and grant proposals* (5th ed.). Thousand Oaks, CA: Sage.

Lofland, J., & Lofland, L. H. (1995). *Analyzing social settings: A guide to qualitative observation and analysis* (3rd ed.). Belmont, CA: Wadsworth.

Madison, D. S. (2005). *Critical ethnography: Method, ethics, and performance.* Thousand Oaks, CA: Sage.

Maggio, R. (1991). *The bias-free word finder: A dictionary of nondiscriminatory language.* Boston: Beacon Press.

Malloy, H. L., & McMurray, P. (1996). Conflict strategies and resolutions: Peer conflict in an integrated early childhood classroom. *Early Childhood Research Quarterly, 11,* 185–206.

Mark, M. M., & Gamble, C. (2009). Experiments, quasi-experiments, and ethics. In D. M. Mertens & P. E. Ginsberg (Eds.), *The handbook of social research ethics* (pp. 198–213). Thousand Oaks, CA: Sage.

Marshall, C., & Rossman, G. B. (2010). *Designing qualitative research* (5th ed.). Thousand Oaks, CA: Sage.

Mastera, G. (1996). *The process of revising general education curricula in three private baccalaureate colleges: A grounded theory study.* Unpublished doctoral dissertation, University of Nebraska–Lincoln.

McAllister, G., & Irvine, J. J. (2000). Cross cultural competency and multicultural teacher education. *Review of Educational Research, 70*(1), 3–24.

McCall, W. A., & Crabbs, L. M. (1925). *Manual of directions for the Standard test lessons in reading.* New York: Bureau of Publications, Teachers College, Columbia University.

McCarthey, S. J. (1994). Opportunities and risks of writing from personal experience. *Language Arts, 71,* 182–191.

McCaslin, M. L. (1993). *The nature of leadership within rural communities: A grounded theory.* Unpublished dissertation, University of Nebraska–Lincoln.

McEwan, H., & Egan, K. (1995). *Narrative in teaching, learning, and research.* New York: Teachers College Press.

Mead, M. (1928). *Coming of age in Samoa: A psychological study of primitive youth for Western civilization.* New York: Morrow.

Meijer, P. C., Verloop, N., & Beijaard, D. (2001). Similarities and differences in teachers' practical knowledge about teaching reading comprehension. *Journal of Educational Research, 94*(3), 171–184.

Melendez, M. C., & Melendez, N. B. (2010). The influence of parental attachment on the college adjustment of White, Black, and Latina/Hispanic women: A cross-cultural investigation. *Journal of College Student Development, 51*(4), 419–435.

Merriam, S. B. (1998). *Qualitative research and case study applications in education.* San Francisco: Jossey-Bass.

Mertens, D. M. (2009). *Transformative research and evaluation.* New York: The Guilford Press.

Mertens, D. M., Holmes, H. M., & Harris, R. L. (2009). Transformative research and ethics. In D. M. Mertens & P. E. Ginsberg (Eds.), *The handbook of social research ethics* (pp. 95–101). Thousand Oaks, CA: Sage.

Mertler, C. A. (2001). *Lessons learned from the administration of a Web-based survey.* (ERIC Document Reproduction Service No. ED 458278)

Messick, S. (1980). Test validity and the ethics of assessment. *American Psychologist, 35,* 1012–1027.

Metzner, B. (1989). Perceived quality of academic advising: The effect on freshman attrition. *American Educational Research Journal, 26*(3), 422–442.

Meyer, R. C. (1996). *Stories from the heart.* Mahwah, NJ: Erlbaum.

Miles, M. B., & Huberman, A. M. (1984). *Qualitative data analysis: A sourcebook for new methods.* Thousand Oaks, CA: Sage.

Miles, M. B., & Huberman, A. M. (1994). *Qualitative data analysis: A sourcebook for new methods* (2nd ed.). Thousand Oaks, CA: Sage.

Miller, D. L. (1992). *The experiences of a first-year college president: An ethnography.* Unpublished doctoral dissertation, University of Nebraska–Lincoln.

Miller, D. L., Creswell, J. W., & Olander, L. S. (1998). Writing and retelling multiple ethnographic tales of a soup kitchen for the homeless. *Qualitative Inquiry, 4,* 469–491.

Mills, G. E. (2011). *Action research: A guide for the teacher researcher* (with MyEducationLab). (4th ed.). Upper Saddle River, NJ: Pearson/Allyn & Bacon.

Morrison, T. G., Jacobs, J. S., & Swinyard, W. R. (1999). Do teachers who read personally use recommended literacy practices in their classrooms? *Reading Research and Instruction, 38,* 81–100.

Morrow, S. L., & Smith, M. L. (1995). Constructions of survival and coping by women who have survived childhood sexual abuse. *Journal of Counseling Psychology, 42,* 24–33.

Morse, J. M. (1991). Approaches to qualitative-quantitative methodological triangulation. *Nursing Research, 40,* 120–123.

Morse, J. M., & Niehaus, L. (2009). *Mixed method design: Principles and procedures*. Walnut Creek, CA: Left Coast Press.

Muffo, J. A. (1986). The impact of faculty research on state and federal policy. In J. W. Creswell (Ed.), *Measuring faculty research performance* (New Directions for Institutional Research, No. 50, pp. 75–85). San Francisco: Jossey-Bass.

Muncey, T. *Creating autoethnographies*. London: Sage.

Murphy, K. R., & Myors, B. (1998). *Statistical power analysis: A simple and general model for traditional and modern hypothesis tests*. Mahwah, NJ: Erlbaum.

Murphy, L. L., Impara, J. C., & Plake, B. S. (Eds.). (1999). *Tests in print V*. Lincoln: Buros Institute of Mental Measurements, University of Nebraska–Lincoln.

Nastasi, B. K., Hitchcock, J., Sarkar, S., Burkholder, G., Varjas, K., & Jayasena, A. (2007). Mixed methods in intervention research: Theory to adaptation. *Journal of Mixed Methods Research, 1*(2), 164–182.

National Center for Educational Statistics. (1997). *Digest of educational statistics 1997*. Washington, DC: U.S. Department of Education, Office of Educational Research and Improvement.

Neff, J. M. (1998). From a distance: Teaching writing on interactive television. *Research in the Teaching of English, 33,* 146–157.

Nelson, L. W. (1990). Code-switching in the oral life narratives of African-American women: Challenges to linguistic hegemony. *Journal of Education, 172*(3), 142–155.

Nesbary, D. K. (2000). *Survey research and the World Wide Web*. Boston: Allyn & Bacon.

Neuman, S. G., & McCormick, S. (Eds.). (1995). *Single-subject experimental research: Applications for literacy*. Newark, DE: International Reading Association.

Neuman, W. L. (2000). *Social research methods: Qualitative and quantitative approaches* (4th ed.). Boston: Allyn & Bacon.

Newkirk, T. (1996). Seduction and betrayal in qualitative research. In P. Mortensen & G. E. Kirsch (Eds.), *Ethics and representation in qualitative studies of literacy* (pp. 3–16). Urbana, IL: National Council of Teachers of English.

Nippold, M. A., Duthie, J. K., & Larsen, J. (2005). Literacy as a leisure activity: Free-time preferences of older children and young adolescents. *Language, Speech, and Hearing Services in Schools, 36*(2), 93–102.

O'Brien, N. P., & Fabiano, E. (Eds.). (1990). *Core list of books and journals in education*. Phoenix, AZ: Oryn.

Olesen, V. L. (2007). Feminist qualitative research and grounded theory: Complexities, criticism, and opportunities. In A. Bryant & K. Charmaz (Eds.), *The SAGE handbook of grounded theory* (pp. 417–435). Los Angeles, CA: Sage.

Ollerenshaw, J. A. (1998). *A study of the impact of a supplemental storytelling (oral narrative) strategy on fourth grade students' understanding of the physics of sound*. Unpublished doctoral dissertation, University of Iowa, Iowa City.

Ollerenshaw, J. A., & Creswell, J. W. (2000). *Data analysis in narrative research: A comparison of two "restorying" approaches*. Paper presented at the Annual American Educational Research Association, New Orleans, LA.

Orona, C. J. (1997). Temporality and identity loss due to Alzheimer's disease. In A. Strauss & J. Corbin (Eds.), *Grounded theory in practice* (pp. 171–196). Thousand Oaks, CA: Sage.

Pachnowski, L. M., Newman, I., & Jurczyk, J. P. (1997). *Immediate data: The World Wide Web as a resource for teaching research methods*. (ERIC Document Reproduction Service No. ED409361)

Padula, M. A., & Miller, D. L. (1999). Understanding graduate women's reentry experiences. *Psychology of Women Quarterly, 23,* 327–343.

Pajak, E. F., & Blasé, J. J. (1984). Teachers in bars: From professional to personal self. *Sociology of Education, 57,* 164–173.

Patton, M. Q. (1990). *Qualitative evaluation and research methods* (2nd ed.). Newbury Park, CA: Sage.

Patton, M. Q. (2002). *Qualitative research and evaluation methods* (3rd ed.). Thousand Oaks, CA: Sage.

Pedhazur, E. J. (1997). *Multiple regression in behavioral research: Explanation and prediction* (3rd ed.). Fort Worth, TX: Harcourt Brace College Publishers.

Perrine, R. M., Lisle, J., & Tucker, D. L. (1996). Effects of a syllabus offer of help, student age, and class size on college students' willingness to seek support from faculty. *Journal of Experimental Education, 64*(1), 41–52.

Persichitte, K. A., Young, S., & Tharp, D. D. (1997). *Conducting research on the Internet: Strategies for electronic interviewing*. (ERIC Document Reproduction Service No. ED409860)

Personal Narratives Group. (1989). *Interpreting women's lives*. Bloomington: Indiana University Press.

Plano Clark, V. L., & Creswell, J. W. (2008). *The mixed methods reader*. Thousand Oaks, CA: Sage.

Plano Clark, V. L., & Creswell, J. W. (2010). *Understanding research: A consumer's guide*. Boston, MA: Merrill.

Plano Clark, V. L., Miller, D. L., Creswell, J. W., McVea, K., McEntarffer, R., & Mickelson, W. T. (2001). In conversation: High school students talk to students about tobacco use and prevention strategies. *Qualitative Health Research, 12*(9), 1264–1283.

Poling, A., & Grosset, D. (1986). Basic research designs in applied behavior analysis. In A. Poling & R. Fuque (Eds.), *Research methods in applied behavior analysis: Issues and advances* (pp. 7–27). New York: Plenum.

Punch, K. F. (1998). *Introduction to social research: Quantitative and qualitative approaches*. London: Sage.

Ramanathan, M. (2006). *Ethics in quantitative research methods*. Short Term Training Program "Ethics in Social Science Research Related to Health," ICMR, New Delhi and CSER, Mumbai, India. Retrieved from icmr.nic.in/bioethics/cc_biothics/presentations/haryana/session61.pdf.

Reichardt, C. S., & Cook, T. D. (1979). Beyond qualitative versus quantitative methods. In T. D. Cook & C. S. Reichardt (Eds.), *Qualitative and quantitative methods in evaluation research* (pp. 7–32). Beverly Hills, CA: Sage.

Reichardt, C. S., & Mark, M. M. (1998). Quasi-experimentation. In L. Bickman & D. J. Rog (Eds.), *Handbook of applied social research methods* (pp. 193–228). Thousand Oaks, CA: Sage.

Reichardt, C. S., & Rallis, S. E. (1994). *The qualitative-quantitative debate: New perspectives* (New Directions for Program Evaluation, No. 61, pp. 5–11). San Francisco: Jossey-Bass.

Reid, R., Hertzog, M., & Snyder, M. (1996). Educating every teacher, every year: The public schools and parents of children with ADHD. *Seminars in Speech and Language, 17,* 73–90.

Review of Educational Research. (1931–). Washington, DC: American Educational Research Association.

Rhoads, R. A. (1995). Whales tales, dog piles, and beer goggles: An ethnographic case study of fraternity life. *Anthropology and Education Quarterly, 26,* 306–323.

Rhoads, R. A. (1997). Implications of the growing visibility of gay and bisexual male students on campus. *NASPA Journal, 34,* 275–286.

Richardson, L. (2000). Writing: A method of inquiry. In N. K. Denzin & Y. S. Lincoln (Eds.), *Handbook of qualitative research* (2nd ed.). Thousand Oaks, CA: Sage.

Richie, B. S., Fassinger, R. E., Linn, S. G., & Johnson, J. (1997). Persistence, connection, and passion: A qualitative study of the career development of highly achieving African American-Black and White women. *Journal of Counseling Psychology, 44,* 143–148.

Riessman, C. K. (1993). *Narrative analysis*. Newbury Park, CA: Sage.

Robrecht, L. C. (1995). Grounded theory: Evolving methods. *Qualitative Health Research, 5,* 169–177.

Rosenau, P. M. (1992). *Post-modernism and the social sciences: Insights, inroads, and intrusions*. Princeton, NJ: Princeton University Press.

Rossman, G. B., & Wilson, B. L. (1985). Number and words: Combining quantitative and qualitative methods in a single large-scale evaluation study. *Evaluation Review, 9*(5), 627–643.

Royal, M. A., & Rossi, R. J. (1999). Predictors of within-school differences in teachers' sense of community. *Journal of Educational Research, 92*(5), 259–265.

Rudestam, K. E., & Newton, R. R. (1992). *Surviving your dissertation*. Newbury Park, CA: Sage.

Rudner, L. M. (1993). Test evaluation [Online]. Available at www.ericae.net.

Ryen, A. (2009). Ethnography: Constitutive practice and research ethics. In D. M. Mertens & P. E. Ginsberg (Eds.), *The handbook of social research ethics* (pp. 229–242). Los Angeles, CA: Sage.

Sagor, R. (2005). *The action research guidebook: A four-step process for educators and school teams*. Thousand Oaks, CA: Corwin Press.

Salant, P., & Dillman, D. A. (1994). *How to conduct your own survey*. New York: Wiley.

Salkind, N. J. (2010). *Statistics for people who (think they) hate statistics* (4th ed.). Thousand Oaks, CA: Sage.

Schmuck, R. A. (1997). *Practical action research for change*. Arlington Heights, IL: IRI/SkyLight Training and Publishing.

Schmuck, R. A. (Ed.). (2009). *Practical action research: A collection of articles* (2nd ed.). Thousand Oaks, CA: Corwin Press.

Schwandt, T. A. (2007). *The SAGE Dictionary of Qualitative Inquiry* (3rd ed.). Thousand Oaks, CA: Sage.

Schwandt, T. A., & Halpern, E. S. (1988). *Linking auditing and metaevaluation: Enhancing quality in applied research*. Newbury Park, CA: Sage.

Self-Brown, S. R., & Mathews, S. H. (2003). Effects of classroom structure on student achievement goal orientations. *Journal of Education Research, 97*(2), 106–111.

Shadish, W. R., Cook, T. D., & Campbell, D. T. (2002). *Experimental and quasi-experimental designs for generalized causal inference*. Boston: Houghton Mifflin.

Shapiro, E. S., & Lentz, F. E. (1991). Vocational-technical programs: Follow-up of students with learning disabilities. *Exceptional Children, 58,* 47–59.

Shelden, D. L., Angell, M. E., Stoner, J. B., & Roseland, B. D. (2010). School principals' influence on trust: Perspectives of mothers of children with disabilities. *Journal of Educational Research, 103,* 159–170.

Sieber, S. (1973). Integration of fieldwork and survey methods. *American Journal of Sociology, 78,* 1335–1359.

Sills, S. J., & Song, C. (2002). Innovations in survey research: An application of Web-based surveys. *Social Science Computer Review, 20*(1), 22–30.

SilverPlatter Information Services. (1974/86–). *Sociofile*. Wellesley Hills, MA: Author.

SilverPlatter Information Services. (1986). *PsycLIT*. Wellesley Hills, MA: Author.

Smetana, J. G., & Asquith, P. (1994). Adolescents' and parents' conceptions of parental authority and personal autonomy. *Child Development, 65,* 1147–1162.

Society for Research in Child Development. (1945–). *Child development abstracts and bibliography*. Washington, DC: Committee on Child Development, National Research Council.

Sociological Abstracts, Inc. (1953–). *Sociological abstracts*. San Diego: Author.

Solomon, D. J. (2001). Conducting Web-based surveys. *Practical Assessment, Research & Evaluation, 7*(19), 1–6.

Spindler, G., & Spindler, L. (1992). Cultural process and ethnography: An anthropological perspective. In M. D. LeCompte, W. L. Millroy, & J. Preissle (Eds.), *The handbook of qualitative research in education* (pp. 53–92). San Diego: Academic Press.

Spradley, J. P. (1979). *The ethnographic interview*. Fort Worth, TX: Harcourt Brace Jovanovich College Publishers.

Spradley, J. P. (1980). *Participant observation*. New York: Holt, Rinehart and Winston.

Stake, R. E. (1995). *The art of case study research*. Thousand Oaks, CA: Sage.

Stake, R. E. (2000). Case studies. In N. K. Denzin & Y. S. Lincoln (Eds.), *Handbook of qualitative research* (2nd ed., pp. 435–454). Thousand Oaks, CA: Sage.

Stanulis, R. N., & Jeffers, L. (1995). Action research as a way of learning about teaching in a mentor/student teacher relationship. *Action in Teacher Education, XVI*(4), 14–24.

Strauss, A. (1987). *Qualitative analysis for social scientists*. New York: Cambridge University Press.

Strauss, A., & Corbin, J. (1990). *Basics of qualitative research: Grounded theory procedures and techniques*. Newbury Park, CA: Sage.

Strauss, A., & Corbin, J. (1998). *Basics of qualitative research: Techniques and procedures for developing grounded theory* (2nd ed.). Thousand Oaks, CA: Sage.

Strike, K. A., Anderson, M. S., Curren, R., Geel, T. V., Pritchard, I., & Robertson, E. (2002). *Ethical standards of the American Educational Research Association: Cases and commentary*. Washington, DC: American Educational Research Association.

Stringer, E. T. (2007). *Action research* (3rd ed.). Thousand Oaks, CA: Sage.

Subject guide to books in print. (1957–). New York: R. R. Bowker.

Swidler, S. A. (2000). Notes on a country school tradition: Recitation as an individual strategy. *Journal of Research in Rural Education, 15*(1), 8–21.

Tashakkori, A., & Teddlie, C. (1998). *Mixed methodology: Combining qualitative and quantitative approaches*. Thousand Oaks, CA: Sage.

Tashakkori, A., & Teddlie, C. (Eds.). (2003). *Handbook of mixed methods in social and behavioral research*. Thousand Oaks, CA: Sage.

Tashakkori, A., & Teddlie, C. (Eds.). (2011). *SAGE handbook of mixed methods in social and behavioral research* (2nd ed.) Thousand Oaks, CA: Sage.

Teddlie, C., & Tashakkori, A. (2009). *Foundations of mixed methods research: Integrating quantitative and qualitative approaches in the social and behavioral sciences*. Thousand Oaks, CA: Sage.

Tesch, R. (1990). *Qualitative research: Analysis types and software tools*. Bristol, PA: Falmer Press.

Theberge, N. (1997). "It's part of the game": Physicality and the production of gender in women's hockey. *Gender & Society, 11*(1), 69–87.

Thomas, J. (1993). *Doing critical ethnography*. Newbury Park, CA: Sage.

Thomas, W. I., & Znaniecki, F. (1927). *The Polish peasant in Europe and America*. New York: Knopf.

Thorndike, R. M. (1997a). Correlational procedures in data analysis. In T. Husen & T. N. Postlethwaite (Eds.), *International encyclopedia of education* (2nd ed., pp. 1107–1117). Oxford and New York: Pergamon and Elsevier Science.

Thorndike, R. M. (1997b). *Measurement and evaluation in psychology and education* (6th ed.). Upper Saddle River, NJ: Macmillan/Prentice Hall.

Thorndike, R. M. (2005). *Measurement and evaluation in psychology and education* (7th ed.). Upper Saddle River, NJ: Pearson Education.

Tierney, W. G. (1993). *Building communities of difference: Higher education in the twenty-first century*. Westport, CT: Bergin & Garvey.

Tuckman, B. W. (1999). *Conducting educational research* (5th ed.). Fort Worth, TX: Harcourt Brace College Publishers.

Turabian, K. L. (2007). *A manual for writers of term papers, theses, and dissertations* (7th ed.). Chicago: University of Chicago Press.

Unger, H. G. (1996). *Encyclopedia of American education*. New York: Facts on File, Inc.

University Council for Educational Administration. (1966–). *Educational administration abstracts*. Columbus, OH: Author.

University of Chicago Press. (2003). *The Chicago manual of style* (15th ed.). Chicago: Author.

University Microfilms International. (1938–1965/66). *Dissertation abstracts*. Ann Arbor, MI: Author.

University Microfilms International. (1987–). *Dissertation abstracts ondisc* (computer file). Ann Arbor, MI: Author.

Valois, R. F., & McKewon, R. E. (1998). Frequency and correlates of fighting and carrying weapons among public school adolescents. *American Journal of Health Behavior, 22,* 8–17.

Van Maanen, J. (1988). *Tales of the field: On writing ethnography*. Chicago: University of Chicago Press.

VanHorn-Grassmeyer, K. (1998). *Enhancing practice: New professional in student affairs*. Unpublished doctoral dissertation, University of Nebraska–Lincoln.

Viadero, D. (1999). What is (and isn't) research? *Education Week, XVIII*(41), 33, 34–36.

Vockell, E. L., & Asher, J. W. (1995). *Educational research* (2nd ed.). Upper Saddle River, NJ: Prentice Hall.

Vogt, W. P. (2005). *Dictionary of statistics and methodology: A non-technical guide for the social sciences* (3rd ed.). Thousand Oaks, CA: Sage.

Wang, J., & Staver, J. R. (1997). An empirical study of gender differences in Chinese students' science achievement. *Journal of Educational Research, 90,* 252–255.

Ward, P. (1999). Chapter 3: Design of the Saber-Tooth project. *Journal of Teaching in Physical Education, 18,* 403–416.

Ward, P., Barrett, T. M., Evans, S. A., Doutis, P., Nguyen, P. T., & Johnson, M. K. (1999). Chapter 5: Curriculum effects in eighth-grade lacrosse. *Journal of Teaching in Physical Education, 18,* 428–443.

Watters, J. J., Christensen, C., Arcodia, C., Ryan, Y., & Weeks, P. (1998). Occasional visits to the kingdom. In B. Atweh, S. Kemmis, & P. Weeks (Eds.), *Action research in practice: Partnerships for social justice in education* (pp. 250–279). London and New York: Routledge.

Webb, E. J. (1966). *Unobtrusive measures: Nonreactive research in the social sciences.* Chicago: Rand-McNally.

Wilkinson, L., and the Task Force on Statistical Inference. (1999). Statistical methods in psychology journals. *American Psychologist, 54*(8), 594–604.

Wilson, H. W. (1929/32–). *Education index.* New York: H. W. Wilson.

Winthrop, R. H. (1991). *Dictionary of concepts in cultural anthropology.* Westport, CT: Greenwood.

Wolcott, H. F. (1974). The elementary school principal: Notes from a field study. In G. Spindler (Ed.), *Education and cultural process: Toward an anthropology of education* (pp. 176–204). New York: Holt, Rinehart and Winston.

Wolcott, H. F. (1983). Adequate schools and inadequate education: The life history of a sneaky kid. *Anthropology and Education Quarterly, 14,* 3–32.

Wolcott, H. F. (1992). *Writing up qualitative research.* Newbury Park, CA: Sage.

Wolcott, H. F. (1994). *Transforming qualitative data: Description, analysis, and interpretation.* Thousand Oaks, CA: Sage.

Wolcott, H. F. (1995). *The art of fieldwork.* Walnut Creek, CA: AltaMira.

Wolcott, H. F. (2008). *Ethnography: A way of seeing* (2nd ed.). Walnut Creek, CA: AltaMira.

Wright, D. B. (1997). *Understanding statistics: An introduction for the social sciences.* London: Sage.

Yin, R. K. (2008). *Case study research* (4th ed.). Thousand Oaks, CA: Sage.

Zeichner, K. (1999). The new scholarship in teacher education. *Educational Researcher, 28*(9), 4–15.

Ziller, R. C. (1990). *Photographing the self: Methods for observing personal orientation.* Newbury Park, CA: Sage.

Author Index

Subject Index